AF594103

Martin Luther and Buddhism

Princeton Theological Monograph Series

K. C. Hanson, Series Editor

Recent volumes in the series

Christian T. Collins Winn, editor
From the Margins: Celebrating the Theological Work of Donald W. Dayton

Ronald F. Satta
Sacred Text: Biblical Authority in Nineteenth-Century America

Anette Ejsing
A Theology of Anticipation: A Constructive Study of C. S. Peirce

Michael G. Cartwright
Practices, Politics, and Performance:
Toward a Communal Hermeneutic for Christian Ethics

Stephen Finlan and Vladimir Kharlamov, editors
Theōsis: Deification in Christian Theology

David A. Ackerman
Lo, I Tell You a Mystery:
Cross, Resurrection, and Paraenesis in the Rhetoric of 1 Corinthians

John A. Vissers
The Neo-Orthodox Theology of W. W. Bryden

Sam Hamstra, editor
The Reformed Pastor by John Williamson Nevin

Byron C. Bangert
Consenting to God and Nature:
Toward a Theocentric, Naturalistic, Theological Ethics

Richard Valantasis et al., editors
The Subjective Eye:
Essays in Honor of Margaret Miles

Caryn Riswold
Coram Deo:
Human Life in the Vision of God

Martin Luther and Buddhism

Aesthetics of Suffering

Paul S. Chung

Foreword by
Jürgen Moltmann

Second Edition

PICKWICK *Publications* • Eugene, Oregon

MARTIN LUTHER AND BUDDHISM
Aesthetics of Suffering
Second Edition

Princeton Theological Monograph Series 80

Pickwick Publications
A division of Wipf and Stock Publishers
199 W. 8th Ave., Suite 3
Eugene, OR 97401

ISBN 13: 978-1-55635-459-5

Cataloging-in-Publication data:

Chung, Paul S.

Martin Luther and Buddhism: aesthetics of suffering / Paul S. Chung. With a foreword by Jürgen Moltmann.

xxvi + 446 p. ; 23 cm.— Princeton Theological Monograph Series 80

Includes bibliographical references.

ISBN 13: 978-1-55635-459-5

1. Luther, Martin, 1483–1546—Views on suffering of God. 2. Buddhism—Relations—Christianity. 3. Christianity and other religions—Buddhism. I. Moltmann, Jürgen. II. Title. III. Series.

BR128.B8 C38 2008

Manufactured in the U.S.A.

In Honor of

Helmut Gollwitzer

and

Jan M. Lochman,

my theological fathers

Contents

Foreword

A FOREWORD IS NEITHER AN AFTERWORD NOR A REVIEW. A FOREWORD should open up the door to a text and make one feel so invited that the book gets read. I will confine my introductory remarks to such an invitation. The work of Paul Chung says much more than the title suggests. The title speaks of a comparison between Martin Luther and (Mahayana) Buddhism in regard to the "Aesthetics of Suffering," but the content provides an extraordinarily rich theology that combines Europe with Asia, the sixteenth century with the twenty-first century, and Christian theology with the history of religion in a postmodern cultural context. I've rarely read such a multi-faceted study. The reader will be instructed extensively and be brought to develop his/her own thoughts in every chapter. One gets no impression of superficiality in any chapter. To the contrary: the author goes to the root of the questions and does not exempt the reader from the "Anstrengung des Begriffs" (Hegel). After reading, I put this book down with great surprise and decided to encourage students and anyone interested in theology in Europe, America, and Asia to urgently and repeatedly read it. Here, "theology of the cross" is radicalized, and the dialogue between Christianity and Buddhism, and also between Asia and the West, is exalted onto a new level.

My contribution in this foreword can only be reserved. I'd like to engage two related pictures: (1) the crucified Christ and the dying, declining Buddha; (2) the cross in the rose, Luther's shield image (Wappenbild), and the Lotus flower, on which the Buddha sits or stands.

The crucified Christ is the living Son of God. He suffered torture in his body, wore a crown of thorns, and was nailed and died on a Roman cross. He suffered in his soul the abandonment of his people, whose high priests delivered him, and the crowd demanded his execution. He suffered betrayal, denial, and curse on the part of his many disciples. Only women kept an eye on him "from afar." He lost his identity as a Jew, as rabbi and teacher, as a friend, and died in human loneliness. On the deepest level, however, his suffering relates to God whom he has called "Abba, dear Father" since his baptism, and whose proximity he has proclaimed to the poor and the sick among his people. He died with the cry: "My God, why have you forsaken me?" This is the experience of hell, as Luther and Calvin rightly interpreted it. The passion of Jesus Christ culminates in the passion of God, the experience of the darkness of God, and the corresponding dark night of the soul. If this passion is "the gospel of the Son of God," as the gospel of Mark states at the beginning (1:1), the Father is also abandoned by the Son in the Father's forsakenness of the Son. The Son suffered the dying in the far distance from the beloved Father, and the Father suffered the death of the beloved Son. These are different pains at the same suffering. What occurred on the cross between God the Son and God the Father embraces the whole suffering of this world and opens up all the hells of torture.

What we perceive in the declining Buddha and the Bodhisattva by contrast, is *dukkha,* divine compassion and sympathy. This is also grounded in self-denial and self-sacrifice, self-emptiness and compassion. With limitless compassion the Buddha takes part in the cosmic suffering of the world, and in so doing he shows his completeness. But he does not cry; no statue shows the Buddha who is distorted by affliction. No one must feel sympathy or compassion with him. Rather, all Buddha statues and pictures show forth wonderful rest and world-transcending spiritual peace. Also, the Bodhisattva who gives up his/her own perfection in order to help the weak shows mildness, compassion, and merciful understanding of the weak who are not yet enlightened. The declining Buddha died a beautiful death on the way to salvation. Christ didn't die a beautiful death, but a death that was frightening even in his own day.

Where do the suffering Christ and the compassionate Buddha converge and diverge from each other? Paul Chung's book pursues an answer to this question. The perfect beautiful Lotus on which the Buddha sits or stands is a primordial symbol of world genesis. This sublime floating flower blossomed, together with the creator of the world, out of primal water. In India there was Brahma, who created the world sitting and ruling on it. Then the Buddha was given to the world. The Lotus flower is the conceptual key to created-creative beauty. Anyone who meditates on it is reminded of Dostoevsky: "Beauty will redeem the world," because beauty has produced everything. The flower of the Lotus is an aesthetics of the beautiful.

Against this, "no stately form or beauty" (Isa 53:2) is to be known in the crucified. "The suffering servant of God" is no image of human beauty. But this image of the savior on the cross does not stand for himself alone, because his background is always drawn in the shining color of the twilight of the resurrection. It is not the cross of the dead, but always the cross of the Christ who was resurrected by God into the new creation. Since medieval times this symbol is represented by a flower: the rose. Luther's shield image shows the cross of Christ in the midst of a blossoming rose. The crucified who redeems the world from sin and suffering is embraced by the leaves of the rose, which points to the beauty of God's new creation. As the Buddha stands on the Lotus blossom of world genesis, so the one who is crucified for the world is set on the petals of the rose of the resurrection of the world. It was not only Luther who saw such a thing in his shield image; the Lutheran philosopher Hegel did the same thing in the nineteenth century. Hegel made a universal Good Friday out of the historical Good Friday and looked for "the rose in the cross of the present," and in so doing, he meant God's reconciliation in the midst of the suffering and affliction of the present. Lotus flower and blossoming rose: What do they say to us about common ground? And what do they say for themselves about the aesthetics of suffering and beauty? We find the answers to these questions in Paul Chung's book. Books also have their own destiny. I hope that this work of Paul Chung will be attractive to intelligent readers and have a lasting impact on ecumenical theology.

Jürgen Moltmann
Tübingen,
July 20, 2002

Preface to the Second Edition

My life between West and East is characterized by an ongoing engagement with the interpretation of theological and philosophical classics of Christian theology and Chinese religions. In the act of interpretation, I hope, what is forgotten and hidden in Martin Luther and Buddhism might be disclosed and revealed. It calls for a creative yet difficult dialogue with two different life-worlds. In this process I am completely open to the irregular, unexpected, and mysterious speech of God. To the degree that I understand Martin Luther and Buddhism in different manners, I will make my interpretive strategy reliable and feasible in order to deepen and improve a Buddhist-Christian relationship. In perception and interpretation of the world of suffering I want to come back to a new terrain of Asian enculturated theology with interest in hermeneutical hybridization and resistance of the other. In so doing, my intellectual journey is always open to the other side of God, speaking through the life-world of "rose and lotus" in suffering and wisdom. God's act of speaking as my symbolic linguistic source gives rise to an aesthetic perception of suffering. My self-understanding of God's speaking is articulated and informed by my lived experience in engagement with people of other faiths and wisdom. Therefore, language, in my interpretation of Martin Luther and Buddhism, is not separable from the living context of my primary articulation of a lived experience with the two beautiful symbols of "rose and lotus," being under the influence of these worlds. Coalescence of multiple horizons in my hermeneutical experience brings together analytical thinking and self-interpretation into a complementarity that is also articulated and expressed in linguistic experience. Through suffering human beings learn the limitations of human existence and the transcendence of God in a genuine sense. This experience of negativity helps one be attentive to the mystery of God's speech event, which, in turn, inspires one's mimetic desire in the quest for God's *utopos*. Therefore, a theology of suffering is a threshold in search of a theology of God's *utopos*. At this juncture, I have revised my previous trinitarian thinking, which was captive to a myth of the Father's kenosis into the Son for the transcendence of God in the Trinity. I appreciate my assistant, Terra Schwerin-Rowe, for her work on proofreading the second edition.

Paul S. Chung
Lent 2007

Dubuque, IA

Acknowledgments

I would like to thank the following for permission in using selected texts:

McGrath, Alister E. *IUSTITIA DEI: A History of the Christian Doctrine of Justification*, excerpts from the glossary. Reprinted with the permission of Cambridge University Press.

For S. J. Samartha's poem, reprinted with the permission of Lutheran World Federation: LWF studies, *Communion, Community, Society* (Geneva: LWF, 1998) 201–2.

Karl Barth, *Church Dogmatics*. Edited by G. W. Bromiley and T. F. Torrance, 1936–62, by the permission of T. & T. Clark.

Brian Davies, OP 1992. Reprinted from *The Thought of Thomas Aquinas* by Brian Davies (1992) by permission of Oxford University Press.

For the glossary of technical terms *Buddhist Spirituality* II, Author / editors: Takeuchi Yoshinori, ed. With James H. Heisig, Joseph S. O'Leary, and Paul L. Swanson by the permission of The Crossroad Publishing Company.

From *Luther's Works* Vol. 1 pgs 58, 126 © 1968 by Concordia Publishing House. Reprinted with permission.

From *Luther's Works* Vol. 10 pg. 237 © 1974 by Concordia Publishing House. Reprinted with permission.

From *Luther's Works* Vol. 11 pg. 318 © 1976 by Concordia Publishing House. Reprinted with permission.

From *Luther's Works* Vol. 15 pgs 303, 308 © 1969 by Concordia Publishing House. Reprinted with permission.

From *Luther's Works* Vol. 21 pgs 113, 328–29, 344 © 1968 by Concordia Publishing House. Reprinted with permission.

From *Luther's Works* vol. 22 pgs 492–93 © 1968 by Concordia Publishing House. Reprinted with permission.

From *Luther's Works* Vol. 25 pgs 135, 260 © 1972 by Concordia Publishing House. Reprinted with permission.

From *Luther's Works* Vol. 7 pg. 217 © 1968 by Concordia Publishing House. Reprinted with permission.

Introduction

THIS BOOK IS DESIGNED TO BRING THE GREAT REFORMER MARTIN LUTHER into dialogue with Asian theology and spirituality, especially that of Mahayana Buddhism. A common basis for interreligious dialogue between Luther and Buddhism lies in the interpretation of *dukkha* (suffering), in which an attempt is made to construct a theological aesthetics of divine suffering and human suffering. Therefore, it is of special significance to contextualize Luther's theological insights and their ecumenical repercussions in an encounter with other traditions. In recent ecumenical conversation, Luther is examined in depth as we see him in his theological struggle and project. In this ecumenical dialogue we perceive well how Luther's thought was grounded in a dimension of human liberative practice and spiritual insights that has been neglected in its authentic sense throughout the history of Lutheranism. In Lutheran-Orthodox dialogue, Luther is seen as the theologian offering us a spirituality of *theosis* from the real aspect of the indwelling Christ present in faith. Moreover, liberation theology has discovered that Luther is conceived as a theologian of solidarity with those who stand for justice and liberation. However, it is not easy to see Luther as the one recognizing and affirming otherness in a postmodern, pluralistic religious context. Of course, there is a good reason for that, because Luther did not live in a world characterized by postmodernity or the contemporary awareness of religious pluralism. In addition, it is noteworthy that Luther was a man of his time, with limitations, weaknesses, and mistakes. Therefore, it would be a perilous project to transplant Luther out of his context for a cross-cultural reading. These truths notwithstanding, Luther may be reread as an important theologian in an interreligious context due to his deep insight into the suffering of God, which has been suppressed in the Christian tradition under the excessive influence of Greek philosophy.

According to John B. Cobb Jr., Luther's insight into the discovery of the Bible and his teaching of grace in particular serve as an inspiration for setting Western theology free from its bondage to Greek formulations regarding Christian beliefs, system, and doctrine. Understood this way, Luther may encourage Christianity to undertake an encounter with otherness by listening to the word of God openly and honestly in our pluralistic context.[1] That being the case, it is still not an easy task to understand, update, and apply Luther's thought in regard to the complex situation of the Asian world and its spirituality. Some of the world's most ancient cultures and sources of religion remain alive in Asia and are still influential. The substance of culture is unthinkable without its religious dimension, especially in Asian societies. Tillich's phrase, "religion is the substance of culture, culture is the form of religion," is profoundly true of Asia.[2]

Buddhist-Christian dialogue shows how important the nexus between culture and religion becomes. Doing theology in an Asian context shows us an interpretation of the gospel different from Western theology. In the process of interreligious dialogue Martin Luther was recalled by Protestant scholars like Tillich and Cobb in the interest of mutual understanding and renewal. Comparing the mystic element in Luther's eucharistic thought to the nature-mysticism of Buddhism, Tillich suggested that Luther's sacramental thinking, while generating a kind of nature-mysticism, may find its influence in the later development of Protestant mysticism, such as pietism and the German romantic movement in a secularized form.[3] Cobb, as we have already mentioned, notices a striking existential resemblance between the emphasis on the grace of Other-Power in the founder of Pure Land Buddhism in Japan, Shinran, and Luther's teaching of justification by faith alone. However, the issue of suffering and universal compassion may be common between Christianity and Buddhism. In Buddhist-Christian dialogue, it is worthwhile to articulate the dimension of suffering coupled with a spirituality of self-emptiness and compassion and praxis for liberation. This aspect is what this book will address in actualizing Luther's understanding of divine suffering in relation to a Buddhist idea of *dukkha*.

The notion of *dukkha* focuses Asian experience in conscious dialogue with the theology of Martin Luther and his ecumenical followers. A theological aesthetics of divine *dukkha* characterizes Asian confessional theology in regard to creation and redemption as well as in recognition of the beauty of otherness. A Latin American liberation theology's call

1. Cobb, *Transforming Christianity and the World*, 139.

2. Tillich, *Theology of Culture*, 42.

3. Tillich, *Christianity and the Encounter of World Religions*, 44.

for a preferential option for the poor would be insufficient in the Asian church and theology, unless it takes into account the wisdom of other religious ways and a liberative dimension of self-emptying spirituality. What shapes my motivation for running into a theological aesthetics arises out of my pastoral experience of the Korean American Lutheran church in Orinda, California. Along the way of a multicultural ministry of the ELCA (Evangelical Lutheran Church in America) I have been engaged in psychological pain, cultural gaps, pessimism, and socio-economic disturbances among my congregation. My pastoral experience has involved a struggle with and compassion for the community of the different, innocent, and suffering. My experience with people in *dukkha* encourages me to pay renewed attention to a feasibility of the aesthetics of the *theologia crucis* as a way of understanding, recognizing, and affirming God's strange but mysterious voice of beauty coming from people of other faiths. A theological aesthetics of divine *dukkha* calls for a prophetic *diakonia* and the need for creative inculturation and contextualization of the insights of Martin Luther in relation to the beauty of otherness. An experience of God's strange beauty in *dukkha* is articulated and explored in this study of Luther and his ecumenical development from an interreligious perspective. The beauty of God's being in trinitarian fellowship, which focuses on the incarnation, life, ministry, and death on the cross of Jesus Christ, expresses from the start the heart of the wounded Trinity. The question "what moves the human heart?"[4] is answered by God's universal compassion and mercy for all living, sentient creatures on the basis of God's suffering love. This comes from Luther's *theologia crucis.* In other words, God's beauty originates with a compassion for divine others as well as the world. Jesus Christ, the crucified and resurrected One, forms an aesthetic model of beauty, suffering, and glory. This aspect leads to a participation in divine life through the liturgy of the word and sacrament, because "whoever sees me sees the Father" (John 14:9). Liturgy, i.e., *Leit-ourgos,* which means the work of the people, is the place where people of God hear the gospel of Jesus Christ, receive the grace of forgiveness of sin, praise the glory of God, and finally are encouraged to become faithful disciples following Jesus' self-emptying life in service of the kingdom of God.

4. García-Rivera, *Community of the Beautiful*, 9. This book provides a theological aesthetics for liberation theology's move toward a balance between a theology of liberation and inculturation and popular religion.

A theology of the cross becomes a premise for the theology of glory, in so doing crossing infinite distance between God and creatures toward God's universal reconciliation with and compassion for the world. *Keine Weltlosigkeit Gottes* (There is no God without world) is what Martin Luther might bear witness to throughout his whole theological program and personal struggle. The Lutheran sense of the rose is well expressed by "a black cross in the midst of a heart surrounded by white roses." For Luther, "the Christian's heart walks upon roses when it stands beneath the cross."[5] In a letter to Lazarus Spengler (1530) Luther articulates his sense of aesthetics toward the theology of the cross in the following way: ". . . such a heart should stand in the midst of a white rose, to show that faith yields joy, comfort, and peace. . . . Such a rose stands in a field the color of heaven, for such joy in spirit and in faith is a beginning of the heavenly joy which is to be: now already comprehended within, held through hope, but not yet manifest."[6]

Given this fact, the Reformation principle of *sola fides, sola Scriptura,* and *sola gratia* can recognize itself in following *solus Christus* in this world. According to Hegel, a philosophical definition of beauty as the sensuous semblance of the idea presupposes the concept of the idea as the concept of absolute spirit. In this regard, "beauty . . . is no mere formula reducible to subjective functions of intuition; rather, beauty's fundament is to be sought in the object."[7] Hegel's aesthetic principle "Truth is concrete" becomes meaningful for a theological aesthetics focused on divine suffering in a *theologia crucis.* For Hegel "both the estrangement and reconciliation" coexist with "having in mind Christ's death upon the cross." "Reason is a rose within the cross of the present," because "the agony of the estrangement and reconciliation have already taken place within history in the suffering God."[8]

Hegel's reflection on the death of God is related to a Lutheran hymn of 1641 in which there is the phrase "God himself is dead." This phrase, according to Hegel, reflects "an awareness that the human, the finite, the fragile, the weak, the negative are themselves a moment of the divine, that

5. Löwith, *From Hegel to Nietzsche*, 19.

6. Ibid.

7. Adorno, *Aesthetic Theory*, 352.

8. Löwith, *From Hegel to Nietzsche*, 17.

they are with God himself . . . This involves the highest idea of spirit."[9] In Hegel's view, the death of God has an essential meaning with respect to the reconciliation between the infinite and finite. Hegel finds an idea of negation in God's being, which constitutes a critical moment in Hegel's dialectical framework.

However, the dilemma of theological aesthetics raises the question to what extent a language of suffering and a language of beauty can be mediated reciprocally in one another. If aesthetic theory forms itself as a way of expressing "the unconscious, mimetically written history of human suffering," a theological aesthetics of *dukkha* appears as a protest against reason's conspiracy and compulsion toward all-encompassing dominion and against a natural scientific optimism of social order and ecological stability without a concern for the victims and the others.[10] If a theory of beauty is grounded in expression of the truth of lived experience, a theory of truth can no longer be metaphysical, or transcendental. Rather, it describes and represents a reality of human life.[11] The aesthetical dimension in Luther's thought will be an objective of this book, in which justification, the *theologia crucis*, the Trinity, and Eucharistic theology will encounter the wisdom of Buddhist spirituality.

Chapter 1 describes Martin Luther in light of religious pluralism with respect to his ecumenical dialogue. A complex situation of doing theology in a postmodern context is introduced and discussed in terms of revisiting and rethinking Buddhist-Christian dialogue. In chapter 2, I deal with the uniqueness of Luther's life and theology in tracing his Reformation principle and his controversies. Luther's theology cannot be adequately understood apart from his spiritual and social biography. His understanding of justification, the *theologia crucis*, and some controversial debates are dealt with in modern Luther scholars' investigations. Characterization of Luther's theology will be made with respect to its ecumenical significance for today. Chapter 3 presents how the teaching of justification is debated in an ecumenical context today. After that we will attempt to discern Luther's significance with an Asian focus concerning his concept of justification in relation to the theology of the cross and the doctrine of two kingdoms.

9. Hegel, *Hegel Reader*, 497f.

10. Adorno, *Aesthetic Theory*, xiii.

11. Cf. Auerbach, *Mimesis*.

In chapter 4 I talk about Luther's theology of the cross in an ecumenical light. Luther's *theologia crucis* grows in prominence especially in Karl Barth and Jürgen Moltmann in a European context, and by Kazoh Kitamori in Japan, and finally in the liberation theology of Latin America. Furthermore, recent talk about the *theologia crucis* in relation to the cosmic Christ will show its relatedness to the Buddhist universal teaching of salvation. This chapter will discuss the significance of the theology of the cross in an interreligious context. Chapter 5 is an attempt to deepen and actualize an Asian trinitarian theology of Divine *dukkha* in dialogue with Luther and modern theologians. The traditional understanding of the humanity of Christ is seen complementarily in light of a Buddhist notion of cosmic suffering (*dukkha*). Trinity and *Sunyata* will be juxtaposed for reconstructing an Asian understanding of the Trinity. In chapter 6 we discuss Luther's eucharistic theology in relation to a Confucian spirituality of ancestral rites. The Western traditional debate about the Eucharist is seen by and large on the basis of spatial dimensions. When eucharistic theology meets Asian spirituality, it needs to be extended to include the time dimension in an eschatological sense. Here is the place where an Asian understanding of ancestors' rites would come to terms with the time dimension of the Eucharist, in which the coming Christ will be the cosmic Lord over all human beings in light of his descent into hell. Given this fact, Luther's language of Jesus' descent to hell will be compared to a Buddhist spirituality of universal compassion. An Asian reading of the story of Lot's wife will meet the Buddhist story of the woman *Janjanup*. A fusion of horizons with an Asian ecclesiology of the other will emerge.

In chapter 7 Luther and Karl Barth are brought into Buddhist-Christian encounter. Karl Barth is a follower of Luther, albeit one with reservations. Luther and Barth have not been fully discussed and integrated into interreligious dialogue. Barth's Japanese disciple, Katzumi Takizawa, responds to Barth's understanding of Japanese Buddhism. We will explore a connection between Karl Barth and religious pluralism. Luther's theological instincts of a cosmic and "universal" dimension will be explored and engaged in a dialogue with the Buddhist notion of *Sunyata*, self-awakening, *Soku*, etc. There will be a focus on three patterns of soteriology in Buddhism with respect to Luther's soteriology. Then I will ask to what extent Luther's idea of justification can converge with and diverge from the soteriology of Buddhism. A dialogue in particular will arise between Luther's justification and a Buddhist concept of justification in Shinran.

In conclusion, Luther and Asian theology will follow the same track, albeit in a different way, in the sense of doxology of God. The kingdom of God in Jesus Christ is not yet realized, but it is on the way. The mystery of the kingdom of God puts Luther and Asian spirituality before the same task of recognizing nature as the creation of God and affirming other religious ways in favor of solidarity with the humiliated and all living creatures *coram Deo et coram Mundi*. It is the theology of creation that entails also a spiritual dimension of doxology, but coming from the *theologia crucis*. In the afterword there will be a discussion of *theologia crucis* and its aesthetics in light of postmodern divinity. God's suffering on the cross revealed Godself as God's great compassion "in, under, and through" all living creatures and highlighted God's preferential option for scapegoats and victims in our postmodern world.

Abbreviations

BC	*The Book of Concord: The Confessions of the Evangelical Lutheran Church,* trans and ed. Theodore G. Tappert (Philadelphia: Fortress Press, 1959).
CD	*Church Dogmatics*, by Karl Barth, 13 vols. (New York: Harper & Row, Edinburgh: T. & T. Clark, 1936–62).
De Tri	Augustine. *De Trinitate*. Trans. Edmund Hill, OP, as *The Trinity* (New York: New City Press, 1991).
Handbuch	*Handbuch der Dogmen- und Thelogiegeschichte* Bd.1. Carl Andresen, Adolf Martin Ritter, Klaus Wesel, Ekkehard Mühlenberg, Martin Anton Schmidt (Göttingen: Vandenhoeck & Ruprecht, 1988).
Inst	*Institutes of the Christian Religion,* by John Calvin. Vols. 20 and 21 of the Library of Christian Classics, ed. By John T. McNeil (Philadelphia: Westminster, 1960).
LW	*Luther's Works,* American edition. Vol.1–30, ed. Jaroslav Pelikan (St. Louis: Concordia Publishing Company, 1955–67). Vols. 31–55, ed. Helmut T. Lehmann (Philadelphia: Fortress Press, 1955–86).
MLBTW	*Martin Luther's Basic Theological Writings*, ed. Timothy F. Lull (Minneapolis: Fortress Press, 1989).
RGG	*Die Religion in Geschichte und Gegenwart: Handwörterbuch für Theologie und Religions-wissenschaft* (Tübingen: J. C. B. Mohr, 1986).
ST	Thomas Aquinas, *Summa Theologia* (New York: Benzinger Bros., 1947).
WA	*D. Martin Luthers Werke. Kritische Gesamtausgabe.* 61 vols. (Weimar: Hermann Böhlaus Nachfolger, 1883–1983).

WA, TR	*D. Martin Luthers Werke: Kritische Gesamtausgabe, Tischreden*. 6 vols. (Weimar: Hermann Böhlaus Nachfolger, 1912–21).
BS I	*Buddhist Spirituality: Indian, Southeast Asian, Tibetan, Early Chinese,* ed. Takeuchi Yoshinori in Association with Jan Van Bragt, James W. Heisig, Joseph S. O'Leary, and Paul L. Swanson in Volume 8 of World Spirituality: An Encyclopedic History of the Religious Quest (New York: Crossroad, 1997).
BS II	*Buddhist Spirituality: Later China, Korea, Japan and the Modern World,* ed. Takeuchi Yoshinori in Volume 9 of World Spirituality: An Encyclopedic History of the Religious Quest (New York: A Herder & Herder Book, Crossroad, 1999).

* The English-language policy is to list surnames last. However, in Korea, what would be the surnames precede what would be the forenames.

He deserves to be called a theologian, however, who comprehends the visible and manifest things of God seen through suffering and the cross.

LW 31:40

Life is full of suffering

The Buddha

1

Martin Luther in the Context of Poverty and Religious Pluralism

Doing Theology in a Pluralistic Context

It becomes an inevitable reality in Asia that a way of dealing with the gospel/culture question turns into a gospel/religions question without further ado. Consider a story about a missionary and a tribal leader: A young missionary worked with a tribal group for several months and then sent a message to his senior colleague asking him to officiate at a baptism as the sign of recognizing them as Christians. The senior missionary arrived and made a plan for baptism on the following day. During the night the tribal council had a serious discussion, and then sent a message of regret that they had decided not to become Christians through baptism after all. Astounded, the senior missionary asked the tribal leaders whether his young colleague had informed them, clearly, of the privileges which they would receive—the forgiveness of sins and the assurance of eternal life in heaven. The leaders responded in earnest that the younger missionary had taught in a proper way about the meaning of baptism as a sacrament. Indeed, the problem was not his, but theirs. They were more concerned about the ongoing relations with their ancestors. They didn't mind the gift of baptism and going to a Christian heaven, but their ancestors would not be there in a Christian heaven, because they were not Christians. This was not acceptable to them, so they wished to continue with their ancestors even after death.[1]

A Christian heaven excluded those ancestors because of their unbelief or unknowing of Jesus Christ, which addresses the high cost of cutting

1. *Reformed World: Break the Chains of Injustice,* vol. 45, no. 4. (December 1995), 177–78.

them off from their traditional culture and spirituality. For Christians, the question of the gospel/culture nexus is often a difficult agenda to handle, because missionaries are afraid of mingling the sacred with the profane. They are afraid of syncretism—in other words, tainting or polluting Christ with the bad elements in profane cultures. In addition, it is believed that non-Western cultures are too inferior to be compatible with or approachable in Christianity. By and large these negative views about the interaction in the gospel/culture nexus have been uncovered and labeled as the arrogance of Western Christianity under the auspices of a Greco-Roman culture. This is also a postmodern challenge to logocentrism.[2]

If culture may be defined as the integrated pattern of human knowledge, belief systems, and corresponding behaviors, culture as a human universal has an essential diversity in the sense that culture varies with time and place. An understanding of universal culture calls for a form of contextual analysis. Theology as a part of culture is a human activity conditioned by its language, context, and diversity of belief systems. Revelation assumes and incarnates itself in human culture.[3] Therefore, theology does not merely fall from the heavens, but is an ongoing dialogue with revelation in its own historical and cultural perspective. Even in the world of the New Testament, various cultural "gospel understandings" are presented in a different way, but with integrative confession of God in Jesus Christ.

Since the Enlightenment, European culture has dominated all others in the American colonial setting in the name of spreading the gospel. A cultural imperialism was by and large camouflaged by mission and evangelism. It distorted cultural and environmental diversity. Indigenous cultures were suppressed, destroyed, and an alien culture was imposed in the name of propagating the gospel. The gospel was at times misused or manipulated as a tool of control and domination in the hands of one Western rationality culture. In this process, Western theology tends to lose sight of differences and distinctive qualities of non-Western cultures in relation to the gospel. The gospel, paradoxically speaking, has served not as good news but as bad, even ominous news in the name of evangelization by suppressing and dismissing the universally relevant insights of other cultures and religious ways for the narrative of the gospel.[4]

2. Cf. Sarup, *Introductory Guide*.

3. Cf. Tanner, *Theories of Culture*.

4. Cf. de Las Casas, *Devastation of the Indies*.

Religion expresses itself first in various aspects of symbol or mythological motifs. It is of social, historical, and ontological character. It is social in that it maintains the interrelation of individuals and groups in terms of religious values and beliefs. It is of historical character in expressing fundamental ontological continuity between human beings and religious tradition. A radical epistemological break with each paradigm is hard to maintain in spiritual life, because of its hermeneutical consciousness coupled with historical, religious, and cultural continuity. Therefore, the way that religion shapes human understanding in relation to history and tradition is not objective and static but dynamic, taking on a life of its own, producing inexhaustible possibilities of meaning.[5]

We focus on the significance of an ontological understanding of religion. From encountering the past and religious traditions, an understanding is rooted in a process of fusion of horizons. Thus in the working of tradition such fusion occurs constantly. From there, old and new grow together again and again in living value without one or the other ever being removed explicitly. As David Tracy insists, "all interpretation is a mediation of past and present, a translation carried on within the effective history of a tradition to retrieve its sometimes strange, sometimes familiar meanings."[6] The concept of a fusion of horizons may well express that human beings are not able to escape from their own historical tradition, and thus history becomes history of effect (H. G. Gadamer) for human beings and life. Different cultures and religions are intermingled and present in the process of understanding. Concerning the complexity of Asian religio-cultural realities, this hermeneutical process is explicitly seen in the co-existence or religious fusion of horizons in Shamanism, Buddhism, Islam, Hinduism, Confucianism, Christianity, etc.[7]

The organized world religions, such as Hinduism, Buddhism, and Islam have long traditions of both scholarship and mysticism. The Asian religions have much in common concerning spiritual, personal, moral, and social life in a humanitarian-cosmological view. These religions have triggered powerful criticism of injustice, inequality, and authoritarianism, as seen in the Indian independence movement led by Mahatma Gandhi, in the human rights struggle of Christianity in South Korea brilliantly

5. Gadamer, *Philosophical Hermeneutics*, xix.

6. Tracy, *Analogical Imagination*, 99.

7. Cf. Kim Kyoung-Jae, *Christianity and the Encounter of Asian Religions*.

propelled by indigenous minjung theology, and in the people's movement against Marcos in the Philippines. In Asia, cultures and religions, in spite of being humiliated and attacked as paganism by the Western missionaries, have prevailed and still remain influential.

In the Asian context of religious pluralism, a Christian's absolute claim of salvation is radically questioned and challenged. Several liberal-minded Asian theologians tend to go beyond the uniqueness of Christianity toward a pluralistic understanding of salvation, in which conversion does not play a role. Unlike liberation theology in Latin America, multi-religious dimensions of liberation remain the core element and become a challenge by demanding the partnership and dialogue of Asian theology and church.

Aloysius Pieris, a Roman Catholic theologian from Sri Lanka, is an experienced theologian in contact with Buddhism and in touch with many multi-religious groups in the struggle for the liberation of the poor. He affirmed strongly that the poor people of Asia are also very religious. According to him, theological reflection in Asia must take both these elements—poverty and religiosity—seriously. Insofar as poverty and religiosity come together in this way, both become liberative. This Pieris regards as the specificity of Asian liberation theology. In view of the evangelizing role of Christians in the encounter with non-Christians, what is more important for him is to bear witness to the spirituality common to all religions. At a theoretical level, core-experience, collective memory, and interpretation are used to help co-existing religions understand each other in a complementary and mutual way. His hermeneutical approach seems close to Dilthey's hermeneutics of trilogy, i.e., experience—expression—understanding.[8]

Interestingly enough, his interest in Asian liberation Christology takes the cross of Jesus seriously in a twofold way: (1) Jesus' struggle to be poor in terms of renunciation of the world, and (2) Jesus' struggle for the poor in terms of renunciation of Mammon organized into powers and principalities. These twofold ascetics make Jesus' way salvific. This aspect does not compete with buddhology, but complements it, so that the gnostic detachment of Buddhism comes to terms with the agapeic involvement of Christianity in a struggle for the liberation of the poor. This principle of complementarity deepens Pieris' concern in constructing an Asian liberation theology. That is to say, complementarity plays an important role in

8. Cf. Palmer, *Hermeneutics*, 107–18.

carrying out interreligious dialogue, with special focus on each religious core-experience of spirituality and liberation.

In Pieris' view, co-experience in Buddhism is gnosis or liberative knowledge, while in Christianity that comes from agape or redemptive love. However, for him both gnosis and agape are necessary, precisely because each in itself is inadequate so as to be a medium not only for experiencing, but also for expressing intimate human moments with the Ultimate Source of Liberation.[9]

Be that as it may, acknowledging the limitations of a point of view does not necessarily tend to relativism or subjectivism. According to Richard Niebuhr, "it is not evident that the man who is forced to confess that his view of things is conditioned by the standpoint he occupies must doubt the reality of what he sees."[10] Niebuhr's critical historical theology expresses a way of formulating a particular religious language in ongoing conversation with the past toward comprehending the future. An attempt to construct an Asian (post) confessional theology in this line involves self-criticism and self-limitation in dialogue with other churches as well as with wisdom from other religious traditions.

In a similar way, Karl Barth stresses, in the context of secular parables of God's reign, that the church can and may expect to hear "true words even from what seem to be the darkest places." True words may be heard even in "openly pagan" religious worlds, because according to the Word of reconciliation God does not deny humans—*Keine Menschenlosigkeit Gottes* (God is not without humans).

An attempt to make Luther relevant to another religious tradition such as Buddhism entails a significant effort to contextualize him. In so doing it can serve a better understanding and transformation of Luther's prophetic insights of *Solus Christus* into a universal dimension for today in an encounter with others.

Reading the scriptures from an Asian angle with a hermeneutic of suspicion (P. Ricoeur) does not necessarily lead to deconstructing or dissolving the gospel. It must not become a mere relative co-mediating thing among other religious truth claims. Therefore, it should go into a deeper understanding of co-experience of the ultimate reality. Unfortunately, once Western culture began to dominate others, starting with the

9. Pieris, "Buddha and the Christ," 163.

10. Niebuhr, *Meaning of Revelation*, 13.

Constantinization of Christianity, the gospel/culture nexus was changed to the power/knowledge nexus. Such a relationship was espoused and camouflaged in the name of establishing the church as the medium of salvation. The exclusivist strategy took no account of any values inherent in other cultures and religions. Indigenous cultures were suppressed and left behind. The reality of exclusivism is still powerful in many Asian fundamentalist Christian circles.

Theology and The Other

Theology is profoundly challenged to face the religious Other and recognize difference. In the Western Christian tradition the Other was labeled in a different way: it was pagan until the sixteenth century, and then unenlightened in the age of Reason. It is called primitive in the nineteenth century, and just different in the twentieth century. A century ago the privileged citizen of any developed Western nation—white, male, Protestant—did not have to confront the Other. Women, slaves, native peoples, and homosexuals were of course not invisible, but we successfully deproblematized, and unrecognized them. The unproblematic nature of otherness in earlier times was a result of the prevalence of what Jean-François Lytord calls "metanarratives."

Metanarrative is a grand story that attempts to explain the complex horizons of the human life-world by way of a totalizing concept. For instance, Kant's concept of transcendental-critical reason, Hegel's concept of absolute spirit, or the Marxist concept of class struggle and liberation are examples. These grand stories dislocate particularity and uniqueness grounded in the human life-world by reducing them into the one universal metanarrative. Metanarrratives shape a view of the world. In the power of metanarratives the voice of the Other is unheard, the presence of the Other as Other is unnoticed. In postmodernity, the abandonment of metanarrative means the encounter with the Other. The category of the Other in postmodernity represents the postmodern spirit of deconstructing modernism and resisting the status quo.[11]

Postmodern thought is characterized by its debate over the problem of modernity inherited from the Enlightenment. The Enlightenment project of modernity was and remains the triumph and mastery of human reason over the external world. At the same time it is by and large caused

11. Cf. Lyotard, *Postmodern Condition.*

by human bondage to technology, ecological devastation, and the exercise of instrumental reason. Reason becomes instrumental, not liberative, even though enlightening. Postmodern thinkers are outraged by the totalitarian arrogance of the Western culture of rationality. The absolute claim of reason is implicit in the mass extermination of the Nazi era, Stalinism, the scientific rationalism of the A-bomb in Hiroshima, the Holocaust, the Persian Gulf war in the Middle East, etc. The certainty of reason is a tyranny, which excludes what is uncertain, what doesn't fit in, what is different. To be sure, reason is indifferent to the Other.

In this regard Emmanuel Levinas has no hesitation in accusing Western philosophy of a totalizing or totalitarian discourse. Here the Other is always reduced to the same, subdued and captured by consciousness. The difference is domesticated, the Many is reduced to One. The task of philosophy is to overcome otherness. To protect the Other's otherness becomes the ethical imperative in face of a gigantic totalizing conspiracy of reason. The Other is not to be translated and comprehended through the rational coherence of language.[12]

To avoid the mistakes in the past there have been a number of theological efforts to pay attention to differences and distinctive qualities of other cultures and religions. Since the 1965 documents of the Second Vatican Council, Karl Rahner and Hans Küng have carried out a groundbreaking paradigm shift in recognizing other religious people outside Christianity as anonymous Christians (to use the phrase of Rahner) or anonymous children of God. Rahner's theory of "anonymous Christians" is not based on natural human desire for union with God, but on the supernatural existential which is built into us by God's free initiative of grace. In other words, God's self-communication in Jesus Christ is the source of our longing search for God. Thus the members of other religious traditions can live as anonymous Christians in the sincere practice of their religious beliefs. This is due to the supernatural existential structure, which comes out of God's universal grace in Jesus Christ.[13] However, Rahner's notion of the "anonymous Christians" would be offensive to non-Christians by forcing them into a category that they do not acknowledge. Would a Christian be happy were he/she to be called an "anonymous Shamanist?"

12. Barber, *Ethical Hermeneutics*, 13; Levinas, *Otherwise Than Being*, 162.

13. Cf. Dupuis, *Toward a Christian Theology*, 143–49.

This inclusivist strategy is ready to accept the values found in other religions. It is, however, inclined to see these as the preliminary stage of preparing for the gospel truth. Since then, much has been said about interreligious dialogue in light of which theological claims of Christian uniqueness are asked to face other religions and spiritualities in a multi-cultural context. There has been an insistence that the church/world dichotomy should be rejected, and that the church should learn from the world and otherness.

The recent shift of interest in ecumenical theology about interreligious dialogue points to the fact that Christianity is required to reflect on the pluralist demands of other religions. A term like "the theology of religions" makes a universal demand to include and integrate all religions and ideologies into the mystery of God as the Great Integrator. Such a pluralistic strategy, rejecting claims for a specific, particular, context-bound way, does not recognize the privilege of Christianity in any absolute sense, and even stresses total rejection of the postmodern incommensurability of religions and ideologies. Pluralism has now become the rule and ideology in welcoming, approving and affirming any ideas or practices. People in a pluralistic context are asked without reservation to enjoy the reality of pluralism. Pluralism that emerges from a situation of religious plurality and intercultural exchange has become "an experiential reality to everybody" in favor of promoting the proliferation of pluralism in both a factual and an ideological sense.[14] However, it would be naïve to assume that a theology of religions is so autonomous as to become a project of reducing all differences of religious languages into one Integrator.

To promote a pluralistic theology of religions, John Hick and Paul Knitter represent an epistemological break with the universal demand of Christianity, calling for the recognition of the validity of salvation in other religions. Christianity is to be given no hermeneutic privilege or normative status within religious plurality. God as great Integrator or Oneness has many different names (John Hick). Christian symbols, dogmas, and belief systems are reduced to represent a relative manifestation of the absolute meaning, or mere symbols of the absolute. It seems that such a claim is not theological, but religious-philosophically oriented. John Hick argued for a Copernican revolution in theology concerning the place of Christianity among world religions. In calling into question the traditional Christian

14. Pannenberg, "Religious Pluralism and Conflicting Truth Claims," *Christian Uniqueness Reconsidered*, ed. Leonard Swindler, 96.

position of salvation through Christ alone (which is according to him Ptolemaic), a Copernican revolution in theology involves a paradigm shift from the dogma of Christianity as the center to the model of God at the center around whom all the religions including Christianity revolve as planets revolve around the sun. Likewise in the works of Wilfred Cantwell Smith or Paul Knitter, the Christian claim to superiority is replaced by other ways of knowing about the one God or the absolute. In so doing, theology needs to encompass within its horizon the spiritual experience of other religions. According to Wilfred Cantwell Smith theology is inseparable from the history of religions: "From now on any serious intellectual statement of the Christian faith must include . . . some sort of doctrine of other religions. We explain the fact that the Milky Way is there by the doctrine of creation, but how do we explain that the Bhagavad-Gita is there?"[15]

Inclusivism of Christianity is challenged so as to embrace and yield to the position of pluralism. The line of Christian inclusivism no longer satisfies theologians of religions such as John Hick and other proponents of a pluralistic position. That is why all the world religions are equally valid as the instruments for salvation. However, the pluralist line of thought is likely to fall prey to the loss of one's own religious identity, even while maintaining and recognizing the otherness of other traditions with sincerity. The pluralist group is blamed for playing down the fact that different religions make conflicting truth claims.

According to Pannenberg, this strategy of pluralism is accused of reviving the old German liberal theology of Harnack and others in the nineteenth century.[16] What is more important for Pannenberg is to take in earnest the final future of God at the center in favor of genuine pluralism in which the Christian has the promise of God in Christ. However, the other religious traditions do not provide that particular eschatological hope. Christian uniqueness in a pluralistic context issues from the eschatological finality of Jesus Christ. Therefore, "the specific character of the Christian faith" is based on "a historical past and related to an eschatological future salvation." That being the case, "the truth claims of the Christian

15. Smith, "Christian in a Religiously Plural World," 100.

16. Pannenberg, "Religious Pluralism and Conflicting Truth Claims," 100.

proclamation are at its basis, and the differences with other religions finally result from conflicting truth claims."[17]

Be that as it may, Raimundo Panikkar among theologians of religions (ordained as a Roman Catholic priest in 1946) has proposed that religious traditions are incommensurable, because human reason is considered to be an insufficient criterion for evaluating religions. It is taken for granted in postmodern circles that reason is a contextual and relative reality, rather than existing as an absolute timeless validating norm or a transcendental reality. Likewise, according to Panikkar, Western theological universal truth claims need peeling away like an onion to show their christic, universal vision in face of the mystery of God from the cosmotheandric perspective. Panikkar's defense of pluralism represents spiritcentrism as insubordinate either to the logocentrism or eschatoncentrism to which Western thought would be attached.

Panikkar symbolizes the history of Christianity in relation to other religions by way of three sacred rivers. Mahatma Gandhi once used a river analogy: "One may drink out of the same great rivers with others, but one need not use the same cup"; "The soul of religion is one, but it is encased in a multitude of forms. My position is that all the great religions are fundamentally equal."[18] Panikkar's metaphor of a river is exemplified up to the point of calling for a pluralistic plunge into the river Ganges. In fact, the rivers of the earth do not meet each other, not even in the ocean, nor do they need to meet in order to be truly life-giving rivers. But where do they meet? It is in the skies—that is, in heaven.[19] His poignant question runs like this; "Does one need to be spiritually a Semite or intellectually a Westerner in order to be a Christian?"[20] Unfortunately, this statement runs in an anti-Semitic direction.

The Jordan stamped Christianity indelibly with its Jewish origin and with all its historical ties to all the particular events of Israel. At this point, Jesus stands for exclusivism. Here Christianity is the only true absolute religion. Likewise, the Tiber in Rome exercises influence on Christianity with its medieval crusades and its imperial mission. It stands for the Western mentality of Christendom, in which all rivers lead to Christianity

17. Ibid., 102.

18. Cf. Demarest, *General Revelation*, 255.

19. Panikkar, "Jordan, The Tiber, and The Ganges," 92.

20. Ibid., 89.

as all roads to Rome. Here inclusivism is made explicit in Roman Catholic official relations to non-Christian religions. However, Panikkar uses the mother river of the Ganges as a symbol for recognizing the otherness of the other religions and thus encompassing all other religions and traditions in Asia, Africa, and Oceania. What is important for Panikkar is the readiness to adopt a pluralistic attitude, flowing peacefully, plunging into the Ganges.[21] The Ganges, which is formed from many sources and runs in diverging outlets, stands for contemporary pluralism. Panikkar's awareness of Christianness comes to the fore instead of doctrinal Christianity or institutional Christendom. Nevertheless, Panikkar's vision of Christianness does not adequately consider the particular-universal dimension of Jewish-Christian tradition.

In an attempt to bring Christianity over the Rubicon into pluralistic theology, Knitter makes note of three principal strategies, that is to say, three bridges across the Rubicon. The first is a "historico-cultural" bridge in the name of historical relativity, in light of which both exclusivists and inclusivists appear presumptuous with their excessive attachment to the truth claim of Christian absoluteness. The second is the "theologico-mystical" bridge in the name of the divine mystery that exceeds human linguistic and conceptual formulation. The third is the "ethico-practical" bridge in the name of justice and peace. It is well expressed by Hans Küng: "no world peace without peace among the religions, no peace among the religions without dialogue between the religions, and no dialogue between the religions without accurate knowledge of one another."[22]

Beyond both the conservative exclusivist approach and liberal inclusivist approach, Paul Knitter calls for a new paradigm of the pluralist position, which means "a move away from the insistence on the superiority or finality of Christ and Christianity towards recognition of the independent validity of other ways. Such a move came to be described by the participants in our project as the crossing of a theological Rubicon."[23]

However, the metaphor of crossing a theological Rubicon (reminiscent of Caesar's crossing of the same river in 49 BCE) is subject to skepticism due to its formidable project of including the Other, differences, and uniqueness within its own integrating framework. In editing *Christian*

21. Ibid., 109.

22. Küng, "Christianity and World Religions," 194.

23. D'Costa, ed., *Christian Uniqueness Reconsidered*, viii.

Uniqueness Reconsidered: The Myth of a Pluralistic Theology of Religions, Gavin D'Costa calls into question whether pluralistic theology is an adequate or even appropriate approach to religious pluralism. According to John Cobb, interreligious dialogue can only take place on the basis of the recognition that each tradition of religion is unique in its own way and has different goals in many instances. His position is summarized as the position against pluralism in favor of "a fuller and more genuine pluralism." Therefore, "normative thinking within each tradition can be expanded and extended through openness to the normative thinking of others."[24]

Critically speaking of a pluralistic theology of religions, Moltmann sheds light on not losing identity, but attaining a deeper understanding of identity in engaging dialogue with other religions. For him, Christian-Marxist dialogue in the European context as a model for interreligious dialogue shows how to deal with issues of ethics, practice, and justice. What is more promising for Moltmann is to bear witness to the truth of one's own religion without falling victim to the relativism of a multicultural society. Dialogue is formed in the following way: "from anathema to dialogue—from dialogue to co-existence—from co-existence to convivence—from convivence to cooperation."[25]

At this point Moltmann proposes a twofold level of dialogue. Direct dialogue has to do with confrontation and comparison of different religious concepts even including the animist religions of Africa, Australia and America. Indirect dialogue has do to with social, political, and environmental issues.[26]

Two tendencies are discernible surrounding the debates about the theology of religions: the first is a blending of the exclusivist and pluralist positions' emphasis respecting the incommensurability of other religious traditions, at the same time concentrating on one's own; the second is a combination of the inclusivist and pluralist options, stressing the value and richness of other religious ways while insisting on the hermeneutical necessity of one's own limitation. The Gadamerian concept of "fusion of horizons" is taken into consideration, maintaining a specific, particular, context-bound way into the diversity of religions. Although I do not recognize the privilege of Christianity in any absolute sense, I am bound

24. Cobb, "Beyond 'Pluralism,'" 86.
25. Moltmann, *Experiences in Theology*, 20.
26. Ibid., 20–21.

to encounter other religions from my own perspective. A theological approach to other religions poses the question of how to encounter the different as different.

The dialogue should not remain at a metaphysical level, i.e., for the sake of dialogue, but needs to be motivated toward renewing and transforming social and ecological conditions threatening life for the sake of practical consequences. Listening to the challenges of other religions would be an integral part of Christian theology in a postmodern context. The dialogical relation with the religions of Asia provides "a similar opportunity for reconceptualization in and through engagement with Eastern wisdom."[27] Without engaging in serious conversation with the other great ways, a Christian systematic theology would be impossible. In interreligious conversation, the Christian learns from searching the different ways of Others for the unfathomable mystery of God in which they experience a universal revelation of God. However, the debate in interreligious dialogue is complicated and provocative, and still has no satisfactory solution. Only further dialogue will tell where it goes with the hermeneutics of suspicion and retrieval.[28]

A Buddhist-Christian Conversation Revisited

Buddhism has gotten more and more into dialogue with Christianity since the Second Vatican Council, which has affirmed a "more dynamic, evolutionary concept of the reality" of the church by putting an end to the long burdened European, Greek, rationalistic theology. In considering the relationship between Christianity and other religions, a conversation is encouraged to prepare for dialogue with religions outside Christianity. On the Protestant side, however, it was Paul Tillich who began to renew and deepen his understanding of Buddhism by his visit to Japan, where he met some eminent Buddhist scholars, Buddhist and Shinto priests, and Christian leaders and missionaries in discussions between Christianity and Buddhism. His book after the trip, *Christianity and the Encounter of World Religions*, may be regarded as the first publication articulating his encounter with Buddhism in a systematic manner.[29] Tillich's approach, based on a dynamic typology of Buddhist-Christian conversation, becomes an

27. Cobb, "Religions," 371.

28. Tracy, *Dialogue with the Other*, 79–83.

29. Cf. Tillich, *Christianity and the Encounter of World Religions*.

example for "making inroads into Buddhist spirituality" in the dialogical-personal way.[30]

However, in accepting Tillich's dialogical approach, Masao Abe makes it possible to facilitate a Christian-Buddhist encounter at a deeper level in which he makes some corrections to Tillich's understanding of Buddhist ideas.[31] Prior to Tillich, it was Karl Barth who dealt with Pure Land Buddhism in Japan in light of the name of Jesus Christ. He saw the grace element in Pure Land Buddhism in a positive way, which has a providential disposition. In Pure Land Buddhism there is a lack of a critical resistance to cultic-ethical righteousness, argued Barth. What is an unsurpassable difference between the two religions is the lack of the name of Jesus Christ. The name Jesus Christ might not be confined to Christianity, but God's eternal Immanuel for the world and the entire human race.[32] It is not the church, but the kingdom of God that makes Christianity a genuine religion before God. Barth's approach is to find symptoms of the kingdom of God in Buddhism, in which God's strange voices outside the walls of Christianity play a decisive role in leading Christianity to self-criticism and radical openness toward the other.[33]

In like manner, Barth's understanding of Buddhism was responded to and corrected by his Japanese disciple Katzumi Takizawa at a deeper level for making clear similarity and difference on both sides. Kim Kyoung-Jae, who is a prolific Korean theologian representing an Asian minjung theology of religions and cultures, thinks a Barthian criticism of Amida faith does not hit the mark of Pure Land Buddhism. Regardless of whether these evaluations are correct, it is worthwhile to note what Barth has contributed for Buddhist-Christian dialogue.

What is Buddhism? Its teaching can be divided in general into three main traditions: Theravada (Hinayana) Buddhism, Mahayana Buddhism (including Zen Buddhism), and Vajrayana Buddhism. After the Enlightenment under the Bodhi tree at Bodhgaya in India, the Buddha first taught Hinayana Buddhism, that is, the Four Noble Truths. After that, Gautama taught Mahayana Buddhism, which put emphasis on the path of Emptiness and compassion. This path is sometimes called

30. Ibid., 38.

31. Abe, *Zen and Western Thought*, 175–85.

32. *CD*, I/2:342.

33. For the strange voice of God outside the walls of Christianity, see *CD*, I/1:55, and IV/3.1:115–25.

the Great Bodhisattva Way, which is well expressed in the vow not to enter the infinite stillness and bliss of *Nirvana* until the last sentient being is released from suffering. Finally, the Buddha taught Zen. Twenty-five hundred monks assembled at the Vulture's Peak to hear the Buddha. He didn't open his mouth at all, and only sat there without any movement. As time went by, he picked up a single flower and held it up. Nobody knew what it meant. Only one monk, Mahakashyapa, smiled broadly from the back of the assembly. Then the Buddha said, "I transmit my true Dharma to you." He gave Mahakashyapa transmission, making him the Buddha's first successor.[34]

The classical answer to the question "what is Buddhism?" is expressed well in terms of the taking of refuge in three supreme realities: the Buddha (literally, the awakened one), the Dharma (the teaching of the historical Buddha), and the Sangha (Buddhist community). These are "the three jewels" beyond all prices. The well known formulation of the Dharma finds its classic locus in the Four Noble Truths: (1) Life is full of suffering (*dukkha*); (2) suffering is caused by craving or thirst for desires of the senses; (3) suffering can be stopped by the cessation of this craving, which means the attainment of *Nirvana*; and (4) there is a path that leads to the cessation of suffering, namely, nirvanic liberation through the practice of the Eightfold path of right view, right thought, right speech, right action, right livelihood, right effort, right mindfulness, and right meditation.[35]

With the Four Noble truths, we come to the relationship between suffering, dependent co-origination, cessation, and the path. That all things are suffering is the basic insight of the Buddha. Everything is impermanent, so everything is always changing. Because we are attached to things, we constantly suffer. There are eight sufferings: the first four are birth, old age, sickness, and death; the last four are being separated from those you love, being in the presence of those you dislike, not getting what you desire, and the imbalance of the five skandhas (aggregates).

Buddhist teaching on suffering, therefore, is based on the fact that everything is impermanent. This is the basic insight into impermanence—no suffering without attachment. When ignorance appears in our mind, the ego appears, and then everything appears. This refers to the teaching of twelve links in the chain of dependent co-origination, which is the second

34. Zen Master Seung Sahn, *Compass of Zen*, 20.

35. *BS* 1, xv–xvi.

Noble Truth. For example, when ignorance disappears, mental formations disappear. When mental formations disappear, consciousness disappears. When consciousness disappears, name and form disappear. Eventually life and death, old age and sickness also disappear, because everything comes from our mind. This is the way to stop suffering, the third Noble Truth.

What is characteristic of Buddhism lies in its realistic perception of the world as it is. Its goal is to overcome a samsaric reality of life and birth cycles entangled in the cosmological *dukkha* (suffering). The Four Noble Truths become manifest in the realistic and acute realization of, and the serious attempt to overcome, the suffering at the heart of which Buddha's teaching lies. By *dukkha* the Buddha means that human existence, including all sentient living creatures, suffers from a fundamental and cosmological alienation because the conditions of suffering and unsatisfaction are correlated with the impermanence of all things, which is chained to the circle of birth and death in the world of becoming (Sanskrit: *samsara*). For Buddhism, real suffering lies exactly in the inclination inherent in human nature to seek after and cling to pleasure, while avoiding and averting suffering. The more we try to cling to pleasure and avoid suffering, the more intertwined and entangled we become in the duality of pleasure and suffering. This is where *dukkha* occurs. When Gautama the Buddha remarks that "existence is characterized by suffering," he refers to "the reality of this non-relative suffering," meaning the whole process constituting suffering.[36]

The path to stopping the suffering is called the Eightfold path. *Sila* (precepts) represents right speech, right action, and right livelihood. Right effort, right mindfulness, and right meditation are represented by *samadhi* (meditation). Right view and right thought are represented by *prajna* (wisdom). There are three basic insights of Buddhism: (1) all compounded things are impermanent; what is unchanging is our true nature; (2) in attaining this world's impermanence we attain that "all Dharmas are without self-nature"; and (3) everything appears out of Emptiness and eventually returns to Emptiness. The world is already completely empty and still. The Psalmist says, "be still and know that I am God," so also Buddhism says "all Dharmas come from complete stillness." This stillness is true Emptiness. It is the nature of our mind and the whole universe. As the Catholic mystic Angelius Silesius says,

36. Cf. Abe, *Buddhism and Interfaith Dialogue*, 74.

The God who is pure emptiness
Is created as form.
Becoming substance, light and darkness
The stillness and the storm.[37]

If the Four Noble Truths and the Eightfold path are basic and central to Hinayana, Mahayana adds the six Perfections (*paramita*) as the core of bodhisattva practice. The six Perfections include a social dimension that is donation and forbearance in addition to the Eightfold path.

Unlike Hinayana, which stresses benefits to the individual alone through its goal of self-perfection, Mahayana asserts that all sentient beings possess the Buddha-nature, the disposition and capacity to attain Buddhahood. They are capable of becoming bodhisattvas through the bodhisattva's vows, self-awakening and the six Perfections. The bodhisattva concept is broadened in Mahayana Buddhism to emphasize that any being (*sattva*) is capable of aspiring to Enlightenment (*bodhi*). The primary goal of Mahayana is to fulfill the bodhisattva vows to bring all sentient beings to Enlightenment.

From here arose Pure Land Buddhism, which is based on the story of the bodhisattva named Dharmakara. He made forty-eight vows of compassion in order to save sentient beings in the world of suffering. The bodhisattva Dharmakara achieved Buddhahood and became Amida after long practice. He is called both the Buddha of Infinite Life and the Buddha of Infinite Light. Since Amida is able to save all sentient beings through his vows, his teaching is of universal character.

A mutual renewal and transformation in dialogue with a school of Amida Buddhism and the Bodhisattva teachings in Japanese Mahayana Buddhism is brilliantly proposed by John Cobb. Interreligious conversation can benefit both religions. Each renews and deepens the other, and both maintain their differences. Cobb brings the teaching of salvation in Shinran (1173–1262), the founder of the true teachings of Pure Land Buddhism, into conversation with Luther's theology of justification. According to Shinran, a human being is only to be saved by the Amida-Buddha and is reborn in the Pure Land. Therefore, it suffices for receiving grace and salvation to recite and pray with the name "Nembutsu" (*Namu-Amidabutsu* = Amen, Amida-Buddha).

37. See Seung Sahn, *Compass of Zen*, 106.

Cobb's interest in carrying out mutual transformation through the praxis of dialogue becomes clear in his insistence that Amida Buddhism can deepen and renew its self-understanding in an encounter with Christianity, as conversely Christianity could with respect to Buddhism. His understanding of a "buddhized Christianity" would occur in being renewed by Christ as the principle of the Transformation. Christ is the Way. Not as in the exclusive Way, but allowing different ways in itself Christ can serve as the inspiration for correcting, renewing, and transforming in every religious way.

Therefore "a Christocentric Catholic theology" gains in prominence for Cobb. The goal is to represent an alternative way beyond absolutism or relativism. Cobb's attempt is a crossing over to Mahayana Buddhism and a coming back to Christianity in favor of mutual transformation. This proves to be a hermeneutic strategy for transforming Christianity through Buddhist insights and achievement without displacing or dislocating the centrality of Christ.[38]

It is David Tracy who pays more attention to the greatest affinity between the Mahayana Buddhism of Nagarjuna (represented and rethought in the contemporary modern Kyoto school of Nishida, Tanabe, Nishitani, Takeyushi, Abe, and others) and French deconstructive post-modern philosophy like that of Gilles Deleuze and Jacques Derrida. Of course, Tracy does not ignore the difference between the Buddhist notion of "not-two" (non-duality)—namely, "a metaphysical, yet anti-metaphysical character" of Mahayana Buddhism—and the French postmodern celebration of Nietzschean difference and dissension.[39] Whereas the deconstructionists strongly affirm difference, the Kyoto school celebrates non-duality. To develop an analogical imagination through Buddhist-Christian dialogue, while engaging in the dialogue as a committed Christian theologian, Tracy proposes to take three elements into account. The primary element is "self-respect" for one's own tradition. Secondly, Tracy accounts for "a self-exposure" to the other religion as the terror of otherness; and thirdly, there must be an attitude of "willingness" on the side of the dialogue partner to allow for the process and challenge of mutual questioning and inquiry. A willingness even to risk one's own understanding "in the presence of the

38. Cobb, *Beyond Dialogue*, 142–3. Cf. Cobb, *Transforming Christianity*, 84.

39. Tracy, *Dialogue With The Other*, 70–71.

other" might constitute the dialogue in an authentic sense.[40] Furthermore, a conversation should be carried out in face of and in recognition of the otherness in which conversion is out of the question. Tracy calls for a mystico-prophetic model to make interreligious dialogue an integral part of all theological thought.[41]

As far as the Buddhist liberation of *Nirvana* is concerned, it comes about through extinguishing the craving deeply rooted in the ego. *Nirvana*, which is an existential awakening to egolessness or selflessness (*anatta* or *anatman*), can be attained only through liberation from craving or attachment to the dualistic view. *Nirvana*, the Middle Way that transcends the very duality of pleasure and suffering, even including that of human beings and divinity, calls for the death of the ego to live the life of the true self. Therefore, a Buddhist *Sunyata* or Emptiness is, according to Abe, neither nihilistic nor monistic absolutism, but dynamic relativism beyond the opposition between relativism and absolutism. In Emptiness everything is realized as it is in its total dynamic reality to be free from God and to overcome Nietzschean nihilism.[42] A Buddhist concept of *Sunyata* comes to the focus in an encounter with a Christian concept of God.

What is the *Sunyata*? The term "Middle Way" in the classic idea of the historical Buddha was presented as a way of avoiding the extreme poles between the right Scylla of "eternalism" and the left Charybdis of "materialistic annihilationism."[43] In so doing, "dependent co-origination"—"relationality" (Sanskrit: *pratitya-samutpada*), the most basic and central idea of Buddhism—has been developed to the extent of indicating that everything without exception is dependent on something else. Therefore, the Buddha bid a farewell to the traditional Upanishadic notion of Brahman as the ultimate power of the universe and in so doing declared that everything without exception is transitory and changeable—perishable.

In its standard form we see twelve links: ignorance, volitional actions, consciousness, psychophysical phenomena, the sense faculties, contact, sensation, thirst, clinging, the process of becoming, birth, and finally pain—and death. It is said that the Buddha began his teaching of the *Sunyata* in the *Avatamsaka*-sutra, which is one of the main sutras of the

40. Ibid., 73; cf. Tracy, *Analogical Imagination*, 446–57.

41. Ibid., 94.

42. Abe, *Buddhism and Interfaith Dialogue*, 79–80.

43. *BS* 1, 11.

Mahayana tradition. According to Theravada Buddhism, the whole world is a realm of suffering. To get out of this suffering one must attain complete Emptiness, *Nirvana.* However, Mahayana Buddhism begins with complete Emptiness. If you attain this Emptiness your suffering will disappear because suffering is also empty. That the world is suffering should be extended to the teaching of Emptiness. In other words, "Mahayana Buddhist teaching begins at this point of complete Emptiness; Hinayana Buddhist teaching culminates in it."[44]

If originally everything is fundamentally empty, everything in the whole universe is the same substance because the substance is empty. This is the insight into existence and nonexistence of the Dharmas. The experience of Emptiness reveals the ultimate truth of the world, just as it is. The Emptiness is truth itself because everything is empty. In this regard, the Mahayana way of teaching takes Emptiness as the starting point where Theravada leaves off.[45] Therefore, the Middle Way refers to the path of Emptiness. Later development of Nagarjuna's Middle Way in India, China, and Korea expanded the definition of *Sunyata* to include "true Emptiness."

The teaching of Emptiness finds its firm logical underpinning on the basis of the Madhyamika tradition of Nagarjuna (ca. 150-250 CE). In demonstrating the Emptiness of all things in dependent co-origination, the idea of Emptiness expresses its aim in overcoming all form of dualistic thinking. The idea of Emptiness is, in fact, the true nature of the real beyond human words or concepts.

However, in so doing it is noticeable that Nagarjuna's logic of Emptiness may be inclined to nihilistic perils. That being the case, a Buddhist understanding of no-self moves in an affirmative sense to realize Emptiness and dependent co-origination through such practices as Zazen meditation rather than retaining the doctrine of the no-self in the negative sense. It would be difficult to see an example in Western philosophy or theology as radical as the Buddhist idea of no-self.[46]

Besides, it seems difficult to lead a conversation between Buddhism and Christianity from the Ch'an (Zen) iconoclastic perspective. "Encountering a Buddha, kill the Buddha. Encountering a patriarch, kill the patriarch.

44. Seung Sahn, *Compass of Zen*, 116.

45. Ibid., 122.

46. Abe, *Zen and Western Thought*, 3–83; cf. Tracy, *Dialogue with The Other*, 75.

. . . Only thus does one attain liberation and detachment from all things, thereby becoming completely unfettered and free." This sounds blasphemous to Christianity.[47] Zen Buddhism never does talk about an absolute, nor does it try to explain Emptiness or a complete world. It refers to a momentary world. In one moment there is everything. In a moment there is nothing. There is no mind, no Buddha, no God—nothing. But there is mind, Buddha, God—everything. Zen Buddhism's goal is experiencing that. How would this insight be reconciled with Christian doctrine?

The Christian understanding of the one God who is essentially transcendent, self-existing as absolute love, grace, mercy, etc., apart from everything relative, is regarded as caught in a state of obsession or false image. A Buddhist notion of *Sunyata* that is grounded on mutual relativity or interdependency is strongly affirmed as the ultimate truth because through the Buddhist awakening we know that everything is mutually related to each and every other thing. According to Abe, this is the essential aspect of a dynamic relativism transcending the opposition between a fixed relativism and absolutism at the heart of which the teaching of dependent co-origination does lie. Given this fact, John Cobb underscores that the absolute Nothingness or *Sunyata* in Buddhism cannot be fused into the Christian faith in the Ultimate Reality.[48]

Be that as it may, we notice that in Buddhist tradition the doctrine of *Trikaya* Buddha has been shaped and developed in the direction of the Yogacara form of Buddhism in response to the nihilistic risks of Nagarjuna's Middle Way. According to Nagarjuna's logical refutation on the basis of the insight on Emptiness, all truth claims are to be called into question, even suspecting the essential doctrines of Buddhism (such as Four Noble Truths) as illusory views. A thorough deconstructive method comes to the fore by the negation and removal of clinging to fixed truths, whereby the experience of self-awakening becomes open in a new way. Although rejecting nihilism, the idea that everything is empty does not allow for maintaining the validity of any doctrinal discourses, even in constant tension with the doctrinal affirmation of dependent co-origination.[49]

Certainly, the essential teaching of the Middle Way of Nagarjuna was affirmed in the context of Yogacara, but in so doing a new attempt was

47. Abe, *Zen and Western Thought*, 187.

48. Cobb, *Beyond Dialogue*, 110–18.

49. *BS*, 1, 204.

made to ground insight into *Sunyata* through a critical understanding of the mind. What is more interesting to Buddhist-Christian conversation is a Buddhist understanding of the three bodies. *The Astasahasrika Perfection of Wisdom* makes a clear distinction between the physical body of the Buddha (*rupakaya*) and his *dharma-kaya*. The contrast of the Buddha's physical form with his *dharma-kaya*, which would lead to disparagement and devaluation of the Buddha's physical body, was introduced to criticize *stupa* worship. The Buddha's Dharma-body replaces the worship of *stupas* containing the Buddha relics after his death. The *dharma-kaya* is the body (or collection) of ultimate truths. The appeal to the spiritual body (*dharma-kaya*) rather than the form-body *(rupakaya*) emerges. Of course, the familiar three-body doctrine is not found in the early *Perfection of Wisdom* or in the writings of Nagarjuna. In accordance with *Astasahasrika*, Nagarjuna mentions a physical body and a *dharma-kaya*. For Nagarjuna it is about neither non-being nor being, neither annihilation nor permanence, neither non-eternal, nor eternal. It may not be categorized in terms of duality. Therefore, it cannot be praised. However, the *Ta-chih-tu lun* (*Mahaprajnaparamita Sutra*) attributed to Nagarjuna by Chinese tradition refers to the *dharma-kaya* as not Emptiness but rather as the supramundane qualities of the Buddha.[50]

Cittamatra texts whose sources are the *Mahayanasutralamkara* and its commentary, and Asanga's *Mahayanasamgraha* generally refer to the Buddha possessing three bodies. The first form of Buddha is *dharma-kaya* or *svahavikakaya,* which is the Essence Body. In other words, it represents the eternal cosmic Buddha-nature, which means the essential or fundamental dimension of the cosmos. The second body is known as *sambhoga-kaya*, the Body of Complete Enjoyment. It is the impermanent body, in fact the glorified body, of the Buddha that appears seated on a lotus throne in a Pure Land preaching the Mahayana to the assembly.

Therefore, the Mahayana sutras are based on the teaching of the Enjoyment Body's preaching, rather than the so-called historical Buddha Siddhartha Gautama. It is the actual Buddha in his supramundane form appearing for the benefit and enjoyment of the Bodhisattvas in mysterious ways. It is the Buddha of Buddhist devotion. The third form is *nirmana-kaya*; the Transformation body, which is incarnated as the historical Buddha, like Gautama Siddhartha. The Transformation body manifests

50. Williams, *Mahayana Buddhism*, 174.

itself in any suitable way. In this regard, Buddhists have no objection to regarding the historical Jesus as a Transformation Body Buddha. It is a manifestation from the Enjoyment Body out of compassion for the benefit of beings in a particular time and space. If Zen Buddhism remains militant-iconoclastic, a Buddha-*trikaya* doctrine must also be out of consideration. If Zen Buddhism sticks purely to the absolute Nothingness in total rejection of reality itself or the phenomenal world, it is likely to fall into abstract reality as the great Korean Buddhist monk Wonhyo warned.[51]

Buddhist-Christian dialogue teaches us that the two religions do not work in the same way, nor in totally different ways, but they are non-dual, "not-two." As the dialogue continues and develops, dialectics between a hermeneutics of suspicion and retrieval would come into focus. A reality of religious pluralism is inevitable especially for Asian Christianity. To become a Christian in an Asian context seems to entail a choice between two options—that is, a militantly exclusive fundamentalist way of rejecting other religions as chimeras, or a tolerant liberal way of relativizing Christianity not only by affirming other revelations and ways of salvation, but also even by running the risk of plunging Christian identity and uniqueness into the pluralistic river. However, there is a need to carry out interreligious dialogue at a deeper personal level so as to seek a unique way beyond exclusivism or pluralistic relativism while remaining a committed Christian with a radical openness to otherness.

A Conversation with Martin Luther in an Asian Context

Given the complexity of doing theology in a multi-religious context, it would be controversial or even dubious to bring Luther to the interreligious agenda from an Asian perspective. As Timothy Lull complains, there has not been enough reading *of* Luther and too much reading *about* him.[52] An attempt to bring Luther into the context of poverty and spiritualities of world religions calls for a hermeneutic of suspicion and retrieval in meeting Luther in an Asian context.

Images of Luther have been caricatured and sometimes distorted, particularly during the Third Reich in Germany. His varied attitude toward the Jews, from "that Jesus Christ Was Born A Jew" (1523) to his work "On the Jews and Their Lies"(1543), was contextually bound and

51. Kim Kyoung-Jae, *Christianity and the Encounter of Asian Religions*, 170.

52. Lull, *Conversations with Martin Luther*, 140.

has aroused heavy debates. In addition, his political theology of the two-kingdom doctrine gave a basis for the political authorities to suppress and destroy those who stood up for the sake of socio-political justice and liberation. Luther's urge of the Princes to "stab, smite, and slay" the rebellious peasants exemplified his notorious political conservatism.[53]

Again, a conservative line was drawn from Luther's political views to the political quietism of German Christians in the Third Reich. However, there is another aspect of progressive thought in Luther himself that is open to social and economic change and is energetic in the creation of education, the public welfare system, and public health. In addition, Luther's political heritage has been developed in various different directions—not only toward the political authoritarianism of Prussia or the Third Reich, but also toward the social democracy of the Nordic countries. We must recognize a prophetic interpretation of Martin Luther by Lutheran representatives of the Confessing church, running counter to Neo-Lutheran interpretations.[54] There is, furthermore, a Marxist reading of Martin Luther.[55] Thus it is difficult to make generalizations about Luther without further ado.

As Heiko Oberman cautions, Luther was a child of his time who cannot merely be transplanted to our emerging, postmodern era.[56] Nonetheless, we see why Luther gains prominence in our current ecumenical dialogue. There is something profound in his thought that is still insightful and provocative to learn from. Interestingly enough, liberation theology in Latin America has recently paid attention to Luther, for Luther can be characterized as the one in favor of the movement of liberation in the age to come.

Even in the eyes of liberation theologians, Luther can be seen as the protagonist who is to bring about a grand process of liberation for future generations. In due respect, Luther is regarded as "a necessary point of reference for all who seek liberation and know how to struggle and suffer for it."[57] From the Latin American perspective, Luther's teaching of justification by grace and faith is highly acclaimed as the radical principle of equality among human beings and of the valuing of each one of them

53. Luther, "Against the Robbing and Murdering Hordes of Peasants" (1525), in *LW* 46:54.

54. Cf. Iwand, *Luthers Theologie*.

55. Cf. Koch, *Luthers Reformation in Kommunistischer Sicht*.

56. Oberman, *Luther*, 314.

57. Shaull, *Reformation and Liberation Theology*, 25.

before God. This teaching stands in opposition to forms of discrimination against persons and limitations on the quality and dignity of their lives.[58]

In the context of African American experience with Luther, theologians and pastors take issue with the European-American understanding of justification, out of which occurs a radical dichotomy between justification and sanctification. Sanctification or social justice should be an integral part of justification. Bringing about justice for the benefit of the victims deepens and actualizes the right relationship between God and human beings, and between human among themselves. Therefore, Luther's doctrine of the two kingdoms is open to criticism because it dichotomizes reality by playing off spiritual liberation against socio-political liberation. There arises a strong demand that the liberating impulse of Luther's teaching on the two kingdoms be rediscovered for those suffering under a socio-political structure of injustice and violence.

Unlike liberation theology, Asian theology, as we have already mentioned, is surrounded with multi-religious spiritualities and their unique claims for the salvific way. Doing theology in an Asian context means struggling with overwhelming impoverishment, on the one hand, and engaging in dialogue with multifaceted religiousness, on the other hand. Poverty and spirituality are inseparable, forming one and the other side of the same coin. This situation is a real challenge for Asian Christians. There is a strong advocacy in Asian theology for accepting the pluralism of religions beyond exclusivism or inclusivism, even as many groups of Asian Christians show preference for the fundamentalism of Western Christianity in the nineteenth century. On the other hand, Panikkar's phrase, "plunge into the Ganges," becomes a popular way for liberal Asian Christians to doubt the universal claim of Christianity.

Luther's sensitivity to others, his limitations notwithstanding, is expressed well in his reflection on the irregular grace of God. Consider Luther's reflection on Ishmael: "For the expulsion does not mean that Ishmael should be utterly excluded from the kingdom of God. . . . The descendents of Ishmael also joined the church of Abraham and became heirs of the promise, not by reason of a right but because of irregular grace."[59]

58. Altmann, *Luther and Liberation*, 5. Regrettably, Altmann does not pay attention to the consequences of Luther's doctrine of justification for his Eucharistic theology.

59. Luther, "Lectures on Genesis chap. 21–25," in *LW*, 4:42–44; cf. *LW*, 1:301.

Taking God's irregular grace seriously, I am interested keenly in retrieving Martin Luther as an irregular thinker from a post-foundational and hermeneutical perspective. According to Luther, the speech action of God is not simply reduced to his regular and confessional (or foundational) theology. As Luther argues, "God has to speak in a different way. If God opens the mouth, and lets a word forward, so it works . . . Also God has grasped, with this short word, the whole of the gospel and kingdom of Christ, so that nobody can eradicate it."[60]

In the Lutheran tradition, Dietrich Bonhoeffer is paradigmatic. He read Scripture in various contexts and the situation of the world in which Christians find themselves. Reminiscent of Luther's statement, Bonhoeffer expresses his marvelous sensitivity to others. "The curses of the godless sometimes sound better in God's ear than hallelujahs of the pious."[61] Luther condemned reason as a whore, and Lukács condemned the Nazis for destroying reason. However in the period of National Socialism, Bonhoeffer found the key to reason in openness to others.[62] In his prison cell Bonhoeffer represents a theology for others—that is, "the excluded, the suspect, the maltreated, the powerless, the oppressed, the reviled—in short . . . those who suffer" outside the walls of Christianity.[63] For Bonhoeffer, as Jesus is for others, so also the church becomes meaningful only when it exists for others. A christological motive for Bonhoeffer's being for others refers to God in human form; that is to say, the man for others is the Crucified.[64]

In the Asian context Luther's theology of the cross was first reformulated through the "theology of the pain of God" (Kitamori) in comparison with the mind of Bodhisattva who suffers with all sentient creatures with great compassion. Kitamori was the first Japanese theologian to engage himself in dialogue with Luther from a perspective of the pain of God in Japanese cultural contexts. The symbol of Buddha seated on a lotus floating upon the lake symbolizes the present reality of *samsara* under the chain of suffering embedded in life, death, and the cycle of rebirth. In the midst of the lake full of agony and suffering a lotus blooms for itself.

60. *WA*, 24, 390, 27v.

61. *AB*, 161.

62. Cf. Lukács, *Destruction of Reason*.

63. *LPP*, 17, cf. Pangritz, *Karl Barth*, 86.

64. *LPP*, 381f.

In like manner, *Nirvana*—the great liberation and Enlightenment—emerges out of samsara and returns to it. The double movement from samsara to *Nirvana* and then from *Nirvana* to samsara expresses a Buddhist symbol of great compassion for all sentient beings in the *dukkha* as the Cross of Jesus Christ symbolizes God's solidarity with and involvement in all living creatures in suffering, with great mercy. However, Kitamori's theology of God's pain remains at an individualistic level, losing sight of the life-setting that suffering is rooted in and comes out of. In other words, he lost sight of the suffering of victims that Korean minjung theology sharpens in the praxis of liberation and in struggle with social injustice.

Asian contextual minjung theologians in South Korea have an ambivalent attitude to Luther—an attitude that is positive to Luther's profound understanding of divine suffering in his theology of the cross, but negative to his political conservatism during the peasant rebellion. They'd rather stand in favor of Thomas Müntzer's revolutionary spirit in approaching social and political issues.

Given this fact, a conversation with Martin Luther, which the author makes an attempt to do, entails a twofold task: a critical dialogue with Luther, and at the same time with Asian contextual theology of minjung and religions. Concerning the Asian religious liberative situation, there has not, in fact, been much attention to Luther. It would be challenging but meaningful to confront Luther with an Asian spirituality of Buddhism. How to read Luther with an Asian sense is at the center of my hermeneutical approach to him. What is needed is not to plant Luther's theology in Asian soil, but to bring Luther's theological impulse into critical dialogue with Buddhist notions of suffering, *Sunyata*, Enlightenment, etc. My interpretation of Martin Luther is contextual and different, related to my East Asian self-understanding and perspective in particular, and to a different social and cultural context in general. In my encounter with people of other faiths, a new meaning of Luther's theology occurs.

What Christianity and Buddhism have in common is their profound understanding of suffering (*dukkha*), albeit each with a different approach to the solution of it. The issue of suffering in Buddhism is an integral part of shaping the uniqueness of a Buddhist spirituality with an emphasis on dependent co-arising and spiritual awakening to the authentic true self that leads to nirvanic Enlightenment. The reason for choosing Martin Luther for this dialogue lies mainly in the fact that it was Luther who initiated the subject of the suffering of God on the cross, in contrast to the theology of glory in medieval scholastic realms. His understanding of divine suffering deserves to be reflected on in a context of social justice and profound religiosity. As Moltmann writes, "at the center of the Christian faith stands an unsuccessful, tormented Christ, dying in forsakenness."[65]

The crucified Christ is taken as the foundation and criticism of Christian theology. The crucified God reveals the compassion of the passionate God and is regarded to be at the heart of Christian theology after Auschwitz. *Theologia crucis* needs to be deepened in Jewish-Christian relations. Auschwitz must elicit a discussion of the theology of the cross accompanied by a postmodern attention to Otherness. A conversation with Martin Luther in an Asian context that features a Buddhist understanding of suffering would be helpful in mutually enriching both traditions in favor of reciprocal recognition, thereby encouraging solidarity with the humiliated and affirmation of the poor in other religions.

65. Moltmann, *Crucified God*, ix.

First should be a cross: black, within the heart, which would have its natural color, that I may remind myself that faith in Him who was crucified makes us blest. . . . Now the fact that it is a black cross mortifies, and is intended to produce pain; yet, it allows the heart to retain its natural color, does not destroy nature, that is, does not kill but rather keeps alive—Justus enim fide vivet, sed fide crucifixi.

Luther's letter to Lazarus Spengler, 1530

2

The Uniqueness of Luther's Life and Theology

Luther's Personal Development

THE THEOLOGY OF MARTIN LUTHER CANNOT BE FULLY UNDERSTOOD without considering his spiritual and social biography, at the heart of which lies his struggle for and discovery of God's justification for all. As all the theological structures and ideas of Luther are inspired and extended by his teaching on justification, so his doctrine of justification becomes the driving force of his whole life-struggle and the larger program of the reformation. Martin Luther (1483–1546) is thought to have been born on November 10, 1483, in a middle-class house in Eisleben, and named after the saint of the day, Martin of Tours, whose festival was on November 11, the day of Luther's baptism. Even though Luther himself was certain about the year of his birth in 1484, his early chronology is not yet clear. In Eisleben Luther began his life and ended it. Luther's parents Hans and Margaret belonged to a rising economic class and after having their second son moved the following year from the vicinity of Eisennach to the neighboring town of Mansfeld, where Luther grew up and went to its city school from about 1490 until 1497. Luther considered Mansfeld to be his hometown and his native land, and he had a deep concern for it until the end of his life.

In his fourteenth year (1496 or 1497), he was sent to Magdeburg for schooling. A year later he was transferred to St. George's School in Eisennach. Luther once told the mayor of Magdeburg that he went to school with the Brethren of the Common Life, which belonged to the lay branch of the *Devotio Moderna*.[1] Although Luther reports that he went to

1. Oberman, *Luther*, 96.

school with the Brethren, almost nothing is known about the school in Magdeburg. Though the Brethren did not maintain a school, they possibly lodged pupils away from home and supervised their school work by providing the dormitory. Here Luther may have been exposed to the influences of this spiritual movement for the first time. The Brethren and their *Devotio Moderna* movement favored patristic literature, particularly that of St. Augustine and St. Bernard.

Johannes Gerson (ca. 1429), chancellor of the University of Paris and an important council theologian, became popular and was regarded as a doctor of the church along the lines with the four great Fathers of the Western Church: Sts. Ambrose, Augustine, Jerome and Gregory the Great. Luther had a great respect for Gerson, calling him "Doctor Comforter." Although the influence of the Brethren on Luther during the period of Magdeburg schooling is not strongly supported by some scholars, Luther as a young professor in Wittenberg was familiar with the writings of the devotional movement. By all accounts, Luther studied and appreciated several writings of the authors in the *Devotio Moderna* in his lifetime. The short period of schooling in Magdeburg for Luther was unlike Erasmus of Rotterdam who as a schoolboy spent nine years with the Brethren in Deventer, because Erasmus rebelled against his schooling.

In the summer semester of 1501 Luther began his study at the University of Erfurt and got his BA in 1502 and his MA in 1505. Erfurt was the commercial center of the fruitful Thuringian basin. The University of Erfurt was founded in 1392 as the fifth German university after Prague, Vienna, Heidelberg, and Cologne. His father intended him to become a lawyer. In 1505, Luther completed the general arts course at Erfurt and was in a position to move on to study law. The University of Erfurt was "a stronghold of the *via moderna*."[2] Among its well-known faculty members were Jodokus Trutfetter from Eisenach and Bartholomew Arnoldi of Usingen. In the summer of 1505 Luther began the study of law.

During his study Luther once was in danger of losing his life. On his way home to Mansfeld in 1503 his dagger pierced his leg, cutting the artery in his thigh. His experience with impending death was intensified by the outbreak of the plague in the year 1505 in which two law professors fell victim to it. Luther would later mention *Anfectungen* that he had as a youth. After the master's examination, Luther became interested in reading

2. Ibid., 114.

the Bible. "When I was a young master in Erfurt, I continually wandered about sadly because of the *Anfectungen* of sorrows, so I devoted myself to much reading of the Bible."[3] Be that as it may, Luther was trained as a nominalist in Erfurt. In defending himself from the nominalist background, Luther once said, "I demand arguments not authorities. That is why I contradict even my own school of Occamists, which I have absorbed completely."[4] However, after 1515, Luther became a strong opponent of his school teaching on grace and justification.

At the end of June 1505, Luther made a trip to his parents in Mansfeld and on Wednesday, July 2, he returned to Erfurt from Mansfeld. As he was near the village of Storterheim, a severe thunderstorm gathered around him. Suddenly, a bolt of lightning struck the ground next to him, perhaps throwing him off his horse. Stunned and terrified, Luther cried out, "Help, St. Anne, I will become a monk!" (St. Anne was the patron saint of miners.) Luther had had his first personal experience with the terrifying presence of the living God. This was a heavenly calling that Luther received in terror. Luther's friend Crotus Rubeanus and his monastic teacher Johannes Nathin used to compare Luther's experience with the conversion experience of the Apostle Paul on the road to Damascus (Acts 9:34). Luther was thoroughly familiar with the ideal of the monastery. In becoming a monk he sought to escape the final judgment and hell: "I took the vow not for the sake of my belly but for the sake of my salvation." "For this reason I too entered the monastery."[5]

As we have already mentioned, the leading figures at the University of Erfurt in Luther's time were members of the arts faculty, Jodokus Trutfetter (ca. 1519) from Eisenach and Bartholomew Arnoldi of Unsingen (1462–1532), who represented the philosophical principles of William Occam (ca. 1349), i.e., nominalism, or in a more exact sense, terminism. The study of philosophy in Erfurt was of overwhelming significance for Luther. "Without Aristotle no one becomes a doctor of theology."[6] Luther once said that he belonged to the scholastic position of the Occamists.

During Luther's time in Erfurt nominalism was very attractive because of Trutfetter and Unsingen, whom Luther later identified as his teachers.

3. Brecht, *Martin Luther: Road to Reformation*, 47.
4. *WA*, 6:195, 4f; cf. Oberman, *Luther*, 120.
5. *LW*, 54:338.
6. Brecht, *Martin Luther: Road to Reformation*, 34.

Trutfetter published his commentaries on almost all of Aristotle's writings in relation to logic and natural philosophy. Likewise, Unsingen published several writings on the subject of natural philosophy and logic, including an exercise on Aristotle's physics and *De Anima*. However, Unsingen did not have Trutfetter's competence, precision, or wealth of ideas. When Luther later mentioned his philosophical sources from the school of the terminists, he meant particularly the area of logic. Nominalistic scholasticism became the first major idea controlling Luther's thinking.

In Luther's time the conflict between nominalism and humanism does not appear as strongly. This was a humanism that stood in peaceful coexistence with scholastic philosophy. Luther's teachers Trutfetter and Unsingen were friendly to this humanism. Nominalistic dialectics and humanistic enthusiasm for language were not in strict opposition to traditional piety and humanistic interests. Students were encouraged to welcome humanism as the herald of a new era, without leaving the sure ground of scholasticism. However, peaceful coexistence between humanism and nominalism in Erfurt did not last. This peace came to an end at Erfurt in 1500, when Nicholas Marschalk began to attack scholasticism, especially in regard to the unspiritual life of monks and the cult of relics.

Early in the sixteenth century Conrad Muti (called Mutian Rufus) had a considerable influence on Erfurt humanism. He was an Erfurt master and had become a doctor of law in 1501 in Bologna, where he was in contact with Italian humanism. He was an important figure in German humanism alongside Erasmus. Unlike the previous Erfurt humanists, he was very critical of the Erfurt scholastics. In 1506 the humanists attacked the educational method of the philosophy faculty in Erfurt. Luther had no personal contact with Mutian until 1515, but later he conceived of him in a very negative way.

Luther was familiar with Crotus Rubeanus (ca. 1539), a humanist who began to attack the scholastic system in collaboration with Ulrich von Hutten. He was one of the authors of the famous anti-scholastic *Letters of Obscure Men*. Through Crotus, Luther was acquainted with Ulrich von Hutten. He in turn remembered Luther as a budding humanist in the Erfurt period.[7] During his study of philosophy Luther's engagement with humanism remained in peaceful harmony with the traditional nominal-

7. Oberman, *Luther*, 124.

istic philosophy. The nominalist heritage gradually gained priority and became dominant over humanism in Luther's thought.

On July 17, 1505, Luther entered the most rigorous of the seven major monasteries in Erfurt, that is, the monastery of the Augustinian Hermits. He chose the way of the Observant Augustinians, who resided in the Black Cloister on the left bank of the Gera River. The Black Cloister is so named for the clothing which the monks wore. This monastery bore the name of Augustine because it adopted the rule ascribed to his name. The order studied the theology of Augustine, the content of which was interpreted from the angle of medieval theology. At the Augustinian eremite cloister, Occamism was predominant in philosophy and theology. Luther, in fact, continued to train himself in the Occamist intellectual tradition during his monastic life.[8] Luther's father was outraged at his decision to enter the monastery and remained alienated from his son for a considerable amount of time. Luther believed that he would never again come out of the monastery. Upon entering the Augustinian monastery, however, he continued his studies as a monk and earned his doctorate at the University of Wittenberg in 1512.

The major reason for Luther's entering the Augustinian monastery was his desire to find a merciful God and his grace, rather than to seek a place of contemplation or study. As a monk Luther accepted the monastic form of life completely. Searching for a merciful God expressed well Luther's spiritual thirst for salvation. He was in a desperate effort to find peace with God. However, he found himself incapable of meeting the requirements prescribed by the righteousness of God. Whereas a God of justice demands complete obedience, Luther found himself incapable of following this obedience, which led him to an experience of overwhelming anguish. "In the monastery I did not think about women, money, or possessions; instead my heart trembled and fidgeted about whether God would bestow His grace on me." "For I had strayed from faith and could not but imagine that I had angered God, whom I in turn had to appease by doing good works."[9]

The new vicar general, John Staupitz (ca.1465–1524), who was appointed head of the German Augustinian Observants in 1503, was then Luther's superior in the order. In his encounter with Staupitz, Luther was

8. Lohse, *Martin Luther's Theology*, 22. For Occam's significance for Luther's Christology and doctrine of the Lord's Supper, *LW*, 37:222–26.

9. *WA*, 47:590, 6–10; cf. Oberman, *Luther*, 128.

led to a Bible-oriented theology focused on discipleship and salvation rather than scholasticism. At times Luther felt a special gratitude to him for the rediscovery of the gospel. "It would not be right for me to forget you or to be ungrateful to you, for it was through you that the light of the gospel first began to shine out of the darkness into my heart."[10]

The Erfurt Augustinian monastery had close links with the University of Erfurt, which allowed Luther to wrestle with the great names of late medieval religious thought—such as William of Occam, Pierre d'Ailly (1350–1420), and Gabriel Biel—in the course of preparation for ordination. Luther had to study the *Sentences* of Peter Lombard and the writing of the Tübingen theologian and nominalist Gabriel Biel (ca.1410–1495), *Exposition of the Canon of the Mass* (*Sacri canonis missae expositio),* which had first appeared in 1499. Biel was indebted to Occam's ideas regarding the doctrine of original sin and grace. According to Melanchthon, Luther learnt Biel and Pierre d'Ailly by heart. Their writings helped Luther deal critically with doctrines such as transubstantiation. These two Occamist theologians were of special significance to Luther.[11] He was ordained as a priest on February 27 or possibly on Easter Saturday, April 3, 1507. He was so terrified with the words of the eucharistic prayer at his first mass that he almost ran away from the altar. A sense of the *mysterium tremendum* of the holiness of God shaped Luther's lifelong concern with the living God.

As the old Luther recalled in his lecture in the book of Genesis, "'And Isaac prayed to the Lord for his wife, because she was barren: and the Lord answered his prayer' (Gen 25:21). A prayer like this, which breaks through the clouds and reaches up to the majesty of God, is not easy. I, ashes, dust, and full of sin, speak with the living, eternally true God. This cannot but cause one to tremble, as I did when I celebrated my first mass. . . . Joyous faith, however, which rests on the mercy and the Word of God overcomes the fear of his majesty . . . and rises boldly above it."[12]

It was on *Corpus Christi* in 1515 that Luther joined, as a priest, in the procession at the newly founded monastery in Eisleben. His sudden consciousness of the presence of Christ the judge overwhelmed him with horror about the sacrament. Confessing his experience to Staupitz, the

10. *WA Br* 3 Nr. 659, 5–8; cf. Lohse, *Martin Luther's Theology,* 24.

11. Lohse, *Martin Luther's Theology*, 23.

12. *WA*, 43:378; cf. Oberman, *Luther*, 137.

latter responded that his thought was not of Christ, because Christ is not present as judge here.[13] For Luther, Christ was seen not as a comforter, or forgiver, but as a tyrant looking like the lawgiver Moses. After the fearful experience with Christ's presence in the Eisleben procession, Staupitz instructed Luther to look at Christ as the suffering one who was on the cross. Luther's *Anfechtungen* (inner struggle) can be explained not as a condition of emotional illness as from the perspective of psychology, but as a condition of being confronted by the living God.

As Luther remarks,

> I myself knew a man who claimed that he had often suffered these punishments, and in fact over a very brief period of time. Yet they were so great and so much like hell that no tongue could adequately express them, no pen could describe them, and one who had not himself experienced them could not believe them. . . . At such a time God seems so terribly angry, and with him the whole creation. At such a time there is no flight, no comfort, within or without, but all things accuse. . . . In this moment, it is strange to say, the soul can not believe that it can ever be redeemed.[14]

To put it otherwise, *Anfechtungen* are related basically to the problem of God's election or reprobation. It was Staupitz who helped Luther to pull out of his preoccupation with the judging Christ and showed him a way out of the terrors of predestination. Staupitz interpreted the experience of separation from God as a sign of being especially near to God. The suffering Christ gives a vivid example of it, the idea of which would be integrated into Luther's theology of the cross. The *Anfechtungen*, which touch the deepest questions of faith about the nature of Christ, predestination, and reprobation, are constitutive for Luther's own new theology. For Luther, spiritual experience or spirituality is deeply connected with his theology.

The Bible is for Luther the foundation on which the church and its tradition are based. However, the interpretation of Scripture did not play an important role at the Erfurt theology faculty. Luther reports that Andreas Bodenstein, who called himself Karlstadt after his birthplace, did not own a Bible when he earned the doctor of theology degree. It was Staupitz who had reinstated Bible study in the monasteries of the reform congregation and put emphasis on the interpretation of the Bible in ap-

13. Brecht, *Martin Luther: His Road to Reformation*, 75.

14. *WA*, 1:443; cf. Brecht, *Martin Luther: Road to Reformation*, 80.

proaching the study of theology. For Luther the Psalter was the book of *Anfechtungen*. It is also the word of God that could deal with and help overcome *Anfechtungen*. In fact, the one who goes through *Anfechtungen* is capable of understanding what the Scripture says.

Like the two larger mendicant orders, the Dominicans and the Franciscans, the Augustinians played a central role in the University of Erfurt. Mendicant monks who would earn the theological degree were to be registered at the University. From the summer semester of 1507 Luther studied theology under Johannes Nathin who held the Augustinian chair of theology at the University of Erfurt. However, Luther did not manage to continue and complete the study of theology in Erfurt, because he had to register due to the summons of John Staupitz at the University of Wittenberg for the winter semester of 1508 to 1509. There he read Aristotle's *Ethics* and earned the grade of *Baccalaureus Biblicus* in the spring of 1509. After earning his first theological degree he was able to take the examination for the degree of bachelor of the sentences as early as the fall of 1509.

In the meantime, he was called back by his Erfurt monastery to teach there. Luther was appointed one of the delegates to Rome for an appeal against the union between the reform congregation and the Saxon provincial order. Both Staupitz and his superior, the general in Rome, were concerned about bringing all the Augustinian monasteries under one central administration. The two delegates began their trip in November 1510. At the first sight of Rome, Luther threw himself upon the ground with the words "How blessed are you, holy Rome!" It was truly holy because of the holy martyrs, dripping with their blood.[15] Luther did not prevent himself from paying pious visits to the holy places and receiving the spiritual blessings connected with them. There was also the *Sancta Scala*, which Christ himself climbed to the palace of Pontius Pilate. To redeem the soul of his grandfather Lindemann or Heine Luder from purgatory, Luther climbed on his knees in the Lateran palace the stairs from Pilate's place, saying the *Our Father* on each step. At the top of the *Santa Scala*, his doubt was not avoidable. "Who knows whether it is true?"

Luther's experiences with Rome were ambivalent. The real mission was a failure. The religious abuses were seen everywhere. However, he also participated in the riches of grace in Rome. The business of the Observant

15. Cf. Kittelson, *Luther*, 59.

Augustinians did not work out as they hoped. The Observant monastery had to decide whether to submit to the authority of the vicar general for Germany, John Staupitz, or retain its relative independence. Luther's brothers in the Black Cloister decided not to submit. However, Luther with his friend, John Lang, was in agreement with Staupitz. The majority of their brothers in Erfurt were angry about Luther's decision. After all, Luther and Lang were supposed to live with Staupitz in the Augustinian house in Wittenberg. Finally in the late summer of 1511 Luther reassumed his study in Wittenberg, and finally earned *Doctor Theologicus* on October 19, 1512.[16] Luther held the chair of biblical theology at the University of Wittenberg from that day until his death.

Luther and the Reformation Breakthrough

The University of Wittenberg was founded in 1502 by Staupitz, who was summoned by Elector Frederick the Wise of Saxony to undertake that task. Luther's Augustinian superior became the first dean of theology and held the chair of biblical theology for ten years. Finally he handed it over to Luther to begin his career as a theological professor in biblical studies. Luther began his lectures over the next five years concerning the Psalms (1513–1515), Romans (1515–1516), Galations (1516–1517), Hebrews (1517–1518), and once again the Psalms (1518–1521). During this formative time Luther was influenced by St. Paul and Augustine. It is not clear when Luther first became preoccupied with Augustine. His comprehensive marginal notes on numerous writings of Augustine from around 1509 show that Luther may have been interested in Augustine as early as at Erfurt. For the preparation of his first lectures at Wittenberg Luther made intensive reference to Augustine especially in *The First Psalms Lecture* (1513–1515) and in *The Lecture on Romans* (1515–1516). What attracted Luther to Augustine is the latter's radical doctrine of sin and grace, the teaching of which is antithetical to Occam.

In the introduction to the *Lectures on Romans*, Luther writes, "The chief purpose of this letter is to break down, to pluck up, and to destroy all wisdom and righteousness of the flesh. . . . No matter whether these works are done with a sincere heart and mind, this letter is to affirm and state and magnify sin, no matter how much someone insists that it does not

16. Schwarz, *Luther*, 118.

exist, or that it was believed not to exist."[17] This view is in contrast to the traditional teaching in which there was a continual cooperation between God and human beings in the process of salvation. Especially when grace is infused, human beings are capable of such cooperation.

It was Augustine who instructed Luther to recognize (semi-) Pelagianism smuggled into the center of the entire Catholic Church. Augustine's anti-Pelagian writings became a theological reason for Luther to fight against the late medieval Franciscan (Occamist) teaching of sin and grace. Unlike the medieval Thomist teaching, John Staupitz, following in the footsteps of Gregory of Rimini, put emphasis on the personal presence of the Holy Spirit and the role of uncreated grace in justification of believers.[18] John Staupitz was the decisive figure for Luther. He led Luther to the crucial turning point concerning the issue of justification. Staupitz was trained in the nominalistic spirit of the *via moderna,* and was strongly inspired by St. Augustine and St. Paul to develop a biblical theology. Human sin, God's grace, and justification through Christ were central themes of his theology, which decisively shaped Luther's ideas. Nevertheless there is not much known about the Augustinian school at Wittenberg, which followed the traditions of the nominalistic Augustinian hermit Gregory of Rimini. However, Luther's exegetical study of St. Paul led him to Augustine. "How can I find a gracious God?" With this question in mind, Luther preoccupied himself with the problem of the righteousness of God, the theme of which is prominent in both the Psalms and the letter to the Romans. The idea of the righteousness of God became a threat bringing only condemnation or punishment to Luther. It was only a punishing righteousness for Luther.

As Luther recalled in the famous preface to the first volume of his Latin works in 1545, the year before his death, the new discovery took place during the time of the indulgence controversy and the Roman canonical trial. After the lectures on Romans, Galatians, and Hebrews, Luther intended to interpret the Psalter anew in late 1518 or early 1519. Luther said that he hated the idea that "in it the righteousness of God is revealed," because he was taught to understand the term "the righteousness of God" in the formal or active sense. That is to say that God is righteous and punishes

17. *LW*, 25:135, cf. Brecht, *Martin Luther: Road to Reformation*, 132.

18. McGrath, *Martin Luther's Theology*, 66–67.

the unrighteous sinner according to the righteousness of God. Luther's difficulty lay especially in the righteous God who punishes sinners.

> I live without reproach as a monk, my conscience was disturbed to its very depths and all I knew about myself was that that I was a sinner. . . . I did not love, nay, I hated the righteous God who punishes sinners. . . . At last, mediating day and by the mercy of God, I gave heed to the context of the words, 'In it the righteousness of God is revealed,' as it is written, 'He who through faith is righteous shall live.'

In reflection on the statement "the righteous person shall live by faith," Luther began to realize that "the righteousness of God is that through which the righteous live by a gift of God, namely by faith." That is to say that the righteousness of God refers to a passive righteousness by which the merciful God justifies us by faith.[19] His breakthrough, which was later called the "tower experience" (*Turmerlebnis*) in his Table Talks, took place in his heated study room located in the third floor of the sewer tower of the Augustinian monastery, and propelled him into the forefront of the Reformation. Now the concept of God the All Terrible became changed into God the All Merciful. Romans 1:17 became truly the open gate to paradise for Luther. His new understanding is affirmed by rereading Augustine's *On the Spirit and the Letter* at the beginning of 1518.[20]

There is no reason for "Christians to do what is inside them" as preparation for receiving sacramental grace. The role of humility for Luther is of special significance. Despairing of one's own ability might be helpful in describing Luther's idea of humility. In the *First Lectures on the Psalms* Luther stressed that absolute humility was a necessary precondition for saving grace. "Humility itself is judgment," to accuse and to judge oneself. Luther even argued that "humility alone saves."[21] The place of humility in the Christian life is of fundamental significance for Luther's life as a monk. As he moved into 1515 and his *Lectures on Romans*, Luther retained the teaching of the *synteresis* or the spark of goodness which can be found in every human being. This is what underlay scholastic theology as the basic organizing principle. "For we are not wholly inclined to evil, because a

19. *LW*, 34:336–38; cf. Kittelson, *Luther*, 134.

20. Oberman, *Luther*,154.

21. *LW*, 10:237; cf. Brecht, *Martin Luther: Road to Reformation*, 128–36.

remnant is left to us which is inclined toward good things, as is evident in the synteresis." This is "the sum of all the vices."[22]

However, in light of God's righteousness, according to Paul, human beings have nothing to offer God. The human condition in the presence of God's righteousness makes Luther approach human humility not in terms of *synteresis*, but in terms of Christ alone. The righteousness of God comes from faith. Faith trusts God's promises. Nothing is more humble than faith. Now Luther intended Christ alone by faith alone, because both humility and faith are gifts of God coming along with the righteousness of God. For Luther, Christ on the cross is the objective fact of our righteousness, grace, and faith. Human strivings have no part in it.

> Now this alone is the right Christian way, that I . . . turn alone to Christ's righteousness, so that I know for certain that Christ's goodness, merit, innocence, and holiness are mine. . . . In his name I live, die, and pass away, for He died for us and was resurrected for us. . . . He in whose name I am baptized, receive the Holy Sacrament, study the Catechism—He will embrace us if only we trust in Him.[23]

We are justified indeed through Christ's suffering, in which God saves only sinners and gives life to the poor and the humble. The humiliation of a sinful person brings that person close to God. Christ's works are weak; the cross of God is hidden from our eyes. In the context of Rom 4:7, Luther brings up the famous formula that the believer is righteous and a sinner at the same time: righteous in a sense that God does not impute sin, but sinner in a sense that the reality of sin still exists in the believer. This idea is in opposition to scholastic theology.

> At the same time he is both a sinner and righteous, a sinner in fact, but righteous by the sure imputation [of Christ's righteousness] and the promise of God that he will continue to deliver him from sin until he has completely cured him. And thus he is entirely healthy in hope, but is in fact still a sinner, but he has the beginning of righteousness so that he continues more and always to seek it, yet realizes that he is always unrighteous.[24]

A human being in need of grace is like one under the care of a physician.

22. *LW*, 25:222; cf. Kittelson, *Luther*, 91.

23. *WAT*, 2, no. 1351; 66, 1–7; 1532; cf. Oberman, *Luther*, 153.

24. *LW*, 25:260.

All salvation comes to us from without. Human beings are bound to be humble and passive before saving grace. What is righteousness for human beings is humility, because salvation is given from outside. The theology of humility and abasement is constitutive for the theology of the cross. In addition, Luther deepened his theology of humility in an encounter with the mysticism of John Tauler and the *Theologia Germanica.* He held high respect for the love mysticism of St. Bernard of Clairvaux, Hugh of St. Victor, St. Bonaventure, and Jean Gerson.

In the *First Lectures on the Psalms* his attitude was positive toward Dionysius's negative theology, but in the *Lectures on Romans* he changed his attitude toward it completely. According to Luther, this mystical theology lost sight of the incarnation, justification, and purification despite the fact that it grasps something important in God's hiddenness. Bernard of Clairvaux was of special significance for Luther's exposition of Rom 8:16. Although Luther in his later years was critical of certain elements of Bernard—especially regarding the strong advocacy of monasticism, subservience to the papacy, and veneration of the Virgin Mary—Bernard was "the starting point for Luther's doctrine of faith and the assurance of faith."[25] Luther was familiar with common mystical expressions such as human departure, being enraptured, groaning, or the tiny spark within the soul. A mystical element was integral in his theology of humility and his own theological interests.

He read Tauler and the *Theologia Germanica*, which is the anonymous writing known as the *Theologia deutsch*. He takes it as a striking example of genuine, personal, living theology. In 1518 Luther published a complete edition of the *Theologia deutsch* by writing a preface: "To boast with my old fool (St. Paul), no book except the Bible and St. Augustine has come to my attention from which I have learned more about God, Christ, man, and all things."[26] Tauler became a signpost in Luther's search for life by faith in the world. The term "happy exchange," which is Luther's favorite term in expressing the relationship between Christ and human being, is borrowed from Tauler and the *Theologia Germanica.* This German mysticism which stands in line with St. Augustine put emphasis on the fact that the goal of human life lies in union with God, but it is totally blocked by original sin. It is Godself who must overcome this situation by his grace. The human

25. Kleineidam, *Universitas Studii Erffordensis*, 239; cf. Lohse, *Martin Luther's Theology*, 25–26.

26. Cf. Hoffman, *Theologia Germanica.*

being is essentially passive in the reception of God's grace, which involves a great dying to one's self in order to realize his or her true life by becoming justified. Everything that belongs to salvation is exclusively divine work because justification takes place when God comes to be present in the human inner being. Tauler becomes for Luther a witness to the hellish experience of *Anfechtungen.*[27]

Tauler's mystical passivity or bold resignation (*Gelassenheit*) runs contrary to scholasticism. Tauler's mysticism influenced his Wittenberg friends such as Karlstadt and Thomas Müntzer. In the framework of mysticism, the terms "groaning" and "rapture" characterize the beginning and the end of the road from painful separation from the world to a joyous union with God. Luther's encounter with Augustinian theology through Johannes von Staupitz, with the mystical component of Tauler, encouraged and confirmed him on his way to a new spirituality and a new way of thinking toward the Reformation.

Luther and Conflict with the Roman Church

Before his Ninety-five Theses (1517), Luther began to criticize the prevailing form of theological education. During his formative period Luther interpreted Augustine in light of Paul, and on the basis of the Paul-Augustine tradition attacked scholastic theology in order to renew the church. Luther's encounter with Augustine might be dated back to the autumn of 1509. On the title page of *Aurelii Augustini opuscula plurima* printed in Strasbourg in 1489, Luther noted, "St. Augustine died in the year of our Lord 433. Now, in the year 1509, that is 1076 years ago."[28] Even though the date of death is incorrect, it shows that Luther studied Augustine in 1509 and discovered the difference between Augustine and Aristotle. In the winter semester between 1509 and 1510 at Erfurt, Luther commented on Augustine's two major works, *De Trinitate* and *De Civitate Dei*: "I find it more than astonishing that our scholars can so brazenly claim that Aristotle does not contradict Catholic truth."[29]

Augustine's theology, though venerated in the church, had been displaced during and after the thirteenth century by the approach of St. Thomas Aquinas (1225–1274). Thomas took his method from Aristotle

27. Cf. Hoffman, *Luther and the Mystics.*

28. Oberman, *Luther*, 159.

29. *WA*, 9:27, 22–24; cf. Oberman, *Luther*, 159.

(384–322 BCE) by way of translation from Arabic. Under the influence of Aristotle, Thomas put emphasis on human reason, and the order and structure of being, without surpassing the mysteries of the faith (such as the Trinity, Incarnation) through the use of human reason. His followers took a further step in stressing human rationality and responsibility even within the realm of grace. This philosophical and theological orientation in which Luther was educated came out of William of Occam (1300–1349), an English Franciscan.

In contrast to Thomas, Luther thought that reason no longer was valid in matters of faith. "To say that Augustine exaggerates in speaking against heretics is to say that Augustine lies almost everywhere."[30] Luther's enthusiasm for Augustine focused on his writings on original sin and humanity's total need for grace in sharp contrast to the late medieval theology that put emphasis on human nature's ability to be in cooperation with God and thereby come to merit salvation on the basis of infused grace. St. Paul also is in support of Augustine's pessimism about human capacities.

Luther's rejection of scholasticism is due to his suspicion that Pelagianism corrupted the whole theological framework. In this framework Luther was aware that, helped by the infusion of grace, a human being, with his or her renewed deeds, becomes righteous before God. According to late medieval teaching, a human being, once restored to a reasonable and natural understanding of God, is capable of overcoming sin and evil on the basis of free will. Consequently he or she can create the good works of the will that please God. Such an ability, led by free will, is required as the preparation for receiving the infusion of grace through sacraments as well as for actualizing habitual possession of grace. Luther's critique of scholastic theology was triggered by the influence of Aristotle as well as the Pelagianizing doctrine of sin and grace. It was done from the standpoint of a Bible-oriented theology along the lines of Paul and Augustine.

Luther was propelled to fame through a series of controversies. The first controversy was centered on the sale of indulgences, which were rooted in the penitential practice of Western Christianity in the Middle Ages. According to Thomas Aquinas the authority over indulgences is assigned to the pope who dispenses the excess merits of Christ and the saints. An indulgence might also be applied to the dead in purgatory in terms of someone's works. In the use of indulgences the sincerity of repentance

30. "Disputation Against Scholastic Theology," *MLBTW*, 13.

began to be threatened, and thus it disrupted the practice of pastoral care. There was emphasis on the indulgence's four primary graces: (1) the complete remission of all sins and the complete forgiveness of punishments of sin and purgatory; (2) the possibility of obtaining a confessional letter for absolution at a time of one's own discretion and death; (3) the possibility of buying a confessional letter in which the dead relatives participate in all the church's goods. In other words, those who donate for the new construction of the Church of St. Peter in Rome "share in all the petitions, intercessions, alms, fasts, prayers, and pilgrimages with their parents who died in love from now on and to all eternity"; and (4) the total remission of all sins for souls in purgatory in terms of the pope's intercession.[31] In fact, indulgences guarantee the entire forgiveness of sins.

In addition, there was an alliance between indulgences of the church and political and commercial interests. At the turn of the sixteenth century the papacy was in severe financial difficulty. Pope Leo X's ambition to complete St. Peter's cathedral came into contact with the politics of Albert, a member of the ambitious House of Hohenzollern. Albert was engaged in constant political struggles. The biggest bank of Germany, owned by the Fugger family, promised to pay Albert for getting the papal confirmation and the necessary dispensation from Leo X. In turn, Leo authorized the sale of the indulgence in Albert's territories to repay the Fuggers and to help rebuild St. Peter's. Pope Leo X's bull of indulgences on March 31, 1515 (*Sacrosancti salvatoris et redemptoris nostri*) is associated with these financial interests from the beginning.

John Tetzel, a Leipzig Dominican who was excellent at the business of selling indulgences, planned this mission with care. Several horsemen, drummers, and trumpeters preceded Tetzel to town after town announcing the imminent arrival of something significant. A copy of the prized indulgence was attached to a makeshift cross and raised above the crowd for all to see. "Do you not hear the voices of your dead relatives and others, crying out to you and saying, 'Pity us, pity us, for we are in dire punishment and torment from which you can redeem us for a pittance?'" Luther took a particular exception to the advertising copy of John Tetzel, who was promoting indulgences: "Once the coin in the coffer rings, a soul from purgatory heavenward springs!"[32]

31. Lohse, *Martin Luther's Theology*, 100; cf. Brecht, *Martin Luther: His Road to Reformation*, 180.

32. Cf. Kittelson, *Luther*, 103.

When John Tetzel tried to sell these indulgences in the Wittenberg region, he irritated Luther considerably. Philip Melanchthon, who in 1517 was not yet in Wittenberg, wrote the first report of this event after the death of Luther. "Induced by Tetzel's selling of indulgences, Luther wrote theses on indulgences and publicly posted them on the door of the church of All Saints on 31 October 1517," according to the university custom.[33] This date is observed as marking the beginning of the Reformation.

For Luther, not indulgences but the cross and mortification belong to the Christian life. The slogan of advertisement "A penny in the box, a soul out of purgatory" was under fire. In defiance of the sale of indulgences Luther proclaimed that the church's treasure was the poor. If necessary, the pope should be prepared to sell the basilica of St. Peter for those in need. Indulgences are meaningless without repentance. One may donate to St. Peter's Basilica voluntarily, but not to get an indulgence. In fact, Luther did not conceive of the theses as his program for rebellion against the pope. Luther himself in 1514 said that from the beginning he did not wish to attack indulgences, but only their misuse. He was not concerned about attacking the pope, but about defending him. In opposition to the indulgences Luther said: "No man can be assured of his salvation by any Episcopal function . . . because the Apostle [Paul] orders us to work out our salvation constantly 'in fear and trembling.'"[34]

Luther addressed a letter to Archbishop Albrecht of Mainz concerning the indulgences circulated under his name. According to Luther, the first and only duty of the bishop is to take care of the people for learning the gospel and the love of Christ. In December 1517, it was proposed that there should be a debate at the University of Wittenberg. In the scholasticistic tradition as a rule disputations served to clarify some complicated academic issue. The archbishop regarded Luther's letter as a direct challenge to his authority and forwarded them with a letter of complaint to Rome.

In addition to Tetzel's furious reaction, another strong opponent to Luther was the theologian John Eck at the University of Ingolstadt. Eck sent Luther his rebuttal of the theses, entitled *Obelisks*, or daggers, in which Eck called Luther a Bohemian, accusing him of disturbing the good order of the church, inciting rebellion among the common people,

33. Cf. Brecht, *Martin Luther: His Road to Reformation*, 200.

34. *LW*, 48:46.

and finally of being a despiser of the pope. In response to Eck, Luther had his *Asterisks*, or little stars, sent to Eck, in which Luther attacked Eck as the person on whom to impale his theses. The *Obelisks* and *Asterisks* necessarily led the two opponents to the disputation at Heidelberg. Luther's insistence in the disputation shows his break with the traditional teaching of God, salvation, and human being rather than dealing with the problem of indulgences. His voice is clear in that "free will, after the fall, exists in name only and as long as it does what it is able to do, it commits a mortal sin."[35]

As a matter of fact, Luther declared that the prevailing theology of scholasticism amounted to damnation. The famous scholastic formula "do what lies within you" falls apart, concerning nothing but an additional sin. Of course, Luther's genuine intention was not to speak against doing something, but rather for turning to Christ in recognition of human sin.

His theology of the cross comes to the fore in sharp contrast to the theology of glory. "A theologian of glory calls evil good and the good evil. A theologian of the cross calls the thing what it actually is."[36] Scholastic theology can no longer conceive of God's alien work and is the enemy of the cross of Christ. God allows Godself to be found in the crucified Christ, which is the real content and meaning of true theology. Martin Bucer, a young Dominican from Alsace, expressed his impression "as if in a dream" that the mocker of indulgences radically opposed the prevailing Heidelberg Aristotelian theology. In a letter to his friends, Bucer announced that "Luther responds with magnificent grace and listens with insurmountable patience. He presents an argument with the insight of the apostle Paul. What Erasmus insinuates he speaks openly and freely."[37]

In the aftermath of the indulgence crisis at Heidelberg, Luther made an effort to explain his theological perspective in the theses in *Resolutions Concerning the 95 Theses,* finished in May 1518. In examining Matt 4:17 in Erasmus's edition of the Greek New Testament, Luther was aware of the difference between the Latin translation and the Greek. According to the Latin, the translation is "do penance, for the kingdom of heaven is at hand," whereas in the Greek it is said, "Be penitent. . . ."

35. *MLBTW*, 39.

36. Ibid., 44.

37. Horowitz, ed, *Briefwechsel des Beatus Rhenamus*, 108; cf. Kittelson, *Luther*, 112.

He concluded, therefore, that doing has nothing to do with salvation, especially in view of indulgences. That being the case, to repent and to do penance are totally different from each other. "When our Lord and Master Jesus Christ said, 'repent' [Matt 4:17], he willed the entire life of believers to be one of repentance" (Thesis 1). Penance is a misleading word. Genuine repentance is not imposed, but granted as a gift. With this idea in mind, Luther makes a move from the critique of indulgences to a general critique of what was central and fundamental to the practice of late medieval religion in his day, because what is at stake is dependent on believing only in the truth of God's promise in Jesus Christ. "Any truly repentant Christian has a right to full remission of penalty and guilt, even without indulgence letters" (Thesis 36). In the *Resolutions* Luther urged that the church must stand in constant self-renewal and reformation. This urgency lies in all of Christendom and is what God eagerly wants and desires.[38]

In the summer of 1518 Luther's trial was officially opened in Rome. The indulgence controversy and the dispute about scholastic theology spread beyond Electoral Saxony eventually to Rome. On August 7, 1518, Luther received the summons of Rome possibly through the papal legate Cajetan in Augsburg. Luther was required to appear within sixty days after receiving the summons. Otherwise, he was threatened with the ban. Sylvester Prierias, a Dominican and the order's watchdog on doctrinal matters, accused Luther of being in error. Prierias had published in June a *Dialogue against the Presumptuous Conclusions of Martin Luther*, "in which the pope is infallible in matters of faith and doctrine. The pope as the highest authority and the foundation of the universal church authorizes even the Scriptures. Whoever says that the Church of Rome may not do what it is actually doing in the matter of indulgences is a heretic."[39]

It was Cajetan who was to take Luther into his custody and bring him before the papal court. Frederick the Wise undertook political negotiations with Cajetan, who then promised not to seize Luther. At the urging of Frederick the Wise, Cajetan applied to Rome for a transfer of Luther's case to Germany. With the help of the elector a hearing for Luther was established in Germany to safeguard his temporal safety.

Afraid for Luther's fate, Staupitz proposed that Luther come to Salzburg in order to live and to die with him. The hearing took place at

38. *LW*, 31:250. Cf. Kittelson, *Luther*, 114.

39. Cf. Oberman, *Luther*, 194.

Augsburg in October 1518 in the house of the Fuggers where Cajetan was living. Cajetan, acknowledged as one of the Dominicans' foremost theologians, felt a need for three points: (1) the treasury of merits; (2) the necessity of faith for justification in terms of sacramental grace; and (3) the papal authority for the sanction of the sale of indulgences. He emphasized especially the power of the pope, which stood above councils, the Scriptures, and the entire church. Therefore Luther was urged to accept the bull *Unigenitus,* which includes the doctrine of merits as the basis for indulgences.

The pope, through the power of the keys, possesses authority over indulgences, extending even to the dead in purgatory. All Cajetan asked Luther to do was say *revoco* (I recant). In the confrontations with Prierias and Cajetan, Luther challenged the sole authority of the pope in the church on the basis of the principle of Scripture. Luther was not convinced by Cajetan's claim that papal authority required Luther to submit to *Unigenitus* and therefore to indulgences, because the decree was contrary to the Scriptures. Unlike the case of the Heidelberg disputation and his triumph there, Luther left Augsburg as a fugitive. Cajetan sent a letter to Elector Frederick and referred to Luther as *fraterculus*, a monk of no account. Frederick was either to send Luther to Rome or to eject him from his territories. In spite of this Frederick decided to protect Luther in his territory until Luther was found convicted of heresy. In December of 1518 Luther published his documentation of the proceedings, the so-called *Acta Augustana* in which he made clear that his explanations of the certainty of faith and justification were divine truth to which even the pope was subject.

Luther's reputation rose considerably in 1519 at the Leipzig Disputation. The political situation after the death of Emperor Maximilian made Pope Leo X approach Luther's case through the mission of Karl von Militz. Von Militz was sent as ambassador and special emissary of the pope to negotiate with Luther. The pope secured a commission to present Elector Frederick with the Golden Rose, a sign of special papal favor. To avoid the election of Maximilian's grandson, Charles I of Spain, as Maximilian's successor, Leo would support the candidacy of Elector Frederick, if only he was in agreement with the pope's request. If Frederick had a favorite cleric in his territories, Leo could grant this person both a cardinal's hat and a wealthy archbishopric. The chief point in the mission of Militz was to have Luther recant his attack on the papal dignity in a more diplomatic manner. The pope would encourage the transfer of the Luther affair to a German bishop if Luther recanted his position. Even Militz took leave of Luther with a kiss and tears. But Luther was not deceived by Militz's "kiss of Judas" and his "crocodile tears." This political maneuvering gave Luther more time.

At the very end of 1518 Eck published twelve theses of his own to defend confession, the treasury of merits, purgatory, and indulgences. After the hearing in Augsburg before Cajetan and the subsequent agreement with Militz to silence, the Leipzig debate with John Eck inflamed Luther's quarrel with the church anew. The debate opened on June 27, with a high mass and a great banquet. On the debate's first day Pope Leo lost one battle: Charles I of Spain was unanimously elected Holy Roman Emperor.

The debate was divided into three rounds of discussion. On June 27 and 28, and from June 30 until July 3 Eck and Karlstadt initially debated, then Eck and Luther from July 4 until July 13 (except for July 10). Then on July 14 and 15, Eck and Karlstadt again opposed one another. What was of epochal significance in the Leipzig debate lay in the conflict over the primacy of the pope. A challenge such as this one had never before happened in the history of Christianity in such a magnitude.

Karlstadt and Eck began with the freedom of the will and the necessity of grace as a presupposition for the doing of good works. Eck insisted that the will is by nature able to cooperate with grace, while Karlstadt denied it. Before Luther engaged in debate with Eck, Luther was allowed to preach on the day of St. Peter and Paul (June 29) at the request of Duke Barim of Pomerania. The gospel appointed for the day was Peter's confession in Matt 16:13–19. Luther's sermon was later published in a more moderate but expanded version. In bringing forth the relationship between the doctrine of justification and the doctrine of the church, Luther insisted that grace is to be taught prior to works. Gifted with grace, a person has the free will to do good works. The office of the keys was given first to Peter. With this, however, Peter represents the church. That is to say, the keys are given to every Christian. The priests are the servants of the power of the keys. The keys are rightly used when one receives grace. One has the grace of God coming from faith, and with it the forgiveness of sins.

It is proclaimed in the office of the keys. Eck considered Luther's sermon, "completely Bohemian."[40]

During the course of a complicated debate over the nature of authority, Eck managed to get Luther to admit that both popes and general councils could err. As Luther had written in the *Resolution Concerning the Authority of the Pope,* Luther pointed out that the Greek church had existed for more than a thousand years before the insistence on papal supremacy. They existed without acknowledging the authority of Rome. Eck declared that anyone who denied the papal authority agreed with Jan Hus, the Bohemian reformer who had been burned at the stake for heresy against the papal authority by the Council of Constance (1415). Luther denied not only the authority of the pope but also that of the councils of the church. Only Christ is the head of the church.

Through the debate with John Eck in January 1519 at the University of Leipzig, which was under the control of Frederick's relative Duke George, a loyal supporter of Rome, Luther himself realized that his theological position was in agreement with John Hus. Eck drove Luther to criticize, beyond the nature of indulgences, papal authority and the historical claims on which it was based.[41] As Luther argued, "It is not necessary for the ordinary man to dispute much about the power of St. Peter or the pope. What is more important is to know how one should use it for salvation. It is true that the keys were given to St. Peter, but not to him personally, but rather to the person of the Christian church. They were actually given to me and to you for the comfort of our consciences. St. Peter, or a priest, is the servant of the keys."[42]

After the entire confrontation between Luther and Eck, the Wittenbergers returned from Leipzig discouraged, considering their stay there a waste of time. However, observers from Bohemia were present at the Leipzig debate. Two theologians who belonged to the moderate Utraquist party of the Hussites were impressed by Luther's direction. The followers of Hus applauded Luther as "the Saxon Hus." Luther, after reading the little book *Concerning the Church* sent by Roždalovsky, a Czech theologian, exclaimed, "We are all Hussites and did not know it!"[43] In

40. Brecht, *Martin Luther: His Road to Reformation,* 319.

41. Cf. *LW,* "Leipzig disputation," 31:318.

42. Cf. *LW,* 51:59.

43. *LW,* 48:153.

spite of agreements at some points between Luther and Hus, however, we should not downplay their differences regarding justification.

Luther and the Struggle for Reformation

In the major treatises of 1519–1521 Luther called for a program of reformation and extended his critique of Roman Catholic teachings. Late in 1519 Luther published *A Sermon on Usury* (expanded as the so-called *Large Sermon on Usury*, 1520) in which the problem of joint stock is brought under critical question. The Fuggers' wealth was based on John Eck's insistence that it is permissible to lend money at five percent. The Fugger family owned the biggest bank in Germany, which advanced the money necessary to support the alliance between the pope and the powerful in the state. Luther was aware of the necessity of the *Zinskauf*, i.e., the leasing of real estate property at a profit of four to six percent in the secular realms. However, he maintained that one may not profit at the cost of the needy. A Christian is summoned to help people in need without getting interest or profit. The way of financing the church in terms of indulgences and offerings must change. Although trade would not function without an interest in profit, Luther advocated a just distribution of burdens and risks. He had a critical sense for the possible abuses of economic life. Luther's economic ideas were further extended in his political and economic writing *On Trade and Usury* in 1524.

In 1519, Luther began to develop his sacramental theology and to express many critical things about the Brotherhoods. In 1520 he began relentlessly attacking the mass as sacrifice.[44] In *The Blessed Sacrament of the Holy and True Body of Christ and the Brotherhoods* (1519), which is his first comprehensive discussion of the sacrament of the altar, Luther makes social and ethical consequences an integral part of his eucharistic theology, in critical view of the late medieval organization of brotherhoods. These were popular, lay-centered renewal groups in his time.

Against the ways of heavy drinking and other excesses of these fraternal organizations, Luther insisted that the true brotherhood and sisterhood that was created by Christ lies in sharing and participating in the bread and wine. What was more important for Luther was that the Supper is not only a means of grace but also a sacrament of love. In Luther's view, reception of love and demonstration of it replace mere self-interest that

44. Cf. "Treatise on the New Testament—that is the Holy Mass."

threatens to destroy fellowship. For Luther, liturgical-sacramental worship entails the renewal of social life. Not group selfishness, but the fellowship of all the saints, lies at the heart of the sacrament. "As love and support are given you, you in turn must render love and support to Christ in his needy ones."[45] In this regard Luther does not, however, relate the Lord's Supper to the doctrine of justification.

In *A Treatise on the New Testament, that is, the Holy Mass*, Luther advanced his ideas of the sacrament by focusing on Christ's original institution, which is the chief element of the Lord's Supper. "God alone—without any entreaty or desire of man—must first come and give him a promise. This word of God is the beginning, the foundation, the rock upon which afterward all works, words, and thoughts of man must build."[46] The Lord's Supper possesses the structure of promise and faith. Considering the gifts of the Lord's Supper as the forgiveness of sins and eternal life, Luther criticized a downplaying of the words of institution in the mass. As a consequence, the sacrament was perverted into a good work. The essence of the mass is not a sacrifice that human beings bring to God. Faith is directed to Christ's sacrifice for us, which consecrates all believers as priests. Luther's idea of the priesthood of all believers comes to the fore in relation to the Lord's Supper.

In reflecting on the situation of the church in comparison to the experience of ancient Israel in Babylon after the fall of Jerusalem, Luther published his famous writing, *A Prelude on the Babylonian Captivity of the Church*. As Luther stated, "to begin with, I must deny that there are seven sacraments, and for the present maintain that there are but three: baptism, penance and the bread. All three have been subjected to a miserable captivity by the Roman Curia, and the church has been robbed of all her liberty."[47]

Encouraged by the remarkable success of this work, Luther followed it up with *The Babylonian Captivity of the Christian Church* (1520). In this wonderful piece of writing, Luther argued that the gospel had become captive to the institutional church. The medieval church, he argued, had imprisoned the gospel in a complex system of priests and sacraments. The church had become the master of the gospel, where it should be its servant.

45. *MLBTW*, 247.

46. *LW*, 35:82, cf. Brecht, *Martin Luther: His Road to Reformation*, 380.

47. *MLBTW*, 274.

This point was further developed in *The Freedom of a Christian*, in which Luther stressed both the freedom and obligations of the believer.

Luther characterized the Babylonian Captivity of the Eucharist in a threefold way: (1) Roman tyrannical withholding of the chalice from the laity; (2) the doctrine of transubstantiation; and (3) Roman understanding of the mass as human work, a propitiatory sacrifice repeating or reenacting the sacrifice of Christ on the altar. Understood in this way, the mass belongs to one of three great abominations, along with the papacy and monasticism. It does not become the means of grace pointing to a gracious God, but a human task of duty and even terror. As a result, the mass as a work of sacrifice was perverted into a money-making scheme. The concept of sacrifice in the canon of the mass obscures the gift-promise character of the supper. For Luther, "the mass is not a work which may be communicated to others, but the object of faith . . . for the strengthening of each one's own faith" to receive the divine promise of forgiveness of sins.[48] What is at stake for Luther is to stress the central significance of the promise and faith. For this he appealed to Augustine's word: *Crede et manducasti* (believe, and you have eaten).

In this regard the sacrament is not effective *ex opere operato* (a completed work that the priest performed by making sacrifice). It is rather called an *opus operans* (a work that God was doing and by which he was feeding his people).[49] However, Luther shared the notion of the Roman Catholic Church that Christ is truly present in the sacrament. More frequent reception of the sacrament by the laity was strongly argued.

In addition to sacramental theology, Luther published three major practical works through which he established himself as a major popular reformer. Luther wrote in German, making his ideas accessible to a wide public. In *A Treatise on Good Works* Luther tried to ground the ethical dimension of his justification. In an exposition of the Ten Commandments, Luther presented faith as the condition for making every work good. Faith is captain of every action because the one who is righteous lives by faith (Rom 1:17). Apart from faith there can be no good works. In this regard God's commandment should be understood. In fact, the grace of justification does not encapsulate human activity, but rather encourages it to be faithful to God's demand. Faith in a gracious God means that one is to be

48. *MLBTW*, 307.

49. Kittelson, *Luther*, 154.

gracious to one's fellow people. Thus Luther expanded Christian ethics on the basis of the doctrine of justification.

In dedication to the emperor and the German nobility Luther published his programmatic writing *To the Christian Nobility of the German Nation Concerning the Reform of the Christian Estate.* Obviously the pope's supremacy over the emperor was rejected. Furthermore, in this writing the pope's superiority is only in regard to preaching and absolution. The indulgence sellers should be driven out of Germany. From the practice of selling indulgences, the pope is the antichrist, no longer most holy, but most sinful. Church reform is to be done out of liberation from Rome's oppressive demands.

The priesthood of all believers plays an important role in dislodging the papacy's monopoly on the exposition of Scriptures. Luther does not refrain from his criticism of the Fuggers who were participating in the economic profit from the sale of offices and indulgences. As in the *Sermon on Usury*, Luther challenged the begging, insisting that every city should care for its own poor. Itinerant beggars, or begging pilgrims, or even the mendicant monks should be responsible for their own living. Luther's proposal was enacted in Wittenberg as an ordinance for common purchase. This system helped get credits for initiating the Reformation's first program of charity and became the model for later evangelical ordinances of community chests. In the appeal to the German nobility, Luther argued passionately for the need for reform of the church as well as the schools. Later Luther developed his proposal *To the Christian Nobility* in the preface to the Leisnig ordinance of a common chest at the beginning of 1523. He also argued that the mendicant monasteries in the cities should be converted into schools. A year later his famous writing *To the Councilmen of All Cities in Germany That They Establish and Maintain Christian Schools* became a milestone in the history of the German educational system.[50] The educational system needed to be reformed. In regard to the immense collapse of schools and church educational institutions, education was reinvented in a society in which humanism coupled with reformation provided a more efficient pedagogical system.

During Advent 1520, Luther gave an exposition of the *Magnificat*, Mary's hymn of praise, the printing of which was completed when Luther was at the Wartburg castle. In the *Magnificat* Luther regards Mary as the

50. *LW*, 45:339–78; cf. Asheim, *Glaube und Erziehung*, 20–87.

model for believers, and above all, the example of God's action, rather than as a mediator between human beings and the judging God. It is God who puts down the mighty and makes something out of nothing. Mary is the powerful example of how God turned the world upside down by choosing the humble and poor. In genuine humility Mary does not think of her own worthiness. It is God's grace that we are to admire in Mary, not Mary's merit. The role of Mary was especially important in Christian piety and devotion of the late Middle Ages. However, Luther's understanding of Mary turned the traditional view of Mary upside down. She does nothing, but God does everything.

God shows Godself as the merciful One. The strong, mighty, and proud are God's enemies. God confronts them as the judge. In contrast, God raises up the humble who are insignificant to the world. True worship does not lie in liturgical celebration of the mass as a human work, but in proclaiming God's mercy and promise in God's incarnate Son. Luther's exposition of the Magnificat reveals the direction in which Luther's understanding of justification moves, that is to say, from below. God who justifies is God on the paths of freedom and liberation especially for the poor and the humble. In the year of 1519 and 1520 Luther's reformatory program is in the spirit of *ecclesia semper reformanda.* Thereby the distinction between clergy and laity was eliminated in favor of the priesthood of all believers. The expression of this becomes manifest in the abolition of celibacy and of monasticism as a special spiritual estate. The reform of the religious and ecclesiastical hierarchy put an end to the centrality of the pope in the church, its finances, and the state.

In the summer of 1520 the crisis leading to excommunication came to a head. The bull threatening excommunication was published on June 24 and was referred to as *Exsurge Domine,* the initial of which was taken from Ps 74:22[23], i.e., "Arise, O God, plead thy cause." It calls God to act against the foxes and the wild boar who are destroying the vineyard of the Lord. It gave Luther sixty days to recant or to be excommunicated. Such acts commonly included a public burning of the heretic's books. While the bull threatening to excommunicate Luther was in process the curia attempted in May to urge Frederick the Wise to take measures against Luther. "If they damn my books and burn them," Luther announced, "I will burn the entire canon law."[51]

51. *WA, Br* 2.137, cf. Kittelson, *Luther,* 150.

To reconcile his position with Pope Leo X, Luther was persuaded to write the treatise *The Freedom of a Christian*. It is usually considered one of the three mains works from the year 1520, with *To the Christian Nobility* and *On the Babylonian Captivity*. However, this treatise did not come to terms with Rome, but further advanced a bold challenge to papal authority.

In *The Freedom of a Christian* Luther argues that nothing external such as the pope, prince, riches, or adversity is necessary or fundamental for human life. In the life we have in Christ a human being is free from all works. Therefore, the Christian is free "to empty himself, take upon himself the form of a servant, be made in the likeness of men, be found in human form, and to serve, help, and in every way deal with his neighbor as he sees that God through Christ has dealt and still deals with him."[52] God humbles the proud. The pope cannot be the vicar of Christ, but only his servant. Luther does not believe in the supernatural position ascribed to him by his flatterers. Leo is considered a wolf among the sheep.

Therefore, Christian liberty comes from the alien righteousness, *extra nos* (outside of one's self), so that the Christian can become free and share everything of Christ in being bound to Christ. As a result, the Christian life is understood as being full of extraordinary freedom, finding its most genuine expression in dedicating one's life for others. For Luther, Christian liberty means no human achievement at all, but rather a gift bestowed from God that is an empowering gift enabling us to be emancipated from obsession with our own self-concern and interest. Human liberation is only possible on the basis of this spirituality coming out of being incorporated into Christ. *The Freedom of a Christian* reaches its climax in its description of the relationship of Christ with the soul as that between bridegroom and bride, whose wedding is faith leading to joyful exchange. In this regard, we understand what Luther means by Christian freedom: "A Christian is a perfectly free lord of all, subject to none. A Christian is a perfectly dutiful servant of all, subject of all."[53] The background of *The Freedom of a Christian* expresses itself in the liberation from *Anfechtungen*, which is experienced in faith. From Luther's perspective, *The Freedom of a Christian* was a sincere, final attempt at reconciliation. However, Luther's

52. *MLBTW*, 618.

53. Ibid., 596.

approach to Christian freedom inevitably led to a thoroughgoing revolution in the church's life and teaching.

By now, Luther was at the center of both controversy and condemnation. On June 15, 1520, Luther was censured by a papal bull, and was ordered to retract his views. He refused, adding insult to injury, by publicly burning the bull. Luther was under threat of papal condemnation when Leo X's bull of June 15 arrived in Wittenberg. Luther burned both the bull and several papal books (including canon law) on December 10 in an act of defiance. This act called into question the entire ecclesiastical legal system on which the condemnation of the bull was based.

He was excommunicated in January of the following year. Again, he refused to withdraw his views. Luther was summoned to appear before Emperor Charles V at the Diet, or Parliament, in Worms (1521). Luther was not allowed to debate or defend, but only to answer the question of whether he agreed to recant the truth of what he had written. Luther responded boldly:

> Unless I am convinced by the testimony of the Scriptures or by clear reason (for I do not trust either in the pope or in councils alone, since it is well known that they have often erred and contradicted themselves), I am bound by the Scriptures I have quoted and my conscience is captive to the Word of God. I cannot and will not retract anything, since it is neither safe nor right to go against conscience. May God help me. Amen.[54]

Luther's position became increasingly serious. Realizing this, a friendly German prince arranged for him to be kidnapped, and took him off to the safety of Wartburg, a castle near Eisenach (May 1521 to March 1522). Even though Luther was in great distress for ten months at the Wartburg castle, he managed to complete the translation of the entire New Testament into German, as well as other significant writings. Luther called his experience in the Wartburg castle his Patmos, in reference to the island in the Aegean where John wrote the book of Revelation. Luther disguised himself now as "Junker Jörg," Sir George. This time was the most productive of his life. During his months of isolation, Luther had time to think through the implications of many of his ideas. By the time he returned to

54. Brecht, *Martin Luther: His Road to Reformation*, 460. The saying "I cannot do otherwise. Here I stand." is affirmed in a late printing. Cf. Brecht, *Martin Luther: His Road to Reformation*, 537.

Wittenberg in 1522 to take charge of the Reformation in that town his ideas were gaining considerable support throughout Europe.

His period of isolation at Wartburg allowed him to work on a number of major reforming projects including liturgical revision, biblical translation, and other reforming treatises. The New Testament appeared in German in 1522, although it was not until 1534 that the entire Bible was translated and published. The Edict of Worms, issued by the emperor shortly after Luther left Worms, declared him an outlaw. The theological faculties of the universities of Paris, Louvain, and Cologne condemned his teaching. Shortly after arriving at the Wartburg castle, Luther made his response to the attack by a Louvain professor, James Latomus (Jacques Masson, ca. 1475–1544). The issue in controversy was the concept of sin. After baptism the remnants of sin still remain in our life. The remnants of sin are to be understood as truly sin, not merely as weakness or punishment as his Catholic opponent taught. No good works are without sin.

Of course, something good is done in the struggle against sin. The whole person was condemned and therefore the whole person was saved. There was no room for Luther to allow for a spark of goodness in which a Christian is inclined to do partially good works by purchasing indulgences. There is no way to attain salvation through doing works of any kind. Unlike Latomus, Luther excluded human cooperation from the process of justification. Luther's rebuttal to Latomus is one of the most clearly systematized expositions of the central Reformation doctrine of grace and human nature before his debate with Erasmus in *The Bondage of the Will.*

While Luther was exiled in the Wartburg castle disguised as Knight George, Andreas Karlstadt (c. 1480–1541), Luther's senior colleague, who was present in the debate with Eck in Leipzig, took charge of the Reform process by taking dramatic iconoclastic action further than Luther himself had done. Karlstadt, former dean of the Faculty at Wittenberg, sought refuge at the Danish court in Copenhagen after the Diet of Worms. After returning to Wittenberg, however, he took over the leadership from Melanchthon, and moved in a direction different from Luther's. For example, according to Karlstadt the usual way of receiving only bread in communion is a sin.

Regardless of the injunction of Frederick, Karlstadt announced that the new form of Holy Communion (distribution of both bread and cup) in the vernacular liturgy would be introduced without priestly vestments. This radical reform led to an almost hysterical crowd at Christmas in 1521.

Without informing the court, Luther made a secret visit to Wittenberg at the beginning of December in order to see the situation there. Students who described themselves as "young, unrestrained, and ignorant Martinians" disturbed the mass in the city church, kept the priests from the altar, and took away the missals.[55] On December 4, students expelled the Franciscans and threatened to stone their monastery.

The radical change, which meant a total break with church tradition, was not acceptable to Luther. As a result, actual violence and destruction were done upon images and altars. The city school was to be closed and the university was on the verge of collapse. Of course, Luther's writing from the Wartburg castle, *The Judgment On Monastic Vows* (1521), is consistent with some changes that Karlstadt made. However, people were not encouraged to destroy religious images and take iconoclastic action against shrines and houses of religious orders. In *On Monastic Vows*, Luther's concern grew from his theory of justification; we don't make a vow to God, but God makes a vow to us. Luther elaborates the contrast between the Bible and eternally binding vows, because "neither the early church nor the New Testament knows anything at all of the taking of this kind of vow."[56]

As for monasticism, in his treatise *To the Christian Nobility* Luther does not want to "let Christian souls get entangled in the self-contrived traditions and laws of men."[57] However, if vows are voluntary, they are not condemned. In other words, vows pleasing to God should be kept, whereas godless vows should be broken in obedience to God. Therefore, Luther's intention was not the abolition of monasticism. If evangelical freedom were preserved, Luther would not be totally against the possibility of vows or monasticism.[58] This was the starting point in changing everything. Luther's orientation toward evangelical freedom is well expressed.

Since Worms, Luther had been thinking of the possibility of an insurrection, but he clearly rejected violence against priests, as that would bring the Reformation into disrepute. Luther indeed understood how people felt the urgent need of reform, but he rejected any disturbances. They are not the proper fruit of the gospel, but brought the gospel into disrepute and

55. Brecht, *Martin Luther: Shaping and Defining*, 30.

56. *LW*, 44:252.

57. *LW*, 44:175.

58. Lohse, *Martin Luther's Theology*, 143.

caused opposition to it. The God of peace was not stirring up a bloody and destructive riot, but a peaceful one. God would accomplish God's judgment without insurrection, so that a justified rebellion of the oppressed was not permissible but forbidden by God. In response to so-called Lutherans in rebellion, Luther argued; "I ask that men make no reference to my name; . . . What is Luther? After all, the teaching is not mine. Neither was I crucified for anyone."[59] In the exposition of the *Magnificat* at Wartburg Luther allowed no justification for a right to revolt. In reference to Luke 1:52, "He has put down the mighty from their thrones," he argues the oppressed are raised up "without any crash or sound."[60] In doing so, Luther opposed the Wittenberg disturbances.

At the same time, the so-called prophets from Zwickau, trades people, claimed to have received direct revelation from the Holy Spirit about the course of reformation. Zwickau was a "pearl" among the Saxon cities well known for its trade, particularly its cloth industry. Before the Reformation, the city was under the influence of Waldensians and Taborites. In 1520 Luther had dedicated the German version of *The Freedom of a Christian* to the city governor, Hermann Mühlpfort. Thomas Müntzer had been recommended by Luther to take the place of the preacher at St. Mary's church while he was on leave. In Zwickau, Müntzer was influenced by Nicholas Storch who possessed a remarkable knowledge of the Bible, especially with emphasis on special, immediate revelations and illuminations. When the city council took action against Storch's teaching, he escaped by leaving the city with his adherents, who made their way to Wittenberg. These people made a powerful impression on Melanchthon with their appeal to divine revelations and visions of the future.

Even rejecting infant baptism, they went so far as to say that scripture is surpassed by direct revelation from the Spirit. Melanchthon was at a loss of what to do and Frederick did not want Luther to intervene for his safety, nor did he want such a change in Wittenberg. Luther's return to Wittenberg (March 6, 1522) meant his responsibility for this disorder and involvement in normalizing the crisis. Luther's letter to Frederick shows how Luther felt about the disorder in Wittenberg, claiming that "the sword

59. Ibid., 32.

60. *LW*, 21:344.

ought not and cannot help a matter of this kind. God alone must do it . . . and without the solicitude and cooperation of men."[61]

What was at stake for Luther in the midst of the crisis was the way reform should be done in accordance with God's Word. The heart of reformation lies indeed in the way it is done, not in eliminating the Mass or distributing communion in both kinds. The changes in every case should be done in a more orderly and systematic way. Preaching was the driving force for Luther to reassert some order and control in the situation of crisis. [62]

> For there are many who are otherwise in accord with us . . . who would also gladly accept this thing, but they do not yet fully understand it. . . . Therefore, let us show love to our neighbors. . . . we must have patience with them for a time, and not cast out him who is weak in faith. . . . So long as love requires it and it does no harm to faith. If we do not earnestly pray to God and act rightly in this matter, it looks to me as if the misery which we have begun to heap upon the papists will fall upon us.[63]

It was Luther's belief that the proclaimed Word that had to illuminate and win people's hearts should replace creating a new order with appeal to enforced measures. Luther was not partial to images, but a general destruction of images must not occur. Faith had to be accompanied by a concern for love, and bold action could not be taken without love. The same thing was done when receiving communion under both kinds. This had to remain optional for the time being. Any sort of compulsion in connection with the gift of the Lord's Supper should not be used. Love and concern for the weak were primary. The *Invocabit* sermons made a profound influence on people in Wittenberg. As far as confession, images, celibacy, and fasting were concerned, Luther's approach was in the spirit of the *Invocabit* sermons.

In this regard, we can understand Luther's position on the destruction of images in spite of his sharp critique of the abuses in venerating images and the saints. Luther's attempt at liturgical renewal in his *Concerning the Order of Public Worship* (1523) focused on three issues: (1) God's Word has been ignored and silenced; (2) fables, lies and legends of the saints are substituted for its place; and (3) worship is misunderstood as a human

61. *LW*, 48:391, 315.

62. Cf. "Invocabit Sermons," *MLBTW*, 414–44.

63. Ibid., 418.

work. What was a more serious defect was caused by the absence of the Word. For Luther, there is no worship without preaching, no matter how brief it is. At the heart of Luther's emphasis on the Word was its interpretation. The Lectionary should be kept, however with the preacher's freedom to alter it. The Word of God should be given great scope and centrality in worship. The Word of God that must hold central place means not only preaching but also the Word of God in the sacraments.

As long as the tradition does not obscure the gospel, it is given the benefit of the doubt.[64] Music is a gift of God that encourages musicians and choir as well as congregation for the worship of God. On the visual arts Luther's position is ambivalent, positive about images (in his treatise on the *Magnificat* in 1521), but negative in the midst of the controversy of early 1522. Later in 1523 Luther proposed an actual order for the Mass in Wittenberg in which the language of the people, vernacular hymns, and the gift-character of the sacrament come to the fore in contrast to the sacrament as human work or sacrifice. He was open to diversity in approaching the liturgy, because, he believed, the spirit of Christ must dominate in the church.[65]

Assumptions of Martin Luther in Controversy

Luther and the Peasant War

Theologically, Luther's life was constantly challenged by fanatics, prophets, the peasant war, and the Jewish religion with which he was deeply entangled in controversy. In this section I will pay attention to Luther's controversial attitude to the Peasants' war, his theological debates with Erasmus and Zwingli, and finally the Jewish question. Serious controversy was not slow to break out. The Peasants' War began in the summer of 1524 with a revolt in the southern part of the Black Forest. Its causes were complex. Since the middle of the fourteenth century there had been a series of peasant uprisings in Europe, and the German Peasants' War was one of them. It reached its climax between March and May of 1525. Poverty had been increasing among the rural population, which caused the urban

64. *MLBTW*, 454.

65. In 1526 he provided "The German Mass" (*LW*, 53:51–90) in which we note that Luther distances himself from earlier Catholic features. In 1544 his document on worship in the Sermon at the Dedication of the Torgau Castle Church (*LW*, 51:331–54) needs consideration for his mature understanding of worship.

lower classes and peasants to revolt in a number of cities. In addition, a considerable share of the taxes due had to be paid to church institutions. The Reformation critique of the church and the economic situation, along with the call for evangelical freedom, gave lower classes reason to engage in social and political disturbances.[66]

Until the beginning of 1525 Luther had confronted economic problems in the question of *Zinskauf* and usury. He was averse to the radical solution of Thomas Müntzer and Karlstadt in which the old church structure were to be destroyed. Instead of leading to a revolutionary extermination, Luther wanted to see things regulated peacefully and appropriately by calling upon the government to prevent a radical solution. In this regard Luther drew a clear line between revolt and Reformation. Thomas Münzter had returned to Muhlhausen where Heinrich Pfeiffer and he held under their sway a new election to the so-called Eternal Council on March 17.

Along with Karlstadt, Thomas Müntzer was the most important opponent of Luther in his own camp. Born around 1489 in Stolberg in the Harz Mountains he became an aggressive supporter of the peasants' cause. Upon Luther's recommendation he worked in Zwickau as a substitute for Ergranus during his vacation, while there he was in heavy conflict with the old believers as well as the Franciscan monks. When the council dismissed him in April 1521, people in the circles of the *Tuchknappen* who were associated with Müntzer continued to preach their immediate revelations and their repudiation of infant baptism in Wittenberg at the end of 1521. They are known as the Zwickau prophets: Nicholas Storch, Thomas Drechsel, and Marcus Thomae. During a stay at Prague, Müntzer attempted to attract Bohemians, but his *Prague Manifesto* met no success at all. In 1523 the council of the rural village of Allstedt called Müntzer, where he succeeded in winning followers from all classes of society. Müntzer's activities between Zwickau and Allstedt raised considerable tension between him and Luther.[67]

However, it is not easy to ascertain the theological relationship between Luther and Müntzer. Some scholars see Müntzer as a more radical pupil of Luther, whereas others regard him as an apocalyptic prophet who was captivated by medieval German mysticism in relation to Bohemian

66. Cf. Williams, *Radical Reformation*, 137–74.

67. Ibid., 120–4; cf. Gritsch, *Thomas Müntzer*.

and Taborite sources. A Marxist interpretation of Müntzer depicts him as the theologian of the revolution. That being the case, in interpreting Müntzer complex elements such as the mystical heritage, Luther's impact, the apocalyptic eschatology of Joachim of Fioris, and his social and political activism are too difficult to be reconciled.[68]

In a letter to Luther, Müntzer attempted to distance himself from the Zwickau prophets. He insisted that he had nothing to do with the riot of the Zwickau *Tuchknappen.* However, Luther reacted negatively and remained intolerant of him. After 1523 Müntzer became a radical opponent of Luther. Luther was accused of proclaiming a faith without mortification, and of ignoring the bitter Christ in favor of a sweet Christ. Luther's teaching of justification was blind to the eschatological task in separating the tares from the wheat without further ado. In the preface to his *Deutsche Evangelische Messe* (in late summer 1524), Müntzer, in exposing the outrage of all idolatry, attacked Luther's Latin *Formula Missae* in which Luther tended to accommodate the weak. Following this, there occurred on Maundy Thursday (March 24, 1524) the burning of the Marian chapel at Mallerbach, which belonged to the neighboring Cistercian monastery in Naundorf near Allstedt.

Since the beginning of 1523, two former monks, Matthew Hisolidus and Heinrich Pfeiffer, had been preaching in Mulhausen for the Reformation cause. Pfeiffer appears to have been close to Karlstadt in many respects. When Pfeiffer was dismissed an insurrection broke out in various sectors. Müntzer worked in Mulhausen without a proper call. Pfeiffer and Müntzer also interfered in an insurrection on 19 September, but they were banished. They then made their way to Nuremberg. Müntzer's direct confrontation with Luther began when Müntzer returned to Mulhausen in the spring of 1525. Mulhausen was threatening to become the center of the revolt in Thuringia. Individuals like Karlstadt and Müntzer instigated disturbances in Tothenburg, Nuremberg, Schweinfurt, and Mulhausen.

When the groups of rebellious peasants in Upper Schwabia joined together in Memmingen at the beginning of March they produced *The Fundamental and Proper Chief Articles of All the Peasantry and Those Who Are Oppressed by Spiritual and Temporal Authority.* This document was also known as the Twelve Articles, and became the most widely known agenda of the Peasants' War. The content of these articles was clearly informed by

68. Cf. Goertz, *Thomas Müntzer.*

the gospel. Along the lines of the spirit of the gospel, the peasants were not revolutionaries. The first three articles—on the freedom to choose a pastor, the partial removal of the tithe, and the abolition of serfdom—were formulated on the basis of Reformation thought. They referenced a number of theologians including Luther, Melanchthon, and Jacob Strauss. However, there was no mention of Müntzer and Karlstadt. Essentially, they sought a peaceful solution to the conflict. However, violent action broke out and reached its high point on April 16 after the capture of Weinsberg.

In response to the Twelve Articles of the peasants' "constitution," Luther published *Admonition to Peace: A Reply to the Twelve Articles of the Peasants in Swabia.* Luther was concerned about the gospel and the common good of state and society. The system of two realms, although separate but related, were biblically based after all. Therefore, Luther rejected revolution for the benefit of the Reformation, but he did not forget to intercede for the peasants' cause with the princes and lords, including the bishops, priests, and monks. They were responsible for the revolt, he argued, because of their resistance to the gospel and exploitation of the common people. The revolt came as God's righteous punishment of the lords. False prophets had already begun to lead people astray toward the political revolution that would later devastate Germany through murder and bloodshed.

From the Twelve Articles Luther recognized the religious and economic demands conditionally and acknowledged the validity of the social complaints for which the government was responsible. Luther also criticized the peasants, warning them against the fanatical and murdering spirits that would call themselves a "Christian Association or union" and appeal to divine right. Luther's political principle was that a Christian is forbidden to resist the government with force, even if the government acts improperly. "No one sits as judge in his own case."[69]

Luther emphasized that the gospel should not be imposed by violence. Therefore, the action of the peasants was completely unjustified when measured against this Christian standard. A Christian who was suffering injustice was to endure it. If the peasants were Christian, they would only pray to God and have God as their helper and savior. This conservative admonition corresponded to Luther's faith and experience. What Luther specifically accused them of was the intention to impose their articles by

69. Brecht, *Martin Luther: Shaping and Defining*, 176.

violence. Even the legitimate demands for the gospel could not be instituted by violence. The conclusion of the work was addressed to both the authorities and the peasants. Both were in the wrong, he concluded. As the authorities were oppressive tyrants, so the peasants were rebels. Both were under God's wrath. Germany was threatened with destruction in a revolt that was out of control.

In fact, Luther's *Admonition to Peace* is not primarily a proposal for a political solution. Rather, it was addressed to their conscience in expression of the same critical consequences for both parties. In recognizing the peasants' demand, nevertheless, Luther did not condone the insurrection of the peasants for the evangelical cause. This conclusion was also based on his idea of two realms. Luther's *Admonition* was regarded as flattering to the princes by betraying the need of peasants who sympathized with the Reformation. Opposition against this admonition was stirred up in the Peasants' War. The conflict then moved into its violent phase.

Visiting Eisleben and nearby cities (April and May 1525), Luther decided to confront the Thuringian revolt in his preaching. He admonished crowds of peasants to keep the peace and condemned their appeal to Christian liberty and the gospel for their justification and violence. As in the *Admonition to Peace* Luther preached the crucified Christ as the model for a Christian attitude ready to suffer. This message was not well received and Luther again found himself in danger because of his sermon. He was rejected, even threatened. The atmosphere was hostile and Luther's *Admonition* did not persuade his opponents. Müntzer's attractive preaching message of the equality of all people gained more and more in popularity.

Since writing the *Admonition to Peace* Luther's attitude toward the peasants had become more critical. After the revolt began he advised immediate action as a warning to them. Luther argued agressively that they broke their oath of obedience to their lords, had falsely appealed to the gospel by starting a revolution, and in so doing, they became robbers and murderers. Luther's confrontation with Müntzer became inevitable. Luther was sure that Münzter was behind the revolt in Thuringia. The two realms of church and state were confused in a way that condoned violence and revolt.

Luther's writing, *Against the Murderous and Thieving Hordes of Peasants,* is overblown in his resentment against Thomas Müntzer and the peasants in the revolt. They violated their oath of obedience to the authorities so God's punishment would be imminent. Moreover, they instigated a revolt of bloodletting and desolation and crime. They were in an emergency state, and it justified everyone in acting against the rebels. The peasants' earlier claim that they were willing to negotiate was a lie. It was Müntzer, the "archdevil of Muhlhausen," who led the peasants astray and was convicted of this devilish work of robbery, murder, and bloodshed. "If the peasants did not lay down their arms, then the princes were to smite, strangle, and stab [them], secretly or openly, remembering that nothing can be more poisonous, hurtful, or devilish than a rebel. It is just as when one must kill a mad dog: if you do not strike him, he will strike you and a whole land with you."[70]

The revolt that was taking place in the name of the gospel was a sin of eschatological perversity. The authorities had every reason and the inherent right to take action against the rebels who deserved death. The rebellion had nothing to do with the Reformation. Evangelical authorities should act in the fear of God, recognizing the revolt as God's deserved punishment upon Germany, and call upon God for help against the devil. As in the *Admonition to Peace* they should offer the peasants an opportunity to negotiate. If it failed, however, they should swiftly take to the sword. "This is the time of the sword and wrath, not the day of grace."[71] A prince was entrusted with the office of imposing punishment with a clear conscience. "A prince can win heaven with bloodshed better than other men with prayer." What is worse, the peasants were forcing others to join with them. Such participants are also guilty. The authorities were obliged to step in for these fellow travelers who were in the bonds of hell and the devil. "Therefore, dear lords, here is a place where you can release, rescue, help. Have mercy on those poor people! Let whoever can stab, smite, slay. If you die in doing it, good for you! A more blessed death can never be yours."[72]

Revolt was intolerable. Luther accused the peasants of breaking faith, revolting, and abusing the gospel. In conclusion, one should flee from the peasants as from the devil himself. It was the right and responsibility of the government to take action. Before that, a Christian government should offer to come to terms. If this failed, clear action should follow.

70. *AE*, 46, 54, 52, 50 (*WA*, 18, 361, 359, 358); cf. Kittelson, *Luther*, 191–92.

71. Ibid.

72. Brecht, *Martin Luther: Shaping and Defining*, 181.

The situation of those who were forced to participate in the rebellion of the peasants called for the government's forceful intervention. As before, Luther was still striving for a negotiated solution. In the publication of the Weingarten agreement between the Swabian League and the peasants in Upper Swabia (on April 22) the peasants disbanded their force and did homage to their lords. The lords renounced any punishment of the peasants. Luther welcomed this solution as a model for restoring the relationship between the lords and the peasants.

On May 15, Philip of Hesse, George of Saxony, and Henry of Brunswick, joined by Counts Albrecht and Ernest of Mansfeld, slaughtered the Thuringian peasants at Frankenhausen. Thousands were killed, and Thomas Müntzer was taken prisoner. Luther was convinced that the rebels would suffer God's punishment. He warned the victorious princes not to presume too much, because they were not righteous, but the peasants were in the wrong. Luther distanced himself from the merciless revenge the lords were taking on their prisoners, and from the victors' misuse of power. It can be noted, however, that Luther lacked understanding for the oppressed and their problems.[73]

Müntzer was a theologian who had divorced the reception of the Spirit from the external Word. Consequently it led him to a revolutionary transformation of the Word into the kingdom of God on the basis of the Old Testament theocentric model. Although Luther had previously been critical of both sides, such a balanced approach was no longer available in the midst of the revolt as it played out. Because the peasants were clearly in the wrong, the authorities had to act mercilessly against them. After some excellent attempts to mediate, Luther, in that controversy, wrote an angry, bitter pamphlet, urging the Princes to smite, slay and destroy the rebellious peasants. It caused Luther's reputation to suffer severely. Luther argued that the feudal lords had every right to end the peasants' revolt, by force where necessary. Luther's writings on this matter had virtually no impact on the revolt itself, but tarnished his image severely. However, something seemed to crack in Luther after the terrible episode of the Peasants' War in 1525. It was the first of many shameful writings.

73. In "An Open Letter on the Harsh Book Against the Peasants," Luther added, "When I have time and occasion to do so, I shall attack the princes and lords too, for in my office of teacher a prince is the same to me as a peasant." *AE*, 46, 75 (*WA*, 18:393); cf. Kittelson, *Luther*, 192.

Luther and Erasmus

In the conflict with Erasmus of Rotterdam over free will, Luther had to defend his theology of justification. In September 1524, Erasmus's *Dialogue on Free Will* (*Diatribe De Libero Arbitrio*) appeared, calling into question Luther's understanding of human nature. Luther's *Bondage of the Will* (*De Servo Arbitrio*) became one of his most important publications and was regarded by Luther himself as among his best works. This was composed mainly in the Autumn of 1525 and was in print by the end of December of the same year. Only once had Augustine spoken of the bound will. By using this title, Luther intended to make clear that he understood himself as the defender of the Augustinian doctrine of sin and grace against Pelagians, old and new. Luther wrote this treatise in the midst of the peasants' revolt and the controversy about the Lord's Supper.

The dispute between Luther and Erasmus had to do with the starting point of Reformation theology concerning sin, and the bondage of the human will with respect to grace. In the debate with Erasmus, Luther further developed his view of sin and the will and in some respects his view of God as well. Erasmus defined freedom of the will as, "a power of the human will by which a man can apply himself to the things which lead to eternal salvation, or turn away from them."[74] Against Luther, he thought that ignorance of freedom of the will easily led to godlessness.

Holding a different opinion about the capacities of free will, Erasmus took issue with Augustine's notion that a free will was capable only of sinning, and with Luther's more radical notion that free will was an empty formula. Because there were tensions among the biblical statements on free will, Erasmus made an attempt to reconcile these statements by a combination of human will and divine grace. That is why Erasmus was very critical of Luther's insistence that a human being is a total sinner without grace.

Of course, Erasmus had no intention of removing grace as the essential way of initiating salvation. Nevertheless, grace does not reject the cooperation of human will. Otherwise God would be accountable for evil. In his relationship with the Reformation Erasmus understood himself to be in a neutral position between Roman Catholic teachings and Luther from the beginning. His problem was navigating between the Scylla and the Charybdis of the two sides. Luther had an "obstinate assertiveness,"

74. Rupp, trans., *Free Will and Salvation*, 47.

lacking moderation and evangelical gentleness. At certain points in his *Diatribe*, Erasmus is supportive of the opinion of the skeptics concerning the authority of Holy Scriptures and the decree of the church.[75]

In reply, Luther affirmed that the Holy Spirit is no skeptic. "It is not the mark of a Christian mind to take no delight in assertions; on the contrary, a man must delight in assertions or he will be no Christian. And by assertion—in order that we may not be misled by words—I mean a constant adhering, affirming, confessing, maintaining, and an invincible preserving."[76] In this light Erasmus is charged with being a skeptic. "Let Skeptics and Academics keep well away from us Christians, but let there be among us 'assertors' twice as unyielding as the Stoics themselves."[77]

Luther was defending the Reformation principle of scripture, according to which scripture as such is clear and requires no exposition by priests, as in Roman Catholic teachings, to overcome possible obscurities. Erasmus' accusation of "obstinate assertiveness" made no sense, because a definitive assertion of the faith belongs inseparably to the confessional character of Christianity. A Christian needs it. "Take away assertions and you take away Christianity."[78] This does not mean that it contains no tensions or even contradictions in detail. Bondage of the will for Luther was not merely a result of the fall (like Augustine) but came from human creatureliness.

For Luther, Christ was seen as the midpoint of scripture. The Holy Spirit interprets himself/herself. The view that Holy Scripture interprets itself, but also that Christ is its decisive content, is the presupposition underlying Luther's conviction that Scripture is clear. The Spirit makes sure claim on our hearts. In *The Bondage of the Will* Luther dealt with the question of Scripture's clarity in much greater detail. According to Erasmus, God had willed that some things reported in Scripture should be inaccessible to us. There was profound significance in the obscurity of such passages.

Luther distinguished three lights (*tria lumina*). In view of the *lumen naturae* Luther dealt with the insoluble problem of how a good person can suffer and a bad person prosper. Further, in view of the *lumen gratiae*

75. Cf. Brecht, *Martin Luther: Shaping and Defining*, 217.

76. *LW*, 33:19–20.

77. Cf. Lohse, *Martin Luther's Theology*, 164.

78. Brecht, *Martin Luther: Shaping and Defining*, 226.

he takes into account the problem of how God can damn a person who is unable to do something good. Finally, the *lumen glorae* will some day bring the solution. In the *lumen gloriae* we will see that God always acts "with the most righteous and manifest righteousness." Even in view of the *lumen naturae* and *lumen gratiae* God is not unjust. For Luther, God's righteousness is revealed in the gospel and seized by faith alone. This core statement of the Bible is clear. Its real content is the revelation of Christ and his work of salvation. The whole Bible must be interpreted on the basis of Christ. The gospel is not hidden in the darkness of a cave.

The essential difference between Erasmus and Luther lies in that Holy Scripture for Luther is clear and unequivocal with the help of the Holy Spirit. All Scripture must be read and interpreted from and toward Jesus Christ. This is an interpretation of the entire Bible in relation to the revelation of Christ. "Remove Christ from the Scriptures and there is nothing left." Through Christ, God and God's design were rendered accessible to everyone, even though there may be passages, statements, and concepts that are obscure to us. However, the gospel is plain and must therefore be taught and preached simply and without skepticism.

Thus, the issue lies in whether a person has the capacity of doing anything for his/her own salvation, or if it is entirely dependent on God's grace and predestination. Luther's concern is to demonstrate that the divine will is independent of the human will. The Son of God had assumed a human body, and in him God had gone through the ultimate depths of death and hell. God's predestination, which might be found in Jesus Christ, meant the reliability of God's promise for human salvation. At this point the human will determines nothing. A human being is like a beast ridden either by God or by the devil. Thus, free choice belongs only to God. It should not be understood as destroying human free will in a moral sense. Only concerning salvation is a human being powerless for the sake of Christ. Not the human approach to God and salvation, but God's approach to us is at the heart of Luther's justification. This is what the Bible teaches us fundamentally.

Therefore, the formula that "a power of the human will by which a man can apply himself to the things that lead to eternal salvation" remained meaningless and obscure. In this regard Luther challenged significant biblical passages used by Erasmus to affirm the free will. After all, God's omnipotence excluded free will. Otherwise, Christ remained a partial redeemer. Luther's exaggerated distinction between *Deus absconditus* and *Deus revelatus* in debate with Erasmus (for instance Ezek 18:23) has been accused of flirting with Marcion's doctrine of two gods.[79] However, Luther's exaggerated statements and remarks in *De servo arbitrio* must be seen and taken from a christological perspective. "If we believe that Christ has redeemed men by his blood, we are bound to confess that the whole man was lost; otherwise, we should make Christ either superfluous or the redeemer of only the lowest part of man, which would be blasphemy and sacrilege."[80]

Luther and Zwingli

Widespread disturbances in Germany were the start of what was seen in retrospect as the Reformation. The Colloquy of Marburg (1529), arranged by Philip of Hesse, was of particular importance. Luther's meeting with Zwingli and others at Marburg in 1529 marked division over the Lord's Supper. The most significant controversy erupted over the very different views on the nature of the real presence held by Luther and Zwingli. Luther's strong commitment to the real presence of Christ in the Eucharist contrasted sharply with Zwingli's metaphorical or symbolic approach to it. Although many sought to reconcile the two views, they eventually came to nothing. This failure led to the permanent alienation of the German and Swiss reforming parties at a time when increasingly adverse political and military considerations made collaboration imperative.

In August 1524, Luther was informed that in Zurich Ulrich Zwingli was interpreting the words of institution symbolically. In a letter to a Reutlingen preacher, Matthew Alber, Zwingli presented his new view of the Lord's Supper. In 1523 he was still ready to come to terms with Luther on the Lord's Supper, but he showed hesitation about the sacrament as an external means of salvation. While, in 1523, Luther clearly rejected the Dutchman Hoen's symbolic interpretation of the words of institution, Zwingli, in 1524, found in Hoen's interpretation help in understanding the Lord's Supper as an act of thanksgiving and confession. The way of interpreting "is" in the words of institution as "signifies" and the spiritual eating of the Lord's Supper on the basis of John 6 were not acceptable to Luther. In his treatise *The Adoration of the Sacrament* (1523) Luther clearly affirmed the real presence of Christ's body and blood in the elements of

79. Cf. Lohse, *Martin Luther's Theology*, 164.

80. *LW*, 33:293.

the Supper, in contrast to Hoen. Against Hoen Luther writes: "In that case one should say: That Mary is a virgin and the mother of God is equivalent to saying that Mary signifies a virgin and the mother of God. Likewise: Christ is God and man; that is, Christ signifies God and man."[81]

For Luther the sacrament is an object of faith as a means of grace. When the Lord's Supper is taken in light of the words of institution it should not be taken symbolically or metaphorically. Christ is able to be in many places and yet remain at the right hand of God. This surpasses human understanding. We have to believe that Christ's body and blood are really present. It is given to the recipient as a gift. The purpose of the sacrament consists in the strengthening of faith and the assuring of conscience. Its fruit is love and communion. The real treasure in the Lord's Supper is Christ himself. However, for Zwingli the object of faith is not Christ's presence in the sacrament, but his death. Nothing external can support faith. "The flesh is of no avail" (John 6:63) is applied to the Supper.

The symbolic and significative interpretation of the *est* in the words of institution ensued. According to Zwingli, eating the body of Christ in the Lord's Supper is an act of cannibalism. From this a clear distinction between the divine and human nature in Christ is drawn. The human nature did not partake of divine omnipresence, therefore the real presence of Christ's body and blood in the Lord's Supper is also excluded. According to Zwingli, the Supper represented a "*commemoratio* by which those who firmly believe they are reconciled with the Father through Christ's death and blood proclaim this life-giving death."[82]

Luther's christological idea of "sitting at the right hand of God" is not confined to a specific place in heaven, but understood in a way that Christ participates in God's omnipotence and omnipresence that permeated all of creation, down to the tiniest leaf or seed. In his sermon of 1526, *The Sacrament of the Body and Blood of Christ—Against the Fanatics,* Luther writes, "We believe that Christ, according to his human nature, is put over all creatures [Eph 1:22] and fills all things. . . . Not only according to his divine nature, but also according to his human nature, he is lord of all things, has all things in his hand, and is present everywhere."[83]

81. *LW*, 36:280.

82. Zwingli *CR* 90, 807, 11–14; cf. Lohse, *Martin Luther's Theology*, 172.

83. *LW*, 36:342.

According to Luther, Christ's humanity and divinity were inseparable. In contrast to the sharp distinction about the human and divine natures of Christ (*alloiosis*, interchange), Luther affirmed his theory of the ubiquity of Christ's humanity on which the real presence of Christ in the Lord's Supper is grounded. The weak point in Zwingli's Christology would cause a perilous bifurcation of Christ's person and his saving work. In order to prove Christ's humanity present everywhere, Luther introduced three different ways of being present: locally in a circumscribed manner, the incomprehensible way in which angels and spirits are present, and the nature of God's being, which fills everything.[84]

Landgrave Philip of Hesse was interested in a unified political front of the evangelicals against the Catholic side. He convened the Marburg Colloquy to reconcile the parties from Wittenberg and Zurich. What was at stake in the colloquy was the words of institution that guaranteed the real presence of Christ's body. Even Luther proposed a compromise in which there would be reconciliation if the opposing party agreed on a substantial and essential presence of Christ's body, but not in a quantitative, qualitative, or local manner. This offer was not acceptable to his opponents because the theory of the real presence of Christ's body undermined their biblical exegesis and spiritualistic orientation. The presence of Christ's body and blood remains as a stumbling block to church unity.[85]

> And although we are not at this time agreed as to whether the true body and blood of Christ are bodily present in the bread and wine, nevertheless the one party should show to the other Christian love, so far as conscience will permit, and both should fervently pray God Almighty that by His Spirit He would confirm us in the true understanding.[86]

Luther and Jewish Religion

By 1527, it was clear that Luther was not a healthy man. Convinced that he had not long to live, Luther married a former nun, Katharina von Bora. Although Luther went on to produce a number of major theological works

84. Brecht, *Martin Luther: Shaping and Defining*, 319.

85. It is shown among recent Zwingli scholars that Zwingli's development of the Lord's Supper in his later stage affirms the real presence of Christ. See, e.g., Gäbler, *Huldrych Zwingli*, 122–23.

86. "The fifteenth Article of The Marburg Colloquy;" cf. Lohse, *Martin Luther's Theology*, 176.

in his later period (most notably a *Commentary on Galatians*), his attention was increasingly taken up with his personal health and the politics of the Reformation struggles. Luther's influence on virtually every aspect of Reformation thought is immense. His approaches to biblical interpretation, gospel and law, the doctrine of justification, the church, and the sacraments remain theological landmarks.

Luther's scriptural hermeneutic was Christ-centered. "Here you will see the swaddling cloths and manger in which Christ lies, and to which the angel points the shepherd (Luke 2:12). Simple and lowly are these swaddling cloths, but dear is the treasure, Christ, who lies in them."[87] The relationship between law and gospel does not refer to the Old Testament simply as law, the New Testament simply as gospel. Luther mentioned for example Genesis or Isaiah as great works of gospel.[88] As the law consists in making requirements, so gospel is related to what God has done for us, by reversing the approach of the law. [89]

> The chief article and foundation of the gospel is that before you take Christ as example, you accept and recognize him as gift, as a present that God has given you, and that is your own. . . . This is the great fire of the love of God for us, whereby the heart and conscience become happy, secure and content. This is what preaching the Christian faith means.[90]

The distinction of law from gospel led Luther to a commitment to preaching Christ with respect to what God has done for us. Luther regarded the gospel of John as "the one fine, true, and chief gospel, and far to be preferred over the other three and placed high above them."[91] Luther's canon within the canon was the gospel of John plus the "gospels" of Romans, Galatians, Ephesians, 1 Peter, and 1 John. He ignored various biblical books (Esther, for example) and warned against the legalistic tendency of James. Luther's radical Christocentrism in understanding the Scriptures becomes manifest in the following remark: "Therefore, if the

87. "Preface to the Old Testament," *MLBTW*, 119.

88. Ibid.,120.

89. Ibid., "How Christians Should Regard Moses," 136.

90. Ibid., "What to Look For and Expect in the Gospels," 106.

91. Ibid., "Preface to the New Testament," 117.

adversaries press the Scriptures against Christ, we urge Christ against the Scriptures."[92]

Luther loved the Old Testament and was one of the first major theologians to trouble himself with learning Hebrew. All through his life he found spiritual comfort not only in John and Paul, but also in Genesis, Isaiah, and especially in the Psalms. Signs of this hope are found in an important early writing: *That Jesus Christ Was Born A Jew* (1523).[93] In this treatise Luther combines a forceful theological defense of the Messiahship of Jesus with calm and generous pastoral advice about how Jews should be treated. In accordance with the belief that there was no other way of salvation for the Jews, he hoped to win some Jews to faith in Jesus Christ. Through friendly, fraternal instruction, Luther emphasized the original preferred position of the Jews over the gentiles in the history of salvation. The Old Testament patriarchs lived in hope of the deliverer.

According to the promises made to Abraham and David, he was to come from their descendents. Mary's virginity was not her own special quality, but was used by God in the work of salvation. The messianic prophecy in Isa 7:14, which spoke about a young woman, not a virgin, bearing a son, was not evidence contradicting Mary's virginity. He demonstrated to the Jews that the obscure messianic prophecies in Gen 49:10 and Dan 9:24–27 could refer only to Christ. Luther's concern is not to integrate the Jews forcefully into the articles of faith about Jesus Christ, as long as they saw Jesus as the Messiah. Christianity was to have patience and refrain from the old accusations against the Jews. In contrast to previous practice, the Jews should be allowed equal rights in society and commerce. Luther dedicated his work to Bernard, a baptized Jew living in Schweinitz. Luther had participated in the baptism of his son in March 1523. In criticizing remaining discrimination against converted Jews, Luther's positive attitude toward the Jews was remarkable during this time.

However, the worst of Luther on the Jews is found in a bitter, angry late writing: *On the Jews and Their Lies* (1542).[94] This conflict with the Jews was based on a theological and exegetical quarrel. In April 1537, the Strasburg reformer Wolfgang Capito, one of Europe's most eminent Hebrew scholars, wrote to Luther to help Josel Rosheim of Lower Alsace

92. *LW*, Thesis 49, 34:112.
93. *LW*, 45:195–229.
94. *LW*, 47:121–306.

in a petition to the elector. In August 1536, the elector Jon Frederick issued a decree banishing all Jews from his territories and forbidding them to pass through them. Anti-Jewish sentiment in Europe was a well-known fact, as Shakespeare's *The Merchant of Venice* attests. In his letter to Josel of Rosheim (1537), Luther expresses his concern in a friendly manner: "My dear Josel! I would most gladly intercede for you with my most gracious lord, both in word and letter, just as my treatise [That Jesus Christ Was Born a Jew, 1523] did great service to all of Judaism." However, Luther showed his bitter feelings about them, "because you and your people have so shamefully abused everything I have done." Christians regarded "this damned, crucified Jew" as the true God, while the Jews regarded him as "a heathen" and even "after his death pray for a Lord."[95]

The Jews' unwillingness to accept the divinity of Jesus and the Trinity, and their practice of usury, led Luther to attack them. Luther's early advocacy for the Jews in *That Jesus Christ was Born a Jew* had been misused, and the Jews had called Christians apostates. Luther was still in favor of benevolent treatment of the Jews in order to win them for the Messiah. "For the sake of the crucified Jew, whom no one will take from me, I gladly wanted to do my best for you Jews, except that you abused my favor and hardened your hearts."[96] In the letter to Josel of Rosheim, Luther stated his positive interest in winning the Jews to the Messiah and added a polemic against the rabbis who rejected the Messiah. Luther admired the Jewish people. Christ was the flower that grew from the beautiful plant of this people.

Nonetheless, nothing changed in his attitude toward rabbinic biblical exegesis. In Luther's view it was totally out of the question to interpret the suffering servant (Isa 53) as referring to the Jewish people. The new covenant was fulfilled in Christ. The Christians became the true Israelites. However, the Jews are not denied life, and the door of grace is not closed. In Paul's earnest affirmation, the Jews are not to be abandoned entirely. Luther's rejection of the Jewish exegesis of the Bible and salvation remained strong, however, and the Pauline expectation for the Jews is not aban-

95. *WA Br* 8, 89–90; cf. Kittelson, *Luther*, 274.

96. *WA, TR*, 3, no. 3596; cf. Brecht, *Martin Luther: The Preservation of the Church*, 337. However, Luther in his "Table Talks" replied in a negative manner; "Why should we give permission to these rascals who injure people in body and property and with their superstitions cause many Christians to fall away?" *LW*, 54.239.

doned. Like papists, Sacramentarians, and Anabaptists, Luther regarded Jews as enemies of the gospel of Jesus Christ.

In *On the Jews and Their Lies* (1542) Luther defended the Christian faith from what he perceived as the madness of the Jews. As he saw it, the faith of Christians should be strengthened to fight against the blasphemies of the Jews. First of all, Luther's confrontation with the Jews came from his teaching on justification. The concluding third part of the book has become notorious and infamous because of modern anti-Semitism. Luther attacked the Jews vehemently, replying to suggestions that Jesus was distorted as a cabalistic magician, that Mary was called a whore or a dung heap, and that Jesus was a freak because he was conceived by Mary during menstruation. For Luther such abuses and curses against Jesus and Mary could be only madness and blindness worthy of God's punishment. Besides, the Jews believed that their Messiah would kill and destroy the Gentiles.

For economic reasons Luther depicted Jews as loafers while Christians had to work hard. The Jews were a plague and a sickness. Luther's solution was to practice a sharp mercy. He justified the use of force and made specific proposals: setting fire to synagogues in which Christ and Christians were reviled, making blasphemy a criminal offense, burning houses of the Jews, treating Jews like gypsies, confiscating and destroying prayer books and Talmudic writings, forbidding rabbis to teach, abolishing safe-conducts through the countryside, prohibiting their involvement in borrowing and lending, forced hard labor for young Jews, and finally, expulsion from the land.

In this light Luther believed that coexistence of the Christian and Jewish religions was impossible. What Luther really intended was the expulsion of the Jews, not their massacre. If the curses and the animosity of Jews against Jesus Christ, Mary, and the Trinity were real, they came from rabbinic interpretation of the Scriptures and their polemics and agitation. There was no sense in talking about mutual toleration or a relationship of coexistence. Even if Luther's proposals were carried out, the Jews would continue to curse in secret. Therefore, the only thing to do was to expel them. The Jew's accusation that Christians worshiped more than one God was an unbearable lie to Luther. The only recourse was a sharp mercy that purged and expelled them. It is no surprise that Nazi propaganda ministers discovered and reproduced this material for their own uses.

Luther's conflict with the Jews was by and large due to a hermeneutical crisis. Taking issue with the vilification of Jesus and also with the Jewish criticism of the differing genealogies of Jesus in Matthew and Luke, Luther made an extensive attempt to clarify the complex relationships of Jesus' lineage. For Luther, both Old and New Testaments testified to the virgin birth and messianism of Jesus. In fighting against the rabbis' critique of the Christian interpretation of the Bible, Luther affirmed that the Old Testament also bore witness to Christ without further ado. The Old Testament should be interpreted on the basis of the New.

In Luther's treatise on *The Last Words of David* he explains that David appealed to a promise of the anointed one by living in accordance with the promise.[97] The anointed one to whom David was speaking was really the triune God, in whom the humanity of Jesus was involved. God's covenant with David (2 Sam 7:11–16 and 1 Chro 17:1–14) did not merely refer to Solomon and the Temple, but pointed beyond them to the Messiah and his kingdom. The doctrine of the Trinity and the divine sonship of Jesus are fully affirmed by the Old Testament. Jewish exegesis could no longer be compatible with Luther's theology. Like all Christian theologians of his time, Luther regarded the Jewish religion in a negative way and hoped for their conversion to Christianity. He was pessimistic about the possibilities and prospects of the Jews, but he never denied them entirely.

In the conclusion of *On the Jews and Their Lies* Luther expressed his wish: "May Christ, our dear Lord, convert them mercifully and preserve us steadfastly and immovably in the knowledge of him, which is eternal life. Amen." Luther's opposition to the Jews was by and large due to scriptural conflict, because Jewish exegesis could not be compatible any longer with Luther's theological interpretation of justification, Christology, Trinity, and finally of the Old Testament. Luther's hatred toward the Jews may have been based on social, economic, or psychological motives, but not on racial prejudices of anti Semitism. Socio-economic, psychological, and racial motives were common, and Luther participated in the attitudes common in his day. As a general rule, I would say that Lutherans today are not responsible for what Luther said five hundred years ago. They are responsible for how they edit and pass on tradition. It would be sufficient to say that Luther was indefensibly wrong in his hostile remarks about Jews. Luther's attitude toward the Jews must be challenged and criticized

97. *LW*, 15:265–352.

in a theological and hermeneutical way, and Luther's mistake must be corrected and improved in light of Christian-Jewish dialogue.[98]

Characteristics of Luther's Theology

Given Luther's life and struggle, we need to delineate what is characteristic of Luther's thought. Luther nourished his theology from reading the scripture, Pauline theology, and the tradition from the church fathers, especially Augustine. In fact, Luther was a man with great respect for the tradition, in spite of his bitter criticism of it. For Luther, theology means nothing other than "*sapientia experimentalis*" (experiential wisdom),[99] which is determined by his triadic formulation: "*oratio, meditatio, tentatio.*"[100] In the dramatic framework of the justification event, Luther sees faith as *vita passiva*, in which *vita activa* with its work or *vita contemplativa* with its speculation should not be self-complacency and self-righteous before God.[101]

What is at stake for Luther's understanding of theology is, therefore, not scholastic, but rather pastoral and spiritual; that is to say, a theology of scripture creates faith and speaks to it. From the theology of the Word of God, Luther's systematic reflection on the catechism comes to the fore. Theology as textual meditation is related to theology as grammar of the language of the Holy Scripture, in which the Spirit plays a decisive role by having its own grammar.[102] For this reason, Luther understands theology not as a science of principle or nature (essence), but as the science of history and experience. Theology is an endless wisdom, because it cannot be learned enough. It refers to a spirituality of humility, obedience, and resistance with respect to the Word of God, God's death on the cross, and God's justice and justification for the individual, the church, and the world.

Luther's understanding of justification was central to his theology. All his important teachings about the doctrine of God, the sacraments, the

98. In "Declaration of the ELCA To The Jewish Community," we read that "in concert with the Lutheran World Federation we particularly deplore the appropriation of Luther's words by modern anti-Semites for the teaching of hatred toward Judaism or toward the Jewish people in our day." Cf. Lull, *My Conversation with Martin Luther*, 150.

99. *WA*, 9:21, 98.

100. Ibid., 30:50, 658.

101. *WA*, 5:11, 166.

102. *WA*, 24:39 II, 104.

theology of the cross, ecclesiology, and the like are deeply related to it. It was the cardinal article separating him sharply from the traditional teaching. Justification comes by grace, for Christ's sake, through faith. There is no doubt that the heart and soul of Luther's Reformation theology was the article on justification. Salvation comes as a free and surprising gift from God who sets aside condemnation and offers a new covenant freely and mercifully to all humanity. This gift cannot be deserved or earned; it can only be received in faith and by trust in the love and kindness of God who offers it. In light of the death and resurrection of Jesus Christ, justification by faith is a matter of death and life.[103] The classic Lutheran definition of justification is to be found in Article IV of the Augsburg Confession (1530). Even though Melanchthon wrote the confession, it had Luther's full approval during his stay at Coburg. After reading the first draft, Luther said, "It pleases me very much and I do not know how I could improve on or alter it . . . for I cannot tread so softly and lightly."[104]

We "become righteous before God by grace, for Christ's sake, through faith."[105] Three prepositional phrases "by grace," "for Christ's sake," and "through faith," taken together explain various aspects of God's justifying work. This is the positive affirmation of what can really happen to us by the grace of God.

> To obtain such faith [the justifying faith] God instituted the office of ministry, that is, provided the Gospel and the sacraments. Through these, as through means, he gives the Holy Spirit, who works faith, when and where he pleases, in those who hear the Gospel. And the Gospel teaches that we have a gracious God, not by our own merits but by the merit of Christ, when we believe this.[106]

Understood this way, his intention in the treatise of *Bondage of the Will* becomes clear. Justification by faith is understood as a matter of death and life. Our separation from God is fundamental and relational; individual sins are signs of a more basic problem, which can be cured only from God's side.

103. Cf. Forde, *Justification*.

104. *WA*, *Br* 5, 319, cf. Kittelson, *Luther*, 233–34.

105. *BC*, 30.

106. Ibid., 31.

> Now, since death, the cross, and all the evils of the world are numbered among the works of God that lead to salvation, the human will thus be able to will its own death and perdition . . . But what is here left to grace and the Holy Ghost? This plainly to ascribe divinity to "free will!" For to will the law and the gospel, not to will sin, and to will death, is possible to divine power alone, as Paul says in more places than one.[107]

God became a man, suffered, and will rule for all eternity. This message is unequivocal. The gospel is plain and must therefore be taught and preached simply and without skepticism. There is no free will pertaining to salvation. However, this negative side of Luther stands in dialectical relation with the positive side of justification—human faith through the grace of God is recalled to love for Christ's sake. We are "rapt to Christ with the sweetest rapture through the Holy Spirit," because "the Holy Spirit is no skeptic, and the things He has written in our hearts are not doubts or opinions, but assertions—surer and more certain than sense and life itself."[108]

Luther's teaching of justification from without leads us to pay attention to God's alien work in the suffering of Christ. Luther's orientation in Reformation theology is best known through his theology of the cross, a term he coined in 1518. It was used in various contexts to articulate his theological vision and goal. Where the theology of the cross was concerned, his orientation was not only against scholasticism, but also against the humanism of Erasmus.

In speaking of the reform at the University of Wittenberg, he said, "our theology and St. Augustine" can be seen adequately in light of the *theologia crucis* stressing what is essential for Christian faith in rejection of scholastic as well as humanistic attempts, such as Erasmus'.[109] If God is present in Jesus at the moment of defeat and rejection, then most of our guesses about who God is and where God is to be found (in glory, in power, in success) are wrong. In an attempt to know God on the basis of God's creation, Luther saw the theology of glory arrive at divine judgment and wrath. God is one whose ways are beyond ours, but who comes to the weak, the marginal, the undeserving. This is Luther's most original contribution to the theology of the cross and its spirituality. In addition,

107. Luther, *Bondage of the Will*, 140.

108. Ibid., 70.

109. *LW*, 48:42.

Luther's spiritual experience of *Anfechtungen* (inner struggle) cannot be taken apart from his theological reflection on the cross, which discerns the omnipotent God not in manifestations of power and glory but in the midst of peril and suffering.

Despite all this, the theology of the cross may not be seen in opposition to a theology of the resurrection. Luther focused on the cross in contrast to scholasticism, which ignored it by turning gospel into law. For him, however, the resurrection is inseparably connected with the cross, so that "a theology of resurrection is the intrinsic complement of a theology of the cross."[110] Luther's theology of the cross expressed well the profound depth of his spiritual experience, and was taken by Dietrich Bonhoeffer in our times to stand in favor of a "world come of age," especially in regard to the suffering of people.

As for the hermeneutical approach to the Scriptures, Christ should be the center. The hermeneutical distinction between law and gospel is the new Reformation formulation of the distinction between law and grace first proposed by Augustine. According to Luther, the law is not merely superseded by the gospel. Rather, in the old as well as the new covenant law and gospel remain in a dialectical relation. In all of Scripture God is encountered as one who demands, orders, and judges, but also loves, gives, and forgives. The right interpretation of the Bible is to hear both of these notes, without confusion in Old and New Testament alike, and to learn from each but understand that gospel/grace/mercy is the bottom line. Luther's own study of scripture was quite original.

> Gospel means nothing else than a preaching and a crying out of the grace and the mercy of God, merited and conquered by the Lord Christ by means of his death. And it is not what is found in books and what is written in letters; rather, it is a voice that resounds in all the world and will, pray God, be shouted and heard in all places.[111]

In Luther's thought there is a dimension of evangelical rejoicing in the law. In the *Preface to the Old Testament* (1523, revised 1545), Luther gives special regard to the Old Testament, which is "the very words, works, judgments, and deeds of the majesty, power, and wisdom of the most high God." The law is not merely conceptualized as having an accusatory func-

110. Lohse, *Martin Luther's Theology*, 39.

111. *WA*, 12:259; cf. Altmann, *Luther and Liberation*, 51.

tion, but also as involving the gratitude of the justified for the grace of Christ. As Luther states,

> Now in the New Testament there are also given, along with the teaching about grace, many other teachings that are laws and commandments for the control of the flesh. . . . Similarly in the Old Testament too there are, beside the laws, certain promises and words of grace, by which the holy fathers and prophets under the law kept, like us, in the faith of Christ.[112]

Luther's understanding of Word and sacraments is deeply rooted in his understanding of the gospel, in contrast to the medieval teaching of the sacraments as human sacrifices/works of the law. Appealing to the union between the Word and sacraments, Luther pays attention to the interconnection between promise (*promissio*) and faith (*fides*). For Luther, baptism is not merely water, but God's command and Word are connected with it. God's Word and command are at the center of understanding sacraments.[113] Likewise for the Lord's Supper, Christ's words of institution are inseparably connected with the real presence of Jesus Christ under the bread and wine, thus the promise is apprehended in faith.

What is characteristic of Luther's eucharistic theology can be well delineated in the following way: it was critical, practical/mystical, speculative (ubiquity), and had a social and communal dimension. Moreover, the eucharistic theology of Luther was not only a means of grace, but also could be reinterpreted in light of a cosmic Christology reflecting on the universality of Christ's body present in the world. According to article VIII of the Formula of Concord it is said that the exalted Lord is not only present bodily in the Lord's Supper, but is also spatially present in general. ". . . [A]lso according to and with this same assumed human nature of his, Christ can be and is present *wherever he wills* (emphasis added), and in particular that he is present with his church and community on earth . . . ."[114]

The right hand of God is not a specific place in heaven, but "precisely the almighty power of God which fills heavens and earth, in which Christ has been installed according to his humanity in deed and truth without any blending or equalization of the two natures in their essence

112. *MLBTW*, 119–20.

113. *BC*, 348, 438.

114. *Solid Declaration,* VIII.78, BC, 606–7.

and essential properties."[115] The cosmic Christ in the Eucharist is of special significance for Asian Christianity as it understands the Lord's Supper in relation to Confucian ancestral rites (cf. chapter 6).

As for the priesthood of all the baptized, Luther's statement of the universal priesthood always served to counter the resistance of the Catholic hierarchy and especially the papacy to demands for reform. In *A Treatise on the New Testament*, Luther expresses his idea of the universal priesthood of all the baptized. "Thus it becomes clear that it is not the priest alone who offers the sacrifice of the mass; it is this faith that each one has for himself. This is the true priestly office, through which Christ is offered as a sacrifice to God, an office which the priest, with the outward ceremonies of the mass, simply represents. Each and all are, therefore, equally spiritual priests before God."[116]

Luther was breaking here with the medieval idea of the hierarchy of estates, according to which the spiritual is above the temporal with the pope at the apex. By contrast, Luther emphasized the independence of the temporal estate, which has its own task from God, and in fulfilling its duty it need not be obedient to the spiritual estate. To establish his view, Luther interpreted the universal priesthood on the basis of baptism or of faith in Jesus Christ. "For whoever comes out of the water of baptism can boast that he is already a consecrated priest, bishop, and pope, although of course it is not seemly that just anybody shall exercise such office."[117]

However, in opposition to fanatics and after 1530 Luther took more seriously the ministerial office for the sake of the church order than the universal priesthood. For Luther the ministerial office had to find scriptural basis affirming that Christ instituted all the offices, including the ministerial office (Eph 4:11). Already in *To the Christian Nobility of the German Nation* Luther mentioned, "the ministry which God has instituted, the responsibility of which is to minister word and sacrament to a congregation, among whom they reside."[118]

Given this, for Luther tension between the universal priesthood and the ministerial office including the Episcopal office was situated contextually and should be discussed in terms of the scriptural basis. Be that as it

115. Ibid., VIII.28, 596.

116. *LW,* 35:100–101.

117. *LW*, 44:129.

118. Ibid., 44:176.

may, in baptism God calls all Christians to a life of witness and service in the world. God can be praised through all vocations, as each Christian seeks to be Christ to his or her neighbor. Christians are called not to hang around the church but to go where they are needed in the world. Human beings find it hard to accept that God is gracious. God therefore presents this message not only in the preaching of the Word but also in baptism, in confession and forgiveness, in the Lord's Supper, and in the mutual conversation and consolation of brothers and sisters. In an Asian context, Luther's idea of the priesthood of all baptized has a conspicuous resonance with the liberative aspect of minjung theology in which a struggle for liberation from Church hierarchy and dominion plays a significant role.

From this perspective the Reformation principle *of ecclesia semper reformanda* (the church has to be always renewed) goes hand in hand with the principle *status mundi renovabitur* (the condition of the world will be renewed). An honest reading of church history from the beginning shows that the problem of corruption in the sixteenth century was not an isolated aberration. Because God's message comes through fallible human persons, the church needs reform in every generation. The Reformation teaching becomes explicit in his last confession: "I am fully conscious and certain that I have taught correctly from the Word of God, according to the service to which God pressed me against my will; I have taught correctly about faith, love, the cross, and the sacraments. Many accused me of proceeding too severely. Severely, that is true, and often too severely; but it was a question of the salvation of all, even my opponents. I was still intending to give all I had to write about Holy Baptism against Zwingli and the contemnors of the sacraments. But God has evidently decided differently."[119]

For Luther the church of Christ was the church of the persecuted, sufferers and the martyrs, who truly bore witness to their crucified Lord through their suffering. As a matter of fact, "the church is the child of the gospel."[120] Let me introduce Luther's ecclesiology by citing his remarks; "In truth, the gospel comes before the bread (Holy Supper) and baptism, as the one most certain and noble sign of the church, because it is only through the gospel that the church is conceived, formed, nourished, born, educated, fed, clothed, ornamented, strengthened, prepared, and

119. Briefwechsel, 66, 27–67, 8, cf. Jonas, I.106, 6f; see Oberman, *Luther*, 322.

120. *WA*, 2:430, 6–7.

sustained. In a word: The whole life and substance of the church is in the Word of God."[121]

Furthermore, Luther listed seven marks of the church: (1) the Word of God; (2) the Sacrament of Baptism; (3) the Sacrament of the Altar; (4) the power of the keys; (5) the calling and ordaining of pastors and bishops; (6) prayer, praise, and thanks to God; and (7) enduring the cross and inner conflict (*Anfechtung*).[122]

Luther's reflection on two kingdoms is related to God's complex impact on the world stands in relation to the three estates or life arrangements. After returning from the Wartburg Luther began to emphasize strongly the necessity of using the secular sword to guard against social disorder. Two realms need to be considered: that of the Word for the pious and that of the sword for the wicked. "Thus, in summary, worldly authority must outwardly rise up and restrain evil, inwardly it must be wise and prudent so that it knows how to temper and moderate its severity in a way that is meek and right."[123]

Luther developed the theme from Matt 3:2: "Repent, for the kingdom of heaven is at hand." The dimension of proclaiming the kingdom of God is important in determining the content of the gospel. However, the earthly kingdom had not been abolished by Christ. Thus Luther comes to the concept of two ways of ruling the believers and the unbelievers through the use of the Word or the use of the sword. They are not opposed to each other. Christian freedom is willing to submit to the government's orders out of love for the neighbor. This has nothing to do with a spirit of servitude and accommodation.

While Christians give deepest thanks for what God had done in Jesus Christ they also know that God continues to rule through creation, that the church has no monopoly on wisdom or goodness for living in this world, and that Christians are often put to shame by those outside the community of faith. The two kingdoms are not separated from each other, but are in a state of mutual responsibility for God's kingdom. In *Temporal Authority: To What Extent it Should be Obeyed,* Luther presented the basis of political power and a Christian relationship to it particularly in regard to the prohibition of Luther's writings and his translation of the

121. *WA*, 7:721, 9–13; cf. Altmann, *Luther and Liberation,* 62.

122. "Councils and the Church," *MLBTW,* 540–75.

123. Brecht, *Martin Luther: Shaping and Defining,* 115.

New Testament in Nuremberg. He did this by dividing people into the kingdom of God or the kingdom of the world. Christians belong to the kingdom of God. They need no earthly sword or law because the Holy Spirit leads them by love and willingness to suffer. However, most people belong to the kingdom of the world. They are compelled under the law by the sword to live in peaceful coexistence.

Therefore there are two realms or ways in which God rules: the spiritual realm justifies the human being before God, and the temporal realm keeps evil in check and preserves peace. The gospel cannot rule the temporal world, it would amount to chaos. Thus, the Sermon on the Mount is directed to Christians as individuals. It does not help in the exercise of a political office. After affirming the necessity of the government for the Christian, Luther limits the power of the government in encroaching on God's kingdom and realm. Temporal laws apply to people's lives and possessions, not to their souls. No temporal ruler should be allowed to make rules about faith so the mandate concerning the confiscation of Luther's translation of the New Testament should not be obeyed. The rulers are not competent to prevent heresy. Heresy could not be countered with force, only with the Word of God. The common people are learning to think so that they would not continue to endure unjust government. Luther's political ethic is an important contribution to the history of freedom of conscience. Government has no power to intervene in spiritual matters because faith is a matter of each individual's conscience. By and large, *Temporal Authority* is the fundamental and most significant document of Luther's political ethics. Characteristic of Luther's political thought was the need to distinguish properly the kingdom of God from that of the world, and yet to relate them to each other.

Like the distinction between two kingdoms Luther also made distinction between the three estates that include the priestly estate (*ecclesia*), the estate of marriage (*oeconomia*) and the temporal authority (*politia*). In all three estates where the papacy has no place at all the Christian must act responsibly, especially in the economic sphere. This is what Luther intended by his reflection on two kingdoms in relation to the three estates.[124]

In this regard, we understand Luther's position on economic issues. After his *Sermon on Usury* of 1520, Luther developed his response to the usury in his sermons on the Ten Commandments in March 1523. The

124. *LW*, 37:364–65; cf. *LW*, "Lectures on Genesis 2:16–17," 1:104.

interest on capital should be shared between creditor and debtor in order to moderate rates of interest. Once the idea that economic activity was incompatible with faith and Scripture was abolished the economic abuses could also stop. Luther's follower, Jacob Strauss, the former Dominican from Basel, criticized economic abuses at length. Strauss held that any profit on capital was displeasing to God and so paying obligations of this sort was sinful. Luther, who was motivated by Strauss, was in favor of abolishing the un-Christian usury, but he did not agree with Strauss's total prohibition of the usury.

Luther enlarged the previous version of his large *Sermon on Usury* in 1524 under the title *On Trade and Usury* on the basis of Deut 15:3.[125] He did not recognize the privilege granted to the Jews of engaging in the business of usury. In principle, Luther affirmed the necessity of trade. But in practice, the merchants' principle of obtaining the highest possible price was incompatible with Christian love. Indiscriminate exploitation of markets was not justified because business was to be run in accordance with the principle of justice and fairness. "There are some who have no conscientious scruples against selling their goods on time and credit for a higher price than if they were sold for cash. Indeed, there are some who will sell nothing for cash but everything on time, so they can make large profits on it. Observe that this way of dealing—which is grossly contrary to God's word, contrary to reason and every sense of justice, and springs from sheer wantonness and greed—is a sin against one's neighbor . . . According to divine law he [the seller] should not sell his goods at a higher price on the time payment plan than for cash. Again, there are some who sell their goods at a higher price than they command in the common market, or than is customary in the trade . . . All such fellows are manifest thieves, robbers, and usurers."[126]

A major problem in trade consists in guaranteeing capital credit. Because people cannot rule the market world with the gospel, the government must provide the regulation for the protection of property. Luther rejected giving surety, speculating in futures, taking advantage of the market situation, and cornering the market except for state stockpiling. Capitalizing on price advantages, manipulating products, weights, or measures are strongly criticized. The economic abuses could not be regulated

125. *LW*, 45:245–310.

126. *LW*, 45:261–62.

either by the law of Moses or by the gospel. Rather they must be curbed according to common sense. Normally five percent interest was allowed, but in bad years it could be reduced. His concern was to warn against greed and the service of mammon. The problems of obtaining and owning property were to be dealt with and regulated by Christians according to the principle of love, and by the authorities according to the principle of common sense. Luther's economic theory accords with his political idea of two realms. Luther criticized the aberrations of economic activity, but he also rejected any legalistic regulation of it. However, Luther was by no means consistent with this principle in his debate with the so-called fanatics as well as in his conflict with the rebellious peasants.

Luther's teaching of justification and the principle of *ecclesia semper reformanda* accentuated God's initiative for the poor and the humble. In his *Commentary on the Magnificat,* Luther took Mary as an example of justification, because she was impoverished and a pregnant woman without marriage. She "actually (became) impoverished and (was) completely wrapped up in poverty so that, without any human help, God alone may do the work."[127]

Luther's perspective from below expressed itself well in his teaching of the priesthood of all believers in which he envisioned women preaching under extreme circumstances, although he rejected any usurpation of the pastoral office. In the reorganization of church affairs of the city of Leisnig, Luther was supportive of the plans for establishing a common chest, calling a pastor on the basis of Scriptures and introducing an order of worship. In reply to this plan (1523), Luther wrote that the mark of a Christian congregation is the pure preaching of the gospel.[128] The church's legal organization is not based on canon law, but rather on God's Word. The congregation has the right to reject the instructions of Catholic bishops and abbots, and to call and install a qualified and gifted person as the pastor. Although cooperation between bishop and congregation was not excluded in principle, a call from the congregation was necessary for exercising the general office of the ministry. The Reformation movement

127. *LW*, 21: 328–29.

128. "That a Christian Assembly or Congregation Has the Right and Power to Judge All Teaching and to Call, Appoint, and Dismiss Teachers, Established and Proven by Scripture," 39: 305–14. In his treatise *To the Councilmen of All Cities in Germany That They Establish and Maintain Christian Schools* (*LW*, 45: 347–78), Luther shows his interest for everyone to read and understand the Scripture.

had the potential to develop from below. Luther wrote a preface to the *Leisnig Ordinance of a Common Chest* in 1523. Here Luther affirmed a congregation's right to choose a pastor and establish a common chest into which the income of the parish, the church, the endowed masses, brotherhoods, alms and bequests were to be combined.[129]

Luther was an attractive figure in his passion for the gospel, his courage for renewal of the church, his communicative powers in speaking and writing. His sense of vocation was expressed in his compassion for the sick afflicted by the plague. Between 1527 and 1529 and then again in the summer of 1542 the plague ravaged the city of Wittenberg. Refusing to leave the city with his colleagues, Luther wrote to his wife in a seemingly coldhearted manner. "Spare me your worrying, there is someone better to worry about me than you and all the angels; he lies in the manger and hangs from the Virgin's teats."[130]

On the other hand, he is a troubled and even frightening figure in his anger, his lack of charity to enemies, and his capacity for violent and highly irresponsible speech under pressure—as with the peasants and the late writings on the Jews. Philip Melanchthon, "Erasmus of Wittenberg," wanted to leave Wittenberg for fear of Luther's ire and his ruthless withdrawal of sympathy. Melanchthon was strongly convinced that Luther's vocation lay in becoming "the charioteer of Israel."[131] In spite of their differences, he was essentially in agreement with Luther. Besides, Luther is a puzzling figure to modern persons in his obsession with the devil and his sense that the world was about to end. Driven by a disturbance between fear of God and abhorrence of the devil, Luther was "a child of his time" whose character cannot simply be transplanted and translated into our postmodern era. Despite mistakes and wrong doings, as Oberman states, "there is something to be learned from trying to imagine Luther as our contemporary because it is his personality and character that are at issue."[132] Luther would invite us to read God's suffering love for us in a different context, where not Luther himself, but Jesus Christ is at issue. A conversation with Luther in a different context calls for a hermeneutical task of actualizing and deepening the gospel of Jesus Christ to whom

129. Luther shows his economic ethics in his treatise, *Fraternal Agreement* (1523), *LW*, 45:186–91.

130. Cf. Oberman, *Luther*, 316.

131. Ibid., 303.

132. Ibid., 314.

Luther bore witness passionately and concretely all his life. The dimension of the gospel for the poor, a new understanding of Jesus Christ as the poor is above all championed by liberation theology in Latin America. Here Luther joins in solidarity with people in need of liberation from social and political oppression.

When it comes to a conversation with Luther in an Asian context, we should focus on poverty and pluralistic religious spiritualities. The subject of Luther and otherness needs to be reformulated from a perspective of Asian contextual and post-foundational theology, which I try to actualize in this book. This is a daring task, in which Luther's theology would be challenged and transformed in encounter with otherness. In such a hermeneutical task of audacity, Luther's theology of the Word of God in action will be retrieved through his irregular and fragmentary concept of God's freedom.

This task will succeed when the gospel of Jesus Christ is deepened and Jesus Christ is more profoundly witnessed in different contexts in favor of life rather than imitating and transplanting Luther's ideas. The significance of Luther lies in his passionate turn to the statement that the just shall live by faith. In other words, in an Asian context surrounded by overwhelming poverty, multi-religious spiritualities, and ecological devastation, Luther may appear as a theologian of life in solidarity with the poor and humble in recognition of the others who unconsciously and indirectly would follow in the footsteps of the kenotic way of Jesus Christ. "In the midst of death we are surrounded by life."[133] This slogan can make Luther's theology of justification relevant today in Asian contexts beyond its topical interest and narrowness.[134]

133. Oberman, *Luther*, 330.

134. Cf. Forde, *Justification*, 81.

If God should be asked at the last judgment, "Why did you permit Adam to fall?" And he answered, "In order that my goodness toward the human race might be understood when I gave my son for man's salvation"

LW 54:385–86

If innumerable beings . . . after hearing my name when I shall have become a Buddha, should direct their thoughts incessantly to being born in my country . . . repent their misdeeds, perform good acts for the cause of Buddhism, and recite sutras, then I will cause them to be born in my country without their going back to hell and the states of animals and hungry ghosts; and if they so wish, I will make them Buddhu by virtue of this vow of mine. If this vow of mine is not realized, then may I not become a Buddha

The Great Amida Sutra

3

Martin Luther and the Doctrine of Justification in Context

THE "JOINT DECLARATION ON THE DOCTRINE OF JUSTIFICATION" AFFIRMS an epoch-making new ecumenical consensus and reconciliation between the Roman Catholic Church and the Lutheran World Federation concerning the understanding of justification, which has historically been a stumbling block to both sides.[1] This declaration was signed on October 31, 1999, Reformation day. In order fully to understand the importance of this statement on justification, it is necessary to take note of the historical development and debates on this doctrine that have played a major role separating the Catholic Church from Protestant churches. In this chapter I discuss justification in a broader ecumenical context and then interact with Luther's theology of justification with respect to its spiritual and socio-economic dimensions. Along the way of this study I will extend and contextualize Luther's theology of justification from an Asian perspective with the focus on justification's relevance to the theology of divine suffering and the language of two kingdoms.

Historical Development and Controversy over Justification

The development of the doctrine of justification in the medieval period is Augustinian in character with reference to the newly accepted categories of the day. Augustine was paid high respect in face of the increasing influence of Aristotle's philosophy. He interprets the Latin term *justificatio* (from Greek term *dikaiosis*) as *justum facere*, which is often referred to

1. Cf. *Joint Declaration on the Doctrine of Justification* (Geneva: LWF and PCPCU, 1999).

as *justificatio coram hominibus* rather than *coram Deo*. His teaching navigates between Manichaeism and Pelagianism. The former rejected the free will while the latter exaggerated its role in the matter of justification and salvation, leading to denial of the need for involvement of any divine grace whatsoever. What was at issue in the debate between Pelagius and Augustine was the understanding of prevenient grace (*gratia praeveniens*). According to Augustine, Pelagius was so against grace that he was in a position to oppose even Christ's grace.[2]

Pelagius (350/354–418) represents the idea that a human being, soul and body, is primarily created good by God and thus is equipped with free will to do good acts freely. Therefore, he understands grace as an external, non-coercive grace of knowledge like knowledge of the Decalogue or the example of Christ. However, what is at stake for Augustine is the priority of grace in understanding justification in a way that does not demolish human will, but rather establishes it. His earlier excessive emphasis on human will in contrast to Manichean's teaching (generally prior to 396) began to be withdrawn in the later framework of establishing the spiritual ascent to perfection through faith in God with the help of infused grace.

In contrast to the Pelagian exaggeration of free will, Augustine affirmed that a human being possesses no liberty at all because the free will is taken captive by sin. It is only available for sin. In so doing, righteousness cannot avail itself and become possible without the help of divine action.[3] Although Adam possessed free will before the fall it was compromised and confounded by sin, and thus became captive to sin. Even though the free will is not lost it needs to be healed by grace. Justification takes place where a human's enslaved will becomes a free will with the help of divine healing grace. Therefore, Augustine's doctrine of free will is to be distinguished from Luther's doctrine of the will in bondage. For Augustine, the captive will is incapable of desiring good or effecting its own justification because of sin and lack of merit. God operates to initiate human justification and thus cooperates with a human will to perform good works, finally bringing justification to perfection. God as the author of justification and holiness operates upon a human will in the act of justification and cooperates with it in the process of justification toward eternal life.

Faith cannot exist without love. Since Augustine, "faith working through love" (Gal 5:6) has been the dominant theme in understanding

2. *Retractationes,* II 42, 68.47, 73. Cf. *Handbuch,* 447–48.

3. Cf. McGrath, *Iustitia Dei*, 26.

the nature of justification. This statement is open to a Pelagian interpretation except for the fact that faith and love are gifts of God. Just as *cupiditas* is the root of all evil, so *caritas* is the root of all good. For Augustine, it is love rather than faith. His teaching on justification includes the event of justification through operative grace and the process of justification through cooperative grace.

Augustine does not distinguish between the double aspects of justification. God's work is not finished and completed once and for all in the single event of justification but requires a perfecting process in which God's cooperative grace is in collaboration with the human free will. In this regard, human righteousness is inherent rather than imputed from without because, although justification originates from God, it is located within human will. Of special significance for Augustine was the interior renewal of the sinner by the grace of the Holy Spirit. In participation in the life of the Trinity the justified sinner is led to adoptive filiation and deification in the process of the justification.[4]

However, Augustine's idea of deification/divinization is unlike that of neoplatonism because it is grounded in adoptive sonship rather than in the divine origin of the soul in its participation of the life of the Trinity. It is Christ alone who realizes our teleological purpose. Augustine's double understanding of justification, i.e., the event and the process, corresponds to the Reformation concepts of justification and sanctification, especially in John Calvin.

The teaching of justification during the medieval period may be regarded as a systematic attempt to understand Augustine encountering Aristotle's philosophy as it was understood at the time. In the case of Thomas Aquinas, justification of the unrighteous originates in an infusion of grace.[5] Four requirements are needed for the process of justification: (1) an infusion of grace, (2) a movement of free choice directed toward God by faith, (3) a movement of free choice directed toward sin, and (4) the forgiveness of sin.[6]

4. Augustine's phrase, "*Deus facturus qui homines erant, homo factus est qui Deus erat*," (Cf. McGrath, *Iustitia Dei*, 32). As Augustine states, "it is clear that because he said that humans are gods they are deified from his grace not born from his substance . . . He who justifies also deifies, because by justification he makes sons of God . . . If we have been made God's sons, we have also been made gods; but this is by adopting grace, not by nature giving birth," (*Hom. on Ps*. 49.1.2). See McGinn, *Foundations of Mysticism*, 251.

5. *ST*, 1a 2ae.113.7.

6. Ibid., 113.6.

The infusion of grace is the efficient cause of the remission of sin. Thomas does not represent a forensic concept of justification, but his understanding of justification as a remission of sin expressly includes the remaining other three elements. That is to say: *infusio gratiae, motus liberi arbitrii, remissio peccatorum*. Thus, a movement of the free will toward God must precede its motion against sin. In other words, the former is the cause of the latter. Justification takes place under the influence of grace as a human being moves toward God by faith in Christ. This teaching is of special significance in his *Summa Theologiae*.

According to Thomas, a human being is transformed from a state of corrupt nature to one of habitual grace through justification and the remission of sin. There is a decisive difference between the virtue of justice and the supernatural habit of justice with the infusion of divine grace. The virtue of acquired justice is conceived as particular or legal justice pertaining to interpersonal relationships between human beings, while the virtue of infused justice comes from God through the infusion of grace. Justification is seen entirely in the context of justice because it is a "kind of rightness of order in people's own interior disposition, namely when what is highest in people is subject to God and the lower powers of their souls are subject to what is highest in them, their reason."[7]

According to Thomas, God's remission of sins means we have repented and changed direction and returned to him. "Now the effect of divine love in us which is removed by sin is the grace by which someone becomes worthy of eternal life, from which people are excluded by mortal sin. And therefore the forgiveness of sin would not be intelligible unless there were present an infusion of grace."[8] As God forgives our sin God does not change God's mind about us—because God is eternal and immutable—but changes our mind about God. A human being that has been accepted or acquitted by God is declared to be righteous. This righteousness is possessed only by imputation from without; but at the same time, justification is regarded as making a difference in people. The first statement is close to Luther in that the Christian who is consecrated by his or her faith does good works that are the fruit of faith alone.

Thomas also asserts that even though one is restored through justifying faith the human is unable to overcome sin entirely. In other words,

7. Ibid.,113.1.

8. Ibid.,113.3.

a human being is not capable of avoiding actual sin after justification. However, justification is in no way a consequence of human works; it is the effect of grace. "In this sense, that good movement of free choice itself, by which someone prepares to receive the gift of grace, is the action of a free choice moved by God . . . The principal agent is God moving the free choice; and in this sense it is said that our will is prepared by God, and our steps are directed by the Lord."[9] For Thomas, justification is "*sola gratia sine operibus precedentibus,*" which means "the grace of God does not presuppose goodness in human beings but creates it." Of course, human deeds are an integral part of justification as an internal process in which a human being strives to reach the final, complete goal.

Unlike Peter Lombard, who identified *caritas* as what is infused into the soul in justification by the Holy Spirit, Thomas stresses a created gift that is caused within the soul by God. That is to say, a supernatural habit. What happens before the sinner is justified? The human being is disposed for the reception of uncreated grace of the Holy Spirit in which a quality of the soul is brought about by the action of grace. It may be termed created supernatural grace. It is still uncertain whether created grace is to be considered the disposition toward the reception of uncreated grace or the result of the reception of uncreated grace. In other words, one can argue whether Thomas deals with the justification on the basis of *analogia entis* (analogy of being) or *analogia fidei* (analogy of faith).[10]

Aquinas does not agree that human beings after the fall are wholly corrupt and incapable of good. According to him, "without grace, people of themselves can know good. Even in the state of corrupted nature, human nature . . . can by virtue of its natural endowments, work some particular good."[11] At the same time, however, he does not forget to insist that "for the knowledge of any truth whatever people need divine help, that the intellect may be moved by God to its act." Therefore, people "need the help of God as first mover to do or wish any good whatsoever."[12] If God alone can impart grace—because it is out of the question that any capability of created nature should cause grace—we need grace even to prepare ourselves for grace.[13] "People can do nothing unless they are moved by

9. Ibid., 112.2.

10. *Handbuch*, 677.

11. *ST*, 1a 2ae. 109.1.2.

12. Ibid.

13. Ibid.,112.1.

God."[14] "So it is clear that people cannot prepare themselves to receive the light of grace except by the gratuitous assistance of God moving them within."[15] In citing Augustine, Thomas says, "God by co-operating with us, perfects what he began by operating in us, since he who perfects by co-operation with such as are willing, begins by operating that they may will."[16]

Understood in this way, Aquinas agrees with Luther that justification is being made righteous from without as the external pronouncement of God. There is nothing necessary on the human part prior to justification. However, he disagrees with Luther in saying that justification relates not merely to the beginning of the Christian life, but to the entire process for Christians to reach the final goal of deification by the help of the co-operating grace.

In the early Latin fathers, merit appears to have been regarded simply as a divine gift to the justified concerning the bestowal of eternal life. The discussion of merit in medieval times, however, centered around the concepts of merit and congruity. Although a human being is not able to merit justification by his or her moral action, his or her preparation for justification could make the subsequent justification congruous or appropriate. The distinction is made between merit in the strict sense of the term (*meritum de condigno*) and merit in its weaker sense of propriety (*meritum de congruo*). When applying the concept of merit to justification, it is *meritum de congruo*. When a moral act is performed outside a state of grace, it may be conceived as an appropriate basis for accepting the infusion of justifying grace. However, the concept of congruous merit has been the target of considerable criticism from the Protestant side. The concept of condign merit expresses the notion that a person has a claim on God to reward human efforts. When a moral act is performed in a state of grace it is worthy of divine acceptation on that basis. The notion of obligation is decisive and essential to the concept *de condigno,* which is thus defined as an act performed by the person placing God under obligation to him or her.

In keeping with the concept of merit, the axiom *facienti quod in se est Deus non denegat gratiam* (God will not deny grace to one who does

14. Ibid.,109.6 ad.2.

15. Ibid.,109.6.

16. Ibid.,111.2. Cf. Augustine, *De gratia et libero arbitrio*, 17. See Davies, *The Thought of Thomas Aquinas*, 270.

one's best) caused confusion within the early Dominican school because of Thomas' radically different interpretation of it. In the *Commentary on the Sentences*, Thomas is inclined to affirm that a human can prepare himself/herself for justification in terms of his or her own natural abilities without the aide of grace. This disposition is meritorious *de congruo.* God is constantly offering God's grace to human beings. In so doing, anyone who does *quod in se est* receives it. Here, Thomas is different than Augustine.

However, in the *Summa Theologiae* Thomas locates this preparation outside human natural abilities, although he continues to insist on the necessity of a preparation for justification. The preparation for justification becomes a work of grace. The axiom is interpreted in such a way that God will not deny grace to those who do their best as long as they are moved and inspired by God to do so. From his early position that the disposition toward justification is meritorious *de congruo*, Thomas comes to a different understanding that there are no merits prior to justification in his later writings such as *De Veritate* or the *Summa Theologiae.*

A critique of the role of supernatural habits in justification comes from Duns Scotus. Scotus understands the dialectical relation between God's absolute power and God's ordained power in a way that by the former (*de potentia absoluta*) God is totally free in God's decisions, while, by the latter (*de potentia ordinata*) God is totally reliable in God's actions. These two relations are maintained simultaneously without contradiction. For him, a supernatural habit or habit of charity is required for justification *de potentia Dei ordinata.* If the necessity of such a habit *de potentia Dei ordinata* is rejected, a human being can be regarded as acceptable to God before penitence. This is impossible because of *potentia Dei ordinata* God requires such a habit for acceptation and justification. However, the habit of created charity may not be regarded as the formal cause of divine acceptation, but as a secondary cause of divine acceptation. From the beginning, God ordained the created habit of charity as the *ratio acceptandi.* In so doing, it derives only from the divine ordination on which the inner connection between acceptation and the habit of charity is based. However, Occam criticizes Scotus' idea that the created habit in justification plays a secondary and derivative part.

According to Occam, God may bypass created habits *de potentia absoluta.* In other words, God may grant eternal life to an individual in the absence of any such habit. God is not dependent on such a created habit. Although God justifies human beings in terms of created supernatural habits, this arises not from the nature of things, but from the divine ordination. This provided a basis for undermining the foundation of the *habitus*-theology. The foundational statement that God could act other than God acts in a normal sense is, according to Occam, interpreted in such a way that God on the basis of absolute power could bypass what God intends to do on the basis of ordained power. Of course, the ordained power of God is none other than the absolute power of God, but a special use of the one power of God. Unlike Scotus, Occam put priority on the absolute power of God according to which God does not need the created grace of habit for justification. Justification is from the *acceptatio* of God, rather than the supernatural created habit of grace, which takes into consideration meritorious human deeds.[17]

On the basis of the theology of the *pactum* (covenant) Occam retains a positive attitude to the axiom *facienti quod in se est*. In terms of the relationship between the inherent value of a moral act and its ascribed value that is based on the covenant between God and the human being, Occam interprets the axiom *facienti quod in se est* up to the point where human disposition is not able to cause justification in terms of its own nature (*ex natura rei*), but in terms of the value ascribed to it by God (*ex pacto divino*).

The voluntarist position that is particularly associated with the later Franciscan school and the *via moderna* considers the meritorious value of human acts to rest upon God's will itself. Moral virtue imposes no obligation upon God. However, a human act can only be meritorious if it is performed in a state of grace. What comes first lies in the divine acceptation.

Occam takes a human act as meritorious, *de potentia ordinata*, if it is performed in a state of grace. However, the meritorious value of that human act is determined only through the divine will. Occam's discussion of congruous merit was influential in the general understanding of the concept of the merit at the time. God rewards moral acts performed outside a state of grace with congruous merit, according to which a person is capable of acting up to the point where God may bestow upon the person a habit of grace. Occam's double understanding of merit on the basis of the dialectical relationship between two powers of God can take a favorable view of moral capacities while simultaneously destroying the notion

17. *Handbuch*, 710–11.

that human acts themselves may be regarded as capable of meriting grace or eternal life. By the concept of *pactum* a human act may be accepted as worthy of grace.

Generally speaking, Occam is charged with teaching (semi) pelagianism because of his excessive emphasis on *de potentia sua absoluta* in which God can pardon sin without the infusion of grace. Even God may accept a human being as worthy of eternal life without a habit of grace or damn him or her without sin. In light of the covenant between God and human beings that provides the basis for understanding the greater ascribed value, human moral acts are capable of meriting justification *de congruo*. This is because God will accept the moral righteousness as a way of justifying human beings. For the *via moderna* the axiom *facienti quod in se est* is taken to mean that God may grant the gift of justifying grace to those who do *quod in se est*. On the basis of this idea, human moral acts which are not distinguished essentially from moral achievements without a habit of grace may be acceptable as merit *de condigno*.[18] In spite of attempts to save the justification of the *via moderna* from a charge of pelagianism, the most vulnerable thing in justification lies in the lack of a role for the incarnation and death of Jesus Christ.[19]

What is characteristic of the medieval understanding of justification is that justification refers not only to the beginning of the Christian life, but also to its continuation and ultimate perfection in a fundamental change in one's nature, not merely one's status. As a matter of fact, there is no such thing as the distinction between justification and sanctification. This distinguishes Reformation teaching, especially that of John Calvin. The Reformation distinction between justification and sanctification would have been untenable to the medieval Catholic theologians because they see justification as involving a real change in the sinner from its beginning to its end. Luther's concern is with assurance through Christ alone in face of God's judgment. What Luther came to believe is that a human being

18. Cf. *RGG*, P–Se, 834. For Luther's early affinity to the *via moderna*. "'Ask, and you will receive; seek, and you will find; knock, and it shall be opened to you. For everyone who asks receives, etc.' (Matt 7:7–8). Hence the doctors rightly say that God gives grace without fail to the man who does what lies within him *(homini facienti quod in se est Deus infallibiliter dat gratiam)*, and though he could not prepare himself for grace in a manner which is meritorious *de condigno*, he may do so in a manner which is meritorious *de congruo* on account of this promise of God and the covenant of mercy (*pactum misericordiae*)." *WA*, 4:262, 2–7, cf. McGrath, *Martin Luther's Theology of the Cross*, 89.

19. McGrath, *Martin Luther's Theology of the Cross*, 57–63.

can be justified before God *extra nos* through the alien righteousness of Christ, which is imputed by grace through faith alone. With the principle that we are *simul justus et peccator*, Luther rejects a righteousness that is essentially inherent in us.

In critical response to such a forensic understanding of justification, Catholics in the Council of Trent saw justification as something that God does rather than declares or imputes. The Council of Trent attempted to define a Catholic consensus on justification against the Protestant challenge, rather than settling controversial debates arising out of the various Catholic schools (Thomist, Scotist, and Augustinian). The Thomists dominated Trent. What was at stake was a total rejection of a meritorious disposition toward justification. However, Franciscan (and Scotist) representatives defended the notion of the necessity of a human disposition toward justification, which is *meritorious de congruo.* A moral act that is performed outside a state of grace, even though not meritorious in the strict sense of the term, may be regarded as appropriate for the infusion of justifying grace. They sought a *via media* between the Pelagian concept of justification *ex meritis* and the Thomist denial of all merit prior to justification. In other words, they were on a middle path between the denial of merit, *de condigno* (a moral act performed in a state of grace is worthy of divine acceptation for that reason), and recognition of merit, *de congruo* prior to grace.

The Council of Trent rejected the view that a sinner may be justified solely by imputation from without while in actuality remaining a sinner. In this regard, justification was seen and defined in light of personal transformation. It also rejected the thesis that justification consists only in the remission of sins. Therefore, the righteousness of believers in justification is not merely the righteousness of Christ. The righteousness that is the basis for justifying human beings is not *imputatio justitiae alienae Christi* in the Lutheran sense, but *habitus divinae gratiae* (habitual grace of God inherent in human beings) in the Augustinian-scholastic sense. This tends to lose God's grace of justification as divine judgment. The grace of justification can be heard in faith which means assurance of salvation.

The significance of Trent is its threefold understanding of justification. The first article of justification implies an initial human transformation from a state of sin to that of righteousness. The second article of justification teaches that a person, once justified, may increase in righteousness and perseverance in the Christian life. The third concerns the justification of lapsed believers by indicating how a person may forfeit justification and regain it through penance. What is at stake concerning a debate between the Lutheran Church and the teaching of the Council of Trent in the sixteenth century, therefore, revolves around a sacramental framework of penance. A priestly absolution (*ego absolvo te*) comes finally after the confession of sin (*confessio oris*), contrition of the heart (*contritio cordis*), and active satisfaction (*satisfactio operum*).

A theological question arises whether or not faith alone suffices, or if, in addition, works are necessary for justification. Justification is thus defined in a transformational sense with an emphasis on alteration in human status and nature. A human being is called through prevenient grace, irrespective of his or her merits, to dispose himself or herself toward justification. As a consequence of human cooperation with God's grace, God begins to justify a human being by the illumination of the Holy Spirit. Faith is to be seen as the beginning of human salvation, the foundation, and root of all justification. This gift of faith, without which it is impossible to please God, may merit justification. Of course it is excluded that human beings may merit justification *de condigno*.

But a Franciscan teaching of *meritum de congruo* should not be explicitly excluded. Although the grace of Christ precedes human effort, the believer, by cooperation with grace, is entitled to merit and to the increasing of grace. Finally, God will bestow eternal life as a reward to those who preserve the grace of justification until the end. Therefore damnation is directed against "a purely extrinsic conception of justification," according to which "the Christian life may begin and continue without any transformation or inner renewal of the sinner."[20]

The Ecumenical Discussion of Justification

Since the Second Vatican Council (1962–1965), ecumenical efforts have been concerned with bridging the Protestant forensic understanding of justification and the Catholic understanding of it as a transformation. The Catholic theologian Hans Küng, in his major study about justification, finds common ground between Karl Barth and the Council of Trent. He argues that if the Council of Trent is interpreted in a Thomistic sense, and if certain aspects of Barth's doctrine of justification are left behind, there is a fundamental agreement between them.

20. McGrath, *Iustitia Dei*, 272.

According to Küng, God's declaration of justification transforms a human being because God's declaration creates the reality that it proclaims.[21] Küng's idea that justification is both declarative and transformative is also ecumenically visible. Küng represents the Tridentine doctrine of justification as teaching no merit at all prior to justification. In spite of several criticisms, Küng has deepened agreement between Roman Catholics and Protestants concerning the doctrine of justification. According to Küng, Roman Catholics and Protestants share a common emphasis on a Christocentric and anti-Pelagian theology of justification.

In 1972 the Malta Report was published by the joint Study Commission of the Lutheran World Federation and the Vatican Secretariat for Promoting Christian Unity. It marks a growing ecumenical consensus on the doctrine of justification. On September 30, 1983, the US Lutheran-Roman Catholic dialogue participants published *Justification by Faith,* a document that has become the departure point in Lutheran-Catholic dialogue on justification. It serves as an inspiring model for contemporary ecumenical reflection and comes to terms with the historical course of these two great traditions, albeit from different theological perspectives. By taking into account perspectives for reconstruction, this document affirms "a fundamental consensus on the gospel." Of course, there are "remaining differences" between the two churches on a number of important aspects of doctrine that are interpreted in a spirit of complementarity, not in a contradictory sense.

"Our entire hope of justification and salvation rests on Jesus Christ . . . We do not place our ultimate trust in anything other than God's promise and saving work in Christ. Such an affirmation is not fully equivalent to the Reformation teaching on justification according to which God accepts sinners as righteous for Christ's sake on the basis of faith alone . . . Yet it does not exclude the traditional Catholic position that the grace-wrought transformation of sinners is a necessary preparation for final salvation." "That work can be expressed in the imagery of God as judge who pronounces sinners innocent and righteous (cf. n. 90), and also in a transformist view which emphasizes the change wrought in sinners by infused grace."[22]

21. Küng, *Justification,* 213ff.

22. *Justification by Faith*, Origins: NC Documentary Service, October 6, 1983, #157–58; 298.

However, the Joint Declaration on the Doctrine of Justification (October 31, 2000) between the Roman Catholic Church and the Lutheran Church, makes the doctrinal controversy and condemnation appear in a new and ecumenical light. What the common understanding of justification articulates is that we are justified through Christ alone, and faith is itself God's gift through the Holy Spirit who works through word and sacrament and at the same time leads believers into the renewal of life toward the eternal life that God will finally complete (article 16). In article 18, we read that "Lutherans and Catholics share the goal of confessing Christ in all things, who alone is to be trusted above all things as the one Mediator (1 Tim 2:5f) through whom God in the Holy Spirit gives himself and pours out his renewing gifts."[23]

However, synergism in preparing for and accepting justification in Roman Catholic theology, even though seen as an effect of grace, needs to be discussed in a more nuanced way with reference to Luther's understanding of justification, which includes "that believers are fully involved personally in their faith, which is effected by God's Word" (article 21). According to Luther, righteousness has, from the beginning, nothing to do with the help of inherent habitual love or of inherent grace. It is Christ himself who is the driving force and connects the effective moment of justification to the forensic moment of it. From the Catholic side, justification remains free from human cooperation, and is not dependent on the life-renewing effects of God's grace. Nevertheless, God's forgiving grace always brings with it a gift of new life. In this dialectical relationship, Catholic understanding of sin (article 29) is embedded in ecumenical compromise with Luther's concept of *simul peccator et justus* based on the *extra nos* principle. A theological understanding of the human sinful condition and a renewal of life within justification needs further discussion, especially with respect to the statement "justification and renewal are joined in Christ, who is present in faith" (article 26).[24]

Understood this way, it is important for us to consider Lutheran-Orthodox dialogues. In parallel with the Roman Catholic-Lutheran dialogue, a Lutheran-Orthodox dialogue concerning justification and theosis has entered into a new phase in which Luther is deepened and actualized through his concept of Christ's real presence in faith.

23. *Joint Declaration*, 16.

24. Ibid., 19.

Given this dialogue, it is pertinent to notice that a forensic understanding of justification is challenged by Luther himself. He does not ignore the twofold dimension of justification in terms of *unio cum Christo* (union with Christ) or *inhabitatio Christi* (Christ's indwelling) in the believer. Luther's idea of Christ's real presence through faith and his notion of cooperation are proposed as an arching bridge between faith and love, in which a combination between the forensic aspect and the effective aspect of justification can be highlighted.[25]

At this juncture, a theology of justification in the *Formula of Concord* (FC) is critiqued due to its one-sided forensic manner, according to which Christ's indwelling reality is understood singularly as a consequence of the forgiveness of sin. The favor (*favor*) of God as the forgiveness of sin and God's gift (*donum*) as God's essential indwelling in the believer are united in the person of Christ who is really and truly present in faith itself.[26]

It is the Mannermaa school at the University of Helsinki that has promoted an ecumenical dialogue between Lutherans and the Orthodox by opening a new quest for Luther's theology. Discovery of an idea of theosis (deification; *Vergöttlichung*) in Luther's own writings initiated on the part of the Mannermaa school has become the inspiration for relating Luther's teaching on justification to the notion of theosis in the Orthodox Church. Theosis can be defined as the belief that the human being has a share in the divine life as it is manifested in Jesus Christ. He or she partakes of "the divine nature" (2 Pet 1:4). This divine nature permeates the human being like leaven, and in so doing restores him or her to his or her original state of *imago Dei*. Of course, it must be remembered that the distinction between God and human beings is made by distinguishing the divine essence from divine energy. Therefore, deification in Eastern teaching means that participation in divine nature is about divine energies rather than about divine essence.[27]

The Finnish-Lutheran dialogue in Kiev in 1977 claimed that there iss a common basis for the idea of justification and deification. According to the document in Kiev 1977 ("Salvation as Justification and Deification"), "it has become evident that both these important aspects of salvation dis-

25. Braaten, *Union with Christ*, 68.

26. Mannermaa, *Christ Present in Faith*, 4–5.

27. This idea is preserved more clearly in the Eastern understanding of the Trinity. Cf. Lacugna, *God for Us*.

cussed in the conversation have a strong New Testament basis and there is great unanimity with regard to them both."[28]

For Mannermaa, the grounding contact point of the Lutheran-Orthodox dialogue consists in Luther's idea of "Christ present in faith" (*in ipsa fide Christus adest).* Christ's presence in Luther's thought is real-ontic. This aspect has been long ignored in Luther research in excessive attachment to neo-Kantian transcendental ideas according to which Christ being present through faith is not a real event, but in its effect on us. At the heart of the doctrine of deification is the idea of real participation in the divine life in Christ. The real-ontic nature of deification in Luther's thought stands in close connection with the classical Eastern teaching that views the words of St. Peter as partakers of divine nature in a real and explicit way. As Lossky remarks, "they leave us in no doubt as to the reality of the union with God which is promised us, and set before us as our final end, the blessedness of the age to come."[29]

Luther, unlike Lutheranism, never distinguishes Christ's person from his work. Christ who is really present in faith means the *forma fidei*, that is, the realization of faith by becoming a link between faith and good work. Christ is both *donum* and favor. If the presence of Christ in faith becomes the grounding principle for Luther's understanding of deification, Luther's Christological concept of *communicatio idiomatum* is imbued with Luther's anthropological understanding of happy exchange.

For Luther, Jesus Christ is the content of justification imputed from without as well as the basis for one's renewal. Hence, Luther's idea of deification in Christian faith cannot be equated with deification in the sense of an ontological mixture between human nature and the divine nature. According to Gal 2:20, what makes Luther's expression of deification possible is the apprehension of Christ, or inhabitation of Christ in us in which there can be no question of a mixture of Christ with faith.[30] Therefore, Osiander's notion of an essential deification of the human being is rejected.

In regard to Lutheran-Catholic ecumenical conversation, the Mannermaa school tried to challenge article 26 specifically by ignoring the real dimension of sin after baptism. As the article from the Lutheran side states, "It [power of sin] no longer is a sin that "rules" Christians . . .

28. Kamppuri, *Dialogue between Neighbors*, 73.

29. Lossky, *Mystical Theology*, 67.

30. *WA*, 40.1, 229 (Luther on Gal 2:16).

Thus this sin no longer brings damnation and eternal death" (article 29). This Lutheran position meets Catholic agreement in article 30. Because, in baptism, Jesus Christ takes away all that is sin in the proper sense, "Catholics do not see this inclination as sin in an authentic sense."[31]

An inclination (concupiscence) no longer separates those who are justified from God. Properly speaking, therefore, it is not sin. With emphasis on the reality of the effective aspect of justification, the Catholic position regards the real character of sin *post baptism* to be overcome through justification. At any rate, in the *Joint Declaration*, generally speaking, a Lutheran position is characterized in forensic terms, while a Catholic position is presented in effective terms. In so doing, the two aspects of justification are described as two different sides of one justification, and in an ecumenical consensus the one comes to terms with the other.

In Luther's thought, the forensic aspect is not separated from the effective aspect in real union with Christ through faith. In fact, the tree does not exist apart from producing good fruit. Therefore, the issue of the reality of residual sin and the view that a Christian is really made righteous needs to be deepened and integrated in terms of the indwelling Christ in the believer's faith. That is where the real union of the believer with Christ is rooted. The doctrine of deification includes the idea of a Christian's life as righteous and sinful at the same time rather than excluding either dimension. Those who are justified take a new path toward deification, which means a process of growing in holiness. As the scriptures witness, "But we all, with open face beholding as in a mirror the glory of the Lord, are changed into the same image from glory to glory, even as by the Spirit of the Lord" (2 Cor 3:18). Deification is made possible under the influence of the Holy Spirit by a deep and sincere faith, together with hope and permeated by love (1 Cor 13:13).[32]

However, the great obstacle lies in how the two dialogue partners perceive the freedom of human will. The Orthodox tradition refers in an ontological sense to the freedom of the human will in cooperation with deification, in contrast to the Lutheran position. Along with the issue of synergism, the idea of deification of the human being (in which a mystical term of spiritual ascension comes to the fore) also remains a stumbling block in Lutheran-Orthodox dialogue. As the Limassol statement (1995)

31. *Joint Declaration*, 22.

32. Kamppuri, *Dialogue between Neighbors*, 75.

addresses, "By baptism and participation in the other mysteries (sacraments) of the church, the faithful are raised to a new life of righteousness in Christ . . . God gives them, in the Holy Spirit the power to pass through purification and illumination of the heart and arrive "with all the saints" (Eph 3:18) at glorification (Matt 17:2; John 17:22; 2 Cor 3:18; 2 Pet 1:4)."[33]

The triad purification-illumination-glorification is unfamiliar to Lutherans because Luther rejected human striving and effort even in cooperation with the Holy Spirit for salvation. He even blamed a theosis based on a mystical threefold way as the work of a beggar, too close to pantheistic union in neglect of christological significance. Although justification can be seen affirmatively from the Lutheran perspective as a real participation in Christ and therefore as having a share in the divine life, the Lutheran-Orthodox dialogue finds it difficult to deal with a mystical triad of purification-illumination-glorification (deification) in regard to justification in Jesus Christ.[34]

When Luther's justification is viewed from a third-world perspective, it supports justice and liberation. Leonardo Boff interprets Luther to celebrate "the incredible discovery of the unlimited mercy of God in Jesus Christ crucified."[35] As a matter of fact, Luther's discovery of justification is a message of liberation from the burden of enslavement, a move from domination toward the gracious forgiveness of God. However, Luther is also challenged by liberation theology in that he was not capable of implementing the significance of his spiritual revolution in the social and political domains. In so doing, those in power and dominion are allowed at ease into the life of the church while still exercising their own interest at the expense of people in need. Luther's failure to be in company with the oppressed peasants during the peasants' war and even his appeal to those in power to suppress them became a notorious example of the problem.

Social and ethical limitations notwithstanding, Luther's opulent message of justification by faith is read well enough to radicalize its core meaning through and through in relation to the revolutionary transformation of life in every way. In other words, justification by faith and grace

33. Ibid., 179–80.

34. Cf. Braaten, *Union with Christ,* 179–80.

35. Boff, "Lutero entre la reforma y la liberacion," 93. Cf. Shaull, *Reformation and Liberation Theology*, 30.

becomes a touchstone in which the empowering and liberating initiative of God can be tested in responding to the cry of the poor.

Altmann, one of the leading liberation theologians in Brazil restores much of Luther's liberating and revolutionary insights that has been downplayed. He makes a concerted effort at a Latin American reading of Luther relevant to the contemporary agenda of massive suffering and social transformation. It is noteworthy that justification by faith and grace includes a radical principle of equality and value among all human beings before God, in which all forms of discrimination and privilege are strongly opposed.

Given this fact, Luther's discovery of justification can be understood adequately against the radical shift from a hierarchical order to the affirmation of personal human dignity on the one hand, and from an institutional system to a community of God's people under the promise of word and sacrament that could be in strong affinity to Christian base communities in Latin America on the other hand.[36] For Luther, the heart of the church is an egalitarian community. No matter what the social class or position, everybody in the church is of equal status and position before God. What the hierarchical institution may be in danger of losing can be found in the Christian base communities in Latin America.

To stress justification as liberation, Altmann argues that the passivity of Luther's teaching of justification should not be used to justify passivity in matters of liberation because the freedom of the believer before God should be expressed in relation to his or her commitment to one's fellows. Life under grace, which is highlighted in justification as costly grace, wants to become alive in the midst of the threatened life of marginalized and exploited people.

In so doing, Luther's doctrine of justification may be regarded as a point of departure for the conversion toward the Liberator God in Jesus Christ. Justification seen in the Latin American situation plays a critical function with respect to the institutionalized church in power and domination and with respect to the radicalism of human dignity in every way. However, although Altmann views justification in the multi-faceted dimensions of Luther's thought, he remains silent about the connection of Luther's justification with his eucharistic theology.[37] Revolutionary praxis is not supposed to be synonymous with salvation, but it should come

36. Altmann, *Luther and Liberation*, 5.

37. Ibid., 37–41.

from our grateful response to the gospel in Jesus Christ in which there is a need to distinguish God's saving grace in Christ from all human efforts pursuing social transformation.

As with the Latin American experience at the 1986 Harare Conference, the African American church took issue with a European-American understanding of justification, which created a radical dichotomy between justification at a personal level and sanctification at a socio-political level. In an African American understanding, sanctification and social justice should be an essential part of justification. Bringing about justice for the victims belongs to the realm of a right relationship between God and human beings, and between human beings themselves. Therefore Luther's teaching of two kingdoms is challenged by the fact that it dichotomizes reality by playing off spiritual justification against socio-political justice.

From there arises a strong demand that Luther's teaching of justification and two kingdoms should be critically reread in favor of those who suffer under socio-economic structures of injustice. An African American hermeneutic of suspicion focuses on the historical understanding and experience with the white European-American teaching of justification by faith alone. Justification should not be separated from being liberated both from personal sin and from social oppression. In this regard, the double aspect of *coram Deo* and *coram hominibus* in one justification is highlighted.

African American experience calls for Luther's doctrine of two kingdoms to be reread and sharpened by an African American understanding of two worlds. Here God employs a twofold reign in the world through the law and the gospel. God rules the world on the left through law, which can be in correspondence with an African American understanding of "this world." God's rule of the world on the right refers to God's justification of the sinner through the gospel corresponding to the "other world" in African American thought. Rather than assent to human authorities (Rom 13) leading to social conservatism and political quietism, African Americans emphasize prophetic activism in favor of a world of freedom and transformation of violent and oppressive structures of the society. The church has a mandate to address God's word to the state reminding it that the state is "to account for and to justify its actions before God" and its role is "to establish law and justice, and maintain peace and security for all persons given to its care."[38]

Luther's theology offers feminist theology a dialogue and mutual partnership because feminist theology is not merely an addition to women's voices and challenges but expresses itself as a complementary point of view. At stake for feminist theology is its opposition to injustice such as sexism, heterosexism, anti-Semitism, ecological devastation, war, imperialism, and etc. What is common to the theologies is that they are grounded in the contextualities of life's particulars in method and character. For example, Luther's formulation *finitum capax infiniti* (the finite is capable of the infinite) provides the basis for vitalizing human particular experience in theological discussion about justification. The incarnation is God's compassion and solidarity with suffering humanity, creation "within the confines of a particular situation."[39]

Luther's justification is not a mere abstract formulation in a dogmatic sense, but is experientially and situationally bound, *coram Deo*, because *ecclesia semper reformanda est*. Woman's experience needs to be in place as a source for theological rethinking. In this regard, Luther's understanding of justification by faith needs to be reformulated so that it is "internally" extended to the relationship between God and the world. All creatures become participants in the grace of God in terms of mutuality, reciprocity, and vulnerability between God and the world.[40] A conversation between Luther and feminist theology implies a willingness to risk one's identity for openness, plurality, and creative vision toward the future "more than we have dared to dream."[41] Regrettably, Luther's *theologia crucis*, which can be a core expression of divine suffering in compassion with all living sentient creatures, remains a negative focus in feminist theology.

A most challenging but promising response to Luther's teaching of justification in a forensic sense comes from Pentecostal circles. Frank Macchia, a highly qualified theologian and ecumenist, casts his critical eye on a "spiritless" understanding of justification among Lutherans, Reformed, and Evangelicals, in terms of his constructive proposal of Spirit

38. Maimela, "Twofold Kingdoms," 105–06. Cf. Bloomquist, *Promise of Lutheran Ethics*, 82–83.

39. Farley, *Tragic Visione*, 116. Cf. Pederson, "Conversations Toward an Ongoing Lutheran Reformation," Nr.1.

40. Ibid., 12.

41. Tracy, *Plurality and Ambiguity*, 79.

Christology. He takes Jesus' experience of the Spirit, especially in his resurrection, as the point of departure in reshaping and deepening the cutting edge of a pneumatological soteriology. In addition, his challenge extends and directs to an alliance of evangelicalism including tongues visible in the Pentecostal conservative circle.

Macchia's heart pulses in a life-transforming experience of the Spirit with respect to the whole of life, that is, human bodily social-cultural existence as well as ecological well-being of the new creation. In openness for and in company with the confessional others, Macchia's ecumenical sense becomes explicit in his attempt to launch a pneumatological reshaping and reorientation of Christology and soteriology. It can also better serve to improve and direct a Pentecostal encapsulation of the Spirit due to its excessive emphasis on "personal receiving" of divine supernatural manifestations such as tongue speaking or physical healing among others, toward the holistic life of the Spirit in creation. Following Miroslav Volf, Macchia takes a "material" understanding of salvation in a Pentecostal context to be more in affinity to soteriology of liberation theologies.[42]

At stake for Macchia's Spirit Christology is to see the resurrection of Jesus in light of the Spirit's work for the redemption and renewal of creation. His serious challenge to Lutheran theology in this regard lies in the theology of the cross. Its meaning would be threatened without reference to Christ's salvific work by the Spirit for the world, he argues. According to him, the meaning of the cross should be more balanced and extended pneumatologically and eschatologically in light of Spirit Christology, which means Jesus' experience of the Spirit as the charismatic Christ. In addition, the meaning of the cross, due to a spiritless understanding of the life and death of Jesus and its related justification, would limit a cosmic dimension of the resurrection to a mere appendage of Jesus' death. A consideration of the resurrection of Jesus seen in light of the power of the Spirit leads to a comprehensive and profound understanding of the Spirit of eschatology and the Spirit of the new creation.

This sounds like Moltmann—of course a Pentecostal version of him. Macchia's passionate critique of justification is concerned more about its forensic dimension, in which there would occur a lack of Jesus' dynamic experience with the Spirit and his prophetic ministry for the proclamation of the Lord's year forever (Luke 4:18). His question may run like this: Would the Reformer's teaching of justification be competent to take

42. Volf, "Materiality of Salvation," *Journal of Ecumenical Studies*, 437–67.

account of God's redemptive justice in Jesus' prophetic ministry? Given this fact, a pneumatological concern about the righteousness of Christ comes to terms with Moltmann's reorientation of justification in terms of the victim-oriented and the solidarity Christology. Herein Moltmann actualizes Blumhard's prophetic sense of God's kingdom. Along the way, Macchia intensely questions the "whereabouts" of the Spirit's work in the forensic understanding of justification.[43] A highly qualified and committed Pentecostal theologian's critical but friendly dialogue with the Lutheran teaching of justification is a real gift for Lutheran theology.

Be that as it may, it remains a question whether a pneumatic understanding of Christology can be sensitive to the resurrection of the crucified, in which we see that the resurrected Christ still bears the scars of suffering on the cross. The Spirit of resurrection cannot properly be understood without the Spirit of suffering love on the cross. Macchia's question about the "whereabouts" of the Spirit's work in Luther's teaching of justification could be more balanced in relation to Luther's language of "happy exchange" in which the understanding of faith and justification is not "spiritless," but is profoundly spiritual and experiential in a personal encounter with the living Christ in the power of the Spirit. The spirituality of *Anfechtungen* in this regard, which is rooted in the Spirit of mortification *coram Deo* may serve as a complementary corrective to the peril of the over-emotionalism of a pneumatic experiential spirituality.[44]

In current ecumenical dialogue, Luther can be contextualized so that Christian faith in Jesus Christ can be taken "in a theologically holistic, ethnically inclusive, and culturally contextual manner."[45] However, when Luther comes into Asian focus, a new conversation between Luther and a Buddhist understanding of justification calls for an attentive sense and listening to "the terror of otherness" whose voices are not only "strident and uncivil," but even ominous to Christianity. Interacting with Luther in light of interreligious dialogue is not merely an intellectual task but is also

43. Cf. Frank D. Macchia, The Spirit Set Us Free: Implications in Pentecostal Tehology for a Pneumatological Soteriology. Paper presented at the AAR/SBL meeting, Denver, CO, 2001.

44. For Luther's openness to charismatic experience and renewal see, "A Simple Way to Pray," in which we are aware that Luther himself experienced a certain prayer of the Spirit. "The Holy Spirit himself preaches here, and one word of his sermon is far better than a thousand of our prayers. Many times I have learned more from one prayer than I might have learned from much reading and speculation," LW, 43:198.

45. Pero, *Theology and the Black Experience*, 266.

a practical one. It is a dialogue in which the good news as the source of new life can be deepened in an encounter with the other religion's spirituality of poverty and liberation. In the next chapter I discuss Luther's teaching of justification and then bring Luther to an Asian context. Later (in chapter 7, "Justification and Other-Power: Luther and Shinran"), I start a conversation between Luther and a Buddhist idea of justification. We seek mutual recognition in a complementary way.

The Many Facets of Luther's Theology of Justification

As we have seen, Martin Luther has been discussed in depth in ecumenical conversations. We saw dialogue between the Lutheran and Roman Catholic Churches concerning the teaching of justification, dialogue between the Lutheran and Greek Orthodox churches, and dialogue between the Lutheran, Episcopalian, and Reformed Protestant churches. In a parallel development, there has been a growing interest in Martin Luther from the perspective of Liberation Theology in Latin America. Leonardo Boff, a leading liberation theologian, characterized Luther as one standing in favor of liberation in the age to come. Bringing about a grand process of liberation, Luther is regarded as "a necessary point of reference for all who seek liberation."[46]

As far as scholastic theology is concerned, Luther's rejection is due to his suspicion of Pelagianism inside scholasiticism. According to late medieval teaching, human beings, once restored to a reasonable and natural understanding of God by the infusion of grace, are capable of overcoming sin and evil in terms of free will in order to cooperate with God and thereby come to earn merit for salvation. Consequently, one can create the good works of the will that please God the most. Such an ability based on free will is required as the preparation for receiving the infusion of the grace through the sacraments, as well as for actualizing "habitual possession of grace." Against the scholastic concept of original sin (*carentia justitiae originalis*, the lack of original righteousness) and the understanding of grace as habitual, Luther brought *peccatum radicale*. Therefore, the Christian life, which Luther characterized as a double movement of sin and justifying faith, is a life of *simul justus et peccator*. Luther said, "it is not true that God can accept man without his justifying grace."[47]

46. Shaull, *Reformation and Liberation Theology*, 25.

47. *MLBTW*, 17.

Viewing Augustine through Aristotelian eyes, Aquinas found it important for the sinner to be forgiven and to respond freely to God with the aid of an infusion of grace. The *justificatio impii* is seen from the effects of grace, and is brought about by the infusion of grace. The notion of grace, in the context of scholastic theology, is treated less as the gracious action of God toward us, and more as something infused into the individual. In speaking of grace as a quality of the soul of the individual, Aquinas sees this quality as the source of the spiritual life, from which the virtues of faith, hope, and charity spring.[48] These virtues, in turn, are the source of meritorious works.

To encapsulate this idea, grace "is the principle of meritorious works through the medium of virtues."[49] Therefore, justification of the unrighteous as a whole becomes possible in terms of the infusion of grace, in which four requirements (the infusion of grace, a movement of free choice directed towards God by faith, a movement of free choice directed towards sin, and the forgiveness of sin) are met. Even though Aquinas did not reject the notion that we are justified because Christ nullified the barriers between God and humans, he thinks of justification as involving the work of grace, which means a movement not merely away from sin. In this regard Aquinas thinks that justification is not only the beginning of the Christian life, but also a continuation of it leading up to the ultimate perfection.

After the argument with Erasmus (1525), Luther began to realize that synergism plays an integral part even in Augustine. Augustine argued that infused grace and human acts alike are required for the process of salvation. Making justification coincide with sanctification, Augustine saw faith operate in fulfilling *ardens caritas*. Far from consenting to semipelagian-scholastic theology, Luther grounds his theology of justification on St. Paul. Luther opposes the *caritas* idealism of Augustine. There is no point of return! Luther's concept of *fides Christo formata* (faith formed by Christ) implies a paradigm shift in radically initiating the Reformation. Therefore, Luther's life and theology were a way of struggle in finding the gospel, and he underwent this in a grand process of liberation.

Where *fides Christo formata* is concerned in the context of Christian freedom and transformation, Luther, in his essay *The Freedom of a Christian*

48. *ST*, 1a 2ae. 110. 2–4.

49. Ibid., 4. 1.

(1520) (regarded as his *magna carta* of the Christian life),[50] stresses the significance of Christian freedom as follows: "As our heavenly Father has in Christ freely come to our aid, we also ought freely to help our neighbor through our body and its works, and each should become as it were a Christ to the other that we may be Christ to one another and Christ may be the same in all."[51]

It is God's grace in Jesus Christ that entirely restores the lost freedom in human beings by incorporating them into Christ, making one flesh with him. In following Ephesians (5:31–32) and Bernard of Clairvaux, Luther takes benefit of faith to mean "unit(ing) the soul with Christ as a bride is united with her bridegroom. By this mystery . . . Christ and the soul become one flesh. And if they are one flesh and there is between them a true marriage—indeed the most perfect of all marriages . . . it follows that everything they have they hold in common, the good as well as the evil."[52] This idea is manifest in dealing with two kinds of righteousness: "Just as a bridegroom possesses all that is his bride's and she all that is his—for the two have all things in common because they are one flesh (Gen 2:24)."[53]

Christian freedom, which comes from the justification of the sinner, insulates human beings from the curse of sin, from being turned toward the self (*incurvatus in se*). The alien or external righteousness is primarily "the basis, the cause, the source of all our own actual righteousness."[54] The spirituality of freedom does not remain in the forensic dimension of justification *extra nos*, because faith, as a decisive work in us, changes us and rebirths us anew. "This righteousness follows the example of Christ in this respect [1Pet 2:21] and is transformed into his likeness (2 Cor 3:18). It is precisely this that Christ requires."[55] The justified person may not be idle and must do works freely only to please God.

Christians who are full of extraordinary freedom find its most genuine expression in dedicating themselves to others. The Christian is free to live in response to the gift bestowed. In this way we become disciples of Christ by acting out our implanted righteousness and freedom through

50. Hütter, "Twofold Center of Lutheran Ethics," In *Promise of Lutheran Ethics*, 40.

51. *MLBTW*, 619–20.

52. Ibid., 603.

53. Ibid., 155.

54. Ibid., 156.

55. Ibid., 158.

love. Therefore, we understand what Luther means by Christian freedom: "A Christian is a perfectly free lord of all, subject to none. A Christian is a perfectly dutiful servant of all, subject of all."[56] In case of excessive emphasis on the first half, forgetting its second half, there occurs a tendency to abrogate God's commandments. However, in case of excessive emphasis on the second half, suppressing the first half, there arises a notorious Lutheran submission to all kinds of political authorities.

But in dichotomization of the two statements a freedom remains for the "internal" spiritual life and then the "external" political and economic life remains independent. From the beginning, Luther's teaching of justification, which is based on a life in union with Christ ("happy exchange"), expresses a dynamic relation of faith to love. In other words, the Christian life is a life in which faith is active in love. The christological hymn (Phil 2:4–11) is the basis for Luther to think that God's own humility in the most radical sense refers to the embodiment of God's freedom in love. God's self-giving love shapes effectively and finally the freedom in humility that we are called to follow in our faith. "This is the evangelical paradigm, the over-arching model of our Christian freedom."[57]

Moreover, justification needs to be articulated in the world, in which every aspect of life becomes the arena of discipleship. Luther's teaching of justification, which is deeply related to the priesthood of all the baptized, can be expressed in all dimensions of human life. In other words, as relevant to personal sanctification and the social-political realm. According to Luther's Christology of conformity, Christ, as the first-born among people, represents "the exemplary person and prototype" for the experience and sufferings of many brothers and sisters. In other words, through the fact that Christ experienced and suffered our predicament we might experience his brotherhood and sisterhood in the midst of our predicament.

In his commentary on the Gal 2:19 (1535), Luther understands the suffering of Christ as a sacrament and an example from an Augustinian perspective.[58] As sacrament this means the death of sin in us. As an example it behooves us to imitate him in bodily suffering and dying. Christ as a sacrament is not imitation-spirituality, but rather is really present in the faith of the believers. The good deeds of a Christian are good fruits as the consequences of receiving the gift of Christ. Therefore, "the Freedom

56. Ibid., 596.

57. Hütter, "Twofold Center of Lutheran Ethics," 41.

58. *LW*, 27: 238.

of a Christian never contradicts God's commandments . . . [but] rejoices in God's Commandments and welcomes them as creaturely ways of embodying our love of God and neighbor."[59]

Justification is of fundamental significance for the realization of a Christian ethical life and for spiritual growth. "Having been justified by grace, we then do good works, yes, Christ himself does all in us."[60] In Luther's understanding of *fides Christo formata* the person of Christ is not separated from the work of Christ. The Spirit is actually present in the faith of the believer and communicates to the person and the work of Christ. Life in the Spirit can show growth, as Luther expresses in a surprising way: "This life, therefore, is not godliness but the process of becoming godly, not health but getting well, not being but becoming, not rest but exercise. We are not now what we shall be, but we are on the way. The process is not yet finished, but it is actively going on. This is not the goal but it is the right road. At present, everything does not gleam and sparkle, but everything is being cleansed."[61]

At this point, we need to pay attention to the role of the Spirit in Luther's thought. Luther characterized the Holy Spirit as the one calling through the gospel, enlightening with spiritual gifts, and sanctifying and preserving in the true faith, "just as he calls, gathers, enlightens and sanctifies the whole Christian church on earth and preserves it in union with Jesus Christ in the one true faith."[62] There is a pneumatological orientation in Luther's *De servo arbitrio*. In line with Augustine's concept of *gratia increata* (i.e., the personal presence of the triune God in the human being through the Holy Spirit), Luther re-appropriates a doctrine of justification in terms of pneumatology. For Luther, the Holy Spirit represents divine initiative in sharp contrast to any notion of the natural capacities of the human *arbitrium*. "*Spiritus sanctis non est Scepticus.*" (The Holy Spirit is not a skeptic.)[63] By using the "*servum arbitrium*" (bound will) Luther understands himself as a defender of the Augustinian doctrine of sin and grace.

59. Hütter, "Twofold Center of Lutheran Ethics," 43.

60. *LW*, 34: 111.

61. *LW*, 32: 24.

62. *BC*, 345.

63. *LW*, 33: 24.

For Luther, the Spirit is present and works in all creation as well as in every human being even in every natural occurrence and is not confined to faith and church. "The Holy Spirit is among humans in a twofold way. First through a universal activity, by which he preserves them as well as God's other creatures. Second, the Holy Spirit is given from Christ to believers."[64] The Spirit, as the third person of the Trinity, is of cosmic character because even natural gifts or activities cannot be understood apart from the activity of the Spirit. As Luther said in his *Lectures on Galatians*, "So all these things are services and fruits of the Spirit. Raising one's children, loving one's wife, and obeying the magistrate are fruits of the Spirit. According to the papists they are fleshly things, because they do not understand creaturely things."[65]

In this regard, Karl Barth emphasizes the role of the Holy Spirit in Luther. Like Calvin, Luther, in his commentary on the Galatians, articulates the testimony of the Holy Spirit in the experience of believers (*Testimonium Spiritus Sancti internum*).[66] Luther describes Christ as the greatest sinner as well as the greatest person in a dialectical way.[67] No one can understand God or God's external means "without experiencing, proving, and feeling it."[68]

Understood in a pneumatological perspective, *fides Christo formata* implies a notion of participation in terms of union with Christ, but not to the exclusion of the external means of Word and sacrament. This union, which we also see in considering Christian freedom, signifies the transformative and effective part of justification. This may be termed in Luther "*solo Spiritu Sancto*" (through the Holy Spirit alone), coupled with *solus Christus*.[69] Therefore, justifying faith does not remain only in receiving forgiveness imputed *extra nos*, but also includes the personal experience

64. *WA*, 39 II, 239, 29–31. Cf. Lohse, *Martin Luther's Theology*, 235.

65. *WA*, 401, 348, 2–5. *LW*, 26: 217. Cf. Lohse, *Martin Luther's Theology*, 236.

66. *CD*, I/1:526.

67. *LW*, 25:277.

68. *LW*, 21:299. Cf. Christenson, *Welcome Holy Spirit*, 117–18. However, The charismatic theology of Lutheranism is not supposed to play off the dimension of external means against living union with Christ. Moltmann suggests expanding the Reformation doctrine of justification in the following way: (1) of emphasizing the justice of God in favor of the victims, (2) of the regeneration of life, (3) of experiencing the Spirit in context of the charismatic powers of life, and (4) of considering eschatological orientation, Moltmann, *The Spirit of Life*, 123–60.

69. Lohse, *Martin Luther's Theology*, 237.

of the real Christ dwelling in us, and furthermore participates in a real sharing of blessing, righteousness, and the life of Christ. Luther's concept of participation finds its expression in the joyous exchange in which Jesus Christ as the greatest sinner of all takes upon himself human sin and overcomes it, and then bestows his divine righteousness on the believer.

As we already mentioned earlier, Luther plays off *fides Christo formata* against *fides caritate formata*. For Luther, faith as the gift of the Spirit refers to the reality of Christ present in faith. He is the only way to salvation, making unnecessary human efforts of love. Christ as the object of faith is not separated from the subject of faith. Christian spirituality experiences Christ really present in faith. This has nothing to do with a supernaturally sublimed love, but rather with Christ himself who speaks, lives, and works in the heart of the believer. In distinction from Eastern theology, Luther puts *liberium arbitrium* against the gracious work of the Holy Spirit, as was manifest in his critical attitude toward Erasmus. That is why Luther strongly opposes all the synergistic tendencies implied by the *facere quod in se est* principle of the nominalists.

From this, Luther reappropriates divinization in light of *fides Christo formata*. He is critical of divinization by works of righteousness or self-propulsion through ever-higher spiritual strivings because that would be the work of a beggar. In his sermon of 1525 Luther says, "Much has been written on the divinization of man, and ladders have been constructed by means of which man is to ascend to heaven . . . However, all these are merely works of a beggar."[70] The human being becomes sanctified and transformed toward God by the power of the Holy Spirit. *Simul justus et peccator*, seen in the perspective of pneumatology, should be reclaimed in relevance to participation in the divine nature because Luther's teaching of the Holy Spirit excludes synergism, while the Orthodox teaching highlights synergism between God and human being. For Luther, not synergism but *fides Christo formata* is the heart of a deification, which has less to do with a changing of human nature into divine nature than with adoption of believers as God's children.

Justification in the Socio-Political Dimension

The medieval phrase *fides caritate formata* signifies human merit for salvation through good deeds and charitable activity, the achievement-oriented

70. Cf. Braaten, *Union with Christ*,92.

piety and account-book mentality. The scholastic phrase *facere quod in se est* (do what lies within you) makes sure a relationship between economic charitable works and the mathematics of salvation, in which the rich of innumerable cloisters and thousands of priests lived primarily by support of stipends and money given for masses to aid souls in purgatory. In contrast to *fides caritate formata*, Luther's *fides Christo formata* puts an emphasis on human vocation in secular works. Here, Luther turns upside down medieval economic teaching based on its understanding of salvation. For Luther human labor is a divine commission in terms of faith. Human works are the masks of God, behind which God continues creation and opposes evil, thereby giving every person the necessities of life.[71]

Luther sees economic justice for the poor against the background of medieval economic teaching in which manual labor was devalued and vocation was limited only to spiritual and ecclesial professions. Luther intended not self-sanctification or almsgiving but prophetic *diakonia* for the poor and the weak, as well as a just social and economic order that would function as a form of worship within the world. In contrast to the medieval two-leveled ethic, Luther's discovery of the significance of the world from the perspective of the gospel led him to challenge the begging of mendicant monks and denounce the usury and exploitive economic practices of early capitalism. Of the greatest necessity for Luther was the abolition of all begging throughout Christendom. From his *Brief Sermon on Usury* (1519) through *Trade and Usury* (1524), to *Admonition to the Clergy to Preach Against Usury* (1540), Luther opposed the expanding monetary system and credit economy: "There is no greater human being on earth than a miser and usurer for he desires to be above everyone."[72] Anyone who manipulates prices in his own interest "springs from sheer wantonness and greed," contrary to God's word, reason, and every sense of justice. "All such fellows are manifest thieves, robbers, and usurers."[73] In the political context, Luther's theological program for the priesthood of all the baptized was radicalized, especially in *The sermon on the Magnificat* (1521), from the perspective of the poor and the humble, which is highly acclaimed by liberation theology.[74]

71. *LW*, 14: 114–15.

72. *WA*, 51:396, 12.

73. *LW*, 45:261–62.

74. Altmann, *Luther and Liberation*, 92–93.

Moreover, Luther's treatise *Temporal Authority: To What Extent it Should Be Obeyed* (1523), was not written to promote uncritical obedience to the secular powers, but to limit obligation of Christians to obey their princes. When the princes tried to ban the buying and selling of the German version of the New Testament Luther wrote this treatise. The political authority should not interfere with the freedom of the conscience because only God rules this matter through his spiritual government. In successive writings such as *The Commentary on the Sermon on the Mount* Luther brought forth a distinction between God's two governments: the spiritual and the temporal realms, which has undergone intense criticism and debate among scholars. Karl Barth was the first to label this Lutheran doctrine "the two-kingdoms doctrine" when he spoke out against the "Deutsche Chisten" in the 1930s who had misused Luther's twofold teaching to justify the Führer Adolf Hitler and National Socialism.[75]

What Barth actually attacked was the political misuse of Luther's teaching. Barth spoke against an interpretation that separated two realms dualistically by ignoring a highly dialectical and paradoxical view of God's twofold reign. Here the life of the church has nothing to do with the secular world, leaving the secular world autonomous on the basis of its own powers and principalities. Therefore, the Christian must submit to them without reservation. Consequently the orbit of the gospel affects only the inner souls of Christians and their fellowship within the church. Thus, the issue of public life was totally untouched by the proclamation of the gospel. Doctrine in such a dualistic context is powerless to offer an ethical basis for resisting tyrannical governments, not only in case of Hitler, but also of many figures in the third world. This is the infamous political quietism attached to the two-kingdoms doctrine. Christianity was to be restricted only to the personal, inner sphere, implying obedience to any kind of political authorities without qualification. However, Luther's understanding of God's twofold rule was not rooted in the model of "Christ against culture" (sectarian), but "Christ and culture in paradox." In fact, Luther handles the twofold rule of God in a dynamic and paradoxical way: the kingdom on the left with the law, the kingdom on the right with the gospel. The twofold rule of God is closely connected to an understanding of law and gospel. Law is not to be sentimentalized into gospel, nor is gospel to be secularized in a new law. The distinction between two entities

75. Braaten, *Principles of Lutheran Theology*, 124.

is not supposed to be a separation but an interaction in paradoxical and creative ways.[76]

Certainly, Luther can sound dualistic and quietistic. "You have the kingdom of heaven; therefore, you should leave the kingdom of earth to anyone who wants to take it."[77] In commenting on Matt 5:38–42 Luther made a distinction of two spheres in the sense of bifurcation. "A Christian may carry on all sorts of secular business with impunity—not as a Christian but as a secular person . . . Thus when a Christian goes to war . . . punishing his neighbor, or when he registers an official complaint, he is not doing this as a Christian, but as a soldier or a judge or a lawyer."[78] However in the larger context of Luther's writings, the two spheres are in profound interaction.

In his commentary on Ps 2, Luther states that Christ rules through the worldly government. Secular realm belongs to the kingdom of God in the sense of office and estates. The state protects the pure doctrine, and cares for the widow, the orphan, and the poor. Finally, the state has to protect against violence and crime in order to promote and establish the peace, which is an analogy of the kingdom of heaven (Cf. Matt 5:9).[79] Gustaf Wingren's remark is also worth quoting: "It is the neighbor who stands at the center of Luther's ethics . . . Vocation and the law benefit the neighbor, as does love born of faith . . . Love born of faith and the Spirit effects a complete breakthrough of the boundary between the two kingdoms, the wall of partition between heaven and earth, as did God's incarnation in Christ."[80]

Moreover, Luther stresses that God is at work in God's secular domains, *oeconomia* and *politia*. Following the Augustinian tradition Luther divided human beings, first of all, into two parts: one under the reign of God, and the other under the reign of Satan (*civitas dei—civitas diaboli*). Luther understands history as the battlefield between God and Satan in an apocalyptic-eschatological perspective. Christians and churches fight

76. Benne, "Lutheran Ethics," 24–25.

77. *LW*, 45:102.

78. *LW*, 21:113.

79. Iwand, *Luthers Theologie*, 300.

80. Wingren, *Lutheran Vocation*, 45. Cf. Childs "Ethics and the Promise," 100. Bonino, in a critical stand against quietistic versions of Luther, agrees with Wingren: "At the ethical level gospel and law, power and love, come together in the life of individual Christians, in whatever stand (social or vocational location) they may find themselves in society," Bonino, *Toward a Christian Political Ethics*, 25.

for their own right when an official institution intervenes to destroy their spiritual mandate. Christians also should be in solidarity with those who work in official institutions to promote the common good and well-being of the people. Therefore, Luther stood apart from the fanatics who would retreat from social life or transform the secular areas of life totally into the kingdom of God by force and violence. Given this fact, a simple separation of the two kingdoms from each other was out of the question for Luther.

Luther attempted to concretize tension between God's kingdom and the power of Satan in various areas of human life. Thereby the Church is called and encouraged to become the co-worker of God in protecting creatures from injustice and oppression, and promoting human life with mutual love and equity. Therefore, "faith active in love" in Luther's thought can be read as "faith active in love seeking justice."[81] Dietrich Bonhoeffer's retrieval of the church's responsibility as prophetic *diakonia* for the political sphere moves in this direction.[82] In the church's social witness Luther's teaching of two kingdoms still retains a prophetic aspect of justice and peace. William Lazareth stresses this point emphatically, claiming that "in short, what Lutherans need desperately today is a prophetic counterpart to the priesthood of all believers. Evangelical Christians will be reverent to God's word as well as relevant to God's world by expressing both their priestly Yes, through faith active in love, and their prophetic No, through love seeking justice."[83]

Luther's Justification Extended into Asian Focus

Even though Luther has gained ecumenical prominence, he is not fully explored from an Asian perspective. In discussion of a Christian attitude toward non-Christian religions we are aware of growing concern to explore the relationship between the gospel and multi-cultural pluralism. However, for Christians, the question of the gospel/culture nexus is often difficult to handle because evangelical theologians are afraid of mingling the sacred with the profane. Syncretism is about adulterating the gospel with neopaganism. However, the gospel was at times misused as a tool of control and domination by Western culture. This colonial collaboration

81. Childs, "Ethics and the Promise," 101.

82. Cf. Ford, "Dietrich Bonhoeffer," 28–34.

83. Lazareth, "Luther's Two Kingdoms," 131.

of Western Christianity is analyzed and comes to light in the liberation theology of Latin America, Africa, and Asia.

Unlike liberation theology in Latin America, whose main issue does is not in dialogue with other religious belief systems, many Asian theologians are concerned more about the issue of interreligious dialogue. For example, Fr. Aloysius Pieris, a representative of Asian religious liberation theology from Sri Lanka, is an experienced theologian in contact with Buddhism and in touch with many multi-religious groups in the struggle for the liberation of the poor. He affirms strongly that the poor people of Asia are also very religious. Theological reflection in Asia must take both these elements—poverty and religiosity—together. When poverty and religiosity come together in this way, both become liberative. Pieris points to this as the specificity of Asian liberation theology different from liberation theology in Latin America.[84] The experience of Western Christianity allied with colonialism is very traumatic for Asia. Many questions and challenges are posed to Western theological methodology and legitimatization of Christian dogmas to construct a planetary theology from an Asian perspective. Given this fact, I focus on some issues related to Luther's theology of justification in regard to Asian complex realities: overwhelming poverty and multi-faceted religiosity.

Luther's Justification and Theology of Divine Suffering

Luther's *theologia crucis*, the essence of the true theology (expressed in the Heidelberg disputation, 1518) is his theological program opposed to a *theologia gloriae*. Theology of the cross refers to the knowledge of God based only on the crucified Christ, whereas a theology of glory refers to the knowledge of God derived from the philosophical and metaphysical principle of scholastic theology. The theology of the cross understands God from divine suffering and pain, and seeks God in the divine weakness and foolishness. It destroys both the theology of glory and human self-righteous moral theology. Rather, the theology of the cross hides God, yet reveals God's hiddenness in the death of Christ. *Deus crucifixus* and *Deus absconditus* are delineated in the theology of the cross. This theological program functions in liberating human beings from *homo incurvatus in se*. However, Luther has often been criticized because he did not develop his theology of the cross social-critically during the peasant rebellion.

84. Pieris, *Asian Theology of Liberation*, 69.

Luther's theology of the cross is reflected and echoed in an Asian context, first of all, by Kazoh Kitamori, a Japanese Lutheran theologian. His theological program focuses on the pain of God. According to him, the pain of God is at the heart of the gospel. Luther's metaphor, "God fighting with God" (*da strydet Gott mit Gott*) at Golgotha combines God's wrath with God's love from the perspective of divine suffering. Therefore, "the essence of God can be comprehended only from the 'word of the cross.'"[85]

However, Kitamori's pain of God is frequently criticized by minjung theologians in South Korea—the so-called Korean liberation theology (Min meaning "people," Jung meaning "mass suffering")—in that he ignored the suffering side of the victims. Like Moltmann, minjung theology agrees to include "both the question of human guilt and man's liberation from it, and also the question of human suffering and man's redemption from it."[86] Moltmann's groundbreaking statement, "The sufferings of Christ are also sufferings of the people (*ochlos*)" has a relevance for the victim Christology of minjung, which develops the concept of *han* in a more profound way than the concept of pain.[87] *Han* is a particularly difficult Korean term to articulate, but is used to delineate the depths of human sufferings rooted in the anguish of a victim on the emotional, social, and even ecological levels.

Minjung theologians generally accept *han* as an important indigenous theological term to understand the relation of divine and human suffering, or forgiveness and sin. Therefore, minjung theology radicalizes the concept of sin from the perspective of the *han* of the victimized. It would underpin the doctrine of justification by the doctrine of justice for the oppressed. In this regard Luther's teaching of justification has been heavily attacked due to its forensic metaphor in which liberating praxis is ignored, on the one hand, and due to its neglect of social relations on the other hand.

From the Roman Catholic camp of Asian religious liberation theology, Pieris develops his Christology in a twofold way: (1) Jesus' struggle to be poor in terms of renunciation of the world, and (2) Jesus' struggle for the poor in term of renunciation of mammon organized into power and principalities. This twofold ascesis make Jesus' way salvific. This aspect

85. Kitamori, *Theology of the Pain of God*, 41.

86. Moltmann, *Crucified God*, 134. Cf. Park, *Wounded Heart of God*, 114–20.

87. Moltmann, *History and the Triune God*, 47.

does not compete with buddhology but complements it. Here the gnostic detachment of Buddhism comes to terms with agapeic involvement of Christianity in a struggle for liberation of the poor. In his view, "religion and poverty in their coalescence offer the cultural context and the liberationist breakthrough for Asian Christology."[88]

Complementarity plays an important role in interreligious dialogue especially concerning each religious core-experience. For example, core-experience, in Buddhism, is gnosis or "liberative knowledge," while in Christianity it is agape or "redemptive love." However, in his view, both gnosis and agape are necessary to each other because each religion is inadequate for experiencing and expressing the Ultimate Source of liberation.[89] What is significant to Pieris is that the theology of forming caritas is revitalized in the option for the poor. Beyond justifying faith, it brings Christianity and Buddhism together so that each religion complements the other in a liberating praxis.

In this context, Luther's theology of justification and theology of the cross are supposed to be rediscovered as the counterparts for an Asian theology and spirituality. In Luther's time, sin was the language that the hierarchical-sacerdotal structure of the church imposed upon the oppressed and the victimized. Luther's radical understanding of justification is expressed in socio-economic terms that could actually help the victims of oppression.

Luther criticizes the economic development of his time. As the political realm belongs to the church's political service to God's universal reign, so economic realm refers to the church's economic service to God who stands in favor of the poor. Luther's theological reflection on God (the first commandment) in reference to the economic realm shows explicitly that mammon is regarded as the chief example of opposition to God. Luther's critique of mammon in his time led to his economic ethics, based on the commandment, "You shall not steal."[90] Therefore, economic issues became an integral part of theological reflection on God. The character of capital, which is in contrast to God, motivates Luther to fight for the sake of the poor and the needy against the capital process and accumulation. Luther

88. Pieris, *Asian Theology of Liberation*, 62.

89. Pieris, "Buddha and the Christ," In *The Myth of Christian Uniqueness*, 163.

90. "The Large Catechism," *BC*, 386–92, 416–20.

portrays the problem of capital expansion with the metaphor of devouring capital.[91]

Luther's teaching of justification cannot be adequately understood without reference to his reflection on economic justice. Psalm 127 provides a basis for Luther to understand that human beings are not the efficient cause in the area of politics and economics, but the instrumental cause, through which God acts. Therefore, they are servants and coworkers with God. Although Luther is not convinced about human cooperation with God regarding justification, he locates human cooperation with God in the care and maintenance of the world. According to Luther, being justified through faith, we further proceed to an active life.[92]

Luther's struggle for economic justice may give an impetus for church and initiative groups to resist violence and injustice, to carry out constructive initiatives for the poor, and to advance ecological sustainability.[93] Luther gives a valid lesson for Asian Christians who struggle with the inequalities of world economy in global capitalism.

Luther's theology of the cross needs to be extended and actualized in the direction of the resurrection of the crucified, in which God's active justification leads to a justice-creating kingdom of God, speaking out against human passive quietism and violence of social structures. God's justification refers to the question about the justice of God in history. God's justification is the justification of creating justice on the side of victims and at the same time, bringing the sinner to righteousness. That being the case, the suffering and death of Jesus Christ in the context of forgiveness of sin *pro me* and *pro nos* should be grounded in and understood from the resurrection of the crucified *pro me* and *pro nos,* especially with respect to God's justice for human life and God's ecological concern for all living creatures.

The new beginning of life seen in light of the resurrection of the crucified leads to the life of forgiveness, reconciliation, and *metanoia* by establishing the justification and compassion of God's grace socially, politically, and culturally. The God who justifies human beings is also in need of God's justification from human beings, that is, human responsibility for God's justice and participation in the life of God full of justice,

91. Cf. *WA*, 53, "An die Pfarrherren, wider den Wucher zu predigen," 331–424. Cf. Marquardt, "Gott oder Mammon," 189.

92. *WA*, 40 I, 447, 22f, cf. Gollwitzer, *Krummes Holz*, 313.

93. Duchrow, *Weltwirtschaft-heute*, 82.

forgiveness, compassion, and love. We remain always sinners in the past. However, we are always created righteous from the future of God. *Simul Justus et peccator* defines a Christian as an eschatological existence in light of the resurrection of the crucified.

God the Father gives Godself not only to us, but also to all creatures. God makes all creation, however small or unimportant, to help and provide the comforts and necessities of life.[94] For the Reformer, faith in God implies that the Creator gives himself/herself to all creatures, by looking after human beings and indeed all creatures generously in this earthly life. Luther states explicitly the eschatological implications of justification. "In the meantime, as long as we live here, we are carried and nourished in the bosom of the mercy and long-sufferance of God, until the great day. Then shall there be new heavens and new earth, in which righteousness shall dwell."[95] Luther's idea of justification is oriented toward the new creation on a cosmic dimension through the work of the Holy Spirit. It is not in contrast to a theocentric-ecological reading of nature in a Lutheran sense.[96] For Luther, God is immanently powerful in nature, in which we see God's dynamic presence and compassionate care "in, with, and through" all living sentient creatures. The whole creation is envisioned as "the mask of God."[97] God the creator is present "with all creatures, flowing and pouring into them, filling all things."[98]

However, the beauty of God's goodness and glory, in other words, the aesthetics of God's glory in nature is more deeply grounded in his teaching of justification. "Now if I believe in God's son and bear in mind that He became man, all creatures will appear a hundred times more beautiful to me than before. Then I will properly appreciate the sun, the moon, the stars, trees, apples, pears, as I reflect that he is Lord over and the center of all things."[99] This is a beautiful text, especially for Asian contextual theology and churches: one that strives to relate our faith and justification to ecological fellowship, in other words to foster an Asian aspiration to harmony and interconnection of human life in nature. For Luther, the Spirit of justification is the Spirit of creation, the Spirit of resurrection,

94. *BC*, 412, 418, 420.

95. *LW*, 25:263.

96. Cf. Santmire, *Travail of Nature*, 128.

97. *WA*, 40:1.94.

98. *LW*, 22:26.

99. *LW*, 22:496, "Sermon on the Gospel of John."

and a final transformation of all things, a new heaven and a new earth. "Then there will also be a new heaven and earth, the light of the moon will be as the light of the sun, and the light of the sun will be sevenfold . . . That will be a broad and beautiful heaven and a joyful earth, much more beautiful and joyful than Paradise was."[100]

For Luther a theological aesthetics relating to nature is not directly commanded because the sun stopped shining and darkness covered the whole land (Luke 23:44). In the dereliction of Jesus on the cross, the crucified is the one who spoke about God's care and goodness about the lilies of the field and birds of the air (Matt 6:25). It is no wonder that Luther affirms the mediatorship of Jesus Christ for creation and preaches a cosmic Christ that would later become a decisive theme in the ecumenical conferences from New Delhi 1961 to Vancouver 1983. Luther's idea of a cosmic Christ is seen in terms of *concretum universale*: Universal not speculative, personal not individualistic, existential in participation in the world.[101] The true Christian foundation of the theology of divine aesthetics (i.e., doxology) comes from the theology of the cross, and the realistic direction of the aesthetics of divine suffering will arrive at an aesthetic doxology that is also a cosmic eschatology.

Luther's theology of the cross is not only anthropological and soteriological, but also universal and cosmic. It thereby becomes a basis for engaging dialogue with religious pluralism in perspective of the cosmic Christ. A non-religious interpretation of the gospel implies a christological interpretation of the world come of age. Thus, universal interpretation of Jesus Christ implies interreligious interpretation of the gospel, by recognizing the mysterious presence of Christ in people of other faiths.

When Luther comes to Asia, the Buddhist teaching of *dukkha* is the counterpart in mutual dialogue. A Buddhist starts with the realization that everybody and everything is in cosmic *dukkha*. The Buddhist solution to it becomes explicit in the great compassion of *Amida* for all sentient beings. We make note of a universal grace of the absolute Other-Power in *Amida* Buddha. According to a Buddhist legend *Amida* Buddha was Dharmakara who lived in India a million years ago. After the Enlightenment, he refused to reside in *Nirvana*. Instead, he made forty-eight vows to save people by bringing them to the West Pure Land. He declared that if his vow was

100. *LW*, 12:119.121 (Luther, "Selected Psalms"). Cf. Santmire, *Travail of Nature*, 131.

101. Bayer, *Schöpfung als Anrede*, 78.

not fulfilled and realized, then he would not become a fully Enlightened Buddha. These vows were made for all who would be born in his land, never returning to the lower realms. Those who believe in *Amida* and wish to be reborn in earnest and with sincerity need to repeat the name of *Amida*, on the condition that they are not supposed to commit the serious crimes of murdering parents, murdering an *Arhat*, doing harm to a Buddha, slandering the Dharma, or causing schism in the *Sangha*.

Some form of Pure Land teaching comes from one of the earliest streams of Mahayana Buddhism. *Amida*—Infinite Light—which is immeasurable, shining in every direction with its radiance, refers to his infinite wisdom, his all-illuminating and infinite omniscience. In terms of his infinite light as wisdom, he exists for the sake of all sentient beings, helping them in many different ways. This compassion is the driving force for Bodhisattva's path. Resulting from deep compassion for the suffering of others, one experiences life-transforming reality and becomes a "Son or Daughter of the Buddhas."[102] The compassion from the depths of our heart extends up to the limits of the cosmos in all directions and for all sentient creatures.

If Luther's justification is seen in the cosmic understanding of Christ, faith is grounded only by the power of the Spirit, not by human strength or reason. If faith is based on the sacraments as God's promise for forgiveness of sins and eternal life, faith is not merely anthropologically relevant, it centers on Jesus Christ in the promise of the sacrament. The Jesus Christ that faith venerates is the crucified and risen Lord who rules the universe.

The meaning of the christologcal hymn in the letter to the Colossians points in this direction: Jesus Christ, the first born of all creation, in whom all things were created, in heaven and on earth, visible and invisible, whether thrones or domination or principalities or authorities—all things were created through Christ and for Christ. Jesus Christ is before all things, and in him all things are held together. However, this cosmic Lord, the first born from the dead who might be preeminent in everything, is the cosmic reconciler and peacemaker between God and all things, whether on earth or in heaven, by the blood of the cross (Col 1:15–20). The universal lordship of the exalted Christ is the Lord of the resurrection of the crucified. The resurrection of the crucified dwells in us by the Spirit and leads us to transformation of life through "the happy exchange." It is also cosmological, culminating in an eschatological transformation of all things.

102. Williams, *Mahayana Buddhism*, 199.

The great compassion of *Amida* can be taken up to God's unselfish cosmic agape in Jesus Christ by becoming an integral part of deepening the aspect of great compassion in Christianity. Therefore, when justification comes alongside Buddhist spirituality of compassion it does not restrict itself to a forensic moment imputed *extra nos*, but beyond that, it refers to God's *mahakaruna* (great compassion) for all sentient beings, which highlights its climax in the death of Jesus Christ on the cross. The Father's *mahakaruna* for the Son as well as for all living creatures in *dukkha* shows himself as God with the motherly mercy and compassion in participation with the Spirit in the Son's death, and in solidarity and unity with everybody and everything in *dukkha*. This understanding of God leads to an understanding of *theologia crucis* that includes and integrates the *han* of Asian minjung and the universal compassion of the Buddha within the framework of an Asian contextual Christology based on divine suffering in affirmation of the lowest of the low outside the wall of Christianity.

The Two-Kingdom Doctrine for Solidarity with and Recognition of Otherness

In Luther's view of the Christ/culture relationship, at issue is the matter of God and human beings rather than that of Christians and pagans. What is important for Luther is that the godly and the ungodly, the life in church and the life in culture, the kingdom of God and the kingdom of the world, the gospel and culture are closely associated, never separated. This is also where the substance of Luther's theory of two kingdoms lies.

Carl Braaten expresses the essence of the doctrine: "This doctrine draws a distinction between the two ways of God's working in the world, two strategies that God uses to deal with the powers of evil and the reality of sin, two approaches to human beings, to mobilize them for active cooperation in two distinctly different kinds of institutions. One is created as an instrument of governance seeking justice through the administration of law and the preservation of order, and the other as an instrument of the Gospel and its sacraments announcing and mediating an ultimate and everlasting salvation which only Christ can give in an act of unconditional love and personal sacrifice."[103]

Luther's doctrine of the two kingdoms has been frequently criticized because others regard him as limiting the claim of Jesus Christ to only the

103. Braaten, *Principles of Lutheran Theology*, 135.

spiritual area and abandoning secular life to the kingdom of the world. Thereby, God's final victory in Jesus Christ is belittled, and so results a false dichotomy and dualistic understanding of the church and the world.

Be that as it may, Luther's two-kingdom doctrine does not make church and state autonomous entities, but subjects the two realms to one universal reign of God. Luther's political thought is contextually understood from a threefold perspective: (1) a critical-constructive participation, (2) a critical-passive resistance, and (3) a critical-active transformation. Luther's genuine concern lies in closely relating the spiritual kingdom to the worldly kingdom and admonishing both of them to stand in line with God's struggle against the world of the devil. To illustrate what the doctrine of two kingdoms means, a diagram is useful.[104]

Regnum Dei

Secular government	Spiritual government
State, Economy, Family	Preaching, Faith, Church
Through law, reason, power	Through Christ, gospel in the Holy Spirit
World person	Christ person

Regnum Diaboli

At the political level, for Luther, there is no alternative to an alliance between the throne and the altar or a confounding of law and gospel. When the secular realm, standing for *regnum diaboli*, opposes the spiritual government, a conflict between them occurs. When the secular world stands for God's reign, correspondence between them occurs. Luther understands life as arranged in three areas (*ecclesia, economia*, and *politia*). These arrangements are divinely imposed mandates rather than the fixed order of creation (*Schöpfungsordnung*). When we see these mandates in light of God's dynamic action in continually creating, and thus being involved in the creatures' life, a complementary relationship between the spiritual realm and the secular realm comes into existence. Justification by faith alone is to be seen within the framework of God's twofold strategy, and also in light of God's dynamic universal reign. It is basically embedded into the life of poverty and suffering on the part of the church proclaiming the gospel of justification.

104. Moltmann, *Politische Theologie, Politische Ethik*, 82–83.

Luther's genuine concern in his reflection on two kingdoms is to develop "political" service to God. As Luther argues for a critical resistance to corruption of the powerful, "the princes and "big shots" find it quite tolerable that the whole world should be criticized if only they themselves are exempted from this criticism. But they must certainly be criticized too and anyone entrusted with the office of preaching owes it to them to point out where they act unjustly and do wrong, even if they protest that such criticism of ruler will lead to rebellion."[105]

When it comes to the economic structure in secular realms, Luther's prophetic critiques convinced even Karl Marx to recognize Martin Luther as a prophetic denouncer of capital accumulation associated with usury. Marx quotes Luther in his analysis of the conversion of surplus-value into capital, saying, "The heathen were able, by the light of reason, to conclude that a usurer is a double-dyed thief and murderer. We Christians, however, hold them in such honor, that we fairly worship them for the sake of their money . . . Little thieves are put in the stocks, great thieves go flaunting in gold and silk . . . Therefore is there, on this earth, no greater enemy of man (after the devil) than a gripe money, and usurer, for he wants to be God over all men."[106]

Furthermore, when seen in light of Luther's irregular thinking based on God's freedom his concept of two kingdoms can provide a theological model of understanding other religions as integral parts of God's reign. God provides secular government even among the heathen and the godless. At this point, Luther's reflection on Ishmael is striking: "For the expulsion does not mean that Ishmael should be utterly excluded from the kingdom of God . . . The descendents of Ishmael also joined the church of Abraham and became heirs of the promise, not by reason of a right but because of irregular grace."[107]

Deepening this statement, I attempt to reconstruct an irregular theology in post-foundational and hermeneutical contour from a Lutheran perspective. "Post-foundational" is, in this context, a descriptive and technical term, which articulates a speech event of God coming from outside the walls of the Christian church. God's word in freedom is beyond the ecclesial foundation. Foundationalism is a term denoting a belief that a philosophy of consciousness can secure sure, certain, "presuppositionless"

105. *WA*, 28:360, 25–28. 361, 33–39. Cf. Duchrow, *Global Economy*, 7.

106. Marx, *Capital*, 649–50.

107. "Lectures on Genesis ch.21–25," *LW*, 4:42–44.

foundations without reference to a particular human situation under the influence of tradition, history, and society. "Hermeneutical" is related to language events of God's word as a history of effect, or a theological "life-world," which affects Christian existence in engaging with interpreting the word of God in the world, society, and world religions.[108]

Luther is attentive to what God could speak to us, which is different from what we would expect. In his "Smalcald Articles" (1537), Luther presents the content of the gospel in a fivefold way. The fifth form of the gospel is "*mutum colloquium and conslatio fratrum*" (mutual colloquium and consolation of brothers and sisters), and Luther's theology of the gospel corresponds to an important explanation of Heb 1:1, according to which "God spoke to our ancestors in many and various ways by the prophets." The Word of God in Jesus Christ cannot be understood apart from God's speech in action through all ages in plural horizons of effect. God's speech points to an open event in the sense of mutual colloquium and brotherly and sisterly comfort. Grounding his concept of the fifth form of the gospel on Matt 18:20, Luther is close to 1 Sam 23:42. "The Lord is witness between you and me forever . . . The Lord shall be between me and you, and between my descendents and your descendents, forever." In the consolation of brothers and sisters, the word of God can be found interpersonally and retains a binding authority in this mutual colloquium. In this regard, Luther is to be understood as a theologian of dialogue, drawing special attention to the dialogical mode of the presence of God and Christ. Luther's theology of dialogue in an irregular sense protects a theology of Lutheran confessions from the dangers of dogmatization, encapsulation, and parochialism. In light of his deliberation of the word of God coming from outside the walls of a Christian church, the irregular perspective in Luther's thinking characterizes Luther as a theologian of eschatological proviso when it comes to his teaching of justification and God's reign.

From this irregular perspective, God's presence is attested by the sun and moon, heaven and earth, and by all of the fruits on earth. If we do not recognize God's presence in the cultural and natural world, it is not God's fault, but our fault. Given this fact, it is worthwhile to note

108. According to Husserl, the all-embracing world horizon that is constituted by a fundamentally anonymous intentionality is distinguished from a concept of the world as it can be made objective by natural science. Husserl calls this phenomenological concept of the world "life-world."

Luther's marvelous sense of "the wonderful and most lovely music coming from the harmony of the motions that are in the celestial spheres."[109] We are encouraged to listen attentively to the beautiful music coming from others. Luther's teaching of justification, when seen in light of God's universal reign and care, has an inclusive implication (cf. particularly his commentary on 1 Tim, and his reflection on Jesus' descent into hell). At a conversational level with religious others the Lutheran Christian has to improve discernment in order to listen to God's mysterious voice, going beyond human foundational and confessional reductionism through acknowledging meticulously the wisdom and religious value found in neighbor religions.

Hence Luther's distinction between the three estates may be seen not only in terms of a socio-political sphere, but may also be seen as extended to the cultural-religious life of people outside Christendom's walls. Christianity is not free to avoid life in culture. Luther regarded common life in culture as the realm in which God and the neighbor could be served. It would be a great error to separate Christian life from culture and retreat to Christian fundamentalism or exclusivism. If teaching and wisdom of other religions stand in favor of God's reign there would be a correspondence between the gospel and other religions. A Christian is to learn to recognize light and wisdom from other religions.

The world of wisdom in creation is not in contrast to God's universal reign. It belongs to it as the sign and guidepost in light of God's reconciliation with the world. In other words, realms of secular government can be reflective of and in correspondence with the grace of God's reconciliation with the world. In this light, Luther's two-kingdoms language can be reappropriated and reread for the language of solidarity with and recognition of the others. In Jesus Christ who died and descended into hell, arose from the dead, and is coming again, nothing can separate the living sentient creature in creation from God's reign in reconciliation. Jesus Christ seated at the right hand of the Father is omnipresent with the Father by the power of the Spirit. Luther's reflection of the dynamism of divine immanence may be read universally and christologically; he is very emphatic on this point, "His own divine essence can be in all creatures collectively and in each one individually more profoundly, more intimately, more present than the creature is in itself . . . It encompasses all things and dwells in

109. *LW*, 1:126.

all."[110] Luther's doctrine of ubiquity refers to a universal Christ because Luther thinks of the right hand of God universally and cosmologically. Christ's body is also everywhere not only according to his divinity but also his humanity. If fact, Christ is "a lord of all things, has all things in his hand, and is present everywhere."[111]

A reading of christocentric inclusivism in Luther can be extended in dialogue with the wisdom of other religions by recognizing the different paths as unique ones. A dialogue between the scriptures and wisdom of others must be a necessary and actual task, as well as an important mission for Asian contextual theology and churches. A Christian in a pluralistic context needs to learn how to speak self-identity without doing any harm to other religious ways. This attitude does not come from secular humanism, but from the radicalism of God's grace in the life, death, and resurrection of Jesus Christ.

For Luther, God is the incomprehensible one who is all-comprehending and embracing. "One cannot comprehend God, yet one senses God's presence, for God lets himself be seen and known by one and all and reveals himself as a good creator who acts for our good and gives us all good things. This is testified to by the sun and moon, heaven and earth, and all the fruits that grow from the earth. But it is not the creator's fault and that of his innumerable good acts that we do not recognize God, as if God desired to be hidden from our eyes. No, the fault lies not with God but with us . . . "[112]

In correcting and critically expanding the Lutheran impasse of Jesus' resurrection, Pannenberg stresses that Christology is rooted in the Easter event. "Therefore, Jesus' resurrection from the dead, in which the end that stands before all men has happened before its time, is the actual event of revelation. Only because of Jesus' resurrection, namely because this event is the beginning of the end facing all men, can one speak of God's self-revelation in Jesus Christ."[113] The resurrection of Jesus should be seen in its historical and universal context, thus becoming the basis for acknowledging that God in Jesus Christ is identical with the God at work in other religious traditions.

110. Cf. *WA*, 23:134. 34–23.136. 36. Cf. Santmire, *Travail of Nature*, 130.

111. *LW*, 36:342.

112. Cf. Schwarz, *True Faith in the True God*, 40.

113. Pannenberg, *Jesus—God and Man*, 129.

At this juncture, it is of especial significance that we interact with Luther's writing against the Jewish religion. Luther's fight against the Jewish religion is not based on racial prejudice or resentment, but on the Jewish "No" to Jesus Christ. Luther's original intention was to see Jesus as the Christ in the history of God's people, Israel. Nevertheless, Luther interprets the entire history of Israel in the Old Testament to be a history of Christ. Christ in Exodus is the basis for Luther to establish a dialogical relationship between the Old Testament and the New Testament. Christ in Exodus, who is God in the Hebrew Bible, can be regarded as the hermeneutical basis for Luther's internal dialogue with the Jewish religion.

In a letter to Justus Jonas (June 30, 1530), Luther writes that he has become a new student of the Decalogue. For Luther, the Decalogue is the dialectic of the gospel, and the gospel is the rhetoric of the Decalogue. The Decalogue is the reason-reflecting ground of the gospel, while the gospel is the assertion, the art of language, the rhetoric of the Decalogue.

Luther's two-kingdom teaching was severely distorted and misused in relation to the Jewish people during the period of National Socialism in Germany. A distorted legacy of the Reformation concerning the Jewish people and their religion can be investigated and corrected in a historical-critical exegesis and in an interpretation of the scripture in terms of the contemporary academic scholarship. Biblical scholarship becomes a helpful corrective to improve and overcome Luther's one-sided understanding of justification and the Jewish religion.

Be that as it may, Luther's statement that Jesus Christ was born a Jew is still a challenge for Christians to get into serious dialogue with people of other faiths. The Jewish "No" to Jesus Christ should be accepted not only in terms of religious tolerance, but also in terms of encouraging an encounter in which we pay attention to the Jewish faithfulness to Torah. In the framework of God's commandment, Luther does not violate the significance of the Torah. Despite his hostile attack on Judaism in his later work, Luther's theology of law takes seriously the Old Testament by discovering the gospel in God's promise granted to God's people in the Old Testament.

What is more important is that in Moses there are the promises of God that sustain faith (Gen 3:15, 22:18; Deut 18:15–16). Therefore, Luther reads Moses for the beautiful example of faith, of love, and of the cross. Seeking Christ and the gospel in both the Old Testament and the New Testament constitutes Luther's creative approach to law and gospel, reading the Scriptures in a dialectical, dialogical, and dynamic way. According to Luther, "Moses is, indeed, a well of all wisdom and understanding, out of which has sprung all that the prophets knew and said. Moreover even the New Testament flows out of it and is grounded in it."[114] Based on God's reconciliation, the human heart begins with feeling kindly and joyously toward God's law. What is surprising is Luther's deliberation of three kingdoms in a fragmentary way.

In "How Christians Should Regard Moses" (1525) Luther attempts to secure a third kingdom for the Jews, in addition to the two kingdoms. "Between these two kingdoms still another has been placed in the middle, half spiritual and half temporal. It is constituted by the Jews, with commandments and outward ceremonies which prescribe their conduct toward God and man."[115] In reflecting on the Christian hermeneutical relationship with Moses, Luther experiments with the following thoughts: another kingdom, half spiritual and half worldly, is grasped by the Jews with the law and with external ceremonies and rituals. Luther is willing to learn from Moses as a moral teacher, not as a lawgiver. Luther allows a space for Judaism as a moral religion without forcing it to be assimilated into the Christian system.

In this regard we to seriously reflect Bonhoeffer's statement: "The Jew keeps open the question of Christ. He is the sign of the free mercy-choice and of the repudiating wrath of God. "Behold therefore the goodness and severity of God" (Rom 11:22). An expulsion of the Jews from the west must necessarily bring with it the expulsion of Christ. For Jesus Christ was a Jew."[116]

Luther's theology witnesses to the gospel in prophetic *diakonia.* It engages in earnest dialogue with other religions and cultures in light of God's reign. Luther was not merely a dualistic thinker, but a dynamic, dialectical thinker who recognized others and otherness. In a process of interreligious dialogue, hermeneutical fusion of horizons (Gadamer) does not allow us to go about syncretizing the gospel with other religions. But such a dialogical process can help us understand the gospel more profoundly from an Asian perspective. Given this fact, Luther's doctrine of two kingdoms

114. *MLBTW,* 130.

115. Ibid.,138.

116. Bonhoeffer, *Ethics,* 90. Bonhoeffer's daring phrase that anyone who cares only for the Jew can also sing Gregorian chant serves as an inspiration for Lutheran Christians in dialogue with Jewish people, as well as with the people of other faiths.

can be reclaimed to promote an interreligious model of cooperation with other religions for bringing justice, peace, and preservation of creation through God's reconciliation with the world of religions.

Such humanity has been made liable and subject to death and hell yet in that humiliation has devoured the devil, hell, and all things in itself

LW 5:219

I am the frog swimming happily in the clear water of a pond, and I am also the grass-snake who, approaching in silence, feeds itself on the frog . . . please call me by my true names, so I can wake up, and so the door of my heart can be left open, the door of compassion

Thich Nhat Hanh

4

Luther and Theology of the Cross in Context

Luther and Medieval Theology

As we have seen from Luther's theological development in relation to scholastic theology (in chapter 3), Luther's understanding of *theologia crucis* cannot adequately be understood without the background of the late medieval heritage with which Luther struggled. Scholastic thinkers—the "schoolmen" as they were called—are often represented as debating earnestly, if pointlessly, how many angels could dance on the head of a pin, or whether or not God is able to create a stone that God cannot lift up, etc. Scholasticism was regarded by the humanists at the beginning of the sixteenth century as pointless, arid intellectual speculation over trivial things. Could God undo the past, by making a prostitute into a virgin? Could God have become a cucumber instead of a human being? These questions were regarded as a frivolous and ridiculous way of debate by the humanists.

To understand the complexities of medieval scholasticism, it helps to distinguish two main streams among the various branches of scholasticism: the one is the realist tradition of the *via antiqua* (Bonaventure, Aquinas, and John Duns Scotus), the other is the nominalist tradition of the *via moderna* (William of Occam, Gabriel Biel, Gregory of Rimini). Generally speaking, the early period of scholastic theology (ca.1200–1350) was influenced by realism, and the later period (ca.1350–1500) by nominalism. Although it is difficult to offer a precise beginning or end, scholasticism is generally regarded as reaching its climax in the period from 1200 to 1500. Scholasticism, as "a particular way of organizing theology," put emphasis on rational justification of religious beliefs and the systematic description of those beliefs.[1]

Nominalism was represented by two groups: the *via moderna* (the modern way) and the *schola Augustiniana moderna* (the modern Augustinian school). The former, which is represented by theologians in the fourteenth and fifteenth centuries, finds its classic formulation in the Englishman William of Occam as the most famous of the nominalists who died in 1349 in exile in Munich. His followers, the Frenchman Pierre d'Ailly, Robert Holcot, and the German Gabriel Biel (who would be regarded as a second Occam), were very optimistic about the human capacity to do everything necessary to enter into a relationship with God. During the fifteenth century, the *via moderna* began to have significant influence on many northern European universities, particularly at the university of Erfurt in Germany where Luther was educated. Luther's theological program for the reformation arose particularly in his response to the *via moderna* of scholasticism. Their excessive emphasis on human will in preparation for salvation was branded as Pelagianism by Luther.

However, writers such as Thomas Bradwardine, Gregory of Rimini, and Hugolino of Orvieto were profoundly pessimistic about the human capacity to enter into such a relationship without the grace of God. In critical response to the soteriology of the *via moderna* at the University of Oxford, Thomas Bradwardine (later archbishop of Canterbury) in his book *De causa Dei contra Pelagium* charged thinkers of the *via moderna* with being "modern Pelagians."

He appealed to Augustine and stressed the significance of his anti-Pelagian writings. His ideas were taken up by Gregory of Rimini at the University of Paris. Being a member of the Order of the Hermits of St. Augustine, Gregory represented an Augustinian view of soteriology in contrast to the Dominicans' appeal to Thomas Aquinas or the Franciscans' recourse to Duns Scotus. Even though Gregory adopted a nominalist view on the question of universals, his soteriology put emphasis on divine initiative in justification along the lines of Augustine. Later, Luther had a great respect for Gregory as the scholastic thinker who did not deviate from Augustine's theology of grace. However, Luther's familiarity with the *via Gregorii* in Erfurt in 1508 through Trutfetter is still debated among scholars.[2] Two different schools of thought (*via moderna* and *schola Augustiniana*

1. McGrath, *Reformation Thought*, 67.

2. Unlike Oberman, McGrath insists that Luther had no knowledge of the theology

Moderna) shared anti-realism in regard to logic and the theory of knowledge, but represented different theological understandings of soteriology and the human will.

During Luther's time at the University of Erfurt (1501–1505), the faculty of arts stood under the influence of representatives of the *via moderna*. After his decision to enter an Augustinian monastery (1505), he was preoccupied with the writings of representatives of this movement such as William of Occam, Pierre d'Ailly, and Gabriel Biel. Particularly Biel's *Commentary on the Canon of the Mass* was a theological textbook for those who prepared for ordination. At that time Luther was inspired by Biel's interpretation of the canon of the Mass.[3]

In the autumn of 1508 Luther went to teach at the newly founded University of Wittenberg in which only *via Thomae* and *via Scoti* (*via antiqua*) were allowed to be taught. However, after the important changes were introduced to the university, the *via Gregorii* (*via moderna*) was permitted to be taught. Even though the *via Gregorii* is arguably identical with the *schola Augustiniana moderna* in a narrow sense, which was the theology at Wittenberg, the *via Gregorii* would be closer to the *via moderna* in an extensive sense.[4] Luther's affinity with the *schola Augustiniana moderna* through John Staupitz at the Augustinian Cloister at Wittenberg would be circumstantial, because the three Augustinian theologians (Nathin, Arnoldi, and Staupitz) who influenced Luther did not belong to the *schola Augustiniana moderna*.

Even Staupitz regarded himself as a representative of the *schola Aegidiana*.[5] Luther, in his letter to his friend Lang (May 18, 1517), reports: "Our theology and S. Augustine are progressing well, and with God's help rule at our university. Aristotle is gradually falling from his throne, and the final doom is only a matter of time. It is amazing how the students dis-

---

of Gregory of Rimini until the time of the Leipzig disputation in 1519. McGrath, *Luther's Theology of the Cross*, 37. Cf. Oberman, *Luther: Man between God and Devil*, 122.

3. *LW*, 54:264.

4. Oberman, "Headwaters of the Reformation," in *The Dawn of the Reformation*, 39–83. According to Oberman, "*the schola Augustiniana moderna*, initiated by Gregory of Rimini, reflected by Hugolin of Orvieto, apparently (was) spiritually alive in the Erfurt Augustinian monastery, and transformed into a pastoral reform theology by Staupitz, as the *occasio proxima*—not the *causa*!—for the inception of the *vera theologia* at Wittenberg," (Ibid., 82). For a critique of this conclusion, see McGrath, *Luther's Theology of the Cross*, 71; McGrath, "Forerunners of the Reformation," 236–41.

5. McGrath, *Reformation Thought*, 79.

dain the lectures on the Sentences. Indeed, no one can expect to have any students if he does not want to teach this theology, that is, lecture on the Bible or on St. Augustine, or another teacher of ecclesiastical eminence."[6]

Luther's relation to late medieval scholasticism is still visible in his understanding of the *synteresis* in his pre-reformation period. However, in launching the reformation break, he was sharply critical of the method of scholastic theology in his "Disputation against Scholastic Theology" (September 4, 1517). Preferring Augustine, Luther addresses his strong criticism of Aristotle's dominance of theology. As a matter of fact, there is no possibility of mentioning good works within human power that could prepare one for meeting and satisfying God. Aristotle's understanding of righteousness and his role in theology, according to Luther, was opposed and inimical to the grace of God. No one could become a theologian without Aristotle when Luther was in Erfurt. Now, however, no one could become a theologian with Aristotle.

In opposition to Scotus and Gabriel, Luther rejects the *synteresis* as point of contact for justification. "Nor is it surprising that the will can conform to erroneous and not to correct precepts."[7] "Indeed, it is peculiar to it that it can only conform to erroneous and not to correct precepts."[8] Rejecting Biel and late medieval nominalism, Luther mounted a wholesale attack on "the entire Ethics of Aristotle" as "the worst enemy of grace."[9] "Briefly, the whole Aristotle is to theology as darkness is to light."[10] Luther rejected any theological claim that human natural capacity can be in cooperation with God for salvation. Luther once wrote that he lost Christ in Scholastic theology. What he learned from them is nothing but ignorance of sin, righteousness, and the whole Christian life. In opposition to a semi-Pelagian view of salvation in nominalism, Luther took a decisive step in launching his *theologia crucis* coupled with his teaching of justification. During the formative time for the Reformation break Luther was deeply influenced by his exegetical study of Psalms and Paul and indebted to Augustine and the German mystics who helped him to overcome *Anfechtungen* and thus lead to his confrontation with all nominalistic claims about human natural abilities and qualities before God.

6. *LW*, 48:42. Cf. Brecht, *Martin Luther: His Road to Reformation*, 171.

7. *MLBTW*, 14, Thesis 14.

8. Ibid., Thesis 15.

9. Ibid., 16, Thesis 41.

10. Ibid., Thesis 50.

Luther and *Theologia Crucis*

It is by and large accepted that *theologia crucis* is the key to Luther's theological method. As Walter von Loewenich writes, "the theology of the cross is a principle of Luther's entire theology, and it may not be confined to a special period in his theological development."[11] *Theologia crucis*, which is the distinctive mark of Luther's whole theology, comes to the fore explicitly in his Heidelberg Disputation of 1518, in which his entire theology is grounded in the crucified Christ.

Prior to the Heidelberg Disputation, however, a theology of the cross was expressed in his sharp response to John Eck. Against Eck's sixth Obelisk questioning Luther's sixteenth thesis on indulgences, Luther attacks Eck, charging that he is ignorant of the theology of the cross.[12] According to Luther, anyone who is ignorant of the theology of the cross loses sight of "the existence of an all-shaking temptation in Christian experience."[13]

The theology of the cross appears to be played off against scholasticism. In Luther's *Lectures on Hebrews* (Heb 12:11) we see the *theologia crucis* mentioned in his gloss on Heb 12:11. God's proper work (*proprium opus*) is hidden from the world, a scandal to the Jews and folly to the Gentiles. God's proper work is only revealed through his alien work (*alienum opus*) in suffering, which is accepted only by faith. A dialectic between proper work and alien work plays a significant role in shaping and influencing Luther's idea of faith and justification. *Opus alienum* as expressed in the cross and sufferings is understood and realized only in the believer's faith.

In the *Resolution* Luther expresses the *theologia crucis* in discussion of thesis fifty-eight, which calls into question indulgences and the merits of the saints and of Christ.[14] "The merits of Christ perform an alien work . . . in that they effect the cross, the labor, all kinds of punishment, finally death and hell in the flesh, to the end that the body of sin is destroyed . . . For whoever is baptized in Christ and is renewed shall be prepared for punishment, crosses, and deaths . . . Just so must we be conformed to the image and the Son of God."[15] In view of a double way of God's operation, God does alien work for the sake of God's proper work, which is hidden

11. Loewenich, *Luther's Theology of the Cross*, 13.

12. *WA*, 1:281–314.

13. Cf. Ngien, *Suffering of God*, 44. Cf. *WA*, 1.281.28–31.

14. *LW*, 31:83–252. *WA*, 1:525–628.

15. *LW*, 31:225.

to the world. In thesis fifty-eight the scholastic theologians are identified with *theologia gloriae*, in which the theology of the cross is abrogated by losing the crucified and hidden God.

However, the theologian of the cross "knows of a crucified and hidden God, concealed not only because he himself is crucified, but also hidden under all the crosses and sufferings of true Christians . . . so that Christ is their light, righteousness, truth, wisdom, and all good, concealed through *sub contrario*, In a crucified God . . . Through his *opus alienum* of judgment he realizes his opus proprium of salvation."[16] The principle of justification by faith comes from Luther's theology of the cross in which the sinner meets the crucified and hidden God on the cross. Given this fact, the works of all people in preparation for grace by free will are blocked and become meaningless. The scholastic principle of *facere quod in se est* is abandoned in a radical way. Instead, a life of discipleship under the cross of Christ comes to the surface; that is, *conformitas Christi*. Without God's *opus alienum* we cannot have hope in God.

In the "Heidelberg Disputation," which is crucial and decisive in Luther's thought concerning righteousness, grace, and justification, Luther puts his theology of the cross in an antithetical stance toward Aristotle and scholastic theology, both of which are characterized by a theology of glory. For Luther, theologians of glory are not competent to recognize how God works in a crucified and hidden manner. If people attempt to speculate on the invisible things of God by way of human reason, they are incapable of discerning God's revelation in the suffering of Christ. Anyone who seeks to approach the invisible things of God through created things does not deserve to be called a theologian. The human sinful condition serves only the misuse of "the best in the worst manner," and seeking to get closer to God through good works.[17] That being the case, the true knowledge of God, according to Luther, can be found in God's self-revelation through Christ on the cross. Therefore, "He deserves to be called a theologian, however, who comprehends the visible and manifest things of God seen through suffering and the cross."[18]

The theology of the cross is to God revealed in the suffering and foolishness of the cross what the theology of glory is to God's omnipotence and omnipresence manifest in created things. Actually, the work of Christ

16. *LW*, 31:223. Cf. Ngien, *Suffering of God*, 46.

17. *MLBTW*, 32.

18. Ibid., 31.

in grace makes human accomplished works pleasing to God. Human righteousness *coram Deo* through faith in Christ is the backbone for understanding Luther's theology of the cross and his doctrine of justification. As a matter of fact, a theology of the cross is a theology of revelation rooted in *solus Christus*.[19] Given this fact, a theology of the cross makes human justification possible only by faith in Christ, because "He is not righteous who does much, but he who, without work, believes much in Christ."[20]

The Aristotelian notion of justice in which moral attitude or habits of action play a significant role is sharply rejected at this point. In the explanation of this thesis in the Heidelberg disputation Luther accentuated our righteousness from the outside. "In such a way is Christ in us by faith. Nay rather than in us he is one with us. Now Christ is righteous and fulfills all the commands of God." The Aristotelian notion of justice that is acquired by improving an appropriate moral attitude becomes meaningless with respect to the justice of God. In *Disputation Against Scholastic Theology* we hear from Luther that "one must concede that the will is not free to strive toward whatever is declared good. This is in opposition to Scotus and Gabriel."[21]

God's revelation is paradoxical and concealed under the cross because human beings are incapable of seeing God directly. Those who know Christ can know God hidden in suffering. But a true theologian comprehends the visible and hinden parts of God in terms of the passion and the cross. In fact, for Luther *Deus absconditus* is to be known only in *Deus revelatus*, that is, in *Deus incarnatus, Deus crucifixus*. God wants to be recognized and known as God hidden in suffering. The shame and humility of the cross is the root and base of true theology and recognition of God. In contrast, the theologian of glory hates the cross and suffering in favor of the glory of works. Such a theology is antithetical to the cross, doubting and rejecting the dereliction on the cross against the self-revelation of God. That is why "a theologian of glory calls evil good and good evil. A theologian of the cross calls the thing what it actually is."[22] Victory over sin and death is made possible only through God's revelation in the weakness of humanity rather than in strength, in the humiliation of the cross rather than in power. Any human effort to get to God not in terms

19. Ibid., 31–32.
20. Ibid., 32.
21. Ibid., 14, Thesis 10.
22. Ibid., 31, Thesis 21.

of God's way of the cross, but in terms of human speculative knowledge is charged with the theology of glory. Luther's paradigm shift in understanding God in suffering and humiliation on the cross brings *Deus crucifixus pro nobis* to the fore.

The practical consequence of a *theologia crucis* strengthens the life of believers under the cross. God is present and active in suffering and *Anfechtungen*; it is here that the living God works out God's justification and salvation. In the midst of *Anfechtungen* we are justified. Sinners are made lovely and righteous because God loves them. However, they are not loved because they are lovely. "As Christ said, 'I came not to call the righteous, but sinners' (Matt 9:13). This is the love of the cross, born of the cross, which turns in the direction where it does not find good which it may enjoy, but where it may confer good upon the bad and needy person."[23]

The *theologia crucis* makes clear God's saving relationship to human beings in terms of suffering and the cross of Jesus Christ. This theology refutes the theology of the medieval church that seeks to ascend to God by speculative and mystical means, and effort on the basis of human achievements. God on the cross says a definitive "no" to all human efforts of merit from God apart from the crucified Christ, but says a definitive "yes" to all human beings on the basis of God's unfathomable love on the cross. The assurance of Christian salvation is grounded on the struggle of divine love against death on the cross. Recognizing God in the shame and humility of the cross belongs to true theology because *Crux sola est nostra theologia.*[24] The theology of the cross becomes a constructive principle for Christian living under the cross because God makes Godself known through suffering. God is active in suffering and *Anfechtungen*. Luther's *theologia crucis* in this regard has something to do with Jesus Christ as the prime sacrament and example. God's redeeming work in Christ becomes the basis for believers' participation in God's grace of justification through faith that does not devalue suffering and *Anfechtungen* under the life of the cross.

Unification Christology and Disjunction Christology

What is characteristic of Luther's Christology lies in his emphasis on its historical approach to God's suffering. In accentuating the divine suffer-

23. Ibid., 48, Thesis 28.

24. McGrath, *Luther's Theology of the Cross*, 1.

ing in Jesus Christ on the cross it is noteworthy that Luther followed the church fathers and ecumenical councils of the ancient church. However, beyond the classic doctrine of two natures, Luther developed Christology with special attention to soteriology, in which the emphasis is not on philosophical teaching about Christ but on a personal relationship with Christ. That is, Christ must be proclaimed, not Christology. Christ himself is stressed in contrast to the Logos Christology of the Eastern church or the philosophical-metaphysical project of scholastic Christology.[25] Before describing Luther's position concerning divine passibility it helps to outline the christological debate relating to two natures in one person of Jesus Christ between the school of Alexandria and the school of Antioch in the ancient church.[26]

Debates of Christology in the ancient church revolved around the way in which God is related to Jesus. In other words, this is about the relation of the divine nature of Jesus to his human nature. From the beginning Christian theology faced the task of clarifying how Jesus is truly God and simultaneously truly man. Since Constantine became Pontifex Maximus, Christianity was under fire by Arius, an Alexandrian priest who was influenced by the left-wing Origenist, Lucien of Antioch. For Arius, Christ was the Logos, the Son of God who existed before God the Father created the world. However, he was not God, and was created out of nothing to assist God in the creation of the world. Therefore, in the beginning there was God alone. Because the Logos was a creature, he could change, enter into history, and unite himself with the human flesh in the person of Jesus. Thus, the incarnation of the Logos was inferior to God the Father.[27]

In clashing with Arius, Alexander, the bishop of the Church in Alexandria who was a right-wing Origenist, insisted that the divinity of the Word incarnate in Jesus should be preserved. When Alexander died in 328 CE, Athanasius succeeded him and continued his theological campaign. He mounted a strong attack upon Arius, claiming that Arius' position would undo the whole reality of salvation. If the mediator is not divine, but rather created by God, this creature can bring no salvation to human beings. This was the core of Athanasius' doctrine of salvation.

25. Cf. The famous principle of Melanchthon in *Loci* where it reads: "*hoc est Christum cognoscere, beneficia eius cognoscere*," (to know Christ is to know his benefits).

26. For a survey of the historical development of Christology in the ancient church, see Braaten, *Christian Dogmatics,* 469–516.

27. González, *History of Christian Thought*, 262–4.

Athanasius, the real founder of Alexandrian Christology, stressed the incorporation of the Logos into Jesus Christ so that the Logos, as the bearer of all of Jesus' functions, offers the basis for all of Jesus' historical actions. "The human in Christ is borne by the Logos."[28] The Logos-*sarx* pattern in Athanasius affirms the unification of the Logos with the flesh and influenced the christological development in the Alexandrian school.

At the Council of Nicea in Bythinia (AD 325), *homoousios*, a term that expresses the oneness of substance between the Father and the Son, was inserted into the Creed of that council, precluding Arian Christology. Thus, Jesus Christ was confessed as "eternally begotten of the Father," "not created," "of the same essence (reality) as the Father (*homoousion to patri*)," "true God from true God."[29] On this basis could the worship of Christ be held, and the reality of the salvation of humanity and the world would be guaranteed. The Nicene Creed became the foundation for understanding the incarnation.

However, the phrase "of one essence (reality) with the Father" sparked a great controversy. The subsequent Christological debates revolved around the issue of how the eternal Son of God, of the same substance as the Father, could become flesh in the person of Jesus Christ. While concepts such as *hypostasis* and *ousia* were used as synonyms at Nicea, the Cappadocians began to develop the teaching of *mia ousia* (one single nature) and *treis hypostaseis* (three persons, or better three modes of being) of God. Although stressing the distinction between the two natures, the Cappadocians, on the basis of a mutual interpenetration of divine and human attributes in Christ, still conceived this unity as a mixture without caution or hesitation.[30]

The new school of Antioch (Diodore of Tarsus, Theodore of Mopsuestia, and Nestorius) developed a Logos-man Christology in which the distinction between the divine nature and the human nature of Christ was held with emphasis on the pure humanity of Jesus (disjunction Christology), while the new school of Alexandria represented a Logos-flesh Christology, in which the two natures of Christ were communicated through each other (*communicatio idiomatum*) in emphasizing the divinity of Christ (unification Christology). Athanasius took the incarnation to its next logical step, a soteriological deification, in which the dynamic of the

28. Pannenberg, *Jesus—God and Man*, 288.

29. Leith, *Creeds of the Churches*, 30–31.

30. Pannenberg, *Jesus—God and Man*, 297.

Logos comes to the fore while the flesh remains only its tool. The unification of the logos with the flesh in the Logos-*sarx* pattern leans toward replacing the human spirit-soul in Jesus Christ with the Logos.[31]

When Nestorius spoke about a mere *synapheia* (fellowship of contact, or conjunction) of the divine and human natures, Cyril of Alexandria attacked Nestorius and contended that the two natures of Jesus are not only conjoined, but also become one, a hypostatic union (*unio personalis*), so that a reciprocal exchange of attributes occurs.[32] For Nestorius, who is regarded as the supposed heretical father of disjunction Christology, Jesus Christ was both fully God and fully human. However, the divine and human natures must be kept distinct in the incarnation. Regarding the union of divinity and humanity in Christ, Nestorius rejected a natural or hypostatic union, which is the foundation of the *communicatio idiomatum*. That being the case, a hypostatic union would bring together two natures to form a third. In Nestorius' judgment, two natures or two persons in unabbreviated form joined in Christ. This scheme of dualism accentuated the divine and the human in their complete difference, which resulted in blocking a real incarnational union of God and humanity in the one person of Jesus Christ. At stake for Nestorius was the conjunction (*synapheia*) or close communion of the two persons. This is the union in the *prosopon*. He was concerned that the hypostatic union as a mixture would confuse and lose the distinction.

Regarding the unity in Christ as a unity of outward appearance (*prosopon*), each *prosopon* of the two natures uniting comes up as a third *prosopon* common to both appearing in the voluntary unity of the man Jesus with God. The two outward appearances that are connected in a third *prosopon* must be neither divine nor human. Although the Logos may have assumed a whole man by uniting himself with the complete man Jesus, their unity was a third thing beside the divine Logos and the man Jesus, both of which are presupposed as already independent. Therefore, the man Jesus was no longer in unity with God. This union was rather a conjunction in contrast to a *communicatio idiomatum*, a doctrine that was found not merely among Alexandrines, but also among the more moderate Anthiochenes such as Theodore of Mopsuestia. For Nestorius, Mary was to be designated only as *christotokos*, mother of Christ, not as *Theotokos*, mother of God. God cannot have a mother. The title "Bearer of God" leads to a confusion of the

31. Ibid., 288.

32. Poehlmann, *Abriss der Dogmatik*, 218.

divinity and the humanity in Jesus Christ. The Antiochene Christology did not succeed in making clear the unity of God and humanity in the man Jesus because of its disjunction of the two natures.

In Alexandria, *Apollinarianism* arose later in the fourth century. Here, the Logos replaced not the human soul in Jesus but the human spirit. Apollinarius, bishop of Laodicea and a friend of Athanasius, together with the Great Basil of Caesarea (ca. 300–379), was a strong defender, not only of the Nicene faith, but also of the Alexandrine theology. Apollinarius affirmed that the Son is distinctly other than the Father (against Sabellianism), but eternally shares the one substance of the Father (against Arianism). He felt his task was to clarify how the immutable Word could unite with mutable humanity. He followed the triple division in Plato and 1 Thess 5:23, in which human nature is composed of body, soul, and spirit or reason. However, according to him, the humanity of Christ assumed in the incarnation was incomplete. Surely the Logos in Christ was truly God, but in the incarnation he did not become wholly human. Although the Logos took upon himself the body and soul of the man Jesus, he took the place of his human spirit. In other words, the Word occupied the place of the spirit. Christ is human because his body and his soul are human, but he is divine because his spirit is the eternal Logos. With Apollinarius the Logos-*sarx* pattern came to its logical conclusion in which the Logos in Jesus replaced the human spirit. His doctrine was repudiated in Alexandria in 362 because it undermined the doctrine of soteriology.

If Christ is not fully human the whole human being cannot be saved. The union of God and human being prevailed in the thought of Gregory of Nazianzus. What is not assumed by God is not redeemed. "If anyone has put his trust in Him as a Man without a human mind, he is really bereft of mind, and quite unworthy of salvation. For that which He has not assumed He has not healed; but that which is united to His Godhead is also saved. If only half of Adam fell, then that which Christ assumes and saves may be half also; but if the whole of his nature fell, it must be united to the whole nature of Him that was begotten, and so be saved as a whole."[33] As is well known, Athanasius, following Irenaeus, maintained: "He became man so that we might be made gods."[34] In his understanding of the incarnation of the Logos, Athanasius strongly defended the no-

33. Gregory of Nazianzus, EP.101 (NPNF, 2nd series, 7:440). Cf. Gonzáles, *History of Christian Thought*, 350.

34. Oratio de inc, 54. Cf. González, *History of Christian Thought*, 349.

tion of deification: not only does God participate in human life, but also human beings were originally created to participate in the divine Logos. Because of this soteriological thesis, the Arians, as well as Apollinaris of Laodicea also, were rejected in that the divine Logos not only took on flesh, but was a complete man with body, soul, and mind.

The logic of *homoousios* in the Council of Constantinople (381) affirmed a simultaneous *homoousios* of Christ with the Father and at the same time *homoousios* with humanity. If the human spirit is displaced by the divine Logos, the deepest spiritual dimension of human existence becomes excluded in that salvation. The reaction to the docetic tendencies of Apollinarianism was also echoed in Nestorius, patriarch of Constantinople. Even though the new school of Antioch accepted the Nicene doctrine of the divinity of Christ, the prominent representatives of this school—Diodore of Tarsus, Theodore of Mopsuestia, and Nestorius—held the traditional Antiochian notion that Jesus Christ was completely human in body, soul, and spirit. For example, against Apollinarius, Theodore of Mopsuestia moved in the direction of the Cappadocians. "Thus Christ must assume not only the body, but a soul as well; the soul had to be assumed first, and then for its sake the body."[35] The pattern Logos-man was substituted for the pattern Logos-*sarx*, in which the whole man, not only the flesh, was assumed. However, the question still remained unsolved: how man and God could be united in the one person of Jesus, how could God dwell among humanity?

The Alexandrian unification Christology in the fifth century was developed by Cyril following Athanasius. Affirming that Jesus' body possessed its human soul (against Apollinarius), Cyril took human nature to be only the garment of the Logos. The Logos assumed human nature at the incarnation, but not that of the individual man Jesus. Jesus' full humanity was threatened. Jesus became individual only through the Logos as the bearer of his concrete behavior.[36] Cyril, in strong opposition to Nestorius as well as in anti-Apollinarian polemic, did not connect Logos and *sarx* directly together, because he insisted that "the natural impartation of life, which Christ's body needs, is no longer attributed to the Logos as Logos, but is appropriated to the soul."[37]

35. Cf. Pannenberg, *Jesus—God and Man*, 288.

36. Ibid., 289.

37. Ibid.

However, human nature is merely "the garment of the Logos." At this point, we perceive that the human nature of Jesus is not an individual human being, but the Logos is united to humanity in general. Although Cyril does not reject the individuality of Jesus' human nature, Jesus for him became an individual human being only through the Logos. This is the place where Alexandrian Christology is in profound contrast to Antiochene Christology.[38]

In contrast to the Nestorians, the patriarch Eutyches of Constantinople, and Dioscuros, Cyril stressed that Christ was Jesus' divine nature, not his humanity. If the Logos found only the universal human nature at the incarnation, how can a Monophysite tendency be avoided? Jesus as God-man was at the root of Alexandrian Christology. Eutycheanism, also called monophysitism, sacrificed the integrity of Jesus' humanity for the sake of his divinity. At the moment of the incarnation it held that there remained only one nature, and so missed the whole point of the incarnation. In the fifth century the ancient church began to struggle with monophysitism and Nestorianism. Already in the council of Nicea (325) the Arian heresy was condemned because it denied the full deity of Christ. In the Council of Constantinople (381), Apollinarianism was rejected because it denied the complete humanity of Jesus. Nestorius and Eutyches struggled with the issue of how to understand that Jesus Christ was fully God and fully human. However, they went too far toward the right in a divine Christ or the left in a human Jesus. Both extremes impaired the real incarnation of God in Jesus Christ.

At Chalcedon (451), christological dogma was formulated as two natures, divine and human, in the one person of Jesus Christ. Church fathers pursued a middle path between the Nestorians (engendering the unity of the person) and the Eutycheans (absorbing the human into the divine). As the Creed of Chalcedon states, Jesus Christ is confessed as being "of the same reality as God (*homoousion to patri*)" with respect to his deity, and "of the same reality as we are ourselves (*homoousion hemin*)" with respect to humanness . . . actually God and actually man, with a rational soul . . . begotten of the Father before the time began," made known "in two natures (*duo physesin*) . . . without confusing the two natures (*asunkutos*), without transmuting one nature into the other (*atreptos*), without dividing them into two separate categories, without contrasting them ac-

38. Gonzáles, *History of Christian Thought*, 365–66. Pannenberg, *Jesus—God and Man*, 289.

cording to area or function (*achoristos*)."[39] The main point was to affirm a true incarnation. Against Nestorianism the creed affirmed that there was no division or separation, and against Eutycheanism that there was no confusion or change between the two natures. However, the creed did not explain how two complete natures could be united in one person, though remaining distinct. For Alexandrians, the omission of the formula "one incarnate nature of the divine Logos" and of the hypostatic union remained unsatisfactory.

Luther's Christology and Divine Passibility

With Chalcedon, Luther interpreted Christology in the Alexandrian pattern. Luther stressed the substantial unity of the divinity and humanity of Jesus Christ with an emphasis on the humanity of Christ. Luther's starting point from below, placing emphasis on the full humanity of Christ, was not short of God's full presence and action in the fleshly life of Jesus Christ. The principle of *finitum capax infiniti* was firmly established. God is fully in Jesus Christ. As Luther notes, "Yet these two natures are so united that there is only one God and one Lord, that Mary suckles God with her breasts, bathes God, rocks him, and carries him; furthermore, that Pilate and Herod crucified and killed God. The two natures are so joined that the true deity and humanity are one."[40]

Following the Chalcedonian formula of two natures in Jesus Christ, Luther spoke of the *communicatio idiomatum*. As Luther argued in his *Confession concerning Christ's Supper* (1528), "it is correct to say that the Son of God was crucified and died for us. But if someone objects that the deity cannot suffer and die, we reply that this is true, but yet because the deity and the humanity in Christ are one person, therefore, on account of such personal union the scripture attributes to the deity whatever belongs to the humanity and vice versa."[41] While Luther preferred the real mutual interpenetration of the two natures in terms of the figure of "the glowing iron,"[42] Zwingli maintained a mere figure of speech in the communication of attributes. In the antithetical positions of the reformers, we see

39. Leith, *Creeds of the Churches*, 35–36.

40. *LW*, 22: 492–93.

41. Cf. Ngien, *Suffering of God*, 71.

42. *WA*, 7:53. Cf. Pannenberg, *Jesus—God and Man*, 299.

again a revival of the controversy between Alexandrian and Antiochene Christology.

There are two heretical ways of referring to the suffering of Christ. In the circles of the Ebionites or adoptionists the suffering of Christ certifies that he was only a human, because God cannot suffer. As far as Christ is merely human, the suffering can be accepted. This axiom stems from the Greek ontological concept of God as unchangeability and impassibility, not from the biblical notion of God. In the circle of the docetists and monophysites, the suffering of Christ is not real, because the divinity of Christ is affirmed. Christ did not really suffer, because he was truly God. Again, the impassible deity in the God comes from Greek metaphysics, not from the biblical living God. However, the God of Israel was free to suffer out of divine love for God's own people. Christ suffered in his person, and this person is God the Son, of one being with the Father. As far as God is incarnated in Christ, the suffering becomes an integral part of the experience of God with humanity. It is also biblically affirmed.

It was important for Luther to confess that Christ suffered and died. This Christ is true God. Therefore, the Son of God suffered. Christ was crucified, according to the human nature. This fact must be attributed to the whole person. This is called *Synechdoche* (that is, when a part of something is used to refer to the whole thing). Luther taught that the whole Christ is really present at the Lord's Supper in terms of *communicatio idiomatum* in the personal union. Ubiquity (an attribute of the divine nature) is communicated to the human nature based on the incarnational union. By contrast, Zwingli found any concept of communication to be merely nominal, a rhetorical figure of speech. He uses the theory of *alloesis* to deny the understanding of the two natures in the personal union. The human Christ cannot be really present in the Lord's Supper, because he is finite and so can be present only in a particular place at a time (*in certo loco*). Zwingli's position is characterized as a *praedicatio verbalis.*[43] His concern lies in safeguarding the transcendence of God and insuring that the Son of God does not suffer and die; only the man Jesus suffered and died. The controversy on the communication of attributes was later expanded to a full-scale war over Christology between the Lutherans and the Reformed.

In keeping with the Chalcedonian orthodoxy Luther emphasized the unity of Christ's person and accused Zwingli of being a Nestorian, because

43. "Formula of Concord," SD VIII, & 40–45, *BC*, 599.

he separated the divine from the human nature in the person of Christ. For Zwingli, passibility of God was out of the question because God is far removed from the experience of suffering. In repudiation of Zwingli Luther contended, "Beware! Beware, I tell you, of the 'Alloesis.' It is the devil's spawn. For in the end it sets up such a Christ that I wouldn't want to be called 'Christian' after him."[44]

For Luther, suffering is in reality communicated to the divine Logos. In the *Schwabach Articles* (1529) Luther expressed his own thinking emphatically. "One should not believe or teach that Jesus Christ suffered for us as a man or as mankind; but because here God and man are not two persons but one indivisible Person, one must hold and teach that God and man or the Son of God truly suffered for us."[45] The person of Christ holds the properties of the two natures, and so one of the two natures is attributed to the whole person.

Even though the hypostatic union suffers in the person of Jesus Christ according to God's human nature, God suffers, because God and man are united in the one Person of Christ without separation. In *The Word was Made Flesh* (1539) Luther interprets *communicatio idiomatum* in such a way that God as God is not capable of suffering, but with respect to man God suffers. As far as God and man in one person cannot be separated, the Christ as true God and true man suffered for us and the whole person died for us. According to Luther, Nestorius' fault was in not admitting a *communicatio idiomatum* between the two natures. God's impassibility then becomes the ground motive of Nestorian Christology.

However, for Luther the *idiomata* of the two natures coincide; they are united and joined. As Luther contends, "We Christians must ascribe all the idiomata of two natures of Christ, both persons, equally to him. Consequently, Christ is God and man in one person . . . namely, Christ has died, and Christ is God; therefore God died—not the separated God, but God united with humanity . . . If it seems strange to Nestorius that God dies, he should think it equally strange that God becomes man; for thereby the immortal God becomes that which must die, suffer, and have all human idiomata . . . On the other hand, whatever is said of God must also be ascribed to the man, namely, God created the world and is almighty; the man Christ is God, therefore the man Christ created the world and is

44. Cf. Ngien, *Suffering of God*, 71.

45. Ibid., 72.

almighty. The reason for this is that since God and man have become one person, it follows that this person bears the *idomata* of both natures."[46]

The heresies of Nestorius and Eutyches stand in opposition. The former would not ascribe the *idiomata* of the human nature to the divine in the one person of Christ, whereas the latter would not ascribe the *idiomata* of the divine nature to human nature. As Nestorius takes only the Man Christ to be crucified, so Eutyches takes only God to be crucified. What is important for Luther was to make a distinction between a communication *in abstracto* and a communication *in concreto*. "If I speak rightly saying that the divinity does not suffer, the humanity does not create, then I speak of something in the abstract and of a divinity which is separated. But one must not do that . . . But one believes in a concrete sense (*in concreto*) saying that this man is God, etc. Then the properties are attributed."[47]

If the divinity is understood in an abstract manner, i.e., not united with humanity in Jesus Christ, God does not suffer. However, if the divinity is understood *in concreto*, i.e., united with humanity, the divinity has a share with the human nature in Christ. What was at stake for Luther was the notion of a real and concrete communication between the divine nature and human nature. Luther emphasizes the fact that according to the humanity, Christ is a creature, yet according to his divinity, Christ is God. Thus are the two natures utterly conjoined in one person. *Extra Christum non est Deus alius*. For Luther, the two natures were distinct, but not separated. The conjoining of the humanity and divinity in Christ was greater and more certain than the conjunction of soul and body. Christ as impassible Son of God was the unity of the immortal divine nature and mortal human nature. Therefore, God and man were crucified under Pontius Pilate.

The Lutheran position was branded the child of Eutycheanism in excessively stressing the unity of the divine-human person, and so running the monophysite risk of mixing the two natures (*finitum est capax infiniti*—the finite is capable of the infinite), while the Reformed position, child of Nestorianism, maintained a clear distinction between the two natures (*finitum non capax infiniti*—the finite is not capable of the infinite).[48]

46. *LW*, 41:103.

47. *WA*, 40:3, 707, 22–27. Cf. Ngien, *Suffering of God*, 76.

48. According to the Calvinist teaching, the Logos, being infinite, must exist *extra carnem* (outside the flesh) not limited by its union with the flesh. This teaching, which was dubbed the *extra-Calvinisticum* among Lutherans, tends to set the Logos apart from

For Luther, it is no wonder that the two natures in Christ communicate their attributes and their properties from the one to the other. They are attached, intertwined, and united to each other. The two natures in Christ hold each other's properties, even sharing them with each other. By humanity's participation in the divine attributes (*finitum capax infiniti*), or by the divinity's incarnation with the humanity (*infinitum capax finiti*), the divine property of ubiquity is communicated to the human nature. The communication for Luther is understood in a way that the mutual change and communication of the divine and human properties take place from the one nature to the other.

Unlike Zwingli, Calvin, even though he did not reject the *communicatio idiomatum* as such, understood it as based not on a direct ontological exchange of attributes between the natures in terms of the divine property of ubiquity, but on a pneumatological communication, in which he stood closer to Luther than to Zwingli.[49] Luther, in fact, emphasized the ubiquity in the Lord's Supper, and opened up a cosmic and universal dimension of the ubiquity that seems, I think, to be more parallel to Calvin's ubiquity in terms of *arcanus Spiritus instinctus*, albeit with a different approach.[50] Luther conceived of the incarnation in a dynamic way, while Calvin spoke of the *communicatio idiomatum* in the actual sense.[51]

Based on the *communicatio idiomatum*, Luther deepened the suffering, even the death of the divinity in Christ. The person of Christ, on the basis of the *enhypostasis* of Christ's human nature in God, is indissoluble from the divine nature, so that what happened to Christ's human nature in suffering is true also of the divine nature. Therefore, even though Luther made use of the phrase "according to His nature," he distanced himself from Nestorius who denied the suffering of Christ in his divine nature. However, Lutheran understandings of Christology met difficulties in the concept of the Christ's kenosis in the seventeenth and eighteenth centuries. The Tübingen theologians such as Johann Brenz maintained a mere concealment (*krypsis*) of the divine attributes during Jesus' earthly life, while the Giessen theologians such as Martin Chemnitz referred to a par-

its enfleshment, while the Lutherans stick to the phrase "*totus intra carnem* and *numquam extra carnem*," (wholly in the flesh and never outside the flesh). See Braaten, *Christian Dogmatics*, 509.

49. *Inst* II.xiv.2ff; Pannenberg, *Jesus—God and Man*, 299–300.

50. Cf. Chung, *Spirituality and Social Ethics*,13–22.

51. Weber, *Grundlagen der Dogmatik, II*, 149, 153.

tial refusal of them (*kenosis*). We see the controversy between disjunction Christology and unification Christology appear again within the Lutheran understanding of Christ's self-emptying. The Tübingen theologians would threaten the reality of Jesus' historical existence for the sake of a mere concealment of the divine attributes, while the Giessen theologians would threaten a full living unity of the human with the divine nature for the sake of renunciation of the use of divine attributes.

In addition, Melanchthon's disciple, Martin Chemnitz, strongly affirmed a real *perichoresis* of natures in using the figure of fire and iron, which prepares the way for the Christology of the *Formula of Concord*.[52] This is the well known formula of three genera of the *communicatio idiomatum*. The first form of *genus idiomaticum*, which was termed in Lutheran Orthodoxy, says that what applies to the divine or human nature can be asserted for the person of Christ as a whole (in case of Zwingli). Therefore, in Christ there are two distinct natures, unchanged and unmixed like oil and water.

The second form of *genus apostelesmaticum* ascribed all actions including the three offices, not to only one of the two natures, but to the person of the Mediator (in case of Calvin). The person of Christ acts in, according to, with, and through both natures. Thus, Christ is mediator and redeemer according to both natures. Jesus Christ shed his blood by human nature, so that the divine nature did not participate in the suffering of Christ.

The third form of *genus maiestaticum* defended the communication of divine attributes of majesty to the human nature itself. Because of the personal union, the human nature received prerogatives in power, glory, and majesty. Such analysis affirms Christ's human nature as really present in the Lord's Supper. This third form was especially important for the Lutheran teaching of the Lord's Supper in antithesis to the Reformed teaching. The inseparable unity of the two natures (divinity and humanity) is attached and imputed to each. Concerning creation, "it is said correctly that 'the man created,' because the divinity, which alone creates, is incarnate with the humanity, and therefore the humanity participates in the attributes of both predicates."[53] Therefore, "the infant lying in the lap of His mother created heaven and earth, and is the lord of the angels."[54] The divine property of omnipresence is communicated to the human nature.

52. "Formula of concord," SD III & 40–45, BC, 598.

53. *LW*, 26:265.

54. Ibid.

In the nineteenth century, Thomasius developed his idea of self-limitation of the Logos in the incarnation, which became a part of the neo-Lutheran Erlangen theology. In the reflection of a self-limitation of the divine Logos in the incarnation, the Son relinquished the relative attributes of divinity. "The humiliation of (Christ) is not a mere concealment, but a real kenosis (=emptying) of . . . divine attributes, namely not only its use, but its possession."[55] This expresses the *genus tapeinotikon* in which the attributes of the human nature of Christ are communicated to the divine nature in contrast to the *genus maiestaticum.* Then Thomasius said that Jesus was not omnipotent, almighty, and omnipresent in the state of *exinanitionis*, which became manifest in the self-limitation of the divinity in Jesus Christ.

However, Thomasius' concept of self-emptying as abandonment by the eternal Logos of his divine glory failed to achieve the concept of Jesus' full divinity, although it affirmed the real humanity of the historical Jesus.[56] Lutheran Christology is said to run in a theopaschite direction in which the second member of the Trinity suffered and died. "According to His nature God cannot die, but since God and man are united in one person, it is correct to talk about God's death when that man dies who is one reality or one person with God."[57]

Given this fact, Luther's *theologia crucis* would be more in line with Alexandrian Christology. It radicalizes the uttermost depths of suffering in the crucified God, and so divine passibility plays a key part in taking seriously the crucified God. What *theologia crucis* brings to the fore is a revolutionary concept of God, far from the scholastic concept of God or from Reformed theology. The hidden God is to be known only in the crucified God in terms of *communicatio idiomatum in concreto.* Suffering, seen from a christological point of view, is not only at the heart of Luther's understanding of the triune God, but is also rooted in Luther's understanding of a cosmic dimension of Jesus Christ that has been downplayed in the historical development of Lutheran theology. After describing Luther's influence on Moltmann and liberation theology in Latin America and Asia, I will come to a cosmic Christ in Luther's thought and then examine *theologia crucis* in interreligious light.

55. Thomasius, *Christi Person und Werk.* II (1855), 216; Poehlmann, *Abriss der Dogmatik*, 229.

56. Pannenberg, *Jesus—God and Man*, 310–11.

57. "Formula of Concord," SD VIII & 40–45, *BC*, 599.

Martin Luther and the *Theologia Crucis* in an Ecumenical Context

Luther's impulse for deepening divine suffering in terms of the theology of the cross has been rediscovered and discussed in an ecumenical context. In the European context, Jürgen Moltmann, above all, brings the significance of the theology of the cross to light, while in Latin America the theology of the cross was actualized and deepened in the struggle with liberation and freedom for the poor and marginalized in the secular realm. In like manner, the issue of suffering is manifested for Asian theologians because of overwhelming poverty and religious pluralism. The crucified God is discussed in light of the crucified people. In what follows we will describe the theology of the cross in an ecumenical context, Asian in particular.

Martin Luther and Jürgen Moltmann

Moltmann comes from the theology of Karl Barth and his followers (Otto Weber, Ernst Wolf, Hans Joachim Iwand), and is influenced by biblical scholars such as Gerhard von Rad and Ernst Käsemann. Bonhoeffer especially was an important figure for encouraging Moltmann, beyond the pale of the Christocentrism of Karl Barth, to struggle with theological issues from a secular perspective. Philosophically, Moltmann was deeply motivated and remained indebted to the Jewish-Marxist philosopher, Ernst Bloch, whose philosophy of hope was echoed and rediscovered eschatologically in Moltmann's theology of hope. Subsequently, he was engaged in Christian-Marxist dialogue, elaborating major social, critical concepts from the Frankfurt School, most members of which are of Jewish origin and background. The Jewish-Christian dialogue plays a significant role in shaping his on-going ecumenical theology in encounter with other religions. Moltmann's work is very much open to Roman Catholic theology, Orthodox theology (especially with respect to his social trinitarian theology), and the liberation theologies of the Third World concerning social prophetic *diakonia* and activism. His theology is characterized by its faithfulness to biblical thought and its relevance to social and political questions and dialogue with other religions.

One of the characteristics that Moltmann gives prominence to in his theology is the question of God's righteousness in view of the suffering and evil of the world. From the beginning, human suffering is the most profound basis for Moltmann's entire theological system. In our daily lives we face the question of theodicy, because it arises out of the "hells of world wars, the hells of Auschwitz, Hiroshima, and Vietnam, and also the everyday experiences which make one man say to another 'You make my life hell.'"[58]

In his *Theology of Hope*, Moltmann challenged an attempt to justify innocent suffering for the sake of contributing to the divine purpose. The resurrection of Jesus should not be used to justify this suffering, but explicitly gives hope and promise for God's final triumph over all evil and suffering. It is the God of the Bible who takes the initiative in encouraging Christian praxis to resist suffering here and now. Therefore, Christian theology is most meaningful when it is in solidarity with present suffering. Bloch's great work, *The Principle of Hope*, served as inspiration for Moltmann in making Christianity the good news of radical hope. The former as a Marxist philosopher tried to concretize the biblical eschatology as a symbol of hope in secular form in which socialism and humanism are directed into the future in accordance with the principle "transcending without transcendence," while the latter focuses on Christian hope in light of divine transcendence.[59]

The resurrection of the dead that is at the heart of Christian eschatology can challenge Bloch's immanent principle of hope. Christianity as radical hope of new life for the dead begins with the promise of the resurrection, the raising of the crucified Jesus by God. The crucified Jesus in his death is regarded as the one who is wretched of the earth, so his resurrection is ready for and open to those who are forgotten, victimized, and wretched of the earth, too. The radical character of the Christian promise of resurrection strengthens Christians to engage in the process of social and political transformation. What makes Christianity eschatological, and what shapes and characterizes the meaning of Christian hope, lies in the resurrection of the crucified Jesus Christ from death. Therefore, resurrection is only adequately understood when seen in context of eschatology coupled with the future of the risen Christ. Moltmann is emphatic: "Christianity stands or falls with the reality of the raising of Jesus from the dead by God."[60]

This aspect shows that God's promise is culminated in the event of resurrection of Jesus in anticipation of the future resurrection of all the

58. Moltmann, *Crucified God*, 220.

59. Bloch, *Principle of Hope*, 210.

60. Ibid., 165.

dead. His resurrection is the center of God's promise of an eschatological new creation of those whom the crucified Jesus as Godforsaken represented. Moltmann's approach to innocent suffering in light of the hope for God's coming future and righteousness is more and more deepened and concretized in relation to God's loving suffering in solidarity with the world in his book, *The Crucified God.* In some ways, Moltmann's Christology is traditional. For example, he uses the Chalcedonian categories of the humanity and deity of Jesus to organize some of his discussion,[61] and he follows the reformers' threefold office of Christ as a regulative principle.[62] In addition, he is heavily indebted to St. Paul and Martin Luther for his general orientation, focusing on the death and resurrection of Christ. He frequently points to Luther's *theologia crucis* with emphasis, as central to authentic Christianity. "Theologia crucis is not a single chapter in theology, but the key signature for all Christian theology . . . It is the point from which all theological statements which seek to be Christian are viewed (W. von Loewenich)."[63]

Moltmanm is critical of some traditional understandings of Christ, because the doctrine of the two natures has been influenced unduly by the Greek philosophical tradition with its excessive emphasis on the immutability and impassibility of God.[64] Moltmann is, in this regard, critical of Cyril of Alexandria who failed to perceive the suffering of Christ in a genuine sense. The error of the Platonic axiom of the essential *apatheia* of God, which Moltmann thinks the patristic theologians of the two natures were caught in, has been a stumbling block that prevented Christian theology from taking seriously divine suffering. At this point Moltmann's affinity with Luther becomes manifest because Luther is the thinker who consistently brings up divine suffering and overcomes the intellectual barrier of hindering God in the death of Christ in light of *communicatio idiomatum* in contrast to Zwingli's *alloesis.*

In fact, the doctrine of two natures cannot articulate and concretize death in God. "Luther's Christology of the crucified God . . . represents an important further development of the doctrine of the communicatio idiomatum and radicalizes the doctrine of the incarnation on the cross."[65]

61. Moltmann, *Crucified God,* 87–98.

62. Cf. Moltmann, *Church in Power of the Spirit,* 75–108.

63. Moltmann, *Crucified God,* 72.

64. Ibid., 227–9.

65. Ibid., 235.

Be that as it may, Luther came too short in understanding the theology of the cross in trinitarian terms. Therefore, Moltmann's task is located in developing a christological doctrine of the Trinity.

Moltmann is most impressed with Jesus' cry of dereliction in Mark 15:34. "Jesus died crying out to God, 'My God, why hast thou forsaken me?' All Christian theology and all Christian life is basically an answer to the question which Jesus asked as he died."[66] In *The Crucified God*, Moltmann explores the God forsakenness of Jesus in the context of a three-fold account of the crucifixion: (1) in relation to Jewish law, Jesus died as a blasphemer; (2) in relation to Roman authority, he died as a rebel; and (3) in relation to God, he died an agonizing death marked by a deep sense of having been abandoned by God.[67] Although Moltmann considers the quotation of Ps 22:1 in Mark 15:34 to be a post-Easter interpretation by the church, it is "as near as possible to the historical reality of the death of Jesus."[68] The death of Jesus abandoned by God the Father is at the core of divine suffering from a trinitarian perspective. Moltmann understands the sacrifice of the Son by the Father (Rom 8:32, Gal 2:20, John 3:16, Eph 5:25) as an indication of God's active involvement in the death of Jesus. In the passion of the Son, the Father himself suffers the pains of abandonment and the death of his "fatherhood." The Father suffers the death of his Son in his love for the forsaken man.

In *The Church in the Power of the Spirit*, Moltmann again introduces the God forsakenness of Christ. "Christ's surrender of himself to a Godforsaken death reveals the secret of the cross and with it the secret of God himself. It is the open secret of the Trinity."[69] "In the action of the Father in delivering up his Son to suffering and to a godless death, God is acting in himself."[70] However, Moltmann's reflection on *paradidonai* (deliver up, hand over, or abandon, i.e., John. 3:16; Rom 8:31f), which leads to the accursed death of the Son at the hands of the Father, should be balanced by Jesus' willing way to the cross out of love for humankind (Cf. Gal 2:20).

As Moltmann's thought has increasingly focused on the crucifixion of Christ and the question of theodicy, he has begun more frequently to

66. Ibid., 4.

67. Ibid., 126–53.

68. Ibid., 146–7.

69. Moltmann, *Church in the Power of the Spirit*, 95.

70. Moltmann, *Crucified God*, 192.

affirm the passion of God and divine suffering. For this reason, Moltmann is criticized as "boldly theopaschite," although he prefers a death in God to the death of God. Most mainstream Christian theologians, at least until the nineteenth century, readily affirmed the impassibility of God. (See, for example, the Westminster Confession of Faith).

Moltmann's theodicy involves the double claim that the passion of God avoids the problem of atheism or theism and also provides a solid foundation for a Christian theodicy. Human suffering is alleviated by the recognition that God suffers with us in the present and that eschatologically our suffering will be transformed into a final joy. What Moltmann is confronted with is traditional theism and protest atheism.[71] A major cause of the development of the theistic view of God was the "axiom of *apatheia*" prominent in Greek philosophy. The religious motive behind the affirmation of the *apatheia* of God was a concern to guarantee the self-sufficiency and perfection of God. The adoption of this principle had disastrous consequences for Christian theology, for it is incompatible with the biblical notion of God's love, wrath, and empathy for the human situation.

Based on divine *apatheia*, there was no honest recognition of the suffering of the cross as divine. The two natures Christology of Nicea and Chalcedon was an unsuccessful attempt, because it affirmed the suffering of Christ only according to the flesh and only in his human nature. Luther's doctrine of *communicatio idiomatum* appeals to Moltmann especially in this regard, because it tries to break through the rigidity of the two-nature Christology dominant in medieval thought. But Moltmann's concern is of a trinitarian character unlike Luther's: "The theological concept for the perception of the crucified Christ is the doctrine of the Trinity. The material principle of the doctrine of the Trinity is the cross of Christ. The formal principle of knowledge of the cross is the doctrine of the Trinity."[72]

In addition, according to Moltmann, atheism notes only the pain and misery of the world and concludes that there is no God. Moltmann recognizes that much modern atheism takes human suffering as the basis for denial of God. Following Ernst Bloch, Moltmann describes the modern version of atheism as "atheism for God's sake" because of its concern for the justice of God.

Despite his sympathetic analysis of protest atheism, Moltmann is critical of it in that protest atheism has gone too far in substituting hu-

71. Cf. Willis, *Theism, Atheism and the Doctrine of the Trinity.*

72. Moltmann, *Crucified God*, 240.

man beings for God as the supreme being. In fact, atheism has misfired because it takes the theistic view of God to be the genuine Christian view. Moltmann proposes his understanding of the passion of God as a way the Christian faith can move beyond the impasse between classical theism and protest atheism. The passion of God is grounded in the passion of Christ and will be fulfilled eschatologically. The companionship of the suffering God encourages and supports the suffering person in the present, and then the consummation of history will produce the final joy. "The history of God's suffering in the passion of the Son and the sighing of the Spirit serves the history of God's joy in the Spirit and his completed felicity at the end."[73]

When Moltmann develops his view of the passion of God, he always places it within the context of the doctrine of the Trinity. He agrees with Karl Rahner's judgment that the distinction between the economic Trinity and the immanent Trinity is artificial and unnecessary.[74] Moltmann sees the Trinity rooted in the passion of Christ. Moltmann, like Barth, secures the ontological ground of God's revelation in Jesus. "As God appears in history as the sending Father and the sent Son, so he must earlier have been in himself . . . The *missio ad intra* is the foundation for the *missio ad extra* . . . From the Trinity of the sending of Jesus we can reason back to the Trinity in origin, in God himself, so that—conversely—we may understand the history of Jesus as the revelation of the living nature of God."[75]

The Johannine emphasis that God is essentially love is crucial for Moltmann's view. He clearly identifies the ability to suffer with the ability to love. A God who is unable to suffer is a loveless God, much like Aristotle's unmoved mover.[76] Moltmann is fond of Bonhoeffer's stress on the suffering of God as the only way God can be experienced in our time. "Only the suffering God can help." "This history of God contains within itself the whole abyss of god-forsakenness . . . All human history . . . is taken up into this history of God, i.e., into the Trinity, and integrated into the future of the history of God. There is no suffering within this history of God which is not God's suffering; no death which has not been God's death in the history on Golgotha."[77]

73. Moltmann, *Church in the Power of the Holy Spirit*, 64.

74. Moltmann, *Crucified God*, 239–40.

75. Moltmann, *Church in the Power of the Holy Spirit*, 54.

76. Ibid., 222.

77. Moltmann, *Crucified God*, 246.

In *The Crucified God*, Moltmann concluded his discussion of his Christology by stressing a political hermeneutics of liberation that will produce a political theology of the cross. This political theology will break the vicious circles of poverty, racial and cultural alienation, and the industrial pollution of nature. Moltmann is especially concerned that Christians engage in a political hermeneutic of the gospel that would activate Christians to struggle against oppression and injustice. Moltmann's "crucified God" may be one of the most provocative and insightful understandings of God in the tradition of Luther's theology of cross, extending Luther for our time.

The Language of the Theology of the Cross from the Underside of History

Liberation theology has a contribution in making explicitly a new methodology for understanding Christian faith and God. It provides a new way for doing theology rather than offering a new theme for theological reflection.[78] What is at the center of liberation theology, at risk of oversimplication, is to take seriously the articulation of faith as a praxis of solidarity with the poor, exploited and marginalized as "members of the proletarian class" in the society.[79]

In the process of liberation, the world is transformed through liberating love, building up a new, righteous society as a gift of the kingdom of God. This can be seen in liberating humankind from what alienates and dehumanizes it. Therefore, theology is conceptualized as "critical reflection on historical praxis" in light of the kingdom of God. It is supposed to be rooted in the context of the suffering of the poor and engaged in the critical reflection on praxis in the midst of the suffering innocent. Liberation theology has no intention of glorifying the poor themselves, but actualizes God's compassion for the poor. "God does not love the poor because they are good, but because they are poor."[80]

A different theological consciousness emerges in an encounter with historical and sociological developments in Latin America (the so-called dependence theory). This encounter on the part of theologians expresses social scientific research and analysis in theological terms. This encounter

78. Gutiérrez, *Theology of Liberation*, 15.

79. Gutiérrez, "Liberating Praxis and Christian Faith," 8.

80. Brown, *Gustavo Gutiérrez*, 83.

offers a new type of theological reflection that can emerge by becoming integral with concrete social and political praxis for transformation.[81]

If theology is to be a critical reflection, the centrality of praxis is affirmed as the first step. Next, theology follows as a critical attitude. Therefore, as a first step, the ecclesial community holds a significant locus in reflecting theologically in respect to social and political problems because "a privileged locus for understanding faith will be the life, preaching, and historical commitment of the church."[82] The centrality of praxis stands in polar tension with a theological reflection developed in isolation from the particular social context in which it is embedded. The centrality of praxis calls for integrating social and political analysis and political and ideological implications of historical praxis critically into theological reflection. In this way, a new critical recovery and retrieval of the Bible and Christian tradition tells us to reread and mobilize and rediscover "the liberating trust of the gospel" and its praxis of liberation in Christian tradition.[83]

The question about Jesus Christ is the touchstone by which any Christian theology should be tested for its authenticity. From the perspective of suffering innocents, God becomes poor in Jesus Christ by pitching a tent in the midst of human history. Jesus Christ, in whom God becomes the poor, means a touchstone encouraging liberation theology to stand in the preferential option for the poor.[84] "He was poor indeed . . . born into a social milieu characterized by poverty. He chose to live with the poor. He addressed his gospel by preference to the poor."[85] Therefore, Jesus the liberator becomes manifest in his liberative message of bringing good news to the poor, in proclaiming liberty to captives, in giving new sight to the blind, in setting the downtrodden free, and in proclaiming the year of the Lord's favor (Luke 4:16–18).

Given this fact, Christology does not remain mere doctrinal formulation, but becomes a new way of articulating the *theologia crucis* and proclaiming God's love to the poor in the struggle for liberation. A Christology from below means a *theologia crucis* in the midst of poor and suffering innocents with whom God is in deep solidarity. Therefore, Christian faith is

81. Bonino, *Doing Theology*, xxvii. Cf. Eagleson, *Christians and Socialism*.

82. Gutiérrez, *Theology of Liberation*, 11–12.

83. Rodriguez, "Theology from the Underside of History," 116.

84. Gutiérrez, *Power of the Poor in History*, 14.

85. Ibid., 13.

born of the life of the poor and reflected theologically from the underside of the poor. This thrust in liberation theology demands a new reading of the salvific message of the Bible.

What is more interesting is a re-appropriation of Karl Barth and Dietrich Bonhoeffer to reread history from the side of the poor. Gutiérrez, in exploring Christian traditions of liberation in the West as well as in Latin American, African, Asian, and feminist contexts, pays special attention to two great western thinkers. A beautiful text of Bonhoeffer that is praised by Gutiérrez is at the heart of his *theologia crucis* expressing solidarity with unjust suffering. "We have learned to see the great events of the history of the world from beneath—from the viewpoint of the useless, the suspect, the abused, the powerless, the oppressed, and the despised. In a word, from the viewpoint of the suffering."[86]

Furthermore, for Gutiérrez, Barth's attraction lies in his keen sensitivity to the situation of exploitation and profound radical understanding of the God who takes sides with the poor. In other words, Barth's socialist praxis during his early pastoral period in Safenwil leads him to have "sensitivity to the new forms of spoliation and exploitation created by a capitalist society." This plays as the driving force in understanding God "as the One taking sides with the poor against the powerful." His theology can be understood as a protest theology challenging "the deterioration of God's word into a "bourgeois gospel." This is also an integral part of Barth's *theologia crucis*, which refers to God's revolution in Jesus Christ.[87] As Barth emphatically says, "God always takes his stand unconditionally and passionately on this side and on this side alone: against the lofty and on behalf of the lowly; against those who already enjoy right and privilege and on behalf of those who are denied it and deprived of it."[88]

In Latin America, the historical Jesus has had an extremely significant role in the face of poverty and injustice. A Christian symbol in Latin America is the crucifix—an image of Jesus nailed to the Cross bleeding and dying. It is found everywhere. Two images of Jesus become manifest. The one is a dead Jesus, depicted as having suffered for the people, exhausted, defeated and powerless. The other is a "celestial monarch" in which Jesus

86. Cf. Gutiérrez, *Power of the Poor in History*, 203.

87. Ibid., 203, 232.

88. *CD*, II/1:386, see Gutiérrez, *Power of the Poor in History*, 160. For the political theology in Barth in relation to the liberation theology, see Marquardt, *Theologie und Sozialismus*; Hunsinger, "Karl Barth and Liberation Theology," 42–59.

as the king reigned in heaven over the cosmos. This cosmic power has been misused as an instrument for sanctioning and legitimating the colonial rule and social political system of the ruling class, being aloof from the image of Christ's sovereignty as a sovereignty limiting and judging all powers in light of the lowly against the mighty (Luke 1:52).

Unfortunately, the two images of a dead Jesus and a powerful Jesus are politically abused to maintain the system of domination and oppression. The dead Jesus is taken to preach resignation and acceptance in the face of oppression and injustice, where the powerful Jesus is supposed to stand only for vindicating the privilege of the powerful in the name of Christ the effectively cosmic monarch. Meanwhile, a political message coupled with the crucifixion of Jesus is efficiently suppressed. To reinstate the suppressed message, it is necessary to see it from the perspective of the poor in the historical experience of liberation, which means a transition through death toward a new, liberative life. The political message from the cross inspires liberation theologians and their sympathizers to represent the praxis of solidarity against injustice and violence rather than remaining in acquiescence, passivity, and detachment.[89]

Understood in this way, theology of the cross in the context of liberation leads to a break with the dominant progressive European theology. At risk of oversimplification, the dominant theology in Western culture, no matter how liberal, progressive, or liberative, has a point of departure from above, from the position of the privileged. It thus remains thought-oriented in affirmation of individualism, rationalism, and capitalism. In contrast, the liberation theology is involved in the liberation process as primary. Theology comes afterwards, as a second act. A new theological focus and language has its roots in the social life of the lowly people in Latin America whose voices and outcries have been long silent and suppressed, but now begin to erupt. This epistemological break characteristic of liberation theology set in motion the poor and the oppressed as the historical subject of liberation. Therefore, "the locus of liberation theology is . . . among the poor, among the native masses, among the popular classes, as agents and creators of their own history."[90]

From this perspective, a critique can be formulated in regard to political theology in a European context. Following in the footsteps of Ernst Bloch more faithfully than political theologians in Western society (for

89. Altmann, *Luther and Liberation*, 15.

90. Gutiérrez, *Power of the Poor in History*, 194.

instance, Metz and Moltmann), liberation theologians especially sought to start the theology of hope from the theology of resurrection as the future of humanity and the world. Therefore, the event of the promise is the beginning of the critique of what exists. When starting the move from a transcendental future to the historical, liberative dimension of incarnation, Moltmann articulates a language of human self-liberation. If theology anticipates what is ahead, liberation theologians argue, it is incompetent to actualize and concretize the reality of the present in light of the hope. From a perspective of liberation theology, Moltmann's theology of hope is limited to the development of socio-critical ethic in engagement with the sin and injustice of institutionalized structures.

According to liberation theology, the death and resurrection of Jesus Christ as hope are present concretely in the form of anticipation. If the hope of overcoming death is not located in historical praxis it would be in danger of remaining a futuristic illusion. At this point, critiques like a smuggled docetism (Alves) or "non-partisan languages" (Bonino) come out in which one may discern a temptation to detachment in isolation from reality. This is a critique by liberation theology aimed at European progressivist theology. "Words, for instance, which Moltmann and Metz use for clues, have their own meanings in terms of the ideological conflicts of the present. Unless they be specified in relation to a concrete world of reference (the imperialist question, the class struggle, capitalism, and so forth . . .), they will specify themselves through the cultural and political context in which they function."[91]In this regard, Gutiérrez criticized Soelle's political theology as the heir of the Enlightenment stemming "from the political consciousness of the modern spirit" rather than "from the world of the oppressed."[92]

In the context of liberation theology, Luther's *theologia crucis*, seen in the perspective of Jesus' active identification with the poor, can have meaning beyond the individual dimension of forgiveness and acceptance. In fact, the theology of the cross, in Luther's view, has to do with his kenosis (Phil 2:5–11). Luther's exposition of the *Magnificat* becomes the basis for concretizing Jesus for the poor in the context of liberation theology.

91. Bonino, *Doing Theology*, 80. For a critical response to Moltmann's theology of the hope and his concept of eschatology on the side of liberation theologians, cf. Alves, *Theology of Human Hope*, 55–68; Bonino, *Doing Theology*, 139–52; Gutiérrez, *Theology of Liberation*, 216–8.

92. Gutiérrez, *Power of the Poor in History*, 219.

In addition, Jesus' descent into the depths of hell may be taken as victory over tyrannical powers and dominion by experiencing "the death of the death."

With Christ, the world should not be the way it is, but be renewed and transformed. In this regard, Altmann takes Luther's interpretation of the second article of the Apostles' Creed to be a corrective to ethical passivity or political quietism prevailing in the Lutheran tradition. "Christ is our abstraction, and we are His concretion."[93] The model of the happy exchange entails spiritual, ethical, and practical consequences. Not an imitation of Christ, but a conformation to Christ is an expression of practical discipleship in humble service of the poor in the world. It is noteworthy that Luther's Christology is not understandable apart from the historical life of Jesus in strong affirmation of divine suffering in Jesus' humanity.

In like manner, theology of the cross in light of liberation theology would be meaningless in isolation from the liberating activity, life, and death of the historical Jesus. As Sobrino says, "rather than viewing the cross as some arbitrary design on God's part, we see it as the outcome of God's primordial option: the incarnation. The cross is the outcome of an incarnation situated in a world of sin that is revealed to be a power working against the God of Jesus."[94]

Be that as it may, a critique of Luther's theology of the cross says that Luther does not support the value of the historical Jesus for the practice of liberation due to his spiritualizing tendency in criticism of historical faith. Jesus' life in solidarity with the poor should not simply be spiritualized toward a mystic "platonic Christ."[95] Luther's failure to reach out to the social and political needs of the poor during the peasant war becomes questionable, and a legitimate target of criticism. However, Luther's sense of Christology through the cross and kenosis of Jesus can provide a combative and dynamic basis for engaging in the struggle for liberation. Especially the insight of conformation with the cross of Christ, in a soteriological perspective, is well recognized by liberating partners in Latin America.

In due respect to the rediscovery of Luther in the light of liberation theology, however, Luther's *theologia crucis* needs to be more engaged not only with the praxis of liberation in a social and political setting, but also with people of other faiths. The full meaning of liberation will be mani-

93. *LW*, 11:318; cf. Altmann, *Luther and Liberation*, 21.

94. Sobrino, *Christology at the Crossroads*, 201.

95. Altmann, *Luther and Liberation*, 23.

fested in Christ's work of restoration of all things. In addition, an understanding of Jesus as the Liberator in the framework of liberation theology is inclined to downplay Jesus as a Jew in solidarity with Jewish minjung *ochlos*. Therefore, Jesus appears as the Liberator beyond his historical, cultural, religious background in which Jesus remains the One who liberated, even removing the poor from the Jewish religion. In fact, from this perspective Jesus means the removal of Jewish religion. This aspect of the *theologia crucis* is not the task of liberation theology, but of Asian minjung theology. Asian minjung theology makes an attempt to rejudaize Jesus as a Jewish born of *ochlos* by actualizing the *theologia crucis* in an encounter with poverty and indigenous religious spiritualities.

Doing Theology and Suffering in an Asian Context

Doing theology on Asian soil cannot be made, but must be born. Asian theology springs from an experience of faith in the midst of surrounding religious world views and in response to their challenges. Asian reality may find Western theology unsatisfactory for a new emerging Asian consciousness and challenge. The task of indigenization of Christianity may not be regarded as "a shallow syncretism" in the negative sense, but "fusion of horizons" in a hermeneutical sense. In Asian context, the theology of the cross is challenged and reformulated in an encounter with socio-political injustice on the one hand and deep spirituality of religious pluralism on the other hand. These are the religious-cultural realities in Asia.

The Christian church cannot afford to avoid the riches of all the great world religions. They offer anthropological-cosmological ways of salvation in their own manner. An indigenous theology finds its roots in the Asian cultural heritage. The Asian religions, Buddhism in particular, which I chose as a counterpart to Christianity, have a tradition of both scholarship and mysticism, and also a path to liberation. In Buddhism there is an emphasis on personal purification and inner liberation. It emphasizes self-realization through meditation and right action in a cycle of birth, death, and rebirth in several lives.

In addition, Pure Land Buddhism in Japan strictly separates itself from the Zen Buddhist tradition with the former's emphasis on the universal grace of *Amida*. There are many eminent figures leading movements for social transformation nourished by Buddhist roots. For example, Thich Nhat Hanh, a Buddhist monk from Vietnam, was very much involved in the peace movement during the war and had to go into exile. He is a Zen Master, scholar, poet, and the author of numerous books. The mindfulness that is the basis of Thich Nhat Hanh's teaching is not flight from the world into the individualistic practice of meditation, but an effort to live consciously in the present. Rather than avoiding society and world, the correct practice of mindfulness, argues Thich Nhat Hanh, can help us bring peace, joy, and release both for ourselves and for society. "If you have compassion, you cannot be rich. You can be rich only when you can bear the sight of suffering. If you cannot bear that, you have to give your possessions away."[96]

The meaning of doing theology in an Asian context may be expressed well in Panikkar's assertion: he left "Europe as a Christian," "found" himself a Hindu, and "returned" as a Buddhist without ever having ceased to be a Christian.[97] This assertion can refer to a hermeneutic trajectory of Asian contextual theology in company with the misery, poverty, and profound spirituality of world religions, which distinguishes Asian theological currents from other European, North American, or Hispanic Latin American cultures. The mutational character of Asian incultural theology in an encounter with the gospel serves as a driving force for concretizing and raising a new form of consciousness in doing theology in Asia. Let me turn to how Asian theological movements understand and actualize the issue of suffering in the spiritual, social, and political realms through their understanding of the theology of the cross. I confine my attention to some theologians in light of the *theologia crucis*, although there are many other important Asian figures.

Kitamori, a Japanese Lutheran pastor and theologian, rose to international prominence primarily due to his book *The Theology of the Pain of God.* Kitamori insists that the pain of God is a fundamental biblical theme and is the heart of the gospel. God is in pain because of the conflict within Godself regarding God's love and wrath. The pain of God is the place where God's wrath and love are united. The wrath of God against sinners and the love of God for sinners cause God's pain. God suffers pain only when God tries to love us. According to Kitamori, love rooted in the pain of God is crucial to the entire Bible. Human pain and divine pain are qualitatively different, but they share a common ground. In this regard,

96. Berrigan, *The Raft Is Not the Shore*, 102; Cf. Amaladoss, *Life in Freedom*, 82.

97. Panikkar, *The Intra-religious Dialogue*, 2.

Kitamori proposes an "analogy of pain" (*analogia doloris*) as the proper way to speak of God. Kitamori further explicates his understanding of God's pain by delineating three orders of divine love; love of God, pain of God, and love rooted in the pain of God. The first order is God's immediate love of those who are worthy. This kind of love is directed toward Christ and humankind before it is affected by sin. The second order is that God feels pain when God responds to human sin. The third order is love rooted in the pain of God. He proposes to include the movement from the historical Jesus to the pain of God and the movement from the pain of God to the historical Jesus.[98]

Kitamori consistently criticizes Western Christianity's over-dependence on Greek metaphysics. He argues that the significance of divine passibility in the biblical sense has disappeared due to the excessive influence of Greek metaphysics on the early history of Christianity. However, pain is in fact experienced by both Father and Son because of their essential unity. Kitamori also criticizes early Christian theology both for its preoccupation with the Incarnation and *homoousios* and for its neglect of the cross. The Western theologian who has influenced Kitamori most heavily is Martin Luther. To a great extent Kitamori's theology is a revival of Luther's theology of the cross in the post-war Japanese situation. In terms of Luther's christological formulation, *communicatio idiomatum,* Kitamori has managed to actualize that the human attribute of suffering is applied to the divinity of God.

He compared the Buddhist view of compassion to the Christian message, but the former falls short of the pain of God in the gospel. Kitamori is convinced that Japanese culture can have a pivotal role in the presentation of the gospel, especially concerning the pain of God. He has struggled with the feasibility and appropriateness of producing a Japanese theology. The Japanese should articulate their faith from their own culture. Kitamori's contribution to the theology of the cross lies in his attempt to develop a "Japanese" theology in his critique of divine impassibility. Along with a strong reliance on Luther's theology, Kitamori's theology is a specifically Japanese view of God.[99]

Minjung theology in South Korea originated among Protestants. Most minjung theologians belonged to liberal Presbyterian schools. What is important in the movement of minjung theology is to reflect on an en-

98. Cf. Kitamori, *Theology of the Pain of God*, 20.

99. Ibid.

gagement in the social and political struggle for the poor. *Min* means people and *jung* means mass. In general, it refers to people who are oppressed economically, alienated politically, uprooted culturally, and impoverished religiously or in other ways. The point of departure is the experience of suffering and liberation in solidarity or identification with the poor, but also in affirmation of the soteriological function of the Christ present in minjung life. Minjung life in Asia can not only be grasped just in social or economic terms, but also in spiritual, cultural, and religious terms as well. The minjung experience of suffering is first of all characterized by *han*, which denotes a feeling of resentment, depression, repressed anger, hopelessness, just indignation, etc.

Minjung theology finds it very important that there is also an interreligious liberative tradition. In the early history of Korea the Future Buddha *Maitreya* was seen as a messianic liberative figure. According to Buddhist cosmology, a Buddha appears in the world to come. Among these, Buddhas Siddhartha or *Amida* are the Buddhas of the present world. If we pray to Buddha *Amida* through the recitation of his name, we will enter his western paradise (Pure Land) after death. But if we pray to Buddha *Maitreya*, who is the Buddha of the coming world, he will help us realize and fulfill the new world on earth.

This is a Buddhist eschatology coupled with a strong apocalyptic transformation that has old roots in the heart of the minjung, especially in Korea. While the rulers promoted *Amida* Buddhism to distract them from social and political issues, the minjung believed in the *Maitreya*. This belief gave rise to many messianic and revolutionary movements. In so doing, it contributed to the revolutionary practice and hope of the minjung in anticipation of a better future. In light of the advent of *Maitreya* it is significant that while *Amida* Buddhism supplanted *Maitreya* Buddhism in China and Japan, the latter survived among the heart of the minjung in Korea. Here, the telos of everything and everyone is united and fulfilled not merely in a dynamic dialectic between transcendence and immanence of *Nirvana*, beyond the cycle of life and death, as Japanese Zen Buddhism would imagine, but in the coming kingdom of *Maitreya* with a strong ethical, messianic, and even revolutionary spirit. The spirituality of *Maitreya* Buddhism is an integral part of actualizing the concern about interreligious dialogue between Christianity and Buddhism for mutual transformation and recognition.[100]

100. Nam-Dong, "Historical Reference," 176–77.

Ahn Byung-Mu, a great New Testament scholar who is regarded as one of the founding fathers of minjung theology, laid the biblical foundations of minjung theology in his study of Mark's gospel. He points to a special category of people called the *ochlos*. The *ochlos* were not just people (that would have been *laos*), but the unorganized crowd that was constantly around Jesus. They were differentiated from the disciples and the ruling classes. They were the despised tax collectors and those considered sinners, either because they were engaged in occupations that were not approved of in civil life, or because they were sick in various ways, and sickness was considered a consequence of sin. Jesus accepted them without any reservation. He ate with them and healed them of their infirmities. Jesus proclaimed to them the coming liberation of God's rule, thus giving them a new hope for life.

Because of his option for minjung and his purification of the Temple, Jesus was eliminated and put to death. But through the resurrection Jesus gave them assurance of new life. In the Old Testament, the exodus is an obvious paradigm for a process of liberation, but minjung appears in various forms. The minjung is also the oppressed people in Egypt whose liberation by God is narrated in the story of the exodus. They are also the oppressed people to whom some of the prophets brought God's promise of liberation. Moses answered the cry of the people, but Jesus was the very cry of the people themselves. In this sense, Jesus is truly a part of the minjung, not just an individual for the minjung. Therefore, Jesus was the personification and embodiment of the minjung and their symbols.

Starting with the life and action of Jesus as a symbol and type of God's saving action in the world and history, minjung theology rereads the history of God's people to discern in it the ongoing action of God "in, with, and through" them. What is theologically unique is the emphasis on the concept of minjung as God's people in the midst of suffering and God's solidarity in companionship with them. Given this fact, Jesus is not an individual hero for the minjung but as one of them in sharing the same fate and destiny with them, which is a true meaning of Christ's kenosis and suffering. This is the aesthetic of suffering and solidarity that minjung theology emphasizes concerning the relationship between God and the minjung. In this regard, Bonhoeffer's theological aesthetics of suffering becomes attractive for minjung theology.

In addition, Ahn's keen interest lies in relating the Last Judgment (Matt 25) to the Jewish people without the historical Jesus. Even though he comes from the school of Bultmann, he is not concerned about an existential encapsulation of Jesus, but rather sees Jesus in light of the history of a suffering Israel. Unfortunately he was not capable of developing his idea of minjung theology to show that the Jewish "no" to Jesus was based on their faithfulness to *Torah*. According to Ahn, the gospel of Mark, after the destruction of Jerusalem in 70 CE, describes "the homeless, driven-out, scattered people of his time who had been deprived of their rights, Jews and Christians."[101] The crucified Christ and the accompanying divine *Shekinah* are present in the *ochlos*. Minjung in this regard is, first of all, the Jews after the destruction of Jerusalem in the year 70 and then Christians and Gentiles, too. There is no point of "expropriation of what is Israel's."[102]

Like Ahn Byung-Mu, Su Nam-Dong (1918–1984), who is respected as the one of the founding fathers of minjung theology, delivered his paper at a meeting of the North-East Asian Theological Association in Tokyo. It shows his future orientation toward minjung theology in company with Bonhoeffer. "If the present church does not recognize the coming Christ in the face of a suffering brother, then it repeats the religious failure of the Hebrew people. They did not recognize the Messiah in the face of Jesus from Nazareth because of their nationalistic Messiah faith and the cosmic eschatology stained with apocalypticism. Christian religion may follow the same tragic footsteps because of traditional Christology."[103]

For him, the scriptural text of Matt 25:31–46 is the point of departure for developing his idea of the suffering minjung in relation to the suffering Christ. In parallel to Liberation theology, he saw the disfigured face of Christ in the real experience of the suffering minjung in the cruel military dictatorship in South Korea of the late 1960s. What is significant for him in minjung theology is four biblical paradigms of event: Exodus, Cross, Resurrection, and Parousia. In this event-oriented model, the Holy Spirit is the driving force in actualizing the historical event of Jesus Christ in the suffering reality of the minjung here and now in eschatological openness. His concern is to testify to, and deepen, the minjung traditions of Christianity in convergence with those of Korean cultural and religious history. He proposed calling his theological hermeneutics a "pneumato-

101. Moltmann, *Experiences in Theology*, 254.

102. Ibid., 261.

103. Cf. Kyoung-Jae, *Christianity and the Encounter of Asian Religions*, 133.

logical-synchronic interpretation" while calling Western theological trends in general a "christological–diachronic interpretation."[104]

In the form of the latter a theological reflection on the atonement carries excessive stress on individualistic overtones of *pro me* or *pro nobis*. However, in the former direction, the Jesus event is articulated with emphasis on its on-going occurrence in our daily lives. The practice of discipleship of the cross means engaging in the struggle for Christ's messianic passion on the side of the minjung as victims afflicted by injustice and violence in our society. As a matter of fact, theology of the cross "*pro me*" should not go into tension with the practical life of forming discipleship in allegiance to the Jesus event in our world. These two views are not contradictory, but in complementarity. There can be no theology of the cross without reference to the continuation of the Jesus event in our life, as conversely there can be no true discipleship of the cross as a Jesus event without the theology of the cross. However, minjung theology stands in preference for a pneumatological-synchronic interpretation with reference to the universality of grace in the cosmic Christ and eschatology. At this point, the theology of the cross is not a "once and for all" event, but continues to form its shape and be concretized in the midst of poverty, injustice, violence, and an encounter with other religious ways.

The interreligious traditions may serve as religious liberative models for inspiring minjung theology to participate in the minjung event in relation to the Jesus event in light of suffering, participation, and compassion. Therefore, divine suffering is not merely related to whether or not God can suffer according to God's nature in a philosophical sense, but is understood historically and socially as the converging point where human suffering is extended and posited in unity with Christ's suffering.

"The crucified God" provides a basis for minjung Christology to sharpen God's atonement aspect not only through God's solidarity with us, but also God's recognition of a universal suffering of all humanity and all creatures in creation through a pneumatological-synchronic perspective. In so doing, interreligious dialogue becomes an integral part of minjung theology for tracing and articulating the minjung traditions between Christianity and the Korean cultural and religious history that has been neglected and suppressed by people in power. This hermeneutical task that Suh Nam-Dong calls the "converging of two stories" is not satisfied

104. Suh Nam-Dong, "Converging of the Two Stories," 78–79; in Kim Kyoung-Jae, *Christianity and the Encounter of Asian Religions*, 134.

with the interpretation of the world, but moves toward transforming it in anticipation of the coming Christ in the universal cosmic sense. Minjung theology is still open to debate among minjung theologians.

In recent decades, it is noteworthy that there has been a paradigm shift from excessive emphasis on the socio-political dimension to an interreligious model from a hermeneutical perspective. It calls for a new emphasis on interreligious liberative models. How, and to what extent, can minjung theology articulate and elaborate minjung as the others outside the walls of Christianity in light of interreligious dialogue?

In a critical dialogue with minjung theology, I once proposed a model of minjung eco-spirituality, in an interreligious context. There is a lack of a relationship between the minjung cosmic Christ and ecological spirituality. It is said that a Korean has a Confucian head, a Buddhist heart, a Shamanistic gut, and a Christian body. In other words, Confucianism is a religion for the mind, Buddhist for the heart and compassion, Shamanism a religion of intuition and spiritual awareness, and Christianity a complex religion of integrating these three religious elements in terms of a belief in God. Regardless of the fact that Shamanism has been severely attacked by other religions due to its superstitious and otherworldly dependence on the cosmic activity of spirits, religions such as Buddhism, Confucianism, and Christianity have flourished on Shamanistic soil.

Although minjung theology discerns a Shamanistic element in the positive sense of relation to the *han* of minjung life, it generally retains a psychological function of relieving *han* through *dan* (release). However, Shamanism as "Archaic Techniques of Ecstasy" (Eliade) is the primordial spiritual matrix of the minjung's spirituality, albeit tainted by its negative element, enabling us to respect all creatures as our fellows in awareness of a divine presence in all creation. Minjung theology seems to be reminiscent of liberation theology in Latin America, especially in regard to the issues of social and political emancipation.

However, a model of social analysis based on a political-economic ideology is not sufficient for a society characterized by the complexity of cultural religious realities. Minjung theology, even though it is critical of, and provocative to, Western theology and its doctrinal formulation and system, tends to vindicate the Euro-American rational system of modernity as the normative principle in perceiving and analyzing the reality of indigenous peoples' life and spirituality. Concepts such as the struggle for progress in history were quintessential to both liberation theology and minjung theology. Since the collapse of the Marxist idea and its experiment, however, the western concepts of rationality and historical progress face skepticism due to having produced and validated industrial technology and neo-colonial international relations, finally amounting to the catastrophe of destroying creation as a whole and ecological devastation around the world.

Unlike the Western European concept of history (conceptualized generally as a linear temporal process on the basis of progress), minjung spirituality is rooted first in the awareness of the Spirit's universal presence in creation and only secondarily in history. A modern anthropocentric concept of history in the Enlightenment project of Western society has little room for a cosmic dimension of Christ because it cannot take into consideration the whole of creation as God's. However, minjung spirituality reflects a positive view of the cosmos as the presence of God's goodness. Special and natural revelation must be seen in dynamic co-relation, because of Christ in culture and culture in Christ. Minjung cosmic Christology is connected to its eco-spirituality in which a *theologia crucis* stands as the driving force in combining pneumatology and cosmic Christology with commitment to Christian faith, hope, love, and radical openness toward others.[105]

C. S. Song, a prolific Asian-American theologian, takes Jesus as the representative of the crucified people in the third world, especially in East Asia. Jesus as the crucified people is the starting point for understanding the theology of the cross. In his attempt to actualize and deepen Jesus' suffering on the cross in solidarity with the people's suffering, a people's hermeneutic plays a significant role. A famous Korean poet of resistance in the 1970s in South Korea, Kim Ji-Ha and his poem, "the Gold-crowned Jesus," help C. S. Song to approach the question of who was the real Jesus. Instead of the traditional concept of "the very God and the very Man" in the Niceno-Constantinopolitan creed, people's suffering becomes the pivotal clue to illuminating who the real Jesus was. In fact, people's hermeneutics replaces christological hermeneutics, which has been normative in shaping the identity of western Christianity from the ancient church up to the present.

To what extent and depth does he articulate a people's hermeneutics in the midst of suffering and make it relevant to the concept of God? For this task he tries to strike a contrast between the God of retribution and

105. For the cosmic Christ, see Moltmann, *Way of Jesus Christ*; and *Spirit of Life*.

the God of Jesus. In relating Job's argument to the God of retribution, C. S. Song argues, God in the biblical sense is in solidarity with those who suffer. His question is raised in a poignant way: Who is the God Jesus cried to on the cross in comparison with God as Abba of Jesus? How can Abba God forsake and destroy his beloved Son? Why does Jesus not address God as Abba on the cross, instead of calling "my God, why have you forsaken me?" At this point, Moltmann's approach based on a theological trial between God and God is untenable for C. S. Song.[106]

His wholesale attack on Western Christianity refers to the fact that not God as Abba, but a "vindictive Deity" or "a remote and hidden God" in an Augustinian-scholastic sense has been normative and excessively influential in understanding God. His understanding of God, in which God does not give up on human beings, no matter how sinful and sinister they are, expresses itself as corrective to the traditional and still influential understanding of Western theology concerning the relationship between the Father and the Son. That is to say, the Father removed the Son for the salvation of all human being. A Pauline soteriology of "deliver up" seems supportive of the brutal satisfaction concept in understanding the distance between the Father and the Son. However, in the story of the prodigal son, we meet without doubt "the waiting father's anguish, pain, and grief."[107] Who is the God of Jesus in striking contrast to the traditional concept of the God of retribution and abandonment? Should not this Abba-God participate in Jesus' suffering by running to Jesus, throwing his arms around him?[108] Should the meaning of the incarnation "the Word become flesh" be more appropriate than the Abba-God on the cross? This is the argument of C. S. Song in bringing forth his *theologia crucis* on the basis of people's hermeneutics.

In so doing, the scandal of the cross is not only a scandal to the Jews, but is also a scandal to God. Jesus' heartfelt prayer in Gethsemane refers in his obedience to the loving God as Abba, not to the stern Judge or God of impassibility. However, C. S. Song's Asian Christology has nothing to do with the trinitarian eschatological theology. It remains an incarnational theology on the basis of suffering, solidarity, and existential identification between Jesus and the people. Unlike Korean minjung theologians, for C.

106. Song, *Crucified People*, 63.

107. Ibid., 76.

108. Ibid., 77.

S. Song, *ochlos* is not seen in relation to the Jewish people. An existential identification between Jesus and the suffering people comes to the surface. Therefore, Christ functions as a mere symbol, not as the divine name, *logos ensarkos* (Logos existing only within the flesh).

According to C. S. Song there are many "Jesuses," not only of Jewish flesh, but of Indian, Japanese etc. His theology of a universal incarnation highlights his assertion that Jesus is the crucified people. Shusaku Endo, a Japanese Roman Catholic Christian, plays a normative role for C. S. Song in approaching the existential, even ontological, identification between Jesus and the people. The ugly, emaciated man on the cross can be present in all human suffering. Therefore, Asian Christians are supposed to discover Jesus among their own people's life in suffering and poverty. Jesus Christ is Christa too because not Christ, but the suffering of Jesus and people is redemptive and sacramental, thus lying at the center of his theology of the crucified people.[109] C. S. Song's theology of the cross turned a Christology from above into a Jesuology from below in a provocative way. He is not concerned about articulating and expounding the aspect of God's solidarity with, and involvement in, the suffering people because the suffering people are themselves redemptive. An anthropocentric liberal existential approach typical of Western theology (for instance Herbert Brown) seems more apt for C. S. Song's theology of the crucified people.

Furthermore, I mention Aloysius Pieris from Sri Lanka who is an ordained Roman Catholic priest. From the beginning of his career he showed a passionate interest in the relationship between Christianity and Buddhism, which has had a long and venerable tradition in his country. He not only is a scholar of Buddhism, but he also has close dialogical and experiential contact with many multi-religious groups by engaging in the struggle for the liberation of the poor. Since graduating from the Pontifical Theological Faculty in Naples in 1966, he became the first Christian ever to be awarded a doctoral degree in Buddhist philosophy at the University of Sri Lanka in Colombo. He is regarded as a leading representative of Asian theology in the authentic sense. He is very close to colleagues among the liberation theologians in Latin America, but different from them in emphasizing the significance of religiosity. "The Asian religious attitude to poverty, even in the context of its march to economic progress, differs from the Latin American attitude as a psychological differs from a socio-

109. Ibid., 210–29.

logical one. In the former, voluntary poverty is a spiritual antidote; in the latter it is a political strategy."[110]

Pieris affirmed strongly that the poor of Asia are also very religious and spiritual. Theological reflection in Asia calls for taking seriously two elements—poverty and religiosity. According to him, doing Asian theology cannot eschew either pole: the third *worldliness* of Asian continent or its peculiarly *Asian* character. "More realistically and precisely, the common denominator linking Asia with the Third World is its overwhelming poverty. The specific character defining Asia within the other poor countries is its multifaceted religiousness. These two inseparable realities constitute in their interpenetration what might be designated as the *Asian context*, the matrix of any truly Asian theology."[111]

The Asian religions, Buddhism in particular, have seen that the craving for material goods leads some to exploit and impoverish others. This craving is countered by the option to be poor, giving up both the desire for material goods and also the actual possession of them. Choosing to be poor leads to the option for the poor in a struggle that leads to liberation from imposed poverty. When poverty and religiosity work together in harmony, a struggle for liberation becomes liberative in a genuine sense. It escapes from the vicious circle to which a struggle for liberation can fall, which can be seen often in liberation movements and groups. The specificity of the Asian liberation theology that Pieris articulates can be found in the life of Jesus. Jesus chooses to become poor in the very act of his birth. "The "option to be poor" becomes a true "following of Jesus" only to the extent that it is also an option for the poor."[112] The kenosis of Christ (which is similar to a Buddhist notion of detachment from craving) becomes meaningful. It is to be followed in humble service to non-Christian people. Not only Christians, but many other believers are following Jesus today in a struggle with the poor by voluntarily becoming the poor. This is the spiritual way to which all of us are called. Where the positive elements of poverty and religiosity meet each other, both can become a driving force for liberation and justice.

Given this fact, Pieris highlights the evangelizing task of Christianity in a twofold sense. The one is solidarity with non-Christians by witnessing to the spirituality common to all religions. The other is to reveal the

110. Cf. Hennelly, *Liberation Theologies*, 203.

111. Pieris, *Asian Theology of Liberation*, 69.

112. Ibid., 15.

Christian uniqueness proclaiming Jesus as the new covenant by participating with the poor against mammon's principalities and powers that create poverty and oppression.[113] What motivates Pieris in this direction comes from "two biblical axioms: the irreconcilable antagonism between God and wealth, and the irrevocable covenant between God and the poor, Jesus himself being this covenant."[114]

In as much as God in Jesus takes the side of the poor and the oppressed, the struggle of the poor for liberation coincides with God's own salvific action. We see that many people from other religions take the option that Jesus took, and in so doing are followers of Jesus in practice much more than those who merely profess a formal allegiance to Christianity. The option to be poor has a messianic and soteriological role in the history of liberation and salvation because God shapes human history via the kenotic way of Jesus Christ. As Pieris emphasizes, "I speak rather of those religious seekers who have opted to be poor in their search for the saving truth and who, during their pilgrimage, encounter Jesus within their own soteriological perspectives."[115]

"The crucified God" is often referred, in Asian perspectives, to a kenotic way of doing something in the struggle of the minjung for a spiritual and social emancipation. In an encounter with a negative, mystical theology in the Buddhist tradition, God's experience is articulated and extended beyond Christianity to the relationship between God and all creatures. Redemption and creation stand not in polar tension, but are understood as one reality of God. God's experience is therefore expressed not merely in the institutional church but in passionate solidarity with the poor and heartfelt concern for all living creatures. Therefore, the church in Asia must abandon its alliance with power through which theology of power-domination and instrumentalization (so called theology of glory) must give way to a theology of humility, poverty, and compassion. This is where an Asian version of doing *theologia crucis* becomes meaningful.

The face of God in Jesus Christ can only be successful if the church participates in Asia's own search for it in the midst of poverty and in company with minjung. The face of God in Jesus Christ can be found in God's condemnation of mammon as the enemy and declaration of Godself in the sacramental presence with the lowest of the low. This is a different face

113. Amaladoss, *Life in Freedom,* 95.

114. Ibid.

115. Ibid., 64.

of God to be sought in the otherness of minjung. Therefore, theology of the cross in Asian contexts takes a step further in recognizing the strident and strange face of God in other religious ways that are characterized by the spiritual kenosis of poverty and resurrection of emancipation. The theology of the cross is liberative in solidarity with the poor, inclusive and open in recognition of other religious ways, dialogical in witnessing to God in the kenosis of Jesus Christ, and co-participation on the pilgrimage in companionship with minjung as anonymous children of Abba, Father.

Luther's Christology in Universal-Cosmic Dimension

In an ecumenical context, a paradigm shift from the quest for the historical Jesus to the quest for the cosmic Christ seeks a well-balanced dialectical relationship between the cosmic Christ and the historical Jesus. The words and liberating deeds of the historical Jesus are not to be ignored, but become the foundational basis for a theology of the cosmic Christ. Since Augustine's theology of "God and soul," mediated through the Enlightenment to the existentialism of Rudolf Bultmann, the secret of theology has become anthropology (Feuerbach). The emphasis on the human being as the transcendental subjectivity over external objects was at the heart of the Enlightenment project. Here, knowledge is certain and objective, and the criterion for certainty depends on human rational capabilities to the neglect of more profound spiritual faculties beyond human reason. "The Enlightenment anthropology" substitutes humanity for God on center stage in history by dislodging God from the world of human affairs.

Jaroslav Pelikan's comment on the loss of the cosmic Christ is relegated to the quest for the historical Jesus. The Enlightenment project, which has been influential on theological discourse in the modern age, made possible and necessary the paramount importance of the historical Jesus by deposing the cosmic Christ.[116] In the ecumenical conference of New Delhi (1961), a Lutheran scholar, Joseph A. Sittler, called for a cosmic Christology based on the cosmic Christ hymn (Col 1:15–20). For him, Christ is the ground of all things, and of the unity of the world. Sittler took a self-critical view of the Western Church's tendency to dualism between nature and grace since Augustine. He therefore encouraged people to take seriously the tradition of the Orthodox Church Fathers,

116. Pelikan, *Jesus Through the Centuries*, 182.

especially Irenaeus' teaching of *recapitulatio mundi,* which encompasses both nature and grace.

According to Sittler, anthropocentrism has subjugated nature to grace, resulting in a threatening crisis of nature. A Christology of nature becomes urgent for theology.[117] From an Asian perspective, a cosmic Christ is reformulated, extended, and challenged, in such a way that the cosmic Christ should be encountered in other religious ways. The cosmic Christ who is present and at work in other religions encourages Christians to listen to, and participate in, them. Since New Delhi, the WCC has recommended a "Dialogue with Men of Other Faiths and Ideologies" in terms of a cosmic Christ.[118]

A cosmic Christology is relevant to ecological concerns and interreligious dialogue. At some point, theology of the cross remains in the background mainly due to its historical narrowness. The historical Jesus becomes, on account of its absolute truth claim for salvation, a stumbling block against other religious truth claims, whereas a cosmic Christology is an open Christology that can recognize other religious ways beyond the parochial setting of the historical Jesus. To what extent does Luther's theology of the cross have to do with its cosmic universal orientation? Luther's theology of the cross cannot be seen as an early form of Luther's theology, but the basic and central idea pertaining to his whole theological framework. In the Lord's Supper controversy, Luther pronounced more clearly his view of the presence of Christ's body and blood "in, with, and under" the bread and wine by setting forth his doctrine of ubiquity in reference to the traditional two-natures doctrine. For Luther, faith in Christ is the spring "from, through, and in which all his theological reflections flow to and from, day and night."[119]

According to Luther, Christology is inseparably connected with soteriology, which is well expressed in Luther's hymn, "Dear Christians, One and All, Rejoice": "But God had seen my wretched state Before the world's foundation, And, mindful of his mercies great, He planned for my salvation. He turned to me a father's heart."[120] There can be no Christology without soteriology, as conversely there can be no soteriology without Christology.

117. Sittler, "Called to Unity," 181.

118. Cf. Knitter, *No Other Name?*, 138.

119. *WA*, 40:1, 33:7–11; cf. Lohse, *Martin Luther's Theology*, 221.

120. Luther, "Dear Christians, One and All, Rejoice," *Lutheran Book of Worship*, Hymn no. 299.

Moreover, Christ is depicted as "a mirror of the Father's heart" in *The Large Catechism* (1529). That is, God revealed God's whole fatherly heart in Christ's person and work. It has been assumed that Abelard's soteriology and Anselm's theory of satisfaction had an impact on Luther's Christology. However, Luther's understanding of Christ's atonement goes a step further than Anselm's notion of satisfaction. In the exposition of the creed's Second Article in *The Large Catechism*, Luther takes Jesus Christ to "restore us to the Father's favor and grace . . . suffer, die and be buried that he might make satisfaction for me and pay what I owed, not with silver and gold, but with his own precious blood."[121] Divine forgiveness and the suffering of Christ are expressed in the idea that Christ becomes a curse for us, because cursed is everyone who hangs on a tree (Gal 3:13).

By receiving the punishment for our sins and setting us from the curse of the law, Christ fulfills and satisfies the will of God expressed in the law. Therefore the suffering of Christ is the foundational basis for satisfaction. In Luther' view, "everything else depends on this satisfaction, including the destruction of the might and the authority of the demonic powers."[122] Distancing himself from the concept of satisfaction, however, Luther's theory of atonement is more reminiscent of Irenaeus's notion of recapitulation: "That Christ has made satisfaction for our sin . . . too little is said of the grace of Christ, and not enough honor paid the suffering of Christ . . . he not only made satisfaction for sin but also redeemed us from the power of death, the devil and hell, and establishes an eternal kingdom of grace and a daily forgiveness even of the remainder of sin that is in us."[123]

Christ's dereliction on the cross, "Eli, Eli, lema sabachthani?," that is, "My God, my God, why have you forsaken me?" (Matt 27:46) can be understood adequately alongside Jesus' descent into hell. Jesus experiences the human predicament: abandonment by God, indeed hell. At the same time, he swallowed up "the power of death, the devil, and hell" for establishing an eternal kingdom of grace. "In short, our sin must be Christ's own sin, or we shall perish eternally." A "wonderful exchange" between Christ and believers takes place in the sense of the union. "Now let faith

121. *BC*, 414.

122. Althaus, *Theology of Martin Luther*, 220.

123. *WA*, 21:264, 27–33; cf. Lohse, *Martin Luther's Theology*, 227.

come between them and sins, death, and damnation will be Christ's, while grace, life, and salvation will be the soul's."[124]

Luther's concept of a wonderful exchange in its affinity to the theosis of Church fathers underscores the transformative, effectual dimension of his doctrine of justification, in spite of its forensic moment. If Christ is really present in our faith, divine involvement in our life and our mysterious union with Christ takes place at a level of profound intimacy. An ecumenical conversation between Luther and Orthodox churches makes Luther's theology of the cross a starting point for discussing the relationship between justification and theosis as well as for a possible reconstruction of the cosmic Christ from the perspective of the theology of the cross.

According to Irenaeus, God works through God's revealing Word. There is one sole God and Father who contains all things and gives being to all things. "If that manifestation of God which comes through the creation gives life to all who live on the earth, how much more does the manifestation of the Father which is performed by the Word give life to those who see God."[125]

For Irenaeus, the economy of the divine manifestations through the cosmic Christ is present to creation from the beginning and reveals the Father progressively. All divine manifestations take place through the Logos who is the visible presence of the Father. In affirmation of Justin's cosmological function of the Logos (*sperma tou logou*), Irenaeus takes the creation itself to be a divine manifestation because all divine manifestations are Logos-manifestations. According to Irenaeus, the cosmic order of creation is not separated from the historical order of redemption. "For by means of the creation itself, the Word reveals God the Creator . . . And these things do indeed address all humans in the same manner, but all do not in the same way believe them."[126] "He is present at every point in time. From the beginning to the Son, present to the creatures whom he has formed, [he] reveals the Father to all those to whom the Father wills . . . therefore in all things and through all things there is one God and Father, and one Word, his Son, and one Spirit, and one salvation to all who believe in him."[127]

124. *LW*, "The Freedom of a Christian," 31:351.

125. Adv. Haer. IV, 20, 6–7; Cf. Dupuis, *Toward a Christian Theology*, 61.

126. Adv. Haer. IV, 6, 5–6. Ibid., 62.

127. Adv. Haer. IV, 6–7. Ibid., 61.

There is no need of dissociating the universe from the personal revelation of the divine logos. The Word of God manifested himself to Adam in the garden, inaugurated the second covenant with Noah, and appeared to Abraham at Mamre, and talked to Moses in his presence. Logophanies in the Old Testament are authentic anticipations of the Christophany.

At this point a serious question is raised: Will the theology of the universal revelation of the cosmic Christ, espoused by Irenaeus, weaken the unique and irreplaceable importance of his historical incarnation? How is it possible to reconcile the universality of God's gracious initiative with a once-for-all historical Christ-event? For Irenaeus, Christ heralded is different from Christ given. The historical Christ who assumed human flesh reaches the climax of the Father's manifestation through the visibility of the Logos. According to Irenaeus, what is important for a cosmic Christ lies in the historical, redemptive, and eschatological sense. This is what he calls "recapitulation," and it expresses the work of Christ as head of a new humanity. Adam is to the head of the old nature what Christ is to the head of the new nature.

The incarnation is the initial stage of the recapitulation of all things by Christ in continuity with what happened before. The incarnation as Christ's recapitulation is a new starting point. It stands in continuation and fulfillment of creation and in anticipation of final consummation. The initial victory of Christ begins in incarnation, not in resurrection. It involves a victory over Satan, and consequently total liberation of the humanity from the power of sin and death. God's incarnation in Christ is the beginning stage of victory over evil so the entire life of Christ is an integral part of recapitulation continuing until the final consummation in eschatological dynamism. Despite strong resistance on the part of Satan that may not be downplayed, the final fulfillment and salvation will be placed under Christ's last victory over the Devil. The church as the body of Christ plays an important part in carrying out an eschatological recapitulation through baptism and the Eucharist, in which the church and people of God are united to Christ.[128]

Luther's emphasis on *creatio ex nihilo* can be understood properly in opposition to the Aristotelian idea of the eternity of the world. The traditional formula of *creatio ex nihilo* expresses God's absolute sovereignty and the World's finitude. Although Luther stresses God's creation of the world in freedom, creatures may share in the struggle against the devil for

128. Cf. González, *History of Christian Thought*, 157–70.

the sake of life. So writes Luther in *The Genesis Lecture*: "God has created all these creatures to be in active military service, to fight for us continually against the devil."[129]

It is noteworthy that Luther rejected without doubt the creature's cooperation with respect to justification, but affirmed it for the activity of all creation. An anthropological reflection on placing God's creatures at the level of "coworkers, not co-creators" is remarkable in providing a dynamic character to Luther's theology of creation in contrast to the so-called orders of creation in nineteenth-century neo-Lutheran theology.[130] In breaking with the medieval idea of putting the spiritual estate above the temporal, Luther has all three estates or hierarchies function in equality, albeit each with a different task in the preservation of life. Although God's commission continues unaltered for preserving creation, the order of creation could expose itself to the danger of perversion and distortion on account of the human sinful condition.[131]

However, article VIII of the Formula of Concord (1580) did not achieve its purpose of reconciling two rival camps, but the christological controversy raged into the seventeenth century between the Lutheran theologians of Giessen and Tübingen. If the human nature of Jesus became ubiquitous in the Lord's Supper, was he also universal in the whole world and in all creation? The Giessen theologians put emphasis on the state of humiliation (*status exinanitionis*) by limiting the use of divine attributes in the earthly Jesus (*kenosis*), while the Tübingen theologians affirmed the doctrine of *krypsis*. (The divine is not only limited to the human Jesus, but also the divine powers were exercised in secret.) Lutheran theology tends to favor the kenotic Christology in which Thomasius coined the term *genus tapeinoticum*, from *tapeinos*, meaning humble and lowly. Here the divine attributes that had to do with the cosmological dimension would be suppressed and abandoned. As part of the kenotic Christology the aspect of *vere deus* was confined and threatened. *Genus tapeinoticum* accentuates the participation of human nature in the divine nature. However, for Luther this term must be used in reference to the affirmation of the divinity of Christ.

Luther himself gives a fresh interpretation to the "emptying" (*kenosis*) (Phil 2:6–7) at the incarnation: Jesus Christ "emptied himself, taking the

129. *LW*, 1:74; cf. Lohse, *Martin Luther's Theology*, 42.

130. *WA*, 47:857, 35, cf. Lohse, *Martin Luther's Theology*, 242.

131. Lohse, *Martin Luther's Theology*, 246.

form of a servant, being born in the likeness of men." Although at the incarnation, in Luther's view, Christ did not leave his Godhead in heaven, he renounced it gradually in his earthly life. "He relinquished that form to God the Father and emptied himself, unwilling to use his rank against us, unwilling to be different from us. Moreover, for our sakes he became as one of us and took the form of a servant, that is, he subjected himself to all evils."[132] Jesus' emptying denotes Jesus' willingness to allow the pains of the human predicament to have an impact on his divine nature.

At this point Luther is different from some kenotic theologians who interpret the incarnation as totally abandoning the divine nature for the sake of earthly human nature. According to Luther, the divine nature was present throughout the earthly life of Jesus, suffering human predicaments and death. "God has suffered, the Man has created heaven and earth . . . that the Servant (Christ) . . . is Creator of all things."[133] Given this fact, we perceive that the doctrine of the *enhypostasis* is affirmed for Luther, implying that the human nature of Jesus Christ has no hypostasis apart from the divine nature.

In contrast to the later Lutheran development of Christology, Luther himself did not lose sight of the dynamic relation between *anhypostasia* and *enhypostasia* by affirming that a divine person assumed human nature.[134] When the view of emptying is dealt with in relation to Jesus' abandonment at the cross, Luther states that on the cross the deity was indeed not separated from the humanity, but Jesus' divinity withdrew and hid. "Such humanity has been made liable and subject to death and hell yet in that humiliation has devoured the devil, hell, and all things in itself."[135] This ex-

132. *LW*, 31:301, cf. Lohse, *Martin Luther's Theology*, 229.

133. *WA*, 39:2, 280, 16–22; cf. Lohse, *Martin Luther's Theology*, 229.

134. At the fifth ecumenical council in Constantinople (553) Leontius of Byzantium, who was one of the neo-Chalcedonian representatives, affirmed the unity of the man Jesus with the Son of God in the formula of *enhypostasis* of Jesus in the eternal logos. The man Jesus has the ground of his human existence (his hypostasis) not in humanity, but in an impersonal humanity of Christ. The designation "en"-hypostasis expresses Jesus' human nature in unification with the Logos from the beginning. However, this teaching cannot be understood adequately apart from the doctrine of *anhypostasis*. *Anhypostasis* as a negation is inseparably connected with *enhypostasis*, which means that Jesus Christ has a personal existence but only in and through the Logos. The contribution of Leontius was to interpret the Chacedonian formulation "in two natures" along the lines of the priority of the Word and the unity of the Word made flesh. Cf. Pannenberg, *Jesus—God and Man*, 338–40; *Handbuch*, 277–270; see further *CD*, 4/2:49–50, 91–92.

135. *WA*, 43, 579, 42–580, 2; cf. Lohse, *Martin Luther's Theology*, 230.

presses God's universal radical grace in the suffering of Jesus Christ toward defeating the devil and the power of death and hell for all creatures.

Luther's doctrine of ubiquity affirms Christ's exalted human nature as present everywhere. His cosmic Christology is well expressed in his 1526 sermon, "The Sacrament of the Body and Blood of Christ against the Fanatics": "We believe that Christ, according to his human nature, is put over all creatures (Eph 1:22) and fills all things . . . Not only according to his divine nature, but also according to his human nature, he is a lord of all things, has all things in his hand, and is present everywhere."[136]

Luther no longer thought of the right hand of God as a particular place in heaven, because Christ's body is everywhere. True to form, the right hand of God is everywhere, although we do not know how that occurs. Understood in this way, Luther's *theologia crucis* can be adequately understood in reference to Luther's cosmic Christology based on the doctrine of ubiquity and in relation to *anhypostais-enhypostasis*. Here, God's presence is saving only in connection with the humanity of Jesus Christ in a universal dimension (Jesus' self-emptying at his incarnation or his abandonment by God at the cross descending into hell). Dogmatically reversed, Luther's Christology, in reinterpreting a patristic tradition of the cosmic Christ, would take a new and creative expression in radical openness to people in the world and effectuation of divine suffering in a cosmological scope.

Unique Narrative of *Theologia Crucis* in Interreligious Context

God's universal grace in Jesus Christ is not about a totalizing meta-narrative in the interest of ruling and subsuming all other religions and cultures into Christianity. God begins with a small narrative of a particular suffering event in the concrete, parochial setting of a historical Jesus. The small narrative manifests itself in the liberating word and action of Jesus of Nazareth. A christological universalism that was awakened among Jesus' disciples after his death and resurrection gains more and more in cosmological and universal significance. For them, the gospel means an invitation to all human beings to participate in God's unselfish cosmic love that takes place concretely and historically in Jesus Christ on the cross. This is not logocentrism supporting the absolute religious superiority of Western Christianity over other religions and cultures without reservation.

136. *LW*, 36:342.

Rather, it points to God's redemptive presence in solidarity with those who suffer, where Christ is also really and truly present. The uniqueness of the gospel should not be totalized and manipulated in the presentation of the regular dogmatics. Rather, the narrative of the gospel might call for the necessity of irregular dogmatics, the task of which listens openly and honestly to the mystery of God outside of the walls of Christianity especially with regard to Christ's presence in, and solidarity with, people in poverty and profound religiosity in anticipation of the final liberation and reconciliation of the coming God.[137]

A Christian grand narrative based on the story of God's action in the eschatological history of Jesus Christ that stands for the salvation and the completion of all living creatures in the cosmos needs not be exhausted by the naiveté of the Enlightenment project in which universally valid truth is sought only by appealing to human reason. The unique narrative of the gospel witnessed by the scriptures lies beyond the bounds of the unfinished project of modernity. Rather, it points us to what God has done, is doing, and will do for us even through different, strange, and ominous voices of otherness. In this regard, the *theologia crucis* should be reflected upon and deepened in light of the resurrection of the crucified Christ for the godless and the innocent in other religions.[138]

In other words, a *theologia crucis* in light of the resurrection of the crucified Christ is eschatologically open in scope toward other voices of God in the world. Jesus Christ is not merely the Lord for the church, but for the world. As Luther stresses, "He (Christ) is the living and immortal image against death, which he suffered, yet by his resurrection from the dead he vanquished death in his life. He is the image of the grace of God against sin, which he assumed, and yet overcame by his perfect obedience. He is the heavenly image, the one who was forsaken by God as damned, yet he conquered hell through his omnipotent love."[139]

In speaking of Luther's *theologia crucis*, we should not ignore the resurrection of the crucified Christ conquering hell through his love. Since Jesus, as one of the Trinity, realizes himself fully through the resurrection, he thus becomes the eschatological hope of all people for the resurrection

137. For the distinction between regular dogmatics and irregular dogmatics, cf. *KD*, I/1:55f. 83. 292ff. *KD* I/2:942f. *KD*, IV/3:147ff.

138. Moltmann, *Crucified God*, 73.

139. *MLBTW*, 645–46.

from the dead.[140] However, the human Jesus, who is the one of the Trinity, is begotten, obeys, and glorifies the Father through the Spirit. Christianity as one of the world religions has its uniqueness through the death and resurrection of Jesus Christ in its eschatological openness. The eschatological future of God's kingdom occurred in the message and history of Jesus. The eschatological kingdom that is proleptically present in the event of Jesus Christ can be seen in the threefold way of pre-temporality, supra-temporality and the post-temporality of eternity.[141] Therefore, Luther's *simul justus et peccator* that is characteristic of Christian existence should be understood as our past and future in God's arms.

A Christian is a person in the movement, in solidarity with non-Christian people, in direction toward God's future. The future of God that appears through the death and resurrection of Jesus Christ as the eschatological power of salvation puts Christianity at a unique place with soteriological significance in encounter with the history of world religions. A theocentric pluralism that brings God as the Integrator to the center of "the universe of faith" would lead to an ahistorical idealism or a naïve relativism in face of social and political issues, resulting in suppressing the unique narrative of divine suffering in Jesus.[142] The universal salvific will of God is not in contrast to the necessary mediation of Jesus Christ. God who is revealed in a decisive manner in Jesus Christ is nevertheless present and at work in other religious traditions in light of the coming future of God. This inclusivist paradigm encourages us with a radical openness to seek "to explore the many and various ways in which God has spoken to all his children in the non-Christian religions." This openness "will lead to the positive fruits of this exploration transforming, enriching and fulfilling Christianity."[143] On the other hand, the exclusive conservative model

140. According to Pannenberg, "the resurrection of Jesus is just as constitutive for the deity of the Father as for the divine sonship of Jesus. Without Jesus' resurrection, the Father Jesus proclaimed would not be God," "Gott der Geschichte," 88. Cf. Jenson, "Jesus in the Trinity," 198.

141. *CD*, II/1:619. For Ted Peters' critique of simultaneity of past, present, and future in Barth's thought, see Peters, *God as Trinity*, 149. In this context, Peters quotes from Barth, "Even the eternal God does not live without time. He is supremely temporal. For His eternity is authentic temporality, and therefore the source of all time. But in His eternity, in the uncreated self-subsistent time which is one of the perfections of His divine nature, present, past and future, yesterday, to-day, and to-morrow, are not successive, but simultaneous," *CD*, III/2:437. 526. II/1:61–62, 608, III/1:71.

142. Hick, *God and the Universe of Faith*, 121.

143. D'Costa, *Theology and Religious Pluralism*, 136.

displacing all other religious ways needs to take more into consideration the eschatological future of God in the life, death, and resurrection of Jesus Christ.[144]

In fact, God's gracious initiative and invitation to the gospel encourages Christians and non-Christians alike to choose life against death rather than pursuing human achievement in our world in the pattern of the Enlightenment. The other face of human life is characterized by Auschwitz, Hiroshima, and all the misery coupled with modern capitalism in the name of progress and scientific rationality.[145] "God for us," who was, is, and will be present from the creation to the consummation of the world and the cosmos, manifests Godself concretely and definitely in the crucified Christ.

At this point, God's unselfish cosmic love encounters the cosmological *dukkha* in all sentient creatures. This aspect of divine Love encountering *dukkha* would lead all religions including Christianity not only to self-criticism in respect to a preferential option for the poor, but also to engaging in the profound religiosity of minjung outside Christianity. Unlike liberation theology, the concern of which lies mainly in stressing a balance between faith and politics within the Christian tradition, Asian minjung *theologia crucis* pursues divine suffering in personal, social, political, and cosmological realms and also in other religious dimensions. In agreement with Luther, it sees the penal suffering of Christ "in his relatedness to the rest of humanity," and agrees that Christ suffered for us "the punishment of the cross as though he deserved it."[146]

In disagreement with Luther, however, it seeks to deepen and actualize God's sacramental presence discernable in the life of the innocent minjung outside Christianity. In fact, the *theologia crucis* stands as a unique convergence of narratives between Christianity and other religions. The *theologia crucis* becomes a hermeneutical filter in encounter with the cross of the innocent who take upon themselves the burden of the sinful world. Jesus who died as one of the Jewish *ochlos* represents God's partisanship for *ochlos*-minjung, innocent victims in the present-day world.

A liberative model of Western class structures need not be transplanted to Asia. Asia is simultaneously ravaged by massive poverty and ecological devastation, and characterized by a religious spirituality of detachment

144. Cf. Braaten, "Place of Christianity," 311.

145. Moltmann, *Crucified God*, 68.

146. Pannenberg, *Jesus—God and Man*, 278.

and self-emptying liberation. Even from a Buddhist perspective the poor do not want to become selfish subjects of history. They seek self-transcendence, detachment in distance from clinging to becoming selfish subjects of history. Empowerment of minjung is not given in the progress of class struggle or a strategy of seeking dominion, but in a spiritual, feminine lifestyle of watercause, in the principle of childlike spontaneity, and in action without attachment to it. Jesus' feminine compassion can be seen in his endorsement of the simplicity of a child (Matt 11:25; 18:5). Nature for Jesus implies God's way of being present, sustaining, and nurturing all. Jesus' self-description as living water (John 4:10; 7:38) provides a striking example of the Taoist source of living water.

Overcoming *dukkha* is not restricted to the historical domain, but is connected to self-emptying transcendence, or a life of living water and spontaneity beyond what is at the phenomenological level—albeit affirming social, political, environmental significance.

In this regard, poverty and the suffering innocent are not merely issues that can be overcome through the struggle for liberation on the basis of political or economic analysis. They refer to other spiritual dimensions of detachment and to a religious spirituality of kenosis in destroying and transcending craving paradoxically so as to become the poor. In this regard, the *theologia crucis* can be reread and re-appropriated in an Asian context with the hermeneutics of suspicion and retrieval in stressing that "Jesus himself is the poor," or "Jesus himself is self emptying."

All liberative attempts and movements can be meaningful when following the spirit of Jesus' poverty and renouncement that is expressed and reaches its climax on his cross. Therefore, a liberative movement and action should be more sensitive to the spirituality of self-immolation so as not to get caught in a vicious circle of reversing the genuine spirituality of liberation that can be unfortunately discerned in the liberation-oriented activism or praxis fetishism inside of the liberative action group. Jesus Christ's "self emptying" attitude is not merely sacramental, but calls for an experiential *Anfechtungen* of social discipleship expressed in the praxis of solidarity with the poor by renunciation of privilege and dominion, and in recognition of Christ's universal initiative in other religious ways. If the affirmation of the uniqueness of God in Jesus Christ is misused to suppress other religious ways, insights, and wisdom, it would betray God's unique narrative of divine *dukkha* for all sentient creatures occurring on the cross, and thus turn the good news into ominous news.

The relativization of Christianity can be meaningful through a radical understanding of the gospel when it encourages Asian Christians to be more faithful and attentive to the prophetic and spiritual elements in other religions in which we learn humbly and openly to listen to God's voice. However, this relativization is not meant to be a relativization of the gospel as such, but rather refers to a self-critique of the institutionalized church toward God's universal reign. There are strange voices from God, whose fatherly heart is the mirror of Jesus' self-emptying way. In fact, Jesus, through the experience of absolute nothingness, becomes unselfish cosmic love for, with, and in all sentient creatures. At this point, a spirituality of Buddhism is not in antithetical contrast to a spirituality of the cross, but profoundly complimentary.

At times, Luther's statement has led Lutherans to affirm theopassianism in which God genuinely suffers. Luther affirmed the suffering of the second Person of the Trinity. Of course, Luther's understanding of divine suffering is not simply to be identified with Patripassianism, the suffering and death of God the Father. In line with Alexandrian Christology, Luther stands closer to the theopaschite tradition in affirming the statement that God and suffering come together in the one person of Jesus Christ.[147] If the Father and the Spirit share the death of the Son, but not in total identification with his death, the reason is for the sake of the world. There can be no God without world, and no world without God. In terms of a critique of religion, people do not merely kill God, but kill the innocent paradoxically. God's unselfish love that is highlighted in the crucified Christ does include the world outside Christianity by integrating it into the wounded life of the triune God. In the crucifixion the absolute nothingness is fulfilled as the absolute infinite love. That is seen clearly in Jesus' detachment from craving or clinging to the omnipotent God as people in his time would expect. As a matter of fact, God's unselfish cosmic love can be adequately understood against the broken Trinity in divine co-participation in and great compassion for the death of the Son.

At this point, Christian agape meets Buddhist *dukkha* where suffering can be overcome and led to final liberation through the suffering love of God. *Dukkha* is not merely of human or all sentient beings, but of divine life. We can perceive motherly pain of God begetting the Son in the Spirit of eternal Life giver. If *dukkha* is seen from the perspective of divine suffering, the Buddhist path to Enlightenment can be seen as complementary

147. Jansen, *Studien zu Luthers Trinitätslehre*, 118–19.

to Christianity due to its radical understanding of detachment and self abrogation. Christian agape, which is realized in Jesus Christ's voluntarily detached renunciation of clinging to God, is not in opposition to the Buddhist concept of self-awakening to realize true self, or the *mahakaruna* (great compassion) that is a capacity of suffering with others.[148]

If the triune God continues its trinitarian being by engaging in and having a share in the death of the Son, the crucifixion of the Son can be regarded as the most radical, and most valuable gospel of God's unselfish love for all living creatures. "God for us" turns upside down even the people's rebellion against God for God's own sake, and radicalizes God's solidarity with people in poverty and profound religiosity in which nothing can sever human beings from God. A theocentric approach is, in the name of transcendental apophatic mystery, not supposed to downplay "God for us and the world in Jesus Christ" in eschatological openness because its weakness would be seen with its excessive emphasis on God's all-transcending monarchy. A balance between the Buddhist insight of *Sunyata* and a Christian theology of *perichoretic* relationality can be fulfilled in considering the divine suffering of Jesus Christ, which does not suppress other different ways to Enlightenment and wisdom, but affirms them in light of the suffering innocent in our midst.

There is no Jesus apart from the cosmic Christ as conversely there is no cosmic Christ without the suffering of the historical Jesus. In this regard, there is no need to distinguish the mystery of God from the historical incarnation. *Deus victor* in Jesus' descent into hell can be properly understood through his death and resurrection as the Christ *Pantocrator* for God's creation and the kingdom of religions in eschatological perspective. The crucified Christ, in destroying the hell of all human beings, means the total cosmic liberation from death and hell and thus rejects any exclusivist or chauvinist attitude from the outset.

In the biblical narratives, Jesus' death is presented as a cosmic event: "darkness was over the whole land" (Mark 15:33); "the sun was eclipsed" (Luke 23:44). "The earth quaked; the rocks were split; the tombs are opened and the bodies of many holy men rose from the dead" (Matt 27:52–53). At the death of Jesus "the veil of the Temple was torn in two from top to bottom" (Mark 15:38). The dialectic of transfiguration and crucifixion insists that cosmic Christ and suffering come together. Even

148. Cf. Lefebure, *The Buddha & The Christ*, 143–66.

after the resurrection the cosmic Christ is always presented with wounds and scars that belong to the historical Jesus, the suffering servant who is persecuted and crucified for announcing the kingdom of God. The post-resurrection confession of the disciples is not merely that "we have seen the historical Jesus after Easter," but "we have seen the Lord," which means the Ruler of the universe—a cosmological title (John 20:18, 25, 21:7; Luke 24:34). The eschatological future should be seen and realized in our struggle for liberation and the praxis of our affirmation of otherness in the apocalyptic midst threatened by ecological devastation and religious intolerance and wars.

In celebration of the cosmic Christ, Paul deepens our union with the cosmic Christ, saying that nothing that exists, nothing still to come, not any power, height, depth, or any created thing, can ever come between us and the love of God made visible in Christ Jesus our Lord." (Rom 8:38–39) The Incarnated Christ is seen in a dialectical relation to the cosmic Christ who is "above all, God for ever blessed" (Rom 9:5). In the context of Colossians (Col 1:15–20), a cosmological Christology is praised wherein in Christ all things were created in heaven and earth visible and invisible. The idea of all things holding together and being reconciled in Christ means a cosmic redemption. In the Pauline kenotic Christology (Phil 2:6–11), the cross of the historical Jesus is central and essential to grounding a cosmic Christ. To understand the cosmic Christ is impossible apart from historical context of the cross and resurrection. However, without seeing a sacramental, cosmological significance of the cross in light of the resurrection, the cross is easily likely to fall into an anthropocentric individualism, or into the individual mystic spirituality of the imitation of Christ. The practical discipleship of the cross should be elaborated in our conformation to the self-emptying way of Jesus Christ.

Luther's *theologia crucis* is radical and revolutionary in that it is enough to know that "Christ went to hell, destroyed hell for all believers, and has redeemed them from the power of death, of the devil, and of the eternal damnation of the hellish jaws." In this regard, Bonhoeffer's actualization of Luther is worth mentioning in that "the curses of the godless sometimes sound better in God's ear than the hallelujahs of the pious."[149] "It means that nothing is lost, that everything is taken up in Christ, although it is

149. Bonhoeffer, *Act and Being*, 160.

transformed, made transparent, clear, made free from the anguish of selfish desire. Christ restores all this as God originally intended it to be."[150]

Minjung theology in South-Korea launched an attack on Western theology in the name of Jesus' unity and identity with the minjung (the lowest of the low). Suffering, or *han* of the minjung is highlighted in seeing Jesus' death on the cross as representative of minjung collective victims. There can be no Jesus without minjung, and vice versa. At this point the issue of justice and righteousness as the minjung event happening on the cross comes to the fore in socio-political perspective rather than justification between God and human being. However, minjung Christology tends to ignore the radical and cosmic dimension of Jesus' death destroying the hell of *han*.

Postmodern theory of language teaches that language is not a reflection of reality but rather a socio-cultural linguistic system. Language can be seen in terms of social constructions reflecting local cultural values rather than becoming objective descriptions of reality. Many postmodern thinkers hold that language should be found or located in the social constructions of particular cultures and historical periods. In so doing, the relationship between humans and reality is constructed in discourse. This is especially true when it comes to speaking of the divine mysterious death in Jesus Christ in an Asian-specific religious context.

The subject matter about "the crucified God" needs to be constructed through social, cultural, religious, and ethnic conventions on Asian soils. Asian confessional theology of divine *dukkha* invites us to develop a critical reflection and praxis of the cosmic Christ toward liberation for the poor as well as revitalizing a discourse of *dukkha* in different cultural religious contexts. The Buddhist language of suffering is welcomed and elaborated to the extent of deepening and renewing a Christian understanding of divine suffering in a new perspective. Conversely, a Christian language of divine death ushers in a new possibility of conversation with a Buddhist way to *nirvanic* liberation through realization of Absolute Nothingness.

A hermeneutic limitation should be set up, so that mutual transformation in encounter with other religions does not take the place of syncretism or relativization, without doing harm to the uniqueness and diversity of other religions. Rather, it enables and encourages each religion to find a deeper understanding of itself. This is an important task of wit-

150. Bonhoeffer, *Letters and Papers*, 170.

ness and dialogue in the Asian context. God does not have many different names (Hick) or many mediators (Panikkar), but one name is enough. In understanding the different as different we come to the inclusive reality of Jesus Christ in other religions and cultures. Interreligious dialogue is not supposed to be the wholesale relativization of other religions by suppressing their unique ways. The issue of religion cannot be totally resolved in terms of "the project of Enlightenment" by pointing to the God as Integrator or subsuming all religious claims by ignoring human different experiential confessions and faiths in historical, particular figures.

However, the name Jesus Christ does not encapsulate religious pluralism in an exclusive sense, but stimulates and dynamizes it in fidelity to one's own tradition by taking sides with God's universal reign for the sake of justice, peace, recognition of other voices in different religions and cultures, and preservation of the creation as our brothers and sisters. Interreligious dialogue stands not merely for the conversion, but also for conversation and cooperation in which the future of all religions will be determined by God's gracious love and God's coming future of *novum*, because "God will make everything new."

In the context of Revelation, animals "glorify and honor and give thanks to the One sitting on the throne" (Rev 4:9) and elders praise him: "You made all the universe and it was only by your will that everything was made and exists" (Rev 4:11). Christ as the Lamb slain for the entire human race is sung and praised in a way that "because you were sacrificed, and with your blood you bought people for God of every race, language, people and nation and made them a line of royal people and priests, to serve our God and to rule the world (Rev 5:9–10). All the living things in creation, everything living in the air, on the ground, and under the ground, and in the sea cry "to the One who is sitting on the throne and to the Lamb, honor, glory and power, for ever and ever" (Rev 5:13–14).

God's eternal *Immanuel* revealed itself in the historical *Immanuel*, and was expanded and enhanced in the cosmic *Immanuel,* inviting all living creatures to God's liberation by swallowing up the power of death. Luther's *theologia crucis* serves as an inspiration for witnessing Christ's kingdom and secular kingdoms as one reality standing in dialectical and eschatological co-existence before God's unselfish love in the mystery of the crucified God. The wounded cosmic Christ whose name is "God-with-them" (Rev 21:3) will be God to all people, Christians and non-Christians alike, by relieving injustice for the many wounded people and creatures on earth and by wiping away all tears from their eyes. The wounded cosmic Christ will be maker of the whole of creation anew. The cosmic Lamb, innocent and slain for the entire creation, with which the eternal *Immanuel* stands in inseparable connection, is the alpha and omega for a *theologia crucis* that is meaningful in encounter with Asian world religions.

Jesus' self-emptying kenosis allows him to accept human nature in support of those who suffer in poverty. Jesus identifies himself with those in suffering in a historical-universal dimension (Matt 25). Dogmatically reversed, from this aspect, we might discern a sacramental identity of Jesus with the victim on the way to Jericho, not merely with the good Samaritan. The point of this story is not about the Good Samaritan, but the victim on the street who is the focus of Jesus' parable. In this regard, the good Samaritan is a good example for doing discipleship in solidarity with the victimized Christ on the street.[151]

Bonhoeffer's idea of the view from below in which "religionless workers and human beings in general" or "the masses" may be justified has a special relevance to Asian understandings of victim Christology.[152] Doing a theology of the cross in an Asian context stands vicariously for "the excluded, the suspect, the maltreated, the powerless, the oppressed, the reviled—in short, those who suffer."[153] In this regard, Asian contextual theology shares Bonhoeffer's call for church's repentance: "The church confesses that she has witnessed the lawless application of brutal force, the physical and spiritual suffering of countless innocent people, oppression, hatred, and murder, and that she has not raised her voice on behalf of the victims and has not found ways to hasten to their aid. She is guilty of the deaths of the weakest and most defenceless brothers of Jesus Christ."[154]

The broken and wounded Trinity participating in the death of the Son is not capable of abandoning or abusing the divine son or child, but just of participating in the Son's eternal decision to do an act of self-emptying for human beings and the world. As a matter of fact, the Father, who eternally joins the kenosis of the Son in the inner trinitarian life, cannot forsake the Son, but co-participates to a different degree. "For this reason the Father loves me, because I lay down my life in order to take it

151. For this insight I am indebted to Ahn Bung-Mu, who repeatedly stressed this perspective during my student years.

152. Bonhoeffer, *Letters and Papers,* 17, 280, 381.

153. Ibid., 17.

154. Bonhoeffer, *Ethics*, 114.

up again . . . but I lay it down of my own accord. I have the power to lay it down, and I have the power to take it up again" (John 10:17–18).

This calls for an explication of how the triune God shares in *dukkha*, divine and cosmic. The unselfish cosmic love of the triune God can be at the heart of the wounded Trinity in Luther's theology of the cross. If the Trinity begins with the crucified God, we have, then, a broken and wounded Trinity. The intra-divine life has a share in the great death of the Son to realize his true self through absolute love. This is where Jesus' self-emptying love meets, in a critical and transformative way, the self-realization and awakening of Buddhism to *Sunyata.* This will be dealt with when Luther and the Trinity meet Buddhist-Christian dialogue.

First, I believe with my whole heart the sublime article of the majesty of God, that the Father, Son, and Holy Spirit, three distinct persons, are by nature one true and genuine God, the Maker of heaven and earth

LW 37:361

Such are that Buddha's supernatural penetrations, such the force of his vow that in the worlds fall ten directions, wherever anyone preaches the Scripture of the Dharma Blossom, his jeweled stupa invariably wells up before that person, his whole body in the stupa giving praise with the words, "Excellent! Excellent!"

Lotus Sutra

5

Luther and Asian Theology of Trinity

I BEGIN WITH THE *FILIOQUE* (THE SPIRIT PROCEEDING FROM THE FATHER and the Son) controversy. Under the influence of Eastern Orthodox theology of the Trinity, Moltmann makes a wholesale attack on Sabellian notes in Western trinitarian theology. Thus, ecumenical challenges to the *filioque* added to the creed of Nicea and Constantinople have a well-known history. The doctrine of the Trinity reaches its climax in God's plan of salvation in the person and the work of Jesus Christ, his incarnation, crucifixion, resurrection, and ascension through the Spirit (cf. Eph 1:3–14). Although there is no explicit mention of the full doctrine of the Trinity (intradivine persons, processions, and relations) in the New Testament, we see that God redeems human beings through Christ in the power of the Holy Spirit. The relationship between the economy and the eternal being of God, i.e., between the economic Trinity and the immanent Trinity, is central and essential to understanding the eternal mystery of God in the economy of salvation.

In what follows we are concerned with describing the idea of the Trinity in its historic and dogmatic development. We will trace the controversy about the Trinity in the ancient church with respect to divine passibility, and then summarize the trinitarian ideas in Augustine. It is necessary to discuss Luther's notion of the Trinity with reference to the ancient church and Augustine. After this, I will turn my attention to Luther's theology of the Trinity and the ecumenical debate on the Trinity with respect to Unitrinity (Karl Barth) and Triunity (Moltmann). In an Asian context the Trinity becomes interreligious in an encounter with the wisdom of world religions. After dealing with Asian "other" Trinity (Panikkar and Lee Jung Young), I will try to construct an Asian understanding of the Trinity in a critical dialogue with Luther's theology. A discussion of the

Trinity and *Sunyata* in a Buddhist-Christian context will be attempted, bringing the *filioque* formula into Asian focus. No doubt Christian theology is inherently trinitarian in content and structure. The Trinity is one central symbol of the Christian community. The emergence of trinitarian theology, albeit grounded in biblical narrative, comes about from the theological heritage of the ancient church. The dogma of the Trinity evolved out of christological debate against Arianism and Sabellianism.[1]

Divine Passibility and Trinity in the Ancient Church

I begin with three patterns of understanding God as Trinity since the post-apostolic period: adoptionism, subordinationism, and modalism. A modalist Trinity was a credible threat to the ancient church. In modalist form, divine passibility was strongly affirmed. In the modalist-type, Father, Son, and the Spirit remain only various names expressing one and the same God. The Spirit and the Son do not have their own pre-existence, because God the Father is incarnated in the Son. So-called "Patripassianism" emerges from the notion that God the Father suffered on the cross. This modalist notion was called monarchianism, because it held absolutely the oneness and monarchy of the one God.

In the second and third centuries it took two different forms: modalist monarchianism (or Sabellianism) and dynamic monarchianism. The former gave modalism its theological foundation. Sabellius became a strong advocate of the modalist theology and held that the Father, Son, and the Spirit were simply serial modes or manifestations of God, or masks that God puts on Godself. In Sabellius' serial modalism, God appears serially in each mode in distinct periods in history: as God the Father in the Old Testament, as God the Son in Jesus, and as God the Holy Spirit since Pentecost.

However, the term *mask* is identical to *prosopon*, the word used in the definition of Chalcedon. The one God takes on three forms. In the form of the Father, God appears as the Creator; in the form of the Son, God appears as the Redeemer; and in the form of the Holy Spirit, God appears as the Sanctifier. This would mean that the same God who manifested Godself as the Father was crucified on the cross in the form of Christ. It excludes any relation or distinction in the triune God. Father, Son, and Spirit are three manifestations or modes of appearance of the One God

1. Moltmann, *Trinity and the Kingdom*, 127.

who is without distinction, unknowable and ineffable to us.[2] To the contrary, dynamic monarchianism describes the Son and Spirit as powers or energies (*dynameis*) emanating from God the Father who is one and has only one visage. Jesus has been made Son of God by the descending of the son-power upon him. Paul of Samosata, elected as the bishop in Antioch (about 260) and an advocate of dynamic monarchianism, interpreted the divine Logos as an attribute of the One God.[3] The single identity of Father and Son (*homoousios*) in this regard is affirmed. Therefore, God exists only as God's wisdom or power in Jesus Christ, and the Logos is not united to the humanity of Jesus.

Against monarchianism, Tertullian contends that the unity of God is balanced by *oikonomia* (*dispensatio*; *dispositio*). God is from all eternity One as the unity that is differentiated in itself. The economy of the divine being expresses the unity and monarchy of God (Father). In so doing, Tertullian insists on God's oneness and God's threefoldness, that is, the *trinitas*, a Latin term that seems to originate from him. According to him, there is only one God "under the following dispensation (*oikonomia*) that the only one God has a Son, God's Word, who proceeded from Godself, by whom all things were made, and without whom nothing was made."[4] The Father and the Son are in distinction, but not in separation. The monarchial idea that Father, Son, and Spirit are the selfsame Person is out of bounds.

According to Tertullian, the plurality of the *trinitas* does not imply a division of the unity. The unity that derives a *trinitas* from itself is dispensed. It should not lead to polytheism. In defending the monarchy, however, he sees the divine substance as tripersonal. The unity of God from which the Trinity is derived is actually administrated or economized by Son and Spirit. Tertullian's opponent Praxeas had upheld that God the Father was the person of Jesus Christ who came down into the virgin Mary and who later suffered. Tertullian's understanding basically excludes this Patripassianism, in a way that not the Father but the Son was born and suffered on the basis of the economy. He introduces the words *substantia* (substance) and *persona* (person). The unity of *substantia* safeguards the *oikonomia* by arranging the three *personae*, Father, Son, and Holy Spirit. These are three not in *substantia,* but in form and manifestation.

2. Ibid., 135–36.

3. Ibid., 132.

4. *Adv. Prax.* II (PL 2, 456); see LaCugna, *God for Us*, 28.

However, there is a subordinationist tendency in Tertullian because the monarchy is the starting point for his Trinity while the Son and Spirit are assigned second and third places. Therefore, he argues that the "Father is the entire substance, but the Son is a derivation and portion of the whole."[5] Since Tertullian, the Western Church has used substance to express common divinity between Father and Son. Person is used to mean each particular being. The term person, because of its translation from *prosopon*, seems suspect in being close to modalism in the eyes of the Eastern church.

However, the distinction between *ousia* and *hypostasis* remains obscure in the Eastern Church. *Ousia* designates not only a particular subsistence, but also the common substance of each particular. This obscurity is the same in the term *hypostasis*, which means literally substance, being used as equivalent to the Latin *persona* to designate the individual members of the Trinity. *Ousia* and *hypostasis* are translated as *substantia* in Latin, and thereby confusion arises. The teaching of the Trinity in the Eastern Church seems close to tritheism in the eyes of the Western Church, whereas Tertullian's formula "*una substantia tres personae*" sounds like modalism to the Eastern Church.

Origen (ca. 185–254) held the position of an eternity of the Son, and at the same time subordination to the Father. This twofold tendency is marked in his thought. For him, the Father, Son, and Spirit are substantially and inherently good, wise, and holy. Although the Son and the Spirit excel all created beings to a degree that allows no comparison, they are co-eternal and divine, not by platonic participation (*methexis*), but by their substance. "They are themselves excelled by the Father to the same or even a greater degree."[6]

Against the modalist monarchial notion held by the bishop Heraclides, Origen tries to safeguard God the Father in the absolute sense by distinguishing him qualitatively from the Son: the Son is not God in the absolute sense, but he is the image of Father's goodness. The Son was generated eternally from the Father "as the radiance of the eternal light."[7] The Spirit was also "the first of all that have been brought into being by God through Jesus Christ."[8] The radical qualitative distinction between

5. *Adv. Prax.* IX (PL 2, 205); see LaCugna, *God for Us*, 29.

6. *Comm. John XIII.* 25; see Heron, *Holy Spirit in the Bible*, 70–71.

7. *De Princ. I. ii. 2–6*; see Heron, *Holy Spirit in the Bible*, 71.

8. *Comm. John II.*10 (6); ibid., 71.

Father and Son remains unresolved for Origen. In a subordinationist note that can be traced from Tertullian, Origen differs from Paul of Samosata in that the former does not reject the divinity of Jesus Christ. Where Origen distinguishes God from the Son to highlight the unity of God, Paul of Samosata safeguards monotheism by coining the term *consubstantial* to designate the relationship between the Father and the Son. This is done, however, at the expense of the divinity of Jesus Christ.

Since the death of Origen, his disciples parted company from each other. The right wing of Origenism took over the aspect of the eternity of the Son in union with the Father, while the left-wing of Origenism put emphasis on the Son being subject to the Father in order to defend against Sabellianism. The teaching of Arius came in this midst. He argued that the Son is not God, but was created by God. Therefore the Son must have had a beginning. "Before he was begotten or created or defined or established, he was not. For he was not begotten. But we are persecuted because we say, 'the Son has a beginning, but God is without beginning.'"[9]

There has never been such a radical subordination since then. In agreement with Origen, Arius argues that the Father begets or generates the Son. In so doing this begetting occurred at a temporal point rather than an eternal movement within the divine life. In assuming that there was a time when the Son was not, Arius concluded that the eternal nature of God is one, not three.[10] God the Father is self-sufficient, eternal, ungenerate without beginning, not subject to emanation. The Son is created, and begotten timelessly before the ages. Therefore, he is neither everlasting nor unbegotten like the Father. If the Father and Son are of the same substance, we have two gods, Arius argued. The motto of Arianism, "there was when he was not," insists that Christ was begotten by God the Father in a time before other creatures. Christ is a creature, even though greater than other creatures. With excessive emphasis on the transcendence of God as the absolute, Arius maintained a strict unitarian monotheism. The subordination of Christ to God is in correspondence to subordination at the level of God's inner life. However, in regard to divine suffering, Arius affirmed that God can suffer in the person of the Logos, even though it is a lesser God who suffers. "He was passible by the Incarnation for if only soul and body suffered he could not have saved the world."[11]

9. LaCugna, *God for Us*, 31.

10. Bettenson, "Letter of Arius to Eusebius," 39.

11. LaCugna, *God for Us*, 34.

In the Council of Nicaea (325), Arius was condemned by the bishops at the council who affirmed that Jesus Christ was not created, but begotten of the substance of the Father, *homoousios* with the Father. By adding consubstantial between Father and Son (upon request of the Emperor Constantine), the Nicene creed safeguarded the divinity of the Son. The Son is "begotten of the Father as only begotten, that is, from the essence of the Father, God from God, Light from Light, true God from true God, begotten not created, of the same essence as the Father."[12] Nicea established the christological basis for a trinitarian theology, but it remained silent about the distinction between Father and the Son, and so tends to lean toward Sabellianism. Prior to Nicaea, *homoousios* was used by Paul of Samosata to mean the single identity of Father and Son.[13]

In the council of Constantinople (381), Arianism was defeated finally by the great effort of Athanasius, who was influenced by the right wing of Origenism. Athanasius understood *homoousios* as substance-unity (*Wesenseinheit*), while rivals of Athanasius understands it as substance-similarity (*Wesensgleichheit*). However, substance-unity without substance-similarity would lead to modalism, whereas substance-similarity without substance-sameness would tend to tritheism. However, in affirmation of the *homoousios* of Nicaea and the axiom of God's impassibility, Athanasius denied the real suffering of the Logos. "The Logos is by nature impassible, and yet because of that flesh which he assumed, these things are ascribed to him, since they are proper to the flesh, and the body itself is proper to the Savior. And while he himself, being impassible in nature, remains as he is, unaffected by them, but rather obliterating and destroying them."[14] In contrast to Arius, who concluded that the Son must be begotten and created, Athanasius proposed a trinitarian monotheism in which the Son is subordinated to the Father in the economy but not at the level of God's inner life.

The Cappadocian theologians (Basil, Gregory of Nyssa, Gregory of Nazianzus) found themselves defending the Niceno-Constantinopolitan creed against the extreme Arians, the Anhomoians led by Eunomius. According to the extreme Arians, the Son is altogether unlike the Father. Likewise, the Cappadocians defended themselves against the left-wing of the old Homoian Arianism (*homoias* = like), according to which the

12. Leith, "Creed of Nicaea," in *Creeds of the Churches*, 30–31.

13. González, *History of Christian Thought*, 267–71.

14. Cf. LaCugna, *God for Us*, 38.

incomparability of Father and Son is declared. While they were moving towards rapprochement with the Nicene Homoousians, a party led by Eustathius of Sebaste was moving in the opposite direction in which a Pneumatomachean tendency is developed. According to them, the Spirit is neither God nor creature, but free.

Against Eunomius, who as a neo-Arian affirmed the radical subordination of Son to Father, Basil distinguished between *God for us* in the economic Trinity and YHWH, in which economy is understood as the condescension (kenosis) of the Son of God to human status. *Oikonomia* is the divine self-expression in salvation history, meaning Jesus' human nature. For Basil, economy means condescension of the Son to human nature by his assumption of human characteristics. In a way similar to Basil, Gregory of Nazianzus and Gregory of Nyssa take *oikonomia* to be identical with the human nature assumed at the Incarnation. What is characteristic of Gregory of Nazianzus is that the *oikonomia* of human nature is "a voluntary self-limitation or accommodation."[15] God's condescension is in favor of human deification. "While his inferior nature, the humanity, became God, because it was united to God, and became one person because the higher nature prevailed—in order that I might become God as far as he has been made human."[16]

By distinguishing between the doctrine of the immanent Trinity and the doctrine of the economic Trinity as expressed by the Cappadocians, the language of the Trinity focuses on the Father's relationship to the Son in the intradivine life of God. In the Cappadocian response to Arianism and Eunomianism we see threads of mystical theology. The knowledge of God's work in the world is only a reflection of what God is, but not what God is. In other words, the nature of God remains unspeakable and unknowable like the hind parts of God that were shown to Moses between the gaps in the cliff (Exod 33:23).

The Council of Constantinople (381), in following the effort of the Cappadocians, affirmed the Trinity as one God existing in three *hypostases* that share one *ousia*. However, the Cappadocians were charged with teaching three gods by their opponents. They began to develop the formula *mia ousia, treis hypostaseis* (God exists as three subsistences in one nature), equivalent to the western *one substantia, and three personae* in a broader sense. Three particular subsistences participate in one divine *ousia*.

15. Ibid., 40.

16. Orat. 29, 19, SC 250:219. LaCugna, *God for Us*, 41.

Ousia is equivalent to what is common to the persons, while *hypostasis* is equivalent to what is proper and distinct. For example, Paul, Jane, and John can equally be called human, and this common nature is the *ousia*. However, particular individuals such as Paul, Jane, and John are each a *hypostasis* of an *ousia*. Paul and Jane (two *hypostases*) share the same *ousia*. Therefore, Paul and Jane are *homoousios* because of having a common *ousia*. Father, Son, and Spirit are distinct *hypostases*, which means individual subsistences of the divine *ousia*. *Ousia* expresses concrete existence (for example, Paul, Jane, and John), the divine *ousia* exists hypostatically (as individual Paul, Jane, and John), and therefore, there is no *ousia* apart from the *hypostases*.[17]

According to Basil, the Father, Son, and Spirit, who are one as three individuals, share a common nature. Even an analogy to three human individuals was drawn by Gregory of Nyssa. Of course, Gregory put great emphasis on "the oneness of the *ousia*, on the mutual indwelling of the three *hypostases*, and on the single cooperating activity of the entire Trinity."[18]

In the close approximation of *hypostasis* and *ousia*, *ousia* is ineffable, but God is manifest in the *hypostases* through the economy of salvation: the sending of the Son and Spirit by the Father. The essence of God is beyond every name. The divinity is only a name, not competent to describe God.[19] Nevertheless, Eastern theology generally tends to emphasize the distinct individuality of the three *hypostases* by safeguarding the divine unity in the respective and distinct origins of the Son and Spirit in and from the Father. This would be called the specter of tritheism.

In addition, the monarchy of the Father is strongly affirmed in that Son and Spirit receive divinity from the source. In so doing, the Father is understood as the ruling principle, the cause of Son and Spirit and the source of divinity. This monarchy is difficult to reconcile with a non-subordinationist trinitarian theology. From a perspective of relation of origin, the Father comes from nowhere, the Son is begotten by the Father, and the Spirit proceeds from the Father. The unknowable God is revealed to us through the economy of incarnation allowing for an economic subordination, because Son and Spirit are sent by the Father. The Father is the one who eternally is begetting the Son. So Father is the name (Begetter) of a

17. LaCugna, *God for Us*, 324.

18. Heron, *Holy Spirit in the Bible*, 83.

19. González, *History of Christian Thought*, 320–21.

relation to the Son (Begotten). In light of the doctrine of relations, the essence of God belongs to the Father who communicates divinity to Son and Spirit. However, the primacy of the Father is not weakened by the notion that Father, Son, and Spirit share a common *ousia*. The unity is based on the *ousia* held in common in which the persons exist perichoretically, mutually permeating one another. "For all the attributes of the Father are beheld in the Son, and all the attributes of the Son belong to the Father, in so much as the Son abides wholly in the Father and in turn has the Father wholly in Himself."[20]

In keeping with the tension between a strong monarchy and a common *ousia*, the Cappadocians made a distinction between divine ousia and the manifestation of God through the divine energies (*energeiai*). This apophatic move of the Cappadocians respects the fact that the *ousia* is incomprehensible in a way that the *hypostases* are not. This apophaticism, which in a way corresponds to the neo-Platonic spirituality of the Eastern tradition, is a basis for furthering the Areopagite's *theologia negativa* and the theology of Gregory Palamas in the fourteenth century.[21]

In addition, the sharp distinction between economy and theology makes it difficult to affirm the divine passibility in the full sense because the Logos suffers according to his humanity, but not according to his divinity. In response to Arianism, talk about the Trinity was focused on the meaning of God's inner being rather than the historical manifestation of God's condescension to flesh. John of Damascus (ca. 675–749) follows the Cappadocians. He argues that the Father, Son, and Spirit are one God and have one nature, neither one *hypostasis* nor one *prosopon*. It is impossible to call three *hypostases* of the Godhead one *hypostasis*, though they are in each other. The Trinity has one nature, one divinity, one power, one will, and one principle, which is recognized and venerated in three complete *hypostases*. In fact, the Trinity is conjoined but unmixed and distinguished but inseparable.[22]

20. R. Deferrari, *Saint Basil*, 227; see LaCugna, *God for Us*, 72.

21. Palamas' doctrine of divine essence and the uncreated divine energies (1296–1539) is regarded as representative of Greek patristic theology of the Trinity. Palamas' distinction between divine essence and energies has remained the standard for explaining the relationship between God's radical transcendence and human experience of the incomprehensible uncreated Light. However, the essential connection between *theologia* and *oikonomia* remains unresolved. Cf. LaCugna, *God for Us*, 184.

The one God is recognized only in the three particular subsistences of fatherhood, sonship, and the Spirit's procession. These three *hypostases* are in each other and have a reciprocal *perichoresis* (*circumincessio*). Though John of Damascus denies subordination in the Trinity emphatically, he affirmed that the Father is the origin (*arche*) of the Son and therefore greater than the Son. Because the Son is inferior to the Father, the Holy Spirit proceeds only from the Father, of course, communicated through the Son. "And we do not speak of the Spirit as from the Son, but yet we call it the Spirit of the Son . . . manifested and imparted to us through the Son."[23]

A subordinationist note between Father and the Son is dominant in the Eastern Church. Moreover, in terms of a distinction between the essence and the energies, God in God's essence remains the incomprehensible mystery, and in this mystery lies the generation of the Son and the sending forth of the Spirit. However, God can be reached by the activity of God's uncreated energies. At the level of energies, the Spirit, reflecting the Son and manifesting the glory incarnate in him, springs primarily "from the same One who is Father of the Son, not proceeds from both of Father and the Son."[24] In the Greek church and ecumenical councils of the ancient church, talk about the Trinity revolves around the priority of YHWH with respect to *God for us,* in which divine suffering does not come to full consideration.

However, at the fifth ecumenical council in Constantinople (553), the purpose was to interpret Chalcedon in such a way as to relieve Nestorian objections. John Grammaticus stresses the hypostatic unity to the point where human nature of Jesus cannot be separated from the divine hypostasis at any single moment. This is the so-called doctrine of the *enhypostasis* of human nature (Jesus) in the divine nature of Christ. Along the way, Leontius of Byzantium, as one of the neo-chalcedonian representatives, affirmed the unity of the man Jesus with the Son of God in the formula of the *enhypostasis* of Jesus in the eternal Logos. The man Jesus has the ground of his human existence not in humanity, but "in" an impersonal humanity of Christ.

The designation "en"-hypostasis expressed Jesus' human nature in unification with the Logos from the beginning. In the doctrine of *enhypostasis*, the Logos-*sarx* Christology tends to ignore Jesus' true humanity. Jesus was a human individual only in his unification with the Logos.

23. Quoted in Heron, *Holy Spirit in the Bible*, 84.

24. Ibid., 85.

Given this fact, the doctrine of *enhypostasis* leads to dyophysitism (from the Greek *dyo physeis*, "two natures"), speaking of two natures in Christ.[25] In response, Jesus' humanity is defined as a timeless substance. However, this teaching cannot be properly understood apart from the doctrine of the *anhypostasis*.[26] The term *anhypostasis* was attacked because it abolishes the true humanity. As a result, this led to the victory of monophysitism.

However, it must be kept in mind that *anhypostasis* as a negation is inseparably connected with *enhypostasis*, which means that Jesus Christ has a personal existence, but only in and through the Logos. If the Word of God is incarnated in the man Jesus Christ, his humanity is not abolished but fulfilled in union with the person, the *hypostasis*, of the Word of God. A tendency of deeming Jesus an independent personality (ebionitism, adoptionism, Nestorianism) would thereby be blocked.

As the Chalcedonian Christology stated, the Word exists in two natures, divine and human. However, the affirmation of two natures in Christ would imply that Christ has two existences, the one divine, and the other human. The contribution of Leontius was to interpret the chalcedonian formulation "in two natures" along the lines of the priority of the Word and the unity of the Word made flesh.

In terms of this doctrine, Leontius was able to hold that the humanity of Christ always exists in unity with his divinity, that is, in the eternal Logos. Through the affirmation that the humanity of Christ exists always in unity with the eternal Word is real humanity, docetism and ebiotism are ruled out. The positive side of this teaching, which rules out docetism, is called *enhypostasis* (existence in the Logos). The negative side is called *anhypostasis* (no other independent mode of existence apart from the eternal Logos), in which ebionitism is ruled out. The incarnated Word is always the preexistent eternal Word, the Son of God who became man (*enhypostasis*). Jesus the Man is always no other than the eternal Son of God (*anhypostasis*). Given this fact, the neo-chalcedonian representatives formulated the God-Man unity very sharply so that "*unus ex trinitate passus est in carne*" (one of the Trinity becomes passible in flesh).[27] The so-called theopaschite debate (519–534) concerned the passibility of God. Luther's understanding of divine passibility in the Trinity is thought to stand in the theopaschite tradition.

25. Cf. Pannenberg, *Jesus—God and Man*, 338–40.

26. *Handbuch*, 277–8; see *CD*, IV/2:49–50, 91–92.

27. *RGG* A–C, 1771.

Augustine and the Trinity

Augustine's theology of the Trinity is concerned with the articulation of one God who is Trinity. The Father, Son, and Holy Spirit are simultaneously distinct and co-essential, one in substance.[28] The three Persons are essential in the intra-trinitarian relations, and Augustine discusses the Trinity in the manner of a theo-psychology of the soul, which is created in the image of the Trinity and longs to return to God. In accepting the Trinity as an article of faith (*fides catholica*), he grounded himself in the tradition of the Cappadocian fathers. He followed the fathers who start from the differentiation of each *hypostasis* and move to the unity of the *ousia*. His difference from Greek theology is that Augustine begins with God's unity of substance, and moves to each differentiated particular. Augustine's concern is to explicate that "the Father, the Son, and the Holy Spirit constitute a divine unity of one and the same substance in an indivisible equality."[29] Being aware of the difference between the Greek notion of "one essence, three substances" (*hypostases*) and the Latin notion of "one essence or substance and three persons," Augustine maintains the unity of the divine essence rather than the monarchy of the Father by staying clear of ontological subordinationism.

According to Augustine, the Father is different from the Son, but not different in substance. This distinction is not one of substance, but of relation. The Father or the Son is not called such with respect to each divinity, but in mutual relationship, or in reference to another. As Augustine states, "Although to be the Father and to be the Son are two different things, still there is no difference in their substance, because the names, Father and Son, do not refer to the substance but to the relation, and the relation is no accident because it is not changeable."[30]

"Unbegotten" of the Father differs from "begotten" of the Son, not in a substantial sense but in a relative sense. However, Augustine made a move to equate person with substance beyond the relative character of a divine person. Therefore the person of the Father is no less than the substance of the Father. "For He is called a person in respect to Himself, not

28. Kelly, *Early Christian Doctrines*, 272.

29. *De Tri*, 1.4.7.

30. *De Tri, 5.5.6.* "But Father and Son together are not greater than the Holy Spirit, and no single Person of the Three is less than the Trinity Itself," (*De Tri 8. 1*); see Kelly, *Early Christian Doctrines*, 272.

in relation to the Son or to the Holy Spirit, just as He is called in respect to Himself, God, great, good, just, and other similar terms."[31]

Augustine's dissatisfaction with using substance for God in the plural would lead to the use of the term "person" with respect to substance and also in relation to the other persons of the Trinity.[32] In fact, Augustine prefers to use "essence" for naming God rather than "substance." If the person is equated with the substance, the essence of the Father lies not only in respect to himself, but also in relation to the Son and the Spirit. So, for Augustine, to be God and to be the Father or the Son or the Spirit is one and the same. Therefore, the relation is not relative per se, but subsists in relation to the essence. Divine persons become related to one another outside God's *oikonomia* in salvation history. In the taxonomy of salvation history, the Trinity has only one relation to the creature, one Principle, as they are one Creator and Lord.[33] The three Persons act as one principle (*unum principium*). "As They are inseparable, so They operate inseparably."[34]

For Augustine, the Trinity in the intra-divine life is the foundation for historical mission. The incarnation is accomplished by the triune God in one indivisible activity. In contrast to the sequence of the emanationist model of the Cappadocians, in which God is characterized by Father—Son—Holy Spirit—world, Augustine's theology of the Trinity is represented as a circle or triangle model. Augustine prefers to take the unity of God as the point of departure in considering the Trinity. His starting point within the unity of divine essence would lead to a dualistic tendency to separate the immanent Trinity from the economic Trinity. According to Augustine, *opera trinitatis ad extra indivisa sunt* (the works of the Trinity in the world are indivisible), God's activity in creation is the work of the whole Trinity. Put otherwise, as each of the Persons possesses the divine nature in a particular manner, so the role in the external and economical operation of the Godhead is appropriated to each of them in terms of each origin as Father, Son, and Holy Spirit.[35]

To distinguish a three-personed Godhead acting in history, he suggested what is called the doctrine of appropriation. That is to say, certain

31. *De Tri*, 7.6.11.

32. Cf. LaCugna, *God for Us*, 89–90.

33. *De Tri* 5.14.15.

34. *De Tri* 1.7.

35. Kelly, *Early Christian Doctrines*, 274.

activities in history are appropriated or assigned to each divine person. Some critical reservations in regard to this idea lie in the fact that the doctrine of appropriation would downplay the aspect of the inter-relatedness of the triune God and put excessive emphasis on individuality of each divine person as Creator, Redeemer, and Sanctifier in historical mission. According to LaCugna, there is no need for a doctrine of appropriation if one starts the theology of the Trinity from the economy of history on the basis of the essential unity of *economia* and *theologia*.[36] That is why "in relation to the creature, the Father, the Son, and the Holy Spirit are one Principle as they are one Creator and one Lord."[37]

Regardless of the fact that incarnation is accomplished by the Father, Son, and the Holy Spirit in one indivisible activity, Augustine has no intention of saying that the Trinity was born of Mary, crucified, and buried, then rose and ascended into heaven. From the perspective of the social doctrine of the Trinity in which *perichoresis* is understood as the sociality of the three divine Persons, Moltmann maintains that "God's triunity precedes the divine lordship." In this regard, Moltmann is critical of Augustine's rule of *opera trinitatis ad extra indivisa sunt* as a one-sided move, and poses a question to it.[38] From the perspective of consubstantiality of the three persons, we may say that the Trinity creates, the Trinity redeems, the Trinity sanctifies. While at the time, creation is appropriated to the Father, redemption to the Son, and sanctification to the Spirit in Augustine's theology.

Thus, in Augustine's theology the Father and Son produce the Holy Spirit, as Son is begotten by the Father. The self-relationality of divine persons is affirmed against the monarchy of God the Father. The Holy Spirit is distinguished from the Father and the Son and inherently related to the Giver and common gift between the Father and the Son.[39] The Spirit's communion with the Father and the Son is consubstantial and co-eternal. The Spirit is also the substance, and is called Love as well as Gift, because God is Giver and Love.[40]

Augustine, in thinking of the role of the Spirit as the bond of love between Father and Son, or a kind of communion of Father and Son

36. LaCugna, *God for Us*, 100.

37. Ibid., 98.

38. Moltmann, *Trinity and the Kingdom*, 93, 198–99.

39. *De Tri*, V. 12.

40. *De Tri*, VI. 7.

(*quaedam patris et filii communio*) attests that the Spirit, of God as well as of the Son, proceeds from both.[41] However, it is not a separate double procession, but a single simultaneous procession from both, in which the primacy of the father is affirmed, because the Son is generated from the father. As Augustine states, "God the Father alone is he from whom the Word is born, and from whom the Spirit principally proceeds. Therefore, I have added the word 'principally' because we find that the Holy Spirit proceeds from the Son also. But the Father gave this also to the Son, not as to one already existing and not yet possessing it; but whatever he gave to the only-begotten Word he gave by begetting him. Therefore, he so begot him that the common Gift should proceed from him also, and the Holy Spirit should be the Spirit of both."[42]

In general, a difference between Greek theology and Latin theology is often referred to as a different emphasis on a Tri-unity of divine persons over a Uni-Trinity of divine essence, or Unity over Trinity. What is more important in understanding Augustine is the fact that his starting point begins from the unity of intra-divine life rather than from the plurality of divine persons within the economy of salvation. He appropriated or assigned certain activities to one or another divine person in order to defend himself against charges of modalism; that is to say, creation to Father, redemption to the Son, and sanctification to the Holy Spirit in terms of his doctrine of appropriations.

From here the individuality is more accentuated than interrelatedness. The doctrine of appropriations is devised to assign an attribute or activity to one of the persons according to taxis of the economy without losing the con-substantiality of the three persons. The immanent Trinity calls for a doctrine of appropriation in regard to the economic Trinity. Some would fault Augustine's theology because in it the Trinity would be unbalanced by undermining the relationship between *theologia* (of intra-trinitarian relations and persons) and *oikonomia* (of the redemptive history).[43] In addition, Augustine's psychological approach to the Trinity focuses on the individual human soul as the true economy in which the

41. Kelly, *Early Christian Doctrines*, 274.

42. *De Tri* XV. 29. Cf. Kelley, *Early Christian Doctrines*, 47.

43. LaCugna, *God for Us,* 97–100. As she remarks, "once the Augustinian axiom that 'works of the Trinity ad extra are one' is affirmed, and the economy no longer gives access to the distinctions of persons, then the corrective of a doctrine of appropriations is needed in order to restore a proprium to each divine person," (Ibid., 102).

capacity to know the Trinity may occur apart from the incarnation.[44] The soul may know God by knowing itself apart from its social relations, even apart from God's economy of redemption. The critique asserts that the distinction of the divine persons in the economy of salvation gives way to an individualistic economy centering on the relationship between God and the soul.

Luther and the Doctrine of the Trinity

Luther's understanding of the Trinity is characterized by its focus on divine suffering. He is aware of the fact that from the ancient church onward there has been a close relationship between the doctrine of the Trinity and the incarnation. Although rejecting Patripassianism, Luther boldly affirms that God suffers in Jesus Christ. The Holy Spirit who works to create faith in Jesus Christ is the Spirit of communication of divine suffering.

As we have already seen in the development of the doctrine of the Trinity in the ancient church, the Latin fathers used *substantia* and *essentia* while the Greek fathers used *ousia*. For expressing the threeness of God the Latin fathers used *persona*, which is equivalent to *hypostasis* for the Greek fathers. Luther's reservations about the word *homoousios* and his dissatisfaction with the concept of *persona* notwithstanding, he knew that there was no better term available in expressing God as the triune God. In a sermon on John 1 in 1537, Luther states, "For want of a better term, we have had to use the word 'person'; the fathers used it too. It conveys no other meaning than that of a hypostasis."[45]

For Luther, the terms such as "trinitas," "Dreifaltigkeit" (threefoldness), "gedritts" (thirds), or "Dreheit" (threeness) would be risky and tempting, even seeming blasphemous because of sounding like tritheism. Luther feels that the ancient dogmatic terms are not rich enough to articulate and express his own concept of the Trinity. Luther's understanding of Trinity becomes manifest and explicit in his writings such as *The Three Symbols or Confession of the Belief of Christ* (1538), *On the Councils and Churches* (1539), and *On the Last Words of David* (1543).[46]

44. Augustine develops *vesitigia Trinitatis* (traces of the Trinity) in analyzing the idea of love to facilitate our understanding of the Trinity. He locates the image of God in the human capacity to remember, understand, and love God, (*De Tri* xiv.15).

45. *LW*, 22:16.

46. Ibid., 34:199ff; *WA*, 50:262–83 ("The Three Symbols"). *LW*, 41:3 ff; *WA*, 50:547, 12ff ("On the Councils and the Churches"), *LW*, 15:265ff; *WA*, 54, 28–100 ("On the Last

The doctrine of the Trinity for Luther belongs to an *articulus fidei* confessed and witnessed by the scriptures. The prologue of John's Gospel especially shows and affirms the doctrine of the Trinity, in which God is three distinct persons yet one God.[47] As far as the Trinity is an article of faith, a new grammar and a new language are required to describe and express God's majesty and mystery in which we can talk about the Trinity adequately and correctly through faith, not through reason and philosophy. In his explication of Ps 33:6, Luther says that three persons—the Lord, God's Word, and God's Spirit—are mentioned even though David confesses no more than one Creator. "The Lord does not do His own work separately, the Word does not do His own work separately, and the Breath does not do His work separately."[48] In following the creed of Athanasius, Luther neither separates the simple divinity nor mixes or confuses the three persons: "God in three persons and three persons in one single Godhead."[49]

In order to avoid tritheism, Luther advocates Augustine's principle, *opera trinitatis ad extra sunt indivisa* (all three personae are one God, acting in full unity in relation to the world). The Trinity, which Luther confesses as the "sublime article of the majesty of God," is along the line of Augustine's fundamental principle concerning a dialectics of distinction but no separation of relationship between the immanent Trinity and the economic Trinity.[50] The immanent Trinity, while necessarily distinguished, at the same time must not be separated from God's economic action toward the world.

As Luther states, according to the scripture "the Father is a different and distinct person from the Son in the one indivisible and eternal Godhead. The difference is that He is the Father and does not derive His Godhead from the Son or anyone else. The Son is a Person distinct from the Father . . . since He was born of the Father from eternity. The Holy Spirit is a person distinct from the Father and Son in the same one Godhead. The difference is that He is the Holy Spirit, who eternally proceeds both from the Father and the Son, and who does not have the Godhead for

Words of David").

47. *LW*, 22: 5.

48. Ibid., 15:302.

49. Ibid., 34:205, "Three Symbols."

50. Ibid., 37:361, "Confession Concerning Christ's Supper."

Himself nor from anyone else but from both the Father and the Son, and all of this from eternity to eternity."[51]

Luther's affirmation of three persons becomes visible in *opera ad intra* in the intradivine life rather than in the economic relations of the Trinity *ad extra*.[52] Luther appropriates Augustine's distinction between *res* (reality) and *signum* (sign), applying it to the revelation of the Son in a modified sense to emphasize that the humanity of Christ is not a mere sign or figure. "The humanity in which God's Son is distinctively revealed is reality, it is united with God in one person, which will sit eternally at the right hand of God."[53] The Holy Spirit is revealed to us in the form of the dove as an image of the Holy Spirit, as God the Father is revealed to us in the form of voice as an image. However, Jesus' humanity is eternally bound to the Son of God in which incarnation affects and sharpens Luther's understanding of the Trinity. "The Father is not known except in the Son through the Holy Spirit."[54]

Therefore, a dialectical relationship between the sign of the voice and the sign of the dove (in the case of Jesus' baptism) is related to sign-reality in the humanity of Jesus. Luther, in his commentaries on Gen 1 and John 1, follows in the footsteps of Augustine and Hilary, taking into account "appropriations" in the expression of Father, Son, and Holy Spirit concerning creation, redemption, and sanctification. At the same time he does not forget to stress the unity of the works of the Godhead. "Nor is it possible in this manner to divide God subjectively, for the Father is not known except in the Son and through the Holy Spirit."[55]

Luther's notion of the Trinity, when seen from the incarnation, comes close to God's Triunity (*Dreieinigkeit*) because an eternal birth of the Son in the *perichoresis* of the immanent Trinity is highlighted in a historical incarnation of the Son in the *perichoreis* of the economic Trinity. However, when his Trinity is seen from the perspective of a single appropriation it is inclined to God's Unitrinity. In other words, there is a striking balance in Luther between the western tendency toward the unity of divine nature and the eastern tendency toward a perichoretic participation.

51. Ibid.,15:303; *WA*, 54:58.

52. Jansen, *Studien zu Luther's Trinitätslehre*, 197.

53. *LW*, 15:308.

54. Ibid., 1:58.

55. Ibid.,1:58.

In his explanation of the Apostle's Creed, Luther's remarks are worth quoting.[56] "For however creating and sustaining all things, atoning for sins, forgiving sins, awakening from death and giving the gift of eternal life are works that no other than God can do, nevertheless there are special works here that are ascribed to each Person distinctly, so that Christians have one simple, certain understanding, that there is only one God, and nevertheless three persons in the one unified Divine Essence."[57] *Homoousios* unity and a primacy of the Father in threefoldness of divine *hypostases* is characteristic of Luther's theology of the Trinity.[58]

In *The Three Symbols* (1538) Luther, quoting Athanasius, says, "The Father is of no one, neither born nor made nor created. The Son is of the Father, not made or created but born. The Holy Spirit is of the Father and the Son, not born or created, but proceeding."[59] Luther affirms the eternal begetting of the Son by the Father by reflecting on Ps 2:7: "The Lord said to me, 'you are my son, today I have begotten or borne you'"[60]

In his commentary on John 15:26, Luther justifies the *filioque* in contrast to the doctrine of Eastern Church, which rejected the procession of the Spirit from the Father and from the Son. Augustine's reflection on the *filioque* becomes meaningful for Luther. "To be sent" and "to proceed" refer to two different aspects of the same action. Therefore the Holy Spirit proceeds from both the Father and the Son. "Just as the Son is born of the Father and yet does not depart from the Godhead, but on the contrary remains in the same Godhead with the Father and is one God with him, so also the Holy Spirit proceeds from the Father and is sent by the Son, and does not depart from the Godhead either, but remains with the Father and the Son in the same Godhead, and is one God with both."[61]

The Father is the origin of the Son, and likewise the origin of procession of the Spirit. The eternal generation of the Son and the eternal procession of the Spirit become presupposition and premise for the mission of the Son and the Spirit for the world. The Son's immanent birth and the Spirit's immanent procession protect Luther from a modalist tendency, and the difference between the Persons is witnessed and affirmed in the

56. *WA*, 41:276, 39–277, 16.

57. Ngien, *Suffering of God*, 241.

58. Lienhard, *Luther: Witness to Jesus Christ*, 165.

59. *LW*, 34:216ff.

60. Ibid., 34:216; 12:49.

61. Ibid., 34:217.

gospel. For Luther, the immanent Trinity stands in symmetry and correspondence with the economic Trinity. If Christ is born physically in our world, he is born eternally in God. If God the Father is the Creator of the world, God's origin and essence must be in Godself from whom the Son and the Spirit come. God's historical revelation in three Persons mirrors and corresponds to God's being beforehand in eternity.[62]

However, for Luther the Trinity is known only by God's act in Jesus Christ and the Holy Spirit. The economic Trinity becomes a basis for deducing the immanent Trinity. In this way the economic Trinity is the self-manifestation and communication of the immanent Trinity. In other words, the immanent Trinity becomes a theological presupposition for the economic Trinity. In reflection of a corresponding relationship between the immanent Trinity and the economic Trinity, Luther states, "Therefore it was indeed fitting that the middle Person was physically born and became a Son, the same who was born beforehand in eternity and is Son . . . The Holy Spirit proceeds physically, the same who proceeds in eternity and is neither born nor Son. And thus the Father remains of himself, so that all three Persons are in majesty, and yet in such a manner that the Son has his Godhead from the Father through his eternal immanent birth (and not the other way round), and that the Holy Spirit has his Godhead from the Father and the Son through his eternal immanent proceedings."[63]

God for us, is, in Luther's view, at the center of understanding the Trinity from which YHWH can be deduced. Luther is not concerned about beginning with the Trinity from the metaphysical speculation about YHWH. This would be a theology of glory. For Luther, a theology of glory is based on human reason, speculation, and works righteousness, which humans use to attempt to reach God. Starting from a concrete, historical act of *God for us* in Jesus Christ, Luther moves to the mystery of YHWH. "The Son shows his eternal birth through his physical birth, and the Holy Spirit shows his eternal proceeding through his physical proceeding. Each of them has an external likeness or image of his internal essence."[64] God eternally is in Godself as Father, Son, and the Holy Spirit even before God created, redeemed, and sanctified. *The opera trinitatis ad extra* and *the opera trinitatis ad intra* can be distinguished but cannot be separated.

However, a point of departure for Luther, unlike Augustine, is God *ad extra*, which is in correspondence with God *ad intra*. An understanding

62. Ibid., 34:218. Cf. *CD*, 1/1:383.

63. *LW*, 34:218.

64. Ibid.

of *theologia* cannot be possible without an understanding of *oikonomia.* A Christian confession of God the Trinity is "the highest article in faith—the articles on which all the others hang."[65] At the same time, the central article of the creeds concerning Jesus Christ, to which all the others attach themselves and refer, is basically trinitarian in its intent. In this regard, Luther's new language of the Trinity (*novis linguis*) can be seen in his affirmation of the Augustinian tradition in a neo-chalcedonian realistic approach to divine suffering in which the speculative tone of the Cappadocian theologians would be avoided.[66] "Whoever comes in touch with the man Christ also comes in touch with the Son of God. In fact, the whole Trinity is found in this man."[67]

A christological approach to the doctrine of the Trinity is compatible with the teaching of justification by faith. In fact, his doctrine of justification has a trinitarian structure. Apart from Jesus Christ who, as "a mirror of the Father's heart," "revealed and opened to us the most profound depths of his fatherly heart, his sheer unutterable love," "we see nothing but an angry and terrible judge." "God has given us his Son and his Holy Spirit through whom he brings us to himself." "But neither could we know anything of Christ, had it not been revealed by the Holy Spirit."[68]

The God who acts to justify, to redeem, and to sanctify us is who God is as Father, Son, and Spirit eternally and beforehand. If the economic Trinity were no less than the self-manifestation of the immanent Trinity, would it be meaningful to distinguish the latter from the former? However, Luther, refraining from metaphysical speculation about YHWH, views God primarily, concretely, and historically in terms of his economic activity. In other words, YHWH should be understood in terms of *God for us*. Here the cross is the theological basis for approaching the Trinity. At this point we see a trinitarian theology of divine suffering, that is, the cross-centered Trinity.

In his trinitarian theology, Luther tries to avoid subordination of the Spirit to the Son, although he recognizes the *filioque*. "Christ was sent by the Father and the Holy Spirit."[69] The Father and the Spirit participate in Christ's act of self-humiliation, and God experiences Son's death. Faith,

65. *WA*, 7:214, 27ff.

66. Cf. Markschies, "Luther und Die Altkirchliche Trinitätstheologie," 79.

67. *LW*, 22:246; *WA*, 46:555; see Ngien, *Suffering of God*, 243.

68. *BC*, 419.

69. *LW*, 17:165.

which is created by the Spirit as a gift of the Spirit, is the justifying faith in the crucified Christ. It is the work of the Spirit that enables faith in the heart of the believers. For Augustine, the Spirit is given to us as grace, and awakens in us love for God. However, Luther takes faith to be the effect of the Spirit instead of love. "The Spirit of prayer (cf. Rom 8:26) draws us to Christ in faith, the Spirit of grace places us in the reality of Christ as his instruments in the work of love."[70] Luther's principle of "*Christo formata fidei*" has a trinitarian relevance and exemplifies the anthropological dimension of faith.

In his quarrels with Karlstadt, Müntzer, and others, what is striking for Luther is an outwardly-inwardly relation. Outwardly, the Spirit works through material signs, i.e., baptism and the sacrament of the altar. Inwardly, the Spirit awakens faith and bestows other spiritual gifts to us. "The inward experience follows and is effected by the outward." In other words, the Spirit is not separated from the outward Word and sacraments. "God has determined to give the inward to no one except through the outward. For he wants to give no one the Spirit or faith outside of the outward Word and sign instituted by him."[71] The Spirit, for Luther, is the mediator and communicator of the real presence of Christ in faith. This is characteristic of Luther's understanding of *ordo salutis.* For attaining the treasure of Christ's salvation, God gives us the Spirit. We know nothing of Christ if Christ is not revealed by the Spirit to "inculcate the sufferings of Christ for the benefit of our salvation."[72]

From here we see that Luther's *theologia crucis* is of trinitarian character, because with respect to God's eternal unity with the Son, God is not an impassable God. Rather in the presence of the Spirit God accompanies the Son's life, death, and resurrection for us. Therefore, Luther takes *conformitas Christi*, that is, participation in the suffering of Christ, to be the work of the Holy Spirit. A spirituality of *Anfechtungen* is based on the work of the Spirit justifying, awakening, and sanctifying us toward a final transformation in an eschatological dynamism. "We are not suffering because of public scandal or vice such as adultery, fornication, murder, etc. Rather we suffer because we hold to the word of God, preach it, hear it, learn and practice it."[73]

70. Ibid., 25:296.

71. *LW*, 40:146.

72. Ibid., 37:365.

73. Ibid., 51:198.

Conformitas Christi presupposes and characterizes our discipleship and participation in the world in willingness to accept God's passion and solidarity for the world. This points to a reality of transformation of human existence that stands under the work of the Spirit through word and sacraments. Therefore, a conformity to Christ is not a medieval idea of *imitatio Christi*, but an active participation of discipleship in the world by proclaiming the gospel of the crucified Christ. Christ as the sacrament precedes Christ as an example, although this does not ignore the significance of our discipleship. "Christ is our abstraction. We are His concretion."[74]

The Holy Spirit creates faith in us and brings us to conformity to the crucified. Christ becomes a treasury of all divine blessings for us by destroying and conquering the curse of all creatures. In sum, the Father gives, the Son atones and reconciles, and the Spirit communicates the redemption of Christ through inward-outward means through which the Spirit "inculcates the suffering of Christ" for our salvation. Luther's Trinity calls for prophetic *diakonia*, discipleship, and willingness to conform to the suffering of Christ in the world.

The Trinity in Ecumenical Context: The Monarchical Trinity or a Social Doctrine of the Trinity

In our discussion of the Trinity in an ecumenical context, we will begin with Karl Barth. Karl Barth provides the most insightful solution for the problem of the Trinity. Although ecumenical conversations frequently touch on the Trinity, I will confine my discussion to Barth and Moltmann because they are influenced by Martin Luther, albeit in different ways. We will focus on two different understandings of the theology of the Trinity in Barth. First of all, Barth presented his doctrine of the Trinity explicitly within the framework of the doctrine of the Word of God in the first volume of his *Church Dogmatics*. Barth developed his exposition of the "triune God" at the very beginning of his discussion of the nature of revelation.[75]

The Word of God has three forms: preached, written, and revealed. The last is the basis for the others. God's being is being in the act, and the specific act is revealing. According to Barth, God reveals Godself. God

74. Ibid., 11:318.

75. *CD*, I/1: 295–489. For Tillich's critique of Barth's priority of the Trinity in systematic theology, see Tillich, *Systematic Theology* III, 285.

reveals Godself through Godself. God the Revealer is identical with God's act in revelation and also with its effect.[76]

Therefore, the event of revelation is the starting point for understanding the Trinity. Revelation is God's self-interpretation. According to Barth, the structure of revelation represents the structure of the Trinity as revealer—revelation—revealedness. "Thus to the same God who in unimpaired unity is the Revealer, the revelation and the revealedness, there is also ascribed in unimpaired differentiation within Himself this threefold mode of being . . . we are set before the problem of the doctrine of the Trinity."[77] In the biblical witness to revelation, Barth emphasized "the three elements of unveiling, veiling and impartation, or form, freedom and historicity, or Easter, Good Friday and Pentecost, or Son, Father and Spirit," because this order shows that revelation must indeed be understood as the root or ground of the doctrine of the Trinity.[78] Any *vestigium trinitatis* (traces of the Trinity) in the created order is out of the question. Jesus Christ is the manifestation of the Father who meets and involves himself with human being in the Spirit. This is the heart of Barth's doctrine of the Trinity.

To defend against *analogia entis* (analogy of being) or *trinitas vestigia* (traces of the Trinity) insinuating themselves into the doctrine of the Trinity, Barth attests that "God reveals himself as the Lord." However, his statement has been criticized by some scholars for the way that Barth deduced the existence of the three divine persons or modes of being from his concept of revelation. According to Moltmann, Barth turns Tertullian's principle *una substantia—tres personae* into "one divine subject in three different modes of being." Barth's starting point in the self-revelation of God concentrates on the subjectivity of God. The three divine modes of being are understood merely as three repetitions in God in his doctrine of the Trinity, not three divine I's but thrice of one divine I.[79]

This is where the problem in Barth's doctrine of the Trinity lies.[80] It would not be trinitarian, but a tautology to view God's threefold nature as eternal repetition or to understand the three Persons as a triple repetition of one and the same God.[81] God's triple reiteration of Godself gains more

76. *CD*, I/1:296.

77. Ibid., 299.

78. Ibid., 332.

79. Ibid., 370.

80. Moltmann, *History and the Triune God*, 131.

81. Ibid., 141.

prominence than God's relation to Godself. Although emphasizing both the unity and the threefoldness with God, Barth tends to give priority to the former.[82]

In the passion of Christ, Barth sees the Father taking a share. For Barth, the cross is where God is most clearly revealed.[83] "The proper being of the one true God [is] in Jesus Christ the crucified."[84] To avoid patripassianism, Barth remarks that we have not a loving, suffering, dying Son without a Father who is involved and shares in him in a different way. "God gives himself, but he does not give himself away. He does not give up being God . . . He does not come into conflict with himself . . . He acts as Lord over this contradiction even as he subjects himself to it."[85] Following in the footsteps of Luther, Barth does not hesitate to affirm the Father's participation in the suffering of the Son. *Theologia crucis* is prominent in Barth's reflection on the Trinity.

Be that as it may, with respect to the role of the Holy Spirit, Barth is charged with ignoring the Holy Spirit as the third Person in the Trinity because the Spirit, as the common bond of love, is regarded as "essence of the relation between these two modes of being of God."[86] The Spirit as the third Person of the Trinity has no independent role with respect to Father and Son. Barth's phrase "God in Christ" often causes an impression of pointing to a binitarian relationship, that is, the Father in the Son.[87] There is a tendency in modern theology to identify the immanent and the economic Trinities in terms of Rahner's rule.

It is not exactly so in Barth; the immanent Trinity can neither be identified with, nor separated from, the economic one. It is Eberhard Jüngel, who develops the dilemma between the aseity of God and the relationality of God on the basis of the principle of correspondence. The title of his book explains that "God's Being is in Becoming." According to Jüngel, relationality exists with the divine being, already within the immanent Trinity in the sense of *perichoresis* before God created a world. In this regard, God's relationship to the world *ad extra* corresponds to the interpersonal relationality within the divine life *ad intra*.

82. Ibid., 139–44.

83. *CD*, IV/2:84–85, 357.

84. *CD*, IV/1:199.

85. *CD*, IV/1:185.

86. *CD*, I/1:480.

87. Moltmann, *Trinity and the Kingdom*, 143.

On the basis of a correspondence between YHWH and *God for us*, Jüngel maintains God's aseity while at the same time affirming God's relation to the world. Following in the footsteps of Barth, Jüngel stresses the oneness of God in which Augustine's axiom, *opera trinitatis ad extra sunt indivisa*, is strongly affirmed. This unity of God is an eternal process of becoming unified rather than a simple undifferentiated unity. God's being is understood essentially as a double relational being in which God's relationship to the world *ad extra* realizes itself on the basis of the interpersonal relationality of God's being *ad intra*, that is, a being related to itself. In fact, Barth's language of *analogia relationis* is at the heart of the principle of correspondence. "The reiteration as God's relation to us is the correspondence to God's relatedness: *analogia relationis.*"[88]

Nevertheless, Jüngel loses sight of Barth's epistemological principle, "*esse sequitur operari*" (God's being is known and explained in terms of God's historical act) in connection with Jewishness of Jesus Christ and God's coming reality. Jüngel's ontological localization of "God's being in becoming" is vulnerable to Barth's insight, according to which God communicates Godeslf in the history of God's coming.

At any rate, Barth, in dealing with God's personality, is afraid of using ego or subject because three egos or three subjects can lead to tritheism. Therefore, he prefers to use *Seinsweise* of God rather than Persons. With the mode of being in mind, Barth distinguishes the three ways in which God exists.

However, because of Barth's emphasis on God's lordship, Moltmann accuses Barth of being a strong advocate of Christian monotheism.[89] Thereby the lordship of God precedes Trinity for the sake of securing the sovereignty of God.[90] But later, in the doctrine of God, Barth asserts that the essence of God is twofold: freedom and love. In other words, God is One who loves in freedom. This entails Barth's socio-political concept of God in the Trinity. In the *Church Dogmatics*, Barth speaks of God as "the fact that not only newly illuminates, but also really transforms reality."[91]

88. Jüngel, *Doctrine of Trinity*, 104. However, Jüngel in his later book, *God as the Mystery of the World*, is in agreement with Rahner's rule in which *God for us* (*oikonomia*) becomes YHWH (*theologia*). At this point, *analogia relationis* (analogy of relation) or the principle of correspondence is meaningless, (Jüngel, *God as the Mystery*, 369–70). For the critique of Jüngel's unqualified agreement with Rahner's rule, see Peters, *God as Trinity*, 96.

89. "With the doctrine of the Trinity, we step on to the soil of Christian monotheism," (*CD*, I/1:354)

90. Moltmann, *Trinity and the Kingdom*, 141.

91. "*Alle und in Allem Alles nicht nur beleuchtenden, sondern real veränderenden Tatsache*

God in the Trinity is not a metaphysical basis for interpreting the world, but the grounding reality for transforming it. This is a political consequence of relating the trinitarian understanding of God to God's love in freedom.[92]

Jürgen Moltmann

Coming from the influence of Martin Luther and Karl Barth, but with a critical stance, Moltmann represents the theology of social trinitarianism. In his famous book, *The Crucified God*, Moltmann gives a trinitarian basis for understanding the meaning of the cross. In doing this, he reversed the soteriological question of "what do the suffering and death of Christ mean for us?" and turned it into the theological question of "what do the suffering and death of Christ mean for God?"[93] His answer is that the Father's pain over the death of the Son. It is one divine passion that leads to the pain of the Father, the death of the Son and the sighing of the Spirit: the passion of love for lost creatures. Moltmann's deliberation points to the death of the "fatherhood" of the Father in the death of the Son that is the basis for the relationality and death in the Trinity. Thus, Moltmann is able to avoid patripassianism because we can see there is a profound death in the Father, but it is a relational death, not an actual death of the Father's being.

In this way Moltmann finds it possible to see the cross on Golgotha at the heart of the triune God, so as to perceive the revelation of God in the crucified Jesus. There is no need to avoid suffering of God because the Father suffers with the Son, but not in the same way.[94] Although Moltmann is critical of the theopaschite position, he prefers to be on the side of theopathy, a term that he coined.[95]

According to Moltmann, the Trinity is actually constituted by the event of the cross. The historical event of Christ is constitutive of the divine life proper. "God suffers with us—God suffers from us—God suffers for us: it is this experience of God that reveals the triune God."[96] Therefore, the God of monotheism can be avoided because of the divine

dass Gott ist," *KD*, II/1:289. Cf. Hunsinger, *Karl Barth and Radical Politics*, 68.

92. Marquardt, *Theologie und Sozialismus*, 230.

93. Ibid., 25.

94. Moltmann, *Crucified God*, 203.

95. Moltmann, *Trinity and the Kingdom*, 25.

96. Ibid., 4.

passibility. Along the lines of Luther, the *theologia crucis* for Moltmann should become trinitarian.

The cross was internal to God's own trinitarian experience. God as Trinity not only affects, but also is affected by the world. From this starting point at the cross, there is no possibility of preserving the traditional distinction between the immanent and the economic trinities. Therefore, Moltmann follows Rahner's rule in rejecting the distinction between the immanent and the economic Trinities. "God's relationship to us is threefold. And this threefold (free and unmerited) relationship to us is not merely an image or analogy of the immanent Trinity; it is this Trinity itself, even though communicated as free grace."[97] From the key standpoint of the cross, he envisaged the Trinity as a trinitarian history of God in the world in which Moltmann, beyond the traditional language of the Spirit as the bond of love, tries to assign independent personhood to the Spirit in a trinitarian history of God in the world.

According to Moltmann, there are three forms in which we know the Trinity. Moltmann calls the first form the monarchical form because it is characterized by the descending order: Father-Son-Spirit, or God-Spirit-Word. It is the scheme to be found generally in the Western theology, according to which all the activity of God in the world comes from the Father, is mediated by the Son and is brought to the final completion in the power of the Spirit. In other words, the Father creates through the Son in the Spirit. Therefore, the Spirit proceeds from the Father and his mission in the Son.[98]

In this monarchical form of the Trinity, the Spirit does nothing of its own but implements the work of the Father and the Son. The Father redeems through the Son in virtue of the Holy Spirit. The Father sends the Son and the Spirit. The Spirit brings to fulfillment the action of the Father and the Son. However, here the personality of the Spirit can hardly be recognized. Becoming the bond of love between Father and the Son, the Spirit appears only as the Spirit of the Father and the Son. This trinitarian form is often seen especially in the case of Karl Barth and Karl Rahner. Both of them take the starting point from the event of self-revelation (Barth) or self-communication (Rahner) of the One God. What is at stake in this form is that "the unity of God precedes the Triunity."[99]

97. Moltmann, *Crucified God*, 240.

98. Moltmann, *History and the Triune God*, 68.

99. Moltmann, *Spirit of Life*, 290.

This movement is characterized by the single movement that proceeds from the Father through the Son in the Spirit. However, Moltmann's strong charge against them is that they express the one divine self in the three modes of Father, Son, and Spirit by identifying the divine subject with the unity and not the plurality in order to avoid tritheism. For Moltmann tritheism has never been a danger to Christian theology. Rather, monotheism is the real danger.

According to Moltmann, Barth's starting point is the lordship of God, which amounts to overemphasis on one personal subject with three modes of being. Moltmann reads Barth's formula of one subject in three modes of being as Sabellian modalism.[100] His disagreement with Barth comes out of the fact that in Barth the sovereignty of God and the notion of God as absolute subject coincide. Therefore, the doctrine of the Trinity is understood as an interpretation of this fact: God reveals Godself as Lord. Inevitably, the Trinity is collapsed into the threefold repetition of a single subject. The result is Barth's alleged modalism (only one divine subject in three modes of being). Like Barth, Rahner describes God as a single divine subject in three distinct modes of subsistence. Rahner's term *Dreifaltigkeit* (Threefold God) needs to be replaced by the *Dreieinigkeit* (three-in-oneness). To Moltmann, *Dreifaltigkeit* is modalistic. However, Moltmann overlooked Barth's use of *Dreieinigkeit.*[101] Despite his critique of Rahner, Moltmann allies himself with Rahner's rule by stating that the cross comes to stand only in the economy of salvation, not within the immanent Trinity. "That is why I have affirmed and taken up Rahner's thesis that the economic Trinity is the immanent Trinity and vice versa."[102]

At this point, Moltmann rejects Barth and Jüngel's *via analogia relationis*, the principle of correspondence. For Moltmann, the monarchical form of the Trinity would be based on "the identity model" in such a way that God's nature is in God's operations. Therefore, this is understood as "the model of a functional doctrine of the Trinity."[103] This is interpreted as a doctrine about the Trinity in the sending. The Father is the sender of the Son and the Spirit. The Spirit is sent by the Father and the Son. This movement expresses the threefold God, or Uni-Trinity.

The second form, which Moltmann calls the eucharistic form, is the direct reversal of the monarchical form of the Trinity in which we give

100. Moltmann, *Trinity and the Kingdom*, 139.

101. *CD*, I/1:423.

102. Moltmann, *Trinity and the Kingdom*, 160.

103. Moltmann, *Spirit of Life*, 292.

praise to God for God's work of salvation. In our praise of God, the Spirit is glorifying the Son and through the Son and together with him the Father till the completion of salvation. In this regard, activity proceeds from the indwelling Spirit and all mediation takes place through the Son and with him to the Father. The Father is the recipient of the thanksgiving and praise from God's creatures. The eucharistic form of the Trinity is characterized by the order of Spirit-Son-Father and here the Spirit is the real subject of an activity in relation to the Son and the Father. In the monarchical form, the Spirit is subordinated to the Father and the Son because of the Spirit's activity from the Father and by the Son in the world.

Likewise in the eucharistic form, the Spirit is subordinated to the Son and the Father because of the Spirit's glorification of them. This form is highlighted by the Orthodox Church in celebration of the Eucharist. The monarchical "sending" Trinity in which the sending of the Son and the Spirit is related to the proclamation of the gospel and doing discipleship in the world is the external basis for the Eucharist because the monarchical form of the Trinity reaches its goal in the latter. Orthodox teaching of *theosis* affirms this direction well. As the *katabasis* (God's descent to human being) has its place in the monarchical Trinity in the sending, so the *anabasis* (Human ascent to God) does in the eucharistic Trinity in glory. This form expresses Triunity.

Both forms of the Trinity belong to the history of salvation. They are transcended brilliantly by the third form that Moltmann proposes, which he calls the trinitarian doxology. The trinitarian doxology gives worship and glory to Father, Son, and Spirit together, following the Nicene creed: "Who with the Father and the Son together is worshiped and glorified." The trinitarian doxology appears, for Moltmann, to secure a freedom of the immanent Trinity in relation to the economic Trinity. In worship and glorification the triune God is loved and praised for God's own sake. In this doxology there is no trinitarian order in which we move from praise of God for God's works to the adoration of God for God's own sake in contemplation of the eternal being of the Trinity itself. This is where the concept of the immanent Trinity finds its life setting.[104]

Here, the Spirit is seen in the Spirit's eternal fellowship with the Father and the Son. The Spirit no longer appears in its temporal order, after or under the Son and the Father. The Spirit appears in its eternal *perichoresis* and perfection. Here, the eucharistic Trinity turns into the

104. Ibid., 302.

trinitarian doxology by transforming thanksgiving into prayer, faith into sight. The eschatological hope begins in anticipation of seeing face to face. The trinitarian doxology is the beginning of seeing God because God's eternal being is the goal of salvation history before God's own works. The church's liturgy aims at reflecting the cosmic liturgy of creation and at corresponding to the divine liturgy of life.

If the Spirit, "together with" the Father and Son, is "at the same time worshiped and glorified," the Spirit is seen in perichoretic fellowship with Father and the Son. Spirit-Father-Son is neither in the monarchical movement of God's self-communication (self-revelation) to human beings, nor in the eucharistic movement of the self-communication of human beings to God. Spirit, together with Father and Son, is "in the self-circling and self-reposing movement of a perichoresis."[105] Trinitarian doxology does not mean the end of the monarchical Trinity and the eucharistic Trinity, but makes their movements complete because the immanent Trinity in the doxological form provides origin for these divine movements. When there is talk in a monotheistic way there is a speaking of God as self-giving. However, the history of Christ is already related in trinitarian terms in the New Testament itself (Rom 8:32; Gal 2:20).

When it comes to the nature of the divine unity Moltmann prefers the concept of the integrative unity (i.e., the *perichoresis* of the divine Persons) rather than an idea of ontological unity in three *hypostases* sharing the same substance. In so doing, he does not use the term *Einheit*, but rather *Einigkeit* or *Vereinigung*, which work better to indicate a process of unifying or integration. "The unitedeness, the at-oneness, of the triunity is already given with the fellowship of the Father, the Son and the Spirit. It therefore does not need to be additionally secured by a particular doctrine about the unity of the divine substance, or by the special doctrine of the one divine lordship."[106] His famous "social doctrine of the Trinity" comes to the fore by beginning with plurality and then affirming its unity.

As for the social Trinity, the Spirit is not merely the love between Father and Son, but is himself/herself a subject and object of the mutual love of the three. The Persons of the Trinity are an enduring fellowship of love, in *perichoresis* of the eternal divine life or *circumincessio* of each other's roles. Therefore, Moltmann does not construct a doctrine of the Trinity on the presupposition of the unity of the Godhead. Rather, he begins with the

105. Ibid., 304.

106. Moltmann, *Trinity and the Kingdom*, 150.

Trinity of the Persons. Then he proposes a concept of divine unity as the communion of Tri-unity. This has often been called a social model of the Trinity in terms of communion and *koinonia*. Perichoretic unity is, after all, an affirmation of differences-in-unity. It underscores the distinction of each Person, yet describes their unity (not oneness). "In the perichoresis, the very thing that divides them becomes that which binds them together . . . The doctrine of the perichoresis links together in a brilliant way the threeness and the unity, without reducing the threeness to the unity, or dissolving the unity in the threeness. The unity of the Triunity lies in the eternal perichoresis of the trinitarian persons. Interpreted perichoretically, the trinitarian persons form their own unity by themselves in the circulation of the divine life."[107]

In this regard, Moltmann does not interpret the unity of the triune God in terms of a concept of divine substance for the sake of maintaining the personal differences. As long as the very difference of the three Persons lies in their relationality of perichoretic eternal life process, the Persons themselves form both their differences and their unity "by virtue of their relation to one another and in the eternal perichoresis of their love."[108] Thereby, they are not supposed to be replaced by three modes of being or the same divine subject.

As far as the immanent Trinity is the purpose and the end of doxology, the distinction between immanent and economic Trinity is useful. The immanent Trinity will be revealed as such when the economic Trinity, complete with the history and experience of salvation, is raised into and transcended in the immanent Trinity at the eschaton. Moltmann understands the unity of God not in terms of rule, as monarchy, but in terms of love and *perichoresis*. His perichorectic doctrine of the social Trinity enables Moltmann to see the unity of the triune God in the eternal *perichoresis* of Father, Son, and Spirit. Communion and fellowship are the nature and the purpose of the triune God.

The perichoretic concept of trinitarian unity helps to overcome the dangers of tritheism and modalism equally. The perichoretic concept of unity combines the threeness and oneness without reducing each to the other and is the true concept of Triunity. Moltmann's perichoretic doctrine of a social Trinity gives the panentheistic text, "God will be all in all" (1

107. Ibid., 175.

108. Ibid., 177.

Cor 15:24), a trinitarian sense. The divine Persons will be truly immanent, as God will be all in all and all will be in communion with God.

For Moltmann, the doctrine of the Trinity is the theological interpretation of the history of Jesus in its eschatological openness through the Spirit. It is necessary to see the history of Jesus, and with it the history of the world, as internal to God's own trinitarian experience. In his later work, unlike *The Crucified God* and *The Trinity and the Kingdom,* Moltmann attempts to justify the doxological nature of theology in contemplation and praise of God as God is in Godself. The immanent Trinity is safeguarded for the sake of an eschatological doxology of the triune God.[109] "It is through the trinitarian doxology that we first perceive the immanent Trinity as it rests and revolves in itself, and whose unity lies in the eternal *community* of the divine Persons."[110]

If the immanent Trinity is the content of doxological theology, Moltmann has to agree that statements about *God for us* must correspond to doxological statements about YHWH. Does this return to Barth's *analogia relationis*? Nevertheless, with more seriousness Moltmann deepens through his open Trinity what Barth set out to do regarding God's interaction with world history. However, Moltmann's continued and overriding emphasis on the plurality of divine subjects is charged with a divine nominalism in neglect of a principle of unity.[111]

Moltmann's social doctrine of the Trinity conceives of God as three subjects in interpersonal relationship with each other—a fellowship of love. Their unity does not precede their distinction, but consists in their community. God's trinitarian history in the world is the salvation history in which the three divine Persons relate to each other and to the world. Therefore, the starting point for the social Trinity must be salvation history, i.e., the history of the Father, the Son, and the Spirit attested to in the Bible. Moltmann calls this orientation a salvation-historical approach to the history of God with Israel, with Christ, and with the church in the power of God's Spirit. Their history is the history of their relationship in

109. Ibid., 161. "The doctrine of the immanent Trinity is part of eschatology as well. The economic Trinity completes and perfects itself to immanent Trinity . . . when everything is 'in God' and 'God is all in all,' then the economic Trinity is raised into and transcended in the immanent Trinity."

110. Moltmann, *The Spirit of Life*, 309.

111. For this critique, see Peters, *God as Trinity,* 109.

community, which Moltmann calls the trinitarian history of the Father, the Son, and the Spirit.[112]

It is a history of changing trinitarian relationships in which the relations between the Persons both affect the world and are affected by the world. Therefore, this Trinity is a process of living relationships of love between the three Persons and open to the inclusion of the world. This is called an open Trinity for a pluralistic world. The Trinity itself must reveal the meaning of the kingdom of God. Moltmann proposes the trinitarian fellowship of the three divine Persons as a model for the true human community that is to both reflect and participate in God's own trinitarian life. He finds the image of God in human community reflecting the interpersonal life of a social Trinity.

This social doctrine of the Trinity enables Moltmann to develop social personalism or personal socialism with regard to society, and to become ecologically communitarian with respect to nature. The social Trinity provides a model for human community in which people are free and tolerant of each other and find freedom in relationship with each other to be different and pluralistic.[113] Moltmann's social Trinity, which is understood as open Trinity for the inclusion of the world, is involved in the pluralistic world in terms of suffering love and solidarity, especially for the sake of those who are poor, weak, and oppressed of this world. This is Moltmann's understanding of "anonymous Christians" outside Christianity in the world.[114]

For further discussion of trinitarian language in relation to the Jewish community, I will attempt to evaluate contributions of Barth and Moltmann in Jewish-Christian relation. When we attempt to understand the Trinity from Golgotha (Moltmann) we are aware that there is a noticeable progress in discussing trinitarian language more in the biblical context. However, from a Jewish perspective, crucifixion is difficult to accept in the place of the Trinity. According to Isa 57:15, ". . . the high and lofty one who inhabits eternity . . . [this One] dwells in the high [transcendent] and holy place [in the Temple of Jerusalem] and also with those who are

112. Moltmann, *History and the Triune God*, 82–84.

113. Boff, *Trinity and Society*, 222f. Boff, in accepting the liberative dimension of Moltmann's Trinity, insisted that society with cooperation and equality among all members is the starting point for trinitarian reflection. Human society in this regard can be *vestigia trinitatis* for understanding the Trinity as the divine society.

114. In Moltmann's conversation with Rahner, see Moltmann, *History and the Triune God*, 110–22.

contrite and humble in spirit . . . ." This threefold indwelling of God transcends all human logic. God is the incomprehensible One beyond human knowledge. In Cabalist tradition there is a ten-level theology. Because of God's incomprehensibility, people attempt to divide God into two or three or ten to make God more easily presented.

We are aware of certain similarities between Christian self-understanding of God, the Trinity, and the *sefirot*. The former refers to three persons of God in all coequality, coeternity, and indivisibility, while the latter is ten manifestations of the Infinite. These two different aspects are considered as the profound mystery of faith. In the *Zohar* (1:32b), we read about a description of the *sefirot*, the manifestations of *Ein Sof*, the Infinite.

> Three emerge from one; one stands in three;
> Enters between two; two suckle one;
> One suckles many sides. Thus all is one.[115]

Christian theologians understand the Trinity in terms of self-communication of God or self-distinction of God. However, the Jews know of no "YHWH," or *homoousious*, *ousia*, etc., in the sense of Greek metaphysical ontology. They rather experience a God who gives Godself to them to be known anthropocentrically through God's manner of revelation. For instance, the Jews talk about God's kindness, mercy, and love, etc. This would be called a dynamic monotheism, or ethical monotheism. Through God's manner of revealing God's attributes to all, a New Testament statement—"God desires that everyone be saved" (1 Tim 2:4)—finds its place in the Jewish way of thinking. In fact, Tetragramm (four Hebrew letters usually transliterated as YHWH) is not replaced by Elohim in the context of the Old Testament. When Christians stopped referring to the God of Israel as YHWH and replaced YHWH with a trinitarian description, Israel, as the people of God, were replaced by the church, the new people of God.

From the Christian side, Karl Barth argues that the Word became Jewish flesh. Israel is an adequate prefiguration of the prophecy of Jesus Christ.[116] Karl Barth develops his teaching of the Trinity by paying attention to the root of a trinitarian teaching of the Old Testament. Barth distinguishes between the hidden name and the revealed name of YHWH. YHWH has revealed God's name in a historical form and made it con-

115. Chanamatt, *Zohar: The Book of Enlightenment*, 21.

116. *CD*, IV/3.1:52.

crete and central in Exodus and in the covenant relationship with Israel. The revealed name is hidden. Jesus enters into the place of the temple (John 2:18–22) and became the temple of his body in which the name of YHWH dwells and pitches (John 1:14). The name Jesus Christ does not stand in competition with the name YHWH. The name of God as Father is revealed in God's messianic Son, and the name is revealed in God's presence and effectiveness in the Spirit of holiness.

For a trinitarian discourse, Barth's epistemological principle "*esse sequitur operari*" is of significance: God's being is explained only from God's historical acts. God's being is in action. Jesus Christ the Israelite-Jewish messianic man completely sanctifies the name of God. In Jesus Christ, the coming of the kingdom of God becomes an eschatological realty of God's promise, and in him the Torah-will of God is done and fulfilled (the second petition of Lord's prayer). Barth's contribution lies in his grounding of the Trinity in the Old Testament (CD I/1) and developing the trinitarian teaching in the framework of the covenant and reconciliation history (CD IV 1–3).

Hans Joachim Kraus constitutes an understanding of the Trinity in orientation for God of Israel, the coming of God's kingdom and the indwelling of God's Spirit.[117] In Israel there is the one God who rules (Deut 6:4). However, God's unity and oneness manifests God's diverse forms of the presence in the history of God's coming. Kraus shares with Barth that the coming of the God of Israel in the diverse forms of God's presence is essentially the root of the doctrine of the Trinity. According to Isa 57:15, God of Israel is also God as the high and lofty one who lives "in the shelter of the Most High" and abides "in the shadow of the Almighty" (Ps 91:1).

The name "God of Israel" is the point of departure and foundation for Christian discourse of the triune God. The secret of the name of God in the history of God's coming is an Old Testament root of the Christian doctrine of the Trinity. This forms the point of departure for Christian self-understanding of God through the revelation of Jesus Christ in the presence of the Holy Spirit: One God in the condescension of Jesus Christ and in the grounding of fellowship in the Holy Spirit. This is a Christian self-understanding of Unitrinity (unity of God in the trinitarian relationship).

According to Kraus, God's being shares itself in the history of God's coming.[118] God pitches the tent in Israel, and God dwells in God's mes-

117. Cf. Kraus, *Systematische Theologie*.

118. Kraus, *Reich Gottes*, 102.

siah, Jesus, in fullness of the Spirit without measure (John 3:34f). God is reconciled to us and the world through Christ (2 Cor 5:18–19). In Christ the fullness of God is pleased to dwell (Col 1:19) and God in the Spirit is present in the internal hearts of believers so that without being born of water and Spirit no one can enter the kingdom of God (John 3:5). This statement stands in reference to Ezek 36:25f. "I will sprinkle clean water upon you . . . A new heart I will give you, and a new spirit I will put within you . . . ." The name Jesus Christ does not mean the end of the name of God in Israel, but a name of the herald fulfilling the Torah-Will of God. God works in our hearts in the presence of the Spirit in the coming of the kingdom of God.

Likewise, Israel accepts a theistic concept of Elohim in interaction with the religious environment. Christian self-understanding of the Trinity finds its justification in its missional interaction with metaphysical-ontological worldview in the Greek culture. However, the metaphysical-vertical teaching of the Trinity needs to be interpreted and formulated in the horizon of God's covenantal-promise history with Israel, Christianity, and all. The name of the God of Israel remains the subject in its predicates of Elohim or Father, Son, and the Spirit.

The Trinity in Asian Perspective

One of the most challenging aspects of the contemporary situation for theologians is plurality, religious, and otherwise. Postmodern thinkers are suspicious of both comprehensive systems that claim to offer universal explanations and "grand narratives" that tell the One True Story subsuming and integrating everyone else's story. Many pluralists are inclined to regard the gospels as metanarratives that have worked a totalitarian suppression of other voices. For many pluralists with a deconstructive orientation, the totalizing strategy of the gospel for hegemony in the Western world is met with a skeptical eye due to its tendency to swallow up the many into one universal story. The situation in post-modernity is one of recognizing the different as different, ending in sheer relativism. Central to the issues at stake is the question of one or many. However, it is not always wise to move to one or many too quickly.

What is the place and function of the doctrine of the Trinity in face of the challenge of religious pluralism? Does the triune God have other names, revealing Godself in other religious ways? Are there vestraces of the Trinity in other religions? Can the Trinity be, in fact, interreligious?

The thought of the Trinity from an Asian perspective is grappled by two theologians. One is Raimundo (Raimon) Panikkar, the most prolific and successful author in the dialogue between East and West, and who is an ordained Roman Catholic priest. The other is Professor Lee Jung Young, who was one of the most creative thinkers from South-Korea. Unfortunately, his sudden death is a great loss to the development of Asian contextual theology, as well as to ecumenical dialogue. In this chapter, I will deal with both theologians' views of the Trinity.

The Trinity in Advaitic Thinking

Perhaps the most daring of Panikkar's attempts at mapping a Hindu-Buddhist-Christian spirituality within a still Christian self-understanding came in his early and ground-breaking little book *The Trinity and World Religions*. Here, he imposes a trinitarian structure on Hinduism and an advaitic structure on Christianity. Both "Trinity" and "advaita" become alternative symbols for the cosmotheandric Mystery of God. The Trinity is central in the thought of Panikkar because it permeates all the other dimensions of his entire thought. As Panikkar says, "the Trinity may be considered as a junction where the authentic spiritual dimensions of all religions meet."[119] In the prominence he gives to the Trinity Panikkar is a classical theologian. Panikkar developed his so-called "advaitic Trinitarianism" out of his dialogue with the advaitic tradition of Hinduism. Yet he wants to be authentically trinitarian in the Orthodox Christian sense of the term. Therefore, the very incommensurability of the two religions becomes a window to the whole of the Trinity in which each religion becomes an indispensable part of the *perichoresis* of God because each represents human spirituality in a concrete and unique manner.

According to Panikkar, the Trinity is a symbolic metaphor for theandrism—"that intimate and complete unity . . . between the divine and the human . . . which is the goal towards which everything here below tends."[120] The theandric insight that is at the center of the Upanishads is expressed well in the statement: "God is in all; all is in God."[121]

The term *advaita* is composed of the Sanskrit root *dv*, which means two, and the alpha privative, meaning "not." Etymologically the term means "not two." Panikkar takes the etymological meaning as his key:

119. Panikkar, *Trinity and World Religions*, 42.

120. Panikkar, *Trinity and the Religious Experience of Man*, 71.

121. Vanhoozer, ed. *Trinity in a Pluralistic Age*, 59.

Advaita simply means "not two." It means for him radically relational, organic, and holistic. What may appear to be two, such as God and the world, can, in depth intuition, be seen as related through complementarity. This is true not only of God and the world but of the mutual relations of the persons in the Trinity. In dealing with the Trinity, Panikkar develops the mystery of the Trinity in the interest of allying Christianity and its spirituality with non-Christian traditions.

Taking his categories from the three classical spiritual paths of the *Bhagavad Gita*, Panikkar treats the way of *karma*, the way of *bhakti*, and the way of *jnana*. Since *karma* means action in the Hindu context, primarily the action of worship, Panikkar treats under this heading the spirituality of the worship of God, whether or not it be through a divine name like YHWH or *Allah*. He next describes the way of *bhakti* or devotion as that of personalism. The way of devotion and love (*bhaktimarga*) is the personalist dimension of spirituality. In the third way, the path of *jnana* or knowledge, is linked to advaitic non-differentiation.

In so doing, Panikkar identifies the Father of the Christian Trinity with the absolute *Brahman* of Hinduism and *Tao* in Taoism. The Father, as such, is the transcendent and the unnamable beyond every name. The focus of Panikkar's trinitarian insight is the universality of the experience and the reality of the triangular consciousness of "I," "Thou," and "We." These are mutually constitutive. No "I" is possible without the "We," which in turn cannot be without the "I" and the "Thou." The "I" can address the "Thou" only in the spirit of the "We." Ultimate Reality consists of the network of relationships among the "I," the "Thou" and the "We." If now we can take an experience like this and apply it to our own understanding of the Trinity, then the point of Trinity is the Son. The Son is the Thou, the absolute Thou. It is only from the Son that we can know about the Father. About the Father himself—in himself—we can say nothing. In the Father, the apophatism (the kenosis or emptying) of Being is real and total. That the Father begets the Son means a total generation in which the Father gives himself totally to the Son. Put otherwise, the Father empties himself into the Son. This is what Panikkar calls "the Cross of the Trinity" or "integral immolation of God."[122]

In contrast to the Christian tradition, Panikkar applies *kenosis*, or self-emptying, to the Father in light of a Buddhist *Sunyata*. The Father has no being, the Son is his being. The source of being is not being. The Father is

122. Panikkar, *Trinity and the Religious Experience of Man*, 60.

the "I," thoroughly transcendent and therefore utterly ineffable. Similarly, the Spirit, i.e., the Spirit of communion between "I" and "Thou," is the "We" of the Trinity: "I" is the source of Being and "We" the ground of Being.

By affirming the deep intuition of Hinduism and Buddhism he develops a radical apophatism, or negative theology, of the Father. The Buddhist experience of *Nirvana* and *Sunyata* may be situated in the essential apophatism of the person of the Father. The Father in the kenosis of Being as its very source can be called the silence of the Father, or *Sunyata.* Panikkar observes that the most diverse religious traditions teach us that God is Silence. Since the Father is wrapped in silence he may seem totally inaccessible to us.

Panikkar turns next to the Son, treating him primarily as person, in a manner that correlates with the spirituality of personalism in the path of devotion or love. He brings to light the personal property of the silence of the Father in polar complementarity with the Son as speech. "The God of theism, thus, is the Son; the God with whom we can speak, establish a dialogue, enter into communication."[123] What Panikkar has in mind is not merely the historical Jesus of Nazareth, but the Christ as the universal Logos who links the infinite and the finite. Christ as a mysterious mediator is present everywhere, especially in other religious traditions. Christ is called the Hindu *Isvara*, the Buddhist *Tathagata*, and even the Hebrew *Jahweh* and the Muslim *Allah* in which we have examples of the Logos-mediator between the absolute and the personal.[124] Next, Panikkar approaches the mystery of the Spirit through the notion of immanence. If the revelation of the Father is the revelation of God transcendent, then the revelation of the Spirit, on the other hand, is the revelation of God immanent.

Panikkar gives credit to Hinduism for a special role in illuminating the mystery of the Spirit. As the Father empties himself into the Son, so the Son holds nothing back from the Father. It is the Spirit who makes the kenotic relation complete and consummated. "If the Father and the Son are not two, they are not one either: the Spirit both unites and distinguishes them."[125] I wonder, however, whether this Spirit is identical as the Spirit of the crucified and raised Christ. Panikkar seems to put more emphasis

123. Ibid., 51.

124. Peters, *God as Trinity*, 75.

125. Panikkar, *Trinity and World Religions*, 61.

on the suffering of God in his Trinity of the Father's kenosis. The Spirit is universally present, so the risen Christ is too. However, Panikkar needs to give more attention to the historical suffering of God in his Trinity. The Spirit as a river of life (John 7:38–39) has sprung from the rock (1 Cor 10:4), which is also the historical manifestation of the Trinity in Jesus Christ the crucified and risen.

In the discussion of the Trinity, Panikkar describes three aspects of the divinity and three corresponding forms of spirituality. Buddhism is the religion of the silence of the Father, since the Father expressed himself only through the Son and of himself has no word or expression. Judaism, Christianity, and Islam are the religions of the revelation of the Son. Western culture is a culture of the Word or Logos, guided by the intellectual logos of the Greeks and the Romans. However, the Orient has other modes of perception such as silence and the sense of immersion in unity. What is at stake for Panikkar's observation is that Buddhism is linked to the silence of the Father and Hinduism to non-differentiation of the Spirit.

In this regard Panikkar extends the trinitarian horizon of Christian thinking toward including consciousness of the world's religions. However, a serious critique can be made of Panikkar. The Trinity is the Christian answer to the identity of God as the one Creator, God as Father, Son, and Spirit, in which divine *perichoresis* is at the center rather than the *perichoresis* of religions. In addition, Panikkar's typological simplification of world religions (Buddhism as a religion of Father, Judaism and Islam as the religion of the Logos) remains a field of critique. He attempts to subsume different spiritualities of world religions into Christian discourse of Trinity. Here the Christian concept of the Trinity appears to be a universal principle of totalizing difference and uniqueness of world religions into which an advaitic logic of identity is subsumed in terms of the meta-narrative of Christianity.

According to his typology, Buddhism has to be classified as a religion of silence of the Father that results in eradication and violation of the Buddhist principle of dependent co-arising and compassion. Judaism, Christianity, and Islam are thus reduced to a religion of the Logos. In so doing, Jewish spirituality centered on the name of God and the importance of oral Torah, Christian openness to mystery of God, and Islamic mysticism are subdued into Panikkar's advatic schematization.

However, pluralism in a genuine sense cannot be properly discussed by artificially inserting non-Christian religions into a Christian discourse of the Trinity. A discussion of pluralism finds its locus in God's openness toward the world in God's self-manifestation in history because YHWH is known and derived from *God for us* in salvation history "only by a configuration of the works of Father, Son, and Spirit."[126] By exploring Reality in depth from the vantage point of the Christian Trinity, and by penetrating further through the Buddhist and Hindu modes of experience of silence and non-differentiation, Panikkar has reached an advaitic trinitarian structure that he calls "radical Trinity." This model of radical Trinity helps to promote a breakthrough in *inter*religious or *intra*religious dialogue. "It is in the Trinitarian possibilities of the world religions, in the striving of each in its own fashion towards a synthesis of these spiritual attitudes, that the meeting of religions—the kairos of our time—finds its deepest inspiration and most certain hope."[127]

The Trinity and the Yin-Yang Symbol

By contrast, in the perspective of Lee Jung-Young, the Asian understanding of the Trinity gains a different character. He proposes an eastern understanding of God based on the *I Ching,* a text widely revered in Asian religious culture. Lee develops a typology of theologies as the context for his theological program. The three main options in Christian theology today are the theology of the absolute, process theology, and the theology of change. The theology of the absolute is, according to Lee, all forms of western theology. These theologians generally understand God by way of the static concept of being that has been inherited ultimately from Greek philosophy.

Although some contemporary theologians have understood God in a more dynamic model, they do not break radically from the static Greek metaphysics. Process theology is, for Lee, a transition type of theology. It stands midway between the theology of the absolute and Lee's own project for a theology of change. Process theology has correctly broken with the dominant Western view of God as static, unchanging, eternal, and impassible. Its worldview is compatible with both Western and Eastern thought. However, process theology presupposes a linear view of time, whereas Lee's view of time is cyclical.[128]

126. Vanhoozer, "Does the Trinity," 66.

127. Ibid., 54.

128. However, Lee's critique of process theology is at times inaccurate. A relational

Lee offers the theology of change as a valid alternative to the theology of the absolute and process theology. Lee's theology is based on the metaphysics of the *I Ching*, or *Book of Changes*, which is a Confucian classic that is popular in Korea, China, and Japan. Most East Asian philosophy of religion could be called commentaries on the *I Ching*, just as Western philosophies could be called footnotes to Plato. The *I Ching* is the classic of change and argues that change is the fundamental characteristic of reality. This change is interpreted through two complementary principles, yin and yang. Yin and yang are two primordial forces that pervade all of reality. "There is the Absolute which produced the two forms, yin and yang; and the yin and yang between them produced all things . . . One yin and one yang constituted what is called Tao."[129] Everything in the world can be categorized into yin and yang. Yin and yang are manifestations of one essence, change. They are not a duality, because the distinctions between them are conditional and existential, not essential.

If change characterizes all of reality, then God is best understood as change itself. This view of God is better, according to Lee, than God as being itself (theology of the absolute) or becoming itself (process theology). Change itself is ultimately beyond human comprehension, but it can be known in its concrete, relative manifestations. With his description of God as change itself, Lee is trying to preserve the dynamic character of God. God manifests Godself in a dipolar process, operating through the yin and yang relational forces. In utilizing yin-yang symbols for the sake of trinitarian thinking, Lee casts a critical view on C. S. Song's unqualified statement about the Trinity as mathematical confusion.[130]

What is at stake for Lee is to bring forth "in" as the inner connecting principle to develop an Asian trinitarian hermeneutics. "In" principle refers to mutual inclusiveness of yin-yang movement. His hermeneutical retrieval of the "in" aspect is decisive and fundamental to understanding what the Trinity essentially means. As he stresses, "yin-yang symbolic thinking, which is also both/and thinking, is none other than one (unity)

theory of God in the framework of process theism is not merely confined and caught in "either-or thinking," but stands in dynamic relationality between God and the world on the basis of a primordial nature and a subsequent nature. In addition, before Lee, it is John Cobb Jr. who turned to a yin-yang way of thinking for reconstructing his Christology in a pluralistic age; cf. Cobb, *Christ in a Pluralistic Age*.

129. *I Ching*, Appendix III, sec. 1, ch.v, 1,2. Cf. Lee, *Trinity in Asian Perspective*, 24.

130. Ibid., 56. Cf. Song, *Reign of God*, 61; and Haight, "Point of Trinitarian Theology," 195.

in three (diversity) as well as three (diversity) in one (unity)."[131] Because of this "in" as the inner connecting principle the reciprocal relation between yin and yang becomes trinitarian in character. As long as two are in one (the great circle), one is in three.

Therefore, one is in two, two are in three, and finally, one is in three. The "in" principle functions also as the "and" principle connecting yin and yang. The coexistence of two complementary symbols is due to the correspondence of the "in" and "and" principles. "Both/and" thinking in terms of the mutually inclusive "in" principle becomes the core concept to approaching the Trinity in different way than Tertullian's formula, *una substantia, tres personae,* or the Cappadocians' formula, *mia ousia, treis hypostaseis.*[132] To avoid modalism in the Western Church or tritheism in Eastern Church the "in" or "and" connecting principle is necessary, Lee argues. The yin and yang process is trinitarian inasmuch as they presuppose change as the ultimate reality. According to the *Tao Te Ching,* "the Tao gives birth to one. One gives birth to two. Two gives birth to three. Three gives birth to all things" (ch. 42).[133]

To construct his inductive approach to the Trinity, Lee's order of Trinity is Son—Spirit—Father. By beginning with God the Son, he sees "incarnation as a fulfillment of Trinitarian process in creation."[134] In equating the Word or Logos as *Tao,* he articulates the ineffable nature of Tao in line with the *Tao Te Ching.* "The Tao that can be told is not the eternal Tao," (ch. 1). "The Tao is like the Great Mother: it gives birth to infinite worlds," (ch. 5). The Logos is also the power of creativity, just as the Tao is. In regard to Christ's kenosis (Phil 2:5–9), Lee asserts that the Tao is empty but inexhaustible, whereby fullness and Emptiness always coexist. "The Word as the Tao, which is also known as I or change, is a ceaseless act of emptying and fulfilling process."[135]

However, Lee lost sight of the dimension of the Father by identifying the Son as the *Tao.* Therefore, the death of Jesus on the cross is totally identical with the death of the Father and of the Spirit. That is, the death of the trinitarian God. Therefore, the inseparability and mutual inclusiveness of yin-yang dialectics are not able to distinguish God in the Trinity

131. Lee, *Trinity in Asian Perspective,* 59.

132. Ibid., 59–60.

133. Ibid., 62.

134. Ibid., 71.

135. Ibid., 73.

as divine Persons.[136] How does Lee understand suffering of the Trinity? Lee grounds his affirmation of divine suffering on God's trinitarian nature as love (agape) and divine empathy. For Lee, divine empathy is a better conceptualization of God's suffering than divine sympathy. God does not merely feel with the human situation; God feels by identifying Godself into the human situation and actively participating in it. This is an aspect of a matri-passianism, which Lee's inductive approach to the Trinity highlights, albeit not by rejecting the patripassian issue. The Son in the Father or the Father in Son is due to the empathy of God, the Holy Spirit. At any rate, the Spirit and the Father died when the Son died on the cross. If so, who is the Father to whom Jesus cried and commended his soul in his last confidence?

Even though Lee starts his trinitarian thinking from Jesus Christ, his theology of the Trinity is not christocentric, but Trinity-centric, because of his yin-yang thinking. The center can be redefined and reinvented again and again according to the recentering process of creativity and change. "The centrality of the Father is marginalized through the Spirit and is recentered in the Son. Just as the cell divides itself to create a new cell, recentering is needed in the process of creativity and change."[137]

Therefore the order of the divine Trinity can be always changeable, although Lee begins his Trinity with the order of Son-Spirit-Father. His understanding of the Spirit as the earth mother or *ch'i* (a Taoist concept of the vital energy or material principle comparable to *prana* in Sanskrit, or *ruach* in Hebrew, or *pneuma* in Greek) reinvigorates and reconstructs a "multi-logical" theology because the Spirit is truly immanent and inclusive of all things in the cosmos. The Spirit-centered approach is in fact inclusive and pluralistic in nature. According to the *Tao Te Ching*, "The Tao is called the Great Mother" (ch. 6); "Named, it is Mother of the thousands of things" (ch.1). "The world has a Source, the Mother of the World. Once you get the Mother then you understand the children. Once you understand the children, turn back and watch over the Mother" (ch. 52).

Following Taoism's preference for the value of feminism, Lee upheld strong ecological and feminist views in his change model of the Trinity. Nevertheless, he does not lessen the preeminence of the Father in the divine Trinity in spite of anti-patriarchal warnings. In contrast to *ch'i*, which

136. Ibid., 83.

137. Ibid., 149.

is the image of the Spirit, God the Father is imagined as *Li*, which is the metaphysical principle in the Confucian tradition.

In sum, Lee's model of a yin-yang trinitarian theology is based on triadic thinking. Change as the Ultimate Reality is the foundation of all existence underlying the yin-yang process. For Lee, the Trinity is described as the relationship among change (Father), yang (Son), and yin (Spirit). In other words, God the Father can be symbolized by change itself, God the Holy Spirit by the power of change, and God the Son by the perfect manifestation of change. On the basis of change, Lee finds "Paterque" (the Son proceeding from the Father and the Spirit), "Filioque" (the Spirit proceeding from the Father and the Son), or "Spiritusque" (The Father proceeding from the Son and the Spirit) in the innertrinitarian relationship of Father, Son, and the Spirit.[138] He fully accepts the trinitarian community as individual members in the *perichoresis* because the concept of *perichoresis* still "presupposes the idea of person as individual, even if person is dynamically conceived as an individual-in-relation."[139]

Instead of *perichoresis*, the yin-yang dialectical process shows a preference for a Taoist penetration into yin and yang by affirming the Father as the ultimate Principle as *Li*. However, Lee put emphasis on *Tao* as "the Mother of the thousand of things" or as Logos of the ineffable *Tao*.[140] Lee's change model of Trinity tends to integrate the divine others into the endless moving dance *ad intra* through the connecting principle of the "in." In excessive emphasis of the "in" connecting principle, there is no freedom of God's future. God's future should be totally collapsed into the immanence of the Spirit. Therefore, Rahner's rule needs to be modified so that the immanent Trinity is in the economic Trinity, and vice versa. However, in excessive emphasis on the Father as the Great Ultimate of *Li* transcending the physical universe of *ch'i*, how could Lee maintain that the immanent Trinity is located in the economic Trinity?

Although Lee shows his preference toward the social model of Trinity with respect to liberation theology or feminist theology, his modalistic direction of Tao is not identical with Barthian modes of being (*Seinsweise*)

138. Ibid., 152; cf. LaCugna, *God for Us*, 277.

139. Ibid., 278.

140. I find Lee's emphasis on Tao as the Mother excessive without qualification in respect to the Father as the Tao. "The Valley Spirit is undying. This is mysterious Femininity. The Abode of mysterious Femininity: This is the Root of Heaven and Earth," (chap. 6). Cf. Lee, *Trinity in Asian Perspective*, 163.

or Rahner's distinct modes of subsisting (*Subsistenzweisen*).[141] Rather than *Dreieinigkeit*, Lee seems to affirm the Uni-Trinity for the sake of the Father as *Li* in spite of stressing the Spirit as *ch'i*, and even the Son as *Tao*. *Perichoresis* is different from, and alien to, Lee's model of yin-yang Trinity. Even though Lee is critical of Whitehead's attachment to Alexandrian theology in process theology, his change model of the Trinity would be seen structurally and formally as having an affinity for the trinitarian thinking of process theism in spite of their differences.

In the framework of process theology the God of process theism has two natures: a primordial nature and a consequent nature. It is generally admitted that process theology is not interested in the value of the threefold manifestation of God that would conform with traditional trinitarian ideas.[142] This is because at times trinitarianism leads to arrogant demands about Christianity with exclusive and restrictive views. Therefore, trinitarian doctrine stands in the way of clarifying and deepening the good news of Jesus Christ in relationality with the word and cosmos.[143] The absolutization of the threeness of God is in fact not biblical. John Cobb's attempt to relativize the Trinity for the sake of God's binity (God as transcendent and immanent) suggests various possibilities within process thought to address God's relationality in light of the Primordial and the Consequent Natures. For Cobb, the binitarian doctrine is more important than trinitarian doctrine, albeit not to the exclusion of the Trinity.[144] The metaphysical understanding of God in process thought that is in favor of the preexistent divine reality still contrasts with Moltmann's attempt to begin the Trinity with the human historical Jesus.

However, Lewis Ford, in translating some issues of the classical doctrine of the Trinity into the conceptuality of Whitehead's philosophy, makes an attempt to set up a correspondence between the Logos with God's primordial nature and the Spirit with God's consequent nature in which the Father exists as the ultimate transcendent source of two primordial and consequent natures (comparable to yin-yang). The Father, albeit simply identical with the change of the *I Ching*, unites the Spirit and the Son. The Logos (yang), who is begotten of the Father before all

141. Lee, *Trinity in Asian Perspective*, 151–2. Cf. Wilson-Kastner, *Faith, Feminism, and the Christ*; Boff, *Trinity and Society*.

142. Cobb, *Process Theology*, 110.

143. Cf. Cobb, *Christ in a Pluralistic Age*, 259–64. "Response to Ted Peters," *Dialogue* 30, no. 3 (Summer 1991), 243–44. Cf. Peters, *God as Trinity*, 219.

144. Cobb, "Relativization of the Trinity," 12.

worlds, corresponds to the primordial nature embracing all eternal objects. Therefore, the Spirit corresponds to the consequent nature as God's receptive activity. The Spirit as the Lord and Giver of life guides or lures all creation, especially human beings, to enable ethical praxis in response to the divine source and finally lead to reconciliation with God. So the ethical must precede the reconciliation with God.

When the Father unites and underlines the other two, the Trinity of process theism is closer to Eastern trinitarianism with its tendency toward subordinationism, but also with implications of God's sociality. Generally, thinkers of process thought tend not to consider the Father as one person with respect to the other two, but rather as the one subjectivity including primordial and consequent natures.[145] Lewis Ford, in constructing a contingent trinitarianism, proposes "a single subjectivity as one actuality with three formally distinct natures" in which the Father is correlated with the primordial envisagement, the Son or Logos with its outcome in the primordial nature, and the Spirit with the inverse or consequent nature.[146]

Joseph A. Bracken SJ, tries to extend Whitehead's metaphysical categories and social understanding of the human person toward a revised social doctrine of the Trinity. In the revision of traditional Whiteheadian scholarship, Bracken affirms, beyond a dyadic structure of God, a tri-personal notion of God for the economic Trinity as well as for the immanent Trinity. What distinguishes process thought from classical trinitarian thought lies in their different understandings of God's sociality.

Therefore, they both affirm that God's being is defined by God's sociality, that is, God's social relatededness, God's essential sociality in the framework of classical trinitarian thought is defined within the Trinity of divine Persons, in which God's relatededness with the world is wholly contingent and independent. In contrast, process thought defines God's essential sociality by relationship with the world. This relationship is "beyond the accident of God's will." Or put otherwise, God cannot exist apart from the God-world relationship. Therefore, for process thought God's sociality is world-dependent, whereas God's sociality is self-sufficient for classical trinitarian thought. Gregory A. Boyd proposes the essential insights of process thought in affirmation of the self-sufficient sociability of God through a trinitarian revision of Hartshorne's metaphysics.[147]

145. Ford, *Lure of God*, 117.

146. Ford, "Contingent Trinitarianism," 44.

147. Boyd, "Self-Sufficient Sociality of God," 73–74.

Joseph A. Bracken SJ makes a proposal on a new understanding of the God-world relationship, using the imagery of a Whiteheadian society as a structured field of activity. God as the Trinity can be conceived of as a three-personal organized society. The one God is, *per se*, the unity of a democratically ordered society, mutually dependent upon the three discrete persons. "A trinitarian understanding of the God-world relationship in terms of hierarchically ordered fields of activity seems quite possible. If the three divine persons, for example, are interpreted as three personally ordered societies of actual occasions that, by their dynamic interrelation from moment to moment, sustain a democratically organized structured society, then their joint field of activity could be said to envelop and support the field of activity brought into existence at every moment by the interrelated activity of all finite actual entities."[148]

In this regard, Bracken emphasizes creativity within a trinitarian context as a principle of intersubjectivity "by virtue of which actual occasions, both finite and infinite, come into existence and are related to one another in terms of various societal configurations."[149] If Lee's trinitarian model of change would meet the Trinity of process theism to improve the social dimension of the yin-yang process not only for the immanent Trinity but also for the economic Trinity, then his Asian Trinity would be in a better position to actualize a panentheism of the *Tao*'s social relatedness to the world from a cosmo-anthropological perspective.

Trinitarian Language in Buddhist-Christian Dialogue

In the context of interreligious dialogue, trinitarian thinking meets *Sunyata*. As Mahatma Gandhi asserts, "One may drink out of the same great rivers with others, but one need not use the same cup."[150] Trinitarian thinking meets a Buddhist aphorism: Do not look at the finger! If you do, you will miss the moon. Look at the moon *through* the finger! Moltmann's theology of "the crucified God" is attractive and stimulating in encounter with the Buddhist insight of *Sunyata*. Masao Abe, one of the great representatives of the Kyoto school, finds an affinity between Moltmann's understanding of kenosis in the trinitarian context and a Buddhist understanding of *Sunyata* as self-emptying dynamic event.

148. Bracken, "The World," 96. See Peters, *God as Trinity*, 118.

149. Bracken, "Panentheism," in *Trinity in Process*, 105.

150. Demarest, *General Revelation*, 255.

Moltmann's contribution, beyond the traditional doctrine of the two natures in the person of Christ, lies in reflecting on the death of Christ in a trinitarian eschatological perspective. It was, first of all, Karl Barth who took into account God's passibility in the theopaschite terms of Luther, albeit with a different orientation than he. However, as Moltmann argues, there is a flaw in his thought concerning the trinitarian interconnection.[151] This is where Moltmann begins to struggle with a Barthian understanding of divine passibility. In putting excessive emphasis on "God in Christ" from the christocentric perspective, Barth is blamed for not taking God's passibility fully into a trinitarian sense. According to Moltmann, it could be more promising and meaningful to deal with the death of Jesus in a trinitarian way because talk of God in relation to the Christ event in christocentric terms is inappropriate. Therefore, "the revolution in the concept of God," which is manifested by the crucified Christ, should be properly articulated in a trinitarian way.[152] The death of Jesus is a trinitarian event among the Father, the Son, and the Spirit.

Moltmann understands the Christ event on the cross in a historical sense, while his resurrection has an eschatological sense. The "history of God" in the death of Jesus contains all the depths and abysses of human history. Therefore, the history of God in this regard is understood as the history of history to which all sentient beings are integrated. All human history is taken up into the history of God, or in other words, into the trinitarian life. On this basis, Moltmann makes the death of Christ relevant to a post-Auschwitz theology. As Moltmann states, "even Auschwitz is taken up into the grief of the Father, the surrender of the Son and the power of the Spirit."[153] Therefore, the trinitarian concept of the "crucified God" prevents Christian faith from falling into a faith in Christian monotheism. However, in due respect for Moltmann's creative project of a trinitarian theology of the cross, Abe begins his critique by calling into question a paradox, that is, "God is dead on the cross and yet is not dead."[154]

This is the paradox where the Buddhist idea of *Sunyata* encounters a Christian understanding of kenosis. At this point, Abe makes an attempt to solve this paradox by introducing the Zen philosophical understanding of *Sunyata* as Zero. Abe questioned whether "the unity of three persons

151. Moltmann, *Crucified God*, 20.

152. Ibid., 204.

153. Ibid., 278.

154. Ibid., 244.

in one God or Godhead" would presuppose the fourth being. In order to resolve the danger of the fourth being in the Trinity, the oneness of the one God is supposed to have the character of Zero. Concerning the Trinity, Abe begins by analyzing the Trinity on the basis of Tertullian's formulation: *Tres personae—una subsantia.*

"The unity of three persons in the one God or Godhead" is a starting point for Abe's consideration of Moltmann's view of the Trinity. Abe calls into question the traditional doctrine of God's two natures in wondering how to understand, "God is dead on the cross and yet is not dead." In the traditional formulation of the Trinity, one God is the *substantia* (or *essentia*), and three persons are *hypostases.* In Abe's view, the distinction between *essentia* and *hypostasis* is indispensable and not to be confused. However, the one God as *essentia* is not completely free from the character of the fourth being. In other words, the trinitarian formulation *una substantia—tres personae* would imply the fourth being in the Trinity. In order to overcome this dangerous tendency, "the one God in the Trinity must be the great Zero that is free even from the oneness as distinguished from the threeness."[155] If the one God is understood as nonsubstantial Zero, or *Nichts*, the divine essence is dynamically self-manifesting, and dialectically relational, so that we can necessarily speak of Father, Son, and Spirit. At the point of great Zero, "the unity and the Trinity of God are fully and harmoniously realized without conflict."[156]

In reducing the one God to Zero, Abe comes closer to Moltmann's model of a social Trinity in which *perichoresis* plays a decisive role as the community in mutual interdependence and interpenetration. Therefore, Abe states his affinity to Moltmann's idea that "the divinity of the Trinitarian God is kenosis. This divine kenosis is being as well as non-being. It is neither being nor non-being. It is the unfathomable secret of love, which one cannot comprehend, but rather only worship in amazement. Because all our notions create idols, only amazement understands the secret of reality."[157] However, Abe's proposal of Zero Trinity leads inevitably to the total kenosis of the Father in the Son's death, in contrast to Moltmann.

At any rate, a traditional understanding of two natures can still become an obstacle for Moltmann in resolving fully the dilemma that "God is dead on the cross and yet God is not dead," even though Moltmann

155. Cobb, et al., *Emptying God*, 24.

156. Ibid., 24.

157. Moltmann, "God is Unselfish Love," in *The Emptying God*, 120.

develops his idea in a trinitarian-eschatological way. The doctrine of the Trinity, in affirming the Great Zero, can be a real resolution to this limbo, argues Abe. Now Abe proposes to understand the Zero as *Nichts* or *Ungrund*, which may be found in an analogy in the Christian mystic tradition such as Meister Eckhart or Jacob Boehme. The real solution to the dilemma in this regard is that the godhead as *Nichts* or *Ungrund* should be affirmed as the Zero point in the Trinity. In so doing, the event of the crucified Christ can be simultaneously understood in christocentric and trinitarian terms. The sonship of Jesus is ultimately rooted in *Nichts* or *Ungrund* as "the godhead in the unity of three persons in one God."[158]

That being the case, Abe has several concepts of God in the Trinity: (1) godhead as Zero, *Nichts* or *Ungrund*; (2) the three persons; and (3) the unity of three persons in one God. Is there really room in Moltmann's concept of Trinity for proposing a fourth being? Does Moltmann's theology of the Trinity affirm the unity of three persons in one God or godhead? As a matter of fact, Moltmann moves from his critique of (semi) Sabellian tendencies in Karl Barth and Karl Rahner toward the *Dreieinigkeit* in the *perichoresis* that could correspond to the Eastern Orthodox pattern of the Trinity by regarding the Father as origin without origin. In following Rahner's rule, there is no room for the fourth being. YHWH does not need to be a great Zero, because YHWH can be known only by *God for us* in Jesus Christ. Three persons in the Trinity operate and work to inhere from the beginning in the perichoretic fellowship that is the core concept for Molmann's model of the social Trinity.

In addition, Abe's affinity to the radical apophatic strand highlighted in Meister Eckhart is challenged by David Tracy. "Eckhart remains the clearest Christian analogue to the kind of radically kenotic interpretation of the Christian understanding of God that Abe articulates."[159] Eckhart's famous formulation, "godhead beyond God," in light of which the name Father, Son, and the Spirit are regarded as inappropriate and insufficient to describe who YHWH is. At first glance, the dialectical language of Eckhart has some striking resemblances to Abe's dialectic of dynamic *Sunyata* or absolute Nothingness.

However, Eckhart's use of analogy is Godcentered because only God can provide the proper analogy. His analogy, unlike Barth's *analogia fidei* (analogy of faith) against *analogia entis* (analogy of being), is radically dia-

158. Ibid., 25.

159. Ibid., 146.

lectical because he related indistinction and distinction, immanence and transcendence in a radical, dialectical way. Moving from radical apophatic detachment toward a final negation of it, Eckhart interprets two aspects of the *bullitio* of divine emergence and relations in the Trinity, and the *ebullitio* of the incarnation of the Logos in the soul of the believer. In this radical apophatic thought, the soul can even break through the godhead and God.

Understood in this way, Eckhart's dialectic, although seemingly close to Abe's language of dynamic *Sunyata*, nevertheless affirms the self-manifestation of the godhead in the radical dialectic between *bullitio* as the Trinity and the *ebullitio* of creatures.[160] Of course, Abe's dialectic of dynamic *Sunyata* manifests itself as wisdom and as companion, which is, however, different from Eckhart's neo-platonic emanation language of *bullitio* and *ebullitio*.

Does Abe's language of dynamic *Sunyata* allow for the logos incarnation itself in the soul or the soul's breakthrough to the godhead in the Neo-Platonic sense? In addition, Abe's speculation of the fourth being in the Trinity, which is the divine essence in Christian trinitarian understanding of God, needs to be corrected by reflection about the relationship between "YHWH" and "*God for us*." *God for us* is the main clue to knowing YHWH. God's essence is dialectically and necessarily self-manifestation of Father, Son, and the Spirit.[161] In this light, Abe is asked to pay more attention to the "intrinsically dynamic, self-manifesting, and dialectical character" of Christian trinitarian thinking, argues Tracy.[162] Therefore, there is no fourth, no Zero, no total kenosis. There is duality between Father and Son or God and creatures, but it does not mean dualism in Christian trinitarian thinking. A Buddhist dialectics is of non-duality, whereas the Christian dialectics is identity-in-difference.

As far as the Trinity is concerned, it has been mainly understood as the relation between *perichoresis* and appropriation. In an emphasis on appropriation, there would be a modalistic tendency running into attachment to the oneness of God, in which the threeness of God would be suppressed. However, in stressing *perichoresis* there would be a tritheistic tendency running into the attachment to the three persons of God, in which the oneness of God would be suppressed. A Christian dialectic of

160. Ibid., 149.

161. Ibid., 150.

162. Ibid., 152.

identity-in-difference still revolves around the tension between Tri-unity and Uni-Trinity. To deal with this dilemma, I would like to propose a threefold understanding of *Sunyata* to deepen the discourse of the Trinity. According to the threefold understanding of the Trinity, God in the appropriation, that is, God the Creator, God the Redeemer, and God the Sanctifier, is a provisional phenomenon of one essential Trinity in the historical sense. However, each God is in relationality of co-dependent arising.

God the Creator is in mutual interdependence and interpenetration with the other divine persons, and vice versa. In complementarity to an appropriation-*perichoresis* relation God's self-emptying appears as the wondrous being underlying oneness of three divine persons. If the divinity is self-emptying as unselfish love, the divinity should have the wondrous being of nonsubstantiality. A social doctrine of Trinity in which the perichoretic community of three persons plays a fundamental role rejects the divine substance as the one God. Therefore, "the three persons are by virtue of the essential surrendering different and yet entirely one."[163] That being the case, the unity of the trinitarian God as *perichoresis* is not the one God, but three different Gods in unity. According to Moltmann, the divine substance as the one God "can only be found in the community of the three divine persons."[164]

However, community or fellowship cannot replace the one God. In order to overcome the dilemma, I propose the unity of God as the wondrous being with respect to the self-emptying of the one God in three persons (a social doctrine of the Trinity). This wondrous being can be called the cosmic unselfish love. In this regard, the origin of relation in the trinitarian relation can meet the wondrous being of *Sunyata* underlying the trinitarian relation of Father, Son, and the Spirit. *Dreieinigkeit* can be fully realized when the trinitarian life is seen in light of the wondrous being of self-emptying in which the monarchial form of the Trinity turns to genuine Trinity in equality and fellowship with divine others. This wondrous being of *Sunyata* can be analogous to Eckhart's metaphor, "Father begetting the son in the womb of the Spirit," which would implicitly point to *dukkha* and *karuna* (compassion) of the Trinity.[165] This is a radically cataphatic dimension implied in the threefold understanding of *Sunyata*.

163. Ibid., 119.

164. Ibid., 120.

165. Cf. Moltmann, *History and the Triune God*, 21–25.

The traditional formulation *opera trinitatis ad extra sunt indivisa*, would propose God's movement from the interiority toward exteriority in a linear progressive direction. However, *opera trinitatis sunt indivisa* not merely *ad extra*, or *ad intra*, but in every direction and respect. There are not two trinities. YHWH is not different from *God for us*. YHWH is in radical relationality with *God for us*, and vice versa. When this God is realized in time and space, this God as the wondrous being of self-emptying manifests Godself as the cosmic unselfish love of Jesus Christ in the Spirit of life like the Buddhahood. This wondrous being makes it possible that the Father and the Spirit co-suffered in a different way from the Son on the cross.

The Trinity in self-emptying (a social doctrine of the Trinity) is not different from the Trinity in wondrous being (trinitarian theism). The wondrous being as the self emptying underlines the unity of three persons. Christian dialectics of "identity-in-difference," oneness in three persons, needs to take into account the wondrous being of the self-emptying that is a radically other cataphatic dimension of the *Sunyata*. In light of the wondrous being, "identity-in-difference" is not different from "difference-in-identity." Uni-Trinity is not different from Tri-unity. This dimension can be fully realized at a time when God comes to us in time and space as the cosmic unselfish love. Christ's kenosis as self-emptying on the cross is not different from the realization of the wondrous being in the resurrection. This is why Jesus' last prayer of confidence becomes, "Father, I commend my spirit into your hands." Without the wondrous being of *Sunyata* there occurs total kenosis of the Trinity. Who is then the Father to whom Jesus on the cross prays?

Therefore, "God died, but yet God is not dead." In the experience of the wondrous being, history is open in radical relationality with the eschaton, all sentient creatures in *dukkha* are taken up and integrated into Christ's suffering on the cross as the cosmic unselfish love. They are children and creatures of God in *Sunyata*. God's essential *dukkha* in the Trinity assumed eternally and beforehand the *humanitas Christi*. This would take up the suffering of all human beings as well as of all sentient beings into God's suffering on the cross. It is continued by the future of God in advent that as renewal of all things includes the past, the present, and the future in a temporal sense. The wondrous being as the cosmic unselfish love is in radical relationality with the self-emptying event of Christ's kenosis. Even in the resurrection, Jesus Christ retains his earthly wounded *dukkha* in the cosmic resurrected body. The future of God is represented by the slain Lamb of God. This is an Asian understanding of the "other" Trinity in light of the wondrous being of the *Sunyata*.

Luther and Asian Trinitarian Theology of Divine *Dukkha*

In recent literature on theology and religious pluralism, the theology of the Trinity has become prominent. Trinitarian theologians who prefer to understand the triune God as divine Persons in relation find it important to deepen God's immanence in history, biological evolution, and ecology. Moltmann attempts to locate evolution within his trinitarian doctrine of continuous creation, in which eschatological panentheism is central. Therefore, Barth's trinitarian theology, which centers on the statement, "God revealed himself as the Lord," has undergone intensive criticism, especially by Moltmann. Moltmann argues that the three repetitions of God lean toward (Semi) Sabellianism or modalism.

Since Karl Barth, debate about the theology of the cross has been focused not only on the economy of salvation, but also on the immanent Trinity. An attempt that is made to secure the freedom and sovereignty of God's unity in terms of the traditional distinction between the immanent Trinity and the economic Trinity or in terms of the principle of correspondence[166] is sharply challenged by the concept of an open Trinity, in which "Dreieinigkeit" (three-in-oneness) is the basis for a social doctrine of the Trinity against the alleged tradition of monotheism.[167]

In elaboration of the question of God's loving suffering, Moltmann affirms Luther's *theologia crucis* as the key signature for all Christian theology. In order to overcome the problem of God's impassibility, Moltmann appreciates Luther for his understanding of *communicatio idiomatum in concreto*, in which the aspect of divine passibility breaks through the rigidity of the two natures of Christology prevalent in medieval thought. Moltmann's theology of the cross is unique in that he attempts to place the passion of God within the context of the doctrine of the Trinity. In his

166. Jüngel, *Doctrine of the Trinity*, 32–33.

167. In agreement with Moltmann, Pannenberg takes the passion of Jesus Christ to belong to the inner-trinitarian life of God as well as to history. However, as far as Moltmann affirms the divine unity, it would be a mistake to repudiate trinitarian monotheism. Cf. Pannenberg, *Systematic Theology*, 335 n. 217.

trinitarian understanding of the *theologia crucis*, it is of special significance for him to take seriously Bonhoeffer's aphorism, "Only the Suffering God can help."

Beyond Augustine, Luther, and Barth, Moltmann rejects a doctrine of appropriations as one-sided with more emphasis on *perichoresis*. He also extends the significance of the *theologia crucis* eschatologically and is eminently concerned about a political hermeneutic of liberation in the struggle with the vicious circles of poverty, racial prejudices, and cultural alienation and ecological devastation.[168] Moltmann's sensibility to ecological problems becomes conspicuous because God creates not only in the beginning, but also preserves through an ongoing creation. Divine involvement in the course of evolution manifests God's action in continuing creation, in solidarity with and compassion for the victims of natural selection. Given this fact, Moltmann's concept of a tripartite creation, *creatio originalis—creatio continua—creatio novum*, can meet the Buddhist idea of the universal compassion of the Bodhisattva, which is expressed in the vow for the redemption of all suffering in the evolution of karma.[169]

From the key standpoint of the cross, he has made a great effort to envisage a trinitarian history of God in the world. Be that as it may, Moltmann still allows a distinction between the immanent Trinity and the economic Trinity for God's sake on doxological grounds. Therefore, his early affirmation of Rahner's rule has undergone various stages in his reflection on the Trinity (for example, the monarchial form of the Trinity, the eucharistic form, and the doxological form). By starting off the Trinity of the Persons, Moltmann prefers to propose a concept of divine unity in the communion of Tri-unity. This has often been called a social model of the Trinity in terms of *perichoresis*, communion, and *koinonia*. After all, divine perichoretic unity is an affirmation of differences-in-unity. The distinction between the immanent Trinity and the economic Trinity will be raised into the immanent Trinity at the eschaton in which "God will be all in all" (1 Cor 15:24).

However, Paul's statement, a favorite in Moltmann's vision of eschatological panentheism, does not support Moltmann's trinitarian theology of eschatology because such a statement points to subjection of Jesus Christ to God. In other words, there is a possibility of two eschatologies, that is, God's eschatology and Christ's eschatology in Paul's concept of eschato-

168. Moltmann, *Crucified God*, 235–49, 325–40.

169. Moltmann, *God in Creation*, 208.

logical consummation with emphasis on the freedom and transcendence of God.

At any rate, Moltmann's vision of a unification in terms of dynamic mutuality and relationality or the *perichoresis* of the divine persons becomes the presupposition for a society organized democratically and cooperatively, which is well-echoed by liberation theology. It would provide a potential *vestigia trinitatis* in pursuing the Trinity in society. For a liberation theology, Boff insists that the economic Trinity is not the whole of the immanent Trinity because the Trinity is absolute, a sacramental mystery beyond what is manifested in its economic history.

However, Boff, along the lines of Moltmann, argues that the monarchy of the Father would lead to a theoretical justification for all injustice and oppression in society. In the framework of liberation theology, divine *perichoresis* provides a basis for building a just society. Equality, mutuality and community, which are core concepts in Moltmann's social Trinity, are re-appropriated to actualize the liberation of the Trinity for a just society in Latin America.[170]

What makes Moltmann attractive to Asian contextual theology lies in his linking of the Trinity to a just society with openness to world religions in that the trinitarian Persons affect the world and are affected by the World. According to Moltmann, the Trinity is a process of living relation of love in suffering among the trinitarian Persons that is articulated in terms of an "open Trinity" from the beginning, to the inclusion of the world, human beings and the cosmos. His social Trinity, which is underlined as an open Trinity, could be involved in a pluralistic world in terms of suffering love for and in solidarity with those who are poor, weak, or the oppressed of the world. They are called "anonymous Christians" in Moltmann's view.

From an Asian perspective, Panikkar structures his reflection on the Trinity in encounter with Hinduism and Buddhism. By emphasizing a radical apophatism of the Father in the Trinity, he affirms the deep intuition of Hinduism and Buddhism regarding the Trinity. According to him, the Buddhist experience of *Nirvana* or *Sunyata* comes to its climax in the founding source of the Father. The kenosis of Being is situated in the essential apophatism of the person of the Father.

That is, the Father may seem totally inaccessible to us. If the Father and the Son are not two, they are not one either. At this point, his advaitic

170. Boff, *Trinity and Society*. Cf. Boff, "Trinity," 75–89.

model of the Trinity ascribes to Hinduism a special role in illuminating the mystery of the Spirit. The Spirit both unites and distinguishes the other two persons of the Trinity. While not rejecting the Logos-centered trinitarian way of thinking, Panikkar also wants to deepen and reconstruct the meaning of the Trinity from outside the Logos, that is, from the silence of Buddhism and the unity of Hinduism. Trinitarian Persons remain in the "advaitic" sense, as not two. The mystery of the Trinity penetrates the Buddhist and Hindu experience of silence and non-differentiation.[171] Thus, the Son, the second Person of the Trinity, is left behind, subject to the Spirit.

His reflection on the cosmic operation of the Spirit takes the Spirit to work in hidden and unknown ways, differently from the Logos. The stirrings of the divine Spirit can carry out its vitality and efficacy independent of revelation in Jesus Christ. According to Panikkar, the Spirit proceeds from the Father and back to the Son, but the Spirit is ahead of the Son. If the cosmic activity of the Spirit can be discerned in other religions, a possible pneumatological pluralism in Panikkar would pave the way to a more authentic understanding of other faiths and religions. Be that as it may, it seems to me that his so-called radical Trinity leans toward ignoring the radicality of the Great Death of God in the authentic historical sense.

Regarding interfaith discourse on Trinity, I have appropriated a Buddhist insight into the cosmic *dukkha* in developing an Asian "staurocentric" (cross-centered) Trinity in terms of articulating a dialectical relationship between the freedom of God and the love of God in Christ in self-limitation. No single English term can be equivalent to the word *dukkha* (du, bad, low: kha, empty, hollow).[172]

Chained into the circle of birth and death in the world of becoming (Sanskrit: Samsara), all sentient living creatures suffer from a fundamental alienation and an ontological isolation from the Ultimate. *Dukkha* is a comprehensive notion encompassing physical, psychic, ontological, and cosmological dimensions of life marking the limitations of all finite, sentient, living creatures in the realities of the samsaric world. Luther's *theologia crucis*, in its interpretation of Christ's suffering as the sacrament and the example, is, in essence, of trinitarian character. According to Luther, that Christ's suffering is redemptive in the cosmic scope might refer to the

171. Panikkar, *Trinity and World Religions*, 5–6, 41–42, 46; Peters, *God as Trinity*, 73–80.

172. Dumoulin, *Understanding Buddhism*, 21–24.

fact that Christ's suffering is assumed and communicated by God for the sake of the world, human beings, and the cosmos.

This would be an important Lutheran aspect of *communicatio idiomatum in concreto* seen from a trinitarian point of view. Christ's humanity is included and assumed in the perichoretic fellowship of the triune God. All sentient living creatures in *dukkha* are allowed "enhypostatically" to be related and exalted to unity with God in trinitarian fellowship. Divine *dukkha* does not come out of the volitional tension between God's love and God's wrath, as Kitamori would expect. Rather, it is expressive of the wounded heart of God in companionship with the Son's way for the world. *Dukkha* offers, as a lived experience of Jesus Christ with his *ochlos*, a space for articulating God's relationality with the world.

Kazoh Kitamori sought to construct an Asian theology of the cross along Lutheran lines. For Kitamori, it is of special significance to present pain as the essence of God and thus combine a metaphor of God the Father begetting the Son with the metaphor of God the Father causing his Son to suffer and die. This is the theology of God's pain that is, in fact, of trinitarian character. Following in the footsteps of Luther, Kitamori, like Moltmann, takes it for granted that the Father's abandonment of the Son is exemplified in an Abraham-Isaac typology.[173] By actualizing Luther's phrase, "God hidden in pain," Kitamori sought to combine the pain of God with the love rooted in the pain of God in an attempt to resolve the tension between God's wrath and God's love.

However, Kitamori's failure of understanding and integrating Luther into an Asian context lies in the fact that he ignored totally the pain of the victims with whom Jesus Christ, as the victim, stands in a sacramental solidarity and presence. Furthermore, his incapability of relating eucharistic theology to Luther's justification is vulnerable because *theologia crucis,* in light of the real presence of Jesus Christ, moves in an eschatological direction toward hope. The liturgy of the Eucharist is at the heart of the liturgy of life, which refers to living the gospel in a spirit of self-abnegation and self-realization of kenotic discipleship.[174] What is worse, there is no way for Kitamori to extend his theology of God's pain to the dimension of cosmic suffering because he remains in an individual, forensic, and anthropological realm. The cosmic ecological significance of the theology of

173. Kitamori, *Theology of the Pain of God*, 47–48.

174. Pieris, *Asian Theology of Liberation*, 5–7.

the cross has become necessary and decisive and gains prominence in view of the ecological devastation in Asia.

In what follows, I will attempt to reconstruct Luther's *theologia crucis* from the trinitarian perspective in the affirmation of the humanity of Christ assumed eternally and beforehand in God's life. God the Father assumed *dukkha* in begetting the Son in the presence of the Spirit, and also historically in the life setting of Israel and people of God in the world. This provides a theology of divine suffering from a trinitarian perspective, one suitable for a Buddhist spirituality of *dukkha*. A Buddhist idea that everything and everybody is in *dukkha* deepens a radical relationality of all things. Eternity is a symbol of time without being identical to it. God's eternal life exists in God's life-world of *perichoresis*, which is a symbol of creatures' life in interconnection.

In Lutheran tradition it has been held that the Son of God communicated his divine majesty and attributes such as omnipotence and omnipresence to his assumed human nature in the incarnation (so-called *Genus majestaticum*). In the course of history, however, there has been an excessive emphasis on the state of humiliation (*status exinanitionis*) (Giessen School) by limiting divine attributes only to the earthly Jesus (*kenosis*). However, in the kenotic Christology of Lutheran theology (*genus tapeinoticum*), the content of the divinity of Christ would be severely challenged and threatened, while accentuating the participation of the human nature in the divine attributes.[175]

Seen from the trinitarian point of view, there is no point in separating the twofold way of humanity's participation in the divine attributes (*finitum capax infiniti*) or divinity's participation in the humanity (*infinitum capax finiti*) in Luther's thought. For Luther, the economic Trinity is taken as the self-manifestation of the immanent Trinity, which becomes also the presupposition for the economic Trinity. Immanently, God already exists eternally as Father in the way of *perichoresis* with Son and Holy Spirit, which means that God's being coinheres and interpenetrates divine others, without dethroning God's transcendence in the Trinity. However, economically God exists as the Creator, Redeemer, and the Sanctifier in the way of appropriations. The doctrine of appropriations, which means assigning an attribute or activity to particular divine persons according to the taxis of the economy, makes for a pronounced separateness and

175. Poehlmann, *Abriss der Dogmatik*, 224–25.

individuality of each divine person. Thus, it is not sufficient to articulate the perichoretic interrelatedness and codependence in the economy of salvation.

In order to complement the doctrine of appropriations, in which individualistic assignment of God to Father-Creator, Son-Redeemer, the Spirit-Sanctifier eradicates the transcendence of God in relation to the Son and the Spirit, I appropriate the meaning of *Tao*, *te,* and *ch'i* symbols to articulate aspects of mutual sharing of the trinitarian life without losing the freedom of God (*Tao*) in view of YHWH and *God for us. Tao* as the unity of the godhead becomes manifest and revealed in terms of *te-ch'i* movement in process of change. However, the *Tao* is *Sunyata* as well as wondrous being, underlying *te-ch'i* manifestation. The significance of a *Tao-te-ch'i* symbol for trinitarian thinking lies in its character of relational dynamism. *Ch'i* (Spirit) is in *te* (Son) and vice versa, in which the transcendental unity of the godhead (*Tao*) is affirmed and, at the same time, the threeness of Father, Son, and Spirit exists in mutual fellowship and communion in terms of change.[176] Nevertheless, *Tao* is affirmed as transcendence in *te-ch'i* relationship.

In the Taoist framework, I am aware of a dynamic triadic movement of *Tao* through *te* in the presence of *ch'i*. The permanent *Tao* reflects a biblical idea of God who "shall be." The *Tao* cannot be named or clearly conceived of in human conceptions due to its character of mystery and transcendence. However, this *Tao* is the life-giving ground and womb for all beings. *Te* lies and abides the *Tao*. So *te* is a realization or expression of the *Tao* in actual and natural loving like a metaphor of watercourse. The *Tao* is the ground or womb from which *te* and *ch'i* originate. All life springs from, follows, and finally returns to it through guidance of *te* and *ch'i*. *Tao*, metaphorically expressed as the mystical womb, is closely associated with the Great Void. The Void is efficacious like a belly and capable of emanating *te* and producing breath, *ch'i*. From the perspective of *Tao* dynamic transcendence in the movement of *te* and *ch'i*, I appropriate a trinitarian meaning of God's transcendence in the historical becoming reality.

Here is God who is in creational-covenantal manifestation through Word and Spirit in the cosmos and history of Israel. Here is God who is in revelational-incarnational manifestation in the Son through the Spirit.

176. Cf. Lee Jung-Young, *The Trinity in Asian Perspective*, 50–69. My concern about freedom of *Tao* in a *te-ch'i* way of thinking is different from Lee's interpretation of yin-yang inclusiveness of the *Tao* in which *Tao*'s priority is dethroned.

Here is God who is in eschatological-doxological manifestation with respect to the eschatological subjection of the Son to God's consummation. The essential Trinity, the metaphor of which is expressed in the laboring pain of the Father begetting the Son in the Spirit of life (to use Tillich's phrase "the mother-quality of giving birth") becomes a theological premise for understanding divine suffering in the framework of *theologia crucis*.[177] As a matter of fact, there is neither the immanent Trinity nor the economic Trinity, but the God of Israel in its manifestation in creational, covenanantal, revelational, and doxological form in historical-eschatological relatedness and openness. All forms are in relationality. The doxological Trinity is not the telos to which other forms of the Trinity move, and no different from the essential Trinity. Each form of the Trinity is not timeless, but related to the world, involving God in history as divine agent in mercy and freedom. God is the archaic source, the forwarding reality (God will be who will be), and the coming reality. Finally, God will be all in all through the subjection of the Son to Father.

The debate of the Trinity has been centered on how to understand the relation of each Person concerning the oneness in threeness (Uni-Trinity) or threeness in oneness (the Tri-unity). The priority of the Father has been affirmed as the sole source and the origin of both the divine essence and the persons of the Son and the Holy Spirit or as one divine *ousia* in terms of a coinherence of relationships. To overcome a monarchial form of the Father in the Trinity between the Orthodox Church and the Western Church, there has been an attempt to emphasize the divine *perichoresis* over the social model of the Trinity. Some emphasize a parabolic or chiastic model in the double movement of emanation and return in preference for imaging a single arrow in double movement descending downward from the Father, through the Son and Spirit to the world, and making an upward ascent through the Spirit and the Son, resting finally with the Father; *a patre ad patrem*.[178]

However, my inculturation model of the Trinity finds it significant to stress relationality with a transcendence of the name of God in light of a double dimension of *Sunyata* as the wondrous being in trinitarian fellowship, and *te-chi* movement. God is relational and personal, *ad intra* as well as *ad extra*, from the essential Trinity to the doxological Trinity. This regards the essential Trinity as not timeless but as expressed in its threefold

177. Tillich, *Systematic Theology* (vol. 3), 294.

178. LaCugna, *God for Us*, 192–3. Cf. Peters, *God as Trinity*, 125–7, 178.

manifestation: (1) the creational-covenantal Trinity, (2) the revelational Trinity, and (3) the doxological Trinity in historical and eschatological relatedness and openness. In light of relationality there is but one Trinity that will be consummated and made perfect in the coming advent of the doxological Trinity. However, YHWH does not merely become one with *God for us* in terms of the principle of correspondence. This is because God is complete and realizes Godself in time and space from God's future including the past, present, and future in a temporal eschatological sense. In other words, there is only one God in various relationships to creation, redemption, and consummation. The traditional difference between immanent and economic Trinities is based on the distinction between metaphysics (*theologia*) and physics (*oikonomia*), or history and salvation.

The immanent Trinity, however, should be identical with the economic Trinity in the movement of the self-communication of God. Otherwise, there would be no self-revelation of God. After all, the Trinity is the mystery of God communicating and revealing Godself in relation to us in creation, in incarnation, and in consummation. The Trinity is, in fact, the comprehensive salvation-drama of God's mystery rooted in God's lived experience with Israel and the people of the world moving from creation to consummation. There is no need to make a distinction between the immanent Trinity and the economic Trinity on metaphysical grounds. It is necessary, however, in light of God's transcendence in the coming future in which the essential Trinity and economic Trinity are related to each other. In a model of God's transcendence in the trinitarian becoming reality and a manifestation regarding God's coming future, the Slain Lamb of God plays a significant role.

Rahner's rule marks a groundbreaking watershed for trinitarian discourse in an ecumenical context. In spite of a conflation or equation between economic and immanent Trinities, in Rahner's judgment, God's aseity is not independent of historical self-relatedness with the world.[179] To what extent do we understand the relationship between them? This is a dilemma. In the case of protecting the divine freedom and absoluteness, the economic Trinity would be subordinated to the immanent Trinity. In the case of protecting the relatedness of the economic Trinity with the world, divine sovereignty and independence would be threatened. A total collapse of the immanent Trinity into the economic Trinity would amount to divine dependence upon the world. For Barth, the economic Trinity is

179. Rahner, *Trinity*, 21–22.

the way to what is known as the immanent Trinity, how God is in Godself, but not by losing the priority of YHWH in transcendence and freedom. Thereby, the correspondence appears between economic and immanent Trinities.

If there is only a correspondence between economic and immanent Trinities, how do we maintain the identity between them? If *God for us* is truly identical with YHWH, there is no need for an *analogia relationis*, or a principle of correspondence. In that case, how do we affirm God's eternity independently of the temporality of the world? Following in the footsteps of Karl Rahner, LaCugna's chiastic model of emanation and return shows an outstanding example of actualizing the aspect of "*God for us*" in which the mystery of YHWH manifests itself from the Father to the Son to the Spirit to the creation and redemption of the world and back again to the return to the Father. It is characteristic of the movement *a Patre ad Patrem*. According to LaCugna, there is neither an economic nor an immanent Trinity because "Oikonomia is the comprehensive plan of God reaching from creation to consummation." *Theologia* refers to "the mystery of God" which "is the mystery of God with us."[180]

In fact, for LaCugna the doctrine of the Trinity lies in an attempt to understand the eternal mystery of God on the basis of the economy of salvation. In following Rahner's rule, she proposes a way to understand the eternal life of God in terms of the historical economy of salvation. Of course, it does not mean that *theologia* should be in total identification with *oikonomia*. Since the Nicene creed, the intradivine relations of the three persons have gone un-related to God's activity in the world. "The result of this was a one-sided theology of God that had little to do with the economy of Christ and the Spirit, with the themes of Incarnation and grace, and therefore little to do with the Christian life."[181] Rahner's core concept of God's self-communication by nature becomes the basis for LaCugna to deepen the mysterious and ineffable God in the manifestation and expression of God in sharing Godself with the world. God in relation is who YHWH is, although God's mystery remains. At any rate, *Deus absconditus* is what *Deus revelatus* is. In this light Rahner's rule is taken up to mean, "theology is inseparable from soteriology, and vice versa."[182] If

180. LaCugna, *God for Us*, 223–4.

181. Ibid., 210.

182. Ibid., 211.

God for us is who YHWH is, LaCugna affirms that God is personal. This does not refer to God as "one person in three modalities, or one nature in three persons."[183]

This indicates the encounter between divine and human persons in the economy of salvation. The mystery of God is not based on God's transcendence, but human incapacity to express fully the saving activity of God. God's self-communication is fully and completely imparted to us. In spite of human participation in divinity, God remains absolute and ineffable because of human incapacity to comprehend what we have experienced. A critique appears in respect to the relation between eternity and temporality.[184] If *theologia* is *oikonomia* and vice versa, how does a chiastic model of *a Patre ad Patrem* understand God's dynamic transcendence in a trinitarian becoming reality in view of God's coming?

In my view, a theological attempt to look for the identity of the economic Trinity and the immanent Trinity is found in an eschatological framework. As Moltmann says, "the economic Trinity completes and perfects itself in the immanent Trinity when the history and experience of salvation are completed and perfected. When everything is 'in God' and 'God is all in all,' then the economic Trinity is raised into and transcended in the immanent Trinity."[185]

Therefore, the immanent Trinity, as the coming Trinity, has to be secured on doxological-eschatological grounds. The identity of economic and immanent Trinity is qualified as "an eschatological convergence."[186] That being the case, would not we still be caught in an unbalanced dualism in an eschatological framework of fixing *God for us* as a move toward YHWH as the telos?

From my perspective, the identity and distinction between the immanent Trinity and the economic Trinity cannot be shifted to a fixed form of God's being "all in all" as the telos. God's eschatological presence realizes itself as the wondrous Being of the Trinity here and now because God's eternal life cannot be understood adequately apart from God's temporal life, and vice versa. God, as archaic source is a forwarding reality in sharing

183. Ibid., 305.

184. For this critique, see Peters, *God as Trinity*, 128. Peters has much in common with LaCugna, albeit in favor of an eschatological convergence between the immanent Trinity and the economic Trinity.

185. Moltmann, *Trinity and the Kingdom*, 161.

186. Peters, *God as Trinity*, 177.

God's life with Israel and people of the world. Therefore, the human Jesus is thought not in terms of *logos asarkos*, but *logos ensarkos*. *Anhypostasis* of Jesus is in inseparable relationality with *enhypostasis* of Jesus.

If we see Luther's Christology and its *communicatio idiomatum* through a Buddhist-Taoist way of thinking the passibility of God in trinitarian sharing fellowship is dynamic because *Tao*, which is the wondrous Being of *Sunyata*, as the principle of the unity of *te* and *ch'i*, underlies God's transcendent unity in differentiation, and simultaneously differentiation in God's transcendental unity. Put otherwise, the wondrous being penetrates and co-inheres in the trinitarian life-world as dynamic movement. Likewise, the genuine freedom of the eschatological being of God expresses itself in its realization as *Immanuel* in the world.

In fact, the purpose of Christian spirituality lies in participating in the life of God through Jesus Christ in the Spirit, and in personal encounter with God's self-communication with us. God's eschatology is neither different nor divorced from God's archaic source and historical temporality, but related to it in a qualified dialectical sense. Only on this basis we can talk about the relation between the eschatological consummation in advent and the wholeness of time. The mystery of God is not merely based on human inability to comprehend what he/she has experienced, but on God's transcendence and freedom in the trinitarian manifestation through the Son and Spirit. The eschatological future that is inclusive of natural and world history transforms temporality into the wholeness of time, and integrates it as an indispensable part of eternity. In so doing, it realizes itself in temporality. This is known to us as the dynamics of divine grace, encouraging a human spirituality of gratitude and humility, and strengthening diaconal discipleship in protest against the culture of death before God and before the world.

The cross of Jesus in the economy of God's saving work is related to God's life. The *theologia crucis*, seen in a trinitarian way, forms an understanding of a middle time. It finds itself between the metaphors of the essential Trinity as God giving birth and the eschatological Trinity as the Slain Lamb. With respect to Protology and future (or eschatology) of God, the *theologia crucis* constitutes a middle of time (a time of grace in an historical context), which is related to the essential Trinity and the eschatological Trinity. God's relationship to the world is also internal to the divine life. The Trinity is open, inclusive, and related to the world. Asian Lutheran thinking of the Trinity in this regard does not confine the relationship between *theologia* and *oikonomia* to a double relationship. Rather, it extends God's transcendence in a qualified trinitarian relationship with respect to essential, economic, and eschatological manifestations, in which God's freedom and transcendence in the midst of *dukkha* stands at the center, realized and epitomized by the subjection of the Son to God who will be all in all.

Therefore, my Asian understanding of Trinity avoids dualistic distinctions regarding God's temporality as a move in anticipation of God's ultimate eschatology. Rather, the essential Trinity is neither different nor divorced from the economic Trinity, as conversely the economic Trinity is neither different nor divorced from the eschatological Trinity. They are in a qualified dialectical and non-dual relationality. When God, as the wondrous Being of the Trinity, comes to and grips us and the world through the power of the Holy Spirit, the coincidence of God's life in Trinity opens up in realizing itself as the Immanuel. This is of special significance to Christian spirituality in the experience of God in the trinitarian life. Everybody and everything can realize themselves as brothers and sisters in unity with God in Jesus Christ in the presence of the Spirit. Counter to Lee Jung-Young's speculation, the radical mutual inclusiveness and unqualified non-dualistic way of thinking in a yin-yang framework need not necessarily lead to a total collapse of the economic Trinity into the immanent Trinity or the immanent Trinity into the economic Trinity.[187]

This would be a logic of assimilation and exclusiveness, thus doing harm to the different as different. The immanent Trinity is not in oneness with the economic Trinity, and at the same time, they are not two. In the same way, the economic Trinity is not in oneness with the eschatological Trinity, but they are not two. They are, however, in relationship, in which God wants to express Godself as the wondrous Being through unselfish cosmic love of Jesus Christ by the power of the Spirit.

There is one God who is seen in threefold manifestation of God's life in the eternal-historical non-dual relatedness. The essential Trinity, the economic Trinity, and the eschatological Trinity are in relationality with each other. Nevertheless, there is a space for the lordship of God. As St. Paul states, "When all things are subjected to him, then the Son himself will also be subjected to the one who put all things in subjection under him, so that God may be all in all" (1 Cor 15:28).

187. Jung-Young, *Trinity in Asian Perspective*, 68.

The mystery of God in trinitarian communion can be known only by God in coming to us in accompaniment with our wondrous experience of it through Jesus Christ in the presence of the Spirit. The Holy Spirit brings God's gracious future into our hearts, so that the crucified and risen Christ of yesterday and the doxological Christ of tomorrow are the basis for our faith as well as our discipleship in following *conformitas Christi* in the world. This is a trinitarian spirituality of *Anfechtungen* in an Asian perspective that is also at the heart of the relation among YHWH, *God for us* and God *in advent.*

From the perspective of God in relationship with divine others, we perceive a metaphor of a laboring pain of the Father begetting the Son in the life of the Spirit. This is the prototype for the divine *dukkha* of the Father in relation to the Son and the Spirit based on the eternal incarnation. This initial incarnation of the Son in God's life reflects on the Father's accompaniment into the Son's way for the world.

God requires and accompanies divine others so that they exist in fellowship. This relationality is relationship in difference. *Perichoresis* is a principle of allowing for different Persons and accompanying divine others in fellowship. However, *perechoresis* does not dethrone a priority of God the Father regarding divine others. This *perichoresis* needs to meet a Taoist framework of God's transcendence (*Tao*) in *te* (Son)-*ch'i* (Spirit) manifestation. In the light of the crucified Christ, the Trinity is a broken and wounded Trinity. The metaphor of the essential Trinity, which denotes God's transcendence in God's life with divine others reaches its climax in the suffering of the Son on the cross. Therefore, the crucified Christ is the realistic expression of the co-suffering of God in the Spirit of *Mahakaruna* (Great Mercy*)*. In this regard, "the deepest ground for the passion of Christ is the pathos of God who for eternity is love."[188]

At this point, we are reminded of the Council of Toledo in 675: "We must believe that the Son was not made out of nothing, nor out of some substance or other, but from the womb of the Father, that is, that he was begotten or born from the Father's own being."[189] Primordially speaking, there is no Son of "God" without God's life. God, as mystic womb of Son, generates the Son and breathes forth the Spirit. God's eternity is not merely God's timelessness. Rather, God's temporality is the symbol of God's life in eternity.

188. Moltmann, *History and the Triune God*, 23.

189. Ibid., 22.

If God's relation to what is outside of God reflects the relation that God has within Godself eternally, God in trinitarian life assumes humanity in terms of the generating pain of the Father in the presence of the Spirit. The eternal begetting of the Son is the eternal ground of sending of the Son in the economy of the historical incarnation. So with the Holy Spirit. The Father's journey into the Son in the Spirit of mercy is the primary ground for the Father's co-participation in incarnation, suffering, resurrection and consummation together with the Son and the Spirit. God the Father co-participates in the mission of divine others. Therefore, God in transcendence is, properly speaking, implicitly related to *humanitas Christi* in both eternal and temporal aspects.

God's passion for Israel and God's solidarity with and mercy for Israel are at the heart of God's covenantal history. The creational-covenantal Trinity articulates the God of Israel regarding the divine *dukkha* in relation to Israel, pagans, and all living creatures in suffering. The Father accompanies his oppressed people of Israel through the Word (Wisdom) and the Shekina's presence, and takes care of other people as well, including all creatures. This image of the Father is in opposition to "the demanding father-image of the God."[190]

The dialectic between transcendence and physical immanence of the name of God has relevance in 1 Kgs 8:13f (the temple as the house for God to dwell), Exod 40:35 (the glory of YHWH filling the tabernacle) and Lev 16:16 (God's indwelling in the midst of people's uncleanness). Jewish thinking is also of incarnational character. If the Christian Trinity does not remove the character name of the God of Israel, if the Trinity does not separate the incarnation of the Word of God in the Jewish Messiah Jesus from the indwelling of God in Israel, a trinitarian understanding of God in the name of the Father, Son, and the Spirit overcomes its suppercessionist and patriarchal-onto-theological language in light of YHWH. In 1 Cor 13:9ff, we are aware of Paul's theology of eschatological reserve. Human understanding of God in the mystery of the Trinity remains partial and incomplete until the complete comes. If the Christian discourse of the Trinity is an interpretation of God in covenant with Israel and the Father of Jesus Christ, it should, first of all, be oriented towards the Old Testament. The Trinity articulates the revelation of the name of God in the threefold historical events: (1) in the coming of God to Israel, (2) in the coming of God into Jesus, and (3) in the coming of God in God's Spirit through the Pentecost to all people of the world.

190. Tillich, *Systematic Theology* (vol. 3), 294.

The God of Israel is not an apathetic God who is incapable of suffering, enthroned high above in heaven without feelings. In the rabbinical literatures there is an abundance of biblical texts and explanations of the Scriptures that speak of God abasing Godself and making Godself the servant of Israel (*shekhinah*). In this regard, the Christian understanding of God in the trinitarian expression bears witness to the One who loves Israel, Christians, and people of the world in reconciliation of Christ, and in freedom of the Spirit.

God in the revelational-incarnational manifestation is in continuation of God of Israel in reaching its climax in the historical death of Jesus Christ on the cross. Jesus enters into the place of the temple (John 2:18–22) and becomes the temple of his body in which the name of YHWH dwells and pitches in fullness of the Spirit without measure (John 1:14, 3:34f). In Christ the fullness of God is pleased to dwell (Col 1:19). The name Jesus Christ does not stand in competition with the name YHWH. God in the Spirit is present in the internal heart of believers. God works in our hearts in the presence of the Spirit in the coming of the kingdom of God. Against the direction of the social doctrine of the Trinity, the triune God needs to be reinterpreted in terms of historical dynamism of the one living God in a biblical and historical sense. God feels sorry about humanity (Gen 6:6, Ps 106:45, Joel 2:13, etc.).

In internal relationship of God to Godself, we are aware of a transcendence of God beyond Godself for the sake of humanity. This transcendence points to God's relationship to self and an eschatological reservation. A dogmatic concept of eternal generation of the Son preserves the special historicity of the Father's name in relation to the Son and the historical activity of a biblical God. The Spirit is promised upon all flesh. The death of the Son on the cross, and the compassion of the Father in the death of the Son through the Spirit, and the resurrection of Christ from the dead all have their dynamism and promise in connection with the name of YHWH in the kingdom of God. So *theologia crucis* and *resurrectionis* can be shaped and developed in the framework of God's covenantal promise and eschatological openness; the God of Israel in the revelation of the Father, Son and Spirit is God who is coming to the world. The concept of theopathy helps us to see that God's omnipotence is expressed clearly in God's comprehensive power to co-suffer. Nevertheless, God is free from the iron cage of theopathy.

Given this fact, God in creation is God in immanence within the process of evolution through the Spirit, allowing for self-limitation and vulnerability to the suffering of all creatures in the process of natural selection. Although nature is a creative process at many levels, through law, chance, and emergence, it is not redemptive at all.[191] If the metaphysics of evolution articulates "the interdependence of all beings in an ecological understanding of the web of life,"[192] it would resonate with a Buddhist idea of mutual interplay and influence of all elements and phenomena with each other in the karmic process of evolution through all of time.[193]

Natural selection does not need to be used one-sidedly to justify the survival of the fittest under the conditions of competitive struggle. Rather, in the process of selection, underlying differential reproduction, and survival we recognize the important relationship between cooperation and competition. However, continuing creation is not supposed to be merely a dynamic process of trial-and-error depending on what has already been there. Rather, chance, law, and history in the process of evolution would be consistent with the will of God's longsuffering by hoping all things and enduring all things (1 Cor 13:7). God is wounded for the victims caused by struggle and suffering, accident, and chance or uncertainty, and they will be restored in God's future, finally.

According to God's covenant with Noah, every living creature comes into God's covenantal relationship. A flood will not violate or destroy the law of earth. The law of nature in its independent and free course belongs to God's promise. God loves the world in God's freedom and promise establishing covenant with all. The sign of God's universal covenant is extended beyond Noah toward all future generations. God is no longer a God of distance or gaps, but a God of establishing covenantal relationship with creation, and allowing God's self-limitation according to this covenant, so that the world of nature is driven by natural law and rhythm, and open to God's promise. God's covenantal promise does not take away the evolutionary freedom of the earth, but places a sign of grace accompanying, transforming, and guiding it to God's universal shalom in Jesus Christ who is the image of God.

God in incarnation, the revealed Trinity, is in continuation of God's life in indwelling in Israel in a creational-covenantal context, reaching its

191. Cf. Barbour, *When Science meets Religion*, 113.

192. Barbour, *Religion and Science*, 249.

193. Nisker, *Buddha's Nature*, 58–62.

climax in the historical form of the cross, that is the Great death of the Son. God's participation in the death of the Son on the cross is none other than an expression of divine pathos from the beginning. The resurrection of the crucified in the cosmic dimension is the beginning of the rebirth of all creatures and the whole cosmos. This is the beginning of an eschatological process of a new creation by God restoring all things.

The cosmic innocent lamb slain for the entire human race is at the center of the doxological Trinity. This name, "God-with-them" (Rev 21:3) will be God to all people, Christians and non-Christians alike, by relieving injustice to many wounded people on earth and by wiping away the tears from their eyes. The doxological Trinity will heal divine *dukkha* in terms of God's *mahakaruna* in eschatological consummation. The wounded Cosmic Lamb will be the maker of the whole creation anew where the essential Trinity will make itself completely and finally and universally revealed to everyone and everything. "Tragedy in God" (Nikolai Berdyaev) can be finally healed by the all-encompassing *karuna* of the slain innocent Lamb of God who takes away the sin of the world.

A divine creativity exists immanently within the whole natural order, without losing divine freedom and purpose. God loves in freedom and self-limitation, and so God creates in immanence within the process of natural selection. Put otherwise, God's immanence in the process of evolution is the God of liberation who was proclaimed definitely and explicitly in the gospel of Jesus of Nazareth (Luke 4:18–19).

An Asian project of liberative pluralism, a just society and postmodern recognition of others can be primordially envisioned in the transcendence of God in divine life in the pain of the Father begetting the Son in the life-giving Spirit. They should also be historically and eschatologically concretized in light of God's future in a doxological Trinity. The eschatological Being of God breaks into our history, expresses loving concern for innocent victims, and proclaims a liberative message of the slain Lamb of God for the poor and the low. God's *novum* begins with the resurrection of the crucified. God's future is in relationality with its coming into the present. Therefore, an Asian theology of liberation for the poor can be meaningful and sacramental in light of God's future with respect to the slain innocent Lamb in the presence of the Spirit in our midst. The slain lamb in the doxological Trinity cannot be fully understood apart from the *dukkha* of victims.

At a minimum, Luther's understanding of the Trinity affirms the primacy of the Father as the fountainhead or wellspring of the Godhead with respect to the order of the persons (in the Eastern tradition) and the *homoousios*-unity in the western tradition.[194] Seen in light of a hermeneutic of double understanding of *Sunyata*, Tri-unity is not totally different from Uni-Trinity. *Perichoresis* is not different from *Sunyata* as the wondrous being of nonsubstantiality. At this juncture, the Father is not only the source or origin of the other Persons, but also the source of the passion and mercy for them.

This metaphor of God's begetting the Son is expressive of God's passion for all. The suffering of all human beings and all sentient living creatures is prototypically related to the pain of God begetting the Son in the presence of the Spirit, but exists enhypostatically in Christ's *assumptio carnis* and death on the cross, in the Resurrection. Finally it is integrated and healed in the eschatological form of the slain Lamb of God. In this regard, divinity's participation in humanity (*infinitum capax finiti*) gives a christological dynamism to humanity's participation in the divine salvation drama and furthermore opens up implicitly an affirmation that all sentient creatures in *dukkha* "anhypostatically-enhypostatically" are related, posited and exalted to God's trinitarian life of mercy and passion, and are also transformed in light of the divine eschatological future.

Therefore, Luther's notion of "God's being beforehand" might be interpreted implicitly as a model of God's transcendence and freedom in the trinitarian relationship with the world and a Trinity open toward accepting otherness outside Christianity because every living creature lives in companionship with the divine life of mercy and passion. God's companionship and presence in the Spirit penetrates their suffering in the midst of socio-political injustice and ecological devastation. God in the Bible is the God whom all living sentient creatures are waiting, groaning, and longing for in the coming of the final salvation (Rom 8:19ff). The God who moves in an open-ended process of continuing creation is, therefore, the God who allows for self-limitation by suffering with the world. Being vulnerable to victimization, God restores and redeems. The God who saves must also be the God who creates, as the God who saves must be the God who restores and gives life.

Luther's *theologia crucis* radicalizes the uttermost depths of the tragedy of God in the crucified Christ in a trinitarian perspective. Divine pas-

194. *LW*, 15:316; *WA*, 54:69.

sibility is central in God's loving suffering and mercy in the crucified Jesus Christ. The crucified Christ in the trinitarian life is, in fact, universal and sacramental in solidarity with and mercy for the lowest of the low.

The *Filioque* in Asian Focus

Much has been said about reconsidering the *filioque* regarding the ecumenical concern for reconciliation between the Orthodox East and the Latin West. The decisive question is about the mode of the Spirit's origin. Does the Spirit proceed from both the Father and the Son (*ex Patre Filioque*) or from the Father alone? The Niceno-Constantinopolitan creed of 381 states that the "Spirit proceeds from the Father." However, Augustine (and later Hilary of Poitiers) conceived of the Holy Spirit as the mutual love uniting Father and Son. Therefore, the Holy Spirit is the Spirit of the two in relationship. That the Spirit is the Spirit of the Father and the Son means the procession of the Spirit from the Father and the Son.

Since the death of Augustine, the *filioque* has become gradually affirmed as an article of faith in official statements since the Council of Toledo in 447 and 589. Controversy between the West and the East erupted when Charlemagne urged that the *filioque* be formally inserted in the Nicene Creed. Rome and Constantinople were rivals in newly Christianized areas of Europe. Even though Pope Leo III believed that the *filioque* was theologically correct, he resisted the demand of Charlemagne to insert the *filioque* into the Nicene Creed. Later in that century, Photius, Patriarch of Constantinople, defended the Orthodox position by insisting that the Spirit proceeds "from the Father alone." According to him, Jesus himself said that the Spirit comes from the Father (John 15:26), not from him. Even worse, the idea of the *filioque* makes the role of the Spirit in co-equality and co-eternity subordinated to the first persons of the Trinity. The West in attachment to the *filioque* would inevitably turn Sabellianism from the Father to the Son and lastly to the Spirit as to his grandson. In strong affirmation of the monarchy of the first Person (*archē*), the representatives of the Eastern Church accused the Latin West of di-theism and semi-Sabellianism. In locating the unity of the Godhead in the Father, Vladimir Lossky remarks, "This is why the East has always opposed the formula of *filioque* which seems to impair the monarchy of the Father."[195]

195. Lossky, *Mystical Theology*, 58.

The final break came when Pope Benedict VIII officially added the *filioque* formula to the Creed, perhaps in 1014. The schism between East and West occurred in 1054. Since then, the *filioque* has became a stumbling block between East and West. The main line of defense of the *filioque* has been developed by Augustine, Anselm in his *De Processione Spiritus Sancti* (1102), and re-articulated by Thomas Aquinas a century and a half later.[196] For the Latin West, the *filioque*, in which God's Spirit is, in fact, the Spirit of Jesus Christ, serves to affirm the unity of God, co-equality, and virtual equivalence of the three persons of the Trinity.

For the Orthodox East, however, the *filioque* inevitably introduces two distinct sources or origins into the Trinity by dissolving the Father's primacy into the Son, and then subordinating the Spirit to them. The Councils of Lyons (1274) and Florence (1438–1439) reaffirmed the *filioque*: "The Holy Spirit proceeds eternally from the Father and the Son, yet not as from two origins, but as from one origin, not by two breathings, but by a single breathing." In agreement with this point, Florence adds that the patristic formula, "from the Father through the Son" does not run counter to an Augustinian line of thought in which the Father, by begetting the Son, also bestows upon him that the Spirit should proceed from the Son as well as from himself. However, this reconciling position was repudiated by the Eastern Orthodox Church.[197]

In the twentieth century, strong suspicion has been raised by Eastern theologians (especially Lossky) for the whole framework of western trinitarian theology from Augustine onwards inasmuch as it tends to Sabellianism in its unbalanced emphasis on the divine unity of God the Father. The *filioque* becomes a trademark for generating this imbalance. The subordination and de-personalization of the Spirit occurs as a result.[198] Western theologians are asked even to disavow the doctrine of the *filioque* and affirm the trinitarian framework of the Eastern Church. Moltmann's social Trinity, for example, has no room for the *filioque* formula, because in it he sees a lack of understanding the Spirit as a distinct and independent person.

According to Moltmann, the *filioque* never expressed the Son in completion of the monarchy of the Father regarding the Spirit, because in the West there is no denying that the Son and the Holy Spirit proceed

196. *ST*, I. qu. 36.

197. Heron, *Holy Spirit in the Bible*, 94.

198. Lossky, "The Procession of the Holy Spirit," 31–53. Cf. Vischer, ed., *Spirit of God, Spirit of Christ*.

from the Father each in different ways. The Father is always the origin of both. Therefore, the *filioque* addition is superfluous.

However, the sole procession of the Spirit from the Father is not expressive of the Spirit's perichoretic relation to the Son. In the eternal generation of the eternal Son, God the Father is always the Father of the Son, but not as the Sole Cause, Moltmann argues.[199] Moltmann's proposal is to affirm the single procession of the Father in the eternal presence of the Son along the lines of P. Boris Bobrinskoy: "*Le Fils éternel n'est pas étranger à la procession du Saint Esprit.*"[200] For Moltmann, in his reflection on the trinitarian doxology that corresponds to the social analogy of the triune God, the Spirit proceeds from the Father and rests in the Son. If the Son is begotten by the Father through the Spirit, the Spirit is always present in the Son in all eternity in accompaniment with, resting in, and shining from the Son.[201]

However, Ted Peters argues that if the *filioque* is seen in light of the Easter Christ, we are supposed to think of the Spirit as proceeding from Jesus Christ.[202] In contrast to Eastern Orthodox theology, the Spirit is the principle of relationship and unity, and also the maintainer of the unity in difference. In rethinking Augustine, Peters stresses that "the Spirit is the condition whereby the generation of the Son is made possible, yet without the Son to whom the Father relates there would be no divine Spirit."[203]

At any rate, the Western Church's inclination in which the trinitarian order of Father, Son, and Spirit is placed "side by side" with each other insists on the Spirit in double procession. In the Eastern Church's tendency of placing the trinitarian relations "one after another," the Spirit proceeds from the Father through the Son. If the single procession of the Spirit from the Father implies that the Son accompanies the procession of the Spirit from the Father, the *filioque* formula is unnecessary, because the single procession is enough to maintain the reciprocal relationship of the Father and the Son. The reciprocal accompaniment that refers to the position of

199. Moltmann, *Trinity and the Kingdom*, 183.

200. Ibid., 184. "The eternal Son is not alien to the procession of the Holy Spirit."

201. Moltmann, *Spirit of Life*, 308.

202. Peters, *God as Trinity*, 66.

203. Ibid. In being positive about Coffey's mutual love theory reaffirming the *filioque* and in the appropriation of Augustine by Pannenberg, Peters sees the Spirit in light of relationality and communality whereby the Spirit as the communion of love enables "the divinity and the precise character of the first two persons of the Trinity." Peters, *God as Trinity*, 70.

the Eastern Church means that the Spirit accompanies the begetting of the Son, and the Son accompanies the procession of the Spirit.

Pannenberg's argument calls into question the relations of origin in terms of his radically dependent relationality of divinity. Pannenberg's starting point for the Trinity, like Barth's, is the analysis of God's revelation in Jesus Christ. However, God as the Trinity is dependent on the future of God's coming kingdom. Jesus Christ reveals the love of God in the form of the anticipation of the future of God's kingdom. Pannenberg, in criticism of Barth's emphasis on God as a single divine subject in three modes of being, calls this Western position, from Augustine, Anselm, and Thomas Aquinas down to Hegel, a "pre-trinitarian, theistic idea of God."[204]

In similarity to Moltmann, Pannenberg constitutes the divine unity through the mutual relations of the three divine persons rather than by positing a single divine subject. This is a relational unity that Pannenberg has in mind. Given this fact, the Eastern doctrine of generation and procession, in which the Father is maintained as the source of divinity, is left behind. Instead, the reciprocally determining relational unity comes to the surface. The identity of divine persons deepens their relations to each other. This dependent divinity of three persons is understood properly as the outcome of personhood in relationship. The unity of Godhead as a unity of integrating love finds itself in the Spirit. Therefore, the personhoods of Son and Spirit are not supposed to be reduced to their relation of origin in generation or procession from the Father. The three persons in God are each totally dependent upon their relation to the others.[205] Put otherwise, "The dialectic of otherness and unity internal to the divine life is virtually the source of the three persons."[206]

204. Pannenberg, "Problems of a Trinitarian Doctrine of God," 251. Jüngel defends Barth's *Dreieinigkeit* against Pannenberg's charge, but is in agreement with him on many trinitarian issues due to Pannenberg's post-Barthian tendencies. Cf. Jüngel, "Nihil Divinitas, Ubi Non Fides," 221 n. 66. Cf.; Peters, *God as Trinity*, 136, 141, 224. In my judgment, however, Pannenberg's affinity to Barth's Trinity lies in his emphasis on God's dominion over the world. As Pannenberg states, "The world as the object of his lordship might not be necessary to his deity, since its existence owes its origin to his creative freedom, but the existence of the world is not compatible with his deity apart from his lordship over it. Hence, lordship goes hand in hand with the deity of God." Pannenberg, *Systematic Theology*, 313. For Moltmann's critique of the monarchy of the Father in Pannenberg, cf. Moltmann, *History and the Triune God*, xviii–xix.

205. Pannenberg, *Systematic Theology*, 1:431. Peters, *God as Trinity*, 139.

206. Peters, *God as Trinity*, 141.

In so far as the Father is affirmed as the main source of the Trinity, the Son and the Spirit are inevitably subordinated, whereby genuine reciprocity would be threatened. In criticism of the Eastern Orthodox emphasis on the priority of the Father, as well as Western emphasis on one single divine subject, Pannenberg, in taking the Trinity to mean a unity of reciprocal self-dedication, understands a radical relationality among the three persons. The Son is totally and fully himself in relation to the Father, and vice versa. The Spirit is totally and fully herself in witness to both in uniting and distinguishing them. From this perspective, there is no relation of origin in the Trinity, because the Father, the Son, and the Spirit are equi-primordial. This makes Pannenberg go beyond the metaphor of begetting or proceeding from a divine origin. Therefore, the *filioque* formula is unnecessary.

Barth's affirmation of the *filioque* is mainly due to maintaining the reciprocity between Father and Son. Barth sees a possibility of direct mystical union of God with human beings coming from the exclusive *ex Patre.* "The *Filioque* expresses recognition of the communion between the Father and the Son. The Holy Spirit is the love which is the essence of the relation between these two modes of being of God . . . the intra-divine two sided fellowship of the Spirit, which proceeds from the Father and the Son, is the basis of the fact that there is in revelation a fellowship in which not only is God there for man but in very truth—this is the *donum Spiritus sancti*—man is also there for God."[207]

The Spirit is the divine person who holds the whole Trinity together. In the doctrine of God, Barth moves to affirm the essence of God in a twofold way: both as freedom and as love. The concept of God as the One who loves in freedom entails Barth's liberation concept of God in the Trinity. For Barth, God is the one who is all in all and who, as such, concerns the totality of human existence. God is "the fact that not only newly illumines, but also really transforms reality."[208] God in the Trinity is not a metaphysical basis for interpreting the world, but the grounding reality for really transforming it. This is characteristic of the liberative dimension in Barth's Trinity.

Given the ecumenical debate over the *filioque*, representatives of the two churches tend to think about the triune God in a double manner.

207. *CD*, I/1:480.

208. *KD*, II/1:289.

How is the correspondence between the Son and the Spirit to be maintained? If the Spirit participates in the generation of the Son, the Spirit proceeds from the Father to the Son and from the Son to the Father.[209] However, when it comes to the *filioque* in an Asian context, the issue is not merely confined to the way of affirming reciprocity between the Son and the Spirit, but is a way of expressing and maintaining God's compassion for *dukkha* in a trinitarian-historical sense. The Spirit proceeds from the Father, origin of mercy and love, and from the Son, the realizer of the Father's suffering mercy in the Spirit of life. God's laboring pain in God's begetting of the Son in the presence of the Spirit is manifested as the wondrous Being of Father, Son, and Spirit.

God's freedom in begetting the Son disavows the monarchial form of the Trinity, that is, "the demanding father-image of the God." The Father's journey into the Son through the mother-quality of giving birth in the life-giving Spirit is in relationality with the wondrous being of the three persons. An Asian staurocentric way of thinking does not need to abandon God's freedom so that a social doctrine of the Trinity in this regard does not lose sight of trinitarian theism. The Son becomes the realizer of God's suffering mercy and love in the Spirit of life. Therefore, the relations of origin in the Trinity should be replaced by a metaphor of God's freedom in fellowship begetting the Son in life-giving Spirit.

If the *filioque* is implicitly related to divine suffering, Jesus Christ, who is a mirror of the Father's heart, revealed the most profound depths of God's sheer unutterable fatherly love not only in terms of YHWH but also in terms of *God for us*.[210] The Spirit, in taking share with motherly pain in the Father's generation of the Son, creation, and participation in his death and resurrection is, in fact, the Spirit of self-communication of the wounded heart of God in the trinitarian life. Therefore, the Spirit proceeds from the Father and from the Son in the presence of the life-giving Spirit from eternity *ad intra* as well as *ad extra*. This Spirit is the Spirit of the trinitarian life which enables all living creatures to live in correspondence to divine life and compassion.

The Spirit, who is the Spirit of fellowship between Father and Son proceeds from the Father and from the Son, an *ochlos* Jew born of God's people. If the *filioque* affirms Jesus' passionate solidarity with *ochlos*, who

209. Heron, *Holy Spirit in the Bible*, 178.

210. *BC*, 419.

was also a historical Jew born of *ochlos* minjung, it is also meaningful for Asian contextual theology. The Immanuel of Jesus Christ through the Spirit becomes the connecting principle between God's *Urfaktum* Immanuel and the eschatological Immanuel of God's being "all in all" in the doxological Trinity. The procession of the Spirit from the Father and from the Son in Spirit's life-giving fellowship implies that the Spirit is the Spirit of solidarity with human suffering, and the Spirit of protesting against social structures of injustice, violence, and cosmic ecological suffering related to it.

The *filioque* becomes only meaningful for Asian contextual theology in so far as it witnesses to God's freedom to suffer in self-limitation for the world, human beings, and the cosmos. In this regard, the Spirit proceeds from the Father, the source of mercy and compassion, and proceeds from the Son, the realizer and fulfiller of the Father's mercy and compassion in the presence of the Spirit *ad intra* as well as *ad extra*.

In this sacrament he offers us all the treasure he brought from heaven for us, to which he most graciously invites us in other places, as when he says in Matt 11:28, "Come to me, all who labor and are heavy-laden, and I will refresh you."

BC 454

The virtue of the common people will reach its fullness when the dead are looked after carefully and sacrifice is extended to the ancestors of the past

Lunyu 1:9

6

Luther and Asian Eucharistic Theology

What shapes and characterizes Luther's ecclesiology is his theology of Word and Sacraments. In this chapter we meet Luther's eucharistic theology in relation to Roman Catholic teaching. Luther's theology of the Lord's Supper, when seen in a time-related and eschatological dimension, will engage the spirituality of ancestral rites that has been controversial until the present in Asian churches and theologies. Would it be possible to deepen Luther's theology of the Lord's Supper in terms of his keen insight into Jesus' descent into hell? If we perceive a real presence of Jesus Christ in the Eucharist in relation to Christ's total liberation, how do we formulate an encounter between Luther and a Buddhist insight of universal compassion? Given this problematic idea, I will make an attempt to reconstruct an Asian ecclesiology in critical dialogue with Luther and bodhisattva's way in which Lot's wife and a narrative of the woman Janjanup are read, filling the gap between Christian and Buddhist traditions.

The Roman Catholic Church and the Sacraments

It is safe to say that Roman Catholic teaching on the sacraments was restated by the Council of Trent (1545–1563), according to which there are seven sacraments instituted by Jesus Christ. They are baptism, confirmation, Eucharist, penance, extreme unction, orders, and matrimony. These are called the sacraments of the New Law in comparison with the sacraments of the Old Law. Insofar as the sacraments of the New Law are causative of grace and necessary for salvation, believers receive the grace of justification through them. In fact, they contain the grace that they signify. Therefore, the sacraments confer the grace through the sacramental action itself, on those who place no obstacles in their way.[1] The English word

1. Leith, *Creeds of the Churches*, 425–26.

"sacrament" comes from the Latin word *sacramentum*, which designates the promise or oath on undertaking responsibility in entering into Roman military service. This term is also used to refer to *mystérion* in the New Testament, which signifies the hidden mysteries of God. Along the way, *sacramentum* came to refer to the Christian rites of baptism and the celebration of the Eucharist.[2]

Since Augustine, sacrament has meant a visible word, that is, a sign of some sacred thing. The sign as something visible (material, procedure of Christian rites, the words spoken) is considered to be the image of the sacred thing as something invisible. Therefore, according to Augustine, a *sacramentum* is a sacred sign that shows forth and brings about what is hidden in a divine revelation. For example, the *sacramentum* of baptism shows forth the fact that those who are baptized are buried with Christ and rise to new life (Rom 6:3–4). Sacraments as signs of Christ were instituted and delivered by himself to the church for ministering to the people of God. Though the Lord only gave us a sign for his body, he did not hesitate to say that "This is my body."

The Christian doctrine that the Eucharist is his body is only to be affirmed on the basis of Christ's promise. Signs are a necessary, but not a sufficient condition for the sacrament because they must also be effected by God. Things are learned by means of signs, but that does not necessary mean that we understand them fully.[3] They are supposed to be performed as the work of Christ himself given to the church. They are administered independently of the spiritual and moral condition of the performer.

For this reason, Augustine rejects the Donatists, who held that the sacraments done at the hands of an unworthy priest fail to confer grace. In response, Augustine insists that a sacrament itself obtains an effect that has nothing to do with the state of the performer. Because the sacrament of baptism seals a person's belonging to Christ once and for all, rebaptism is unnecessary. It was Peter Lombard who insisted that there were precisely seven sacraments, and Lombard focused the teaching that Luther criticized and amended.

From the beginning of the ancient church there have been groups representing a realistic concept on the one hand, and a symbolic-spiritual concept of the Eucharist on the other hand. However, these different understandings in the church fathers are not in strong opposition but in

2. Cf. Pelikan, *Growth of Medieval Theology*, 204ff.

3. Rist, *Augustine: Ancient Thought Baptized*, 32–33.

complementarity. A symbol realizes itself in the reality.[4] However, in the Middle Ages there arose a conflict between realists and symbolists. The realists Paschasius Radbertus and Lanfranc stood in opposition to the symbolists Ratramnus and Berengar of Tours. In the mid-800s, Ratramnus (a monk from the monastery of Cobie in France), in response to the highly realistic view of his fellow monk Radbertus, insisted that "there is a difference between the spiritual flesh which is consumed in the mouth of the faithful and the spiritual blood which is daily presented to believers to drink, and the flesh which was crucified and blood which was poured out."[5] Although a change takes place in the Eucharist where the bread and the wine become the body and blood of Christ, according to Ratramnus, however, "the elements 'become' Christ's flesh and blood in the sense that he gives nourishment through them because under the cover of material things the divine power secretly dispenses salvation on those who faithfully receive then."[6]

Some two hundred years later, Berengarius of Tours, when following in the footsteps of Ratramnus, was urged to change his symbolic-spiritual opinion after years of controversy and to sign the following statement (1059): "I Berengarius . . . anathematize every heresy, especially that of which I have been accused, which attempts to argue that the bread and wine which are placed on the altar are after consecration solely a sacrament and not the true body and blood of our Lord Jesus Christ . . . I agree . . . that the bread and the wine . . . are not merely a sacrament, but also the true body and blood of our Lord Jesus Christ; and that they are sensibly—not merely in a sacrament, but in truth—handled by the hands of the priests and broken and crushed by the teeth of the faithful."[7]

Again in 1079, Berengarius was forced to declare that "I Berengarius believe that the bread and wine which are placed on the altar are substantially changed through the mystery of the sacred prayer and the words of our Redeemer into the true and proper and life giving flesh and blood of Jesus Christ our Lord, and that after consecration they are the true body of Christ which was born of the Virgin . . . and the true blood of Christ which flowed from his side; and this not only through the sign and power of a sacrament, but in the authenticity of their own nature and in the

4. Thurian, *Mystery of the Eucharist*, 40.

5. Cited by Heron, *Table and Tradition*, 93–94.

6. Ibid., 94.

7. Ibid., 94–95.

truth of their own substance."[8] The substance of the bread and wine are changed into the substance of the body and blood of Christ, even though the ordinary bread qualities ("accidents") remain. Put otherwise, the bread and wine, upon consecration by the priest, are transformed in substance into the body and blood of Christ, and in so doing Christ becomes bodily present before us. The doctrine of transubstantiation thus entered into the theology of the church, and finally became the dogma of transubstantiation in the Fourth Lateran Council (1215).[9]

In the Council of Florence (1438–1445) Lombard's idea of seven sacraments was sanctioned. Like Lombard, Thomas Aquinas was in agreement that there are seven sacraments celebrated by the church. For Aquinas a sacrament is not merely a sign of what cannot be seen by the physical eye but also a process by which something is actually effected. For example, the water of baptism by itself is not a sacrament, but is when applied to someone who is thereby incorporated into the passion and death of Christ. Therefore, "the term 'sacrament' signifies the reality which sanctifies [and this means] that it should signify the effect produced."[10] Furthermore a sacrament is "a sign of a sacred reality inasmuch as it has the property of sanctifying people."[11] Therefore, "the perfection of the sacrament is not in the water by itself but in the application of the water to someone—the act of washing."[12] In this regard, Aquinas goes on to say that sacraments are genuine causes of grace. The materials used in the sacrament are things used by God in showing forth and bringing about grace.

Aquinas distinguished the sacraments of the New Law from the sacraments of the Old Law. The New Law causes grace and is "appropriated as manifestations of a grace that is already present," whereas the old "fulfilled the function of prefiguring grace," but not of causing grace.[13] The new is effective *ex opere operato,* through the deed performed, while the old is

8. Ibid., 95.

9. "[Jesus Christ's] body and blood are truly contained in the sacrament of the altar under the figures of bread and wine, the bread having been transubstantiated into His body and the wine into His blood by divine power." Cf. Leith, ed., *Creeds of the Churches*, 58.

10. *ST*, 3a. 60.3 ad.2.

11. Ibid., 60.2.

12. Ibid., 66.1.

13. Ibid., 61.4 ad.3. Cf. In the Doctrine of the Seven Sacraments of the Council of Florence (1483–1545): "[The sacraments of the Old Testament] did not cause grace, but foreshadowed the grace that was to be bestowed solely through the passion of Christ. Our sacraments, however, not only contain grace, but also confer it on those who receive them worthily." Leith, *Creeds of the Churches*, 60.

effective *ex opere operantis*, through the activity of the performer. As a sign, a sacrament has a threefold function. "It is at once commemorative of that which has gone before, namely the Passion of Christ, and demonstrative of that which is brought about in us through the Passion of Christ, and prognostic, i.e. a foretelling of future glory."[14] Through his passion, Christ, as the principal cause of grace, inaugurated the rites of the Christian religion by offering himself as an oblation and sacrifice to God. This grace is the form of our sanctification, and the telos of sanctification is eternal life. In this special way the sacraments of the church receive their power from the Passion of Christ. According to Aquinas, the sacrament is instituted by Christ as a means of human sanctification.

However, Aquinas also believed that things in nature do not have, by themselves, an intrinsic power to sanctify. In other words, sanctification cannot be determined by any human authority such as religious leaders. Aquinas takes into consideration two factors in the question of the sacraments: divine worship and human sanctification. The former involves human activity with respect to God while the latter involves divine activity with respect to human beings. "Since, therefore, human sanctification lies under the power of God who sanctifies, it is not for us to decide of our own judgment which materials are to be chosen or us to be sanctified by. This rather is something which should be determined by divine institution."[15] Although sensible things have of their very nature a certain aptitude to signify spiritual effects, "it is by divine institution that a special determination is imparted to this aptitude restricting it to one special significance."[16]

For Aquinas, the sacraments are the visible expressions of the on-going relationship between God and Christians. They are means expressing the mutual love between God and human beings that tell that Christians participate in and benefit from what God did in the life, death, and resurrection of Jesus Christ. They effect what they signify. Therefore, they "constitute sensible signs of invisible things by which people are sanctified."[17] In this regard, "it is necessary for human salvation that people should be united in the name of the one true religion. Therefore the sacraments are necessary for the salvation of people."[18]

14. *ST*, 3a. 60.3.
15. Ibid., 60.5.
16. Ibid., 64.2 ad.2.
17. Ibid., 61.3.
18. Ibid., 61.1.

Above all, Aquinas is called the eucharistic theologian of the Catholic Church. For him, the Eucharist is the sacrament of the Church's unity. "There is one bread, we who are many are one body, for we all partake of the one bread" (1 Cor 10:17). The Eucharist constitutes the goal and consummation of all the sacraments, and so highlights the spiritual life.[19] In celebration of the Eucharist, Christ continues to spread out the effect of the incarnation in time. The Eucharist contains the source (the life of Christ) of its effect (the life of grace), which is the union of Christ with his believers.[20] By means of the Eucharist believers are "brought to spiritual perfection in being closely united to Christ who suffered for us."[21]

The Eucharist, according to Aquinas, signifies three things. The first commemorates the passion of the Lord in regard to the past. In the present sense, the second refers to the unity of the church into which people are brought together through the Eucharist. It has also a third significance in regard to the future: "It prefigures that enjoyment of God which will be ours in heaven." In terms of the Eucharist, believers take to themselves "the godhead of the son."[22]

For Aquinas, Christ is truly present and truly received. The celebration of the Eucharist is simply the sacrifice of Christ. "The celebration of this sacrament is a definite image representing Christ's passion, which is his true sacrifice . . . by his sacrament we are made sharers in the fruit of the Lord's passion."[23] In this context, Aquinas quotes from St. Augustine: "It is impossible to unite people within a religion of any name, whether true or false, unless they are kept together by means of some system of symbols or sacraments in which they all share."[24]

Following in the footsteps of Augustine, Aquinas stressed that "it is profitable to receive daily so as to gather its fruits daily."[25] Those who receive the Eucharist receive the grace of forgiving any sin on the basis of Christ's Passion. Aquinas is very emphatic that Christ is truly present in the Eucharist, because Christ is sacramentally contained in the Eucharist in the sense that the real body of Christ and his blood are in the sacrament.[26] In

19. Ibid., 63.6.
20. Ibid., 79.5.
21. Ibid., 73.3 ad. 3.
22. Ibid., 79.1 and 3a. 73.4.
23. Ibid., 83.1.
24. Ibid., 61.1.
25. Ibid., 80.10.
26. Ibid., 73.5.

the literal sense, not only the flesh, but the whole body is under the sacrament. The change involved in the Eucharist is miraculous because God is able to change the whole being of a thing. "The complete substance of this is changed into the complete substance of that." Because this is a substantial change, it is called by a name proper to itself—"transubstantiation."[27]

Given this fact, Aquinas rejects a symbolic interpretation of the eucharistic presence. In mentioning Berengarius of Tours (ca.1040–1480), Aquinas attributes to him a symbolic understanding of the presence of Christ in the Eucharist.[28] However, the real body and blood of Christ in the sacrament are known only by our faith, which is based on the authority of God. In the Synoptic Gospels we hear Jesus' words, "This is my body," in the narrative of Lord's Supper. We need to take our Savior's word on faith.

According to Aquinas, the substance of bread and wine change into the body and blood of Christ after the words of consecration by the celebrant. However, the words of consecration do not result in a change of accidents, but only in a change of substance. With this idea in mind, Aquinas is distinct from the declaration of Berengarius in which the bread and wine on the altar become, after consecration, not only a sacrament, but also the true body and blood of our Lord Jesus Christ. Aquinas goes on to say that the body of Christ is removed from all possibility of change and the substance of the bread is no longer present.[29] Even though Christ is really present in the accidents after the consecration, he is not supposed to become a prisoner of the Tabernacle. Aquinas distinguished the substance from the dimensions, in saying that the dimensions of bread and wine are not changed into the dimensions of Christ's body. "The substance of Christ's body or of his blood is in the sacrament as a result of the sacramental sign; not so the dimensions of his body or of his blood."[30]

What is at stake for Aquinas is twofold. First, it is important that all the accidents of bread and wine remain to our sense after the consecration so that the flesh and blood of Christ is given to us under the appearances of things. Therefore we are not supposed to eat the body of Christ as human body and drink blood of Christ as human blood. Secondly, in taking

27. Ibid., 75.5.
28. Ibid., 75.1.
29. Ibid., 77.7.
30. Ibid., 76.2.

the body and blood of our Lord in the visible presence, we increase the merit of faith.[31]

The Eucharist is a mystery in the sense that God is a mystery, because the Eucharist is the real presence of God. Through the Eucharist there exists a union between God and believers whose relationship is on-going and thoroughly real. In this mysterious union Christians take share in the life of God as the Son of God lives in the Father's giving of himself. The Roman Catholic doctrine of the Eucharist was given decisively in the formulation of the Council of Trent (1564). "By the consecration of the bread and wine a change is brought about of the whole substance of the bread into the substance of the body of Christ our Lord, and of the whole substance of the wine into the substance of His blood. This change the holy Catholic Church properly and appropriately calls transubstantiation."[32]

Luther and the Sacraments

In the early Middle Ages the Eucharist came to be removed from the lives of ordinary people. Daily communion by the laity was very uncommon. According to the Fourth Lateran Council (1215), the believers must receive communion at least once a year. Until the Reformation, the doctrine of the Lord's supper was not "Take and eat" and "Take and drink," but "Gaze on the Host and find your salvation in the gazing."[33]

According to the medieval sacramental theology and practice, the culminating point of the sacrament occurred at the moment of consecration when the bread and wine are changed into Christ's body and blood. This idea was also endorsed by Aquinas. That being the case, the transubstantiated body and blood replaces Christ's presence in the sacrament. The substantial presence in transubstantiation gains in prominence and the worshiper would have heard the announcement of the priest *hoc est enim corpus meum* (this is my body) at a certain point, upon the elevation of a wafer. It is said that Christ became bodily present at this point. The Eucharist became our thanksgiving to and intercession with God. What is most distinctive in the shape of the medieval liturgy is our offering *(oblatio)* or sacrifice *(hostia, sacrificum)* to God for our sin. What shaped the Eucharist was the emphasis on the human approach to God, that is, the priest offers to God a sacrifice for sin on our behalf. In this way the

31. Ibid., 75.5.

32. Leith, *Creeds of the Churches*, 432.

33. Davies, *Thought of Thomas Aquinas*, 363.

language of sacrifice and oblation replaced the language of the presence in the sacrament.

In his early stage, Luther fiercely debated the teaching of the sacraments in his explanation of the Ninety-five Theses (1518). At stake for him was not sacrament, but the faith that justifies. At the Augsburg hearing Cajetan affirmed this position. After his appearance before Cajetan, Luther began to deal with the question of the sacraments in more detail. In three of Luther's sermons on the sacraments from 1519,[34] Luther gave an account of the sacrament in terms of sign, its meaning and faith. Luther put emphasis on the mutual relation between the word of promise and the faith receiving it. In contrast to Cajetan, Luther insisted that "the forgiveness of guilt is not within the province of any human office or authority, be it pope, bishop, priest or any other. Rather it depends exclusively upon the word of Christ and our own faith."[35] Luther's view of the universal priesthood of all the baptized is stated clearly in saying that where there is no priest, each individual Christian, even a woman or child, does as much.

In light of *simul justus et peccator*, simultaneously saint and sinner, Luther is critical of the Catholic notion that sin no longer exists after baptism. He argues that baptism is an external sign in which the content of the divine promise is shared. The sacrament establishes a covenant between God and human beings to which our faith is related. In *The Blessed Sacrament of the Holy and True Body of Christ* Luther defines the form of the bread and wine as the sign, its meaning or effect as the fellowship of all the saints, and faith as a personal belief in salvation. As the idea of covenant is central to the baptism, so the idea of fellowship or communion is to the Lord's Supper. The forgiveness of sins is the special gift of the Supper in which the words of institution play a major role. In addition, Augustine's idea of *sacramentum* and *exemplum* is interlaced in terms of fellowship. "It is Christ's will then, that we partake of it frequently, in order that we may remember him and exercise ourselves in this fellowship according to his example."[36] "In this way we are changed into one another and are made into a community by love. Without love there can be no such change."[37] However, Luther was in disagreement with the scholastic

34. Cf. Luther, "The Sacrament of Penance, The Holy and Blessed Sacrament of Baptism, and the Blessed Sacrament of the Holy and True Body of Christ, and the Brotherhood."

35. *LW*, 35:12.

36. Ibid., 56.

37. Ibid., 58.

teaching of *opus operatum,* which said that if the sacrament is performed correctly, the sacramental action is, in itself, salutary independent of the priest's own state of grace. What Luther polemicized against is the notion that the *opus*, in itself, is pleasing to God.

In his interpretation of the words of institution, Luther put a special emphasis on the relation of promise to faith. Faith is understood as the adequate answer to the promise whose content is the forgiveness of sins and eternal life. Luther defined the relation between the bread and wine as the body and blood of Christ in regarding "his own flesh and blood under the bread and wine."[38] Consubstantiation means the bread as the body of Christ, and the wine as the blood of Christ without reference to transubstantiation.

In the treatise, *The Babylonian Captivity of the Church* (1520), he attacked the Mass and its three captivities. First, he disputed the reservation of the cup, then the doctrine of transubstantiation, and finally the abuse of the mass in terms of the idea of sacrifice. He gave special priority to the promise over the sign: "in every promise of God two things are presented to us, the Word and the sign, so that we are to understand the Word to be the testament, but the sign to be the sacrament. Thus in Mass, the Word of Christ is the testament, and the bread and wine are the sacrament."[39] He turned Augustine's phrase (*Crede et manducasti*) to good account. The divine promise and faith are at the heart of interpreting the sacrament.

Concerning the Lord's Supper controversy, it was Karlstadt who first publicly stated a view other than Luther's. According to Karlstadt, Christ's words of institution are not to identify Christ himself in the bread and wine. Rather, Jesus Christ points his finger at his own body saying, "this is my body." Prior to Karlstadt, the Dutch humanists Cornelius Honius (Hoen, influenced by Wesel Gansfort) and Erasmus expressed the thesis that the words of institution should be understood in the significative sense. That is to say, the bread and wine "signify" Christ's body and blood. In addition, the Bohemian Brethren, following Luther's position in the Leipzig Disputation (1519), paid homage to Christ in the elements of the Supper, albeit rejecting the scholastic doctrine of transubstantiation. They stated that Christ's true body and blood are present in the Supper, although this presence is spiritual.

In his treatise *The Adoration of the Sacrament* (1523) Luther claimed that the real presence of Christ's body and blood is in the elements, pro-

38. Ibid., 86.

39. *LW*, 36:44.

ceeding from the words of institution. In contrast to Honius, Luther writes in emphatic terms: "If . . . a person can say the word 'is' means the same as the word 'signifies' . . . in that case one should say: That Mary is a virgin and the mother of God is equivalent to saying that Mary signifies a virgin and the mother of God. Likewise: Christ is God and man; that is, Christ signifies God and man."[40] The real presence that lies at the heart of Luther's teaching on the Lord's Supper was launched against Karlstadt, and later against Zwingli.

For Zwingli, the starting point was that nothing creaturely can support faith. That the flesh is of no avail (John 6:63) is applicable to the understanding of the Supper. Zwingli's attachment to the significative interpretation of the *est* in the words of institution comes from Hoen. In rejecting the doctrine of transubstantiation, as well as the idea of the real presence, Zwingli attacked believers of such teachings as cannibals or carnivores.

What was at stake for Zwingli was that the Supper represented a *commemoratio*. Zwingli appealed to John 6:63 in support of his significative interpretation. However, for Luther the meaning of the words of institution "est" could not mean "signifies." The fundamental question of God's presence in the incarnate Christ and in the Supper was indissolubly connected with Luther's christological concept of the unity of the divine and human nature. On the basis of an Antiochene Christology, however, Zwingli strictly divided the divine and human natures. Christ suffered according to the human nature, not his divine nature. The idea that Christ is present in the Supper according to his human nature is in opposition to the majesty of God. He gives much emphasis to the words: "Do this in remembrance of me," compared to the words of institution, "this is my body; this is my blood." Remembrance notes a valid presence of the Lord, not merely the idea of a saving significance of Christ's death. Against Luther's Christology of *communicatio idiomatum*, he accentuated an *alloesis* (interchange) in which the difference between two natures should in no way be confused or mixed.

To clarify how to conceive the presence of Christ's exalted human nature in the elements of the Supper, Luther developed his doctrine of ubiquity after 1526. Against the traditional notion that Christ's exalted human body since the ascension was present at a specific place and thus could not be present on earth, Luther stressed his idea of ubiquity: "We believe that

40. *LW*, 36:280.

Christ, according to his human nature, is put over all creatures (Eph 1:22) and fills all things . . . Not only according to his divine nature, but also according to his human nature, he is lord of all things, has all things in his hand, and is present everywhere."[41] In following Occam and Biel's teaching of ubiquity, Luther rejected that the right hand of God is confined to a particular place in heaven: " . . . that Christ's body is everywhere because it is at the right hand of God who is everywhere, although we do not know how that occurs. For we also do not know how it occurs that the right hand of God is everywhere."[42] During the Marburg Colloquy (October 1529), Zwingli agreed to the formulation, "sacrament of the true body and blood of Jesus Christ" concerning the real presence while Luther did not reject spiritual partaking of the body and blood.[43] However, Luther in his mature years strongly defended the idea of the real presence of Christ's body and blood in the elements of the Supper.

As we already mentioned, for Augustine sacraments are visible and external signs of an invisible, internal, and divine reality. The Word of Christ makes the sacramental action a sacrament of justification and salvation. However, the Donatists, a schismatic church in fourth-century North Africa, claimed a pure line of clerical succession by ordination in contrast to bishops who had lapsed during persecution. The efficacy and validity of the sacrament is dependent on the spiritual state of the performer of the sacramental rituals. Thus, unworthy bishops could not administer valid sacraments. Augustine vigorously opposed this position of the Donatists.

The scholastic teaching of *opus gratum opere operato* as effective sign mediates the grace of God through the completion of the ritual act, regardless of those who do not please God. The grace is imparted effectively by ritual act of the performer in the sacraments of the New Testament. Augustine's defense of the efficacy and validity of Baptism and Eucharist against Donatists was unilaterally understood as depending on the grace-conferring power of the sacramental rite itself, *ex opere operato* (by the work performed).

Connecting himself to Augustine, Luther claimed not sacrament per se but faith in the promise of Christ in the sacrament justifies. For Luther, such expressions as *opus operatum* and *opus operantis* are in vain because

41. *LW*, 36:342, "The Sacrament of the Body and Blood of Christ."

42. Cf. *LW*, 37:214 "Confession Concerning Christ's Supper."

43. It is attested that Zwingli tended to affirm the real presence of Jesus Christ in the elements in his later years. Cf. Gäbler, *Huldrych Zwingli*, 123.

faith is the focal point in receiving grace from the sacrament. However, faith-connection with the sacrament is not a spiritualizing tendency in Luther's thought. For Luther, faith was not a human work, but belonged to the indispensable act of the Spirit. If faith is understood as a human *opus*, Luther's core teaching of justification by faith alone can also remain a human work. When losing sight of faith as the *donum* of the Spirit, faith is easy to understand as a human spiritual effort cooperating with the grace of God. When putting apart the connection of faith with the sacrament in the co-relative sense that is also a divine act, the scholastic teaching of the Lord's Supper degenerated into a meritorious *opus* instead of God's gift of grace.

The position that Luther held in his struggle with Roman Catholic doctrine becomes meaningful insofar as we come to terms with his double definition of faith. Sacraments in Roman Catholic doctrine are not the gift of a gracious God for our salvation, but *opera*, human works through which to get access to merit. Sacraments as human *opera* have nothing to do with faith, but are open to everyone without mortal sin. Through the sacramental action itself, grace is conferred upon "those who place no obstacle in the way."[44] Luther attacks such an idea as heresy.

For Luther, faith is related to the sacrament as God's gracious act. The aspect of correlation between faith and sacrament become more visible and explicit in his struggle with the Anabaptists and the Spiritualists. These people made the priority of God's action in the institution of the sacrament unnecessary, and consequently the administration of the sacraments became totally dependent upon human faith. They averted the other dimension of faith apart from the human side, that is to say, faith as total obedience or surrender to the priority of God's gracious action in the sacrament. As Luther had a different understanding of sacrament from that of Roman Catholic teaching, so he also had a different understanding of Christian faith from that of the fanatics. It is worth noting that Luther is not concerned about the spiritualization of the sacrament, but the sacramentalization of the Christian faith in the most genuine sense of the word.

For Luther, *fides qua creditur* (the subjective aspect of faith) can become, therefore, meaningful only insofar as it is seen in the light of *fides quae creditur* (the objective aspect of faith). This tension is placed dynamically and dialectically in the pneumatological act of salvation. Luther sought to

44. *WA*, 1:544.

understand the sacrament from the gospel point of view. As Christ is truly present, and faith and love (all empirical piety) become possible through the Spirit, so the Spirit manifests itself in the external means (especially proclamation of the Word, two sacraments). A word apart from the power of the Spirit remains only a letter, a law. The means of the Spirit is the Word. With the help of the Augustinian distinction between the outward and the inward Word, Luther considered the outward Word as the word of the Scripture, the inward Word as God's own voice by the Spirit. By contrast, *littera-spiritus*, law-gospel is of decisive importance for Luther's hermeneutical position towards scripture, as well as to the sacraments.

In Luther's understanding of the sacrament, the key is law and gospel, about *opus* and *fides*, about *officium* and *beneficium*.[45] For Luther, gospel itself is *promissio*, which is effected by the Spirit. In every sacrament a divine *promissio* is at the heart of accompanying and fulfilling the sacrament. A divine *promissio* is what makes the sacrament a sacrament. Faith is human obedience to receive this *promissio*. Faith cannot work without a *promissio*. The outward means serves to fulfill this *promissio*. In understanding the word of the sacrament as *promissio*, faith forms the real connection between the word and the external element. Therefore, faith in the *promissio* is to receive the external elements (bread and wine) as the confirmation of the *promissio*.

The real presence of the living Christ is the basis for a correlation between *promissio* and *signum*. God is present in his *promissio,* which can only be accepted by faith. The character of the *promissio-fides* correlation excludes every impersonal concept in the scholastic teaching of the sacrament. In the sign of the supper, our whole life is placed under the power of the living Christ by the power of the Spirit to conquer sin and death, because the body and the blood of Jesus given for our sins are under the bread and wine, given to us as nourishment for the forgiveness of sin and eternal life. They are the signs that establish and sustain the church as the eschatological people of God. The sign is connected with the *promissio* of the sacrament. The signs of baptism and the Supper are therefore only a part of the humanity of Jesus.

After his resurrection and ascension, he is present among us. The confirmation of the promise in the sign effects salvation to those who receive by faith, but condemnation to the unbelievers. The Word and the sacrament are not two different or competing means of grace. There is

45. *LW*, 35:93, and *LW*, 36:35–37. Cf. *MLBTW*, 257, n. 39.

no sacrament without the promise, no Word without the promise. The Spirit makes the external word God's promise, the sign confirmation of the promise. They are the signs which establish and sustain the church with the eschatological people of God.

The sacrament of the Eucharist is union with Christ in a specific manner. The symbol of the Lord's Supper is the physical eating and drinking of the body and the blood of Christ under the bread and wine. Its significance is forgiveness of sin and the guarantee of eternal life in real union with Christ. It is God who also gives the symbol and realizes its significance. The symbols of baptism and the Lord's Supper must be seen in their mutual connection. The Lord's Supper in real union with Christ under bread and wine is to be offered to the baptized, who entered into the real union with the living Christ by death and resurrection in baptism. What we meet in the sacrament is the living Christ himself as the real sacrament in the *promissio* by the power of the Spirit. On the basis of the promise, the ubiquity of Christ's body is possible. Body and blood cannot be understood in the tropological sense concerning Paul's statement (1 Cor 10:16), because Paul does not speak of spiritual participation, but rather of physical participation in the body and the blood of Jesus Christ. Body and blood are the true body and blood themselves. Tropological interpretation is impossible: "This is my body" comes from God and no one may dare add or take away a single letter.

Concerning the eschatological dimension in the Lord's Supper, Luther relates the Lord's Supper to "the living and acting God himself who draws us into his all-embracing, eschatological, saving act."[46] In other words, Christ himself who comes to the Supper is the Lord over time through his death and resurrection. Without resurrection, the Lord's Supper becomes only a tragic Supper in remembrance of the crucified. The real presence in the Lord's Supper needs to be seen in light of the resurrection of the crucified.

It is of significance to embrace both dimensions of space and time in the Supper from an eschatological perspective. Interestingly enough, Ted Peters characterizes the Lutheran position as incarnationalist with regard to Christ's presence in the Eucharist. He also insists that there is a time-related dimension; what is present in the sacrament are the present, past and the future, because the kingdom of God comes ahead of time in the sacrament, "partially but proleptically." In spite of differences and conflict

46. Prenter, *Spiritus Creator*, 171.

of views, it is the work of the Holy Spirit who unites and incorporates us with the salvific accomplishment of Jesus Christ.[47]

The Holy Spirit, who will finally fulfill the *eschaton* as God's great promise, embraces the spatial as well as time-related dimension in the Lord's Supper. In fact, the heavenly body of Christ is alien to the New Testament, but what is at stake is the anticipation of Jesus Christ from heaven in an eschatological sense, not speculation about Jesus Christ existing spatially in heaven (Phil 3:20ff). As people of Israel understand themselves in the Passover feast as partakers of "once and for all" liberation at the Exodus and at the same time of the coming liberation, so the church is also to regard Jesus Christ himself in the Supper as the presence of the coming Lord over time. Therefore, the Lord's Supper signifies the anticipation of the saving feast of the *eschaton*.

Martin Luther and Asian Sense of the Eucharist

With the eschatological dimension in mind, I would like to emphasize the cosmic significance of the Eucharist in Luther's thought in an encounter with the Asian spirituality of ancestral rites. Ancestral worship is regarded by many scholars to be the root of all world religions. The family holds a central place, especially in Confucian culture, in which reverence and glorification of one's ancestors belong to the greatest duty as well as the honor of the living family of descendents. Confucius approves the cult of the ancestor within the framework of filial piety and social moral stability. With good reason, however, Confucius banned any speculations about the state of the departed. "To devote oneself earnestly to one's duty to humanity, and, while respecting the spirits, to keep away from them, may be called wisdom."[48] In response to the question of a disciple about the life after death, Confucius said, "While you do not understand life, how can you know about death?"

With emphasis on ancestral worship, Confucius is recorded as saying that "now filial piety is seen in the skillful carrying out of the wishes of our forefathers, and the skillful carrying out of their understandings. In Spring and Autumn they repaired and beautified the temple-halls of their fathers, set forth their ancestral vessels, displayed their various robes, and presented the offerings of the several seasons. They occupied the places of their forefathers, practiced their ceremonies, and performed their music.

47. Peters, *God—the World's Future*, 292.

48. *Analects*, VI, 20, quoted in Sherley-Price, *Confucius and Christ*, 80.

They reverenced those whom they honored and loved those whom they regarded with affection. Thus they served the departed as they would have served them alive; they served the dead as they would have served them had they continued among them."[49]

In this regard, filial piety is, extending beyond death, expressed in terms of ancestral rites that play a profound role in the bonding of the nation, the family, the religion and the culture. Thus, filial affection is strengthened, interpersonal good manners are fostered, and social stability is maintained. In other words, the cult of the ancestors does not mean necessarily worshipping the spirit—as it looked to the eye of Western missionary—but its proper meaning is to give honor to the departed, and in so doing furnish opportunity for the family to be strengthened in solidarity and to live peacefully in the permanence of the family.

In the Christian tradition, the communion of saints shows a proper relationship of living and departed in the eternal life of Jesus Christ. The duty and privilege of prayer for the departed has been certainly recognized from an earliest Christian tradition. For example, St. Augustine prays for the soul of his saintly mother, Monica, and encourages all readers of the book to "remember her at the altar."[50] However, the veneration of departed saints becomes questionable when a certain soteriological function is added to the communion of saints. In light of the Reformation, rediscovery of *solus Christus*, the interpretation of the communion of saints does not mean the veneration, but fellowship with the saints. The idea that the church is a "fellowship not only in space but also in time" challenges spiritually and eschatologically any historical provincialism and parochialism and further affirms emphatically the departed within the communion of saints in light of the cross and resurrection of Christ. In remembrance of Jesus, we are encouraged to seek the kingdom of God and God's justice (Matt 6:33) in solidarity with the least of his brothers and sisters.[51]

The *communio sanctorum,* which can mean communion in the holy things in the terminology of the Greek liturgy, refers to the participation in the Holy Sacraments. The eating and drinking in the sacrament do not, however, produce in themselves great effects, but "the words for you and for the forgiveness of sins" are anchored, beyond the Eucharist, in the mystery of Christ that is accompanied by the bodily eating and drinking.[52]

49. Ibid., 81.

50. Augustine *Confessions* IX.37.

51. Lochman, *Faith We Confess*, 211–12.

52. *BC*, 352.

According to Luther, the Eucharist refers to the truly real presence of a ubiquitous Christ that is based on the mighty acts of God.

For example, the Great Prayer of Thanksgiving in the Lutheran Book of Worship begins with creation, highlights redemption and moves in expectation of the consummation of all things that are not yet, but are to come. The salvation drama includes the witness of creation (Gen 1, Ps 104), the christological completion (in Col 1:15ff) and vision of eschatological consummation in Rev 21. The God of the holy meal is the God who is "in, with, and, under" all things, not merely with human beings, and finally recapitulates all things in the vision of the New Heaven and the New Earth. The Son, when he comes again to make all things new "as victorious Lord of all," is eschatologically identified as the One who will come in power "to share with us the great and promised feast." The eschatological promise for the renewal of all things is made complete and whole in the Son as the slain Lamb of God. The Lord who is host at this cosmic banquet is the Lord of all, the *Pantokrator* in whom all things in both heaven and on earth are gathered up (Eph 4:6). The crucified and risen Christ is present truly and really as the cosmic Christ, not only in, with, and under the eucharistic element, but with the people gathered, encompassing the whole space of congregation and ever expanding the whole earth and the entire cosmos. The great cosmic banquet that is yet to come is itself experienced and realized here and now in eschatological openness.[53] This is the cosmic aspect of the "cloud of witnesses" in the communion of the Lord's Supper.

Understood in this way, the cosmic Christ who destroyed the power of death and hell by descending into hell is the Lord over all things. Jesus' descent into hell is a necessary context for developing an encounter between Luther's sense of the Eucharist's presence and the Confucian spirituality of filial relationship associated with ancestral rites. As for the Confucian teaching, there has been misunderstanding that the spirits of the departed exercised strong influence upon the prosperity and wealth of the living family on the basis of the due observance of ancestral rites.

As a matter of fact, the Confucian concern is not to stress the power of the spirits to enjoy the food and materials offered by the descendents. If the ancestral rite is not meant to be the veneration of the departed, but rather fellowship and communion with our beloved parents, then filial piety is the cornerstone of Confucian culture, and thus beyond a tradi-

53. Santmire, *Nature Reborn*, 89–92. Cf. *Lutheran Book of Worship*, 69.

tion or custom it becomes "a constituent element of Asian spirituality." It is stressed that filial piety is "the summit of all virtues" coming from Heaven.[54] "The virtue of the common people will reach its fullness when the dead are looked after carefully and sacrifice is extended to the ancestors of the past."[55] Confucius, in fact, is thought not to have cared about any belief in personal immortality or in the power of spirits exercising influence upon the life of their descendents. What is more at sake for Confucius himself lies in his emphasis on the solidarity and continuity of the family, which can be strengthened and preserved by the memorial acts of ancestral rites.

The memorial act of the ancestors does not merely mean offering food and materials. It leads to the perfection of human virtues. A Confucian sense of eternity existing in self-cultivation as well as in the collective and spiritual life of the family would not be in strong opposition to a Christian understanding of eternal life in Jesus Christ who is the resurrection and the life. At this juncture I propose an Asian sense of the eucharistic presence of the cosmic Christ in the celebration of the Lord's Supper that can include a memorial act for our ancestors who died without having known the historical Jesus. This expresses God's *Mahakaruna* (great compassion) in the Eucharist for people outside the walls of Christianity. This also refers to an Asian ecclesiology of solidarity with and companionship of the other.

The Protestant Church in Korea is positive and friendly to the *Baptism, Eucharist and Ministry* document on the Eucharist on many issues. In light of the Eucharist as communion of the faithful, they take *sanctorum communio* to mean Christian responsibility in the world. This encourages the church to seek righteous relationships and *diakonia* in social, economic, and political life in the world, challenging "all kinds of injustice, racism, separation and lack of freedom."[56] As the Korean church report shows, the frequency of the Eucharist is restricted to three or four times per year. Although the Korean church stressed the social and political significance of the Eucharist, she did not relate it to the inclusive meaning of the Lord's Supper for people outside Christianity.[57]

54. Yao, *An Introduction to Confucianism*, 203.

55. Ibid., 202.

56. Thurian, *Churches respond to BEM*, 162.

57. Although Calvin interpreted Jesus' descent into hell (*Inst* II.16.10), in the sense of expressing "the spiritual torment that Christ underwent for us," the Korean Presbyterian church remains silent about the omission of the formula Jesus' descent to hell in a Korean version of it. The point for Calvin was that Christ paid "a greater and more excellent price

Western missionaries, from the beginning, strongly asked the Korean people to cut off their indigenous cultural heritage in order to become Christian. The most controversial issue to this day remains ancestor rituals. This rite was banned and labeled an abomination, in the spirit of the Deuteronomistic hostility to idols. Western missionaries were adamant on this issue. This militant iconoclasm at the heart of the missionaries' gospel became a principle of exclusivism in evangelizing Korea. It challenged and demolished any indigenous spiritual and cultural values and traditions. Simply put, to become a Christian meant to become a person who followed strictly an evangelical way of life implanted and imposed by the missionaries. What is worse, the formula "Jesus descended to hell" was removed, because this formula would remind or mislead Korean people to affirm Christ's universal outreach for people beyond Christianity. A popular slogan expresses the crusade mentality of evangelization: Jesus is the only means of salvation or heaven, but people outside the knowledge of Christ or even without having known him are in the hell of eternal damnation.

In struggling with this implanted gospel, some Asian theologians attempt to re-appropriate the meaning of the Lord's Supper. For example, in reconstructing a Christology for Asian peoples, C. S. Song, a representative of Asian theology from the "third eye" and a prolific writer, takes the Lord's Supper to be the people's Supper, thereby emphasizing the social-critical and life-giving character of the meal in the light of Asian peoples' tragedy and pain. However, in his project we perceive that Christ's promise disappears, and only the people's fellowship and communion remains. It comes to the fore without relationship with the cosmic Christ destroying the *han* of hell, and without the fellowship of the cloud of witnesses. Even though he tries to bring ancestor rites at a funeral feast in relation to *sanctorum communio*, he neglects just who is coming eschatologically and cosmically in the people's fellowship of the Supper. In my judgment, C. S. Song should have been more attentive to the one who vitalizes a deeper understanding of life "as a communal event from the past to the future through the present" from the Asian perspective.[58] At the very least, the ancestor rite is deeply connected with Asian people's understanding of the

in suffering in his soul, the terrible torments of a condemned and forsaken man." This is the place where the lowest humiliation of his suffering takes place. Cf. Lochman, *The Faith We Confess*, 143–46.

58. Song, *Jesus, The Crucified People*, 205.

Ultimate. That being the case, it would be more meaningful to celebrate the Lord's Supper more frequently as a people's supper with a cosmic Christ and in remembrance of his inclusive radical grace in explicitly descending into hell and thus embracing our ancestors who have not known him.

In addition, C. S. Song's project of Asian political theology, in which a story of the Lady Meng serves as a paradigmatic model of resistance for the powerless, touches also on a Confucian filial piety and integrity. Following in the footsteps of C. S. Song, S. C. Yuen makes an attempt to read the story of the lady Meng in light of a Chinese spirituality of *qing-hèn* in which a rhetorical analysis of Lam 1 is made from a Chinese perspective.[59] The tragic story of Lady Meng in Chinese minjung tradition, seen from the dynamics of *qing-hèn*, provides a basis for an Asian theology sharpening a dimension of political resistance, transformation, and new life for the minjung. Etymologically, the Chinese word *qing* is a combination of heart and beauty. *Qing* refers to good or beautiful heart. *Hèn* (equivalent to Korean word *han*) is etymologically a hardened and bitter heart. For Chinese culture *qing-hèn* is related to each other in a more balanced way than the Korean sense of *han*. A story of the Lady Meng symbolizes the protest of the powerless against the oppression and exploitation of the ancient imperial rule of China. The story offers the powerless hope of transformation and new life.

In ancient imperial China there was an emperor, Chin Shih Huang-Ti, who was afraid of invasion by the Huns into his territory. In order to defend against attack, the emperor decided to build a wall protecting the whole northern frontier of China. However, the construction of the wall made no progress. The advice of an ingenious scholar was that a man called Wan should be sacrificed. The emperor dispatched his soldiers to seize a man named Wan who was just sitting with his bride, Meng, at his wedding feast. After her husband's innocent death, Lady Meng attempted to find his body in vain. Her desperate effort without success made her cry out.

After hearing this weeping, the wall was affected and collapsed in order to carry back her husband's bones. The emperor, curious about Lady Meng, ordered his men to bring her before him. Struck by her marvelous beauty, the emperor decided to make her one of his empresses. Aware of the emperor's proposal as inevitable destiny, Lady Meng accepted it, but asked that her husband should be honored at a solemn burial service. Once

59. Yuen, "Reading Lamentations 1 in Light of Qing-hèn," 114–27.

her request was granted by the emperor, she began to curse the emperor on the terrace, and jumped from terrace into the river. Irritated, the emperor ordered his men to cut up her body into pieces and grind her bones to powder. But the little pieces changed just then into little silver fish, and the soul of faithful Lady Meng lives forever.[60] This story is not merely the voice for a people's political theology. It symbolizes a familial piety and integrity between husband and wife and extends to a relationship between the living and the dead. Jesus Christ, in the celebration of the Eucharist, is the One who is in solidarity with and affirmation of the innocent sufferer, who includes and transforms innocent people of other faiths.

In elaborating on the concept of "the wounded heart of God" from a minjung perspective,[61] Andrew Sung Park deals with Luther's *theologia crucis*. However, his treatment of Luther remains superficial because he ignores the cosmic dimension of Luther's thought in relation to Jesus' descent into hell. In my view, Luther's *theologia crucis* can serve as a starting point for deepening an encounter with Confucian spirituality. In reconstructing an Asian understanding of eucharistic theology in terms of cosmic and eschatological events, it is primarily important to see Jesus' descent to hell from the biblical perspective. The main New Testament passage is 1 Pet 3:18f, where Christ "preached to the spirits in prison, who formerly did not obey."

Moreover, "the gospel was preached even to the dead" (1 Pet 4:6). There is similar direction found in Eph 4:6, where Christ "also descended into the lowest parts of the earth." Jesus' descent into hell is reaffirmed by the statement in Revelation that Jesus Christ has "the keys of Death and Hades" (Rev 1:18). The meaning and the intention of these passages, even though controversial, are that the work of Christ was not merely confined parochially to historical reality, but also extended universally and cosmically to those who died before Christ was born.

Luther, following the patristic tradition, viewed the descent to hell as Christ's victory over the power of sin and death, which means a breakthrough of his triumphal procession. Luther took Jesus' descent to hell to be the subjugation of Satan, with all powers and the domain of death turned over to Christ.[62] What was at stake for Luther was a cosmic soteriology of total liberation, embracing not only the social-historical dimen-

60. Cf. Song, *Tears of Lady Meng*, 1–23.

61. Park, *Wounded Heart of God*, 114–16.

62. *BC*, 414.

sion, but also the cosmic universalistic dimension. However, in Lutheran theological tradition this intention was unfortunately dealt with only in reference to the individual metaphysical context.

Luther and Asian Other Ecclesiology

Luther's reflection on Jesus' descent into hell becomes a basis for deepening God's great compassion for the total liberation of people who died without having known the historical Jesus. This aspect can be the driving force for an Asian sense of the eucharistic presence of the cosmic Christ that includes a memorial act of the ancestors related to a filial piety. At the same time, it refers to an Asian understanding of ecclesiology. Given the cosmic dimension of Luther, an inclusive dimension of Jesus Christ meets a Buddhist spirituality of compassion, i.e., bodhisattva.

For Luther, the human being justified by God is called to live in personal-social relationship with others. Luther's teaching of justification and its related eucharistic theology are not merely based on an abstract individual faith, but active in love in all areas of human life in which a Christian discipleship in witnessing to God's grace in Jesus Christ and *diakonia* for the needy are realized. An expression of Christian solidarity and accompaniment with others is particularly expressed in the economic realm where cooperation and the interplay of economic exchange and distribution are done with a sense of equality and love. Despite Luther's original insights, his teaching of justification and his related theology of the Eucharist have been directed in a forensic and individualistic way. The priesthood of all believers, which is rooted in the justification of all believers, points in the direction toward solidarity, recognition and fellowship with others in the community of creation.

The Asian sense of individuality arises only in relation to community. In other words, the individual is understood as a part of community. Especially in Mahayana Buddhism, we make note of the individual's interconnection with the community. In a bodhisattva's vows, the enlightened one postpones individual nirvanic salvation for the sake of the others in suffering and hardship. This is the highest virtue in Buddhism: to give up a privilege of winning an individual salvation in favor of compassion and solidarity with others. The Buddha's original compassion through the ideal of bodhisattva admonishes that the one voluntarily delays and sacrifices his or her own elevation to Buddhahood in order to lead all living sentient beings in the universe to *Nirvana*. This is expressive of the Buddhist core spirituality of *Mahakaruna* (Great Compassion). The most moving compassion of the inspiration and hopes of a bodhisattva are found in Śantideva:

> May I be the doctor and the medicine
> And may I be the nurse
> For all sick beings in the world.
> Until everyone is healed.
>
> May a rain of food and drink descend
> To clear away the pain of thirst and hunger
> And during the aeon of famine
> May I myself change into food and drink.
>
> I become an inexhaustible treasure
> For those who are poor and destitute;
> May I turn into all things they could need
> And may these be placed close beside them (3:8–10). [63]

This is an embrace of the other, maintaining the absolute alterity of the other's face. A mutual transformation comes from an interaction between people who are different; it does not seek to synthesize them into a unified norm of mutual understanding. A bodhisattva suffers for suffering, as God in Jesus Christ suffers for suffering. A Buddhist sensitivity to others enables the hermeneutics of the other, a reading of what is unsaid and repressed and unproblematized in the world of text. The openness to the religious dimension of the other deepens and transforms the Asian church and theology, because without the other's wisdom the church and theology render Christ its exclusivist domain.

This calls for a dynamic of kenotic discipleship in which we pay more attention to the ethical imperatives of the church for others, especially in opposing the violence of totalization. To be ready to hear the core claim of the other, kenotic discipleship is needed, in which following Christ is not possible apart from openness to the religious dimension of others. Hearkening to the invitation of the religious other belongs to a faithful discipleship and kenotic Christology. This is an Asian understanding of Luther's ecclesiology.

For Christians, the God who is revealed in Christ is unique and absolute. It is through Christ that Christians come to a greater understanding of the mystery of God. Yet, this mystery that revealed itself truly, uniquely

63. Quoted in Williams, *Mahayana Buddhism*, 203.

and unsurpassingly in the suffering of Jesus Christ can be found in the wisdom of the others, through which Christians better understand and live out their commitment in the conviction and company of others. In other words, Jesus Christ as the Lord of the world can be found and heard from the strange voices of the others in the world. In this regard, Levinas is worth considering: "The presence of the face coming from beyond the world but committing me to human fraternity, does not overwhelm me as a numinous essence arousing fear and trembling . . . The face of a neighbor that I meet in proximity signifies for me an unexceptionable responsibility, preceding every free consent, every pact, every contract. It escapes representation; it is the very collapse of phenomenality."[64]

With special sensitivity to others in mind, an Asian theology tries to read the story of Lot's wife (Gen 19:1–29) as a way of filling the gap between Western theology and Asian hermeneutics. Samuel Cheon, a promising Old Testament scholar in South Korea, reads the story of Lot's wife in terms of a traditional legend of *Janjanup* in Korea. The story of *Janjanup* is thought to be imported from China to Korea. This story is compared to the story of Lot's wife. There was an old man who was very rich, but stingy and selfish. One day, a Buddhist monk asked for alms by beating a wooden bell. The rich man had absolutely no intention to donate. "I have nothing to give you," he said selfishly. The monk begged and begged. "If you offer a handful of rice and even just a penny, you will live long and eventually go to the paradise." In face of the monk's irresistible begging of alms, the rich man was bothered and outraged. Rushing into the stable and taking up a heap of ox dung with a shovel, he gave it to the monk. "There, take this and leave immediately."

Without saying a word, the monk respectfully received the ox dung by opening his sack. When he turned around, the voice of a woman, the daughter-in-law of the old rich man, came back with a tone of urgency: "Please wait a minute!" In happening to overhear the conversation between these two people, she was filled with sympathy. Offering a large gourd with rice from a pot to the monk, she asked him to forgive her father-in-law's attitude. Standing silently for a while, the monk began to tell her, "At noon tomorrow rain would come in torrents, the middle of your front yard would be flooded, the household of the old man including all people in the village would be punished, you should keep it to yourself, just go up to the mountain nearby to take refuge, you should not look back if

64. Levinas, *Otherwise than Being*, 147–48.

something terrible is heard behind your back." At noon the following day rain poured forth and flooded the front yard. Remembering the words of the monk, she took her baby on her back and began to climb up to the mountain nearby. When a bolt of thunder struck behind her, she, with the child on her back, turned around, forgetting the warning of the monk. Stunned by the sight, she turned into a stone out of fear. Since then, no one has dared to touch the stone, lest the misfortune should befall them.

Samuel Choen attempts to contextualize the theodicy question in terms of reading and comparing a story of Lot's wife and a story of *Janjanup*, the woman turned to stone with her baby. According to him, Lot's wife is not supposed to be blamed as wicked. Her punishment still remains a mystery, even reflecting the suffering of the innocent. In the biblical story, the reason why Lot's wife is selected is by and large based on her background from an unrighteous group such as a Canaanite family.[65] Was Lot's wife really punished and cursed because of her being wicked? At least from an Asian hermeneutics, this is not possible, because Lot's wife is seen as a figure of the embodiment of compassion with her community. Why are the innocent suffering? That still belongs to the mystery of God. However, the issue of theodicy is only met in compassion with the people in suffering.

An Asian hermeneutic of scriptures and Eucharist is non-dual, an embracing of the others. What is at stake for Luther's principle of *sola scriptura* is based on *was Christum treibt* (what drives to Christ), in which the gospel of Christ is at the normative center of authority, that is to say, the canon within the canon.[66] If *was Christum treibt* is the key principle for reading and understanding the scriptures, then an Asian sense and experience in getting access to the scriptures supports God's non-dual compassion and solidarity with all living creatures. This act of reading is in service of promoting the full humanity of marginalized peoples, thus revitalizing a prophetic-liberating tradition in the scriptures as well as in other narratives of God's solidarity with the others in a universal historical framework. Listening to the text is to encounter God "in, with, and through" the diversity of voices in the scriptures as well as in the company of other religious wisdom.

In this regard, an Asian hermeneutic for challenging exclusive, oppressive, and patriarchal texts and readings meets a postmodern call for

65. Choen, "Filling the Gap," 19.

66. *LW*, 39: 193.

ethical responsibility to the others. For Luther, there are "no fixed rules for the interpretation of the Word of God, since the Word of God, which teaches freedom in all other matters, must not be bound [2 Tim. 2:9]."[67] That Luther's theology passionately comes out of concrete struggles connecting life to theology is well attested.[68]

From a Buddhist perspective of non-duality, there is no point in separating theory from praxis, God from creatures, woman from man, etc. What an Asian hermeneutic seeks for the unsaid and the repressed in favor of the others should not be misunderstood as an attempt to idealize the others without qualification. Challenging any attempt at demonizing or totalizing the others, it pursues the embrace of them with a core conviction that God can speak to us in a different way. In the midst of troublesome texts, which are imbued with social, cultural, and religious complexities, to listen to the Word of God comes from human experience with *keine Weltlosigkeit Gottes* (no God without the world) in Jesus Christ or with a Buddhist universal compassion. The Lutheran principle that the finite is capable of the infinite is not to be read in contrast with the Buddhist principle that the infinite is also capable of the finite. It is biblically affirmed. In this regard the claim that "scripture interprets itself" should explain how the scripture interprets God's strange and different voice coming from a context where people in other social, cultural, and religious locations live. We hear it from "the swaddling clothes and the manger in which Christ lies."[69]

In filling the gap between the story of Lot's wife and the story of *Janjanup*, a fusion of horizons can occur, to the point where God's righteousness and compassion are vindicated by respecting the innocent in the mass guilt for the universal redemption of the wicked. Even the guilty may be redeemed by the presence of the innocent. God's justice and mercy become valid in God's involvement in human affairs.[70]

For Luther, Lot's wife was undoubtedly a believing and saintly woman. Luther boldly affirmed that a story of Lot's wife is not about condemnation of the woman, but about an example that gives instruction for us. Although she was overcome by human weakness, she suffers a temporal

67. Ibid., 31:34; cf. Luther, "The Freedom of a Christian."

68. *MLBTW*, 1–2.

69. *LW*, 35:236; cf. Luther, "Preface to the Old Testament."

70. Loader, *A Tale of Two Cities: Sodom and Gomorrah in the Old Testament*, 46–47.

punishment. In other words, her soul is saved. At a minimum, for Luther, Lot's wife was not condemned for this reason.[71]

The reason why Lot's wife looks behind Lot and becomes a pillar of salt is found by most commentators without difficulty in that she disobeyed the angel's command. Lot's "pillarized" wife plays a role in disturbing God's justice for the innocent. A pillar of salt stands as a disturbance or distraction to the commentators in general, but it makes a great difference to women, poets, and people of other cultures. In Kristine Batey's poem,Lot's wife has a reason to turn her attention to what is behind Lot, because she cooked the meals and raised her daughters and visited her women neighbors in Sodom.

> It is easy for eyes that have always turned to heaven
> not to look back;
> those that have been—by necessity—drawn to earth
> cannot forget that life is lived from day to day.
>
> ---
>
> On the bread of the hill, she chooses to be human,
> And turns, in farewell—
> And never regrets the sacrifice.[72]

God's concern about the cry of distress or cry for help (*zeaquah*) of Sodom and Gomorrah and their serious sin and violence (Gen 18:20-21) can be seen in parallel with many who are oppressed and suffering. The cry for help is in contrast to total punishment; it appeals to God's compassion for those innocent sufferers, through whom God would express God's *mahakaruna* for redeeming even the wicked. It is only Lot who is depicted as an insincere and self-centered individual. His wife may become a paradigmatic symbol corresponding to God's concern for those who cry for help in distress and anguish.

When it comes to the pillar of salt, salt is seasoning and used for preserving the food, for the cereal offerings woman renders ready for man to take to the shrine (Lev 2:13), and for purifying bad drinking water (2 Kgs 2:20–21). Salt preserves Lot's wife's pillar, which symbolizes tears, sorrow, and anguish for the others and cry for help in distress to heaven. It represents a wounded heart for the women and children of Sodom.[73] That

71. *LW*, 3,299.

72. Batey, "Lot's Wife," in *Alive Now!* (January/February 1988), 27, quoted in Mckenzie and Haynes, *To Each its Own Meaning*, 222.

73. Mckenzie and Haynes, *To Each its Own Meaning*, 223.

being the case, Asian readings of the text drive us to form interpretations that provide an encompassing account of the text, not by totalizing but by valuing difference and multivocality. It seeks to raise that which was left behind as the untruth, the irrelevant, and the excluded subsisting in the other side of history. In a similar vein, S. J. Samartha, an Indian theologian, expresses an Asian sense to the text of Lot's wife.

> Why did I look back?
> Because my neighbors were out there.
> When, during the birth of my first child
> I cried out in pain
> The women were there.
> They held my hands, wiped my brow,
> Gave me water to drink.
>
> ---
>
> When my little girl hit her foot against a stone
> And broke her toe nail,
> My neighbors came with some crushed leaves
> And put them round her toe.
> My daughter smiled through her tears.
> And where was Lot?
>
> ---
>
> My neighbor's husband walked three miles
> To get water. And he gave us some.
> Why did I look back?
> Because I wanted to perish with my neighbors
> Rather than be saved without them.[74]

Along the same lines, an analogous imagination of Asian minjung theology makes out two traditions of Buddhism in the story of *Janjanup*. Here a Buddhist monk would appear to be the embodiment of Buddhism as a state religion. Buddhism as the state religion has served the ruling class, losing its core teaching of universal compassion in the course of Korean history. Its teaching revolves around a patriotic, legalistic manifestation of Buddhahood in the service of the powerful, in which good deeds for the state are emphasized in contrast to bad deeds for the state.

However, *Janjanup* would appear as the symbolic figure of a bodhisattva, rather than following the Buddhist line of exclusivism. She embodies a communal compassion with all living creatures in the community. An Asian sense of community is inclusive, communitarian and other-directed. Would it be wrong to read Luther's language of Jesus' descent into hell

74. Quoted in Seong-Won, "'You do not see the Forest for the Trees,'" 201–2.

from a Buddhist hermeneutic of compassion rather than a mythological motif? Couldn't we see Lot's wife in relation to Jesus' heartfelt sorrow and compassion in the face of Jerusalem? In Luke 13:34 the ministry of Jesus is likened to a hen that "gathers her brood under her wings." At this juncture, we see an image of God with "the mother-quality of giving birth"[75] in Jesus Christ that can be appropriated for Asian other-ecclesiology.

Jesus' radical openness for and solidarity with the others is revealing in his parable of the Good Samaritan (Luke 10:25–37) in which Jesus includes the religious other. From the beginning, the adjective "good" for a Samaritan (generally despised with a sneer) is an oxymoron for Jesus' audience. Jesus' universal compassion reaches its climax in his last forgiveness. Jesus' radical openness to others characterizes the Asian church. His openness is symbolically manifested in the form of Lot's wife and breaks with the demanding father-image of the church. Furthermore, it embodies fellowship and solidarity with others, and corresponds to "the mother–quality of giving birth" in pain.

In anticipation of the participation of the Gentiles in the coming eschatological salvation (Luke 11:31f, Matt 8:11f), and along the lines of this reflection, Pannenberg states: "Jesus overcame this torment, the depth of the fate of death, for all men who are bound up with him."[76] According to Moltmann, "The Crucified God" is with us in our experience of hell. Therefore, hell and death are resolved once and for all in God. As St. Paul praises, "'Where, O death is your victory? Where, O death, is your sting?' . . . But thanks be to God! He gives us the victory through our Lord Jesus Christ." (1 Cor 15:55, 57). Jesus on the cross, experiencing the present wrath of God against the world without God, embraces the future of God's wrath and the hell of the future, too. This is radical grace, the most costly grace, which can be bestowed only by God through divine suffering of the victim and his wounded heart.[77] This is the place where God's most vulnerable and gracious heart is highlighted in terms of what has been done for all human beings.

Luther stressed expressively the radicality of God's grace in a sermon on "preparing to die" (1519). For him, "Christ's life overcame my death

75. Tillich, *Systematic Theology*, 294.

76. Pannenberg, *Jesus—God and Man*, 274. Pannenberg's remark is worth quoting: "The symbolic language of Jesus' descent into hell expresses the extent to which those men who lived before Jesus' activity and those who did not know him have a share in the salvation that has appeared in him," Ibid., 272.

77. Moltmann, *The Coming of God*, 251–53.

in his death, that his obedience blotted out my sin in his suffering, that is love destroyed my hell in his forsakenness."[78] "So then, gaze at the heavenly picture of Christ, who descended into hell (1 Pet 3:19) for your sake and was forsaken by God as one eternally damned when he spoke the words on the cross, *"Eli, Eli, lama Sabachthani*!—my God, my God, why hast thou forsaken me?"—(Matt 27:46). In that picture, your hell is defeated and your uncertain election is made sure . . . Seek yourself only in Christ and not in yourself and you will find yourself in him eternally."[79]

Given this fact, Jesus Christ crucified and risen sharpens "the universality of Christ's saving work" for all and empowers an ecumenic pluralism that, beyond radical pluralism, is meant to supply a perspective of assuming "responsibility for its corresponding unity."[80]

However, ecumenic pluralism should take more seriously the explosive and driving power of divine suffering. Our participation in the communion of saints leads to our participation in the suffering of Christ in the world, not only for transforming self, society and culture, but also for inspiring our ecumenic pluralistic diversity in the midst of the world's suffering. The Christian understanding of the universal grace of God in Jesus Christ is not one with a bodhisattva's universal mercy, but not-two. In striking a balance between the story of Lot's wife and the story of a woman called *Janjanup*, it is noteworthy that "the horizon is a range of vision that includes everything that can be seen from a particular vantage point. Applying this to the thinking mind, we speak of narrowness of horizon, of the possible expansion of horizon, of the opening up of new horizons."[81]

The Christian and the Buddhist (or no matter what other religious communities they are) may need each other to better understand their own conviction and expand their horizons, thereby modifying and transforming them in encounter with each other. Notwithstanding, they remain different. Religious difference does not need to be regarded as a stumbling block, but as an impetus for better understanding and enriching the divine life to which all living creatures belong and are invited. I understand this position as a non-relativistic, inclusive pluralism toward which Luther's extraordinary sense of the gospel might be reread and rediscovered in favor of an Asian sense of other ecclesiology.

78. *MLBTW*, 648.

79. Ibid., 644–45.

80. Cf. Peters, *God—the World's Future*, 334–56.

81. Gadamer, *Truth and Method*, 269.

God is no such extended, long, broad, thick, high, deep being. He is a supernatural, inscrutable being who exists at the same time in every little seed, whole and entire, and yet also in all above all and outside all created things

LW 19:228

All sentient beings without exception have the Buddha-nature: Tathagata (Buddha) is permanent with no change at all

Nirvana Sutra

7

Re-visitation of Martin Luther and Karl Barth in Interreligious Dialogue

The Baar Statement of the World Council Churches (1990) encouraged Christian theology to improve concern about other religions and take issue with interreligious dialogue in exploration of the theology of religious pluralism. The theology of religions has become more and more attractive, but also controversial in its encounter with postmodern thought and hermeneutic theory. In the circle of theology of religions, Martin Luther and Karl Barth have undergone intensive criticism for their conservative-evangelical attitude toward world religions. Barth's understanding of other religions is often criticized as a model advocating the conservative position, the content of which would imply an exclusive attitude. His theology of revelation along the lines of Reformation thought is generally regarded as inappropriate for engaging a constructive dialogue with religious pluralism today.[1]

Be that as it may, Martin Luther's theology of the cross was well received and echoed especially by Kitamori in the Japanese post-war context. In his book *Theology of the Pain of God*, Luther's idea of divine suffering is actualized in encounter with Buddhist ideas of compassion. In addition, Katsumi Takizawa (1909–1984), under the influence of Nishida, a founding representative of the Kyoto school in Japan, went to Karl Barth at Bonn in 1933, where he took issue with the notion of the "God-human relation" in Barth's thought from a Buddhist perspective. In this chapter, I will first introduce and evaluate Takizawa's reading of Barth and then deal with Barth's high Christology in an encounter with Buddhist insights. Secondly, Luther's thought will be presented in regard to some Buddhist ideas such as *dukkha* coupled with faith, salvation, and ecology. Thereby,

1. Cf. Knitter, *No Other Name?*, 80–96.

an understanding of Luther's theology will be appropriated for Buddhist-Christian dialogue to the point where both traditions can be renewed and deepened.

Karl Barth in Buddhist-Christian Dialogue

In his reading of Barth, Takizawa finds some important elements in affinity to Zen Buddhism, and the school of Amida Buddhism as well. According to Takizawa, Barth's Christology, in keeping with the *Urfaktum* of human beings and of creation, corresponds to the universal *Sunyata* of Zen Buddhism. This *Urfaktum* means the true I-self of Zen Buddhism, which already existed from the foundation of the world. Concerning Barth's doctrine of creation and reconciliation, whose starting point is Immanuel, Takizawa identifies Immanuel with the *Urfaktum* of creation and human being. As the true I-self is found in every person, argues Takizawa, so Immanuel as *Urfaktum* becomes manifest in the historical Buddha as well. In keeping with Barth's notion of inclusive universalism of reconciliation (*CD*, IV/3), Takizawa rejected Barth's early exclusive connection of the Word of God to the person of the worldly Jesus (*CD*, I/1), which would cause a misunderstanding of "Offenbarungspositivismus."[2]

What Takizawa takes seriously lies in the twofold way in which the contact of God with the human self needs to be distinguished: the primary contact is God's ubiquitous presence with human beings, regardless of the fact that they are ignorant of this unity between God and themselves. However, this primary contact of God with self becomes possible by God's coming to us. Thus, human beings are allowed to live in conscious accordance with God's will, which is termed the secondary contact of God with self. The primary contact of God with human self existed even before the appearance of the historical Jesus. Therefore, the event of Jesus alone, in Takizawa's view, should not be regarded as the exclusive ground for the salvific relationship between God and human beings. It can be only a spiritual event to accept Jesus Christ as the Son of God; thus it takes place only in the faith of believers. Therefore, if Christian theology restricts "God with us" merely to the historical Jesus, it remains human arbitrariness.[3]

Jesus' salvific role is to the person in the Hebrew tradition what Gautama Buddha is to the person in the Indian tradition. As far as salva-

2. For the controversy over *Offenbarungspositivismus* between Barth and Bonhoeffer, cf. Pangritz, *Karl Barth in the Theology of Dietrich Bonhoeffer*.

3. Takizawa, "*Was hindert mich noch getauft zu werden*," 37.

tion is grounded, first of all, on the primary contact of God with the human self, this much is in common between Christianity and Buddhism. What is, therefore, important for Takizawa is that Jesus Christ is not fully graspable in terms of the so-called historical Jesus. Understood in this way, the historical-scientific picture of Jesus of Nazareth is not enough. What is at issue is interpreting and reproducing the being and work of the man Jesus under the influence and presupposition of his resurrection. From this perspective, the being and work of the true God are fundamentally identical with the being and work of Jesus. Jesus' disciples were illumined and profoundly enlightened to the truth by his words, actions, and death, in which they recognized the hidden Lord in his whole person, and thus Jesus' real and unique relationship with God is possible. Even though historical-critical method and interpretation are highly skeptical of the historical reality of Jesus' resurrection, it does not become an obstacle to what Takizawa develops in terms of his Buddhist Christology considering *Urfaktum* Immanuel. The disciples, who were illumined and enlightened to the hidden secret and core concept of the person Jesus, began to reinterpret the fleshly life of Jesus as the complete sign of the Truth by way of their narratives and preaching.

According to Takizawa, we know Jesus through gnostic and mystic illumination, which is also an integral part of the Buddhist core concept of a Triple body. What faces us in the human Jesus illumines and enlightens the deeper, more real, original nature of God. The life of Jesus, which is seen and described by the eye of the evangelists, is more than the historical reality of Jesus. Rather, the evangelists see divine nature and human nature as actually becoming one in Jesus. This Enlightenment and illumination of the faith is, in Takizawa's view, true to Christians as well as Buddhists. This is the gift bestowed by God to those believers in both religions.

For Christians, this event of Enlightenment has something to do with the name of Jesus Christ. However, the effect of the Truth happening in Christ places the exclusive meaning of the historical Jesus under relativization, even if the Truth and salvation are bound to the personal encounter with Jesus Christ. At this point, Takizawa is concerned about developing the Buddhist Christology beyond the classic dogmatic pattern of Christology in the Western Church. His concern is to point to the Greater One to whom the whole person of Jesus bears witness.[4]

Interestingly enough, Takizawa depicts this One as the *Urfaktum* Immanuel, God with us (*Urbund*), the One between God and human

4. Takizawa, *Reflexionen*, 76–87.

beings long before the historical Jesus came. For Takizawa, that is a core concept of Karl Barth's theology. What we recognize in Jesus Christ is the performance and fulfillment of *Urfaktum,* God with us, which is, of course, unknowable to us without Jesus Christ. It is not, however, restricted to the human Jesus. The God who was in Christ (2 Cor 5:19) was beforehand, is present for today, and will remain the eternal God with us all.[5]

From this perspective, Takizawa challenges the traditional teaching of Christology. His question revolves around the question of how to assess the name of Jesus Christ in light of the *Urfaktum* Immanuel. Following in the footsteps of Barth, he relates the name Jesus Christ to the original relationship between God and human beings. That is to say, in Takizawa's understanding of the *Urfaktum* Immanuel, the name Jesus Christ is not totally identical with Jesus Christ himself in the historical sense. Thus, Takizawa extends Barth up to the point of relativizing the historical Jesus in favor of the divine original relation to human beings. In this way Takizawa tries to provide a ground for a *theologia naturalis* coming from the Barthian *Urfaktum* Immanuel.[6]

Recalling the Chalcedonian formulation, there is no Jesus without the *logos* (*Anhypostasis*). There is Jesus as the one who lived, suffered, died and was resurrected through the *logos* of God (*Enhypostasis*). This is typical of Western thought, which sticks to the original, essential unity between the human Jesus and the *logos* of God. Takizawa's criticism is aimed at the self-righteous "I" (thinking subject), which has long influenced and manipulated Western philosophy and theology.

The attempt to construct Western Christology by an essential unity between Jesus and God has blocked, according to Takizawa, the possibility of independence of the human Jesus apart from the unity with the eternal logos of God. This fact is unacceptable, not because of its Western thought, but because of its total ignorance of the *Urfaktum* that precedes the human Jesus. This fact results in strictly limiting the universal, cosmic *Urfaktum* of God with us only to a historical-geographical fixed point. Takizawa takes a Barthian formulation, "God is beforehand in Godself" to mean transcending the name Jesus Christ. In a Buddhist manner, Barth's core teaching of the immanent Trinity may be compared to *dharmakaya*, the Essence Body.

At times, Karl Barth is not exempt from his critique, in spite of Takizawa's sympathy with and respect for him. Takizawa's concept of the

5. Marquardt, *Das christliche Bekenntnis zu Jesus dem Juden*, 28–43.

6. Takizawa, *Reflexionen*, 86.

universal Christology can be understood in a Buddhist way. Takizawa, in introducing his contemporary Zen master Hisamatsu, actualizes the I-Self relation. Zen Buddhism, which teaches overcoming the self through meditation, can be helpful in deepening Western thought about Christology.

Here, there are two points in dialectical relations: limit point and contact point. According to the limit point, the ordinary I-Self is negated and killed. However, according to the contact point, the new free subjectivity of human beings occurs without cooperation on the part of human beings. Human beings can become free and come to their own nature, not through works or deeds, but rather originally and essentially as selfless Self. By way of illustration, the Buddha is not meant to be the person Siddhartha, but the illumined nature. Buddha and the ordinary human are one, and at the same time, not in oneness. Being righteous and being sinful are neither two, nor one. This is what Zen Buddhism teaches about the fundamental situation of human beings. That is to say, human beings exist basically not apart from Buddha, whether or not they know it. This is Buddhist non-duality (*soku*-ordinary human beings-relation).

Shinichi Hisamatsu (1889–1980), one of the leading figures of the Kyoto School, has blamed Christianity for original sin, which ignores the fundamental situation of human beings rooted in Buddhist *soku.* At this juncture, Takizawa identifies Buddhist *soku* with the *Urfaktum* Immanuel without reservation. God does not deny human beings when they deny God, regardless of how hostile or alien they are. *Theanthropological* unity, to use Barth's phrase, opposes God's absolute denial of human beings.[7] Of course, Takizawa thinks of the *Urfaktum* in relation to the biblical-historical name of Immanuel. The concept of Takizawa is not in a Buddhist manner, but in a Hebrew manner. In so doing, he thinks of the Immanuel as a Buddhist. His contribution is that he radicalizes the significance of Jesus Christ even to the point where the fundamental experience of every human being, even in other religions, becomes meaningful in the second Immanuel of Christ, which is found in Jodo-shin-Buddhism. With a Barthian orientation in mind, he paves the way, however, for a christological foundation of religious pluralism in light of a Buddhist concept of *dharma-kaya.*

7. Barth, *Evangelische Theologie*, 3.

Barth's Christology in Context of Religious Pluralism

Barth uses the *extra calvinisticum* (Christ outside human flesh) to discuss the relation of *enhypostasis* ("existence in") and *anhypostasis* ("no other mode of existence") in approaching the *assumptio carnis* (assumption of the flesh), which is the basis for constructing his universal Christology. It is well known that in his early stage he repudiated all attempts at a natural theology. As the incarnate Word is the eternal Son of God who became flesh (*enhypostasis*), so Jesus the human is none other than the eternal Son of God (*anhypostasis*).[8] Even during the confrontation with Emil Brunner, and the "Deutsche Christen" in the Nazi regime, he took into consideration strange voices of God outside the walls of Christianity. His reflection of "Gott kann," which encompasses the idea that God can make Godself known to human beings outside of Christianity, is reminiscent of a nominalistic trend and becomes deeply coupled with his Christology. This, in a sense, corresponds to a Buddhist insight of *dharma-kaya* (formless Self) to which Takizawa should have paid more attention.[9] Barth urged the church to listen attentively to the strange and even ominous voices with a humble attitude and radical openness, because through these voices God can lead Christianity to self-criticism and responsibility for a social and political agenda. As Barth states in a provocative tone, "God may speak to us through Russian communism, a flute concerto, a blossoming shrub, or a dead dog."[10] God's speech event, in an irregular and provocative manner, challenges us to understand that the boundary between the church and the secular world can still take a different course from what we would expect.

Moreover, Barth, in his later thought, moves in a different direction regarding the human nature of Christ. In other words, God has implicitly assumed the humanity of all human beings, not a single individual. Within humanity, the church exists *anhypostatically* and *enhypostatically* in Jesus Christ as the second form of his one existence. Finally, "Jesus Christ will be the *totus Christus*—Christ with his Christendom."[11] Barth's universal character of Christology becomes visible in the typology of Adam and Christ in Rom 5: "Not only Christians, but all persons are included in the realm of Christ's effectiveness. Dogmatically reversed, this means that the reality of Christ is the framework and realm in which human beings as

8. *CD*, I/2:163f.

9. Cf. Clausert, *Theologischer Zeitbegriff*, 85–93.

10. *CD*, I/1:55.

11. *CD*, IV/2: 59f.

such are included."[12] This would refer implicitly to the inclusive dimension of *assumptio carnis* in Barth's thought.

Understood in this way, the human species exists *enhypostatically* in Christ. At this point, there is no difficulty in affirming Marquardt's interpretation that Barth would run in a direction of expanding and completing the christological *anhypostasis* through an anthropological *enhypostasis*. That is, the *enhypostasis* of the *humanitas*, of the collective human species in the person of the incarnate Word.[13] At this juncture, we see an idea from the left wing of Hegel in Barth's thought in the way that he understands Christ as the representative of the collective human species (*Gattungswesen*).

Socio-political orientation becomes an integral part in constructing his Christology, in which the content and impulse of natural theology is reappropriated and deepened in terms of a theology of revelation, and later concretized in his teaching of universal reconciliation. Christ's divinity is to a theology of revelation what his humanity is to the content of natural theology. The incarnation of the eternal Word is not merely restricted to the human Jesus, but includes the humanity of Jesus, implying that of all human beings: "In Jesus Christ it is not merely one human, but the *humanum* of all humans, which is posited and exalted as such to unity with God."[14] Therefore, it is of special significance to note Barth's remark in his interview with the *Brüdergemeinde* in 1961 that he later reintroduced the *theologia naturalis* via Christology. We have to speak about it in a different way from the theology of nature. That is to say, in a christological way.[15]

If Barth takes Christ's humanity as a representative of the *enhypostasis* of the human race, if the entire human race exists in the hypostatic unity with the eternal Son of God, the possibility of a universal Christology emerges. If the pre-existent eternal Word exists not apart from, but in relation to the historical act of incarnation, Takizawa needs to pursue Barth's Christological *anhypostasis*, which is expanded and completed through the anthropological *enhypostasis*, from the perspective of *theoanthropology* encompassing socio-political realms. At this juncture Barth's construction of the humanity of Christ's *enhypostasis*, seen from the social-political, and historical perspective, continues to be actualized in relation to universal,

12. Barth, *Christus und Adam*, 50, quoted in Diem, "Karl Barth as Socialist," 129.

13. Marquardt, *Theologie und Sozialismus*, 267.

14. *CD*, IV/2:49.

15. See Maquardt, *Theologie und Sozialismus*, 263.

cosmic "lights and words" coming from other religions and cultures. What sense would it make to speak of Barth in relation to religious pluralism? To what extent would Barth recognize pluralistic claims of divine revelation?

Karl Barth's inquiry into secular parables of the truth (*CD*, IV/3.1) is generally regarded as a response to Calvin's understanding of the hidden, secret impulse of the Spirit. Unlike Calvin's approach to the otherness of Christianity based on the universal cosmic work of the Spirit,[16] Barth prefers to deal with pluralistic issues in terms of his universal cosmic Christology (the prophetic work of Jesus Christ, *CD*, IV/3.1). Barth's concern is to dialectically combine the word of Jesus Christ with various claims to truth in a pluralistic society. According to him, in the world reconciled with God in Jesus Christ, God cannot abandon any secular sphere. Even from the mouth of Balaam we recognize the well-known voice of the Good Shepherd, which should not be ignored despite its sinister origin.[17] Forms of secularism or pluralistic claims to truth ought to be regarded as signs and guideposts pointing to the Word of Christ to whom other cultures and religions are enhypostatically related.

This is not an exclusive position, but inclusive with radical openness to the strange voices outside the walls of Christianity. Profane words and lights are regarded to be as true as the one Word because God is active also in other religions and cultures. The reconciliation of God is not only for the church, but for the world. Therefore, the church has the task of examining closely whether these profane words and lights are in agreement with Scriptures or church tradition or dogma, whether the fruits of these words outside Christianity are good and their effects in the community are positive. At this point, Barth is even positive to "dangerous modern expressions like the revelation of creation or primal revelations" in light of the cosmic Christology.[18] However, Hans Küng complains that Barth corrected his former positions without publicly admitting it, unlike the later *Augustine of Retractions*.[19]

Be that as it may, this is the continuation of Barth's teaching of the strange voices of God outside the walls of the church in relation to the universal reconciliation of Jesus Christ, which Barth had consistently attempted to clarify from his early stage on. In this regard, a dialectical

16. Cf. Chung, *Spirituality and Social Ethics*, 13–24.

17. *CD*, IV/3.1:119.

18. *CD*, IV/3.1:40.

19. Küng, *Does God exist?*, 527.

relationship between Lutheran *est* and the Reformed *but* plays a significant role in shaping and directing Barth's thought. Barth takes the divine work of reconciliation neither to negate the divine work of creation, nor to deprive it of meaning. The work of Jesus Christ does not take from the creation its cosmic lights and language of wisdom. There is no point of tearing asunder "the original connection between creaturely *esse* and creaturely *nosse*."[20]

In light of reconciliation, nothing is separated from God. Religious truth claims within the created cosmos are placed in parallel with the Word of Jesus Christ, in which mutual recognition can be done, and thereby the otherness outside Christianity exists as a partner witnessing the work of God's reconciliation with the world. This is the inclusive Christology of Barth with pluralistic openness.

Martin Luther in Buddhist-Christian Dialogue

The core of Buddhism is generally expressed in the four marks of existence: the impermanence of all conditioned things; the universality of *dukkha*; the absence of a permanent, eternal self; and attainment of nirvanic Enlightenment. From the formal approach, we notice generally that a Buddhist realism sees things as they are, which does not seem alien to Luther's realism of *theologia crucis*, albeit with a striking difference in emphasis on salvation. Both the First Sermon and the discourse on non-self Buddha remain silent about the ultimate reality of selfhood. Later, in conversation between the Greek king Menander and the Buddhist monk Nagasena, non-self teaching is strictly opposed to the atman philosophy of the Upanishads. Nagasena's candid denial of the existence of the soul became the orthodox teaching for *Hinayana* Buddhism.

This is a Buddhist version of negative theology. In view of the three-fold body doctrine, Buddhism would still have a problem in identifying the Ultimate Principle (Christ) with the historical point (Jesus) once and for all, because Buddha body (*dharma-kaya*) manifests itself in many and various historical individuals. The denial of the individual self of Jesus as the mediator seems to polarize Buddhism and Christianity.

In the Buddha's time a spiritual quest was seen and characterized as the search for liberating a person's self in searching for being identical and united with Brahman. A personal union with Brahman as the eternal, ultimate reality was the popular pattern in Hinduism. What characterizes

20. *CD*, IV/3.1:139.

and distinguishes Buddhism from the traditional Vedic idea of Brahman as the sole foundation underlying the universe is Buddha's rejection of Brahman as an imaginary construction. Rather, the ideas of dependent co-origination, impermanence (*anyta*), and no-self (*anatman*) entail rejecting both transcendence and immanence.

The principle of dependent co-origination as the Middle Way stresses that there is neither transcendence, nor immanence, nor middle position—nothing whatsoever more real lying beyond or behind the interdependence of everything in the universe. This nothingness, which cannot be compared to somethingness, is the absolute Nothingness, a term that is favored by the Kyoto school in Japan. This absolute Nothingness is beyond any dualist contrast between nothingness and somethingness. The core teaching of Buddhism is to realize this absolute Nothingness in terms of dependent co-origination and the Middle Way.[21] From a *Mahayana* standpoint Buddhism distinguishes the empirical ego from the authentic true self. This is "metanoesis" for Buddhism in representation of "the true meaning of enlightenment to the truth of religion."[22]

The true self, which is, therefore, of special significance to primitive Buddhism, is oriented toward the attainment of nirvanic liberation. In other words, the self, chained into mutual interdependence and universal relationality, extends beyond the empirical ego to the dimension of the cosmos. The true self of Buddhism is the active subject of morality (*sila*) for responsible moral and religious action, whereas the true self of the Upanishads or Vedanta philosophy remains a metaphysical entity. The true self is interconnected with the attainment of liberative *Nirvana*. Enlightenment, depicted as a realization of the unity between one's self and the entire cosmos of Buddhahood, would mean that one's true self is in unity with the cosmic Ultimate, none other than the cosmic Buddha body (*dharma-kaya*).

Therefore, "everyone and everything is in suffering" is not merely the indicator of expressing Buddhism as fundamentally a pessimistic or nihilistic teaching, but rather points to the ontological, cosmological liberative path leading to *Nirvana*. In a similar way, for example, St. Paul in the Epistle to the Romans gives a clear picture of the condition of human being as well as all living sentient creatures under need and distress in anticipation of the eschatological unity with the coming Ultimate. With

21. Ives, *Divine Emptiness*, 50–52.

22. *BS*, 1, introduction, xx.

focus on sin as the source of suffering he evokes the cosmic pain of everybody and everything in subordination to impermanence (Rom 7:14–20, 8:19–22).

By the same token, the distinction between empirical ego and true self is also of special significance for Luther. His spirituality of the theology of the cross, which is influenced by German mystics like Tauler, embraces, beyond a forensic moment of justification, a profound spiritual dimension of *Anfechtungen* (inner struggle) or *Gelassenheit* (disinterestedness) in understanding Christian faith in relation to *Christusförmigkeit* (Christ-conformity). In fact, Luther's forensic concept of justification is interconnected with its transformative and effective dimensions.

Luther's doctrine of justification includes our freedom and discipleship in the world. Luther's spirituality of *theologia crucis* is not polarized from the spirituality of the Great Death in Buddhism that aims to overcome selfish ego-centeredness in favor of attaining the true authentic self of *dharmakaya*. A Buddhist remark is striking: "How is it that one who has died the Great Death is now on the contrary living?" The Great Death is necessary to attain freedom and salvation. What the Buddhists hear in such biblical texts as "it is no longer I who lives, but Christ who lives in me" (Gal 2:20) is the imperative of dying to the empirical, provisional ego. Following in the footsteps of St. Augustine, Luther understands Jesus Christ as the sacrament, which is inseparably connected with Jesus Christ as the example. It implies the metanoia of turning from empirical, egocentered craving toward the authentic Self of Jesus Christ in his sacramental example of self-emptiness. Christ's path of kenotic Emptiness is not only a sacrament but also an example for the Christian to follow.[23]

In addition, Luther's idea of "wonderful exchange" implies a concept of the unitive marriage between the sinful empirical ego and the true self of Christ, because faith unites the soul with Christ so as to become one flesh (Eph 5:31f). Christ is full of grace, life, and salvation whereas the soul is full of sins, death, and damnation. This is neither one, nor two, but is the non-dual principle between Jesus Christ and the human being in Luther's theology. The true self of Jesus Christ comes to us so as to set us free from *dukkha*.

In this process a Great Death occurs in a Christian sense. In order for the true self of Christ to live, my empirical ego should die. To a vivid image of the most perfect marriage Luther does not ignore the spiritual

23. *LW*, 27:238.

dimension of the Great Death that is essential to Buddhism. In this regard, we know how Luther understands Christian freedom. "A Christian is perfectly free lord of all, subject to none. A Christian is a perfectly dutiful servant of all, subject to all." From here Masao Abe finds a striking resemblance between Luther and Buddhism. However, the essential difference between them lies in the fact that Luther's thought is anthropocentric, while Buddhist *Sunyata* has no center or circumferential limitation. In the boundless openness of *Sunyata*, the freedom of the Buddhist is found in the awakening to this *Sunyata*.[24]

In general, Buddhists take the cross as a sign of the will to dominate and rule, which is precisely opposed to the Buddha's sinking silence into *Nirvana*. Especially in the eye of D. T. Suzuki, the Christian symbol of the cross leads necessarily to a Christian will to power and dominion. He has a pronounced abhorrence of the idea of Christian atonement through blood. Buddhist resistance to the Christian symbol of the cross is partially justified only in view of the historical crusade that has misused the dimension of self-emptying spirituality of the cross for the sake of dominion and manipulation, excluding other ways.[25]

But Luther's idea of *theologia crucis* shows God's self-emptying love for all human beings rather than promoting a Christian interest in political power and rule in the name of the cross. The superficial, inconstant, ever-changing ego is contrasted with the depths of the soul, which touch the eternal. The encounter with the self here immediately opens up an encounter with the God who is utterly other and the Creator of the finite self. However, the Buddhist intuition of self does not work this way, but opens onto the *Sunyata* as the Great Self.

Kenosis and *Sunyata*

In Buddhist-Christian dialogue the kenosis of Christ is the focus. A Christian understanding of God meets, intersects, and clashes with the Buddhist core teaching of *Sunyata*. The emptying God is the fundamental idea of Christian doctrine, just as the emptying *Sunyata* is for Buddhist teaching the path to liberation. Of course, there have been many different interpretations of key Buddhist notions such as *Nirvana*, *Sunyata*, and *dharma-kaya*, even among Mahayana Buddhist traditions in China, Japan, Korea and Vietnam. What mainly differentiates the Christian idea of God

24. Ives, *Divine Emptiness*, 54.

25. Ingram and Streng, *Buddhist-Christian Dialogue*, 32.

as the Ultimate reality from a Buddhist *Sunyata* as the *dharma-kaya* is the Buddhist rejection of a Christian monotheistic or trinitarian concept of God. Based on dependent co-origination, even the ultimate does not exist by itself. The Great Self, which is understood as the ultimate reality, is called the non-duality principle. However, the true meaning of *Sunyata* is affirmative in the non-substantial existence of non-existence in spite of sounding negative. That is why *Sunyata* is called Suchness, Body of Truth.

In this regard, excessive emphasis on *Sunyata* as "the absolute Nothingness" would tend to lose the dynamic dimension of self-emptying *dharma-kaya* underlying the world and all living sentient creatures. If God's self-negation entails God's self-transcendence in spite of the world as God's creation in God, would it be possible to see God merely as *das Nichts* or the absolute Nothingness, to transcend and surpass all relations from a Buddhist perspective? Is this absolute Nothingness exempt from dependent co-origination?

In the Buddhist-Christian dialogue Masao Abe emphasizes the subject of the kenosis of God as the most important and essential. He believes that the notion of the kenotic God endorsed by the Buddhist notion of *Sunyata* would help Christianity to overcome its monotheistic character. In examining the Pauline text of Phil 2:5–8 he first comes to the idea that Christ's kenosis and his abnegation have to be understood as complete, radical, thoroughgoing, and total. At this point he understands *homoousios* between the divinity and humanity of Jesus Christ in one person "as nondual function of self emptying or self-negation."[26] Abe continues to relate the kenosis of Christ to the kenosis of God in terms of dependent co-arising. When the kenosis of Christ occurs here, the kenosis of God also occurs.

If God the Father is not self-emptying, the self-emptying of the Son is insufficient and inconceivable. At this point, Abe rejects any idea of transcendence of the Father in the kenosis of the Son on the basis of *homoousios*. Therefore, he is critical of Barth's concept of *theologia crucis*, which affirms *theologia gloriae* within it. However, Abe's exegesis of the Philippians text on the basis of the total interconnection and identification between the kenosis of Father and the kenosis of the Son is seriously challenged and attacked by some Western theologians, especially by Hans Küng. According to Küng, the Philippians hymn only refers to the kenosis

26. Ives, *Divine Emptiness*, 33.

of Jesus Christ. If the father empties himself in the sense of a Buddhist *Sunyata*, who wakes up Jesus from death to the resurrection? This is a significant flaw in Abe's "Buddhist exegesis of the Christian texts."[27] Would not Masao Abe, in boldly affirming the kenosis of God the father, avoid running into implicitly "monophysitic patripassianism" from a Christian perspective?[28]

Considering Phil 2:5–8, Abe takes Christ's kenosis not only to imply "a radical and total self-negation of the Son of the God," but to have its origin in the kenosis of God the Father. The self-emptying of the Son of God can be, properly speaking, understood in relation to the self-emptying of God the Father. That being the case, how can Abe distinguish Father from Son in spite of maintaining a substantial unity between Father and Son, while still affirming the divine double kenosis? Even in a Buddhist perspective of double negation, the Father is neither one with the Son, nor two with him. Nagarjuna's philosophy of double negation does not say that *Nirvana* is totally identical with *samsara*. Rather it affirms that *Nirvana* is not different from *samsara*, and vice versa.

In a Christian context, divinity is not totally identical with humanity in one person of Jesus Christ, but also not totally different from it. The distinction between Father and Son may be affirmed in a Buddhist perspective. Otherwise, Abe's understanding of *Sunyata* falls victim to the endless dancing of self-emptying without separation or distinction. A Christian notion of distinction, yet no separation (*distinctio sed non separatio*) is more promising for interreligious hermeneutics in encounter with the Buddhist notion of *Sunyata*. In contrast to Abe's interpretation of *Sunyata*, Küng states that there is "a clear indication of a major paradigm shift in Buddhism" concerning the concept of *Sunyata* from Nagarjuna's *pratitya-samutpada* to the Yogacara doctrine of Buddhology. Given this fact, Abe's perspective on the kenosis of God is partial and insufficient because it is based only on a very specific Buddhist paradigm in which the *Madhyamika* is interpreted by a specific Zen philosophy.[29]

Abe's dialectic between love and *das Nichts* lets him further assert God as an all-loving God. God, as *das Nichts,* is in total identification with everything in the universe: the *Sunyata* is in you, you are in *Sunyata*. In more emphatic terms, *Sunyata* is you. You are *Sunyata*. This is the Buddhist

27. Ibid., 214.

28. Ibid., 213.

29. Ibid., 219.

teaching of self-deification in relation to Enlightenment. At this point an apophatic concept of the Godhead above or beyond God as the darkness of the Godhead (Meister Eckhart) comes into juxtaposition with Abe's *Sunyata* on the basis of the absolute Nothingness, or to be more precise, the all inclusive (dynamic) Emptiness (*Sunyata*) of Buddhism.

However, in Buddhist teaching *dharma-kaya* is not totally identical with the other two bodies. What is more at stake for Abe is the direct, immediate relationship between God as the self-emptying reality and the world and human beings in terms of the cosmotheandric unity of a dynamic all inclusive *Sunyata*. In order to attain this Enlightenment, one does the spiritual exercises of Zen meditation in aid of self-realization.

Although Abe is reluctant to accept "a Buddhist exegesis of the Christian texts," his understanding of the dialectic between self-emptying and self-fulfillment reminds us of Nagarjuna's teaching of dependent co-origination from a Japanese Zen perspective. If Emptiness is seen as the ultimate reality through the "not one, not two" principle, in order to avoid monotheistic or dualistic ways of thinking in Christian thought, this doctrine of the Middle Way should take the further step of negating God's self-emptying dynamic cosmotheandric unity and identification with the world in favor of becoming "not one."

In criticizing *Abhidharma* Buddhism, Nagarjuna provides a thorough philosophical foundation for the Middle Way by rejecting the eternalist view as well as the nihilistic view. Based on the *Prajnāparāmitā* (the Perfection of Wisdom Sūtras), he affirmed "not being, and not not-being." The negation of being and the double negation alike mean the negation of non-being as the denial of being. The negation of the negation truly reveals the Emptiness as the ultimate reality free from being and non-being. Therefore, Emptiness as *Sunyata*, or God's self-emptying in Christian terms, transcends and embraces both Emptiness and Fullness in a dynamic constant mode of activity. It is formless because it is totally free from both form and formlessness. Therefore, in *Sunyata*, Emptiness as it is is Fullness, and Fullness as it is is Emptiness, formlessness as it is is form, and form as it is is formless.[30]

Because true Emptiness, which empties even itself is absolute Reality, and this Reality lets all existents truly be, everyone and everything is involved in a Buddhist pantheism, which is grounded on a dynamic activity of emptying everyone and everything including itself. The boundless

30. Abe, *Buddhism and Interfaith Dialogue*, 141.

openness that Abe prefers to use for describing the actual reality of *Sunyata* results in a Buddhist ultimate Reality that deconstructs any centrism such as anthropocentrism, cosmocentrism and even theocentrism. The center is everywhere. Therefore, a Buddhist notion of God as the absolute openness of *Sunyata* is only at liberty to move from the kenosis of the authentic self to fullness of non-being, and vice versa. This is the true nature of God as the *Sunyata* from which all divine attributes stem. How would it be possible for the "absolute Nothingness" as the negation of negation to reveal itself in the form of a historical individual? Only through dynamic negation of negation? Is it unselfish love?

In order for God to be liberated totally from the divine *dukkha* that is clinging to God as the absolute being, God cannot still remain God and at the same time totally identify with the kenosis of Christ. The God who remains transcendent or eternal in distinction from the kenosis of the Son, even in forsaking the Son on the cross, is caught up in incompleteness. It is not the true God. Divine *dukkha* can be solved only by freeing Godself from divine craving to become self-existing absolute being, while God remains *Nichts, Ungrund,* or the absolute Nothingness, because kenosis and pleroma are the reality of *Sunyata* embracing positivity and negativity. This is why Abe wants to propose an understanding of a kenotic God for Christianity in his specific philosophical paradigm of Zen Buddhism.

From this perspective, Abe is critical of the traces of dualism in Catholic theologians such as Karl Rahner and Hans Küng. They are attached to impassibility and immutability in God when they reject the kenosis of God or "the crucified God." Without reflection on God's passibility, we have great difficulty in struggling with the problem of the holocaust at Auschwitz. In this regard, Moltmann's theology of the crucified God is more promising and attractive to Abe, albeit with a different orientation.

Dukkha and Divine Suffering

In following Luther's *theologia crucis,* Moltmann interprets the Christ event on the cross from a uniquely trinitarian perspective by emphasizing the suffering of God's Fatherhood in the death of the Son. "So the new Christology which tries to think of the death of Jesus as the death of God must take up the elements of truth which are to be found in kenoticism (the doctrine of God's Emptiness of himself) . . . The Son suffers dying, the Father suffers the death of the Son . . . The fatherlessness of the Son is matched by the Sonlessness of the Father."[31] In agreement with Moltmann, Abe, however, roots the sonship of Jesus ultimately in *Nichts* or *Ungrund* as "the Godhead in the unity of three persons in one God." In light of *Nichts* as Godhead, the event of the cross of Jesus can be understood properly as the event of an unconditioned and boundless love.[32] How can the *Nichts* or *Ungrund* be passible as the Godhead beyond the God in the sense of Christian mystics?

Luther's understanding of divine suffering looks very insightful in light of the Buddhist notion of *dukkha*. Luther took with great seriousness the concept of the *communication of attributes* in *concreto*. For us, then, the kenosis (Phil 2:6–7) is depicted as Jesus' attitude of self-sacrifice allowing the impact of cosmological *dukhka* on his divine nature. That God genuinely suffers leads Luther to affirm theopassianism. That is, divinity has something do with *dukkha*. The cross is central in God's action and revelation, therefore suffering for others is what God has done in Jesus Christ. The death of God the Son is then integral to the Trinity. For God, *dukkha* is not merely an issue to be overcome through renunciation of craving, but an integral part of Godself as absolute love in freedom in an eternal trinitarian relationality.

Suffering for others is an integral part of the calling of those who would share in God's life. The self-emptying of God the Father becomes manifest in the motherly suffering of the Father's begetting the Son in the power of the Holy Spirit. God does not remain merely in the absolute Nothingness, or Godhead above God, but moves in the dynamic love of intra-divine *perichoresis* in assuming the humanity of Christ into the inner trinitarian life. This is not monistic, but trinitarian theism, in which the *assumptio carnis* in Luther's view would implicitly entail God's assumption of the cosmological *dukkha* of all sentient creatures through self-emptying, while yet remaining in trinitarian *perichoresis*. God is to *dukkha* what Buddha is to Mara, the tempter. The basic and fundamental solution does not merely come from the insight into Emptiness, but from God's mysterious action of self-emptying in Jesus Christ for everybody and everything.

If God the Father and God the Spirit have a share in the death of God the Son, the trinitarian life finds itself in a dialectic between God's being and God's non-being through allowing and assuming the *dukkha* of death into the trinitarian life. If we take "the crucified God" as the starting

31. Moltmann, *Crucified God*, 204, 205, 243.

32. Ives, *Divine Emptiness*, 48–49.

point for discussing the Christian concept of God, God is neither monistic nor dualistic, but a trinitarian unity, while remaining "not one, not two," concerning the relationship between Father and Son. The Buddhist teaching of the triple body is inclined to a monistic attachment to *dharma-kaya* that is not in full relationality with the other two bodies. In this regard the Christian term of *perichoresis* needs to meet a Buddhist doctrine of triple body. The triune God in *perichoresis* asks for a Buddhist to rethink of *dharma-kaya* in full relationality with the other two bodies from the perspective of dependent co-origination.

From a Christian perspective, God in the Trinity wills in freedom to be affected by the world, by assuming *dukkha* in God's intradivine life. The unselfish love of God begins with the broken wounded Trinity in which Jesus Christ realized himself to become the authentic self of cosmic unselfish love. The self-realization of the Son of God takes place in his kenosis, in which God the Father and the Spirit co-participate in a different way. Here, we find a non-duality in the kenosis of the Son in perichoretic relationship with Father and the Spirit. In this regard, a Christian concept of Father causing the Son to die on the model of an Abraham-Isaac typology is replaced by a new paradigm of God the victim in which the Father co-participates in the kenosis of the Son and is in solidarity with the Son the victim. Luther implicitly asserts that the wounded Trinity points to the dimension of God the victim who assumed the *dukkha* eternally and beforehand, and also assumed the *dukkha* of everybody and everything historically. Theological attempts to resolve the Father-Son relation on the cross are proposed by the model of God's giving love in sharing the death of the Son, or the Father's co-suffering the death of the Son.

The wounded Trinity in *dukkha*, which is the basis for a victim Christology of minjung as the people of God, is from the beginning the *Urfaktum* Immanuel in trinitarian relationality. There can be no world without God, as conversely God cannot be the true God without the world. In the crucifixion absolute Nothingness overwhelmed Jesus Christ. He realized divine *dukkha* by turning the absolute power of Nothingness into absolute love, from the cosmological power of death to the eternal, new life through the power of resurrection.

Dukkha and Ethics

From a Buddhist perspective *dukkha*, impermanence, and no-Self form and constitute the fundamental basis for Buddhist ethics. The goal of overcoming *dukkha* in oneself and others is the central concern of Buddhism. The natural human feeling of sympathy for others and solidarity with them in the situation of *dukkha* needs to be discussed in relation to the aspect of victimhood. The Buddha is reported to have remarked, "Having traversed the whole world with my thought, I never yet met with anything that was dearer to anyone than his own self. Since the self of others is dear to each one, let him who loves himself not harm another."[33] What is more promising for a Buddhist ethics is the practice and vision of Thich Nhat Hanh from Vietnam. Vietnamese Buddhism has been shaped by the interplay between the Theravada Buddhist tradition and the Mahayana Buddhist heritage of China. What is fundamental for Nhat Hanh's whole vision and practice are the earliest Mahayana sutras and the later Hua-Yen School of Chinese Buddhism. The Heart Sutra, one of the early *Prajnaparamita* Sutras, expresses his core vision of "inter-are."[34]

In a Buddhist-Christian dialogue, Abe's understanding of *Sunyata* is ethically powerless concerning the victim in *dukkha*, such as in the Holocaust or in the genocide during the Japanese colonization in China and Korea. As Borowitz argues, Abe's proposal that the Holocaust ultimately has no significance should be strongly rejected even from a Buddhist perspective. Clearly, the opinion that there is "no utterly fundamental distinction between the Nazi death camp operators and their victims" is gravely offensive to the victims.[35] A metaphysical logic of *Sunyata* as the absolute Nothingness does not justify it.

Unlike Abe, Thich Nhat Hanh applies the insight of Emptiness to the question of social justice, and sees the social system of a society working as a unity. "Wealth is made of non-wealth elements, and poverty is made by non-poverty elements."[36] A poor girl is pressed to become a prostitute because the entire structure of the society supports wealthy families at the cost of the poor. We must see the prostitute in non-prostitute people and the non-prostitute people in the prostitute on the basis of inter-being. Genuine solidarity with the victim and breakthrough in social justice are a more inclusive, non-dualistic framework in which there is no need to take sides, but to do justice to both sides. Even Buddha and the tempter Mara need each other. The overcoming of discriminating consciousness

33. Harvey, *Introduction to Buddhist Ethics*, 34.

34. Hanh, *Heart of Understanding*, 3.

35. Cobb and Ives, *Emptying God*, 83.

36. Ibid., 33.

leads to perfect freedom. This transformation of our consciousness is an indispensable foundation for the work towards peace and justice in the world. Wisdom and compassion are inseparable. The wisdom of insight into inter-being expresses itself in compassionate action in the world. This vision encourages us to become deeply involved in the quest for peace and efforts to help victims and refugees.[37]

Luther's image of God on the cross would enable us to develop God in a wounded Trinity in favor of the victim. Jesus Christ who entered into the human world was willing to take the burden of world's *dukkha* on himself as the Lamb of God as the scapegoat. This insight becomes fully explicit in relation to a postmodern notion of God. Luther's idea of God in light of the postmodern theory of the scapegoat is expressed implicitly in his exegesis of the gospel of John (John 1:29), where he makes it explicit: The Lamb of God is given to us as God's present. In this regard he stands for the justice of all who believe in him. Christ satisfied the demand of the law under the reign of the tyranny of the law. As the scapegoat, "he was oppressed and He was afflicted . . . Like a lamb that is led to slaughter" (Isa 53:7). The Lamb of God who takes away the sin of the world became the victim, and after all, a curse for us. In so doing, the grace to free us from the demand of the law is given.[38]

Jesus, the one who bears the sin of the world, represents the innocent otherness of the minjung who suffer and so he bears the sin of the world, subject to the violence and murder of the scapegoat mechanism and the hypocrisy of a self-justified social and political infrastructure. Luther's metaphor of God the victim on the cross leads to Jesus as the final scapegoat implying that God was willing to suffer as the victim of human scapegoating. In so doing, justification is meant to be justice for the sake of the innocent victim of otherness in the violent mechanism of the human self-justified social and economic order.[39]

At this juncture, I am keenly aware of Luther's ethical solidarity with the poor, the economically weaker, and the marginalized in his society of early capitalism. Luther's socio-ethical reflection on the economic life and its structural arrangements can be seen and are discussed in his alternative reflection on God or mammon. His critical stance against usury penetrates his early position in his *Small and Great Sermon on Usury* (1519/1920) and

37. Lefebure, *Buddha & The Christ*, 160–62.

38. Muhlhaupt, *D. Martin Luthers Evangelien-Auslegung*, 76.

39. Cf. Peters, *God—The World's Future*, 159–64.

Trade and Usury (1524), until the later writing of *Admonition to Clergy That They Preach against Usury* (1540).

Like the devouring capital, Luther argues, the usurers are eating our food and drinking. Such people are denounced as a dangerous class, even depriving them the right to be called human. Luther's treatise *Admonition to Clergy That They Preach against Usury* (1540), was admired by Karl Marx in the latter's denouncing of the Christian character of capital accumulation, concentration, and monopoly, which is the basis for Christian colonialism. Luther integrates economic issue in terms of his theological reflection on God in the first commandment. Luther's prophetic stance for anti-mammon in the period of early capitalism constitutes an essential motive for his *theologia crucis* in solidarity with the victim, the marginalized, and the scapegoat in our society.[40]

In addition, for Luther, there was a tension between the emptying God and the ubiquity of Christ's body. In following the Alexandrian tradition, he gave a clear interpretation of the emptying at the incarnation. His exegesis of Phil 2:7 runs like this: Jesus Christ emptied himself, taking the form of a servant, being born in the likeness of men, and being found in human form. "At the incarnation Christ did not leave his Godhead in heaven, but in his earthly life he renounced it. The divine person assumed human nature, in so doing, "God has suffered, the Man has created heaven and earth . . . that the Servant (Christ) . . . is Creator of all things."[41]

However, Luther did not interpret Christ's self-emptying as some kenotic theologians do, who at the incarnation focus on a strictly human nature in abandonment of the divine nature. However, in allowing suffering of human nature, the divine nature is present throughout the earthly life of Jesus. After all, God genuinely suffers. Jesus' experience of suffering as a human being is at the same time a divine experience.[42]

Notwithstanding, in accepting the doctrine of the *enhypostasis* and *anhypostasis*, Luther runs into the ubiquity of Christ in a cosmic and universal sense in the treatment of the problem of Jesus' kenosis at the cross. His understanding of the cosmic Christ's body at the right hand of God

40. In *Large Catechism* Luther contrasts God with mammon, which represents money and property. Luther's ideological critique of the powerful in monopoly capital is imbued with his confessional statement of God. Cf. Luther, "Large Catechism," in Kolb and Timothy, *BC*, 387–91, 418.

41. *WA*, 39 II, 16–22; cf. Lohse, *Martin Luther's Theology*, 229.

42. Following Luther, Moltmann affirms the suffering of God as death in God rather than the death of God. Moltmann, *Crucified God*, 205.

has to do with Christ's humiliation in the self-emptying at the incarnation. In other words, the cosmic Christ is not one with the kenosis of Jesus, but not two with his abandonment. "We believe that Christ, according to his human nature, is put over all creatures (Eph 1:22) and fills all things . . . Not only according to his human nature, he is a lord of all things, has all things in his hand, and is present everywhere."[43]

Luther's concept of the cosmic Christ would better approximate a universal Buddhahood in *Hua-yen* Buddhism rather than the self-emptying God in Japanese Zen Buddhism. Where the cosmic *dukkha* is, the cosmic Christ is also. This issue will be discussed further in the next chapter in dealing with three patterns of soteriology in Buddhism. Be that as it may, the affinities between Buddhists and Luther at the existential level are striking, in spite of the divergences at the level of soteriological explication.

Three Patterns of Soteriology in Buddhism

In the various forms of Mahayana Buddhism one can find diverse understandings and emphases regarding salvation. They can be classified as three different types: Faith-based, self-awakening, and cosmos-based. The place to begin is with the three-body (*trikaya*) doctrine. From it we will see how Buddhism shapes its soteriological concept and works in threefold patterns. After the Buddha's death, his disciples began to idealize the Buddha-body in relation to his historical existence. This has continued to be a predominant practice for centuries in the Mahayana tradition.

As we have already seen, according to Nagarjuna, what is dependent co-arising is called emptiness, not what is emptiness is dependent co-arising. However, the Emptiness is represented by words, and that is the Middle Way. Everything in the universe should be negated for *Sunyata* to appear. If this aspect cannot be represented by words, the *Sunyata*-human relation remains totally negative. Through his distinction "not different from" (*Nirvana* is not different from *samsara*, *samsara* is not different from *Nirvana*) he would imply that *Sunyata* is the principle of *Nirvana* and *samsara*. Where Nagarjuna's distinction between *Nirvana* and *samsara* is accepted as the total identification between them without any medium, the dimension of religious practice disappears, thus leading to an uncritical affirmation of the existence of phenomenal world (*prapanca*). This position is unsatisfactory to Yogacara thinkers.

43. *LW*, 36:342.

The Yogacara, or mind-only school founded by Asanga and Vasubandhu (fifth century), is seen often as reacting against the nihilistic perils of Nagarjuna. However, the essential teaching of Madhyamika philosophy is affirmed in relation to the doctrine of mind. Nagarjuna has rejected all theory as illusory in the dialectics of double negation of Emptiness. This insight into Emptiness called into question all truth claims, even the Four Noble Truths. The most central Buddhist doctrine would be branded as illusory. In this regard, the focus on negation and removal was constantly in tension with the affirmative value of dependent co-arising. Although Madhyamika Buddhists explicitly rejected nihilism, they claimed also to affirm neither being, nor nothingness, nor even the absolute Nothingness.

In navigating between the perception of nihilism and the monistic assertion of the ultimate, non-empty reality, Asanga seeks a path toward the realization of consciousness from illusion to awakening. What is characteristic of a Yogacara analysis of the structure of consciousness lies in the container consciousness (*alaya-vijnana*). The Yogacara thinkers go on to reaffirm that within the dependent co-arising Emptiness does exist. Put in other words, being that is born of essentialism is apprehended anew in the context of Emptiness. "Therefore all things are said to be neither empty, nor not empty, because of being, non-being, and being—and this is the middle path."[44]

From beginning with the two-truth theme of Nagarjuna, now the wondrous being of Emptiness is reaffirmed as the nonessential being of empty dependent co-arising. In this sense the three-body (trikaya) doctrine is particularly favored in the Yogacara tradition. A similar account is given in *The Awakening of Faith in the Mahayana,* which was almost certainly composed in China in the sixth century CE. However, for Asanga and Vasubandhu, the fundamental *dharma*-body as well as two other bodies are not reality beyond the scope of Emptiness.

Dharma-kaya is Dharma (Truth) itself without any personal character that is universal and eternal, completely formless and empty. *Sambhoga-kaya,* which is supra-historical or non-historical, has fulfilled Dharma as the reward-body unlike *dharma-kaya.* However, *sambhoga-kaya* is unlike *nirmana-kaya,* the transformation-body who is no less than the historical Buddha in the person of Gautama, existing in many and various forms. Amida Buddha and Mahavairocana Buddha are very important forms

44. *BS,* 1, 208.

of *Sambhoga-kaya* among them. Amida Buddha is a *sambhoga-kaya* on whom Pure Land Buddhism is based with its virtues of immeasurable life and light, while Mahavairocana Buddha is a *sambhoga-kaya* whose virtues as the Great Luminous One are wisdom and compassion. These two Buddhas have been praised and worshiped as the central Buddhas by Pure Land and Esoteric Buddhists for many centuries. However, both Amida and Mahavairocana are different manifestations of one and the same *dharma-kaya*, which is in fact the formless and boundless reality of Emptiness. Besides Amida and Mahavairocana, there are many different *sambhoga-kayas* in the form of Buddhas and Bodhisattvas.

As for *nirmana-kaya*, Gautama Buddha is merely the first historical instance of innumerable forms of the transformation-body throughout Buddhist history. Alongside Gautama Buddha, from the perspective of the threefold body doctrine, Indian masters like Nagarjuna (around 150–250 CE), Chinese masters such as T'ien-t'ai Chi-I (531–597), Japanese masters such as Kukai (774–835), Honen (1133–1212), Shinran (1173–1262), Dogen (1200–1253), and Nichiren (1222–1282), etc., are regarded as *nirmana-kaya* in place of Gautama Buddha. This strikingly shows that the worship of various *nirmana-kaya* is more conspicuous in Japanese Buddhism than in Chinese or Indian Buddhism.

Without *dharma-kaya* as the formless and boundless reality of Emptiness, *sambhoga-kaya* and *nirmana-kaya* cannot appear, although the threefold body of Buddha is different but not divided. The Buddhist doctrine of *dharma-kaya* courts monistic perils if it is seen as the sole ground of Emptiness. For example, Gautama as the first Awakened One in his transformation-body was in oneness with the formless *dharma-body* and invisible reward-body, although Buddha himself strongly denied the vedantic notion of the eternal reality, no matter whether it is the absolute One or absolute Nothingness.

There have been two explicitly different streams noticeable in the Mahayana tradition of Buddhism in view of the soteriological process: *sambhoga-kaya*-centered forms of Buddhism in favor of salvation through the unconditional compassion of Amida Buddha (especially Pure Land Buddhism)—which will be discussed in comparison with Martin Luther's teaching of justification—and *dharma-kaya*-centered forms of Buddhism in favor of salvation through dynamic realization of formless Dharma as *Sunyata*, which is often referred to the self-awakening based type of soteriology. From this type we can talk also about the model of the self-awakening or the universal Buddhahood in cosmological significance. Let's turn first to this model.

Sunyata and Self-Awakening

In the First Sermon, the Buddha presents his *Dharma* as the Middle Way between the extreme of eternalism and materialistic annihilationism. In Buddha's teaching, dependent co-arising is the essential character of the phenomenal world, which accounts for the genesis of *dukkha*. In Buddha's own realization, faith played little part in contrast to established faiths based on authority and tradition. However, faith (*saddha*), in the sense of heartfelt inner commitment to the spiritual life, is an essential part of Buddhism. Buddhist faith is conative, not cognitive. In the *Vimalakirti* sutra, *Sunyata* is called "the baseless base." Though itself being empty, it is the basis for everything. Realization of *Sunyata* means realization of this nothingness and at the same time realization of everythingness. It is simultaneously negation and affirmation. Therefore, the expression of *Sunyata* necessarily takes a paradoxical form. "You should beg alms not to receive alms."[45] This teaching of Emptiness was given by Nagarjuna, who in his *Mulamadhyamaka-karika*, established a radical logical underpinning.

Different from the teaching of Pure Land Buddhism, the Middle Way of Nagarjuna (ca.150–250 CE), the founder of the *Madhyamika* or Middle School has played a profound role in shaping a Buddhist understanding of salvation through the self-awakening to the *Sunyata*. Although under the influence of early *Prajnaparamita* (Perfection of Wisdom) literature, his idea is original and creative in several important ways. His most important work, the *Mulamadhyamakakarika*, is a religious text aiming at understanding Emptiness by means of logic. In order to obtain Enlightenment one must annihilate one's deeds and mental defilements, which arise from mental constructs. Mental constructs arise from *prapanca*, i.e., the entire world of language. *Prapanca* is annihilated in Emptiness. Emptiness, which is nothing but ultimate truth, awaits the religious practice of human beings. Ultimate truth of *Sunyata* is not independent of these practices. For the final liberation (*moksa*), all the elements of the mundane world, mental defilements, deeds, and material causes should be negated for the transmundane *Nirvana* to appear. His famous theory is based on the Eightfold negation: "neither origination nor cessation, neither permanence nor impermanence, neither unity nor diversity, neither coming nor

45. *BS*, 1,157; cf. Eckhart's formulation, "You pray to God to be free from God."

going." This double negation in terms of 'neither nor' rejects two opposing and contradictory poles of affirmation and negation.

According to Nagarjuna, one attains final liberation "when deeds and mental defilements have been annihilated."[46] Deeds and mental defilements arise from mental constructs, so mental constructs form *prapanca*, which is coterminous with the entire world. To annihilate it is to negate the entire world. Therefore, *prapanca* can be annihilated only in Emptiness, which is no less than the ultimate truth. To realize the ultimate truth, *prapanca*, as the obstacle that stands in the way of the Enlightenment must be annihilated through human religious practice. In *Abhidharma* thought, the *dharmas* as the principle constituting the world cannot be annihilated, because what is to be negated are only the mental defilements. However, for Nagarjuna all elements of the earthly world, including mental defilements and the material causes of the world, are to be negated for *Nirvana* to appear and be attained. What is fundamental to Buddhism is the theory of dependent co-arising, which, as a type of relation, views that everything exists in dependence on other things.

In so doing, there is no ground for existence in itself. It is what is called *pratitya-samutpada*. What Nagarjuna intends to do is to approach Emptiness in proving the invalidity of everything existent by way of the relation of dependent co-arising. His view is expressed well in these remarks: "If everything is empty then the four noble truths are also non-existent. You do not know the purpose of emptiness, and the meaning of emptiness." "What is dependent co-arising we call emptiness. That is representation by words and that is the middle way."[47]

Nagarjuna distinguishes between the mundane world and the ultimate truth in terms of the direction of religious practice. Unlike *Abhidharma*, Buddhism, which puts the two realms far apart, for Nagarjuna the distinction between the world of transmigration and Enlightenment is not so far apart. "Transmigration is not different from nirvana. Nirvana is not different from transmigration."[48] Due to the positive side of *Sunyata*, Nagarjuna still remains in dualistic thinking by distinguishing *Nirvana* and *samsara* and by emphasizing the religious practice on the human side.

When Emptiness is applied to *dharma-kaya*, the *dharma-kaya* as *Sunyata* or Emptiness is neither existent nor not-existent, neither fulfilled

46. *Mulamadhyamakakarika* (Stanzas on the Middle Path, hereafter: MMK), xviii, 5a. Cf. *BS*, 1, 189–201.

47. *MMK*, xxiv, 18; cf. *BS*, 1,193.

48. *BS*, 1, 194.

nor unfulfilled. Its character is always dynamic emptying itself, which can be adequately understood as the constant activity of emptying everything, including itself. Based on the dynamic constant activity of negating and emptying reality, *Dharma* body takes a form of *sambhoga-kaya* (reward-body) and *nirmana-kaya* (transformation-body) not by losing its reality of non-substantiality. How can the impersonal emptying reality incarnate itself in the historical, personal forms of individuals?

At this point, Abe recognizes that the negative theology of Meister Eckhart's "Godhead above God" may be exemplified as the clearest and Christian analogue to the Buddhist idea of Emptiness as absolute Nothingness. The Buddhist-Christian dialogue may encourage Christians to return to the radically apophatic mystical tradition, which has been neglected and repressed in favor of the cataphatic theological tradition. However, a Buddhist return to the samsaric world disallows both the God of classical theism and the panentheistic God of process theology, and even is exempt from the eschatology of Judaism and Christianity because of an all-pervasive dependent co-origination.

According to the aspect of *Sunyata,* the true salvation is neither in Buddha nor *Nirvana*, but exactly in the individual realization of *Sunyata* as the absolute Nothingness by way of dependent co-arising. Understood in this way, Gautama Buddha did not accept the Vedantic notion of Brahman underlying the ultimate principle of the eternal self (*Atman*). Rather, Gautama Buddha put emphasis on *Anatman* (no-self) and dependent co-origination to realize the *Dharma-kaya* or the Truth; everything in and beyond the universe is interdependent, co-arising, and co-creating. Nothing can exist independently or be self-existing. In other words, everything without exception, even including divine Buddha, is relative, relational, non-substantial, and changeable. The realization of the non-substantial Emptiness of everything as absolute Nothingness cannot be possible without the doctrine of dependent co-origination.

This Buddhist idea is, as a rule, seen in the following formulation: when this exists, that comes to be; when this does not exist, that does not exist, when this is destroyed, that is destroyed. This mutual dependence is applied not only to everything in the universe, but beyond the universe to the nature of absolute Nothingness as *Sunyata.* From the perspective of dependent co-origination, a Christian understanding of God's self-existing deity is open to serious question because the one God as Being-Itself must be overcome and negated in order for the true absolute to appear as absolute Nothingness through double negation. Therefore, absolute

Nothingness is the ultimate Reality, which may be the religious ground for salvation.

What is the absolute Nothingness as the principle beyond the one absolute God? Is it the emptying zero-point? Because the term "absolute" seems, however, inappropriate even from the perspective of dependent co-origination. The absolute Nothingness must be dependent and realized in human self-realization of one's true self in which *Nirvana* is *samsara*, and conversely *samsara* is *Nirvana*: "In order to attain wisdom, one should not abide in samsara; in order to fulfill compassion, one should not abide in nirvana."[49] All reality is present in every entity of suchness, and every entity of suchness pervades the whole of Emptiness. Therefore, the center is everywhere.[50] In this Emptiness, *Nirvana* and *samsara* are not two. All human efforts obsessed with a self are revealed as a mere nihility, because there is no God, no self, and no real *Nirvana* or a real *samsara*.

The dynamic movement from *samsara* to *Nirvana* and from *Nirvana* to *samsara* is at the heart of the true *Nirvana* in Mahayana Buddhism, which would imply social-ethical consequences. In maintaining *Sunyata* as the principle of God's kenosis, Abe challenges the Christian obsession with the one absolute God in saying that "God the Father who does not cease to be God in the self-emptying of the Son of God is no true God."[51] Given this fact, *Sunyata* is also seen as the religious ground for a Buddhist metaphysical foundation in replacing dependent co-origination by the dynamic emptying principle of the absolute Nothingness.

That being the case, Christian faith in the personal God is not enough. The human sinful condition and human finitude are so deep and so radical that they cannot be overcome even by divine involvement in human affairs. Neither the divine Other-Ppower, nor the faith in divine mercy, but the realization of absolute Nothingness overcomes the human sinful condition. One's self-awakening to the true Self may lead to human Enlightenment and salvation, transcending every form of subject-object duality such as good-evil, life-death, righteous-sinful, etc.

At this point, *dharma-kaya* as the reality of *Sunyata* is reversed into the authentic self of humanity. This is the aspect of divinization from a Buddhist soteriology, in which there occurs the total identification between the *Sunyata* as the *dharma* and the true self of human being. Paradoxically,

49. Abe, *Buddhism and Interfaith Dialogue*, 237.

50. Abe, *Zen and Western Thought*, 223–31.

51. Abe, *Buddhism and Interfaith dialogue*, 216.

the *dharma* body gives way to human self-awakening by being totally dependent on human self-awakening. Self-awakening is not merely a human way to the divine *Sunyata*, but it seems to become *Sunyata* in the sense that *Sunyata* is co-dependent in the self-awakening power of human being.

A Buddhist critique of the Christian concept of the one God is extended to Jesus Christ as the one mediator between God and human being. Interestingly enough, Jesus Christ may be regarded as a symbol of the Buddhist idea of independent causation, in which Jesus is fully accepted as a Buddha or as an Awakened One.[52] However, Jesus Christ is one mediator, that is, one manifestation of *sambhoga-kaya* because *dharma-kaya* remains only *das Nichts*. How can *dharma-kaya* remain *das Nichts* in distinction from *sambhoga-kaya*, while in total self-emptying of it? According to the Buddhist teaching of dependent co-origination, what causes suffering is mainly due to the human disposition to substantialize objects and the human self as permanent and absolute substances. The substantialization of one's own religion would run the risk of religious imperialism. This phenomenon can be seen not only in the history of the religious wars of Christianity, but also in the Nichiren sect in Japanese history.[53]

In order to be free from *dukkha*, human being should be awakened to *Sunyata*, that is, the non-substantiality of everything, including self and Buddha. This Buddhist insight of soteriology leads not, therefore, to faith in the Buddha, but to the teaching of no-self (*anatman*) and self-awakening to *Dharma*. Therefore, the teaching of dependent co-origination that implies the absolute Nothingness not in the sense of the underlying principle of the identity of everything in the universe, but in the sense of "Boundless Openness" or "Formless Emptiness" enables a dynamic way and unity for opening and reinvigorating the ways of religious pluralism without calling for a particular form of absoluteness. Distancing sharply from Pure Land Buddhism, Abe proposes the model of a *dharma-kaya*-centered soteriology based on dynamic "Boundless Openness" or "Formless Emptiness," which can be regarded "as the ultimate ground for all religions and as the basis for a dynamic unity in religious pluralism."[54]

According to him, there is a distinction between the principle and manifestations; *Dharma-kaya* as Boundless Openness manifests itself as the formless and boundless reality of Emptiness or openness, which

52. Abe, *Zen and Western Thought*, 189.

53. Abe, *Buddhism and Interfaith Dialogue*, 30.

54. Ibid., 34.

is the distinctive mark of Buddhist *Sunyata. Sambhoga-kaya* as God revealed itself as Yahweh, Allah, Isvara (Siva, Vishnus, Brahman), or Amida. *Nirmana-kaya* as the Lord reveals itself as Jesus, Muhammad, Krshna, or Gautama. On the basis of this Buddhist universal inclusive framework of the triple-body doctrine, Abe tries to interpret *Sunyata* as the universal principle embracing various forms of God and Lord for their ultimate ground without abolishing different ways and peculiarities of their Gods and Lords.

At the same time, the absolute Emptiness that abnegates and empties all the various kinds of manifestation asks them to return to "Boundless Openness." Understood this way, a radical apophatic theology in Christian tradition is taken to be more in affinity with the Buddhist concept of *Sunyata*. Abe clearly expresses this affinity in his remarks, "God is 'dazzling darkness,' because in God, who is infinite love, self-emptying as-it-is self-fulfillment, self-fulfillment as-it-is self-emptying. *Sunyata* is 'dazzling darkness' because in *Sunyata*, which is boundless openness, samsara as-it-is is nirvana, nirvana as-it-is samsara."[55]

The model of self-awakening to *Sunyata* brilliantly proposed by Masao Abe has no room for the grace of an Other-Power or awakening of faith in his preference for a combination of the doctrine of dependent co-arising and Japanese Zen, in which a possible combination between Pure Land doctrine and other Mahayana Buddhist traditions in China and Korea or Vietnam is completely out of consideration. In general, Abe's "positionless position" tends to an attachment to *Sunyata* as "the absolute Nothingness," boundless and dynamic, while stopping the logical consistency of co-dependent negation. In fact, *Sunyata* is not absolute, relative, boundless, bound, dynamic, or static seen in terms of dependent co-arising. "Do not be attached to any dharmas of non-duality, for there is neither unity nor duality."[56]

A long standing *Madhyamika/Yogacara* conflict was synthesized especially by the Korean master Wonhyo (617–686) on the basis of the doctrines of *Hwaom* Buddhism. Abe's model of *Sunyata* and self-awakening is seen by most Asian Buddhists in China and Korea as a partial description of Buddha nature from a particular Japanese Zen perspective. In Buddhist tradition the aspect of faith is essential because the *Treatise on*

55. Ibid., 148.

56. *Avatamsaka Sutra;* cf. *BS*, 1. 384.

the Awakening of Mahayana Faith, which is attributed to Asvaghosa, has been regarded as the seminal text for East Asian Mahayana Buddhism.

Wonhyo, while exploring the aspect of awakening of faith through his central hermeneutic concept of the *ch'e-yong* formula (essence-function or substance-operation), made a great contribution to harmonizing all dialectical contradictions and polarized opposites (for example, the One and the many, subject and object, *Nirvana* and *samsara*, faith and self-awakening), and illustrating the inseparability of mediation and wisdom, or faith and self awakening. If self-awakening must precede the attainment of *Sunyata*, the *Sunyata* can become the object of religious practice that we would discern in Abe's proposed soteriology.

Wonhyo's interpretation of the *Awakening of Faith* on the basis of ch'e-yong hermeneutics is well expressed in the remarks: "One might say it is 'something,' yet because of it, every thing is empty. One might say it is 'nothing,' yet through it all the myriad things arise."[57] The *ch'e-yong* device works together with the dialectic of opening (*kae*) and sealing (*hap*). For example, "everything is empty because of it" represents sealing, while yet, "myriad things arise through it" represents opening. "Unfolding without complicating; sealing without narrowing, establishing without gaining, refuting without losing" is what lies at the heart of the *Awakening of Faith*.[58]

The Mahayana Buddhist notion of faith is interpreted not as a dualistic subject-object or "faith in" construction, seen dominantly in theistic religions, but as "faith-of" on the basis of a *ch'e-yong* formulation. At this point, the essence of Mahayana arouses faith. Instead of a "faith-in" construction prevailing in dualistic thinking, an act of faith seen from the hermeneutic of essence-function construction is of essential soteriological significance in the Mahayana Buddhist tradition, unlike the Zen Buddhist tradition in Japan.[59]

If One Mind is the essence (*ch'e*), faith is function (*yong*), so that One Mind and faith cannot be separated. Wonhyo goes on further to describe the characteristics of the Mahayana notion of faith by using an essence-attributes-function (*ch'e-sang-yong*) formulation in line with his earlier basic description of the essence-function construction. Faith is simply the function of One Mind, which arises at the root of Mahayana faith.[60]

57. *BS*, II.70.

58. Ibid.

59. Sung-Bae, *Buddhist Faith*, 35–42.

60. Ibid., 38–39.

One Mind is explained in terms of Three Greatnesses (*ch'e, sang, yong*). *Ch'e* signifies the absolute dimension of One Mind, while *sang* and *yong* denote different aspects of the phenomenal dimension of it. This would imply a threefold understanding of the *Sunyata*, which we have already discussed in regard to the Trinity. According to Wonhyo, faith does not require an object, but is governed by the non-dual *ch'e-yong* (faith-of) construction. Buddha represents *ch'e* (essence) related to the absolute level of One Mind, while *dharma* is *sang* (attribute), and *sangha* is *yong* (function) related to the phenomenal level of One Mind. To attain self-awakening of *Sunyata*, awakening of faith is essential, because "faith that the Truth really exists is faith in the greatness of essence (of Suchness) . . . If one can awaken these three faiths, one can enter the world of the Buddha's Dharma, produce all merits, be free from all demonic states, and attain the Peerless Way."[61]

From a Christian perspective, however, Yahweh cannot be identified with the revelation of *sambhoga-kaya* as God, as Abe would speculate. If God as the dazzling darkness is infinite love, or *Sunyata*, is the *Sunyata* supposed to be identical with God as the infinite love? Unfortunately, Abe is quite confused about the Christian understanding of a radical apophatic theology. Meister Eckhart's linguistic perplexity in approaching "Godhead beyond God" or "the very desert of the Deity" transcends the Trinity of Christian revelation, because this is the immobile unity, rest and solitude "pure of all being."[62] The soul as spiritual substance possesses a divine spark, or "*Grund*." For a true union with God to come about, a human being must detach himself/herself from all that is not God. In entering into the divine intellect, the soul would know the purity and freedom of the deity, which is the essential aspect of soul's clinging "by its innermost depths to the Deity."[63]

Self-abnegating and emptying love for God leads to self-discovery and Enlightenment. Therefore, abandonment of self and the release of the soul toward the attainment of Godhead is the end of the soul. To stress such unity with God, and at the same time, to differentiate between "god" and "godhead," the soul must exceed God to go farther toward the abysm of pure Deity. God acts and empties Godself, but the Godhead as the One does not. The detachment and self-negating poverty leads to the

61. Ibid., 73–74.

62. Petry, *Late Medieval Mysticism*, 172.

63. Ibid., 173.

One in ineffable union beyond nominal attributes of God. The perfect identity between the human and divine will is sought, as the soul begins with the total emptying of the self. "Abgeschiedenheit, union-producing detachment and disinterested withdrawal from all that is not God, is the one necessary emphasis," for Meister Eckhart.[64]

Thus we understand Eckhart's paradox, "pray to God to be free from God." Eckhart's nothingness may not be identical with the absolute Nothingness of Zen thought.[65] The Godhead as the One is distinct from all reality, and it makes the divine reality immanent to all reality. Eckhart interprets the *bullitio* of the emergence of divine relations in the Trinity and the *ebullitio* of the birth of the eternal logos in the soul on the basis of dialectics between indistinction and distinction. As McGinn states, "Eckhart conceived of *exitus-reditus* as the fundamental law of reality taught by the Bible, both in *toto*, as found in the scriptural presentation of creation and consummation, and in individual verses (e.g., Eccl 1:7: . . . *ad locum unde exeunt flumina, revertuntur, ut iterum fluant*—'The rivers return to the place from whence they flowed, so that they may flow again')."[66]

The Godhead manifests itself in the distinct *bullitio* as the Trinity, and in the *ebullitio* of the creature. How and why does dynamic *Sunyata* discloses itself as wisdom and as compassion in the Buddhist sense? Tracy's suggestion for the Buddhist awareness of *Sunyata* to develop itself as "ultimate source-wisdom-compassion" would be more appropriate not for the absolute nothingness of the Kyoto school, but for the *ch'e-yong* hermeneutics of Wonhyo.[67]

Furthermore, Jesus Christ as the dynamic identity between self-emptying and self-fulfillment is not degraded to a mere historical figure. He lives in perichoretic relationship with God the Father and the Spirit in historical, eschatological openness. He is *vere Homo, vere Deus*. His humanity is not separable from his divinity. Christian agape flows from the self-emptying of Christ, in the *assumptio carnis*. Therefore, love, in the Christian sense, is grounded on divine detachment of self-emptying, not "a positive attachment," as Abe would speculate.[68] Of course, Abe agreed that Zen's criticism of Christianity in terms of dependent co-origination does not necessarily do justice to the essence of Christianity.

64. Ibid., 176.

65. Tracy, *Dialogue with the Other*, 88.

66. McGinn, *Mystical Thought of Meister Eckhart*, 72.

67. Ibid., 93.

68. Abe, *Zen and Western Thought*, 225.

However, the model of self-awakening proposed by Abe would run the risk of an anthropocentric "inward turn" with de-emphasis on social-political events in the outside world, ecological well-being, the eschatological future of the world, and all living creatures. This is liberation theology's vigorous criticism of Abe. According to Knitter, Buddhism tends to ignore concrete socio-economic analyses because it is preoccupied with overcoming dualistic thinking between good and evil, life and death. The priority of gnosis, or contemplative knowledge, leading to the non-dual reality of Enlightenment, even though including *karuna* or agape, might downplay a prophetic, ethical responsibility merely by remaining in quiet, contemplative sitting.

In addition, from a South-Korean *minjung* theological perspective, Japanese Buddhism appears in negative focus because of its historical non-political consciousness and attitude during the Japanese period of colonialism. It has no interest in taking responsibility for the crimes of the Second World War, comforting women, and all the other victims. In fact, the Japanese Buddhist idea of *Sunyata*, while remaining an effort to achieve non-duality between life and death, is not concerned about *dukkha* of nihility in a social-economic sense.

Would it be wrong to interpret the concept of *Sunyata* as implicitly including divine *dukkha* or *mahakaruna* in its dynamic activity of self-emptying kenosis? Is a Buddhist concept of *dukkha* vulnerable to being captive to the relativistic vicious circle of dependent co-arising logic concerning the question of good and evil, or the poor in the world? Should Buddhist compassion be confined to universal compassion by downplaying the socio-historical dimension of life? As John Cobb suggests, the Buddhist judgment needs to broaden and enrich itself positively toward the relief of suffering in a heightened concern for ethics and history. What is more necessary is to recognize particular differences in regard to the Buddhist teaching of interdependence.[69]

A Buddhist transformation of the world, society, and all creatures would be clearer if it took seriously the divine, cosmological aspect of *dukkha*. Where there is *dukkha,* there is the self-emptying kenosis of *Sunyata* in which *Sunyata*, as boundless openness, is interconnected with *dukkha.* Therefore, a Buddhist position that "you cannot change the world unless you sit" is seriously challenged by the liberative Christian position that you cannot sit unless you change the world."[70] Given this fact, it is

69. Cobb and Ives, *Emptying God*, 95.

70. Abe, *Buddhism and Interfaith Dialogue*, 231–35.

worthwhile to take note of Aloysius Pieris' Asian theology of liberation. According to Pieris, Jesus' salvific way is characterized in a twofold way. First is Jesus' renunciation in his struggle to be poor, and second is Jesus' open denunciation of mammon in struggle for the poor. The first form of Jesus, which focuses on interior liberation, is well symbolized by the Buddha under the tree of gnosis. The second form, which calls for a fundamental change in human relations and the social structures of injustice and violence, does not compete with buddhology, but complements it. In the path of liberation, Christians participate with Buddhists "in their gnostic detachment (or the practice of voluntary poverty)" and Buddhists participate with "Christians in their agapeic involvement in the struggle against forced poverty."[71]

Dharma and Ecology: Hermeneutics of Nature

Seen in light of the current environmental crisis Buddhism becomes a religious aspiration for understanding our attitudes toward nature and ourselves as creatures of nature, embedded in life cycles and dependent on ecosystems. In environmental circles it is generally agreed that the devastation of the earth is mainly due to the Christian narrative of cosmogonies or soteriology in which the natural world was created only for the benefit of humans or the soul, thus alienating the natural world. This anthropocentric perspective of Christianity ignited the ethos of capitalism by making possible the enormous material achievement of industrialization based on technology and science, but at the same time leading to the earth's fatal crisis. This environmentalist perception of Biblical theology is greatly disputed. In Biblical narratives nature is neither to be worshiped nor trashed. One might well find license to trash nature in some texts of Western Gnosticism, a very world-deprecating religion. Unfortunately, Christianity has usually been compromised in the direction of Gnosticism. In general, environmentalism (as a nature religion) dislikes Christianity because Christianity has a historical character and is often compromised by exilic religion.

A counterpart to the negative interpretation of *Sunyata* in terms of the absolute Nothingness, which we have traced and discerned from Nagarjuna to the modern Kyoto school of philosophy, with its positive interpretation of Emptiness, would be *Sunyata* in terms of universal Buddha-nature. This teaching maintains the notion that all sentient creatures hold

71. Pieris, "The Buddha and The Christ," 175.

the potential to attain Buddhahood. Precisely on the basis of Emptiness, which means the lack of any self-existent and substantial Being, all beings can attain Buddhahood. Emptiness as the nature of reality is expressed in the famous chapter on Noble Activity: "True reality is the Tathagata, and the Tathagata is true reality; true reality is emptiness and emptiness is true reality; true reality is the Buddha-nature and the Buddha-nature is true reality."[72] Buddha-nature, like Emptiness, which is neither self-existent nor a substantial reality, is what is neither produced by causes nor produced without a cause. From this comes Buddhahood as "the natural abiding nature" of all beings, by which one can spontaneously awaken to this fact and realize one's authentic inherent Enlightenment.

In Mahayana schools of Buddhism such as *Hua-yen* a remarkable interconnection of reality is seen in images such as the jeweled net of Indra. Each jewel is reflective of all the others in the universe. In like manner the Buddha-nature, which is fulfilled in the natural world, is expressed by the Zen garden in East Asia. In recent years, socially and environmentally engaged Buddhists and Buddhist sympathizers have been playing an active role in protecting the environment in both Asia and the United States. For example, it is said that a Buddhist priest in Japan who is deeply engaged in the ecological green movement once erected a sign stating that the trees have "Buddha-nature."[73]

The Middle Way teaches a spiritual movement through the insight of illusory being into the non-being of Emptiness, lest any essentialist view be smuggled in. However, the Yogacara school has argued that by negating all understanding in the two-truth theme of Nagarjuna, Emptiness is "the other-dependent pattern underlying the illusory genesis of views." Emptiness does exist in the context of "the other-dependent unreal imagining of everyday thinking"[74] for the reaffirmation or realization of being in the context of *Sunyata*. "Therefore all things are said to be neither empty, nor not-empty because of being, non-being, and being—and this is the middle path."[75] Asanga interprets "Buddhas" as being "characterized by the non-existence of existence." Therefore, *dharma-body*, which refers to "emptiness as its essence," can be properly described as the essence of awakening that implies the nonessential being of empty dependent co-

72. Cf. Swanson, "The Spirituality of Emptiness," 76.

73. Tucker and Williams, *Buddhism and Ecology*, Introduction.

74. *BS*, 1.208.

75. *Madhyantavibhaga* 1.2, quoted in *BS*, 1, 208.

origination because the ultimate reality remains transcendent to any conditioned conventional reality.[76] Thus the non-existence of existence is the ultimate stage of awakening that can be attained by *Sunyata*.

Understood in this way, Yogacara thinkers such as Asanga and Vasubandhu paved a way to understand the *dharma-body* (*dharma-kaya*) as "the existence of non-existence" under the scope of *Sunyata*, which would be called the cosmic body filling and pervading the cosmos. The dharma body that means the essence of Buddhahood is the hidden principle of reality common to all Buddhas and transcendental to their multiplicity, beyond the grasp of mind. Free from any notion of essentialism, dharma-body is wisdom attained in terms of contacting the ultimate realm of *Sunyata*.[77] According to the *Nirvana sutra* all-sentient beings possess the Buddha-nature, so that two teachings of universal Buddha-nature and cosmic Buddha-body are interrelated. The cosmos, therefore, in all its parts is identical with the Buddha.

Under the influence of Taoist ideas in China, the Mahayana Buddhists in the T'ien-t'ai school tried to extend the logic of Mahayana universalism to the extent that the distinction between sentient and non-sentient should be abandoned. Therefore, Buddha-nature is ascribed not only to plants and trees, but also to dust particles. When introduced to Japanese soil, Buddhism met the indigenous religion of Shinto in which the whole world, sentient and non-sentient beings alike, is understood equally as offspring of the divine that are inhabited by divine spirits (*kami*). The idea of Shinto promotes a Buddhist universalism of Buddha-nature in a more striking way.

For Kukai (774–835), the idea of the Buddhahood of all phenomena gains in prominence. In calling the natural elements the *samaya*-body of the Buddha, he elaborates a relation of the *samaya*-body's participation into *dharma-kaya*, albeit not in total identification with it. "The existence of the Buddha (Mahavairocana) is the existence of sentient beings and vice versa. They are not identical but are nevertheless identical; they are not different but are nevertheless different."[78] However, *dharma-kaya*, which is beginningless and endless, would not transcend the totality of all things because of its non-identical identity or non-different difference.

In sharing many ideas with Kukai, it was the philosophy of Dogen (1200–1253) that radicalizes the identification of the *dharma-kaya* with

76. Swanson, *Realm of Awakening*, 64; cf. *BS*, 1, 208.

77. *BS*, 1, 208–10; Abe, *Buddhism and Interfaith Dialogue*, 142–43.

78. Quoted in Parkes, "Voices of Mountains, Trees, and Rivers," 114.

the phenomenal world. For him, the Buddhist principle of the *Nirvana sutra* is reread. The sentence, "All sentient beings without exception have Buddha nature," is retaken up to the point where, "All is sentient being, all beings are Buddha nature."[79] Dogen's understanding of Buddha-nature is quite unique in the history of Japanese Buddhism. He reversed the traditional line of Buddhism from the *Nirvana sutra*: "All sentient beings without exception have the Buddha-nature: Tathagata (Buddha) is permanent with no change at all." This is the essential standpoint of Mahayana Buddhism. Rather than all things possessing or manifesting or symbolizing Buddha-nature, however, Dogen reinterprets Kukai's identification of the *dharma-kaya* with all things to be the identification of all things and Buddha-nature.

Therefore, Dogen runs in the other direction, in which "all are sentient beings, all beings are (all being is) the Buddha-nature; Tathagata is permanent, non-being, being, and change."[80] As a rule, all nature has the capacity for becoming Buddha, that is to say, attaining Enlightenment. After his Enlightenment Sakyamuni stated, "Wonderful, wonderful! How can it be that all sentient beings are endowed with the intrinsic wisdom of the Tathagata?"[81] According to the traditional reading of this passage, all living beings possess the Buddha-nature as inherent to themselves as the ontological potentiality of realizing and fulfilling themselves by becoming Buddhas. This might implicitly bring Buddhism close to a homocentric position since only a human with self-consciousness is able to realize and fulfill "the nature of generation-extinction as such."[82] In this respect, the non-homocentric dimension is not completely separated from the homocentric one in the Buddhist teaching of liberation.

According to Dogen, however, Buddha-nature is not meant to be a mere potentiality or a divine seed within all living beings. All beings, living as well as non-living, are originally Buddha-nature. By putting emphasis on the fact that all beings are the Buddha-nature, Dogen twists generation-extinction in the biological sense into appearance-disappearance, or being-non-being, in the cosmological sense. As far as the human liberation from the samsaric cycle of birth-and-death is concerned, it only becomes possible in terms of doing away with the appearance-disappearance or be-

79. Dogen and Shobogenzo, *Dogen zenji zenshu*; cf. Abe, *Zen and Western Thought*, 25.

80. Ibid., 27.

81. Ibid., 32.

82. Ibid., 31.

ing-non-being relation. Here, Dogen bids to radicalize the environmental-cosmological dimension of Buddhism. Thus the universe is proclaimed as the actual body of Buddha. The absolutist connotation of the idea of the *dharma-kaya* is avoided. One would not expect natural phenomena to expound the nature of Enlightenment only in anthropocentric terms, but also in cooperation between the worlds of the human and the non-human, which implies "the twin activities of the Buddha-nature and emptiness."[83] A passage from Dogen is insightful: "Delusion is seeing all things from the perspective of the self. Enlightenment is seeing the self from the perspective of the myriad things of the universe."[84]

The sutras, for Dogen, therefore, are meant to be the entire cosmos and universe itself, "they are the self and others, taking meals and wearing clothes, confusion and dignity."[85] In this regard, a cosmocentric perspective transforms the human fundamental attitude toward the natural world in which all natural beings and non-beings such as mountains, rivers, and the great earth, etc., are experienced as manifestations of one's true self as *dharma-kaya*. The reverence paid to the person of the Buddha is now transferred to the cosmos and all its parts in the sense of pantheism in that the Buddha can be found in every grain of rice, or even those of hundreds of grasses and thousands of trees in deep identification with the Buddha-nature. The Buddhist sense of Buddha's presence in the cosmos serves as an inspiration for environmental awareness and co-existence. However, a critique arises from ecological awareness where, because everything is in Buddha-nature and Buddha-nature in everything, the human abuse of nature might be also considered as the manifestation of Buddha-nature as much as uncultivated mountains and unpolluted rivers.

If *Nirvana* were not different from the samsaric reality of an imperfect world, would there not be any need for activity, not to mention activism for intervention in protecting or saving nature from environmental devastation? If a wall, a tile, or a stone, no matter how total being Buddha-nature or non-being Buddha-nature or Emptiness Buddha-nature is defined as Buddha-nature in terms of Dogen, how can we fight against the polluted rivers or the earth full of radioactive waste because of their manifestation of Buddha-nature? In general, there is not sufficient attention paid to the

83. Hee-Jin, *Dogen Kigen—Mystical Realist*, 256; cf. Tucker and Williams, *Buddhism and Ecology*, 118.

84. Tucker and Williams, eds., *Buddhism and Ecology*, 170.

85. Quoted in Hee-Jin, *Dogen Kigen*, 97; cf. Tucker and Williams, *Buddhism and Ecology*, 118.

victims of creatures due to a Buddhist emphasis on non-duality between *Nirvana* and *samsara* and vice versa, in which a Buddhist peril of a non-ethical position may be discerned.

From a theological point of view, the idea of creation can be helpful in getting out of such a Buddhist cul-de-sac. The human crisis in ecology is related to the spirit of domination, which is ascribed to the Christian attitude of conquering nature in the seventeenth century and afterward. In the time of ecological crisis it has been alleged the Christian tradition in the West has become questionable and is even accused of being ecologically bankrupt in the eyes of ecologists, nature writers, poets, and eco-feminist theologians among others.

For instance, according to Rosemary Ruether, Christianity understood as the heir of neoplatonism, along with Judaism, is accused of alienating, dominating, and rejecting nature for the sake of spirit. She maintains that "the classical doctrine of Christ . . . which fused the vision of the heavenly messianic king (Jewish apocalypticism) and the transcendent *Logos* of immutable Being (Neoplatonism), was a synthesis of the religious impulses of the late antique religious consciousness, but precisely in their alienated state of development."[86] The primary concerns have been social and theological—but not ecological. The theme, "justice, peace, and the integrity of creation" comes along with the prayer, "Spirit of God Renew the whole Creation."[87]

In Lutheran circles, it was Joseph Sittler who addressed his cosmic Christ to the "Call to Unity" in the World Council of Churches in New Delhi, in 1961. His cosmic Christology has been redeveloped by Moltmann and by Paul Santmire's project of "Nature Reborn" within the Lutheran tradition.[88] Luther's marvelous sense of nature appears in his usage of a metaphor from an ancient Greek sage. He bemoans his time, saying that "we have become deaf to what Pythagoras aptly terms this wonderful and most lovely music coming from the harmony of the motions that are in the celestial spheres."[89] "The lovely music of nature," which is at the heart of Luther's aesthetic of creation, signifies wonderment of nature that gradually strengthens our faith. Luther's understanding of justification and Christian faith grows from our wonder and amazement at creation, in which we hear a music coming from the "celestial spheres."

86. Ruether, *Liberation Theology*, 115; cf. Santmire, *Travail of Nature*, 1–2.

87. Cf. Kinnamon, *Signs of the Spirit*.

88. Cf. Santmire, *Nature Reborn Theology*.

89. *LW*, 1:126.

This would be God's beauty in the universe that can be heard and discerned outside the walls of Christianity. We are encouraged to regard God's wonderful and lovely music more attentively because Christian faith without wonderment would be reduced to a deaf faith. Relating Christian faith to marvel, wonder, awe, and reverence, Luther deepens his reflection on God's mysterious presence in, with, and through all living creatures. Luther's ecological theology takes its point of departure from reflection on God's work in all things. God's constant preservation of creation is an on-going act of new creation (*creatio continua*). The almighty power of God must be present everywhere, "even in the tiniest leaf of a tree."[90] God's penetrating presence in all things does not contradict the freedom of God to transcend the world. God's presence in all creatures as God's masks and disguises cannot be properly understood apart from the fact that "God remains free to give."[91]

Luther's anti-Zwinglian polemic should be reread in a cosmic perspective of God's work in the universe. "There is no one and nothing other than God himself who is in all things everywhere."[92] Therefore, Jesus Christ can be present in, with, and under the elements of the Lord's Supper. So, God the Creator works in with, and through all creatures. The Holy Spirit works together with Father the Son.

For Luther an ecological theology cannot be properly understood without understanding the Holy Spirit. God's all-embracing activity is mediated through the Spirit. God as the Spirit is present and at work in a twofold way, universal and ecclesiological: "The Holy Spirit is among humans in a twofold way. First through a universal activity, by which he preserves them as well as God's other creatures. Second, Holy Spirit is given from Christ to believers."[93] What Luther is interested in as to God's engagement in all creation is services and fruits of the Spirit, because everything and everyone are creatures of God. Their natural creatureliness is to be seen in pneumatological terms. A pneumatological understanding of creation that would be explicityly trinitarian may avoid a concept of God as the monarchical ruler of creation by neglect of mutual relationship between God, human beings, and all creatures. According to Luther, the

90. *LW*, 37:57f.

91. Althaus, *Theology of Martin Luther*, 109.

92. *LW*, 37:57–63.

93. *WA*, 39 II, 239, 29–31; cf. Lohse, *Martin Luther's Theology*, 235.

world was created by the entire Trinity in the Unity, not only by God the Father.

"God will be all in all" through the Holy Spirit. The Spirit as immanent divine presence is highlighted in bringing Jesus Christ, crucified, resurrected, "on the way" to us. The phrase, "Solo Spiritu Sancto" (Through the Holy Spirit alone), for Luther may actualize the meaning and scope of *solus* Christus *principally* in the direction of discipleship of Christ in mundane life, and *universally* in the direction of sharing death of all living creatures, especially death of the victimized creation.[94] "Nothing is so small but God is still smaller, nothing is so large but God is still larger, nothing is so broad, but God is still broader, nothing so narrow but God is still narrower and so on. He is an inexpressible being, above and beyond all that can be described or imagined."[95] The omnipresence of God, which implies the freedom of God, is present in the suffering of all living creatures. Thus, Christ's presence is not merely limited to the elements of the Lord's Supper, but can be seen in the victims.

What is extraordinary for Luther's theology of creation is the fact that God is in cooperation with human beings for the preservation of creation, while rejecting this cooperation in regard to justification. "All creatures are God's larvae and mummery that he will let work with him and help in all sorts of creating, but that he otherwise can and does do without their help, so that we cling only to his word."[96] They are invited to God's future in the new creation of all things. The end of the world is not the darkness of death or hell, but the new creation of all things. God's Spirit moves human beings and the cosmos open to the future of God.

What shapes Luther's idea lies in the promise of God with us, Immanuel. For Luther, the Creator is constantly penetrating, overflowing into the created world, and filling the cosmos. "It is God who creates, effects and preserves all things through his almighty power and right hand, as our Creed confesses. For he dispatches no officials or angels when he creates or preserves something, but all this is the work of the Divine power itself. If He is to create it or preserve it, however, he must be present and must make and preserve His creation both in its innermost and outermost aspects."[97]

94. Ibid., 237.

95. *LW*, 37:228.

96. *WA*, 17 II, 192, 28–31; cf. Lohse, *Martin Luther's Theology*, 213.

97. *LW*, 57:57.

Luther's theology of "God with us" is not confined merely to parochial settings, but is deeply rooted in the cosmic dimension of Christ. This is the cosmic Christ in whom "all things hold together." He "makes peace with all things by the blood of his cross" (Col 1:17–20). Luther's teaching about the ubiquity of the risen and ascended Christ needs to be revitalized to cope with the ecological crisis. Luther's understanding of God's space is concretely in the baby on Mary's lap and at the same time universally even in a grain of wheat. God's space is not limited by the space of the world. Rather, "God is substantially present everywhere, in and through all creatures, in all their parts and places, so that the world is full of God and He fills all, but without His being encompassed and surrounded by it."[98] For Luther, God is not one-dimensional, being merely limited to the elements of the Lord's Supper. "His own divine essence can be in all creatures collectively and in each one individually more profoundly, more intimately, more present than the creature is in itself; yet it can be encompassed nowhere and by no one. It encompasses all things and dwells in all, but no one thing encompasses it and dwells in it."[99]

That being the case, Luther identifies heaven with the real presence of God, so that the earthly Christ is at the same time in the heaven. Luther's understanding of the real presence in the Lord's Supper affirmed Christ's being at the right hand of God. The right hand side of God, which means God's omnipresence and omnipotence, affirms that Jesus Christ as the second person of the Trinity according to his humanity takes full participation in the attributes of divine nature. Therefore, the body of Christ is everywhere in heaven and on earth. The right hand side of God is not localized in heaven, but understood just as God's omnipotence and omnipresence of God in heaven as well as in the earth. Where God is, Jesus Christ is. It is taken for granted that the Lutheran divinization of heaven was one of the premises leading to an atheistic critique of heaven, especially by Feuerbach.

However, Luther did not lose sight of the other side of God. No single spatial preposition is sufficient to describe God's presence permeating the cosmos and at the same time the radical immediacy of divine presence even in the grain of wheat. As H. Paul Santmire remarks, "God's glory is

98. *WA*, 23:134. 34–23. 136.36; cf. Santmire, *Nature Reborn*, 82. See further Bornkamm, *Luther's World of Thought*, 189.

99. *LW*, 57:57. Moltmann's panentheism, i.e., God's creation of the cosmos within the divine being needs to meet the outside of God in Luther. Cf. Bouma Prediger, *Greening of Theology*, 114–9.

too great and God's immediacy in all things too mysterious to allow such a one dimensional, literalizing theological predication."[100] For Luther there is no way of separating the historical Jesus from the cosmic Christ who can be discerned in the theological projects of cosmic Christology. The crucified God is recognized, praised, and glorified as both the cosmic Lord and the slaughtered Lamb of God. The death of Christ may be extended to the death of all sentient beings.

The *dukkha* of Christ, if I am not mistaken, may be present through the Holy Spirit in the cosmic death of all things inflicted by violence and injustice in our times. His suffering and dying the death of all the living is not merely done once and for all, but will continue in our eco-prophetic awareness inspired by the *Spiritus Creator*. The universal death of Christ for creation provides the basis "for an all-embracing reverence for life,"[101] because God "killed death by death, punishment by punishment, sufferings by sufferings, disgrace by disgrace . . . these wonderful works as to their root and cause were done in Christ's suffering."[102] Christ as a victim who is present in the Spirit is in deep solidarity with the victims among all living creatures protesting the social ecological structure constantly producing injustice, violence, and death.

The experience of God's reconciliation in the death of Christ reaches its climax in the biblical statement that "God was in Christ reconciling the world to himself . . . If anyone is in Christ, he is a new creation; the old has passed away; behold, everything has become new" (2 Cor 5:19, 17). For Luther, justification in Christ is inseparably connected with the new life of the Holy Spirit, because the Spirit offers and applies to us the treasure of salvation in Jesus Christ by his sufferings, death, and resurrection. "Therefore, to sanctify is nothing else than to bring us to the Lord Christ, to receive this blessing, which we could not obtain by ourselves."[103]

Therefore, the practice of discipleship of the cross is to be concretized in the struggle for the affirmation of life of all sentient beings regardless of their enmity and alienation, not being conformed to this samsaric world but to Jesus Christ in the universe. For Luther, Christ restoring our freedom in terms of the remission of sins is the One who "makes

100. Santmire, *Nature Reborn*, 84.

101. Moltmann, *Way of Jesus Christ*, 256.

102. *LW*, 11: 377–78.

103. *BC*, 415–6.

our state better than the state of Adam was in Paradise."[104] God's future can be experienced as the true anticipation of God's eschaton in hope of God's activity of making all things new. For Luther, the eschatology is transformed through the new relation to God, which has begun with justification, so the doctrine of justification sharpens its contour in relation to eternal judgment.[105] Given this fact, a theocentric-ecological reading of Luther's theology of creation needs to be extended in a trinitarian way, to include God in Jesus Christ by the power of the Spirit who "creates, effects and preserves all things through his almighty power and right hand."[106]

Our feeling and experience involved in majesty and beauty of God inspires our genuine cosmic hymn of praise to God who is present in all things. Eschatology for Luther means that the day of imminent judgment becomes a day of coming salvation, which is grounded in justification in Jesus Christ. The message of God's last judgment as the great invitation of evangelization encourages the church and the people of God to stand for what the kingdom of God means. We are all God's. God calls for a new life of participating in God's creation. "That will be a broad and beautiful heaven and a joyful earth, much more beautiful and joyful than Paradise was."[107]

Understood this way, a world-affirming reading of Luther would not be in contrast with my sense of how a Buddhist voice could make sense of *dukkha* and affirm life in this world. Although this position entails some tension in Buddhism, a world-affirming reading of Buddhism would be meaningful in an encounter with Luther.

Justification and Other-Power: Luther and Shinran

Shinran (1173–1262) is regarded and revered as the founder of the school of the true teaching of the Pure Land, which is often referred to merely as Shin Buddhism. It is the dominant Japanese lineage, although the Chinese Pure Land's representative Shan-tao (613–681) describes his teaching in the same terms. Shinran's uniqueness in Buddhist tradition is his paradigm shift from self-awakening to *Nirvana* toward the universal grace of the absolute Other-Power in Amida Buddha. In studying the various strands of Pure Land teaching proposed by his teacher Genku Honen and the

104. *LW*, 1:100.

105. Lohse, *Martin Luther's Theology*, 334.

106. *LW*, 37:57f.

107. *LW*, 12:12.

general Pure Land teaching in major Mahayana traditions, Shinran articulated his teaching as "true teaching of the Pure Land" (Jodo Shinshu). In so doing, he based his teaching on the tradition of Pure Land Buddhism from Honen: from India to China, and then from Korea to Japan.

Before we discuss Shinran's doctrine, it is necessary to turn our attention to Honen (1133–1212). He met the Pure Land devotion while he was being taught by scholars at Nara in Japan. His understanding of Buddhism is articulated only in the three disciplines of "percepts, concentration, and wisdom," though there are many doctrinal systems in Buddhism. During his formative period he was troubled by the awareness that the more he attempted to practice the three disciplines, the more he found himself failing in them. He confessed that he could not even observe a single precept or deepen his concentration, not to mention obtain wisdom. The decisive turning point, which would put an end to Honen's struggle, finally occurred in 1175 in his reading of a commentary on the Meditation Sutura. "Whether walking or standing, sitting or lying, only repeat the name of Amida with all your heart. Never cease the practice of it even for a moment. This is the very work which unfailingly issues in salvation, for it is in accordance with the Original Vow of that Buddha."[108]

This passage led Honen to abandon other practices and instead focus on reciting the name of Amida. The exclusive practice of *nembutsu* itself thus became central and fundamental to Honen's teaching. His most significant contribution consisted in adopting the Pure Land and discarding other teachings of the established schools. For Honen, it is about choosing self-reliance on one's own power or on Other-Power. Liberation from the *dukkha* entangled in the cycles of birth and death that is engraved at the heart of Buddhist teaching is located by means of two teachings—that of the Holy Path and that of the Pure Land.

However, Honen's way is not revolutionary, because the scriptural basis is found in *The Larger Sukhavatiyuha Sutra*. "May I not gain possession of perfect awakening if, once I have attained buddhahood, any among the throng of living beings in the ten regions of the universe should single-mindedly desire to be born in my land with joy, with confidence, and gladness, and if they should bring to mind this aspiration for even ten moments of thought and yet not gain rebirth there. This excludes only those who have committed the five heinous sins and those who have revived the True Dharma."[109]

108. Coates and Ishizuka, *Honen: The Buddhist Saint*, 187, quoted in *BS*, II, 205.

109. Gomez, *Land of Bliss*, 167; cf. *BS*, II, 207.

Pure Land Buddhism is an integral branch of Mahayana Buddhism. Its central basis lies in the Three Canons dealing with the forty-eight primal vows of Amida Buddha. According to Buddhist tradition (in *Larger Sutra of Immeasurable Life*), Amida Buddha was Dharmakara who lived in India a million years ago. After the Enlightenment, he refused to reside in *Nirvana*, instead, he made forty-eight vows to save people by bringing them to the West Pure Land. The Three Canons of Pure Land Buddhism were translated and introduced to China around the fifth to the seventh century and to Korea by Wonhyo who himself made a commentary on the Amida sutra. The teaching of Pure Land Buddhism was finally introduced to Japan.[110]

Honen interprets this to mean that all those who invoke his name will be saved, because the Buddha's holy intention is in selecting *nembutsu*. This is the vow of the Buddha. In association with Honen, Shinran, however, in his own experiential perspective, interprets the Pure Land teaching as justified historically in the meaning of Amida Buddha's primal vows, confirmation of rebirth in the Pure Land, and Enlightenment in terms of the *nembutsu* of true faith that is central to Sakyamuni's teaching. Going beyond the several streams of Pure Land teaching from China to Japan, he was strongly convinced that the final Enlightenment could be attained not through the self-striving discipline, but through the principle of absolute Other-Power, which is expressed in Amida Buddha's forty-eight primal vows in the *Larger Pure Land Sutra*. According to Shinran, all human activity is entangled with ego interest that cannot be ended sufficiently for achieving Enlightenment as the goal of Buddhist spirituality. "With our evil natures hard to subdue, our minds are like asps and scorpions. As the practice of virtue is mixed poison, we call it false, vain practice."[111]

Shinran maintained that human effort is incapable of purifying itself sufficiently to achieve Enlightenment. As we already have mentioned, Honen stressed that *nembutsu* means exclusive invocation. "It is nothing but the mere repetition of the 'Namu Amida Butsu,' without doubt in His mercy, whereby one may be born into the Land of Perfect Bliss. The mere repetition with firm faith includes all practical details . . . Thus (one) should fervently practice the repetition of the name of Amida, and that alone."[112]

110. Cf. Kyoung-Jae, *Christianity and the Encounter of Asian Religions*, 172.

111. Bloom, *Shinran's Gospel of Pure Grace*, 28 29.

112. *BS*, II, 264.

However, Shinran, though practicing *nembutsu* for many years as a monk on Mount Hiei, did not feel nearer to Enlightenment, so he abandoned the *nembutsu* itself as a practice or means to attain Enlightenment. The more the impure mind tries to purify itself, the worse we are doomed to fail. Therefore, the self-power of the practitioner is overwhelmed and negated by the Other-Power of Amida. A spirituality of trust should be transformed into a spirituality of obedience.[113] Human works and conduct such as meditation and the study of sutras become meaningful only when done out of thankfulness and gratitude for having been liberated and enlightened by the power of Amida rather than for the purpose of attaining Enlightenment.

If deliverance is completely dependent on the power of the Buddha's realized vows, Pure Land soteriology does not merely focus on rebirth in the Pure Land in terms of trust in Amida and the recitation of the nembutsu, but retains the aspect of altruism because the pursuit of Enlightenment has its goal in working for the deliverance and Enlightenment of all sentient beings.

Given this fact, Shinran's reinterpretation of the soteriological process with emphasis on the absolute Other-Power does not mean that people are simply passive with respect to ethical life. If the religious life is understood as an expression of gratitude for the Buddha's compassion and the assurance of our final Enlightenment through our faith/trust in the Buddha's vows, the concrete manifestation of this gratitude is the recitation of the name of Amida Buddha. However, gratitude beyond recitation is expressed by a compassionate concern to share the teaching with others.

Of course, ethical duty is not necessary for salvation, not to mention causative of it, but a means by which the compassion of the Buddha becomes real in the world. Shinran's sensitivity to ethical responsibility and respect for other faiths is extraordinary. He triggered a strong criticism of Buddhist institutions and clergy for not representing Buddhist compassion and wisdom. Therefore, they are criticized as outwardly Buddhist but at the same time as inwardly heathen. He once stated, "When a rich person goes to court, it is like throwing a stone into water, while for a poor person it is like throwing water into a stone."[114]

To be compassionate with the poor, to say the *nembutsu* in favor of the welfare of society is also grounded in a cosmic and universal soteriol-

113. Ibid.

114. *BS*, II, 234.

ogy of the Buddha's compassion. According to Shinran the religious experience and trust are characterized by two types of deep faith. There is one dimension in which a person is aware of spiritual ailment and incapacity, and another that is articulated in faith, in unconditional compassion, and wisdom of Amida Buddha, who embraces all beings without abandoning them. As a matter of fact, the deeper the awareness of one's sinful condition grows, the more abundant and absolute the assurance of Buddha's compassion and grace becomes.

With the absolute Other-Power in view, Shinran stresses "sincerity, faith, and aspiration," which are in unity resulting from Amida Buddha's universal grace. They are required for rebirth in the Pure Land. Faith or trust is crucial for the understanding of practice and soteriology, which is only endowed by Amida. In addition to the concept of faith, Shinran asserts that Amida is the Eternal Buddha by virtue of the twelfth and thirteenth vows. The Bodhisattva Dharmakara became Amida Buddha, which means Eternal Life and Infinite Light, which pervades the cosmos and becomes manifest in the aspiration for Enlightenment or deliverance in all beings.

Shinran made a distinction between *dharmakaya*-as-suchness and *dharmakaya*-as-compassionate means. Amida Buddha was manifested as *dharmakaya*-as-compassionate means out of the formless, nameless *dharmakaya*-as-suchness. Amida Buddha, appearing in the form of Bodhisattva Dharmakara, stated the forty-eight vows of great compassion, and after having fulfilled the vows, he finally became the Buddha of Immeasurable Light and Life. Therefore, Amida Buddha can be called a mediator—if we use a Christian metaphor—between the formless Buddhahood and all sentient living creatures in the world of *samsara*. The primal vow is thus the expression of the embodiment of Amida's *karuna* and *prajna*. However, Amida Buddha for Shinran is not merely the manifestation of the *dharmakaya*-as-suchness, but Sakyamuni Buddha is also the most important of such manifestations including the possibility for human beings to become mediators.

What is distinctive in the concept of faith in Shinran is that faith/trust as the realization of Buddha-nature is placed and seen in Amida's compassion and promise to deliver all beings, as is well-expressed in his vows. This teaching expressed itself in human experience, inspired to become Buddha for the deliverance of all beings. For Shinran, like Luther, a forensic meaning of faith is connected with the belief in the name of Amida that is *extra nos* imputed to us as meritorious and efficacious for us. At the same time this objective dimension refers to an inner transformation of one's mind that is seen as the strong self-evident truth and assurance of the universal vows of Amida for deliverance.

In general, Pure Land teaching is regarded as *upaya*, a skillful device or subsidiary path to Enlightenment to help people attain birth in the Pure Land by reciting the name in an easy way, while the essential religious rigorous spiritual discipline and practices leading to Enlightenment are the meditations and monastery life. In reversing this relationship totally, Shinran insisted that even meditation and morality are the *upaya*. When all human efforts fail, people could be open to and trust fully in Amida's vows. The eighteenth vow of Amida, corresponding to the stage of true faith, is the cause and basis for deliverance, not one's self-awakening practice. Thus the self-discipline-oriented paths to Enlightenment are regarded as subordinate or a preparatory stage for trust in and surrender to Amida's promise of salvation. In highlighting his teaching of absolute Other-Power, Shinran is critically engaged in other teaching of contemporary Buddhism, for example, by indicating that self-striving discipline or self-awakening to *Sunyata* is inferior to our assurance of Amida. This is ensured in the eleventh vow: "May I not gain possession of perfect awakening if, once I have attained buddhahood, the humans and gods in my land are not assured of awakening, and without fail attain liberation."

Because everybody receives their faith equally from Amida Buddha, the spiritual equality of all the faithful is affirmed. Shinran's decision to marry publicly, and give up monastic precepts, and his critique of the contemporary Buddhist Order may be based on his teaching of equal priesthood of all believers in light of the universal grace of Amida Buddha. Faith for others seeks the welfare and deliverance of others that is based on the Buddha's true mind of compassion and wisdom. That is the essence of faith. Religious life for Shinran is seen in a twofold sense.

Negatively, the soteriological process is only grounded on the absolute Other-Power excluding self-striving human effort and self-awakening to *Sunyata*. Positively, religious life is expressed as gratitude for the Buddha's compassion, grace, and assurance of our final Enlightenment in terms of the faith. This gratitude, beyond the recitation of the name of Amida Buddha as a means to attain Enlightenment, is characterized by a compassionate concern for and solidarity with others. An ethical praxis is not a good deed for receiving merit, but intends to share and make real Buddha's compassion with others in society.

A paradigm shift from the egocentric character of religious effort to its altruistic nature marks Shinran's interpretation of soteriology on the basis of universality of the Buddha's vow. Let me conclude the universal teaching of salvation in Shinran by comparison with a remark of Honen: "Even sinners enter into the life of nirvana, how much more the righteous? (Honen) while if the righteous enter into the life of nirvana, then how much more in the case of sinners? (Shinran)."[115]

The difference between Honen and Shinran lies in the point of fact. For Shinran an evil person possesses the capacity to receive Amida's grace of salvation, that is, Buddha-nature. The statement—that an evil person attains birth, so naturally a good person will also—would run counter to the primal vow of Amida Buddha. If a good person attains birth through the self-power, it would be in contrast to Amida's primal vow. Therefore, abandoning attachment to self-power and entrusting oneself wholeheartedly to Other-Power, one will enter the life of *Nirvana* in the Pure Land. For this reason, Shinran said that "even the virtuous man is born in the Pure Land, so without question is the man who is evil."[116]

In the practice of Buddhism there are three main methods: meditation, visualization, and Buddha's-name-recitation. The method of meditation is a difficult practice, whereas visualization (contemplation) is a very subtle method. However, Buddha's-name-recitation is a quick and easy method. Nobody makes a mistake with this method. "Putting worries aside, you may therefore proceed with a decisive heart."[117]

Opponents of the Pure Land doctrine are mostly of Ch'an (Zen) lineage who maintain that Pure Land spirituality is dualistic because of its sharp distinction between this life and the next. The debate inside the Buddhist traditions has been long and complex. In the middle stands an option that combines faith in Amida and Ch'an meditation in China, Korea, and Vietnam. Whereas in Japan the Pure Land and Zen are strictly separated from each other. Karl Barth notices that there is "a holy providential disposition" in the faith in Amida Buddha.[118]

Let me now compare Luther's understanding to Shinran's understanding of universal salvation through faith alone. As a matter of fact, justification for Luther is the doctrine on which the church stands or falls

115. Kyoung-Jae, *Christianity and the Encounter of Asian Religions*, 172.

116. Keel, *Understanding Shinran*, 31.

117. Thien-An, *Buddhism and Zen*, 89; cf. *BS*, II, 266.

118. *CD*, I/2: 340–44.

(*articulus stantis et cadentis ecclesiae*).[119] This article is the central article of salvation for Luther. The teaching of justification, when properly understood, is faith in Christ. Faith in Christ for Luther, however, implies a double meaning of being declared righteous by God on the one hand, and of being acquitted, renewed in terms of the divine promise and grace on the other hand. The event can be understood adequately as a process extending over all of life in eschatological openness. In the first place, Luther put emphasis on *sola fidei* in God who justifies the unrighteous and reckons him/her as righteousness. And next, faith is described as the reception of divine promise. At this point, faith is not understood as human work or repentance to receive divine grace. Rather, "Justification is received by faith, that is, in the shape of faith."[120] The alien righteousness of Christ is intended to express the freedom of divine grace rather than the scholastic idea of grace as *habitus*.

The double dimension of justification, that is, imputation of Christ's righteousness in the forensic sense, connected with a process of transformation, is solely grounded on Jesus Christ who is present in faith, because the justifying faith "takes hold of and possesses this treasure, the present Christ."[121] Christ who is really present in faith is the subject and object of justification and at the same time, the ground for effective transformation of human life. Everyone who believes in Christ is *de jure* righteous because of Christ, while everyone who believes in Christ is *de facto* sinful because of Christ. "The righteous man himself does not live; but Christ lives in him, because through faith Christ dwells in him and pours His grace into Him, through which it comes about that a man is governed, not by his own spirit but by Christ's."[122]

For Luther, Christ encompasses the beginning of justification and the goal of it. Luther's formulation of *simul justus et peccator,* therefore, sees human work in light of Christ in a twofold sense. In an affirmative sense, human work is necessary and active in faith, but in a negative sense it is not enough to cause salvation. The goal of Luther's teaching of justification is purely grounded "on the promise and truth of God, which cannot

119. *WA*, 40 III, 352, 1–3.

120. Althaus, *Theology of Martin Luther*, 230–31.

121. *LW*, 26:130.

122. *WA*, 2, 502, 12–14; cf. Lohse, *Martin Luther's Theology*, 262–63.

deceive," rather than on neglect of the significance of human effort.[123] In this regard, John Cobb recognizes a striking resemblance between Shinran and Luther concerning justification.[124]

If Amida's grace is for Shinran the sole ground for salvation, if the act of *nembutsu* and faith are given to us by Amida Buddha *extra nos*, and if faith as entrusting involves the conversion and transformation of the heart from self-power to Other-Power, then faith is very difficult to realize. If this is the case, faith is even more difficult to realize than "perfect fruit of enlightenment," because of the human sinful situation.[125] Therefore, Shinran found himself in his understanding of faith, totally saved and yet totally lost. This paradox of religious experience is compared to Luther's concept of *simul justus et peccator*. This refers to the similarity in difference. Be that as it may, Shinran's understanding of faith as a gift of Amida seems to presuppose Buddha-nature in all human beings and is connected inseparably with it. Faith in Shinran's thought should be realized in fulfillment of Amida's vows. If an evil person comes to *Nirvana*, his/her Buddha-nature should be in accord with Amida's compassion in the sense of identification between *Nirvana* and *samsara*.

Paradoxically speaking, Amida's grace can be realized only through the Buddha-nature in human beings. The nondual identity between *samsara* and *Nirvana*, or Amida and human beings comes from faith rather than Buddha-nature that receives, realizes, and fulfills *Nirvana*. However, in matters of justification and salvation, Luther would oppose *imago Dei* (or to use the metaphor *imago Buddha* in a Christian way) as the point of departure capable of receiving, realizing, and fulfilling the grace of God.

In addition, Luther's forensic concept of *simul justus et peccator* cannot be properly understood without its effective and transformative dimension of justification. The real presence of Christ, i.e., the *inhabitatio Christi* in a believer, is a central motif in Luther's understanding of justification. Instead of an inherent, habitual quality, *fides Christi* comes to the surface, i.e., Christ who inhabits a Christian through faith. Unlike Shinran, whose interest is not in the real presence of Amida Buddha, the union with Christ in Luther's theology includes both a relation to Christ and unity with him.

123. *LW*, 26:387.

124. Cobb, *Beyond Dialogue*, 102.

125. Keel, *Understanding Shinran*, 112.

Justification is connected with the fact that Christ is really present and has become one with the sinner. The idea of union is central and basic to an explanation of Luther's relation between the forensic and the effective aspect of justification. If Christ, as the *favor Dei*, articulates the forensically declared righteousness, Christ as the *donum Dei* elaborates the aspect of effective righteousness. Because there is still residual sin in human beings in a post-baptismal sense, justification, like the process of salvation, in trembling and fear is based on Christ's forensic and effective work and is in need of the renewal effected by the Holy Spirit.

Moreover, in the matter of soteriology Luther's experience of *Anfechtungen* is quite different from Shinran, albeit there would be an existential resemblance. Luther's experience with God's wrath and love on the cross of Jesus Christ is historical, concrete, and experiential, while Shinran's faith in the Other-Power, which is based on the myth of the bodhisattva named Dharmakara, is not much concerned about the history. Unlike the story of Jesus Christ, the Amida story is more metaphysical, more spiritual than objective, historical reality, and factual. Furthermore, Luther's understanding of divine suffering on the cross tends to elaborate divine immanence in deep solidarity with people who suffer, rather than a manifestation of absolute Nothingness. The Buddhist perspective on salvation is not in accord with a sacrificial image of the nailing and blood on the cross.[126] Therefore, this is an example of difference in similarity.

Unlike Shinran, Luther does not downplay the soteriological significance of the sacrament as God's compassion at the phenomenological level. If salvation comes from the absolute Other-Power of God, our faith in God in the forensic dimension is not in polar tension with faith in God in the unitive sense. It may be rather understood as "essence-function" (*ch'e-yong*) hermeneutics in Wonhyo, in which faith is not merely seen as dualistic thinking, but as a sharing with God through participation in God's compassion, which is highlighted in celebration of the sacrament. The Lord's Supper is the crystallization point of faith that means God's gracious condescension excluding all works-righteousness makes it possible for human beings to be in "happy exchange" with God. It is an important aspect of Luther's teaching of justification and salvation that

126. Ibid., 177.

might more correspond to "essence–function" (*ch'e-yong*) hermeneutics of Wonhyo rather than Shinran's forensic understanding of salvation.[127]

For Luther, Christ arouses faith like the Mahayana does in Wonhyo. This faith is expressed concretely as faith active in love, in which Jesus Christ is understood as the sacrament-model not only for salvation imputed *extra nos* but also for the subject of faith in union enabling the praxis of discipleship (*sacramentum-exemplum*) in service of all creatures in the world. Given this fact, human activity and discipleship are not separated from faith in justification. "If he finds his heart confident that it pleases God, the work is good, even if it were so small a thing as picking up a straw."[128] An ethical consequence of faith does not lie in gathering merits by doing good work, but, "it is a pleasure to please God," serving "God purely for nothing."[129] "Faith desires to be the only service of God," "when the work is done in faith and by faith."[130]

In addition, Luther's theological aesthetics of justification are expressed in his marvelous sense and wonder of "traces of divinity" in all creatures. A Christian faith, when it is not attentive to the beautiful music of God, that is "the lovely music of nature" in creation, it becomes a deaf faith.[131] In realizing the grace of Christ in a unitive sense of "happy exchange," human beings are awakened and enlightened to the praise of God's beauty in all living sentient creatures, reflected even in the smallest followers.[132] As Heiko Oberman states, "It is highly precarious to separate the mystical tissue from the living organism of Luther's spirituality."[133] Luther's aesthetics of God's beauty in creation points to God's kenotic way to incarnation. "God himself is personally present in all things, without which presence even God could not have become [human] nor one person made of divinity and humanity."[134] Furthermore, faith in God the Creator leads to a faith in God's power and wisdom of raising the dead, that is, the

127. Kyoung-Jae, *Christianity and the Encounter of Asian religions*, 78–79.

128. "Treatise on Good Works," (1520) in *Works of Martin Luther*, 189.

129. Ibid., 191.

130. Ibid., 198.

131. *LW*, 1:126.

132. Ibid., 54: 327.

133. Churchill, "This Lovely Music of Nature," 186. For a relationship between Luther and mysticism, see Hoffman, *Luther and the Mystics*; and see also *Theologia Germanica*.

134. *LW*, 37:63.

resurrection of the dead.[135] God's grace in the creation reaches its climax in the Christ event, which is the highest expression of God's justification for all.

If Luther's teaching of justification is seen and discussed in the context of a universal salvation, our salvation by grace is a gift of God (Eph 2:8; Rom 3:24). At least in Pauline theology, God's grace is of universal character, and knows no bounds. That Christ died for all (2 Cor 5:15) refers to the fact that all will be made alive in Christ (1 Cor 15:22). Furthermore, the act of righteousness of one leads to acquittal and life for all (Rom 5:18). The expression *apokatasis panton* (Acts 3:21) refers to the fulfillment of God's promise rather than universal salvation. Eph 1:10 says, "to unite all things in Christ, things in heaven and things on earth." Col 1:20 says "to reconcile to himself all things, whether on earth or in heaven, making peace by the blood of his cross." In reflection upon Phil 2:7–8, Luther emphasizes the "becoming like" other men on the part of Christ, but in relation to the *herlickeyt* (*Herrlichkeit:* glory) of Christ's divinity.[136] For Luther, Christ "flows, pours, and illumines and works in all creatures, and fills all things."[137]

We hear from the cosmic hymn of Christ "that at the name of Jesus every knee should bow, in heaven and earth and under the earth, and every tongue confess that Jesus Christ is Lord, to the glory of God the father" (Phil 2:10f). All enemies will be put under Christ's feet (1 Cor 15:25). Finally, God may be all in all (1 Cor 15:28). This biblical universalism is also expressed well in the statement that "God has consigned all men to disobedience, that he may have mercy upon all" (Rom 11:32). Who does all refer to? To non-Christians as well as Christian?[138]

However, we cannot avoid biblical talk about a double outcome of judgment (Matt 7:3f) or confessional exclusivism (John 14:6). Salvation will apply to some people excluding others because of the lack of faith. The gospel in miniature (John 3:16) identifies faith with eternal life and disbelief with damnation. Without reference to faith, only good works determine whether a person goes to heaven or to hell (Matt 25). Salvation

135. Ibid., 4:120–21.

136. Ibid., 52:86–87.

137. Ibid., 52:63.

138. Peters, *God—The World's Future*, 352–56; cf. Moltmann, *Coming of God*, 240–43. For the discussion of universal salvation, Barth, "Vergangenheit und Zukunft," 37–49; cf. *CD*, II/2:33.94ff, 295f, 417; and Rahner, *Foundations of Christian Faith*, 444.

is "for everyone who has faith" (Rom 1:16). Those who sin against the Holy Spirit will not be forgiven, "either in this age or in the age to come" (Matt 12:32). "He who believes and is baptized will be saved; but he who does not believe will be condemned" (Mark 16:16). We hear talk about hell (Mark 9:45), eternal fire prepared for the devil and his angels (Matt 25:31–46), everlasting fire that is not quenched (Mark 9:48), and the rich man in Hades while the poor man Lazarus is in Abraham's bosom (Luke 16:23). There is a state of being lost (*apoleia*) in Phil 3:19 (1 Cor 1:18, 1 Cor 2:15, etc.).

Universal salvation and a double outcome of judgment are biblically attested in mutual tension. However, according to Luther, we sinners are saved only by God's gracious act in Christ. In addition, this grace comes to us while we are *still* sinners. Christ's saving work is definitely for all. God our savior "desires everyone to be saved." "This is an exclusive proposition that is expressed in universal terms . . . He causes all men to be saved."[139] Luther interpreted the verse in 1 Tim 2:4 in such a way that God desires all people to be saved. In so doing, Luther would tend to affirm a universal dimension of *sola fidei*.[140]

An implication of the universality of justifying grace in Luther's thought should be sharpened in regard to his concept of *theologia crucis* and Christology. If justification is solely based on the death of Jesus Christ for the entire race, a reflection of the crucified Christ should be dealt with in accordance with what Christian faith stands and falls for concerning the universal dimension of God's death for the salvation of human beings and all living creatures. This is the theme to which I now turn my attention in explanation of the relationship between theology of the cross in an encounter with the Buddhist concept of *soku*.

Theologia Crucis and the Logic of *Soku* in Encounter

The Fathers of the Greek and Latin churches had developed a Christian theology in response to Hellenistic culture by explicating Christian faith in terms of the categories of Greek philosophy, particularly Plato and Aristotle. It was Luther who turned to a new paradigm of *theologia crucis*

139. *LW*, 28, 260.

140. See the Lutheran doctrine of single election in "Formula of Concord" XI, 46. Based on God's reconciliation in Christ with the world, Bonhoeffer, in reference to Gerhardt, hopes that Christ restores all as God originally intended it to be, (*LPP*, 170).

for rethinking Christian theology. The apostle Paul was fundamental to Luther, particularly the words, "to know nothing except Jesus Christ and him crucified" (1 Cor 2:2). The symbol of the crucified Christ is "a key metaphor" in Luther's thought, which interprets him as, "the mirror of the Eternal." Jesus was the "mirror of the fatherly heart of (God), apart from whom we see nothing but a wrathful and terrible judge."[141] Justification is divine grace flowing from the symbol of the cross in which Jesus Christ as the mirror of the eternal revealed what the hidden God truly means, through his life, death, and resurrection.

From a Buddhist perspective, Luther's idea of theology of the cross might be echoed in the Buddhist philosophy of Kitaro Nishida, the leading representative of the Kyoto school in Japan, who proposes "the principle of reversibility" as his logic. Nishida's principle is expressed well in the following: "There are sentient beings because there is the Buddha; there is the Buddha because there are sentient beings. There is the world of creatures because there is God the creator; there is God because there is the world of creatures."[142]

For Nishida, the irreversible reality of God implies that God's absolute Nothingness or the reality of dynamic emptying becomes at the same time God's irreversible ground for the human experience with love, freedom, grace, and mercy as the reversible side of God. In Luther's terms, the *Deus absconditus* is the source of the *Deus revelatus*. Just as conversely, the *Deus revelatus* is as the mirror of the eternal, the manifestation of the *Deus absconditus* for the human experience of God's attributes. Nishida's principle of reversibility concerns the identity of opposites in the sense of "not one, not two."

This non-duality, which would correspond to Luther's understanding of Divine suffering in the one person of Jesus Christ, abolishes a pendulum between dualistic and monistic trains of thought in the Western Christian tradition. Other than in the concept of self-emptying double movement in *Sunyata* or absolute Nothingness, Nishida seems to move in affirmation of "absolute charity boundlessly embracing even those who stand against it" without hesitation, when it comes to the incarnation of the absolute as "a nothing constituting the self-negating ground" for the world.[143]

141. *BC*, 419; cf. Pelikan, *Jesus Through the Centuries*, 158.

142. Honda, "Encounter of Christianity," 219.

143. Ibid., 221.

Nishida's logic of absolute charity in the sense of divine absolute love for the world does not need to downplay Jesus Christ, which is at the heart of God's irreversible response to the reversible world in terms of absolute charity. The logic of absolute charity, which manifests itself in the relation of reversibility-*soku* (literally, identity-irreversibility) or irreversibility-*soku*-reversibility, serves as an inspiration for rethinking the meaning and significance of "the crucified God" in an Asian context because it points to the eternal Immanuel in a biblical way.

Be that as it may, Nishida does not ask what kind of historical mediator would reveal the absolute charity of God even for those who stand against it. Buddha-nature, which affirms that everything is the self-negating manifestation of the Absolute, is, therefore, grounded on a *soku* relation between God and the world in a cosmotheandric sense. This notion of inter-relationship between God and the world is not merely Buddhist, but biblical. In other words, the *theologia crucis* is the revealing mirror of the cosmotheandric *soku* between God and the word and all sentient creatures. It is to be understood as the highlighting point where divine charity is sharpened in an encounter with divine *dukkha*.

With respect to the devil as God's antagonist, Luther sometimes sounds like a dualist. However, what is essential for Luther is to affirm divine ultimate power even to the point of using the devil for the divine plan. That is to say, the devil ultimately serves God, even as death is an instrument in God's hand. In effect, the devil is involved in everything, opposing God's will by doing harm to the world and human beings. The reason why God conceals Godself behind the dark powers is to humble us. Although death and sin belong to *regnum diaboli*, reformation is seen as a final, apocalyptic struggle in favor of *regnum Dei*, "so that he (Jesus) might destroy him who has the power of death, that is, the devil" (Heb 2:14).

Luther's understanding of Christ's atonement is exemplified in line with Gal 3:13: "Christ redeemed us from the curse of the law by becoming a curse for us," as it is written in Deut 21:23: "Cursed is everyone who hangs on a tree." In Luther's view, an innocent Christ suffers the curse in our place, and in so doing he set us free from the curse of the law. The strange work (*opus alienum*) of law and wrath is in the service of God's proper work (*opus proprium*) of grace and forgiveness leading eschatologically to salvation. Luther's understanding of Christ's work is of a universal character.

God's proper work is grace and forgiveness in triumph over the enemies of God, the end of which lies in the service of the divine economic plan of salvation. The demonic powers such as sin, death, and finally Satan do not continue to be absolute enemies of God eternally. The atonement of Jesus through satisfaction encompasses the might and the authority of the demonic power and places them under divine power. As Paul Althaus remarks, for Luther "everything else depends on this satisfaction, including the destruction of the might and the authority of the demonic powers."[144]

Jesus' abandonment in experiencing God's wrath and death and hell is vividly heard in Jesus' dereliction on the cross. Luther's concept of *Deus absconditus* is revealed finally and fully in *Deus revelatus,* in which a cosmotheandric unity between God and all living creatures is "enhypostatically" attributed to the cosmic Christ in affirmation of the universal, absolute agape even for those who stand against it. Through Christ, God is involved in the predicament of the cosmos, for humans and all sentient beings at a level of deepest intimacy. "In short, our sin must be Christ's own sin, or we shall perish eternally."[145]

Following in the footsteps of Luther's understanding of the descent into hell, Jürgen Moltmann, in his reflection on Christian eschatology, attests a tradition of the universality of God's grace, especially from the Blumhardts via Swiss religious socialism (Hermann Kutter and Leonhardt Ragaz) to Karl Barth, in regard to the restoration of all things. Universalism as the confession of hope leads not to a political quietism, but to hope for God's kingdom on earth by active participation in social justice and ecological awareness in anticipation of the final redemption of human beings as well as restoration of nature in the new creation. "The confession of hope has slipped through the church's fingers . . . Behold, everything is God's! Jesus comes as the one who has borne the sins of the world. Jesus can judge but not condemn. My desire is to have preached this as far as the lowest circles of hell, and I will never be confounded."[146]

Given the universality of God's grace in Jesus Christ, Moltmann focuses Luther's theology in this direction. However, article XVII of the Augsburg Confession rejects a universal reading of Lutheran tradition

144. Althaus, *Theology of Martin Luther*, 220.

145. *LW*, 26:278, Luther, "Commentary on Galatians."

146. Blumhardt, *Ansprachen, Predigten, Reden, Briefe* II, 131, quoted in Moltmann, *Coming of God*, 254–55.

in sharp contrast to Anabaptist teaching that "the devil and condemned men will not suffer eternal pain and torment."[147] Moltmann attests the true Christian foundation of the hope of universal salvation rooted in the theology of the cross in Luther. Therefore, "the realistic consequence of the theology of the cross can only be the restoration of all things."[148] For Luther, hell is not a special space, not even in the underworld. It is rather "an existential experience, the experience of God's anger and curse on sin and godless being."[149] When Christ was dying on the cross, he experienced not God's present anger over the godless world, but his future wrath and future hell.

As we already have seen, Luther stands closer to a cosmic Christ as conceptualized by a patristic writer such as Irenaeus in his notion of re-capitulation.[150] Luther's theology of the cross provides the basis for the universality of God's grace in favor of inseparable unity between God and all sentient beings in terms of divine *dukkha* occurring in the death of Jesus Christ, which can be meaningful in an encounter with the Buddhist logic of *soku*. Christianity and Buddhism are "not one or two." Rather they have a common witness to God's eternal Immanuel, even outside of the walls of Christianity. This is the most essential aspect of the gospel occurring in the crucified God that Luther witnessed to. God is God for us who stands in poverty and religiosity in terms of his mirror of the fatherly heart in eternity.

The final salvation envisaged by Revelation has to do with the elimination of all dehumanization and suffering and the fullness of human well being and that of every living thing, not just that of human souls. The universal dimensions of the cosmic Christ includes not only the faithful Christians but also those whose names were registered in the book of life in the final judgment according to their solidarity with the cosmic Christ identifying himself with the poor and the victimized. He is making the whole of creation anew (Rev 21:5). The wounded cosmic Christ will be the healer of so many wounded ones on earth, Christian and non-Christians alike, afflicted by injustice and violence.

147. *BC*, 38.

148. Moltmann, *Coming of God*, 251.

149. Ibid., 252. According to Pannenberg, "Christ's descent into hell is a way of expressing the universal significance of Jesus' accursed death, vicariously suffered," (*Jesus—God and Man*, 269ff). Moltmann, *Coming of God*, 252.

150. Cf. Peters, *God—The World's Future*, 227.

This is the divine *soku* for the entire race and all living sentient creatures, and it could be the divine universal grace of justification stemming from the crucified God in an Asian context surrounded by poverty and profound religiosity. "[God] is present everywhere, in death, in hell, in the midst of our foes, yes, also in their hearts. For He has created all things, and He also governs them, and they must all do as He wills."[151] God can forget nothing that he has created, because he will restore all. This is the cosmological-*soku* significance of Luther's *theologia crucis.*

151. *LW,* 19:68.

8

Conclusion

In this writing I am interested in articulating a hermeneutical theology of interfaith dialogue in engagement with this issue of suffering by interpreting and actualizing Luther's theology as it encounters (Mahayana) Buddhist wisdom. According to Hans Urs von Balthasar, a theological aesthetics begins with the expression that God's glory appears. Thus, God's beauty leads the beholder out of the previous existence into a participation in God's mission in Christ in the presence of the Spirit.[1]

However, when it comes to God's appearance in Christ's life and death, a theological discourse on aesthetics is not sufficient without reference to God's loving pain in solidarity with those who suffer. Luther's thinking is rooted in God's embrace of Christ's suffering, which is a basis for his discussion of cross, Trinity, Eucharist, and other areas of his theology. Buddhist reflection on suffering is well expressed in the first Noble Truth: everything and everybody is in *dukkha*. Without reference to the issue of suffering, it is hard to fully grasp Buddhist epistemology of relationality, practical wisdom, and ethical compassion. In an hermeneutical process of fusion of two different horizons, Lutheran theology of suffering and Buddhist wisdom I move in a direction of theo-political interest in emancipation with respect to immanent and prophetic critique of interfaith relation in favor of the poor who suffer under the global reality of economic injustice.

If theological aesthetic is constructed upon the relationship between God's glory and Christ's suffering, this aesthetics undermines an artificial beauty that is produced in a life-world under colonization and reification. If a theological theory of beauty is a theory of perception (in its etymological root), theological aesthetics can not be possible without the

1. Cf. Balthasar, *Seeing the Form*.

perception of a reality of suffering at the personal level as well as at the social and global level. The idea of truth as disclosure (*a-lētheia*) is not properly understood apart from the divine art of the speech event to others. Thus, God's communication in Christ can be concretized in attention to the ugly faces of others, through which God speaks to us in completely different manner.

Given this fact, my theological approach to aesthetics of suffering assumes a character of hybridity in taking seriously the interconnection between a *theologia crucis* (God's love) and a *theologia verbis* (God's freedom). At this point, my attempt is to reinterpret and retrieve Luther as an irregular and thought-provoking thinker for the direction of God's universal reign in the world of world religions. In other words, I emphasize that God may speak to us through the different, strange, and even ominous voice stemming out of religious others. A reflection of divine beauty in an interfaith context becomes a primary hermeneutical perspective for me in order to understand Luther's theology of God in Christ in relation to a Buddhist concept of suffering, nature and ethical compassion. God-world-relationship in a salvific dramatic framework, is, for me, therefore, based on God's speech communication through Israel, the church, and the world rather than an analogy of being or an analogy of faith.

"But you, who do you say that I am?" (Mark 8:29). Publicly, Jesus calls himself into question among his disciples. Martin Luther once referred to this question in a poignant way: "That our Lord Jesus Christ was a Jew by birth." Unlike his controversial, later anti-Jewish writings, Luther, full of gratitude, was sympathetic to and passionate for Israel because they gave us Jesus. Our Lord Jesus Christ was not only a Jew by birth, but also a dead and risen Jew who rules us and the world for today. Under the sway of the Western Greek metaphysics, great attention has been paid to Jesus' relationship with God and God's relationship with Jesus.

However, Asian minjung theology prefers Jesus as a man in his social place, i.e., his social dimensions with his people, the *ochlos*. Reading from the Bible in the synagogue of Capernaum, Jesus proclaims his mission: "The Spirit of the Lord is upon me, because he has anointed me to bring good news to the poor. He has sent me to proclaim release to the captives and recovery of sight to the blind, to let the oppressed go free, to proclaim the year of the Lord's favor" (Luke 4:18–19).

In pursuing this prophetic liberating line and direction an Asian post-confessional theology understands the poor, captive, the blind, the oppressed as the *ochlos* of God. This continues to represent the risen Jesus as Jewish minjung in the ongoing relationship with the minjung of God in the world, and in particular, the Asian context. From the perspective of the *ochlos*, Jesus is seen in his social biography in relationality with his people.

First, from the life of the Jewish people of *ochlos*, who burdened the sin of German Christians during the National Socialism, then from the life of the minjung, who burden the sin of the superpowers of the world under economic globalization, Jesus becomes truly God and truly human for Asian people. Unlike traditional christological dogma (*vere Deus, vere homo*), Asian post-confessional theology retrieves a social dimension of Jesus within the framework of his people, the *ochlos*, in the interest of complementarity. In this regard, an Asian minjung theology focuses the identity and meaning of Jesus Christ as a representative of the *ochlos* in the world, especially with respect to poverty and world religions. The particular claim of the gospel with the crucified Christ was foolishness to the Greeks, and remains a stumbling block to many contemporary Hellenized Christians who feel ashamed of the cross. To the Athenians in front of the Areopagus, St. Paul bears witness to *Solus Christus* in a conviction that everybody lives, moves and has his/her being in the universal reign of God (Acts 17:22, 27b, 28). Therefore, the particularity of Christ cannot be fully understood apart from its dimension of embrace of the others.

As F. W. Marquardt restates Luther's profound insight about the Old Testament, Luther knew fulfillment in the world of the Old Testament. His contemporaries minimized the remark about Christ in the Old Testament as unessential, merely a symbolic way of expression. Luther, in this regard, may have more potentiality than his later writings against the Jewish people.[2]

In his sermon on Gen 22:18 Luther says very clearly that God speaks in a different way from us. Even with short words God includes the whole gospel and the kingdom of Christ so that nobody can describe and understand it adequately. Even Luther advocates an opinion that the holy fathers have expressed all scriptures in the proverbs. We cannot abstract from scripture, but we must integrate ourselves into that new world of the scripture.[3] Luther's strong concern about the law of God becomes explicit in his insistence that faithful people in the Old Testament have faith in

2. Marquardt, *Das christliche Bekenntnis zu Jesus*, Bd. 2, 231.

3. *WA*, 24:390, 27.

Christ as we have. The holy fathers become paradigmatic examples for Christian faith. Abraham was justified in his faith in the word of God and God's *promissio*, just as we are justified in faith in Jesus Christ, the incarnate form of the one word.

In Christ our righteousness is fulfilled and the future is eschatologically present. In faith we might experience the unity of the one word of God and know it together with the faithful of the Old Testament who already experienced God's *promissio* and faithfulness. For Luther, Abraham is the cardinal example of evangelical life (*summum exemplum evangelicae vitae*).[4] What is important in the Old Testament is not only the future, but also the perfected action of God, which is the principle of underlying and ensuring for all the future, then and now. According to Luther, the future of God cannot properly be understood apart from the perfected action of God for the present and the future. In his sermon on Gen 1, Luther thinks that the beginning of the world is, for God, as near as the end. A thousand years are like one day in the sight of God. Adam, who was created in the first day, will be born as the last man. If we see the world from the beginning to the end, all forms of time are interconnected in the sight of God.[5] The temporality of God is bound to history, to Israel and Jesus of Nazareth. The history of God has an open perspective to the future of God. The faith of Abraham is accepted like our faith in the sight of God. The eschatological promise of God, which has become in the reality of Jesus Christ, is of liberative, prophetic character.

Given this fact, an Asian post-confessional and post-foundational theology, which I try to reconstruct in this book, is distinguished from Asian minjung liberation theology because the former is interested in rereading and reinterpreting Christian tradition in critical dialogue with it and in engagement with the wisdom of other religions. Minjung Theology is not much concerned about a Western theological framework and concepts, instead taking a point of departure from the minjung spiritual experience of suffering, self-transcendence (*dan*) and liberation. My approach to Asian contextual theology is theological-dialogical in conversation with Luther and his followers in ecumenical context. It is hermeneutical-liberative in an encounter with a Buddhist insight of *Sunyata* and universal compassion. It is inclusive in its embrace of the others without doing harm to otherness, and postfoundational in recognition of the different as different. In this

4. *WA*, 57.III, 236, 4f. (*A Lecture on Hebrew*, 1518). *KD*, I/2:81. Cf. Whöle, *Luthers Freude an Gottes Gesetz*, 33–42.

5. *WA*, 24.25.16f.

regard, Asian post-confessional theology takes seriously Christian-Jewish dialogue and its theological ecumenical development as a paradigmatic example in relevance to Christian understanding of the others. This points to a direction in concert with "our urgent desire to live out faith in Jesus Christ with love and respect for the Jewish people."[6]

As long as Jesus is understood as the Liberator from the established Judaism, Asian liberation theology is inclined, by and large, to get along with the anti-Jewish tendency originating from Western tradition. In the framework of Asian minjung theology, the law of Moses has lost meaning. In other words, Israel and the Jewish religion are reduced to pharisaic religion in contrast to Jesus as the Liberator. Jesus appears as a destroyer of Jewish religion. In contrast, Asian post-confessional contextual theology, inspired by Luther's insight into suffering, meets the Buddhist insight of *dukkha* and takes a point of departure in understanding the relation between Jesus and Jews by taking seriously Luther's keen formulation, "Jesus was a born Jew." This is not the removal of Jesus' Jewish background, but bringing him to the house of Israel is at the center of Asian post-confessional theology in particular.

The incarnation of God in human flesh is made concrete in becoming a Jew. It is important to see and read the gospel in a new light from the angle of the oppressed, because from this perspective the gospel can be lived and practiced in *conformitas Christi* in the world. This perspective should be revitalized in an encounter with Jesus as *ochlos* minjung who suffered together in their under-history. Luther characterized Christian faith not by human effort, but by the work of the Holy Spirit. "I believe that I cannot by my own reason or strength believe in Jesus Christ my Lord, or come to Him."

If our faith is based on the Spirit of God, we don't need to compare our Christian belief with others. We don't believe our belief itself, because God in Jesus Christ by the power of the Spirit is at the center of it. The Christian mission in an Asian context, first of all, is to witness Jesus' message of liberation for people in need. Proclamation of the year of the Lord's favor means social discipleship in service of God's loving compassion for the poor, the captive, the blind, the alienated, and the oppressed. This liberative praxis comes not from our own reason or strength, but from faith active in love by our witnessing to God's righteousness, peace, and loving concern about all sentient beings by the power of the Spirit. Justification

6. Lull, *My Conversation with Martin Luther*, 150.

by faith alone refers not to the selfish private encapsulation of God's salvation in Jesus Christ in the interest of excluding and condemning others, but refers to God's radical grace in Christ *extra nos* and a universal dimension of the Spirit in favor of them. "The wind blows where it chooses" (John 3:8).

God the creator is also for people in other religious ways. Christ the redeemer does not block the universality of God's grace to others, but concretizes its dimension historically and highlights eschatologically God's compassion with them. The universal scope and significance of Jesus Christ is characteristic of aesthetics of the gospel. The uniqueness of Jesus of Nazareth, which is the highest expression of God's plan of salvation, becomes manifest especially in his passionate solidarity and compassion with others, that is, the deviant, the irrelevant, the marginalized, the oppressed, all in all, the lowest of the low who are *ochlos* of God, minjung.

Bonhoeffer's reflection in his prison papers is worth remembering: "Jesus is one whose only concern is for others." That is, the human for others.[7] Furthermore, Bonhoeffer states a necessity of the church's repentance: "She was silent when she should have cried out because the blood of the innocent was crying aloud to heaven . . . The Church confesses that she has witnessed in silence the spoliation and exploitation of the poor and the enrichment and corruption of the strong."[8]

If we see Jesus within the framework of the life of the Jewish people, Jesus in an Asian context is not confined or a thrall of a Western rationality culture of logocentrism. The spirit of that logocentrism is, by and large, seen in control of everything, to the exclusion of difference or otherness. It would subsume all narrations under one unified metanarrative.

Asian Christians should learn to confess Jesus Christ as our Lord without doing harm to or even condemning other religious ways in which the risen Christ is at work in compassion and solidarity with people in poverty and profound religious devotion outside the walls of Christianity. The eschatological kingdom eschatologically present in Jesus appears and is active in various ways of other religions. In the history of world religions Jesus holds a unique place as the key to the future of the world and its salvation on the basis of his death and resurrection, but without the exclusivism of other religious ways, nor falling into the sheer relativism of neo-liberal pluralists.

7. Bonhoeffer, *Letters and Papers*, 237–38.

8. *Ethics*, 113.115.

The risen Christ is not one with the universal Buddha, but not two. A strange, even uncomfortable, ominous voice stemming from others could serve as an inspiration for setting us free from being captive to the excessive project of the Enlightenment, and leading us to a humble attitude and radical openness toward God's eschatological reign over the world. When it loses God's other voice, a Christian faith falls into the gray zone of a deaf faith. Asian post-foundational theology leaves Jesus open in anticipation of God's future, which is at the same time in relationality with our world of *samsara*. Witness to God's love in relationality with the world, dialogue with other religious ways towards co-existence and pro-existence in the service of God's eschatological kingdom, and finally mutual transformation through hermeneutical conversation toward God's future are all parts of the encounter of Luther with Asian world religions.

In this regard, the theological language of God's saving grace in Jesus Christ is not based on a scientific objective claim seeking one equivocal meaning of the gospel, because the reader cannot discover and recover the meaning of the gospel as it actually was. However, this effective history does not necessarily lead to sheer relativism or a pluralist theology of religion. A Christian theology of religions does not in fact stand in opposition to pluralism itself, because God is the One who accepts the world's pluralism and integrates all its variety and pluriformity through God's universal grace in Jesus Christ into the coming kingdom of God.

The interfaith conversation is meaningful in so far as it gives rise to a common language and improves a mutual enrichment and transformation without doing harm to other areas in which dialogue participants have never been. Meaning is not merely what the author intended, something to be received passively. The conversation with others is likened to a game in which we do not even take the initiative of getting into the game. As David Tracy says, "In every game I enter the world where I play so fully that finally the game plays me."[9] This game of conversing with others produces an "intensification process" that can lead to a reflective distancing from the relativity and inadequacy of all religious beliefs.

Through this hermeneutical circle, participants return to their own religions experiencing them in a more profound way. "The language game" (Ludwig Wittgenstein) is the social and cultural context of meaning. This calls for an analogical imagination, which plays a pivotal role in dialogue with others. Meaning appears as the text and the reader participates in a hermeneutical dialogue in which a fusion of horizons occurs.

9. Tracy, *Analogical Imagination*, 115.

A Buddhist *advaitic* language does not agree to ultimate and absolute truth claims, because human language will always be a limited tool, not unequivocally identical with the Truth, nor dissimilarly distanced from it. In this regard, I find a Buddhist remark meaningful: "Do not look at the finger! If you do, you will miss the moon. Look at the moon through the finger!" Advaitic language is also analogical, telling us something but never telling us everything of the ultimate Truth. Participants in interfaith dialogue recognize "the possibilities of approaching the conversation among the religious traditions through the use of an analogical imagination"[10] in which we can approach the experience and different worlds of other religions with respect and honor.

An analogical imagination enables participants to witness their uniqueness, to get into dialogue with mutual humility and openness, and finally helps to enrich and renew each tradition before the future of God. "If I have already lived by an analogical imagination within my own religious and cultural heritage, I am much more likely to welcome the demand for further conversation."[11] With this basic tone in mind, my concern about reading Luther is not to discover the one and only meaning of Luther's theology, but to experience a fusion of horizons in encounter with Luther and Western mainline thinkers influenced by him.

A reading of Martin Luther in Asian context does not merely mean a hermeneutic task, but is directed toward a practical discipleship in recognition of a religious spirituality of poverty, spiritual detachment, and solidarity with others in suffering. The kingdom of God as the new beginning is realizing itself here and now in eschatological openness. An eschatological reservation need not be read as mere passivity, but as a confession of hope in the expectation of the future of God who will make everything new. The future of God is not merely on the way, but is realizing itself in presence with us as the eternal, present *Immanuel*. The future of God who has come impinges on the present. He is and was and is to come (Rev 1:4, 1:8; 4:8). Time can be properly understood as a dialectical tension between a coming and a becoming in struggle for liberation and recognition of otherness in terms of the eschatological moving. The nonduality of *kairos* makes the future of God present in distinction from *futurum* as *adveniens*, as coming to us.[12]

10. Ibid., 449.

11. Ibid., 451.

12. Lochman, *Lord's Prayer*, 50.

Asian minjung theology inspired, to a large extent by D. Bonhoeffer, has a point of departure from the presence of Christ in solidarity with people of poverty and in affirmation of other religious ways. Asian minjung Christology is a solidarity Christology recognizing other religious truth claims from the perspective of a risen *minjung* Jesus Christ by incorporating into it spiritual liberative elements of other religions in protest against the massive poverty, sexual exploitation, racial, and religious discrimination. Liberation, in this context, is not merely confined to a white-dominated concept of class struggle based on social and economic analysis. The ways to liberation are to be affirmed in a plural sense of not doing harm to the uniqueness of each way. The difference is different, but a conversation with the different produces a common basis to enrich and renew the encounter of two stories: By discovery of the *ochlos* minjung we meet Jesus the *ochlos* Jew.

In encounter with Jesus as the *ochlos* Jew, we discover his risen presence and compassion with the Asian *ochlos* of God. This hermeneutical process helps the Asian church and theology to deepen a fundamental message of Jesus in a biblical way, while at the same time recognizing the social life of minjung in other religious ways that is seen explicitly and vividly in poverty and profound religiosity in a universal christological way.

Let me illustrate with a story that took place in a public cemetery in Canada. There was a white family visiting the grave of their departed. They placed some flowers on the grave in memory of their loved one. They bowed in silence for a while. Some yards apart from it, an Asian family prepared rice and fruits for the departed and knelt and bowed in memory. Curiously, one of the white family members approached the Asian family asking whether the departed would return to eat the rice in front of the grave. The Asian person, a little surprised, responded to him by asking back whether the white departed would also return to sit and smell the flowers near the grave. To Asian people, a bowl of rice symbolizes a deep spiritual life in on-going communion with the ancestors more than a bunch of flowers do.[13]

Rice and flower are not one, but not two, as a way of expressing a memorial act for the beloved departed with loving concern about eternal life. The Lord's Supper celebrates the most expensive grace of God and invites us to an open invitation of Jesus Christ as the coming future of God who will recapitulate a struggle for liberation and a communion and

13. Kyoung-Jae, *Christianity and the Encounter of Asian Religions*, 160–61.

embrace not only the Christians but the Jewish people and the righteous of all the nations. A hermeneutic of recognition could strengthen individual Christians to be more faithful and committed to the triune God by listening to the others and beautifying itself. Such a hermeneutic deepens a profound sense of amazement and wonderment of the gospel from an encounter with the others. "Every authentic conversation" takes place in this encounter.[14]

The meaning of Luther finds itself not in applying him literally to the Asian church, with an expository interest, nor in transplanting him into an Asian scene without a challenge. Luther becomes meaningful in a critical encounter with contemporary Asian aesthetic consciousness. An attempt to reactualize Luther from an Asian perspective is, in fact, to be understood as a conversation with him in mutual understanding and transformation in favor of solidarity with and recognition of otherness. Our common witness is not about Luther himself, but the One whom Luther has passionately witnessed to in his lifelong struggle. Jesus Christ as the future of God locates himself not only "in, with, and under" the sacrament, but also finds himself in the middle of time, especially in the universal presence and solidarity with the others outside the walls of the church who are the lowest of the low in poverty and deep religiosity. It is Jesus Christ who is "the same yesterday and today and for ever" (Heb 13:8). The kingdom in Jesus Christ who has come has to do with our past, present, and future.

Luther's in-depth understanding of God's suffering through his *theologia crucis,* albeit recognizing its weakness and limitation in his time, still offers a basis and insight for Asian contextual theology to engage in critical reflection on praxis, social and religious, in light of the divine *dukkha* of the Trinity. Bonhoeffer's "beautiful text" is a gift to us, but with an Asian reorientation: A hermeneutic from the perspective of those who suffer[15] finds its genuine meaning in engagement with people of other faiths who suffer under the economic globalization of late capitalism.

Martin Luther, one of the great expositors of the Lord's prayer, laid special emphasis on the petition, "thy will be done" in regard to the work of God. "In this petition you will notice that God bids us to pray against ourselves. In that way he teaches us that we have no greater enemy than

14. Tracy, *Plurality and Ambiguity*, 93.

15. Bonhoeffer, *Letters and Papers*, 17, quoted in Gutiérrez, *Power of the Poor in History*, 231 (in a different translation).

ourselves . . . Therefore, we are asking for nothing else in this petition than the cross, torment, adversity, and suffering of every kind, since these serve the destruction of our will."[16]

I accept this marvelous statement as a calling for *metanoia* in respect to our fellow humans in other religions and cultures and our fellow creatures in the midst of environmental devastation. Folding our hands in prayer is the beginning of revolt against the disorder of the world (Karl Barth) by turning to *metanoia* toward the future of God who has come in Jesus Christ. Humanity and the world should be renewed and transformed in Jesus Christ as the total Liberator. In fact, the future of God's kingdom does not merely come, nor do we come into the kingdom. Those who wander in poverty and suffering "love earth and God in one."[17] The kingdom of God is given to them, because they can believe in the future of God. The prayer of the church for the kingdom of God forces her into fellowship and solidarity with the children of earth and the world and pledges her to be in faithfulness to the earth even to hunger and to death in cosmological *dukkha*.

Luther's tone of the restoration of all things through his radicalization of Christ's descent into hell can be reread in an Asian sense as: (1) struggle for liberation in a social and political sense, (2) recognition of the presence of Christ in the minjung who suffer, and (3) affirmation of other religious paths to liberation in light of God's compassion for all. Luther's *theologia crucis* as a public theology will reach its climax in the total liberation of God to whom Christ finally subjects himself so that God may be all in all (1 Cor 15:28). Given this fact, "The true Christian foundation for the hope of universal salvation is the theology of the cross, and the realistic consequence of the theology of the cross can only be the restoration of all things."[18]

In this regard, theology of the cross goes hand in hand with theology of doxology. The gospel invites us not to look at ourselves, but at the God of promise in Jesus Christ, who can never deceive us. Theology of doxology liberates us from our existence curved egoistically into self and encourages solidarity with the poor and affirms otherness and joyful fellowship with all sentient living creatures and creation. The doxology of God is not merely located within the framework of a theology of glory. Rather,

16. *LW*, 42, "An Exposition of the Lord's Prayer." Cf. Lochman, *Lord's Prayer*, 78.

17. Bonhoeffer, "Dein Reich komme," 3:270. Cf. Lochman, *Lord's Prayer*, 45.

18. Moltmann, *Coming of God*, 251.

the glory of God is inseparably connected with the history of Jesus, the *ochlos* Jew. Cross and resurrection are, in this connection, of paramount importance because the glory of God is the glory of the crucified, the glory of self-emptying cosmic unselfish love for the world. The glory of God is humankind being made fully alive (*Gloria Dei vivens homo*). "Thine is the kingdom and the power and the glory."

This is a prayerful expression of total liberation taking place in Jesus Christ toward all sentient creatures in *dukkha*. This is celebrated in a liturgical ministry of Word and sacrament with freedom, joy, and compassion. This dimension of doxology leads us to uprighteous marching.[19] Without the dimension of doxology, our praxis in struggle for liberation and affirmation of otherness would be in danger of becoming a legal works-righteousness. "Consider the lilies of the field, how they grow; they neither toil nor spin; yet I tell you, even Solomon in all his glory was not arrayed like one of these" (Matt 6:28–29).

At this point, we are reminded of Luther's marvelous sense of wonderment at God's mysterious presence in all things. "Ever since the fall of Adam the world knows neither God nor his creation. It lies altogether outside of the glory of God. Oh, what thoughts [humans] might have had about the fact that God is in all creatures, and so might have reflected on the power and wisdom of God in even the smallest flowers!"[20] Luther's theology of nature tells that God comes to us in the creature, but not that the creature comes to God. This would refer to eschatological pan-en-theism, which posits "God as including the world in the divine being but without exhausting this being."[21]

Nevertheless, Luther does not ignore the other side of God's freedom in transcendence when it comes to God's relationality with the world. Those who know God also know, understand and "love the creature, because there are traces of divinity in the creature."[22] That being the case, the fall of Adam and the world is invited to be on the transformative path to the gospel of Jesus Christ, because it is Christ who "makes our state better than the state of Adam was in Paradise."[23]

19. Cf. Gollwitzer, *Krummes Holz—Aufrechter Gang.*

20. *LW*, 54: 327; cf.1:141.

21. Peters, *God—The World's Future*, 123.

22. *LW*, 4:195.

23. *LW*, 1:100.

Theology of the cross, with its starting point in the suffering of Christ, is, in fact, seen as the foundation and fulfillment of the theology of doxology, in which all creation becomes the source of praise and gratitude in expectation of God's presence here and now, and God's *Mahakaruna* (Great Compassion) with us in the cosmos. Redemption and creation are not separated from each other, but interconnected with each other in the death and resurrection of Jesus Christ in whom we are in hope of the coming God's future. This is aesthetics of divine suffering in Luther. We Asian Christians like to pray and sing together with Luther that "thy kingdom may prevail among us through the Word and the power of the Holy Spirit . . . until finally the devil's kingdom shall be utterly destroyed and sin, death, and hell exterminated, and that we may live forever in perfect righteousness and blessedness."[24]

24. *BC*, 427.

Afterword

The Theologia Crucis *and the Aesthetics of Suffering in Postmodern Divinity*

Luther's theological aesthetics of God's glory in Christ's suffering love lays a basis for reshaping and redirecting motives of Asian post-confessional theology toward a different understanding and transformation of Luther. When Luther encounters a postmodern context, he can best be understood by challenging and transcending him. His doctrine of justification, theology of the cross, Trinity, law and gospel, eucharistic theology, and two kingdoms theory among others are seen at the point of the death, resurrection and reconciliation of the crucified Christ, the scope and reach of which is of inclusive, universal character allowing and tolerating other ways. If aesthetics are a way of expressing a theory of beauty or a theory of perceiving that is instructed by the beautiful form, it could be said that a theological aesthetic is perception of the manifest glory of God in Christ-form. As an idea of truth refers to disclosure, God's glory, divine beauty discloses itself in the life and ministry of Jesus Christ who was crucified with a tormented, ugly, and scapegoated face. Participation in the life of this executed God becomes questionable and a scandal from the beginning.

A theological aesthetic of divine beauty is for Luther based on the idea that the appearing form of Christ relativizes all worldly measures of beauty and even turns them upside down. Trinitarian form of *theologia crucis* calls for a postmodern sensitivity to the others in which ethical responsibility for the others precedes ontology by decentering the individual, empirical ego toward the true self of Christ. The Christian, through the gift of the Spirit, is fully incorporated into the life-transforming reality of Christ. From a christological basis of the beautiful, sublime exchange between God and human beings, the Christian enters into a daughter's and son's relationship with the triune God in a nondual way. In the beautiful form creation already offers a reflection of divine glory in expectation of a final transformation of all things. Luther's marvelous sense of sublime beauty and goodness of God in nature becomes manifest in his praise of God in nature. "If God were to withdraw his hand, this building [the creation] would collapse . . . The sun would not long return its position and shine in the heavens, no child would be born; no kernel, no blade of grass, nothing at all would grow on earth or reproduce itself if God did not work forever and ever."[1]

Jesus Christ died, risen, and coming is the source of making every living creature more true, better, and beautiful *coram Deo*. In following and pursuing divine beauty, it would be absurd to sentimentalize and even trivialize the harsh demands that the path of the cross can imply. Divine beauty and glory of the Lord on the basis of Christ's sacrifice is for Luther the primary lens for interpreting God's work in Jesus Christ for the world. A christological basis for a theology of aesthetics may adopt a language of *analogia fidei* for the sake of analogy of the others in God's justification. God justifies Godself first of all in the sacrifice of Christ.

God's justification is the best expression of God's solidarity and accompaniment with the divine other. *Analogia fidei* in God's justification entails essentially God's justice for and solidarity with victims including the ontological dimensions of analogy of the other. This refers to a language of God's politics. No adequate Christian theology can be achieved without the inclusion of divine beauty in its paradoxical form as a part of theological reflection. Aesthetics other than reason gives a priority to a holistic way of life. The beauty of God that highlights its glory of death and resurrection of Christ expresses itself not only in the inner divine life, but also becomes concrete in a historical and ecological concern for all living sentient creatures.

Theologia crucis would become a basis for Hegel's reflection on the death of God. Envisioning the death of God as God's sacrifice, a death for Hegel points to divine self-emptiness, which is the highest expression of reconciling love. "The death of Christ is the vision of love itself—not love merely for or on behalf of others, but precisely divinity in this universal identity with other beings, death. The monstrous unification of these absolute extremes is love itself."[2]

In the death of Christ, reconciling love appears as devouring death in which all are reconciled, God is at home with Godself in humanity, God's

1. *LW*, 22:26, *Sermons on the Gospel of John (Chapters 1–4)*.

2. Hegel, *Lectures on the Philosophy of Religion*, 125.

substitution for others challenges all dominion and bondage, and further concretizes a sublime idea of God's recognition of the others by becoming self-divesting divine love. A Hegelian language of struggle for recognition between master and slave,[3] seen in light of Christ's sacrificial death, might become an expression of an ethical mutuality or responsibility of Luther's *theologia crucis*. Reconciling love, which is the highest expression of Christ's self-emptiness, for Luther may be extended to the point of deepening struggle or praxis of discipleship for recognition of the face of others.

The aesthetics of suffering in the postmodern context is found and recommenced in Christ the victim who is expelled by the culture of violence. In this context Christ could become the scapegoat in allowing himself to be expelled by the reason of violence. *Theologia crucis* in a christological and trinitarian setting cannot avoid the relationship between God the expelled, and humanity the expeller, which reveals the victimage processes underlying the meaning of human culture in our society. John's Prologue refers to the Passion of the Logos in the trinitarian life because the darkness of the world does not comprehend him, and his own people do not receive him. The discourse of expulsion in the framework of the Johannine Logos parallels the word of John the Baptist: "Here is the Lamb of God who takes away the sin of the world" (John 1:29).

Jesus as the scapegoat who is victimized by mob violence radically transformed the God who expels in the story of Adam and Eve, into a God who only suffers violence and expulsion. This points also to the transforming power of the powerless *han,* the aesthetics of which is found in Jesus Christ the victim. This insight is shared as a common basis between post-foundational minjung theology and postmodern divinity of God the victim.

A Nietzschean metaphor of choosing "Dionysus instead of the Crucified" becomes meaningful when it takes into account choosing "the crucified in favor of Dionysus." Jesus is the Son of God insofar as he cut out and eliminated through his love radically the victimage process as the founding dynamic of culture. His unselfish cosmic love, which becomes manifest in his ontological universal title of the Lamb of God, abolishes the mechanism of self-justification and scapegoating, and transforms radically a craving for mimetic desire into a spirituality of self-sacrifice in welcoming hospitality for others. The Logos of expulsion will always be

3. Hegel, *Phänomenologie des Geistes*, 141. Cf. Chung, *Karl Barth und die Hegelsche Linke*, 174–81.

the antidote to the reason of violence. Jesus becomes a hostage for others to the point of suffering and dying.[4] In the idea of the crucified Christ, I discover my passivity in relation to the infinite. As the infinite comes to the finite, so the infinite interrupts my consciousness so that it finds itself in my ethical responsibility for others.

That Jesus becomes a hostage for others disrupts the complacency and self-sufficiency of human wisdom, leading to ethical responsibility for others. In this regard, the *theologia crucis* in postmodern perspective remains a constant reminder inspiring Christianity to be sensitive and attentively responsible in relation to others.[5] According to Levinas, the God revealed in a Jewish-Christian tradition of spirituality manifests Godself only in the traces as seen in the Moses' experience with God in the Exodus (Exod 33). Approaching God in this regard does not mean following these traces but coming to the Others.[6] Likewise for Luther, otherness of God is not a comfortable otherness. In encounter with the hidden God, God as Other in life of Joseph and Moses refers to God's back, the dark side of God. However, the Christians are advised not to speculate on the divine dark traces, but trust in the divine promise of Jesus Christ the incarnated in Jesus from Galilee. The experience of God as Other for Luther shapes a social ethic for others who bear the face of Christ.[7]

The aesthetics of suffering reveals the scapegoat principle is rooted in God's perichoretic "inter-being" with divine others. The term aesthetics refers to judgments of value concerning beauty. God's beauty becomes explicit in perichoretic fellowship of love, freedom, and *diakonia* by abolishing monarchial rule of abandonment and violence. However, beauty and love can be in encounter at the place where they are essentially anchored in the loving compassion of God in Jesus Christ for all sentient being. Here is God's desire in trinitarian life to seek the lost. Divine desire by searching challenges a capitalist desire by lack, which makes "all of desire teeter and fall victim to the great fear of not having one's needs satisfied."[8]

Luther, on the basis of *communicatio idiomatum,* has maintained the fact that God, who has created everything and is still above and beyond it, is not only the highest but also the lowest. In the midst of *maxime*

4. Girard, *Things Hidden Since the Foundation of the World,* 271–3.

5. Levinas, "God and Philosophy," in *The Postmodern God: A Theological Reader*, ed. Graham Ward, 60.

6. Levinas, *Die Spur des Anderen*, 235,

7. *LW*, 7:103ff.

8. Deleuze and Guattari, *Anti-Oedipus, Capitalism and Schizophrenia*, 28.

contraria Luther takes God to be not in contrast to the divine others, but in correspondence to a trinitarian fellowship and communion.[9] Jesus' kenotic way on the cross is a voluntary way of loving identification with the desolate and the abandoned. In the dark night of humanity God has passionate compassion with everybody and everything by compassion for them. This is the foolishness of God who destroys the wisdom of the wise. "In the wisdom of God, the world did not know God through wisdom. God decided, through the foolishness of our proclamation, to save those who believe" (1 Cor 1:21).

God transcends suffering through experiencing it. Thus God's transcendence is concretized in God's reconciliation and peace with the world. God creates everything anew by protesting the violence of the world through the future of God. The world of violence is not able to evade the *karuna* (compassion) of God, it is not radical enough to resist God's profound Yes to us. Jesus, who takes away the sin of the world, is the Christ who destroys the logic of hell by his descent into hell. Christ's resistance to eternal damnation is at the heart of the *theologia crucis*.[10] The aesthetics of postmodern divinity is not grounded in the wisdom of secular humanism, but in the foolishness of God's grace for those who are unable to believe, for all the adherents of other religions. As love is God's *karuna* with the lost, so *dukkha* is God's transforming grace of destroying the hell of violence.

The crucified Christ suffers in seeing the irrational horror of the victimage process in the Holocaust, the Stalin era, Vietnam, the Gulf war, etc. God's transcendence is not timeless, but dialectical in its negation and affirmation of the aesthetics of suffering. God transcends Godself by not transcending God's suffering because God is suffering love in freedom. The sacrifice of the scapegoat relativizes the structure of violence and its self-justification by challenging what is hidden in our human society. Therefore, aesthetics refers to the revealing of the beauty of God in the midst of what is hidden and covered. God's beauty becomes explicit in loving suffering *in se* as well as for us. It leads to the aesthetics of Christian existence, restricting a super place of the ego as the center of human subjectivity.

9. "*DEUS, qui creavit omnia, et est supra omnia, est summus et infimus. . . . Sunt enim in eadem persona maxime contraria.*" Luther, *Vorlesungen über 1. Mose, 1535–1545*. cf. Jüngel, "*Die Wahrnehmungen des Anderen in der Perspektive des christlichen Glaubens* (1997)" in Jüngel, *Indikative der Gnade—Imperative der Freiheit*, 215.

10. Moltmann, "The Logic of Hell," 46.

That being the case, theodicy is located and becomes meaningful in the Son's way into the far country, in which the victimizing mechanism and hominization prevail, allowing his expulsion inflicted by the violence of human culture. God's justice is the justice of compassion, of enduring the punishment on the cross, through which God justifies human beings in sin. In the face of Christ's death no person can justify themselves. The justification event takes place in the overcoming and dissolution of the past and the promising and transformation of the present in light of God's future. God's future in our midst protests a present reality of suffering and the structure of victimization. It takes sides with those who suffer and are scapegoated. The promise of God is antithetical to "the Capitalist promise of 'production' based on the vast and undefined chaos of the quotidian tongue where no promise can be a certainty."[11] Theodicy is not supposed to be merely a language game of rationalization. It should be seen historically and concretely in light of a protesting God in the innocent sufferer against status quo of the world.

God seeks and joins the godless in their experience of god-forsakenness, and thus resists human agony and calls into question a concept of gods. This comes from God's promised eschatological transformation where God's presence and promise turn into the time of resistance. The aesthetics of suffering does not allow suffering itself to become *self-righteous*, but moves us to engage in the protest against present conditions, and in praxis towards God's liberated future. The human being in God's promise is located and exists in the struggle against sinful conditions and hope for the eschatologcally promised future of God. The freedom of the justified expresses itself along the lines of God's liberated future, not only freedom from the status quo, but freedom for God's future. "The *pro-missio* of the kingdom is the ground of the *missio* of love to the world."[12] The promise of God is universal, but it revealed itself in the *missio* of divine love that is, in the life, death, and resurrection of Jesus Christ who is the basis for the *missio* of divine love to the world. Therefore, it is of special significance to be committed to the promise in a sense that God's *pro-missio* needs to be reread and rewritten in encounter with the otherness of God in the world.

The aesthetics of *simul justus et peccator* shows God's action of affirming the human being in the past culture of violence as God negates the

11. Ward, ed., *The Postmodern God*, 309.

12. Moltmann, *The Theology of Hope*, 224.

mechanism producing self-righteousness and scapegoating. Therefore, a Christian has existence in the movement of hope, which is a basis for *anthropologia crucis*, that is, a postmodern political theology of recognition. Human experience with this God, although it seems to be mad and foolish in the perspective of the world, has an eschatological horizon. The point of theodicy is not intellectual explanation or logical clarification, but rather God's promise that is fulfilled in the innocent sufferer, a promise that continues with God's act of compassion in solidarity with those who suffer, abandoned by the world. Therefore, a Christian understanding of theodicy begins with the compassing and protesting God in the innocent sufferer who turns upside down the God of the Grand Inquisitor by challenging any human wisdom of rationalizing theodicy. Therefore, theodicy is not about "grand narratives" "such as the dialectics of Spirit, the hermeneutics of meaning, the emancipation of the rational or working subject, or the creation of wealth." Rather, theodicy as "incredulity towards metanarratives"[13] begins with the question of the foolishness and madness of God. The insanity of the Cross, in which Christ is often referred to as a madman, was "a wisdom which drowned in the 'rationality' of the world."[14]

The path to enlightenment leads through the landscape of madness and foolishness. This is an inspiration in doing postmodern theology in face of suffering of the world. The history of madness (M. Foucault), which is alienated and imprisoned by the culture of reason, finds itself in God's foolishness. "To believe in God in spite of the Holocaust and to understand the possibility of redemption in spite of Holocaust"[15] has to do with the crucified Christ in favor of Dionysus. When a rational understanding of innocent victim fails, a spirituality of divine foolishness begins. Christ, who is seen to a generation unbelieving (Mark 9:19), is proclaimed to the Jews as offense and to the Gentiles as a folly. However, the folly of God is wiser than human wisdom. The weakness of God is stronger than human strength (1 Cor 1:23-25). God chose the weakest of the weak in Jesus Christ to shame the strong. By nullifying the false fullness of reason, Christ becomes self-emptying, by which he became fullness for us.

The human being can live at peace with God on the basis of the death of the scapegoat, which is God's foolishness and madness. This history of God stands for a history of madness, one that refers to others alienated,

13. Lyotard, *The Postmodern Condition*, xxiii, xxiv.

14. Pickstock, "Asyndeton: Syntax and Insanity," 311.

15. Bauckham, ed., *The Theology of Jürgen Moltmann*, 96.

suppressed, and unproblematized by the timelessly valid and recognized human wisdom full of rationality and reason. The saving grace of the cross is the hermeneutic filter that penetrates and encourages our spirituality of poverty and self-renunciation to side with God's foolishness and to sharpen an image of the humiliated humanity of God for a postmodern divinity. As "my neighbor's material needs are my spiritual needs,"[16] so my wealth is the cause of a young prostitute in Manila.[17]

Spirituality of inter-being tells us that God can be found in the face of the marginals, the others, and the suppressed. Insight into emptiness leads to the enlightenment of overcoming of all discrimination. "To be is to inter-be." God is "inter-being." At this point, a Buddhist concept of *dukkha* turns into a Buddhist aesthetics of co-existence and pro-existence of all living creatures. God's inter-being with Christ is the basis for Christ's resurrection and reconciliation. Death in Christ is not different from resurrection in God. God becomes a victim in Christ, that of the crucified one in whom and by whom God restores peace between humankind and Godself. Therefore, God the victim becomes God the eternal Life. The Christian gospel, which has the point of departure in God's scapegoat inscribes figures of self-sacrifice and resistance on the world of politics. This aesthetics of politics is a politics of resistance for the reverence of life. The passion of Christ is a consequence of his divinity as the Son of God rather than being a cause of his divinity.

The power of the resurrection drives the aesthetics of suffering toward the spirituality of deepest resistance against the human culture of injustice and rebellion and anchors it in the eschatological promised future of liberation and transformation. This refers to a theological quest of God's utopia in critical engagement with an iron cage of instrmentalized reason and rationality.

Minjung, the suffering people of God, retain their place in God's protest and challenge to the social structure of violence and injustice that legitimates dominion and privilege at the cost of the innocent victims. The crowd who scorned Jesus and added humiliation to Jesus is of the culture of violence while the minjung are powerless, the innocents belonging to the Son's emptying way in allowing their own expulsion. Jesus is in inter-being with his innocent people from the beginning. So, the minjung become the people of the Lamb of God who takes away the burden of the strong

16. *The Postmodern God: A Theological Reader,* ed. Graham Ward, 49.

17. Lefebure, *The Buddha & The Christ*, 160.

and powerful. In this regard, *theologia crucis* refers to the replacement of an old Athens with a new Jerusalem, a deconstruction of metaphysical onto-theology in expectation of the eschatology of a Jew, a slain Lamb. It has nomadic joy with the suffering, but with sociality and responsibility to others. It is not concerned about totalizing or repressing other voices and differences into one universal metanarrative, but recognizes the different as different.

Therefore, an Asian post-confessional theology in postmodern context not only reads scriptures, but also reads the wisdom of the world religions and makes a concerted effort to discern and listen to God's all-embracing reality of love and compassion manifest in Christ for the world. This is constitutive of a hermeneutics of otherness, the ésprit of which characterizes humility and *Anfechtungen* coming from our remembering God's otherness. God's revelation comes as the divine truth to us, but human understanding of it remains partial and provisional. God is not absent from the cross, because one does not speak ("My God, my God, why hast thou forsaken me?") to one who does not exist there. God in a form of crucifixion appears to be a stranger, that is, otherness of God. For Luther, the otherness of God, the hidden God always manifests Godself in the divine other in the concrete and particular place. Rejecting the other is a denial of God's manifestation in the other.

The divine other who assumed the condition of a slave indicates God's all-embracing love. A postmodern theology of embrace calls for a turning to the other, a participation and recognition in the otherness of the Other, in which the totalizing power of domination and exclusion must be scattered and broken. As in the story of the prodigal son in Luke 15, we make note of the sin of the elder brother who rejected an embrace and has a lack of compassion; he is incapable of embracing the otherness of the prodigal younger brother. Exclusion of the other is a denial of God's *Mahakaruna* for the others.

Luther sees Jesus' dereliction through his descent into hell. The logic of hell is integrated and taken up into the wounded heart of God in the trinitarian life. The humanity of Jesus of Nazareth is the humanity of God, so the death of Jesus is in God's passion. Jesus enters the human predicament and he experiences abandonment by God. Nevertheless, the crucified Christ, in the midst of the sufferings of his agony still experiences the beautifying vision of God: "Father, into your hands I commend my spirit" (Luke 23:46). This is the last hope of Christ and his minjung. Even when

God is absent to our senses, God can be at our nearest. This is the *experimentum crucis.* In the experience of the crucified Christ, an aesthetic of suffering has a spirituality of *anthropologia crucis* in which we meet God's inseparability from his people. Suffering becomes meaningful when it is seen in the light of the event of Easter. The final transfiguration of our suffering comes from the crucified one who is risen bearing in his glory the stigmata of his Passion. *Theologia crucis* does not reject *anthropologia gloriae,* but strengthens it to remain in eschatological hope and in praise of the slain Lamb of God. This doxology of a *theologia crucis* shares with others who follow Jesus' emptying way in other traditions. He lives today from the future fulfillment of God's promises—when an existence of lowest of the low is accepted.

God the victim in Jesus Christ remains a scandal to mimetic desire related to the violence of others or craving related to *dukkha.* The real meaning of the resurrection is encountered in following the footsteps of Christ in face of the culture of violence. Christ abolished the curse of violence and death and established peace and reconciliation with God. Jesus remains a stumbling block to our complacent self-satisfaction. He is a divine Brother and Sister with the minjung of folly, and thus, is in solidarity with their way of bearing the sin of the wise in the world, that is, the exploitation and violence of those in power and privilege. After all, "the stone that the builders rejected has become the chief cornerstone" (Ps 118:22; Luke 20:17).

Bibliography

Primary Sources

Luther, Martin. *D. M. Luthers Werke: Kritische Gesamtausgabe*. 61 vols. Weimar: Hermann Böhlaus Nachfolger, 1883–1983.

———. *D. Martin Luthers Werke: Kritische Gesamtausgabe, Tischreden*. 6 vols. Weimar: Hermann Böhlaus Nachfolger, 1912–1921.

———. *D. Martin Luther Evangelien-Auslegung*. Edited by Erwin Muhlhaupt. Göttingen: Vandenhoeck & Ruprecht, 1961.

———. *The Bondage of the Will*. Translated by J. I. Packer and O. R. Johnson. Westwood, NJ: Revell, 1957.

———. "Dear Christians, One and All, Rejoice." In *Lutheran Book of Common Worship*, Hymn no. 299. Minneapolis: Augsburg, 1978.

———. *Luther's Works*, American edition. Vol. 1–30, edited by Jaroslav Pelikan. St. Louis: Concordia, 1955–1967. Vols. 31–55, edited by Helmut T. Lehmann. Philadelphia: Fortress, 1955–1986.

Secondary Sources

Abe, Masao. *Zen and Western Thought*. Edited by William R. Lafleur. Honolulu: University of Hawaii Press, 1993.

———. *Buddhism and Interfaith Dialogue*. Edited by S. Heine. Honolulu: University of Hawaii Press, 1995.

Adorno, Theodor W. *Aesthetic Theory*. Translated and edited by Robert Hullot-Kentor. Minneapolis: University of Minnesota Press, 1997.

Ahn, Byung-Mu. *Draussen vor dem Tor: Kirche und Minjung in Korea*. Edited by W. Glüer. Göttingen: Vandenhoeck & Ruprecht, 1986.

Althaus, Paul. *The Theology of Martin Luther*. Translated by R. S. Schultz. Philadelphia: Fortress, 1979.

Altmann, Walter. *Luther and Liberation: A Latin American Perspective*. Translated by Mary M. Solberg. Minneapolis: Fortress, 1992.

Alves, R. *A Theology of Human Hope*. Washington DC: Corpus, 1969.

Amaladoss, M. *Life in Freedom: Liberation Theologies from Asia*. Maryknoll: Orbis, 1997.

Anderson, Gerald H. and Thomas F. Stranski, eds. *Christ's Lordship and Religious Pluralism*. Maryknoll: Orbis, 1981.

Anderson, C., A. Martin Ritter, K. Wesel, E. Mühlenberg, and M. A. Schmidt. *Handbuch der Dogmen und Theologiegeschichte* Bd.1. Göttingen: Vandenhoeck & Ruprecht, 1988.

Asheim, Ivar. *Glaube und Erziehung bei Luther: Ein Beitrag zur Geschichte des Verhältnisses in Theologie und Pädagogik*. Pädagogische Forschungen 17. Heidelberg: Quelle und Meyer, 1961.

Auerbach, Erich. *Mimesis: The Representation of Reality in Western Litreature.* Princeton: Princeton University Press, 2003.

Balthasar, Hans Urs von. *Seeing the Form*. Vol. 1, *The Glory of the Lord: A Theological Aesthetics*. Translated by Erasmo Leiva-Merikakis. San Francisco: Ignatius, 1982.

Barber, Michael D. *Ethical Hermeneutics: Rationality in Enrique Dussel's Philosophy of Liberation.* New York: Fordham University Press, 1998.

Barbour, Ian G. *Religion and Science: Historical and Contemporary Issues*. San Francisco: Harper, 1990.

———. *When Science meets Religion*. San Francisco: Harper, 2000.

Barth, Karl. *Kirchliche Dogmatik.* 13 vols. Munich: Kaiser, 1932. Reprinted, Zurich: Evangelischer, 1938–1965.

———. *Church Dogmatics*. Edited by G. W. Bromiley and T. F. Torrance. 13 vols. Edinburgh: T. & T. Clark, 1956–1977.

———. *Evangelische Theologie im 19. Jahrhundert.* Theologische Studien 49. Zürich: Evangelischer, 1957.

———. *Die christliche Dogmatik im Entwurf.* Munich: Kaiser, 1927.

———. *The Humanity of God.* Translated by J. Thomas and T. Wieser. London: Collins, 1967.

———. *Gespräche* 1964–1968. Edited by Eberhard Busch. Zürich: Theologischer, 1997.

———. "Vergangenheit und Zukunft: Friedrich Nauman und Christoph Blumhardt." In *Anfänge der dialecktischen Theologie*, edited by Jürgen Moltmann, 37–49. Munich: Kaiser, 1962.

Bauckham, Richard. *The Theology of Jüren Moltmann*. Edinburgh: T. & T. Clark, 1995.

Bauma-Prediger, Steve. *The Greening of Theology: The Ecological Models of Rosemary Ruether, Joseph Sittler and Jürgen Moltmann*. Atlanta: Scholars, 1995.

Bayer, Oswald. *Schöpfung als Anrede: Zu einer Hermeneutik der Schöpfung*. Tübingen: Mohr, 1986.

Benne, Robert, "Lutheran Ethics: Perennial Themes and Contemporary Challenges." In *The Promise of Lutheran Ethics*, edited by Karen L. Bloomquist and John R. Stumme, 24–25. Minneapolis, MN: Fortress, c1998.

Bennett, John C., ed. *Christian Social Ethics in a Changing World.* New York: Association, 1966.

Berrigan, Daniel and Thich Nhat Hanh. *The Raft is Not the Shore*. Boston: Beacon, 1975.

Bettenson, Henry. *Documents of the Christian Church*. 2nd ed. London: Oxford University Press, 1963.

Bloch, Ernst. *The Principle of Hope*. Translated by N. Plaice and P. Knight. Oxford: Blackwell, 1986.

Bloom, Alfred. *Shinran's Gospel of Pure Grace*. Tuscan: University of Arizona Press, 1965.

Bloomquist, Karren L., and John R. Stumme, eds. *The Promise of Lutheran Ethics*. Minneapolis: Fortress, 1998.

Boff, Leonardo, "Lutero entre la reforma y la liberacion." *Revista Latinoamericana de Teologia* (January–April 1984) 83–101.

———. *Trinity and Society.* Translated by Paul Burns. Maryknoll, New York: Orbis, 1988.

Bonhoeffer, Dietrich. *Act and Being: Transcendental Philosophy and Ontology in Systematic Theology*. Edited by W. W. Floyd Jr. Translated by H. Martin Rumscheidt. Minneapolis: Fortress, 1996.

———. "Dein Reich Komme." In *Gesammelte Schriften* 3. Munich: Kaiser, 1960.

———. *Letters and Papers from Prison*. Edited by Eberhard Bethge. Translated by Reginald H. Fuller. Revised by Francis Clarke et al. New York: Macmillian, 1972.

———. *Ethik*. Edited by Eberhard Bethge. Munich: Kaiser, 1963.

Bonino, J. M. *Toward a Christian Political Ethics*. Philadelphia: Fortress, 1983.

———. *Doing Theology in a Revolutionary Situation*. Philadelphia: Fortress, 1975.

Bornkamm, Heinrich. *Luther's World of Thought*. Translated by Martin Bertram. St. Louis: Concordia, 1958.

Braaten, Carl. *Eschatology and Ethics*. Minneapolis: Augsburg, 1974.

———. *Principles of Lutheran Theology*. Philadelphia: Fortress, 1983.

———. "The Place of Christianity Among the World Religions: Wolfhart Pannenberg's Theology of Religion and the History of Religions." In *The Theology of Wolfhart Pannenberg: Twelve American Critiques, with an Autobiographical Essay and Response*, edited by Carl E. Braaten and Robert Jenson. Minneapolis: Augsburg, 1988.

Braaten, Carl, and Robert Jenson, eds. *Christian Dogmatics*. Philadelphia: Fortress, 1984.

———. eds. *Union with Christ: The New Finnish Interpretation of Luther*. Grand Rapids: Eerdmans, 1998.

Braaten, Carl, and Philip Clayton, eds. *The Theology of Wolfhart Pannenberg: Twelve American Critiques, with an Autobiographical Essay and Response*. Minneapolis: Augsburg, 1988.

Bracken, Jospeh A., SJ, and M. H. Suchocki, eds. *Trinity in Process: A Relational Theology of God*. New York: Continuum, 1997.

Brecht, Martin. *Martin Luther: His Road to Reformation, 1483–1521*. Translated by James L. Schaaf. Philadelphia: Fortress, 1985.

———. *Martin Luther: Shaping and Defining the Reformation, 1521–1532*. Translated by James L. Schaaf. Philadelphia, Fortress, 1994.

———. *Martin Luther: The Preservation of the Church, 1532–1546*. Translated by James L. Schaaf. Minneapolis: Fortress, 1999.

Brown, Robert M. *Gustavo Gutiérrez: An Introduction to Liberation Theology*. Maryknoll, New York: Orbis, 1997.

Busch, E. *Karl Barth: His Life from Letters and Autobiographical Texts*. Philadelphia: Fortress, 1976.

Calvin, John. *Institutes of the Christina Religion*. Vols. 20–21, Library of Christian Classics. Edited by John T. McNeil. Translated by Ford Lewis Battles. Philadelphia: Westminster, 1960.

Childs, James M., Jr., "Ethics and the Promise." *The Promise of Lutheran Ethics* 100.

Choen, Samuel, "Filling the Gap in the Story of Lot's Wife (Genesis 19:1–29)." *Asia Journal of Theology* 15, no. 1 (April 2001).

Christenson, Larry, ed. *Welcome Holy Spirit*. Minneapolis: Augsburg, 1987.

Chung, Paul. *Karl Barth und die Hegelsche Linke*. Bern: Peter Lang, 1994.

———. *Spirituality and Social Ethics in John Calvin: A Pneumatological Perspective*. Lanham: University Press of America, 2000.

———. "Karl Barth and Inter-religious Dialogue: An Attempt to Bring Karl Barth to Dialogue with Religious Pluralism." *Asian Journal of Theology* 15, no. 2 (2001) 232–46.

Churchill, Steven L., "This Lovely Music of Nature: Grounding an Ecological Ethics in Martin Luther's Creation Mysticism." *Currents in Theology and Mission* 26, no. 3 (June 1999) 183–95.

Clausert, Dieter. *Theologischer Zeitbegriff und Politisches Zeitbewusstsein in Karl Barths Dogmatik dargestellt am Beispiel der Prolegomena*. Munich: Kaiser, 1982.

Coates, Harper Havelock, and Ryugaku Ishizuka. *Honen: The Buddhist Saint*. Kyoto: Chionin, 1925. Reprint, New York: Garland, 1981.

Cobb, John B. Jr. *Christ in a Pluralistic Age*. Louisville: Westminster John Knox, 1975.

———. *Beyond Dialogue: Toward a Mutual Transformation of Christianity and Buddhism*. Philadelphia: Fortress, 1982.

———. "Beyond 'Pluralism.'" In *Christian Uniqueness Reconsidered*, edited by Gavin D' Costa, 81–95. Marynoll: Orbis, 1996.

———. "The Religions." In *Christian Theology: An Introduction to Its Traditions and Tasks*, edited by Peter C. Hodgson and Robert H. King. Philadelphia: Fortress, 1985.

———. *Transforming Christianity and the World: A Way beyond Absolutism and Relativism*. Maryknoll: Orbis, 1999.

Cobb, John B. Jr., and Christpher Ives, eds. *The Emptying God: A Buddhist–Jewish–Christian Conversation*. Maryknoll, New York: Orbis, 1998.

Cobb, John B. Jr., and David R. Griffin. *Process Theology: An Introductory Exposition*. Louisville: Westminster John Knox, 1976.

Cochrane, Arthur C. *The Church's Confession under Hitler*. Philadelphia: Westminster, 1962.

Connor, Steven. *Postmodernist Culture*. Oxford: Basil Blackwell, 1989.

Davies, Brian. *The Thought of Thomas Aquinas*. Oxford: Clarendon, 1993.

D'Costa, Gavin, ed. *Christian Uniqueness Reconsidered: The Myth of a Pluralistic Theology of Religions*. Faith Meets Faith Series in Interreligious Dialogue. Maryknoll: Orbis, 1996.

———. *Theology and Religious Pluralism: The Challenge of Other Religions*. Oxford: Basil Blackwell, 1986.

Deferrari, R. *Saint Basil. The Letters*. New York: Putnam's, 1926.

Deleuze, Gilles and Félix Guattari, *Anti-Oedipus, Capitalism and Schizophrenia*. London: Athlone, 1984.

Demarest, Bruce. *General Revelation: Historical Views and Contemporary Issues*. Grand Rapids: Zondervan, 1982.

De Las Casas, Bartolomé. *The Devastation of the Indies: A Brief Account*. Translated by Herma Briffault. Baltimore and London: The Johns Hopkins University Press, 1992.

Diem, Hermann, "Karl Barth as Socialist: Controversy over a New Attempt to Understand Him." In *Karl Barth and Radical Politics*, edited and translated by George Hunsinger. Philadelphia: Westminster, 1976.

Dillenberger, John, ed. *John Calvin: Selections from His Writings*. Bozeman, MT: Scholars, 1975.

Dupuis, Jacques, SJ, *Toward a Christian Theology of Religious Pluralism*. Maryknoll: Orbis, 1997.

Duchrow, Ulrich. *Global Economy: A Confessional Issue for the Churches?* Translated by David Lewis. Geneva, Switzerland: WCC, 1987.

———. *Weltwirtschft—heute: Ein Feld für Bekennende Kirche*? Munich: Kaiser, 1986.

Dumoulin, Heinrich. *Understanding Buddhism: Key Themes*. Translated by Joseph S. O'Leary. New York: Weatherhill, 1994.

Eagleson, John. *Christians and Socialism*. Maryknoll: Orbis, 1975.

Farley, Wendy. *Tragic Vision and Divine Compassion*. Louisville: Westminster John Knox, 1990.

Flannery, Austin, O.P., ed. *Vatican Council II. The Conciliar and Post Conciliar Documents*. Dublin: Dominican, 1975.

Forde, Charles E., "Dietrich Bonhoeffer, the Resistance, and the Two Kingdoms." *Lutheran Forum* 27, no. 3 (Augus 1993) 28–34.

Ford, Lewis S. *The Lure of God*. Philadelphia: Fortress, 1978.

Forde, Gerhard O. *Justification by Faith: A Matter of Death and Life*. Pennsylvania: Sigler, 1990.

Foucault, M. *Power/Knowledge: Selected Interviews & Other Writings, 1972–1977*. Edited by Collin Gordon. New York: Pantheon, 1972.

Frankforter. *The Theologia Germanica of Martin Luther*. Translated by Bengt Hoffman. New York: Paulist, 1980.

Gadamer, H. G. *Philosophical Hermeneutics*. Translated and edited by David E. Linge. Berkeley: University of California Press, 1976.

———. *Truth and Method*. 2d ed. Translated by Joel Weinsheimer and Donald G. Marshall. New York: Crossroad, 1989.

———. *Wahrheit und Methode: Grundzüge einer philosophischen Hermeneutik*. Tübingen: Mohr/Siebeck, 1960.

Galling, Kurt, ed. *Die Religion in Geschichte und Gegenwart: Handwörterbuch fur Theologie und Religionswissenschaft*. 3rd ed. 6 vols. Tübingen: Mohr/Siebeck, 1957–1965.

García-Rivera, Alejandro. *The Community of the Beautiful: A Theological Aesthetics*. Minnesota: Liturgical, 1999.

Gäbler, Ulrich. *Huldrych Zwingli: Leben und Werk*. Munich: Beck, 1983.

Gendle, Nicholas. *Gregory Palamas: The Triads*. Translated and edited by John Meyendorf. Ramsey, NJ: Paulist, 1983.

Girard, René. *Things Hidden Since the Foundation of the World*. Translated by Stephen Bann and Michael Metteer. Stanford, CA: Stanford University Press, 1987.

Goertz, Hans-Jürgen. *Thomas Müntzer: Mystiker, Apokalyptiker, Revolutionär*. Munich: Beck, 1989.

Gollwitzer, Helmut. *Reich Gottes und Sozialismus bei Karl Barth*. Munich: Kaiser, 1972.

———. *Krummes Holz—Aufrechter Gang: Zur Frage nach dem Sinn des Lebens*. Munich: Kaiser, 1970.

———. *Befreiung zur Solidarität: Einführung in die Evangelische Theologie* Munich: Kaiser, 1984.

Gomez, Luis O. *Land of Bliss: The Paradise of the Buddha of Measureless Light*. Honolulu: University of Hawaii Press, 1996.

González, Justo L. *A History of Christian Thought: From the Beginning to the Council of Chalcedon*. Vol. 1. Nashville: Abingdon, 1970.

Grenz, Stanley J. *A Primer on Postmodernism*. Grand Rapids: Eerdmans, 1996.

Grieve, Wolfgang, ed. *LWF Studies: Communion, Community, Society: The Relevance of the Church*. Geneva: The Lutheran World Federation Department for Theology and Studies, 1998.

Gritsch, Eric W., ed. *Encounters with Luther: Colloquia, 1985–1989*, vol. 4. Gettysburg: Institute for Luther Studies, 1990.

———. *Thomas Müntzer: A Tragedy of Errors*. Minneapolis: Fortress, 1989.

Gutiérrez, Gustavo, "Liberating Praxis and Christian Faith." In *Frontiers of Theology in Latin America*, edited by Rosine Gibellini. Translated by John Drury. Maryknoll: Orbis, 1974.

———. *A Theology of Liberation*. Maryknoll, New York: Orbis, 1973.

———. *The Power of the Poor in History.* Maryknoll: Orbis, 1984.

Habermas. J. *The Philosophical Discourse of Modernity: Twelve Lectures*. Translated by Frederick G. Lawrence. Cambridge, MA: MIT Press, 1987.

Haight, Roger. "The Point of Trinitarian Theology." *Toronoto Journal of Theology* 4, no. 2 (Fall 1988), 191–204.

Hanh, Thich Nhat. *The Heart of Understanding: Commentaries on the Prajnaparamita Heart Sutra*. Edited by Peter Lewitt. Berkeley, CA: Parallax, 1988.

Harvey, Peter. *An Introduction to Buddhist Ethics*. Cambridge: Cambridge University Press, 2000.

Hegel G. W. *Lectures on the Philosophy of Religion, III*. Edited by Peter C. Hodgson. Translated by R. Brown, P. Hodgson, and J. Stewart. Berkeley: University of California Press, 1984.

———. *Phänomenologie des Geistes*. Edited by Johannes Hoffmeister. Hamburg: Meiner, 1952.

Hennelly, Alfred T., SJ, *Liberation Theologies: The Global Pursuit of Justice*. Mystic, CT: Twenty-Third, 1995.

Heron, Alasdair I. C. *The Holy Spirit in the Bible, the History of Christian Thought, and Recent Theology*. Philadelphia: Westminster, 1983.

———. *Table and Tradition*. Philadelphia: Westminster, 1983.

Hick, John. *God and the Universe of Faith*. New York: Macmillan, 1973.

Hick, John, and B. Hebblethwaite, eds. *Christianity and Other Religions*. London: Collins, 1980.

Hick, John, and Paul Knitter, eds. *The Myth of Christian Uniqueness: Towards a Pluralistic Theology of Religions*. Maryknoll, New York: Orbis, 1987.

Hodgson, Peter C., and Robert H. King, eds. *Christian Theology: An Introduction to Its Traditions and Tasks*. Philadelphia: Fortress, 1985.

Hoffman, Bengt R. *Luther and the Mystics: A Re-examination of Luther's Spiritual Experience and His Relationship to the Mystics*. Minneapolis: Augsburg, 1976.

———. ed. *Theologia Germanica of Martin Luther.* New York: Paulist, 1980.

Honda, Masaaki, "The Encounter of Christianity with the Buddhist Logic of Soku: An Essay in Topological Theology." In *Buddhist-Christian Dialogue: Mutual Renewal and Transformation*, edited by Paul O. Ingram and Frederick J. Streng. Honolulu: University of Hawaii Press, 1986.

Hood, Robert E. *Contemporary Political Orders and Christ: Karl Barth's Christology and Political Praxis*. Allison Park, PA: Pickwick, 1985.

Horowitz, Adalbert, ed. *Briefwechsel des Beatus Rhenamus*. Leipzig: Teubner, 1886.

Houlgate, Stephen. *The Hegel Reader.* Oxford: Blackwell, 1998.

Hunsinger, George. *Disruptive Grace: Studies in the Theology of Karl Barth*. Grand Rapids: Eerdmans, 2000.

———. *How to Read Karl Barth; The Shape of His Theology*. New York: Oxford University Press, 1991.

———. "Karl Barth and Liberation Theology." In *Disruptive Grace*, by George Hunsinger, 42–59. Grand Rapids: Eerdmans, 2000.

Hütter, Reinhard, "The Twofold Center of Lutheran Ethics: Christian Freedom and God's Commandments." *The Promise of Lutheran Ethics* 40 (1998) 31–54.

———. ed. and trans. *Karl Barth and Radical Politics*. Philadelphia: Westminster, 1976.

Ingram, Paul O., and Fredrick J. Streng, eds. *Buddhist-Christian Dialogue: Mutual Renewal and Transformation*. Honolulu: University of Hawaii Press, 1986.

Ives, Christopher, ed. *Divine Emptiness and Historical Fullness: A Buddhist-Jewish-Christian Conversation with Massao Abe*. Valley Forge, PA: Trinity, 1995.

Iwand, Hans J. *Luthers Theologie*. Edited by Helmut Gollwitzer, et al. Vol. 5, *Nachgelassene Werke*. Munich: Kaiser, 1983.

Jansen, Reiner. *Studien zu Luthers Trinitätslehre*. Frankfurt: Peter Lang, 1976.

Jenson, Robert, "Jesus in the Trinity: Wolfhart Pannenberg's Christology and the Doctrine of the Trinity." In *The Theology of Wolfhart Pannenberg*, edited by Carl E. Braaten and Philip Clayton. Minneapolis, MN: Augsburg, 1988.

Jüngel, Eberhard. *The Doctrine of Trinity: God's Being is Becoming*. Grand Rapids: Eerdmans, 1976.

———. *God as the Mystery of the World*. Grand Rapids: Eerdmans, 1983.

———. *Indikative der Gnade—Imperative der Freiheit: Theologische Erörterungen IV.* Tübingen: Mohr, 2000.

Kamppuri, Hannu, ed. *Dialogue Between Neighbors: The Theological Conversations between the Evangelical-Lutheran Church of Finland and the Russian Orthodox Church 1970–1986.* Helsinki: Luther-Agricola Society, 1986.

Keel, Hee-Sung. *Understanding Shinran: A Dialogical Approach*. Freemont, CA: Asian Humanities, 1995.

Kelley, J. N. D. *Early Christian Doctrines*. New York: Harper & Row, 1978.

Kim Hee-Jin. *Dogen Kigen—Mystical Realist*. Tucson: University of Arizona Press, , 1975.

Kim Jong-Won. "Daisetz T. Suzuki and Paul J. Tillich: A Comparative Study of Their Thoughts on Ethics in Relation to Being." ThD diss., Graduate Theological Union, Berkeley, CA, 1973.

Kim Kyoung-Jae. *Christianity and the Encounter of Asian Religions: Method of Correlation, Fusion of Horizons, and Paradigm Shifts in the Korean Grafting Process*. Uitgeverij Boekencentrum: Zoetermeer, 1994.

Kinnamon, Michael, ed. *Signs of the Spirit: Official Report of the Seventh Assembly*. Grand Rapids: Eerdmanns, 1991.

Kitamori, Kazoh. *Theology of the Pain of God*. Richmond, VA: John Knox, 1965.

Kittelson, James M. *Luther: The Reformer*. Minneapolis: Augsburg, 1986.

Klappert, Bertold. *Israel und die Kirche: Erwägungen zur Israellehre Karl Barths*. Munich: Kaiser, 1980.

———. *Die Auferweckung des Gekreuzigten: Der Ansatz der Christologies im Zusammenhang der Christologie der Gegenwart*. Neukirchen: Neukirchener, 1981.

Kraus, Hans J. *Reich Gottes: Reich der Freiheit. Grundriss Systematischer Theologie*. Neukirchen-Vluyn: Neukirchener, 1975.

———. *Systematische Theologie im Kontext Biblisher Geschichte und Eschatologie*. Neukirchen-Vluyn: Neukirchener, 1983.

Knitter, Paul. *No Other Name? A Critical Survey of Christian Attitudes toward the World Religions*. Maryknoll: Orbis, 1985.

———. *One Earth Many Religions: Multifaith Dialogue & Global Responsibility*. Maryknoll: Orbis, 1996.

Koch, Gerhard Hans. *Luthers Reformation in Kommunistischer Sicht*. Stuttgart: Quelle-Verlag Stuttgart, 1967.

Kolb, Robert, and Wengert Timothy J., eds. *The Book of Concord: The Confessions of the Evangelical Lutheran Church*. Minneapolis: Fortress, 2000.

Kröger, W. "Befreiung des Minjung: Das Profil einer protestantischen Befreiungstheologie für Asien in ökumenischer Perspektive." *Ökumenische Existenz Heute* 10. Munich: Kaiser, 1992.

Krusche, Werner. *Das Werken des Heiligen Geistes nach Calvin.* Göttingen: Vandenhoeck & Ruprecht, 1975.

Küng, Hans. "Christianity and World Religions: Dialogue with Islam." In *Toward a Universal Theology of Religion*, edited by Leonard Swindler. Maryknoll: Orbis, 1987.

———. *Does God Exist? An Answer for Today.* Translated by Edward Quinn. New York: Vintage, 1981.

———. *Justification: The Doctrine of Karl Barth and a Catholic Reflection.* Philadelphia: Westminster, 1981.

LaCugna, C. M. *God for Us: The Trinity & Christian Life.* San Francisco: Harper & Row, 1991.

Lazareth, William H., "Luther's Two Kingdoms Ethics Reconsidered." In *Christian Social Ethics in a Changing World*, edited by John C. Bennett. New York: Association, 1966.

Lee, Jung-Young. *The Trinity in Asian Perspective.* Nashville: Abingdon, 1996.

Lefebure, Leo D. *The Buddha & The Christ: Exploration in Buddhist and Christian Dialogue.* Maryknoll: Orbis, 1993.

Lehming, H., J. L. Walter, M. Loerbroks, and R. van der Vest. *Wendung nach Jerusalem: Friedrich-Wilhelm Marquardts Theologie im Gespräch.* Gütersloh: Kaiser and Gütersloher, 1999.

Leith, John H. *Creeds of the Churches: A Reader in Christian Doctrine from the Bible to the Present.* Louisville: John Knox, 1982.

Levinas, Emmanuel. *Otherwise than Being.* The Hague: Martinus Nijhoff, 1981.

———. *Die Spur des Anderen.* Alber-Broschure Philosophie Series. Translated by Wolfgang Nikolaus Krewaui. Freiburg: Alber, 1983.

Lienhard, Marc. *Luther: Witness to Jesus Christ.* Translated by J. A. Bouman. Minneapolis: Augsburg, 1982.

Lindbeck, Carter. *Beyond Charity: Reformation Initiatives for the Poor.* Minneapolis: Fortress, 1933.

Loader, J. A. *A Tale of Two Cities: Sodom and Gomorrah in the Old Testament. Early Jewish and Early Christian Traditions.* Edited by T.J. Barrda and A. S. Van der Woude. Netherlands: Kok, 1990.

Lochman. J. M. *The Faith We Confess: An Ecumenical Dogmatics.* Translated by David Lewis. Philadelphia: Fortress, 1973.

———. *Living Roots of Reformation.* Minneapolis: Augsburg, 1979.

———. *Unser Vater: Auslegung des Vaterunsers.* Gütersloh: Gütersloher, 1988.

———. *The Lord's Prayer.* Translated by Goeffrey W. Bromiley. Grand Rapids: Eerdmans, 1990.

Loewenich, Walther von. *Luther's Theology of the Cross.* Translated by Herbert Bouman. Minneapolis: Augsburg, 1982.

Löwith, Karl. *From Hegel to Nietzsche: The Revolution in Nineteenth Century Thought.* Translated by David E. Green. New York: Holt, Rinehart and Winston, 1964.

Lohse, Bernhard. *Martin Luther's Theology: Its Historical and Systematic Development.* Translated and edited by Roy A. Harrisville. Minneapolis: Fortress, 1999.

Lossky, Vladimir. *The Mystical Theology of the Eastern Church.* London: James Clarke, 1957.

Lukács Georg. *The Destruction of Reason.* Translated by Peter Palmer. London: Merlin, 1980.

Lull, Timothy F., ed. *Martin Luther's Basic Theological Writings.* Minneapolis: Fortress, 1989.

———. *My Conversations with Martin Luther*. Minneapolis: Augsburg, 1999.

Lyotard, Jean-Francois. *The Postmdoern Condition: A Report on Knowledge*. Minneapolis: University of Minnesota Press, 1984.

Macchia, Frank D. "The Spirit Set Us Free: Implications in Pentecostal Theology For A Pneumatological Soteriology." Paper presented at the AAR/SBL meeting, Denver, 2001.

Maimela, Simon S., "The Twofold Kingdoms: An African Perspective." *Theology and the Black Experience*, 105–6

Mannermaa, T. *Der im Glauben gegenwärtig Christus*. Hannover: Lutherisches, 1989.

Markschies, C., and Trowitsch, M, eds. *Luther—Zwischen den Zeiten*. Tübingen: Mohr/ Siebeck, 1999.

Marquardt, F. W. *Das christliche Bekenntnis zu Jesus dem Juden: Eine Christologie*. Vol. 1. Munich: Kaiser, 1990.

———. "Gott oder Mammon: Theologie und Ökonomie bei Martin Luther." In *Einwürfe 1*. Munich: Kaiser, 1983.

———. *Theologie und Sozialismus: Das Beispiel Karl Barths*. Munich: Kaiser, 1972.

———. *Verwegenheiten: Theologische Stücke aus Berlin*. Munich: Kaiser, 1981.

———. *Was dürfen wir hoffen, wenn wir hoffen dürften?: Eine Eschatologie* Vol. 1.II.III. Munich: Kaiser and Gütersloher, 1993.

Marx. Karl, *Capital: A Critique of Political Economy*. Vol. 1. New York: Modern Library, 1906.

McGinn, Bernard. *The Foundation of Mysticism: Origins to the Fifth Century*. New York: Crossroad, 1994.

———. *The Mystical Thought of Meister Eckhart: The Man from Whom God hid Nothing*. New York: Crossroad, 2001.

McGrath, Alister E., "Forerunners of the Reformation? A Critical Examination of the Evidence for Precursors of the Reformation Doctrines of Justification." *Harvard Theological Review* 75, no. 2 (April 1982) 219–42.

———. *Iustitia Dei: A History of the Christian Doctrine of Justification*. Cambridge: Cambridge University Press, 1998.

———. *Martin Luther's Theology of the Cross*. Oxford: Blackwell, 1990.

———. *Reformation Thought: An Introduction*. Oxford: Blackwell, 1999.

McKenzie, Steven L., and Stephen R. Haynes, eds. *To Each Its Own Meaning: An Introduction to Biblical Criticisms and their Application*. Louisville, KY: Westminster John Knox, 1999.

Milner, Benjamin. *Calvin's Doctrine of the Church: Studies in the History of Christian Thought*. Leiden: Brill, 1970.

Mokrosch, Reinhold and Herbert Walz. *Mittelalter:* Vol. 2, *Kirchen-und Theologiegeschichte in Quellen*. Neukirchen: Neukirchener, 1989.

Moltmann, Jürgen, ed. *Anfänge der dialektischen Theologie I*. Munich: Kaiser, 1962.

———. *The Church in the Power of the Spirit: A Contribution to Messianic Ecclesiology.* Translated by Margaret Kohl. London: SCM, 1977.

———. *The Coming of God: Christian Eschatology.* Translated by Margaret Kohl. Minneapolis: Fortress 1996.

———. *The Crucified God: The Cross of Christ as The Foundation and Criticism of Christian Theology*. Translated by R. A. Wilson and John Bowden. Minneapolis: Fortress, 1993.

———. *Experiences in Theology: Ways and Forms of Christian Theology*. Translated by Margaret Kohl. Minneapolis: Fortress, 2000.

———. *God in Creation: An Ecological Doctrine of Creation.* Translated by Margaret Kohl. London: SCM, 1985.

———. *Gott in der Schöpfung: ökologische Schöpfungslehre.* Munich: Kaiser, 1985.

———. *History and the Triune God: Contributions to Trinitarian Theology.* New York: Crossroad, 1992.

———. "Is 'Pluralistic Theology' Useful for the Dialogue of World Religions?" In *Christian Uniqueness Reconsidered,* edited by Gavin D'Costa, 149–56. Maryknoll: Orbis, 1996.

———. *Kirche in der Kraft des Geistes: Ein Beitrag zur messianischen Ekklesiologie.* Munich: Kaiser, 1975.

———. "The Logic of Hell." In *God will be All in All: The Eschatology of Jürgen Moltmann,* edited by Richard Bauckham.

———. *Politische Theologie, Politische Ethik.* Munich: Kaiser, 1984.

———. *The Spirit of Life: A Universal Affirmation.* Translated by Margaret Kohl. Minneapolis: Fortress, 1992.

———. *The Theology of Hope: On the Ground and the Implications of a Christian Eschatology.* Minneapolis: Fortress Press, 1993.

———. *The Trinity and the Kingdom of God: The Doctrine of God.* Transated by Margaret Kohl. London: SCM, 1981.

———. *The Way of Jesus Christ: Christology in Messianic Dimensions.* Translated by Margaret Kohl. London: SCM, 1990.

———. *Der Weg Jesu Christi: Christologie in messianischen Dimensionen.* Munich: Kaiser, 1989.

Nam-Dong, Suh. "Converging of the Two Stories." In *Christianity and the Encounter of Asian Religions,* by Kim Kyoung-Jae. Zoetermeer: Uitgeverij Boekencentrum, 1994

———. "Historical Reference for a Theology of Minjung, in *Minjung Theology.*" In *Christianity and the Encounter of Asian Religions,* by Kim Kyoung-Jae. Zoetermeer, Uitgeverij Boekencentrum, 1994

Ngien, Dennis. *The Suffering of God According to Martin Luther's 'Theologia Crucis.'* New York: Peter Lang, 1995.

Niebuhr, H. Richard. *The Meaning of Revelation.* New York: Macmillian, 1941.

Nisker, Wes. *Buddha's Nature: Evolution as a Practical Guide to Enlightenment.* New York: Bantam, 1998.

Oberman, Heiko A. *The Dawn of the Reformation: Essays in Late Medieval and Early Reformation Thought.* Edinburgh: T. & T. Clark, 1986.

———. *Luther: Man Between God and the Devil.* Translated by E. W. Schwarzbart. Doubleday: Image, 1992.

Palmer, Richard E. *Hermeneutics: Interpretation Theory in Schleiermacher, Dilthey, Heidegger, and Gadamer.* Evanston: Northwestern University Press, 1969.

Pangritz, Andreas. *Karl Barth in the Theology of Dietrich Bonhoeffer.* Translated by Barbara and Martin Rumscheidt. Grand Rapids: Eerdmans, 2000.

Panikkar, R. *The Intra-religious Dialogue.* New York: Paulist, 1978.

———. "The Jordan, The Tiber, and The Ganges: Three Kairological Moments of Christic Self-Consciousness." In *The Myth of Christian Uniqueness: Towards a Pluralistic Theology of Religions,* edited by John Hick and Paul Knitter. Marynoll: Orbis, 1996.

———. *The Trinity and the Religious Experience of Man.* New York: Orbis, 1973.

———. *The Trinity and World Religions.* Madras: The Christian Literature Society, 1970.

———. *The Unknown Christ of Hinduism.* Maryknoll, New York: Orbis, 1964.

———. *The Unknown Christ of Hinduism: Towards an Ecumenical Christo-phany*. Rev. ed. London: Darton, Longman and Todd, 1981.

Pannenberg, Wolfart. *Jesus—God and Man*. Translated by Lewis L. Wilkens and Duane A. Prieve. Philadelphia: Westminster, 1968.

———. "Der Gott der Geschichte." *Kerygma und Dogma* 23 (1977) 76–92.

———. "Religious Pluralism and Conflicting Truth Claims: The Problem of a Theology of the World Religions. " In *Christian Uniqueness Reconsidered: The Myth of a Pluralistic Theology of Religions*, edited by Gavin D'Costa. Maryknoll: Orbis, 1996.

———. *Systematic Theology*, vol. 1. Translated by Geoffrey W. Bromiley. Grand Rapids: Eerdmans, 1984.

Park, Andrew S. *The Wounded Heart of God: The Asian Concept of Han and the Christian Doctrine of Sin*. Nashville: Abingdon, 1993.

Parkes, Graham, "Voices of Mountains, Trees, and Rivers: Kukai, Dogen, and a Deeper Theology." In *Buddhism and Ecology*, edited by M. E. Tucker and D. R. Williams. Cambridge, MA: Harvard University Center for the Study of World Religions, 1997.

Pederson, Ann. "Conversations Toward an Ongoing Lutheran Reformation." *Currents in Theology and Mission* 24, no. 1 (February 1997).

Pelikan, Jaroslav. *Jesus through the Centuries: His Place in the History of Culture*. New Haven: Yale University Press, 1999.

Pero, Alberto, and Ambrose Moyo, eds. *Theology and the Black Experience: The Lutheran Heritage Interpreted by African & African-American Theologians*. Minneapolis: Augsburg, 1988.

Peters, Ted. *God as Trinity: Relationality and Temporality in Divine Life*. Louisville: Westminster John Knox, 1993.

———. *God—The World's Future: Systematic Theology for a New Era*. 2nd. ed. Minneapolis: Fortress, 2000.

Petry, Ray C, ed. *Late Medieval Mysticism*. Philadelphia: Westminster, 1957.

Pickstock, Catherine. "Asyndeton: Syntas and Insanity. A Study of the Revision of the Nicene Creed." In *The Postmodern God: A Theological Reader*, edited by Graham Ward, 297–317. Oxford: Blackwell, 1997.

Pieris, Aloysius, SJ, *An Asian Theology of Liberation*. Maryknoll: Orbis, 1988.

———. "The Buddha and the Christ: Mediators of Liberation." In *The Myth of Christian Uniqueness: Towards a Pluralistic Theology of Religions*, edited by John Hick and Paul Knitter. Maryknoll: Orbis, 1987.

Pohlmann, G. Horst. *Abriss der Dogmatik: Ein Kompendium*. Gütersloh: Gütersloher Mohn, 1990.

Prabhu, Joseph, ed. *The Intercultural Challenge of Raimon Panikkar*. Maryknoll: Orbis, 1996.

Prenter, R. *Spiritus Creator: Luther's Concept of the Holy Spirit*. Philadelphia: Muhlenberg, 1953.

Price, Leo S. *Confucius and Christ: A Christian Estimate of Confucius*. New York: Philosophical Library, 1951.

Rahner, Karl. *The Trinity*. Translated by Joseph Donceel. New York: Crossroad, 1998.

———. *Foundations of Christian Faith*. New York: Seabury/Crossroad, 1978.

Rist, John M. *Augustine: Ancient Thought Baptized*. New York: Cambridge University Press, 1999.

Ruether, Rosemary, R. *Liberation Theology: Human Hope Confronts Christian History and American Power*. New York: Paulist, 1972.

Robinson, J. M. ed. *Theology as History*. New York: Macmillan, 1967.

Rodriguez, José David, "Theology from the Underside of History: The Perspective of Liberation Theology." Vol. 4, *Encounters with Luther: Lectures, Discussions and Sermons at the Martin Luther Colloquia*. Edited by Eric W. Gritsch. Gettysburg, PA: 1990.

Rupp, Gordon E., trans. *Luther and Erasmus: Free Will and Salvation*. Vol. 17, *Library of Christian Classics*. Philadelphia: Westminster, 1969.

Rusch, William G., and Daniel F. Martensen, eds. *The Leuenberg Agreement and Lutheran-Reformed Relationships: Evaluations by North American and European Theologians*. Minneapolis: Augsburg, 1989.

Samartha, Stanley, SJ, *Courage for Dialogue*. Maryknoll: Orbis, 1982.

Santmire, Paul H. *The Travail of Nature: The Ambiguous Ecological Promise of Christian Theology*. Minneapolis: Fortress, 1985.

———. *Nature Reborn: The Ecological and Cosmic Promise of Christian Theology*. Minneapolis: Fortress, 2000.

Sarup, Madan. *An Introductory Guide to Post-Structuralism and Postmodernism*. Athens: The University of Georgia Press, 1988.

Schleiermacher, Friedrich. *The Christian Faith*. Edited by H. R. Mackintosh and J. S. Stewart. Edinburgh: T. &. T. Clark, 1928.

Schwarz, Hans. *True Faith in the True God: An Introduction to Luther's Life and Thought*. Translated by Mark William Worthing. Minneapolis: Augsburg, 1996.

Schwarz, Reinhard. *Luther*. Göttingen: Vandenhoeck & Ruprecht, 1986.

Seong-Won, Park. "'You do not see the Forest for the Trees.' Asain Spirituality and Community." LWF Studies, *Communion, Community, Society* (Geneva: LWF, 1998).

Shaull, Richard. *The Reformation and Liberation Theology: Insights for the Challenges of Today*. Louisville, Kentucky: Westminster John Knox, 1991.

Sia, Santiago, ed. *Charles Hartshorne's Concept of God*. Dordrecht: Kluwer, 1990.

Sittler, Joseph A., "Called to Unity." *The Ecumenical Review* 14 (October–December 1961) 181.

Smith, Wilfred Cantwell. "The Christian in a Religiously Plural World." In *Christianity and Other Religions*, edited by John Hick and Brian Hebblethwaite. London: Collins, 1980.

Sobrino, Jon, SJ, *Christology at the Crossroads*. Edited and translated by Sister Caridad Inka and John Eagleson. Maryknoll: Orbis, 1973.

Sobrino, Jon, and Ignacio Ellacuria, eds. *Systematic Theology: Perspectives from Liberation Theology*. Maryknoll, New York: Orbis, 1996.

Song, C. S. *The Crucified People*. New York: Crossroad, 1990.

———. *Jesus and the Reign of God*. Minneapolis: Fortress: 1993.

———. *The Tears of Lady Meng: A Parable of People's Political Theology*. Geneva: World Council of Churches, 1981.

Sung-Bae, Park. *Buddhist Faith and Sudden Enlightenment*. Albany: State University of New York Press, 1983.

Suzuki, D. T. *Zen Buddhism and Its Influence on Japanese Culture*. Kyoto: Eastern Buddhist Society, 1938.

Swanson, Paul L. "The Spirituality of Emptiness in Early Chinese Buddhism." In *BS I*.

Swindler, Leonard, ed. *Toward a Universal Theology of Religion*. Maryknoll: Orbis, 1987.

Takizawa, Katsumi. *Reflexionen über die Grundlage von Buddhismus und Christentum*. Bern: Peter Lang, 1980.

———. "*Was hindert mich noch getauft zu werden.*" In *Das Heil im Heute: Texte einer japanischen Theologie*. Goetingen: Vandenhoeck & Ruprecht, 1987.

Tanner, Kathryn, *Theories of Culture: A New Agenda for Theology*. Minneapolis: Fortress, 1997.

Tappert, Theodore G., ed. and trans. *The Book of Concord: The Confessions of the Evangelical Lutheran Church*. Philadelphia: Fortress, 1959.

Thein-An, Thich. *Buddhism and Zen in Vietnam in Relation to the Development of Buddhism in Asia*. Edited by Carol Smith. Los Angeles: College of Oriental Studies, 1975.

Thomas, Aquinas. *Summa Theologica.* Translated by the English Dominican Fathers. New York: Benzinger, 1947.

Thomasius, Gottfried. *Christi Person und Werk*. In *Abriss der Dogmatik*, by Pohlmann, G. Horst. Gütersloh: Gütersloher Mohn, 1990.

Thompson, John. *Christ in Perspective: Christological Perspectives in the Theology of Karl Barth*. Grand Rapids: Eerdmans, 1987.

Thurian, Max. *The Mystery of the Eucharist: An Ecumenical Approach*. Translated by Emily Chisholm. Grand Rapids: Eerdmans, 1983.

———. ed. *Churches respond to BEM.* Vol. 2, *Official Responses to the "Baptism, Eucharist and Ministry" Text*. Geneva: WCC, 1986.

Tillich, Paul. *Christianity and the Encounter of World Religions*. Minneapolis: Fortress, 1994.

———. *Systematic Theology.* 3 vols. Chicago: University of Chicago Press, 1951–1963.

———. *Theology of Culture*. Edited by R. C. Kimball. New York: Oxford University Press, 1959.

Tracy, David. *The Analogical Imagination: Christian Theology and the Culture of Pluralism*. New York: Crossroad, 2000.

———. *Dialogue with the Other: The Inter-Religious Dialogue*. Grand Rapids: Eerdmans, 1990.

———. *Plurality and Ambiguity: Hermeneutics, Religion, Hope*. New York: Harper & Row, 1987.

Tucker, M. E., and D. R. Williams, eds. *Buddhism and Ecology*. Cambridge, MA: Harvard University Center for the Study of World Religions, 1997.

Vanhoozer, Kevin J., "Does the Trinity Belong in a Theology of Religions? On Angling in the Rubison and the 'Identity of God.'" In *The Trinity in a Pluralistic Age: Theological Essays on Culture and Religion*, edited by Kevin J. Vanhoozer, 41–71. Grand Rapids: Eerdmans, 1997.

———. ed. *The Trinity in a Pluralistic Age: Theological Essays on Culture and Religion.* Grand Rapids: Eerdmans, 1997.

Vischer, Lukas, ed. *Spirit of God Spirit of Christ; Ecumenical Reflections on the Filioque Controversy*. Geneva: WCC. 1980.

Volf, Miroslav. "Materiality of Salvation: An Investigation in the Soteriologies of Liberation and Pentecostal Theologies." *Journal of Ecumenical Studies* (Summer 1989) 437–67.

Ward, Graham, ed. *The Postmodern God: A Theological Reader*. Oxford: Blackwell, 1997.

Weber, Otto. *Grundlagen der Dogmatik II*. Neukirchen: Erziehungsvereins, 1987.

Wendel, F. *Calvin: Origin and Development of His Religious Thought*. Translated by Philip Mairet. Durham: Labyrinth, 1987.

Williams, George Husntson. *The Radical Reformation*. Kirksville: Truman State University Press, 2000.

Williams, Paul. *Mahayana Buddhism: The Doctrinal Foundations*. London: Routledge, 1989.

Willis, W. Waite, Jr. *Theism, Atheisim and the Doctrine of the Trinity: The Trinitarian Theologies of Karl Barth and Jürgen Moltmann in Response to Protest Atheism*. Atlanta: Scholars, 1987.

Wilson-Kastner, Patricia. *Faith, Feminism, and the Christ*. Philadelphia: Fortress, 1983.

Wingren Gustaf. *Credo: The Christian View of Faith and Life*. Translated by Edgar Marson. Minneapolis: Augsburg, 1981.

———. *Lutheran Vocation*. Translated by Carl C. Rasmussen. Philadelphia: Muhlenberg, 1957.

Yao, Xin-zhong. *An Introduction to Confucianism*. Cambridge: Cambridge University Press, 2000.

Yuen, Royan S. C. "Reading Lamentations 1 in Light of Qing-hen: A Rhetorical Analysis from a Chinese Perspective." In LWF Studies, *The Role and Interpretation of the Bible in the Life of the Church in China*. Vol. 3, China Study Series (June 1997) 114–27.

Zen Master Seung Sahn. *The Compass of Zen*. Edited by Hyon Gak Sunim. Boston: Shambhala, 1997.

Journals and Documents

The Constitution of the Presbyterian Church (U.S.A). Part 1: Book of Confessions. Louisville, The Office of the General Assembly, 1991.

Currents in Theology and Mission. Vol. 24, no. 1 (February 1997 / June 1999). Vol. 26, no. 3 (June 1999).

Joint Declaration on the Doctrine of Justification. Geneva: LWF and PCPCU, 1999.

Lutheran Book of Worship. Minneapolis: Augsburg, 1978.

LWF Studies, The Role and Interpretation of the Bible in the Life of the Church in China. China Study Series 3. June 1997.

Glossary of Technical Terms

Buddhism

The Glossary of technical terms is borrowed from *Buddhist Spirituality,* Vols. 8 and 9 of *World Spirituality: An Encyclopedic History of the Religious Quest,* ed. by Takeuchi Toshinori in association with James W. Heisig, Paul L. Swanson, and Joseph S. O'Leary. New York: Crossroad, 1999. Sanskrit (S), Pali (P), Chinese (C), Japanese (J)

Amitabha S.; Amita C.; Amida J.
The Buddha of measureless light; also called Amitayus, the Buddha of measureless life. Before becoming a buddha, he was a monk called Dharmakara, who vowed to welcome into his Pure Land in the west all who called on his name.

Anatman S. Anatta P.
No-self, non-ego, the absence of atman.

Atman S.
Ego, a permanent self.

Avatamsaka. S.; Hua-Yen C.; Hwaom.
"Flower-adornment," name of Mahayana sutra and school.

Bodhi S. P.
Awakening; Enlightenment; the conquest of ignorance through the awakening to perfect wisdom.

Bodhisattva S.; Bodhisatta P.
One who undertakes the path to Enlightenment; one who strives to attain the wisdom of the Buddha; a future Buddha; a compassionate being.

Dharma S.; Dhamma P.
Teaching; element; the ultimate constituent of existence; the law that governs all things; the essence or nature of a thing, and hence by association the things themselves; the ultimate truth as taught by the Buddha.

Dharmakaya S.
The Body of Dharma; the body of truth; the totality of the teachings of the Buddha; the eternal essence of the Buddha; the cosmic body.

Dukkha S.; Dukkha P.
Suffering, pain, disquiet, strife, ill, disvalue; the nature of human existence.

Garbha S.
Womb, matrix, seed.

Jnana S.
Knowledge, wisdom.

Karuna S. P.
Compassion.

Madhyamika; Madhyamaka S.
The "middle path" school of Buddhism founded by Nagarjuna.

Mahakaruna S.
Great compassion, the compassion of a Buddha.

Mahavairocana S.
The cosmic Buddha, identical with the Dharmakaya.

Mahayana S.
"Grand Vehicle"; the path of those Buddhists who choose to strive for Buddhahood rather than arhatship, as opposed to Hinayana ("little vehicle") Buddhism.

Maitreya S.
The future Buddha dwelling in the Tusita paradise.

Moksa S.
Liberation; release from karma-governed existence.

Nirmanakaya S.
The body of transformation; the historical incarnation of the Buddha.

Nirvana S.; Nibbana P.
The final state of release following enlightenment; the extinguishing of the flame (of delusions or passionate desires); the final goal of the Buddhist path.

P'an-chia C.
Classification of doctrines.

Paramita S.
Perfection; virtue, of which there are traditionally six or ten. The six are charity (dana), observation of the precepts (sila), patience (ksanti), diligence (virya), meditation (dhyana), and wisdom (prajna).

Prajna S.
Knowledge or Wisdom of the truth attained in enlightenment; the perfect comprehension of the totality of all existence; consummate wisdom; liberating knowledge of the nature of human existence.

Prapanca S.
Verbal constructs or fabricating; the false dichotomy that is necessarily involved in making a verbal statement.

Pratitya-samutpada S; Paticcasamuppada P.
Dependent co-arising; co-origination; dependent origination.

Rupakaya S.
The physical body; the body of form.

Samadhi S.
State of meditative absorption.

Sambhogakaya S.
The body of enjoyment; the body of recompense.

Samsara S. P.
This world of transmigration; the turning of the wheel of birth and death.

Sunyata S.; Sunnata P.; Kung C.; Ku J.
Emptiness; the lack of any substantial being; the fundamental Buddhist conception of ultimate reality.

Sutra S.
Thread; scripture, authoritative text; the first basket of the Tripitika.

Tathagatagarbha S.
The womb, embryo, matrix, of Buddhahood; the innate potential to attain Buddhahood.

Tathata S.
Suchness; the way things are; true reality.

Upaya S.
Skillful means used by the Buddha and by bodhisattvas to help oneself and others realize enlightenment.

Yogacara S.
The consciousness-only school of Buddhism, founded by Asanga and Vasubandhu.

A Glossary of Latin and Greek Theological Terms

The Latin terms are borrowed from Alister E McGrath, *IUSTITIA DEI: A History of the Christian Doctrine of Justification* (Cambridge: Cambridge University Press, 1998).

Acceptatio divina
Divine acceptance. The divine act by which God grants human beings eternal life. In medieval theology, the term is used to emphasize the fact that human salvation is ultimately dependent upon the divine decision to accept him, rather than any quality (such as a created habit) that the indi-

vidual may possess. It should be emphasized that *acceptatio divina* should not be confused with *acceptio personarum*: this latter term is used by Julian of Eclanum and others to refer to the idea of divine favoritism, which is rejected in favor of the divine *aequitas*.

Attritio

An imperfect natural form of repentance for sin, which arises out of fear of divine punishment.

Communicatio Idiomatum

An attribute of the divine nature is communicated to the human nature or vice versa based on the incarnational union. Therefore, the finite is capable of the infinite. This is characteristic of Lutheran Christology during the debate with the Reformed Christology.

Contritio

A perfect form of repentance for sin arising out of love for God, to be distinguished from *attritio*. *Contritio* is usually regarded as being possible only with the assistance of divine grace.

Enhypostasis/Anhypostasis

Leontius of Byzantium used this pair of terms to elucidate Chalcedonian christology. The humanity of Christ always exists in unity with his divinity. The humanity of Christ, which always exists in unity with the Logos, is real humanity. Apart from the divinity there is no such humanity. The positive side is called *enhypostasis*, whereas the negative side is called *anhypostasis*.

Extra Calvinisticum

This term, often used as a noun, denotes that the Logos must exist outside the flesh. This Reformed teaching (unlike Lutherans) put emphasis on the distinction of the divine nature from the human nature in one person of Jesus Christ.

Facere quod in se est

The requirement laid upon a human being by God if he/she is to dispose himself/herself towards the reception of the gift of grace.

Gratia gratum faciens

A habitual gift of grace that renders the viator acceptable to God, and that may not coexist with a state of mortal sin.

Habitus

A permanent state or disposition within the viator, to be distinguished from a transitory act. The habit of grace is understood to be a created form within the soul of the viator, intermediate between the divine and human natures, through whose influence the viator is changed to become more like God. The *habitus gratiae* is often referred to as *gratia creata*, to distinguish it from the uncreated grace (*gratia increata*) of the Holy Spirit.

Meritum de condigno

Merit in the strict sense of the term—i.e., a real merit, a moral act performed in a state of infused grace, and worthy of divine acceptation on that account.

Meritum de congruo

Merit in a weak sense of the term—i.e., a half credit, a moral act performed outside a state of infused grace, which, although not meritorious in the strict sense of the term, is considered an appropriate ground as a fitting reward for the infusion of justifying grace (*gratia prima*). The concept is generally discussed in relation to the axiom *facienti quod in se est Deus non denegat gratiam.*

Pactum

The covenant between God and a human being that governs the theology of the *via moderna*.

Perichoresis

John Damascene in the eighth century used the term *perichoresis* to highlight three divine persons as being-in-one-another in terms of permeation without confusion. The term expresses the coinherence and immanence of each divine person in the other two. Three divine persons inhere mutually in one another and exist by relation to one another.

Potentia Dei absoluta

The absolute power of God—i.e., the possibilities open to God before God entered into any decisions concerning his/her course of action, which led him/her to establish the ordained order through creation and subsequently redemption. It refers primarily to God's ability to do anything, subject solely to the condition that the outcome should not involve logical contradiction.

Potentia Dei ordinata

The ordained power of God—i.e., the established order of salvation, which although contingent, is totally reliable. The dialectic between the absolute and ordained powers of God was used by the theologians of the later Franciscan school, the *via moderna,* and the *schola Augustiniana moderna* to demonstrate the contingency of the implication of created habits of grace in justification.

Viator

Literally, wayfarer or pilgrim. The traditional medieval term used to refer to the believer on his way to the heavenly Jerusalem.

Index